Patty O'Gorman

Physical Education
for Elementary School Children

Physical Education
for Elementary School Children

An Illustrated Program
of Activities for
Kindergarten to Grade
Six

Glenn Kirchner
Simon Fraser University

Fourth Edition

wcb

Wm. C. Brown Company Publishers   Dubuque, Iowa

Contents

Part 5 Gymnastic and Movement Activities

Part **6** **Dance and Movement Activities**

Preface

The central purpose of this book remains the same as for the previous three editions: to provide a basic text for teaching physical education to elementary school children.

The changes that have been made, coupled with the inclusion of several new chapters, reflect a more individualized and exploratory approach to teaching young children. As teachers, we have learned that a humanistic approach in physical education is not solely the use of exploratory methods or new activities. Rather, it is a system of teaching that draws upon both structured and exploratory methods as the need arises. Such an approach calls for structured skills and direct teaching methods when there is a need to ensure that a particular skill or behavior pattern is acquired efficiently and effectively. At other times, the appropriate approach is one that stresses methods that will enhance self-direction and effective interpersonal relationships.

To provide this type of learning environment, the writer has attempted to present both structured and exploratory teaching strategies throughout this book. It is hoped that the format will bridge the gap between the "formal" approach and the "movement education" emphasis within the elementary school physical education program. Both approaches have merit and should be exploited by all teachers. Therefore, both viewpoints are presented in an integrated framework that should prove useful as an easy reference for both students and practicing teachers.

Part I of this book describes the purposes of the contemporary physical education program and outlines the basic characteristics and needs of young children. The purposes of the program and the characteristics of children, in turn, become the guidelines for the arrangement, content, and emphasis of each of the remaining chapters.

Part II is concerned with human movement. It provides the reader with an understanding of the main concepts of movement, the importance of posture and fitness, and the basic skills and movements that are appropriate for elementary school children.

Part III provides the information necessary to plan, organize, teach, and evaluate a physical education program. Although there are many "how to" suggestions in this important part of the text, each chapter is presented in such a way that each teacher can choose the methods, techniques, and organizational procedures that best fit her style of teaching.

Parts IV, V, and VI can be considered the resource areas of the book. Part IV contains a variety of individual and team game activities for primary and intermediate grades. Part V includes comprehensive coverage of gymnastic and movement activities that are performed on the floor, with small equipment, and with large apparatus. Part VI covers rhythmic activities, traditional and contemporary dances, and creative movement. Throughout these sections are suggestions for teaching these activities through both direct and indirect methods.

Part VII provides information about several important aspects of the physical education program, including how a variety of activities can be taught within the limitations of the typical classroom. Exceptional children are also discussed, and suggestions for dealing with their handicaps are provided. Part VII also shows how physical education can be correlated with other subjects in the elementary program.

The reader will note throughout the book the general use of the pronouns "she" and "her" when referring to the teacher. Feminine references are used for the sake of simplicity and consistency. Likewise, the pronouns "he" and "his" are used in reference to the student, although feminine pronouns are used, of course, when describing the girl students shown in illustrations.

This edition contains approximately four hundred new photographs and more than two hundred new line drawings which clarify the new content and methods of instruction. The reader will also note references to films throughout the book. These films, produced under the writer's direction, illustrate how physical activities are taught through a variety of strategies.

A glossary has been added to this edition, and the appendixes, as in past editions, include information about supplementary references, audiovisual resources, and equipment and supplies. This material will provide greater understanding of the general subject of physical education and can be used to enrich the movement experiences of elementary school children.

A revised and enlarged instructor's resource manual accompanies this text. It provides a summary outline of each chapter, along with teaching suggestions and evaluative techniques. The purposes are to give a quick overview of each chapter and to acquaint the teacher with the updated written and audiovisual resources that are available.

Acknowledgments

Each edition of this book has been the result of my involvement in experimental programs with school districts to test new activities and teaching strategies. I wish to express my sincere appreciation to School District No. 43 in Coquitlam, British Columbia, and particularly to the principal and teachers of Ranch Park Elementary School for their generous assistance throughout the preparation of this book. A very special note of appreciation is extended to Mr. Ian Andrews, Mr. Al Byers, Mr. Norman Ellis, Mrs. Sherry Fulton, Mrs. Cheryl Humphries, Mr. George Longstaff, Miss Margaret Robinson, and Mrs. Paulette Strim.

A wise writer also listens to his colleagues. To each teacher, professor, and student who has sent me information and suggestions, I hope this edition reflects, in no small measure, your excellent ideas. I am particularly indebted to the following reviewers for their suggestions and contributions: Elizabeth Ann Arink of Pennsylvania State University, Mary Irene Bell of Eastern Michigan University, Leon Greene of the University of Kansas, Viola Holbrook of Mankato State University, Elba Stafford of the University of Wisconsin-Madison, and Ray A. Stinar of Towson State University.

It would be a major undertaking to acknowledge individually all of the children who appear in the illustrations. To each and every one of these children, my very special thanks. I add a special note of appreciation to Mr. Lowell F. Turner and the boys and girls of Columbia School in Seattle, Washington, for their fine efforts. And I must express an acknowledgment to Diana Cheng, Danny Cheng, Deanne Cowlin, Paul Kirchner, Randy Smith and Ricky Smith, who appear in numerous individual poses.

The many drawings in Parts IV, V, and VI were drawn by Mr. Bill Schuss, a very talented and patient artist. Finally, I wish to thank Mrs. L. Libby for typing the manuscript and my wife, Diane, for all her help throughout the preparation of it.

Physical Education and the Growing Child

Part **1**

Part I is designed to provide teachers with a basic understanding of the meaning and purpose of physical education and the characteristics and needs of young children.

Physical Education in the Elementary School Curriculum

1

The Purposes of Physical Education

The Teacher and Physical Education

The Format and Approach of This Book

During the past two decades, the physical education program for elementary school children has undergone extensive changes in both content and teaching methods. These changes are the result of a growing body of knowledge about children's growth and development and a shift toward a more humanistic philosophy of education.

Numerous studies have been conducted to determine the effect of exercise on such factors as bone and muscle growth, perceptual-motor efficiency, and academic achievement. These investigations clearly indicate that young children must receive appropriate exercise on a daily basis to ensure that their bodies grow and develop in a normal, functional manner.

Long-term studies such as the Vanves program (Albinson and Andrews 1976), in which one-third of the school day was devoted to physical education, have shown dramatically that children with strong and healthy bodies tend to do very well academically. These studies, however, do not imply that increases in strength, endurance, or motor coordination will increase a child's intelligence. They simply demonstrate that children who are physically fit, who possess good motor control, do well in academic subjects. These investigations also show that strong and robust children can meet everyday personal and social pressures and challenges with relative ease.

The changing philosophy and curriculum of elementary education in general is also directly affecting the nature and direction of physical education. On one hand, current and future teachers of elementary school children must emphasize the mastery of subject material and the development of key cognitive processes. On the other hand, the trend toward more humanized schools makes it imperative that each teacher recognize the individuality of each learner and create a learning environment in which students and teachers interact in a personalized manner.

A humanized school is one in which the environment sets the stage for successful personal encounter; where ideas, facts, and feelings are expressed freely and openly. It is an environment where learning activities integrate the personal interests of the students with the goals of the school (Schmuck and Schmuck 1974).

Another national trend that has had a profound effect on physical education is the movement toward equal opportunity or access to all aspects of a public education. In physical education, this means that every child must be given an equal opportunity to participate in physical activities in the instructional program, as well as in all school-sponsored intramural and interschool activities. One implication of this major change is that boys and girls within each elementary grade will be taught together. Hence, the selection of activities, as well as the choice of instructional methods, will be determined in no small measure by this non-sex grouping procedure.

Such challenges of a dynamically changing elementary education program should be incorporated in the purposes of elementary school physical education, which will be given in the following section. These purposes become the basic criteria for the selection of content and the methods of instruction that are emphasized in this book. Also discussed in this chapter are the competencies that a teacher should possess to teach this important subject to elementary school age children. And the remaining parts of this book contain information about the foundation of human movement, ways of developing and teaching physical education programs, and resource materials for each elementary grade.

The Purposes of Physical Education

The primary purpose of education in general is to help each child develop to his or her full potential. This potential includes the development of a child's cognitive skills of thinking, learning, and communicating thoughts and ideas. It also includes development of a variety of closely related affective skills that the child needs to formulate attitudes and feelings about himself and others. And finally, it includes the full development of a child's psychomotor skills of moving, for utility and grace—with creative expression, when desired. (See film "Physical Education for Children," Appendix A). Physical education, as an integral part of an elementary school curriculum, can contribute to these general educational goals in a unique and effective way.

1. To Enhance Physical Growth and Development

Every child is born with certain inherited characteristics that determine his approximate height, weight, and general physique. Environmental factors such as proper nutrition, amount of sleep, exposure to disease, and general parental care will also affect the child's growth and development.

But, in addition to these factors, there is substantial evidence that normal growth and development of bone, connective, and muscle tissue occur only when a child receives adequate and continuous exercise throughout his growing period. Regular exercise, for example, increases bone width and mineralization (Rarick 1973). Similarly, lack of exercise can severely limit the potential growth of other bodily systems and organs.

2. To Develop and Maintain Maximum Physical Fitness

Since the release of the Kraus-Hirschland report in 1953 there has been a substantial effort by the medical and physical education professions to

Figure 1.1

3. To Develop Useful Physical Skills

All movements that are used in everyday activities, such as walking, dodging, and climbing, as well as those highly complex skills involved in sports, gymnastics, and dance activities, may be classified as "useful physical skills." Other terms, such as *neuromuscular* or *motor skills,* are also used to designate this type of physical performance.

The one thing that all these skills have in common is that they have to be learned. Therefore, our task as teachers is to assist each child in developing and perfecting the wide variety of motor skills that will be used in everyday activities and in future leisure pursuits.

The values of efficient and skillful movements, particularly in sports and dance, are many. A child who demonstrates ease and grace of movement is usually physically fit and well adjusted among his peers. Furthermore, a child who is skillful in an activity such as basketball or swimming will not only experience a great deal of enjoyment through participation, but also will usually keep up with the activity for many years. This lesson should be well understood by adults, for we generally participate in activities in which we show a reasonable degree of skill; rarely do we actively pursue or enjoy a sport that we cannot master at least in part.

convince the public of the importance of exercise and physical fitness to children, youth, and adults. There is now a large body of scientific evidence to support a program that will help each child develop and maintain an optimum level of physical fitness.

We know that children who possess the optimum level of physical fitness will normally reach their maximum levels of growth and development. Physically fit children do not show undue fatigue in daily activities and have sufficient reserve to meet emergencies. Children who are physically active are less prone to emotional disturbances and are normally well adjusted and generally outgoing. Proper weight is also adequately maintained by normal children who are continually involved in vigorous physical activity. And finally, physical fitness is a prerequisite for satisfactory performance in sports, gymnastics, and other vigorous activities.

All of these factors that demonstrate the importance of physical fitness stress striving for and maintaining optimum levels of strength, cardiorespiratory endurance, and other related fitness components as a means of achieving optimum growth, better health, and maximum performance.

Figure 1.2

4. To Develop in Socially Useful Ways

According to the platform statement of the American Alliance for Health, Physical Education and Recreation (AAHPER), a socially mature person is one who works for the common good, respects his peers' personalities, and acts in a sportsmanlike manner. Implicit in this is the fundamental principle that democratic citizens must possess a deep sense of group consciousness and cooperative living. Physical education, through team games and other group activities, can foster desirable social behavior. But game situations that require loyalty, honesty, and fair play can promote desirable behavior patterns only if they are intelligently organized and directed. A physically fit and well-coordinated child is a valuable asset; however, the individual who does not possess desirable social traits cannot realize or contribute to the broader ideals of a democratic community.

Figure 1.4

5. To Develop Wholesome Recreational Skills

During the past seventy years we have witnessed unbelievable changes in the social and economic structure of this country. The average work week has been reduced from sixty hours to fewer than forty, and there are strong indications that the next few years will bring an even shorter work week. Rapid transportation, urbanization, and automation in the home and in industry have given us leisure time never before experienced in a modern society. But these changes have also created a challenge to use leisure time for the betterment and well-being of self and community.

Enjoying wholesome physical recreation is an expressed need of contemporary society. Thus there is a need to educate children so they have knowledge and appreciation of skills that can be used in their daily activities, as well as contributing to a sense of creativity and relaxation and providing a means of filling the ensuing years with wholesome physical activity. The task may appear to be overwhelming to elementary school teachers; however, it is their job to lay the foundation for the development of many recreational skills that may be perfected in later years.

Figure 1.3

6. To Develop Intellectual Competencies

Intellectual competency involves the cognitive skills of acquiring a vocabulary, and joining words, phrases, and sentences to express meaning and to communicate thoughts and ideas. On the highest order, it involves the ability to understand, develop, and communicate concepts and ideas. In elementary school education, the development of intellectual competency has generally been delegated to classroom activities, with physical education seen as a way to develop fitness, motor skill, and a variety of social and emotional traits.

Physical education *should* be predominantly physical in nature; it is not, however, an experience that is void of vocabulary, of concepts, of a need to exercise and nurture the child's thinking processes. Every physical activity has a rich vocabulary. Games, dances, and gymnastic movements require the child to think, remember, and conceptualize. Developing a movement sentence in gymnastics, for example, requires the child to plan each movement in a sequential pattern, to remember, and to improve by exploring and evaluating new ideas through movement. Likewise, individual and team games provide a medium within which the young performer develops concepts relating to space, gravity, force, direction, and time.

The teacher should not view physical education as an academic discipline. But she should see it as a medium of movement within which vocabulary, concepts, and the thinking processes of each child should be developed through effective teaching strategies and the appropriate selection of physical activities.

7. To Develop Creative Talents

Contemporary education stresses the development of creativity at all levels of public education. Creativity, however, is a difficult concept to define. A work of art such as a painting, sculpture, or musical score is creative in that it is uniquely different in composition, color, or form. In physical education we define creativity in terms of the way in which a movement or series of movements is performed or by the degree of inventiveness of a movement.

Gladys Andrews says that creativity is what the individual thinks, feels, sees, and expresses in terms of himself and in his own way (Andrews, Saurborn, and Schneider 1960). Since every child has an inherent ability to be creative, the physical education program should provide numerous opportunities for each child to explore and express his creativity through movement.

Figure 1.5

Figure 1.6

Figure 1.7

8. To Enhance a Child's Self-image

Self-image is essentially the feelings a child has about himself. Each child develops feelings about his intellectual abilities, his popularity among his peers, and his ability to perform physical activities. If there is reasonable success in each of these dimensions, the child normally will have a positive feeling about his personal worth. A child who has this positive feeling is generally eager to attempt new challenges.

However, the child who constantly experiences failure in any of these areas will normally have a very low opinion of himself. This too often leads to withdrawal or other forms of undesirable behavior. Classroom teachers clearly understand the implications of such a child's problems in learning tasks and in getting along with his classmates.

Physical education can be either one of the most beneficial or one of the most harmful environments for a child to develop a positive self-image. If the activities are presented in such a way that each child, regardless of his physical ability, can achieve a measure of success, his feelings about himself are enhanced. One needs only to see a young child perform a successful roll or swim his first few strokes to observe the joy of success and the eagerness to try again. On the other hand, a child who is repeatedly required to attempt movement skills that are beyond his capabilities generally develops a negative attitude.

Since self-image is one of the most important factors in learning motor skills, physical education activities must be presented in such a way that every child achieves some success. New methods and techniques described in later chapters can assist teachers in providing this type of program for all children.

These broad purposes indicate what the goals of a modern physical education program should be. Perhaps the unique contributions of physical education are physical fitness and motor skill development. The need for a physically fit nation, from childhood through adulthood, has been emphasized by presidents of the United States, members of the medical profession, and countless leaders in business and education. The inherent values of motor skill development, from the standpoints of both worthy use of leisure time and the positive contributions of physical activity to long-term mental health, must be considered of equal importance.

But, the development of intellectual competencies through physical education should also be emphasized, as with art, music, or any other aspect of the curriculum. All subject areas can and should develop each child's intellectual abilities. Similarly, the development of a child's creativity or the enhancement of his self-image is not the sole responsibility of one teacher or one subject area. Physical education simply is a unique medium within which the personal and creative expressions of children can be developed through movement.

Physical education as a subject in the elementary school curriculum thus must not be considered merely as a means of "training the body." It must be thought of as an integral part of the total curriculum with similar goals and unique contributions.

The Teacher and Physical Education

These purposes of physical education are essentially a reflection of the needs of the individual and contemporary society. From the viewpoint of society, there are certain skills, knowledge, and attitudes that we believe all children should learn. On the other hand, we consider self-direction, expressed in terms of individuality of thought and action, as being equally important. Thus the task of the teacher becomes one of providing an environment within which she can give direction and the substance of learning while providing an opportunity for each child to develop self-direction commensurate with his maturity and ability.

The contemporary approach to teaching physical education can best be described as an eclectic one. There are situations, for example, when a direct teaching method is clearly needed. Learning a new skill that has an element of risk of injury requires a careful progression of skill development and adherence to safety procedures which only the experienced teacher can understand. Thus the skill is presented in a more formal and direct manner. Once the children have demonstrated sufficient competence in the skill, however, more indirect methods can then be used to encourage variation in the movement skill or to combine the newly acquired skill with other skills in a child's movement repertoire.

Each learning situation in physical education will vary according to the children's abilities and maturity and the nature of the learning task. At times, the direct teaching method is called for, while at other times, even within the context of a single lesson, problem solving and creative expression should be encouraged. Therefore, the approach that any teacher uses in her physical education program should not be dominated by a direct or an indirect method of instruction, but characterized by a blending of direct and indirect, or problem solving, teaching strategies, with each emphasized according to the nature of the learner and the learning task.

Figure 1.8

Qualities of Good Teaching

The general qualities of "good" teaching have been presented by numerous authorities and apply to physical education as well as any other subject. It is the writer's personal feeling that genuine enthusiasm by the teacher for the value of physical education is the most critical factor in making this subject a true educational experience.

If classroom teachers are convinced of the value of well-conceived physical education programs, they will seek ways of implementing them. In many ways the classroom teachers are the ideal persons to plan and teach their own physical education programs.

A great many words have been written about the advantages and disadvantages of specialist teachers handling all physical education in the elementary school. The fundamental truth is, however, that for the foreseeable future classroom teachers must assume the responsibility for this subject area. Physical education is handled in this manner now in more than 80 percent of all elementary schools.

There are many other desirable and sometimes necessary characteristics for teaching physical education. Although the following list is incomplete, if a teacher possesses these qualities, there is more than a reasonable chance that the physical education period will be enjoyable and educational.

1. A teacher should want to acquire more competence in teaching physical education.

Classroom teachers are normally required to take one or two professional courses in physical education. This, of course, is inadequate preparation for teaching all the areas of this subject, so it is necessary for teachers to gain new skills and insights through additional courses, texts, films, and other in-service media.

Probably of equal importance is that the teacher "have the courage to be imperfect and enjoy it." No teacher can be an expert in every subject. What is more important is the courage to try new ideas and teaching methods, however insecure one might feel. A child's attitude toward a teacher is not based entirely on the teacher's overall competence; it is based on the very simple premise that the child and the teacher are jointly engaged in the search for knowledge and understanding. It is, in essence, a mutual respect for each other's abilities and efforts. When children know the teacher is trying something new for their benefit, they, in turn, will respond in a mature and understanding way.

2. A teacher should possess a sense of humor.

The writer is often tempted to place this quality at the top of the list. Teaching is very hard work, but it is also a very rewarding profession. The ability to laugh at one's own inadequacies and "gentle" errors is vitally important for the maintenance of sanity and perspective in the day-to-day task of teaching. This is particularly important to classroom teachers who work long hours in confined quarters with children who are extremely demanding of one's patience and understanding. The need for a sense of humor is equally important, if not more so, for the teacher of physical education.

3. A teacher should possess an optimum level of health.

Teachers obviously need to maintain good physical and mental health. Without them, the pressure of teaching becomes too demanding, with serious consequences to both teacher and student. Because physical education is physically demanding, a teacher who lacks strength and stamina will tend to neglect this area of the curriculum, with a loss to both the teacher and the class. New teaching methods do not require a high level of motor skill on the part of the teacher. They do, however, require physical effort and enthusiasm.

The Format and Approach of This Book

This book has been organized to provide the reader with a systematic presentation of the knowledge and skills required to teach physical education to elementary school children. Part I attempts to provide the rationale and direction for a well-balanced physical education program. The basic knowledge of the structure and function of a growing child and important mechanical and movement fundamentals are described in Part II. Part III contains the information necessary to translate the purposes of physical education into an effective program of instruction. Parts IV, V, and VI have been carefully arranged to provide not a balanced program of activities but also a variety of approaches that can be used in presenting these activities to various age levels. Part VII provides additional information about the effective use of the classroom for physical education, instructional ideas in dealing with exceptional children, and ways of correlating physical education with other subjects.

The reader will not find a separate chapter dealing with Movement Education. What she will find is a blending of the concepts, principles, and skills of movement education along with other contemporary approaches used to teach games, dance, and gymnastic activities.

The Child and Movement Experiences

2

Physical Growth

Psychological and Social Development

The Exceptional Child

The central focus of contemporary education is to help the child develop to his full potential. As teachers of physical education, we must understand children's growth and development stages in order to choose appropriate activities and movement experiences wisely.

For example, a cursory knowledge of the young child's bone growth clearly indicates that vigorous daily exercise is necessary for normal development of bone tissue. Such knowledge also shows that excessive weight bearing or the severe blows that accompany a sport such as contact football are harmful to virtually every elementary school child. Likewise, knowledge of the growth of muscle tissue, and of heart and respiration rates, provides insight into the correct amount and duration of exercise for children in the primary and intermediate grades.

Physiological changes, however, are not the sole basis on which to select activities or teaching methods. Psychological changes involving self-image, attention span, and motivation and sociological changes relating to peer group importance also have significant implications for the physical education program.

This chapter will give a thumbnail sketch of important physical, psychological, and social changes that young children experience. A few important implications of these changes for primary and intermediate physical education programs are also provided. A brief discussion of the exceptional child concludes this chapter.

Physical Growth

The physical growth and maturation of an elementary school child's bone, muscle, and other tissues can be described as steady and consistent. Boys and girls gain approximately two inches in height and six pounds a year from age five to twelve, as illustrated in the accompanying table. There is virtually no major difference in height and weight between boys and girls from age five to eleven. During grades five and six, however, girls begin to show early signs of puberty, with marked changes in their physical features (breasts and pelvic girdles), as well as a marked increase in height and weight.

Table 2.1 Average Height and Weight of Elementary School Children

Boys and Girls	Height	Weight
Boys—5 years	42 to 46 inches	38 to 48 pounds
Girls—5 years	42 to 46 inches	36 to 48 pounds
Boys—6 years	44 to 48 inches	41 to 54 pounds
Girls—6 years	44 to 48 inches	40 to 53 pounds
Boys—7 years	46 to 50 inches	45 to 60 pounds
Girls—7 years	46 to 50 inches	44 to 59 pounds
Boys—8 years	48 to 53 inches	50 to 67 pounds
Girls—8 years	48 to 52 inches	48 to 66 pounds
Boys—9 years	50 to 55 inches	55 to 74 pounds
Girls—9 years	50 to 54 inches	52 to 74 pounds
Boys—10 years	52 to 57 inches	59 to 82 pounds
Girls—10 years	52 to 57 inches	57 to 83 pounds
Boys—11 years	54 to 59 inches	64 to 91 pounds
Girls—11 years	54 to 59 inches	63 to 94 pounds
Boys—12 years	55 to 61 inches	70 to 101 pounds
Girls—12 years	56 to 62 inches	72 to 107 pounds
Average Gain	2 inches a year	6 pounds a year

Bones

The bones of an elementary school child are undergoing continuous change in length, width, and general composition. The long bones, such as the humerus (upper arm) and femur (upper leg), have one center of growth in the middle of the bone called *diaphysis* and one or more centers at each end of the bone called *epiphysis*. Growth occurs both from the center of the bone toward the ends and from the ends toward the center. Bone maturation is complete when these centers merge into a solid bone.

Boys and girls from age five to approximately eleven show a steady increase in the growth of bones. During this period, however, the bone structure is still relatively weak and flexible. As a child reaches puberty, bone growth appears to be more rapid; this is quite evident with eleven and twelve-year-old girls in grades five and six.

There is sufficient scientific evidence to indicate that exercise is necessary during these formative years for normal bone growth. According to Dr. C. S. Houston, "If we are active, our bones will be well mineralized and both bones and muscles will be strong." It has also been shown that long periods of inactivity will cause some decalcification of bones (Albinson and Andrews 1976). The result of this demineralization is a weaker and more brittle bone, and hence one that is more susceptible to fractures and other injuries.

Skeletal Muscles

The skeletal muscles of young children are undergoing rapid changes in size and strength. An initial rapid growth in muscle tissue occurs between ages five and six. However, from age seven to eleven or twelve, there is a relatively gradual and continuous growth of muscle mass. By age twelve, the average child has nearly doubled the amount of muscle tissue he had at age six. Experts in the growth and development field indicate that increases in the size and strength of muscles, particularly in children in the middle elementary grades (grades three to five), make this a period of restlessness for most children. As with all other systems of the human body, muscle tissue must be exercised if its full potential is to be reached.

The majority of physical fitness norms show that boys are slightly stronger than girls between the ages of five and twelve. These differences are not the result of an inherent difference in muscular systems, but are normally due to social factors—boys have been encouraged to participate in vigorous activities, while girls have leaned toward less active and physically demanding activities.

But this difference clearly is being reduced by social and cultural changes during the past decades, along with the current policy of giving equal time to the sexes in all publicly supported sport and physical activity programs. In fact, in many contemporary physical education programs, any previously observed differences in strength and general physical fitness levels in this age range have virtually disappeared.

Once they reach puberty, however, boys begin to show significant increases in muscle mass and strength, and physiological changes in girls create proportionately less muscular mass and more fatty tissue. These changes, coupled with other structural changes in both sexes, produce a major difference in the strength of boys and girls as they enter adolescence.

Heart and Lungs

The growth of the heart (cardiac muscle) and lungs is almost proportional to the growth of bones and muscles throughout the elementary school years. The pulse and breathing rates gradually decline throughout the primary grades, and by age nine, the pulse rate is rarely above ninety beats a minute. Respiration rate is approximately twenty a minute.

Easy fatigue and rapid recovery are characteristic of this age.

By age twelve, the pulse rate is normally between eighty and ninety beats a minute and the respiration rate is between fifteen and twenty a minute. Children between nine and twelve have more endurance, although girls with early signs of puberty may tire sooner.

The general structural and maturational changes that occur between the ages of five and eleven or twelve are gradual and approximately equal with boys and girls. Normal and optimal levels of development of bone, muscle, and other tissues depend upon daily vigorous physical activity appropriate to each child's age and maturity. Specific recommendations for primary and intermediate physical education programs follow. (Each area is thoroughly discussed in later chapters.)

Primary Physical Education Program (Five to Eight Years)

1. Participation in vigorous activity, particularly running, climbing, and jumping, is necessary, with provision for frequent rest intervals. Long periods of inactivity during the school day should be discouraged; recess and periodic breaks throughout the school day should be characterized by vigorous and total body movement.
2. Provide for manipulation (catching, throwing, kicking, etc.) of various sizes of balls. Begin with relatively slow speeds and short distances. Gradually increase speed, distance, and use of small objects as skill develops.
3. Plan numerous activities involving quick changes of speed and direction. Games and stunts involving speed, dodging, and changing of direction should be provided for all children throughout this age range.
4. Postural development is a particular problem for children in this age group, and the problem has been intensified in the past few decades by excessive television viewing and general sedentary living. Teachers should be constantly aware of children's sitting and walking postures and should plan activities for general postural development.

Intermediate Physical Education Program (Nine to Twelve Years)

1. Provide vigorous activities, emphasizing cardiorespiratory endurance, for longer periods. Although some girls, particularly those who have reached the early stages of puberty, may be disinterested in vigorous activities, normal growth and development of the heart and lungs are dependent upon vigorous, continuous activity.
2. Provide for posture and strength development. Although all muscles need consistent exercise of an overload nature, special attention should be given to activities involving the arms and shoulder girdle, back, and abdominal area. Provide for more self-testing activities which develop strength in these areas.
3. Lack of flexibility in children of this age appears to be due to their type of activity, rather than structural or growth reasons. Therefore, movements that enhance flexibility are called for. Encourage self-testing activities, particularly those involving stretching and the use of small equipment and large apparatus.

Psychological and Social Development

Children's personal and social characteristics, as well as their physical growth and development, must be considered when planning a physical education program. The next two sections describe some of the more common personal and social characteristics of children in the primary (kindergarten to three) and intermediate (four to six) grades. Specific implications of these characteristics for the physical education program are also provided.

Primary School Children (Five to Eight Years)

These years might well be called the age of conflict. At times the child is still quite individualistic, self-assertive, and independent; then without reason, he may reveal a willingness to share and cooperate. By age seven, adult approval is more important to him than that of his classmates; but by eight, there is a shift to participation in and importance of "gang life." This is quite obvious in the child's interest in group games, team spirit, and team loyalty.

Although the dominant interest is in organized games, children also develop a sense of personal achievement, which becomes quite evident in their increased attention span and desire to practice specific skills. These children are still very mobile and imaginative, and they are keenly interested in rhythmical sounds. They enjoy expressive movements of all kinds. They are, however, easily excited, sensitive to criticism, and strongly in need of approval and close supervision (Cowell and Hazelton 1955).

The following summary, although far from complete, provides important guidelines for the development of any physical education program involving this primary age group.

Additional information may be found in the selected references.

1. Provide a large variety of activities within any instructional period. Games should be simple in purpose, rules, and directions.

Figure 2.1

2. Provide content and teaching methods that foster creative movements (creative games, dance, and movement education).
3. Provide various forms of dance experiences, including singing games, folk dances, and creative dance. Musical accompaniment to gymnastic activities is also strongly suggested, such as with rope skipping and other types of activities.
4. Provide for numerous individual activities in which immediate success is possible for all children, regardless of ability. But, since children at this age need peer acceptance as well as adult approval, there should be planned experience involving sharing, team play, and group cooperation.
5. The spirit of adventure—climbing a rope—and testing of one's ability obviously should be encouraged. But at the same time, the teacher must instill within the child a concern for his

own safety, as well as a general awareness and concern for the safety of others. Extensive use of the movement education approach with gymnastic activities is clearly indicated.

6. The whole group should not be punished for the wrongdoings of one child. Children recognize inconsistencies in degrees of punishment, so teachers should be consistent and fair in the type and amount of discipline. Because of the social awareness and inherent fairness of children, group control through self-discipline should be stressed.

Intermediate School Children (Nine to Twelve Years)

Physical maturation influences the social and psychological development of children in this age group, creating a period of transition and differentiation in the interests and behavior of both boys and girls (Arnold 1968). Generally speaking, both sexes are becoming quite conscious of their bodies, although for different reasons.

Boys tend to be sloppy in their dress and are more concerned about their physical fitness and skill development. They are keenly interested in vigorous competitive sports and show a strong concern about their peers and a great deal of confidence in adults. Hero worship, particularly for well-known athletes, is the rule rather than the exception. On the other hand, girls are becoming concerned with their personal femininity. Such activities as general body mechanics and social dance are now often more important than vigorous and rough team sports. Early signs of tomboyishness generally give way after the beginning of puberty. Both sexes are easily excitable, demanding, and enthusiastic, and constantly seek peer loyalty and independence.

There is no magic line separating one age from another; teachers of grades four to six are aware of the tremendous diversity in psychological characteristics of these children. However, as with the younger age range, there are some basic considerations that should be made when planning a physical education program for children in the intermediate grades.

1. Provide activities that are more complex and challenging. With individual and team games, allow time to learn and practice skills, rules, and complex team strategy. Allow time with dance and gymnastic activities to develop complex and creative movements.

2. Children should be taught motor skills, as well as an understanding of the related concepts and principles that apply to these motor skills and movement patterns.

3. Through the problem-solving method, test and challenge the child's intellectual ability with movement tasks.

4. Carefully select activities commensurate with emotional development. Emotional outbreaks in tense game situations are normal and, in some situations, desirable.

5. Both the activities and the teaching methods must take into consideration the independence that is a natural tendency for children of this age group. Teacher-directed

Figure 2.2

approaches should not be completely abandoned, but they should be blended with approaches that call for greater freedom and responsibility by the child.

6. Special attention should be given to groupings that will provide identification and foster team cooperation and loyalty.
7. Provision should be made within both the instructional and extraclass programs for children to participate in activities that involve their own sex and both sexes.
8. Extensive opportunities should be available for boys and girls to plan and direct activities. This contributes to the development of cooperation, leadership, team loyalty, and friendships.
9. If children, particularly in the fifth and sixth grades, are mixed by sexes, special care should be taken when asking girls to demonstrate skills or movements. Although girls are normally more graceful than boys in gymnastic-type movements, they tend to be embarrassed when asked to demonstrate. Boys, however, are normally more proficient in ball skills and do enjoy demonstrating. The essential task for teachers is to understand and appreciate the differences that normally exist between boys and girls of this age level.

The Exceptional Child

The exceptional child is defined in contemporary education as a child who, in one way or another, deviates from the "normal" intelligence, physical health, or behavior of the "average" or "typical" child. This definition includes the intellectually gifted, the physically gifted, the physically handicapped, the slow learner, and the social deviant. Approximately 12 percent of the school population falls within this group, and each type of gifted child requires some form of special attention (Jarvis and Wootton 1966).

In physical education, as in all other subjects, it is necessary first to distinguish the types of "gifted" individuals.

Figure 2.3

The Physically Gifted Child

Few writers in the physical education field have attempted to define what is meant by a physically gifted child. Yet, by observation of performance and analysis of programs, the contemporary meaning is quite clear. A child who possesses a unique ability in sports, dance, or gymnastics may be described as physically gifted. In individual and team sports, the gifted child is recognizable as a member of the school team. The gifted dancer, gymnast, or swimmer is a member of a school or community club.

These special talents are also recognized within the physical education program of an elementary school, in both instructional and extraclass programs. If all children are given a well-rounded program, special activities for the physically gifted would appear to be in harmony with the educational philosophy and principles of contemporary elementary school programs. Consider the following when providing special programs for the physically gifted child:

1. All phases of the physical education program should be given fair consideration and emphasis.
2. Gifted children should be expected to do a great deal of planning, executing, and evaluating of classroom activities.
3. Higher standards of achievement are established for gifted children.

4. Gifted children should be encouraged to expand their interests and enrich their experiences through participation in special-interest clubs in the school or community.
5. Specialists in sports, dance, and gymnastic activities should be used within the physical education program. A specialist is defined as a qualified person recognized by the school who is capable of teaching his special talent. A parent who has special talent and qualifications in folk dance would meet this criteria.

The Physically Handicapped Child

A normal, healthy child can be defined as one who is free of disease and physical handicaps. Conversely, a handicapped child is one who has an acute or chronic disease, such as rheumatic fever, or is handicapped because of a birth or hereditary malformation. Handicaps of the latter type include hearing loss, cerebral palsy, and an extensive list of orthopedic malformations that impair physical performance (Mathews, Krause, and Shaw 1962). A more extensive discussion of physically handicapped children is included in Chapter 28.

Contemporary educational philosophy adheres to the fundamental principle that a child in school is educable. Therefore, whenever it is physically and psychologically feasible, the physical education program should provide desirable experiences for the physically handicapped child.

The handicapped child's limitations and needs obviously must be determined by such experts as physicians, corrective therapists, and psychiatrists. Furthermore, these authorities should make specific recommendations about the type of physical experiences that these children should have. For example, a child who has cerebral palsy but with limited impairment might be permitted to participate in physical activities involving gross motor movement, such as simple games and certain dance experiences. But movements involving rapid hand-eye coordination, such as throwing and catching skills, may be too great a task for the spastic child.

Teachers have demonstrated keen insight in virtually all learning experiences involving handicapped children. Within the regular classroom situation, children with sight and hearing losses are placed in more advantageous seats. The epileptic child is no longer kept at home, nor is his condition concealed from his peers. Likewise, the physically handicapped child must be integrated into daily physical education activities to the limits of his capacity.

The scope of the handicapped child's program must be based to some degree on the following considerations:

1. The type of exercise should be specified by a competent medical adviser.
2. The type of activities should be appropriate to the child's capabilities and needs.
3. A physical education specialist should be consulted for assistance in developing corrective and remedial programs.
4. The program should allow the child to experience immediate success and enjoyment.
5. Whenever feasible, the extent of a child's handicap should be explained to his peers.
6. The program should include activities that are of long-range recreational value.

The information in this chapter should provide a basic understanding of the nature and importance of a child's growth and development when planning a physical education program. Part II presents additional information about the structure and function of movement and the basic skills and movement fundamentals for children in the primary and intermediate grades.

Nature and Analysis of Movement

Part II deals with three important aspects of human movement. Chapter 3 provides a basic understanding of the structure of a growing child's body and how the fundamental laws of gravity, motion, and force affect a child's movement skills. Chapter 4 discusses the importance of maintaining good posture and an optimum level of physical fitness. The last chapter in Part II describes and illustrates the basic movement skills that are appropriate for children in the primary and intermediate grades.

Basic Structure and Mechanics of Movement

3

The Skeletal System of Young Children

The Muscular System of Young Children

The Basic Mechanics of Movement

This chapter provides information about the important aspects of a child's growth, development, and performance. The first two sections briefly describe the main bones and muscles that are involved in young children's everyday physical activities. The third section explains how the laws and principles of gravity, motion, and force affect all human movements. The information in this chapter will provide classroom teachers with a basic understanding of the physical structure of a young child and the interrelationship between his movements and the laws and principles of gravity, motion, and force.

The Skeletal System of Young Children

The functions of the skeletal system are to protect the soft tissues of the body, such as the brain, spinal cord, and internal organs, and to provide the general framework of the body. The bones support the weight of the body and serve as an anchor, or attachment, for the skeletal muscles.

The bones of an elementary school child develop in much the same way as a tree grows. In the long bones, such as the humerus (upper arm) and femur (upper leg), growth in length takes place at both the center and ends of the bone. As the bone grows, it gradually becomes ossified, or hardens. This process begins about the second month of the embryo's life and continues well into adult life.

Growth of Long Bones

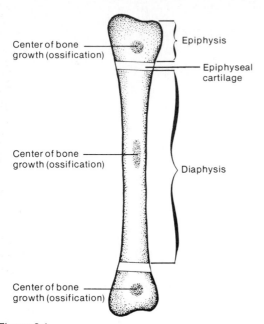

Center of bone growth (ossification)

Epiphysis

Epiphyseal cartilage

Center of bone growth (ossification)

Diaphysis

Center of bone growth (ossification)

Figure 3.1

The bone structure of an elementary school child is still relatively soft and flexible and normally can absorb many jars or blows without fracturing the bones. However, severe blows such as those experienced in contact football and excessive weight bearing on any joint should be avoided. But since the ends of the bones and other connecting tissues around the joints are extremely supple, the child can bend and stretch all parts of his body well beyond what even the most fit adult can do. The yoga-like positions shown in figures 3.2 and 3.3 illustrate the potential flexibility of young children.

The drawings in figure 3.4 of the skeletal system of a twelve-year-old boy identify the bones that form the basic structure of the child's framework. These diagrams provide a basis for understanding how the muscles are attached, the importance of good posture, and the interrelationship of bones, joints, and muscles in the young child's physical activities.

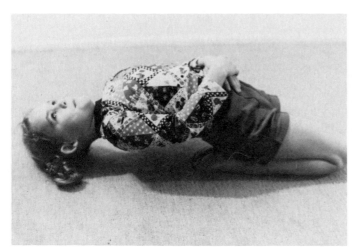

Figure 3.2

Figure 3.3

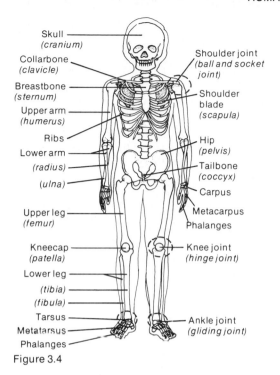

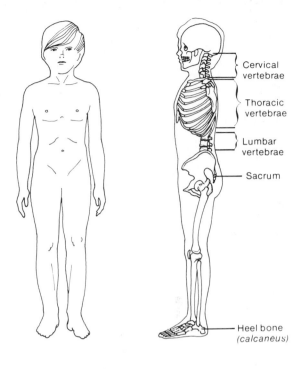

Figure 3.4

The Muscular System of Young Children

The human body contains three types of muscles. *Involuntary,* or smooth, muscles form the muscular portion of the internal organs and function automatically rather than under the direct control of the brain. The *cardiac* or heart, muscle performs its unique function under the involuntary control of the brain. The *voluntary,* or skeletal, muscles are attached to the bones and are under the direct control of the brain. It is the latter type of muscles that we are directly concerned with in physical education, although all muscles are indirectly affected.

A skeletal muscle is made up of bundles of muscle fibers that are enclosed in a sheath of fibrous tissue called *fascia.* At the end of the muscle is a non-contracting fibrous tissue called a *tendon* (fig. 3.5). The tendon normally is attached to a bone or ligament. When a nerve impulse is received by a muscle, the fibers con-

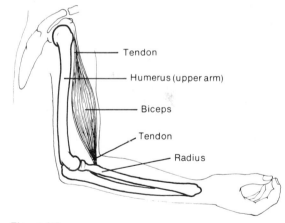

Figure 3.5

tract, causing the muscle to become shorter and thicker. This action is illustrated when a child flexes his arm, causing the biceps to become shorter and thicker. Muscle fibers can only contract, so the antagonist triceps muscles must contract in order to extend the arm.

3

The drawings in figure 3.6 of the same twelve-year-old boy illustrated on page 23 will help teachers locate the main skeletal muscles. The names, such as deltoid, quadriceps, and gastrocnemius, may be difficult to pronounce, let alone remember, at first. But with practice, teachers can soon recognize these main muscles. Knowing these muscles, their general locations, and their main purposes will help the teacher choose appropriate exercises and movement patterns for her students.

Children in the intermediate grades are keenly interested in their bodies. The physical education lesson, therefore, should involve more than learning the skills of physical activities. Take time to explain the main structures of the body and why exercise is important for the normal growth and development of bones, muscles, and other systems.

The Basic Mechanics of Movement

There are basic laws and principles that affect the performance of all movements of the body. The laws of gravity, for example, affect balance and the adjusting of position while moving. The human body is a living machine; it converts food into energy and expends the energy in movement. If the human body is kept in optimum condition and is moved in accordance with the principles of force and motion, expenditure of energy will be proportionate to the task. But if an individual fails to adjust to the laws of motion and force, he will expend too much energy and fail to achieve maximum results.

It is difficult for teachers who have not studied kinesiology (the science of human move-

GENERAL LOCATION OF MUSCLES

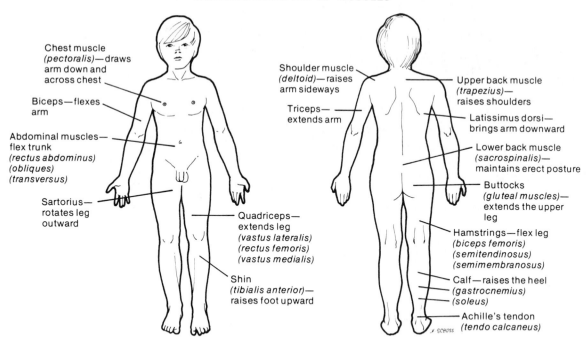

Chest muscle (pectoralis)—draws arm down and across chest

Biceps—flexes arm

Abdominal muscles— flex trunk (rectus abdominus) (obliques) (transversus)

Sartorius— rotates leg outward

Quadriceps— extends leg (vastus lateralis) (rectus femoris) (vastus medialis)

Shin (tibialis anterior)— raises foot upward

Shoulder muscle (deltoid)—raises arm sideways

Triceps— extends arm

Upper back muscle (trapezius)— raises shoulders

Latissimus dorsi— brings arm downward

Lower back muscle (sacrospinalis)— maintains erect posture

Buttocks (gluteal muscles)— extends the upper leg

Hamstrings—flex leg (biceps femoris) (semitendinosus) (semimembranosus)

Calf—raises the heel (gastrocnemius) (soleus)

Achille's tendon (tendo calcaneus)

Figure 3.6

ment) to understand all the important mechanical principles of human movement. They should, however, understand a few important principles concerning balance, force, and motion and be able to apply them when teaching skills and movement patterns.

Balance

Balance is the ability of the body to maintain a stationary position or to perform purposeful movements while resisting the force of gravity. Our first consideration then is the "law of gravity," which is the natural force that pulls everything toward the center of the earth. Most important to balance is that gravitational pull always occurs through the center of the weight or mass of an object. Applied to the human body, the

center of gravity is that point around which the weight is equally distributed in all directions. The human body is in balance when all forces acting upon it equal zero. The child in figure 3.7 is lying on his back with all his muscles in a state of relaxation. His body is not resisting gravity; therefore the center of gravity is the point in the middle of his body weight, indicated by the white circle.

In figure 3.8 the center of gravity is in the middle of the hips. The child is maintaining a state of equilibrium, or balance, through the tension he is applying to his anti-gravitational muscles (the large muscles of the trunk and legs). When his arms are raised, as illustrated in figure 3.9, the boy's center of gravity also rises. If the boy relaxes those muscles, he will fall to the ground, obeying the law of gravity.

Figure 3.7 Center of gravity in middle of body weight (indicated by white circle)

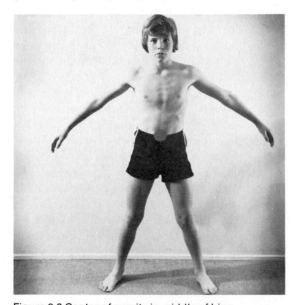

Figure 3.8 Center of gravity in middle of hips

Figure 3.9 Center of gravity raised by raising of the arms

3

Figure 3.10 Wide base of support   Figure 3.11 Narrow base of support   Figure 3.12 Dropping center of gravity closer to base of support

Principle: The wider or broader the base of support, the more stable the body. This principle is extremely important in balance stunts. For example, in figure 3.10 the hands and head of the child performing a headstand form a wide triangle, or broad base of support. The center of gravity is located through the hips and head and midpoint between the hands. By comparison, the child's hands in figure 3.11 are almost in line with the shoulders, thus greatly reducing the base of support.

Teachers will observe that a child performing a headstand this latter way will not hold the position for very long, since even a slight movement is enough to cause him to fall to the side, backward, or forward. The latter can result in a severe strain on the neck muscles, as well as a hard thud.

Principle: The closer the center of gravity to the base of support, the greater the stability. The child in figure 3.12 has assumed the same position as in figure 3.10 but has kept his knees bent, thus dropping the center of gravity closer to his base of support. This example shows that a wide base of support, coupled with a low center of gravity, will help in the performance of numerous balance stunts.

In sports, a stable position might be required when meeting an oncoming force, such as a large ball. A large utility ball thrown with force could knock a young child off balance if he is standing upright with his feet close together, as in figure 3.13. He has a narrow base of support and a high center of gravity. But in figure 3.14 he has spread his legs and bent his knees, giving him a wider base of support and a lower center of gravity.

There are, however, numerous skills in games, sport, and dance activities where an unstable base of support is desirable—necessary, in fact—to perform the skill correctly. The principles of gravity still apply. Sometimes one must deliberately shift the center of gravity to an unstable position so he can move quickly. When the gravity line reaches a point outside the base of support, the individual will fall in that direction.

This is what happens when we walk or run; we shift our weight forward in order to move. The sprinter in a crouched starting position (fig. 3.15a) leans forward considerably, shifting his center of gravity forward (fig. 3.15b). In addition, he has raised his hips higher than his shoulders to increase further the "unstable" position toward the direction in which he intends to move and to place the strong hip muscles in a position to contract effectively.

These principles of gravity are normally taught to elementary school children in academic courses. If these concepts are also explained to children in a meaningful way using their own bodies, they will understand the mechanical advantages of the principles and apply them in sports, games, and other daily activities.

Motion

The laws of motion described by Sir Isaac Newton in the seventeenth century apply to all movements of both animate and inanimate objects. In physical activity, Newton's three basic laws of motion are important in understanding how, where, and why the body should move, as well as how to project or receive an object.

Figure 3.13 Narrow base of support and high center of gravity

Figure 3.14 Wide base of support and lower center of gravity

3

Figure 3.15a Center of gravity indicated by white circle

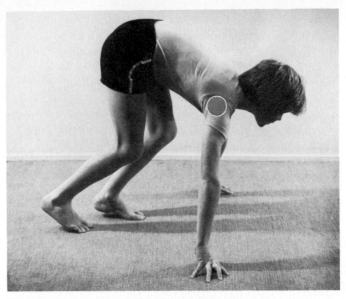

Figure 3.15b Center of gravity indicated by white circle

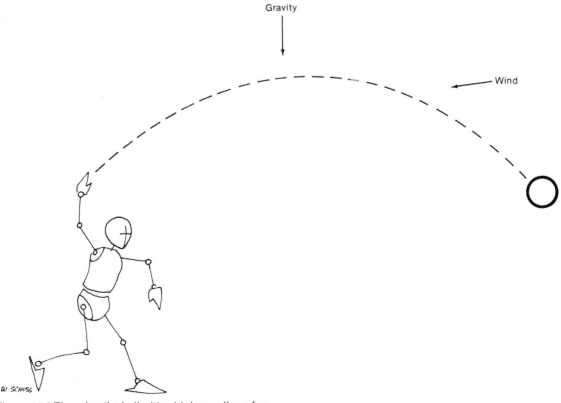

Figure 3.16 Throwing the ball with a high arc allows for the effects of gravity and wind.

Law of Inertia

The law of inertia: An object will remain in a state of rest and an object in motion will remain in motion at the same speed and direction unless acted upon by a force. Inertia is directly proportional to the size or mass of the object and its velocity. This means that the greater an object's mass and velocity, the more difficult it is to change its direction or motion. The force that changes an object's motion or direction could be gravity, wind, another object, or the contraction of muscles.

An understanding of this law is extremely important for performing physical movements. For example, a ball thrown toward a target will move in a straight line and at uniform speed until the force of gravity or wind causes it to change direction (fig. 3.16). Thus a child must learn to adjust to or compensate for these forces in all throwing and striking activities.

Another example for understanding and overcoming the effects of the law of inertia is dribbling a soccer ball. The ball will not move until it receives an external force—the foot. It takes force to start the ball moving (overcoming mass); however, so long as the ball is kept in motion, the effect of inertia is minimal. Performing continuous sit-ups and keeping up a steady running or swimming pace are also good examples of overcoming the effects of inertia.

Law of Acceleration

The law of acceleration: When an object is acted upon by a force, it will move in the direction of that force. The resulting change of speed (acceleration) of the object will be directly proportional to the force acting on it and inversely proportional to the mass. To illustrate this second law, consider a volleyball player executing a high "floating" serve (fig. 3.17a). The force exerted is relatively gentle and is behind the ball, producing a slow acceleration. The second serve (fig. 3.17b) is a more forceful hit behind the ball, causing a rapid acceleration. In this case,

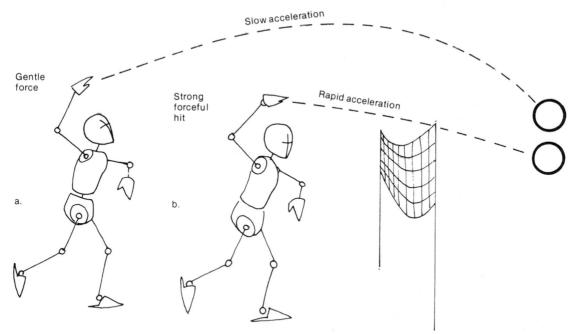

Figure 3.17

a. Gentle force exerted by volleyball player produces slow acceleration

b. Strong, forceful hit causes a rapid acceleration

3

the acceleration is directly proportional to the force. If the player makes the same forceful hit with a tennis ball, it will have a greater acceleration because its mass is much less than a volleyball's. Acceleration in this example is inversely proportional to the mass of the ball.

Law of Action-Reaction

The law of action-reaction: For every action there is an equal and opposite reaction. The tug-of-war (fig. 3.18) can be used to illustrate this law to elementary school children. The distance that Team A moves backward is equal to the distance that Team B has been forced to move forward. And in swimming a child moves forward by pushing backward against the resistance of the water. The water is pushing the child forward with a force equal to the force that he is exerting in his backward body movements.

Although this principle is relatively hard to explain to children, and at times to adults, it applies to all movements directed away from a hard surface. For example, when a child jumps

Figure 3.18

up to tip a basketball, the floor pushes back with a force equal to that which the child has exerted downward through his feet. There is an equal and opposite reaction. Also, to receive the maximum reaction force, the surface that the force is exerted against must be stable. For instance, a hard surface (fig. 3.19a) allows a runner to push off with a maximum thrust because there is an equal and opposite reaction between the foot and the hard surface. But on a grass surface (fig. 3.19b) or soft mud or sand (fig. 3.19c), the surface gives and thus decreases the force that propels the runner forward.

Types of Motion

There are two basic ways the human body or an object can move—in a *linear,* or translatory, motion and in a *rotary,* or angular, motion. All forms of motion, human or mechanical, are linear, rotary, or a combination of the two.

Linear Motion

A linear motion is the movement of a body or an object as a whole in a straight line with uniform speed. Examples are the human body being carried by another object, such as a car or skis. In this type of motion, the body takes on the same motion as the object carrying it. The human body can also move in a linear pathway, as in a walking or running movement; this, however, is a pathway of movement that is the result of the rotary action of the leg at the hip joint.

Rotary Motion

Rotary motion is a movement that traces an arc or circle around an axis or a fixed point. As the radius of the circle becomes smaller, the rotary speed increases. For example, in the first phase of a forward roll, the radius is large because of the partial extension of the legs and trunk (fig. 3.20a). As the performer tucks and rolls, he is decreasing the radius (fig. 3.20b). When the roll is completed, the legs and trunk are extended, thus lengthening the radius and slowing the forward motion (fig. 3.20c).

Law of Action-Reaction

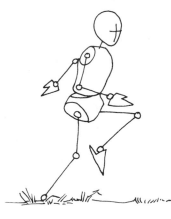

a. Hard road provides a stable surface.

b. Grass field gives, thus reducing force.

c. Soft sand or mud gives even more, with a much greater decrease in force.

Figure 3.19

Rotary Motion

a. Slow rotary speed
Figure 3.20

b. Shorter radius and faster speed

c. Larger radius and slower speed

Virtually all physical skills involve a combination of linear and rotary motions. Movements normally begin with a rotary action of the body, then transfer to linear speed. In running, for instance, the rotary action of the legs at the hip joints is converted into linear speed to move the body forward. Similarly, as a ball leaves the thrower's hand it is converted from the rotary motion of the arm and shoulder into a linear motion. As the ball travels through the air the motion begins to change into a curvilinear motion because of the forces of gravity and air resistance. Curvilinear motion follows a curved pathway, rather than the true arc or circle of rotary motion.

Force

According to K. F. Wells, force can be felt and its effect can be seen and measured, but force itself, like the wind, is invisible (1971). Force is the effect that one body has on another. This can be the movement of one body by another, such as a child throwing a ball, hitting a softball, or volleying a ball. Force can also be the stopping of one body by another, such as the tackler who stops the ball carrier. Finally, force can be resistance against movement, such as the performance of isometric exercises or a wrestler in a defensive position preventing his opponent from moving him. Force, then, is the push or pull exerted against something.

There are several principles relating to the production, direction, and absorption of force that teachers should understand in order to help children execute movement skills with ease, efficiency, and safety.

Production of Force

The total effective force of a movement is the sum of all forces produced by the muscle groups applied in the same direction and in a proper sequence. The jump-reach stunt illustrated here shows this principle, as well as related factors that must be considered when executing any forceful movement.

Any muscular action that is intended to move the body weight must have a firm base of action (stability). The child in figure 3.21a has his legs spread reasonably apart and his knees bent to lower his center of gravity. More force is available from strong muscles than from weak ones, and the flexed-knee position will allow the boy to begin his jump by contracting his thigh muscles, the strongest muscles of the body. As stated earlier, the total effective force of the movement is the sum of all forces produced by the muscle groups in the same direction. This means that the jump should be executed in a continuous movement, beginning with the extension of the legs, then stretching upward (fig. 3.21b), and finally, fully extending the body (fig. 3.21c).

In all forceful movements, continuity or flow from one part through another and the timing of each muscle group contraction are prerequisites for achieving maximum results. One only needs to swing a softball bat forward to understand the importance of continuity and the cumulative effect of a properly executed forceful action.

Direction of Force

When initiating a forceful movement, the force should be directed through the center of the body weight toward the object. In the jumping procedure illustrated in figure 3.21a, the weight of the body is directly over and midway between the feet. When making a forward movement, the force should be applied through the center of weight and in the direction in which it is intended to go. In figure 3.22 the center of gravity is too high and too far back to gain maximum force. By bending and leaning forward (fig. 3.23), the child shifts his weight forward in the direction of the intended forceful action.

Perhaps one of the most important areas of concern is the application of force when lifting heavy objects. "Lift with the legs and not the back" is an overriding principle.

The child in figure 3.24 is attempting to lift the trunk, but his center of gravity is too high and too far forward. When he applies force, it will be upward and backward, decreasing the maximum forces that could have been applied in

a

b

c

Figure 3.21

Figure 3.22 Center of gravity (white circle) too high and too far back

Figure 3.23 Center of gravity shifted

3

Figure 3.24 Center of gravity (white circle) too high and too far forward

Figure 3.25 Center of gravity lowered and moved closer to object

an upward direction. He is also in a vulnerable position, as too great a strain may be placed on his back muscles. The potential force of the leg muscles in assisting the upward movement is almost negligible here. But in figure 3.25 the child has moved his center of gravity closer to the trunk and, lower, by flexing his legs. A forceful movement can now be made by extending the weight upward.

Absorption of Force

When it is necessary to absorb the impact of a forceful movement or object, the shock should be spread over as large an area as possible or as long a distance as possible or both. (Bunn 1955). This principle applies to receiving a blow, landing from a height, or catching or trapping a ball. The essential point is to gradually decrease the force of the movement or object. In figures 3.26b

and 3.26c the gymnast has landed, flexing his knees to absorb part of the downward and forward momentum and using the remaining forward momentum to execute the forward roll. He has gradually and systematically dissipated the forward momentum.

Other examples of gradually spreading the shock of a forceful movement are catching an oncoming ball with arms extended forward, then recoiling the arms, or a football player who rolls after falling on the ball.

The principles relating to balance, motion, and force are important considerations when teaching virtually every skill and movement pattern. Children should learn these principles through their own performances and with the teacher explaining the basic concepts in a meaningful way.

Absorption of Force

a   b   c

Figure 3.26

Posture and Physical Fitness

4

Age, Height and Weight

Posture

Physical Fitness

Methods of Assessing
Physical Fitness

Improving Posture and
Physical Fitness

Cumulative Assessment of
Physical Fitness

Most elementary teachers know that it is important for their students to have good postures and to maintain optimum levels of health and physical fitness. Their role, then, is to determine their students' physical status and plan appropriate activities. This chapter presents methods of assessing health and physical fitness and outlines activity programs and evaluative techniques available to classroom teachers.

In most school districts medical examinations are required on a regular basis. The classroom teacher should be made aware of the results, particularly for children with such conditions as rheumatic fever or birth anomalies who may require special considerations in the physical education program. There are other periodic evaluations that the teacher can make to help her understand and plan for each child's growth and developmental needs. Several of the more important assessment areas are described in this chapter, along with special programs for improving posture and physical fitness.

Age, Height, and Weight

A periodic record of age, height, and weight can be an important aid in assessing the child's normal growth. It should be recognized, however, that most height and weight tables available are based upon age and do not take into consideration such factors as physiological maturity and bone density. Therefore, these tables should be used only as guidelines. The important factor in height-weight assessments is detecting radical changes through the school year. Thus it is wise to take such measurements at least twice a year, and preferably three times (see the cumulative physical fitness record on page 67).

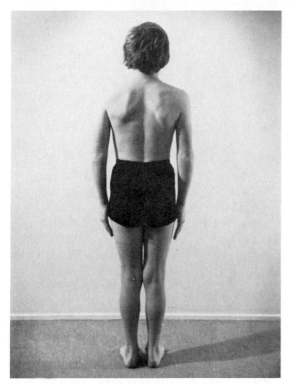

Figure 4.1 Good posture

Posture

Parents, teachers, and school officials have always been concerned about children's postures, particularly since there appears to be a strong relationship between such factors as perceptual acuity, emotional health, and general fitness. Slanting desks, adjustable chalkboards, and improved lighting were all installed to enhance and maintain correct posture. But chronic television viewing and inadequate daily exercise for many children have continued to produce numerous postural problems, which are readily detectable and can be corrected by vigorous exercise.

Good Posture

There is no clear definition or standard of "good" posture that can be applied to all children, whether they are standing, sitting, or moving. Standing posture is judged by the alignment

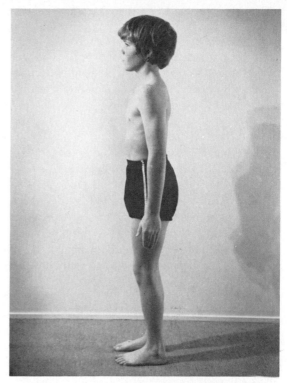

Figure 4.2 . . . natural curves of the body are moderate

of body segments. The child in figures 4.1 and 4.2 has good posture because his body segments are evenly balanced over the base of support. Viewed from the side, the plumb line runs from a little in front of the ankle through the knee, pelvis, shoulders, and ear. In this position the natural curves of the body are moderate, with the head, shoulders, pelvis, knees, and feet balanced evenly on each side of the line. Viewed from the back, the plumb line runs midway through the head, vertebrae, and hips, and equidistant between the feet.

If a child has good posture, a minimum contraction of anti-gravity muscle groups is required to keep his body erect and balanced. But when a child slouches, his upper back muscles must contract to shift the body to the correct posture. If he continues to slouch, his muscles will gradually adapt to that position and he might have a chronic poor posture if it is not corrected.

4

Common Posture Problems

Most of the typical posture deviations of young children can be observed and corrected with proper exercise. The following deviations can be observed when the child is standing beside a plumb line.

Round Back (Kyphosis)

A round back, or kyphosis, is a marked increase in the curve of the upper back (fig. 4.3). The head and shoulders are usually held in a forward position, and the backward curve of the upper body causes the pelvis to tilt forward slightly and the knees to bend somewhat. This condition places an increased strain on the upper back muscles and shifts the weight of the body to the front of the foot.

Hollow Back (Lordosis)

Hollow back, or lordosis, is an exaggerated forward curve of the lower back (fig. 4.4). The most common signs are a protruding abdomen, a swayback, and hyperextension of the knees.

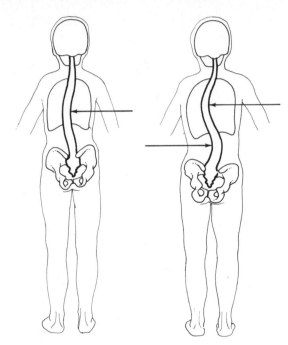

Figure 4.5 Lateral curvature (Scoliosis)—C-type curve, left, and S-type curve, right

Lateral Curvature (Scoliosis)

A lateral curvature, or scoliosis, can be C-shaped, extending the length of the spinal column, or S-shaped, with a small curve on the upper back and a compensating curve on the lower back (fig. 4.5). The C-shaped curve is normally toward the left since most children are right-handed and tend to lean to the weaker side. This comes from the constant elevation of the right arm and the tendency to lean toward the left side of the desk while writing and performing other sitting activities.

Methods of Assessing Posture

In the majority of elementary schools, the classroom teacher is in the best position to assess her students' postures. Most teachers are genuinely concerned about the way a child sits at his desk and how he moves in his daily activities. For most teachers, the evaluation of posture is primarily one of continual subjective observation. When she notices a major change in a child's posture, the teacher brings in the school nurse

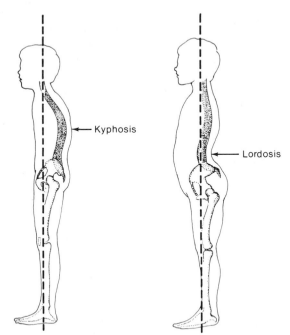

Figure 4.3 Round back (Kyphosis)

Figure 4.4 Hollow back (lordosis)

or parent to determine whether the change is due to a muscular weakness or to other factors, such as nutrition, eyesight, or an emotional disturbance.

If a teacher wishes to use a simple screening test, she might consider the side- and rear-view plumb line test. The accompanying posture chart can be used in various ways, depending on the interests of the teacher, the ages of the children, and the time available. Most teachers can complete the test in the classroom.

Posture Chart

Name: _____

Date: _____
First Evaluation: _____
Second Evaluation: _____
Third Evaluation: _____

Key to score:

Normal	0
Slight	1
Moderate	2
Severe	3

Side View	First Evaluation	Second Evaluation	Third Evaluation
Body Lean: Forward			
Backward			
Forward Head			
Round Shoulders			
Round Dorsal Curve			
Protruding Abdomen			
Hyperextended Knees			
Back View			
Head Tilt:			
to right			
to left			
Shoulder:			
lower on right			
lower on left			
Bow Legs			
Knock Knees			
Feet pointing out			
Feet pointing in			
Curve of Vertebrae:			
C curve			
S curve			

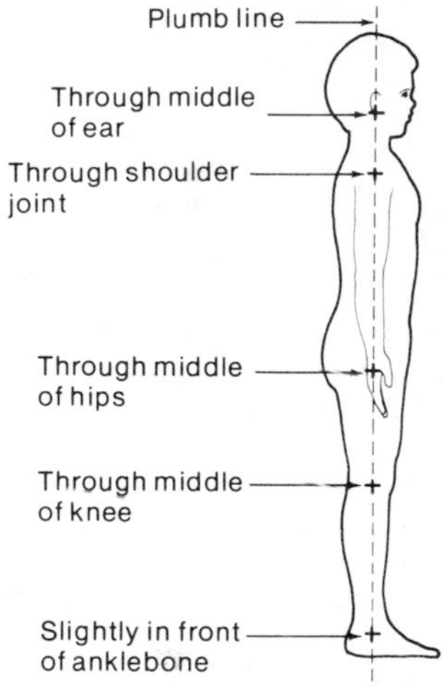

Plumb line
Through middle of ear
Through shoulder joint
Through middle of hips
Through middle of knee
Slightly in front of anklebone

Figure 4.6 Side view

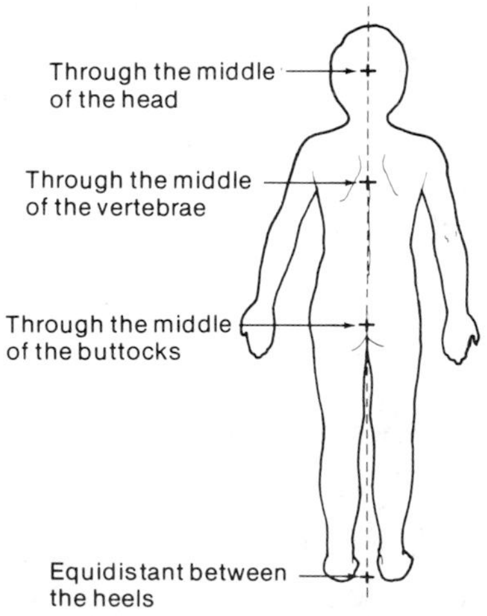

Through the middle of the head
Through the middle of the vertebrae
Through the middle of the buttocks
Equidistant between the heels

Figure 4.7 Back view

4

Physical Fitness

There has been a major emphasis on physical fitness for elementary school children during the past two decades. The President's Council on Youth Fitness has done much to make the public aware of the physical fitness needs of children, youth, and adults. National and state physical education organizations have provided consulting services, testing manuals, and program guides and have sponsored numerous workshops and conferences for teachers. The results of all this interest are improved programs and a general increase in the physical fitness level of elementary school children.

Accompanying this interest and improvement has been a continuous problem within the profession to define "physical fitness" and to earmark the aspects of fitness that should be stressed in an elementary school physical education program. One of the most all-inclusive definitions of physical fitness was given by a representative group of the American Alliance for Health, Physical Education and Recreation (AAHPER 1976).

Fitness is that state which characterizes the degree to which the person is able to function. Fitness is an individual matter. It implies that ability of each person to live most effectively with his potential. Ability to function depends upon the physical, mental, emotional and social components of fitness, all of which are related to each other and mutually interdependent.

Many elementary teachers would agree with this definition, and would say that they contribute to one or more of these general areas of fitness in the classroom. There is general agreement in physical education that "physical fitness" is just one aspect of total fitness.

The definition, however, gives little guidance as to what aspects of fitness should be stressed in the physical education program. A definition for the physical education program, therefore, is necessary before any program can be designed. So we describe a physically fit child as one who possesses adequate strength and endurance to carry out daily activities without undue fatigue and still has sufficient energy to enjoy leisure activities and to meet emergencies.

Components of Physical Fitness

Although there are differing views about which basic components of physical fitness should be measured, the majority of the published test batteries include most of the elements described in this section. A low score on such tests indicates that the child does not possess the strength and vitality to carry out everyday experiences and to respond to emergencies. It can reveal not only a lack of exercise but also possible nutritional needs or congenital or temporary illnesses that could be the cause of low fitness.

Strength
Strength is defined as the amount of force that a muscle or group of muscles can exert. The importance of developing and maintaining muscular strength cannot be overemphasized. Without sufficient strength, the other components of physical fitness—endurance, flexibility, agility, neuromuscular skills—cannot be developed to their full potential.

Endurance
Endurance is the ability to continue a muscular effort over a prolonged period. There are two basic types of endurance in physical performance, muscular endurance and cardiorespiratory endurance. Muscular endurance is the ability of the muscles to continue to function over a period of time; it is primarily dependent upon the strength and physiological condition of the muscle groups involved in the movement. Cardiorespiratory endurance is the efficiency of the heart, circulatory systems, and lungs while performing a continuous movement over a period of time.

Power
Power is the capacity of the body to apply maximum muscular contraction at the quickest possible speed. It is an explosive action in which

maximum muscular force is released at maximum speed. Power is fundamental to performing such skills as jumping, kicking, and throwing.

Flexibility

Flexibility is the range and ease of movement of a joint. The amount of flexibility is dependent upon the structure and nature of the joint(s) involved, the nature of the ligaments surrounding the joint and the extensibility of the muscles relating to the joint. Although flexibility appears to be more of a specific quality relating to one or more joints in a particular movement, it is considered as a general quality in elementary school programs. If a child has a relatively high degree of flexibility he can absorb an on-coming force or blow through a wider range of movement. Flexibility, or suppleness of movements, is also a prerequisite in performing many gymnastic and creative dance movements.

Agility

Agility is the ability to move or shift the body in a different direction with speed and efficiency. Agility is essentially the interrelationship of speed, strength, and coordination and, as such, it involves both innate capacity and training. It is important in gymnastics, track and field, and all individual and team game activities, and is a prerequisite safety skill for the child's everyday play and work experiences.

Speed

Speed is the ability to perform successive movements in the shortest period of time. Speed, like agility, is, in part, innate, yet can be improved through practice.

Methods of Assessing Physical Fitness

There is a wide variety of standardized physical fitness test batteries for elementary school children; some of the more commonly used ones are listed in the accompanying chart. Each

teacher should consult with the local supervisor of physical education or the respective State Department of Public Instruction to determine which test battery should be used.

If no standardized test is recommended, the teacher should evaluate the tests listed on the basis of the following considerations. The test should be a reliable and valid measure of the basic components of physical fitness. Each test item should be readily adaptable to the varying, and sometimes unique, conditions that exist in many elementary schools. Available facilities, the ages of the children, and the size of the class must also be considered. Finally, each test item should be highly motivating and, so far as possible, free of elements that could cause accidents or injury.

Improving Posture and Physical Fitness

As defined earlier, physical fitness is the possession of adequate strength and vitality to carry out daily activities and meet emergencies. In its broadest meaning, then, physical fitness should be considered as a means to an end rather than an end in itself.

Playing a vigorous game such as basketball or soccer requires a high level of endurance. If a child, or the class, does not possess sufficient muscular and organic endurance to play the game, the teacher should take appropriate remedial measures—longer warm-up periods involving continuous movement. Likewise, a boy who cannot perform the "skin-the-cat" on the horizontal bar may well need additional shoulder girdle strength rather than a correction in his motor skill pattern.

Not only is physical fitness important for performance of motor skills, but a high level of physical fitness also is usually indicative of optimum physical and mental well-being. Children with abundant physical vitality generally are organically sound, mentally alert, and socially well-adjusted. For these reasons, classroom teachers should test children early in the school

Table 4.1 Physical Fitness Tests for Elementary School Children

Name of Test	Approp. Age or Grade Level	Items Contained in Test Battery	Source
President's Council Youth Physical Fitness Screening Test	Ages 6-17	Pull-ups Sit-ups Squat thrusts	Youth Physical Fitness. U.S. Government Printing Office, Washington, D.C. 1967
AAHPER Youth Fitness Test	Grade 5-College	Pull-ups Sit-ups Shuttle run Standing broad jump 50-yd. dash Softball throw 600-yard run-walk	AAHPER 1201 16th Street Washington, D.C.
New York State Physical Fitness Test	Grades 4-12	Posture test Target throw Modified push-up Side-step 50-yard dash Squat stand Treadmill	Department of Education, Albany, New York
Elementary School Physical Fitness Test	Ages 6-12	Standing broad jump Bench push-ups Curl-ups Squat-jump 30-yard dash	A description of this test battery and accompanying norms for each age level may be found in Kirchner, *Physical Education for Elementary School Children,* 2nd ed. 1970, Chapter 19.
Oregon Motor Fitness Test	Grades 4-6	Push-ups (boys) Knee touch sit-ups (boys) Flexed arm hang (girls) Curl-ups (girls) Standing broad jump	State Department of Education, Salem, Oregon
Canadian Physical Performance Test Manual	Ages 7-17	Sit-up Standing broad jump Shuttle run Flexed arm hang 50-yard run 300-yard run	Canadian Association for Health, Physical Education and Recreation, 333 River Road, Vanier City, Ontario, Canada

year to determine general and specific areas of weakness and then select appropriate activities to correct these deficiencies.

The procedure and activities described in the following sections will help the teacher evaluate her class's current level of physical fitness and select appropriate physical activities to meet individual and group needs.

Determining Areas of Need

Each class should take a physical fitness test during the first few weeks of the school year. Once the scores are recorded on a class score sheet, a general diagnosis of the class can be made. In the following illustration, both boys and girls scored well above average in the standing broad jump and the thirty-yard dash, so little additional emphasis would need to be given to activities that would improve power and speed.

	Power	Strength and Endurance			Speed	Total
	Standing Broad Jump	Bench Push-ups	Curl-ups	Squat Jumps	30-yard dash	Physical Fitness
Boys	70% above average	90% below average	60% below average	90% below average	75% above average	65% below average
Girls	75% above average	92% below average	70% below average	95% below average	80% above average	70% below average

TEST ITEMS

On the other hand, the poor results of the middle three tests involving strength and endurance reveal a definite need for activities that will increase the strength and endurance of the arm and shoulder girdle and the abdominal and leg muscles. In the majority of cases where the scores of the three middle test items are low, the total physical fitness score also is low. So by increasing the performance in these three items, the total fitness score obviously will also show a proportionate increase.

An individual analysis can also be made of each child to determine specific areas of weakness. Any child who has extremely low scores on all the test items should be referred to the school nurse or family doctor for additional diagnosis. Low scores, particularly for a child who appears to be healthy, often indicate that the child could be suffering from nutritional deficiencies or a temporary illness. If competent medical authorities say the diagnosis is simply lack of adequate exercise, appropriate remedial steps can be taken by the teacher and parent.

The plumb line test for posture can also be used in conjunction with a standardized physical fitness test. A basic screening test for posture will determine general areas of weakness and detect children who may need to be referred to their family physicians.

Selection of Appropriate Activities

Physical education teachers face the multiple purposes of providing vigorous physical activities, teaching motor skills, and providing experiences that will foster intellectual and social development. No single activity can accomplish all these goals. Furthermore, no single activity can contribute to all of the basic components of physical fitness described earlier. The value of the accompanying chart is that it shows how various activities contribute to these basic elements.

To illustrate the use of the chart, let us assume we have tested a fourth grade class in September and found results similar to those shown in the preceding score sheet. The class definitely needs activities that will increase the strength and endurance of the arm and shoulder girdle and the abdominal and leg muscles. During the first few months of the school year, pleasant weather and student interest would indicate that an outdoor activity would be the most suitable choice. The teacher had decided to begin with a four-week unit on soccer activities, but note in the chart that soccer as a "team game" is a low contributer to strength. So, recognizing this inherent weakness of the soccer activity and the need for activities involving strength, the teacher should emphasize warm-up exercises that develop strength in the arm and shoulder girdle and abdominal and leg muscles.

4

Other units of instruction involving games, dance, and gymnastic activities should be analyzed for their potential contribution to physical fitness. Once the inherent limitations of the activity are known, supplemental activities can be included to meet the physical fitness needs of the class.

Specialized Exercise Programs

There are several types of physical fitness activities and programs that can be used either as a supplement to the regular physical education lesson or as a special remedial program. Remedial programs can be designed for a special remedial class or as an individualized program that a child can do during the regular physical education period or at home. The type of exercise program that is selected, however, should be based upon the following three principles of exercise (Clarke and Clarke 1963):

1. The exercise or activity should be adapted to the individual's exercise tolerance.

This means that the child should be able to perform an exercise or activity without undue discomfort or fatigue. There are several cues to determine the child's exercise tolerance. One is to check the scores on a physical fitness test, particularly for those parts that are similar to the exercises in the physical fitness program. If a child's performance in arm and shoulder girdle strength tests was low, the teacher should expect an initial low tolerance in push-ups and pull-ups. With practice, the child's strength will improve, along with his tolerance level. Perhaps the single best means of determining a child's tolerance to an activity is the teacher's own judgment based upon such factors as the child's breathlessness, slow recuperation, and excessively sore muscles.

Table 4.2 Activities for Posture and Physical Fitness

Type of Activity	Strength		Endurance		Power		Speed		Agility		Flexibility		Posture	
	H.	L.	H.	L.	H.	L.	H.	L.	H.	L.	H.	L.	H.	L.
Game Activities														
Relays		x	x		x		x		x			x	x	
Tag Games		x	x		x		x		x			x		x
Simple Team Games		x	x		x		x		x			x		x
Individual and Team Games		x	x		x		x		x			x		x
Dance Activities														
Fundamental Skills		x		x		x		x	x		x		x	
Singing Games		x		x		x		x			x			x
Folk Dances		x		x		x		x	x			x	x	
Creative Rhythms		x		x	x			x	x		x		x	
Gymnastic Activities														
Conditioning Exercises	x		x		x				x		x		x	
Vaulting Box	x		x		x			x	x		x			x
Balance Beam		x	x			x	x		x		x		x	
Rope Skipping	x		x				x	x	x		x		x	
Horizontal Bar	x		x		x				x		x		x	
Climbing Rope	x		x		x				x			x	x	
Stunts and Tumbling	x		x		x		x		x		x		x	
Swedish Gym	x		x		x				x		x		x	
Climbing Cube	x		x		x				x		x		x	
Overhead Ladder	x		x		x				x		x		x	
Agility Apparatus	x		x		x				x		x		x	

2. *The exercise or activity should require an overload performance for each individual.*

An overload performance requires the individual to exert more than his normal effort. If the child can do four chin-ups, an overload performance would be to require him to try five or six. We can increase the overload in endurance activities by reducing the time it takes to run a certain distance or by increasing the distance and holding the time constant.

3. *The exercise or activity should provide for progression.*

This principle is closely associated with the previous two. Any planned exercise program must begin where it is comfortable or within the tolerance level of the child. From there, the program should gradually overload the muscles to increase strength or to increase the demands upon the heart and lungs.

The following exercise programs adhere to these basic principles of exercise. The type of program the teacher selects will depend upon the needs of her class or the individual child who may need a special type of posture or physical fitness program.

Jogging

Jogging is an easy or relaxed run that does not place undue fatigue upon the runner. It is one of the most effective and enjoyable means of improving muscular and cardiovascular endurance. If taught correctly, elementary children—including first graders—can participate in jogging activities in the gymnasium, on the playing field, or in a cross-country setting.

The proper form is like that of a distance runner, with the body erect and relaxed and the arms swinging in an easy manner. The heel of the foot should contact the ground, the foot should then rock forward to a gentle push off the front of the foot.

Before introducing jogging to the elementary school physical education program, it should be presented to young children as a recreational activity. Jogging should not be seen as a prerequisite to competitive cross-country running; rather, it should be seen as an activity in which the child can derive enjoyment and success as he increases the distance he can run without undue fatigue or strain. This means each child should set his own goals. And other activities should be interspersed with jogging, since young children may become bored with the same jogging pace and with such tracks as "around the gymnasium" or "around the outside of the playing field."

The basic approach used to teach children to jog is to have them begin with a walk. When they feel ready, they can begin to jog as far as they can without feeling overfatigued or out of breath. Once the children learn to pace themselves to a jog-walk-jog pattern, introduce a few basic calisthenics that can be performed halfway through the walk. Introducing these exercises early in the jogging program is not only beneficial in developing strength and flexibility, but it will also improve the child's running ability.

After a few days of basic jog-walk-jog activities, introduce the "scout's pace." Have each child jog 110 yards, walk 55 yards, jog 110 yards, continuing the pattern as long as possible. The actual distances can be adjusted to the child's or the class's ability and condition.

As soon as the majority of the children can jog a reasonable distance, such as a mile, introduce other jogging activities into the program, such as "hash running" (page 371), orienteering (page 215), or establishing a 100-mile club, all of which involve enjoyable recreational jogging. The 100-mile club is a program in which each child keeps his own jogging "log" or record sheet. He might receive a certificate when he reaches 100 miles; however, if the jogging program has been introduced correctly the child should find that completing 100 miles is valuable in itself and he has little need for a badge or certificate.

Circuit Training

Circuit training is repeating one or more exercises as many times as possible within a time limit. A simple circuit would be doing six push-ups, ten curl-ups, and eighteen toe touches within two minutes. The number and type of exercises are optional and the variations, unlimited.

This type of conditioning exercise program has many advantages, particularly for the self-contained classroom teacher. In the first place, circuit training allows for individual differences. In the example that follows, the number of repetitions of each exercise is determined by each child, not by the most physically fit child in the class. And one of the most important administrative advantages is the time limit. The teacher determines how much time she wants to devote to circuit training, then proceeds to develop a tailor-made program to meet the needs of her class.

An example is provided to show how to develop a circuit for each member of your class.

Step No. 1: Determine how much time you want to spend on the circuit. Time might range from six to ten minutes; our example is six minutes.

Step No. 2: Select appropriate exercises. Let us assume the teacher has administered a physical fitness test (page 42) and has noted that the majority of students show low strength and endurance in the arm and shoulder girdle (bench push-ups), abdominal muscles (curl-ups), and leg muscles (squat jumps). The circuit

training program thus should contain exercises that will improve these weaknesses. The four exercises shown in the following chart and in figures 4.8-4.11 would meet these needs.

No. 1 Bicycle

Figure 4.8 Rest body weight on head, shoulders, and elbows. Raise trunk and legs and place hands on hips. Extend left leg straight up and flex right leg. Simultaneously lower left leg and extend right leg. Start movement with a slow cadence and gradually increase speed.

Exercises	Maximum Number	Training Dose No. 1 (¼ dose)	Jan. 15	Jan. 16	Jan. 17	etc.
1. Bicycle (legs)	16	4				
2. Push-ups (arms and shoulders)	8	2				
3. Head raiser (trunk)	6	2				
4. Chest raiser (trunk)	11	3				

No. 2: Push-ups

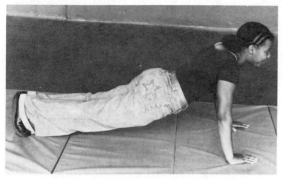

Figure 4.9 Begin in a front lying position, with hands approximately shoulder-width apart and fingers pointing forward. The head should be a few inches off the floor. Extend arms while keeping the back and legs in a straight line.

No. 3 Head Raiser

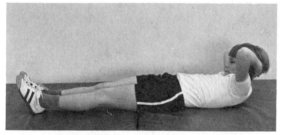

Figure 4.10 Begin in a back lying position, with legs together and hands laced behind neck. Keep seat and legs on floor and raise head upward and forward.

No. 4 Chest Raiser

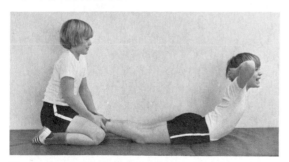

Figure 4.11 One partner assumes a front lying position with his hands laced behind his head. The "anchor" man holds his partner's feet down and places his hands just above the ankles. Lower partner raises head and chest off the floor and keeps elbows sideward throughout movement.

Step No. 3. Determine the maximum number of repetitions for each exercise. This is the first day involving exercise. Start with exercise number 1, the bicycle. All children attempt to do the exercise as many times as they can in one minute. Record the number of repetitions under the maximum number column in the sample chart. Let us assume this is the chart of a fifth grade girl who has performed sixteen bicycle repetitions. Immediately following this test, let the children rest for one minute. Next, have them do as many push-ups as possible in one minute. Let them rest for one minute and continue the procedure to the head raiser and chest raiser.

Step No. 4: Set the training dose. The training dose (see chart) is the actual number of repetitions the child will perform when she starts her circuit program. It might be one-quarter, one-half, or three-quarters of the maximum number. As a suggestion, start with one-quarter of the maximum number as the child's first training dose. Place these numbers in the first training dose column. Now the child is ready to perform her circuit without any rest between each exercise. In other words, she must try to complete the following three laps of exercises in six minutes:

Lap No. 1	Lap No. 2	Lap No. 3
4 bicycles	4 bicycles	4 bicycles
2 push-ups	2 push-ups	2 push-ups
2 head raisers	2 head raisers	2 head raisers
3 chest raisers	3 chest raisers	3 chest raisers

Step No. 5: Attempt to complete the circuit. Each child has six minutes to complete the circuit. Let us assume this girl has completed one lap in two minutes. Now, without rest, she starts her second lap. This lap takes her 2½ minutes, leaving 1½ minutes to complete the third lap. She immediately starts her third lap and gets to exercise number 2, the push-ups, when the whistle blows. Record her results under the appropriate date. She completed two laps and was on exercise number 2 of the third lap, so "3-2" would be recorded under the date and opposite push-ups.

Step No. 6: Continue step number five until the child can perform three laps within the time limit. Then increase each exercise by one repetition. Our girl would now do five bicycles, three push-ups, three head raisers, and four chest raisers.

The length of time the teacher devotes to a circuit training program depends upon several factors. The most important consideration is the class's physical fitness needs. If the class scored low on the physical fitness test, it would be wise to require a daily circuit for five to six weeks. The teacher might also want to design a ten-minute circuit to be performed in the classroom on those days when her class does not have access to the gymnasium. In this case, she should consider student interest and change the exercises in the circuit each month.

There is a wonderful opportunity here to help the child who scores extremely low on the physical fitness test. First, attempt to determine the reasons for the low fitness, such as extreme obesity or chronic lack of exercise. Design a circuit for the child to do at home. This may involve drawing stick figures to explain the exercises and sending a short note to the parents or interviewing them. The results may be tremendous if the teacher shows an interest, making periodic checks with the child and the parents.

Obstacle Course

An obstacle course is an arrangement of small equipment and large apparatus designed to improve one or more of the components of physical fitness. Commerical obstacle courses normally include apparatus to climb, balance upon, vault over, and crawl through. This type of apparatus is basically for use outdoors and normally is permanently anchored to the ground. Homemade obstacle courses using the natural building materials of a region have become very popular in many elementary schools. They are generally built by parents and usually have a theme, such as a western fort or outpost, space travel, or a jungle trek.

Portable obstacle courses can be made with the equipment and apparatus available in the school. These courses have several advantages —they can be arranged in different patterns, and they can be located in a gymnasium or on the playground. Following is an indoor obstacle course that requires a minimum amount of small and large apparatus used in an imaginative and constructive way.

Each child tries to complete the course as quickly as possible. The items along this obstacle course contribute to physical fitness in the following ways:

1. Mount Everest: Climbing improves strength and power.
2. The Snake: Running through the hoops, placing alternate feet in them, improves agility.
3. The Tunnel: Crawling through improves strength and endurance of the arm and shoulder girdle.
4. Hurdles: Jumping over them improves leg power.
5. Superkid: Climbing the rope as high as possible improves strength in arm and shoulder girdle.
6. Tightrope Walk: Walking across balance bench improves balance.
7. The Maze: Hopping through beanbag course improves strength and power of legs.
8. Leapfrog: Straddle jumping over traffic cones (or milk cartons) improves the power of the legs.

Assign one child to start at each station in order to provide maximum participation and avoid confusion and collisions. On the "go" signal each child tackles the task at his station, then continues through the obstacle course until he has completed all eight tasks. If you can duplicate stations two, seven, and eight, it would be possible to begin with two students at each station.

Children thoroughly enjoy indoor and outdoor obstacles courses. Once the students understand the basic purpose of an obstacle course, they should have an opportunity to plan their own. Their designs are usually very imaginative and more demanding than the "teacher-designed course."

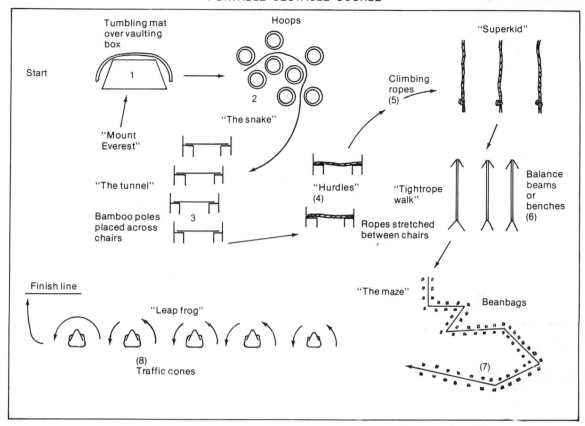

Conditioning Exercises

Conditioning, or calisthenic, exercises have traditionally been used as a warm-up activity at the beginning of a physical education lesson. The fundamental purposes of these exercises are to develop physical fitness and to prepare the body for the main activities of the lesson. Normally, the warm-up begins with a vigorous activity, such as running around the gymnasium, followed by exercises for the neck, arm and shoulder girdle, trunk, and legs. The warm-up period normally lasts about five to ten minutes; however, time allotments vary from class to class.

The following suggestions can make the conditioning exercises effective and enjoyable:

1. Demonstrate the exercise, then have the class perform it slowly so each child can learn the correct form and cadence.

2. Once the children know the exercise, let them do the repetitions at their own rates. This is particularly important when performing flexibility exercises, since children's body structures and potential ranges of movement vary.

3. Add variations to each exercise. For example, "trunk bending forward and backward" can be changed on each forward movement by such directions as "through the legs," "to the left side," or "with right foot in front."

4. Change the basic set of exercises on alternate days.

5. Develop a program of running, stopping, performing an exercise, then running again. Continue the pattern through a series of exercises.

6. Intersperse basic conditioning exercises with yoga or isometric exercises.

The exercises in figures 4.12 to 4.26 are arranged according to neck, arm and shoulder girdle, trunk, and leg exercises. Select one exercise from each category for each warm-up activity. These exercises can also be used for individual remedial programs, performed by children within the regular physical education period or recorded on a "take-home" sheet with the suggested number of repetitions. Parents receiving this information usually make sure their children do the exercises and sometimes even do them with their youngsters.

Neck Exercises

a

b

Figure 4.12 *Head Circling*

a. Begin with the feet apart, arms at sides, shoulders square (not elevated), and head resting on the right shoulder.

b. Rotate head backward, sideward, forward, and back to starting position. Reverse directions and repeat movement.

a

b

Figure 4.13 *Head Pull*

a. Stand with feet slightly apart, back straight, chin on chest, and hands behind head. Elbows should be pointing straight ahead.

b. Lift head up and back and stretch elbows sideways and backward. This exercise may be varied by resisting with the hands as the head shifts back.

a

b

Figure 4.14 *Head Push*

a. Begin in a back lying position with knees bent and hands behind the head.

b. Push head forward and upward, allowing the chin to touch the chest.

Arm and Shoulder Exercises

a

b

Figure 4.15 *Arm Rotators*

a. Stand with feet together, back straight, and arms extended sideways.

b. Rotate arms forward, upward, and backward in a circular movement. Gradually increase the size of the circle and change direction of arm movement after three or four rotations.

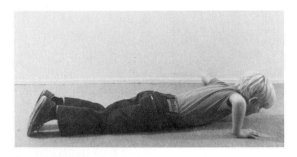

a

b

Figure 4.16 *Push-ups*

a. Begin in a front lying position with hands approximately shoulder-width apart and fingers pointing forward. The chin should be a few inches off the floor.

b. Extend arms, keeping the back and legs in a straight line. Vary this exercise by raising one leg as the body is raised off the floor. Also, instead of lowering the body straight down, lower it to one side.

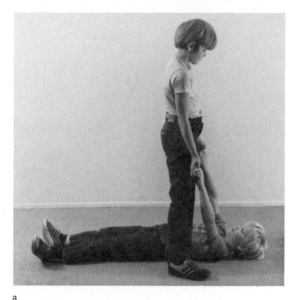

a

Figure 4.17 *Pull-ups*

a. One partner assumes a back lying position with the arms up. The other partner stands with his feet placed opposite the shoulders of the partner on the floor and extends his arms down. Both lock hands.

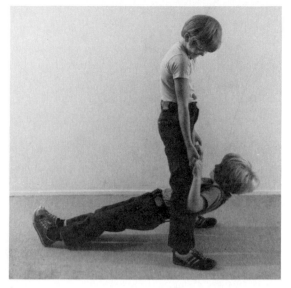

b

b. The standing partner holds his arms straight while the lower partner pulls his body up.

Trunk Exercises

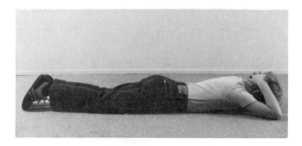

a

Figure 4.18 *Chest Raising*

a. Begin in a front lying position with legs straight and fingers laced behind the head.

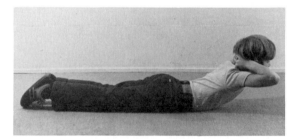

b

b. Keep legs on the floor and raise head and chest. Vary the exercise by keeping the head down and raising the legs or by raising the head and legs together.

a

b

Figure 4.19 *Side Toe Touch*

a. Stand with legs well apart and straight. Bend the trunk forward, extend the right arm backward and upward, and touch the right foot with the left hand.

b. Keep trunk bent forward and reverse arm positions.

a

b

Figure 4.20 *Curl-ups*

a. Lie on the back with knees bent and together and fingers laced behind the neck.

b. Keep the hands behind the neck and raise up and forward until the head or elbows touch the knees.

a

Figure 4.21 *Side Benders*

a. Stand with legs apart, right hand resting on right leg, and left arm raised above the head.

b

b. Drop left arm and raise right arm over head, then bend toward the left side.

a

Figure 4.22 *Side Stretch*

a. Sit on the left hip and extend both legs. Extend left arm and place left hand on the floor.

b

b. Place right hand on the hip and raise the body, keeping the left hand and feet on the floor until the legs and trunk form a straight line.

Leg Exercises

a

b

Figure 4.23 *Pull and Stretch*

a. Sit with legs apart, back straight, and hands resting on the floor beside the knees.

b. Bend the trunk toward the right side and grasp the foot with both hands. Repeat with the left side.

a

b

Figure 4.24 *Treadmill*

a. Lie facedown. Push off the floor with the arms to the elevated push-up position. Keep one leg extended and draw the other leg forward until the knee is under the chest.

b. Reverse leg positions in a continuous and simultaneous action.

a

Figure 4.25 *Squat Jump*

a. Begin in a crouched position with arms at the side of the legs and fingers resting on the floor.

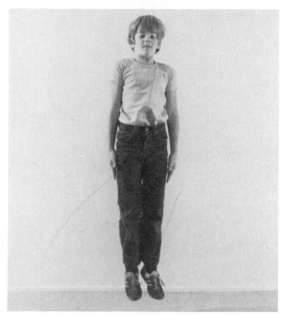

b

b. Push off mat and extend body until the feet are about four to six inches off the mat. The arms should remain at the sides for balance. Return to starting position and repeat.

a

Figure 4.26 *Jumping Jack*

a. Stand with arms at sides.

b

b. Simultaneously jump to a straddle position and raise arms overhead. Return to the original position and repeat. Vary the exercise by jumping to a stride position and changing position of feet on each jumping action.

Cat-Stretch

a. Begin in a kneeling position on all fours.

b. Inhale and rock slightly back and lower chest, trying to touch the throat to the floor.

c. Exhale and arch upward like an angry cat.

Figure 4.27

Yoga Activities

The yoga exercises in this section (fig. 4.27 to fig. 4.38) are a westernized version of an ancient Indian system of exercise. These exercises are basically stretching movements, performed much slower than calisthenics. The purpose of yoga exercises is to improve physical and organic health and the power of concentration. These exercises are also extremely good for developing flexibility and good postural habits.

Children from kindergarten to grade six thoroughly enjoy doing the animal-like movements of the yoga program. Since the movements are performed according to each child's ability, they can be used as an alternate form of warm-up activity, in the classroom, or at home under the parent's guidance. The following basic program will illustrate a few of the more popular movements. Additional exercises may be found in the references in Appendix A.

Basic Yoga Program

Every yoga program should begin with a warm-up activity and include a balance, a fitness, and a breathing exercise. The last exercise in the routine should be a relaxation pose. The accompanying sample program provides a guideline.

Individualized programs can be designed to help children with recognizable muscular weaknesses or posture problems, or to "calm down" a hyperactive child. Remember that a child need only stretch as far as he can; suppleness will improve with practice.

Sample Yoga Program

Warm-up	Rub, rock, roll, and cross-leg stretch
Balance	Wheel
Fitness	Cat Stretch
Fitness	Cobra
Fitness	Locust
Breathing	Breathing
Relaxation	Curling Leaf

Warm-up Activities. Warm-up movements should be quick and gentle. Begin by rubbing the body all over with the hands to increase circulation. Next, with knees slightly bent, hang down from the waist. Finally, rock back and forth on the back, then form a cross-legged position. Other warm-up poses are shown in figures 4.27 and 4.28. Hold each position about five seconds.

d. Inhale and bring right knee toward the head.

e. Exhale and stretch leg backward and upward and return.

Sun Salutation (Fitness)

a. Begin with hands together.

b. Inhale as the arms are raised up and back.

c. Exhale and bring arms forward and down. Try to keep legs straight.

Figure 4.28

Yoga Poses. The yoga poses in figures 4.29 to 4.38 are a few examples of balance, fitness, breathing, and relaxation poses. See the bibliography at the end of the book for additional exercises.

Cobra (Fitness)

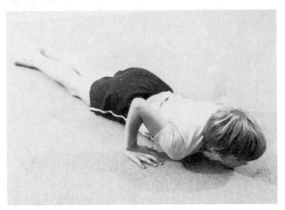

Figure 4.29a Start with body straight and hands at side of body.

Figure 4.29b Inhale and bring head up and back. Exhale and return to starting position.

Lion (Fitness)

Figure 4.30 Kneel with hands on thighs. Bend forward, slide fingers to floor, open eyes as wide as possible, and stick tongue out as far as possible, trying to touch the chin.

Bow (Fitness)

Figure 4.31a Start facedown with hands on floor. Inhale and grasp ankles.

Figure 4.31b Exhale and arch upward.

Crow (Balance)

a. Squat with hands about a foot apart.

Figure 4.32

b. Exhale, bend forward, press inside of knees against elbows, and lift toes off floor.

c. Variation: begin with hands spread far apart.

Locust (Fitness)

a. Start facedown with hands at side of body.

Figure 4.33

b. Inhale and raise one leg. Exhale and lower leg.

Plough (Fitness)

Figure 4.34a Lie on back with body straight, arms at sides, and palms down.

Figure 4.34b Exhale and raise legs up and over the head, and stretch toes away from the body.

c. Advanced: Repeat, raising both legs at once as high as they will go.

Warrior (Fitness and balance)

a. Begin in an upright kneeling position with knees together and feet spread apart.

b. Exhale and lower body until the back rests on the floor. (Use hands for support.)

c. Continue to full arch, resting palms on floor.

Figure 4.35

Wheel (Balance)

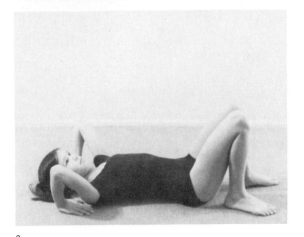

a

Figure 4.36

a. Lie on back with knees bent and arms curved so that palms are flat on the floor beside the chin, with the fingers pointing toward the shoulders.

b

b. Exhale, raise body, and rest head on floor. Take a few breaths.

Curling Leaf (Relaxation)

Figure 4.37a Kneel with legs together, seat on heels, and back of hands on floor.

Figure 4.37b Slowly lower head and slide hands backward. Remain in this position with head resting on the floor and chest against the knees.

c

c. Exhale and continue upward arch.

Complete Breathing (Breathing and Relaxation)

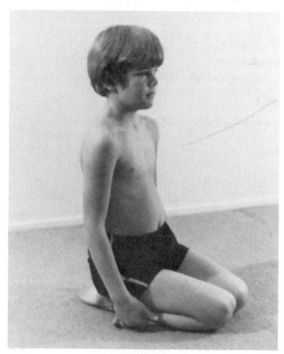

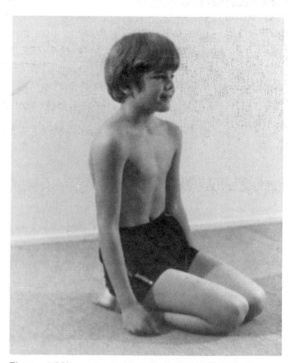

Figure 4.38a Sit on crossed legs (or in a crossed-leg position). Slowly inhale through the nose, gradually expanding the rib cage and pushing abdomen out. Take about 10 seconds to fill lungs. Hold breath for a few seconds

Figure 4.38b . . . then slowly exhale, pulling in the abdomen.

4

Isometric Exercises

Isometric exercises are contractions of muscles involving a push-pull or twist against an object that does not move—such as pushing one hand against the other or holding the hands behind the head and pushing the head against the resistance of the hands. These exercises help develop strength; little, if any, muscular endurance is involved.

Several examples of isometric exercises are illustrated on page 575-77. If this type of exercise program is conducted in the gymnasium, additional exercises involving partner activities, wands, and individual ropes may be designed to increase the strength of muscle groups.

Cumulative Assessment of Physical Fitness

The cumulative physical fitness record shown plots a child's performance on each test item at the beginning and end of each school year.* Such a cumulative record will produce extremely desirable results for teachers, children, and parents if all teachers in the school adopt it. Plotting a child's performance at the beginning and end of each school year provides an insight into the effectiveness of the physical education program, as well as a record of specific improvements made by the child. Another value of the cumulative record is its diagnostic and predictive ability. This is illustrated in the six-year-record of "Mark Brown." (The letters "S," "P," and "R" stand for score, point, and rating.)

In analyzing Mark's performance in relation to his height and weight gains, it becomes quite evident why he showed a definite decline in all items in the spring test during his eighth year: He was simply too heavy for his age and height. However, during the second phase of his ninth year, his record shows a significant increase in height and a loss of eighteen pounds. The record, and the fitness graph, also show an increase in all physical fitness items from his ninth through twelfth years. With this type of record,

each succeeding teacher could understand Mark's potential and set appropriate goals for him within each grade level.

The value of a cumulative record of physical fitness extends beyond physical education. School nurses and parents can refer to the record for answers about sudden changes in height, weight, and physical performance.

How to Construct a Cumulative Record

Before adopting any cumulative record, a committee of teachers, administrators, medical supervisors, and possibly parents should prepare a form including agreed-upon items. Items such as skill performance, attendance, and information about social adjustment also could be included on the form. Care should be taken to develop a form that is informative, yet simple in its instructions and efficient in its recording. The following suggestions will help in developing a useful and practical cumulative record:

1. Involve representatives of all personnel who will eventually use the cumulative record.
2. Record all pertinent data immediately after each test.
3. Establish a standard procedure for recording and storing records.
4. Establish a procedure for transferring records to succeeding teachers.
5. Establish a policy for forwarding complete cumulative records of sixth graders to their junior high schools.
6. Establish a policy of periodic review of the cumulative record and make appropriate additions and changes as dictated by the needs of the program and other pertinent factors.

*The cumulative record was developed by Larry Merlino, Federal Way Public School District, Federal Way, Washington.

Cumulative Physical Fitness Record
Ages 6—12

Name: ___Mark Brown___
Address: ___113 Broadway Street___
School: ___Broadway Elementary___
Test: ___Elementary School___
___Physical Fitness Test___

Grade | Teacher
1. _____
2. _____
3. _____
4. _____
5. _____
6. _____

Age	Ht. In.	Wt. Lbs.	Test No.	Date	Standing Broad Jump			Bench Push-ups			Curl-ups			Squat Jump			30-yard dash			Total Physical Fitness	
					S	P	R	S	P	R	S	P	R	S	P	R	S	P	R	P	R
6	48	53	1	Sept. 1975	29	36	4	4	34	5	8	48	3	9	39	4	7.5	37	4	194	4
	49	55	2	May 1976	32	40	4	10	45	3	12	53	3	12	44	4	6.7	47	3	229	3
7	51	59	1	Sept. 1976	38	43	4	14	48	3	15	52	3	16	46	3	6.5	45	3	234	3
	52.5	62	2	May 1977	47	55	2	20	54	3	20	56	2	22	52	3	5.7	57	2	274	3
8	53	63	1	Sept. 1977	57	62	2	27	58	2	30	59	2	33	58	2	5.1	60	2	297	2
	53	85	2	May 1978	43	44	4	11	43	4	14	48	3	9	35	5	6.3	39	4	209	4
9	53.5	86	1	Sept. 1978	44	42	4	12	45	3	16	48	3	11	37	4	6.0	37	4	209	4
	56	68	2	May 1979	50	50	3	20	53	3	23	53	3	24	50	3	5.3	53	3	259	3
10	57	74	1	Sept. 1979	55	52	3	22	54	3	28	53	3	30	51	3	5.0	52	3	262	3
	58	79	2	May 1980	60	58	2	27	57	2	33	57	2	34	54	3	4.9	55	2	281	2
11	58	80	1	Sept. 1980	64	58	2	31	59	2	35	55	2	36	53	3	4.7	56	2	281	2
	59	85	2	May 1981	68	63	2	37	63	2	40	57	2	40	56	2	4.5	60	2	299	2
12	61	90	1	Sept. 1981	72	64	2	39	64	2	43	62	2	42	58	2	4.4	62	2	310	2
	61.5	93	2	May 1982	79	71	1	44	68	1	46	66	1	48	64	2	4.1	68	1	337	1

4

TOTAL PHYSICAL FITNESS

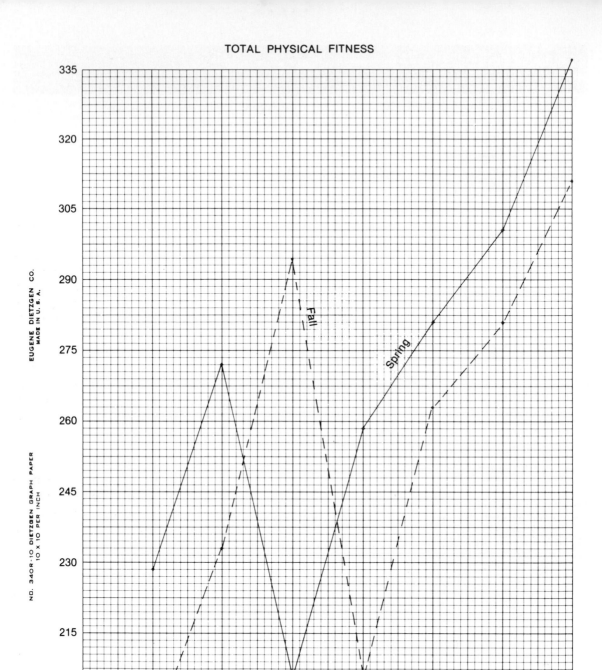

Basic Skills and Movement Fundamentals

5

Movement Concepts and Skills

Locomotor and Nonlocomotor Skills

Basic Game, Dance, and Gymnastic Skills

There have been numerous attempts during the past few years to provide a simple classification system for the skills involved in the elementary school physical education program. Prior to the introduction of movement education concepts to the elementary program, skills were usually classified as locomotor and nonlocomotor skills, or as basic sport, dance, and gymnastic skills. After movement education was introduced, its concepts and skills were treated as a separate entity, and a movement education unit was taught much like a folk dance or basketball unit. Other teachers virtually abandoned locomotor and nonlocomotor skills and the basic game, dance, and gymnastic skills and adopted the classification system used in movement education.

The vast majority of elementary school teachers, however, saw merit in both the traditional and movement education approaches and integrated the best of each into their programs. The author of this book, like many of his colleagues, recommends the integrated system of classifying skills. This eliminates "opposing camps"—one camp being more structured, the other more experimental in its approach to teaching physical education activities.

All children need to acquire the basic locomotor and nonlocomotor skills—running, jumping, turning, and so on—because they are the foundation for the more advanced game, dance, and gymnastic skills. The primary program emphasizes the development of these skills through a variety of activities, using both direct and indirect teaching methods. Some children, particularly at the primary level, can acquire these basic skills informally through individual exploration. As children progress to the intermediate grades, they become interested in acquiring the skills and knowledge of more structured activities such as basketball, track and field, and square-dance movements. These skills too can be presented in a formal, systematic manner or they can be taught using an informal, exploratory approach.

Perhaps the most important contribution of movement education to the physical education program is the unstructured characteristics of its concepts and skills. When children learn what their bodies can do, how they can move, their movement abilities are greatly enhanced. Movement education concepts and skills initially were emphasized in gymnastics and creative dance. Today, however, these skills are blended in a variety of ways with other activities in the physical education program. The amount of emphasis placed on movement skills and exploratory teaching strategies depends upon the emphasis and direction of the program.

The chart that follows illustrates how the three broad categories of skills are related. For example, the teacher who wishes to stress a specific locomotor skill, such as running, may use a variety of directed activities to emphasize correct placement of the feet and coordinated movements of the arms. But when the teacher wishes to stress change of direction or speed,

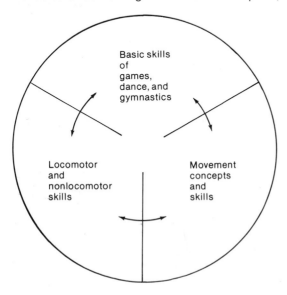

she may incorporate movement skills into the learning process to complement the child's movement ability. Likewise, playing soccer involves basic kicking and dribbling skills but it also involves the child's understanding of two movement education skills—space awareness and his relationship to other players.

This chapter describes the basic skills involved in the three general categories of movement. The reader will note later in the activity sections in Parts IV, V, and VI that each game, dance, and gymnastic activity is complemented by one or more skills from the other two categories of movement.

Movement Concepts and Skills

Movement education skills are grouped under the elements of *body awareness, qualities, space awareness,* and *relationships.* Body awareness refers to what the body can do—the shapes it can make, the way it balances, and the transfer of weight from one part of the body to another. The element qualities describes how the body can move, and includes skills relating to speed, force, and flow of a movement. Space awareness describes the spatial aspects of movement, as well as skills relating to moving in different directions and to different levels. Relationships refer to the connection between the body and other performers or the body and small and large apparatus. (See film, "Introducing the Elements of Movement Education," Appendix A.)

Body Awareness

Body awareness is essentially the ways in which the body or parts of it can be controlled, moved, and balanced. This involves three main elements: the shapes the body can make, the ways the body can balance, and the ways the body can transfer weight from one position to another.

Figure 5.1 Stretched shape

Figure 5.2 Curled shape

Shapes the Body Can Make

The human body is capable of forming an infinite variety of shapes. The three basic types of shapes described here form the framework upon which the child learns the ways that he can stretch, bend, and twist his body.

Stretched and Curled Shapes

A stretched shape (fig. 5.1) is an extension of the whole body or a part of it in a variety of directions. For example, a child can stretch upward, to the side, or through his legs. A curled shape (fig. 5.2) results from an action that flexes or bends the body or a part of it.

Wide and Narrow Shapes

Wide and narrow shapes, like curled and stretched ones, are contrasting shapes. A wide shape requires the legs or arms or both to be away from the trunk in some way. In contrast, the arms or legs must be close together or in a thin line with the trunk in a narrow shape. Both are illustrated in figure 5.3.

Figure 5.3 Wide and narrow shapes

Twisted Shapes

A twisted shape can be performed in two ways. One way is to hold one part of the body in a fixed and stabilized position, such as on the floor or apparatus, then turn the body or any part of it away from the fixed base. In figure 5.4 the body is stabilized, thus restricting the degree of twisting. A twisted shape can also be made when one part of the body is held in a fixed position while the other part turns away from the "fixed" part, producing a twisted shape. Although it could be argued that the latter is a "turn" (usually defined

5

Figure 5.4 Twisted shapes

Figure 5.6 Use a hoop and see if you can discover a balance position with two parts outside the hoop and two parts inside.

Figure 5.5 Can you take the weight on three parts of your body?

Figure 5.7 Find a balance position on the vaulting box using two parts of your body.

as a rotation of the body with the loss of a fixed contact), the synonymous use of "twist" and "turn" is quite acceptable with young children. The refinement in meaning can be made later.

Balance or "Weight Bearing"

A second important aspect of body awareness is balancing or "taking the weight" on different parts of the body. A child can balance on one foot, his head (as in a headstand), or other parts of the body. Figures 5.5 to 5.7 illustrate how the body can be used to answer specific challenges.

Transfer of Body Weight

a   b   c

Figure 5.8 Transfer of body weight

Transfer of Body Weight

The third aspect of body awareness is the transfer of weight from one part of the body to another, which occurs in all human movement. In walking, the transfer of weight is from one foot to another; in a cartwheel, it is from the hands to the feet; and in movement skills, it is from one part of the body to another (fig 5.8).

Qualities

Qualities refer to how the body moves or adjusts to such factors as time, force, and flow.

Time

Time describes the speed of a movement. At one end of the scale, such movements as a sprint to second base or a quick flick of the hand in a creative movement sequence require increased speed or quickness (fig. 5.9). At the other end of the scale, such movements as a slow, controlled relaxation of the trunk and muscles as the child slowly sinks to the ground require a slow or sustained movement.

But time is more than the simple difference between a quick and a slow movement. It is the ability to move at varying speeds and to change pace as the mood or playing situation dictates.

Figure 5.9 Speed or quickness

Force

The quality of force is the effort or tension that is involved in a movement. When a child leaps over a box, he is performing a strong, thrusting action in order to gain enough height and distance to clear the box (fig. 5.10). But in dance, a child shifts his arms lightly from one side to the other to describe something that is very light or gentle (fig. 5.11).

Flow

Flow describes how a movement or series of movements is linked in a purposeful action. *Bound flow* occurs when movements in a series are stopped with the balance maintained, then continued to another static movement. For example, a child performing a tumbling routine shifts from a roll to a shoulder stand and holds his balance position momentarily before lowering his legs and trunk in preparation for another roll (fig. 5.12). Movements that move smoothly from one to another are described as *free flow*.

Figure 5.10 Strong force

Figure 5.11 Light or gentle force

Flow

a

b

c

Figure 5.12 Bound flow

Space Awareness

All the space in a gymnasium or playing field that can be used by a child or group of children constitutes *general space* (fig. 5.13). *Personal* or *limited space* is the immediate area the child can use around him (fig. 5.14). When a child is challenged to "bounce a ball in his own space" or to perform a series of balance positions while remaining inside a hoop on a box or turret, he is using his personal space.

Another aspect of space awareness includes an understanding of the direction and pathway of movement. A child must learn the meaning of directional movements—forward, backward, sideways, and diagonally. He also learns to move in different pathways—around, across, and over. And finally, he learns to move to different levels—high, medium, and low.

Relationships

The fourth element of movement involves the relationship of an individual or group to other performers or to objects. Perhaps the easiest relationship to understand is that of one performer to another, as when partners perform matching or contrasting movements or shapes (fig. 5.15).

A child can also perform a movement with small equipment or large apparatus. His relationship to the equipment is *manipulative* when the equipment becomes an extension of the child, as when he performs a series of movements while holding or contacting a hoop or beanbag. In contrast, the relationship with the equipment is *nonmanipulative* when the child

Figure 5.13 General space

Figure 5.14 Personal or limited space

Figure 5.15 Relationship of performers

5

Figure 5.16 Relationship with equipment

Locomotor and Nonlocomotor Skills

The fundamental locomotor and nonlocomotor skills are the foundation for developing everyday utilitarian and safety skills and are the building blocks for all specialized skills involved in games, dance, and gymnastic activities.

The seven locomotor skills are described and illustrated first in this section. The discussion of each skill includes the mechanical principles involved in its proper execution, common faults, and suggested activities. The nonlocomotor skills then will be treated similarly.

Locomotor Skills

The first five locomotor skills described—walking, running, leaping, jumping, and hopping—represent the skeleton upon which the child begins to develop complex movement skills. Although skipping and sliding (or galloping) are combinations of several of the first five skills, they are described as separate locomotor skills.

Walking
Walking is the transfer of weight from one foot to the other while moving forward or backward. One foot must always be in contact with the floor. The right arm swings forward with the left leg; the left arm moves foward with the right leg (fig. 5.17).

Application of the Principles of Movement

Balance. Walking has been described as a continuous process of gaining and losing balance. This means that a new base of support must be established for each step. Although stability is directly related to the size of the base of support, too wide a base, as illustrated here, will produce a weaving gait, causing the body to move from side to side. When one foot is placed directly in front of the other, the base of support becomes too narrow, making it difficult to maintain balance. The most suitable placement is for the inner edges of the feet to fall along a straight

performs shapes, balance positions, or movements on or over the equipment (fig. 5.16).

Finally, the concept of relationships of individuals and groups is illustrated through leadership and cooperative movement tasks. Movement ideas can be presented in a variety of ways to allow a child to perform in a group as an individual, as a leader, or a cooperative member of the group.

Chapter 21, "Stunts, Tumbling, and Movement Skills," provides a basic procedure for introducing these movement skills into a stunts and tumbling program. A similar pattern is followed in Chapter 22, "Stunts and Movement Skills with Small Equipment," and in Chapter 23, "Stunts and Movement Skills with Large Apparatus." And in Chapter 26, "Creative Dance Activities," movement concepts and skills are used as a basic vocabulary for the development of a wide variety of creative dance and movement ideas.

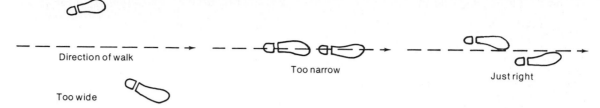

Direction of walk

Too narrow

Just right

Too wide

line, allowing the center of gravity to shift directly over the base of support and preventing unnecessary swaying movements.

Inertia. Since a body at rest will remain at rest unless acted upon by an external force, inertia must be overcome at every step.

Momentum. A body in motion will continue in motion unless acted upon by an external force. The forward motion initiated by the backward thrust of the leg is directed forward through the trunk. An unchecked forward movement would carry the trunk beyond the forward base of support too quickly and would result in a fall forward or a shift to running. To counteract this, the front leg momentarily restrains the forward motion of the trunk to allow a smooth transfer of weight as the back leg begins to move forward.

Production of Force. Since the total effectiveness of a movement is the sum of all forces, properly synchronized leg and arm movements are essential.

Direction of Force. Force that is initiated from the back leg should be directed forward and upward through the center of the body weight. If the direction of force is too vertical, the walk will be bouncy and inefficient. If the force is primarily horizontal, the walk will be a shuffle.

Absorption of Force. In order to absorb the impact of a forceful movement, the shock should be spread over (1) a large area, (2) a long distance, or (3) both area and distance. In walking, the force should be gradually dissipated by transferring weight from the heels to the outer edges of the foot toward the toes.

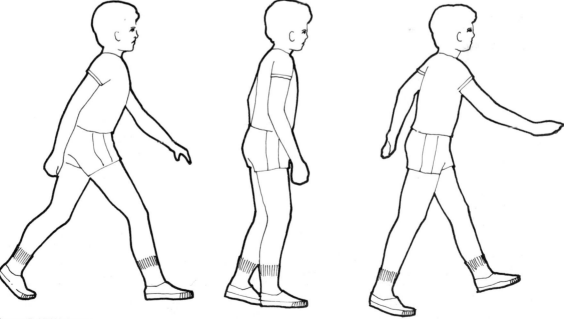

Figure 5.17 Walking

5

Common Faults in Walking

1. Walking with toes turning inward (usually called *pigeon-toed*).
2. Walking with toes turning outward (usually called *duck walk*).
3. Dragging the heel instead of distinctly pushing upward and forward from the toe. This is illustrated by scuffing of the heels.
4. Walking with poor posture, such as with an exaggerated forward, backward, or sideward lean.
5. Walking with an incorrect arm action. In this case, the right arm, rather than the left, comes forward with the right foot. No arm action or letting the arms hang may also be noted.
6. Walking with stiff knees (goose steps). This is usually accompanied by a stiff arm swing.

Walking Activities

1. Walk informally about the room. This should be an easy, relaxed walk that is natural to the child.
2. Same as (1), but in a circle.
3. Same as (2), but with a change in direction.
4. Walk in different ways—short or long steps, fast or slow, hard or soft, high or low.

5. Change speeds. Start slowly, walk at a moderate speed, then briskly, moderately again, slowly, then stop.
6. Walk on the heels with exaggerated arm movements.
7. Walk on tiptoes.
8. Walk slowly for balance (use two, three, or four beats per measure).
9. Walk sideward by crossing one foot in front of the other.
10. Do pantomimes of a "happy" or "sad" walk, of carrying a heavy or light load, of a young man or old man.
11. Combine walking with other locomotor skills. Begin with a walk, then shift to a run, then back to a walk. Repeat with another locomotor skill, such as a skip or slide.
12. Walk on painted lines, balance benches, planks, and other available apparatus.
13. Walk in step with a partner. Begin walking together slowly, then increase speed, change direction, or use other locomotor movements.

Running

Running is the transfer of weight from one foot to another with a momentary loss of contact with the floor by both feet (fig. 5.18).

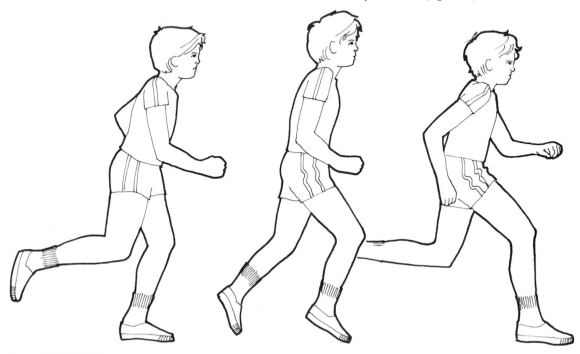

Figure 5.18 Running

Application of the Principles of Movement

Inertia.   The problem of overcoming inertia is, of course, greatest at the takeoff and decreases as the child gains speed. Begin the run from a crouched position to gain maximum speed in the shortest period of time; this allows maximum force to be exerted in a horizontal direction.

Momentum.   Any increase in momentum is directly proportional to the force producing it. In running, the greater the power of the backward leg drive, the greater the forward acceleration.

Direction of Force.   In running, the body lean should be about twenty degrees from vertical. This slight forward lean will keep the center of gravity ahead of the forward foot as it contacts the ground. This will allow the backward extension of the leg to propel the body in a nearly horizontal direction, producing the greatest forward speed and minimizing the inefficient upward movements of the body. Any lateral movements of the body will also restrict forward momentum. To minimize lateral movements, the knees should move directly forward and upward and the arms should swing forward and backward.

Absorption of Force.   In long-distance running, the heel of the foot touches the ground first, and the force is gradually dissipated through the outer edge of the foot toward the toe. In sprinting, the ball of the foot should contact the ground first. This permits the force to be absorbed by slightly flexed hips, knees, and ankles.

Common Faults in Running

1. Running with the heel touching the floor first, followed by a "rocking motion" forward to the ball of the foot. In sprints and dance activities the running step should be performed on the ball of the foot or on the toes.
2. Throwing the legs out to the sides on the forward motion.
3. Running with the toes turning in (pigeon-toed).
4. Running with the toes turning out (duck waddle).
5. Inadequate knee bend in forward and upward direction.
6. Incorrect arm action. In this case, the right arm, rather than the left, comes forward with the right foot.
7. Running in a vertical or erect position, directing too much force upward rather than horizontal.

Running Activities

1. Run informally around the gymnasium.
2. Run with short or long steps.
3. Run with a high knee lift.
4. Run backwards.
5. Change speed—begin slowly, then run at a moderate speed, then run fast.
6. Run on the heels or tiptoes.
7. Run and change directions.
8. Run with a partner, keeping in time.
9. Combine running with other locomotor skills —run, walk, run, slide, and so on.
10. Run around obstacles, such as other children, chairs, or beanbags.
11. Do pantomime running—run like a tall man, a dog, an elephant.

Leaping

Leaping is the transfer of weight from one foot to the other. The toe of the takeoff foot leaves the floor last, while the ball of the landing foot contacts the floor first (fig. 5.19, page 80). The main difference between a leap and a run is that with the former there is a longer loss of contact with the ground, as well as greater height and distance.

Application of Principles of Movement

Since a leap is essentially the same as a run, the same mechanical principles apply. In addition, the following principles are important in producing a maximum leap.

Momentum.   Since momentum is directly proportional to the force applied, the performer should take several running steps before leaping. The increased momentum gained by the run will produce a higher and farther leap.

5

Figure 5.19 Leaping

Direction of Force. The height of the leap is directly proportional to the angle of takeoff, as well as to the backward force of the takeoff leg. To gain maximum height, decrease the angle of takeoff and exaggerate the forward and upward movement of the arms.

Common Faults in Leaping

1. Taking off and landing with stiff knees and ankles.
2. Bending the trunk too far forward on takeoff, producing an exaggerated forward movement on landing.
3. Failing to swing the arms forward and upward.
4. Landing on the heels or flat-footed.
5. Landing on both feet.

Leaping Activities

1. Run a few steps, then leap. Alternate the takeoff foot.
2. Leap for height and distance.
3. Hop in place a few times, then leap forward or sideward.
4. Combine leaping with other locomotor skills —run, leap, walk, and so on.
5. Leap over obstacles—rope, beanbag, hoop.
6. Perform a series of consecutive leaps without breaking stride.

Jumping

Jumping is the transfer of weight from one foot or both feet to both feet (fig. 5.20).

Application of the Principles of Movement

There are two types of jumping movements: one for height, such as the vertical or high jump, the other for distance, such as the standing or running broad jump. The basic mechanical principles for leaping apply also to jumping movements; specific principles follow.

Jumping for Distance. To gain the greatest distance, the jumper should take off with the greatest forward speed and upward thrust. The running broad jump requires maximum speed prior to takeoff; the standing broad jump requires a maximum forward and upward swing of the arms. The angle of takeoff should be about forty-five degrees. As the jumper begins to descend, the arms and body should be brought forward, with the knees bent and feet parallel.

The resulting forward momentum will prevent the body from falling back upon landing and will allow the forward momentum to gradually dissipate through the flexed knees and forward arm movements.

Jumping for Height. Maximum height depends upon several important factors. The angle of takeoff must be as close to vertical as possible. The hips, knees, and ankles should be flexed in the starting position to permit maximum force to be directed upward by the forceful extension of the strong leg muscles. Additional height is also gained by an accompanying forward and upward movement of the arms.

Common Faults in Jumping

1. Taking off and landing with stiff knees and ankles.
2. Leaning the upper part of body too far forward or backward on the takeoff.
3. Not synchronizing the arm swing with the upward or forward movement of the legs and trunk.
4. Landing on the heels or flat-footed.
5. Landing on one foot.
6. Landing with the trunk bent too far forward, producing an exaggerated forward movement upon landing.

Jumping

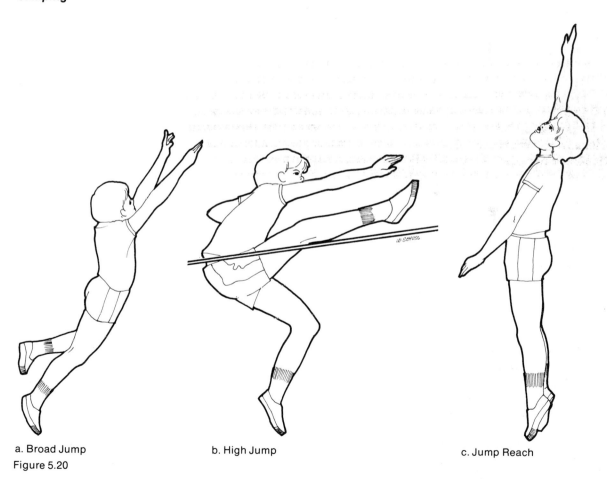

a. Broad Jump

Figure 5.20

b. High Jump

c. Jump Reach

Jumping Activities

1. Jump with feet together and gradually spread legs with each jump.
2. Jump forward, sideward, and backward.
3. Begin jumping from a crouched position and gradually increase the height of each jump.
4. Jump over small equipment, such as ropes, beanbags, and hoops.
5. Jump up and mark the wall with chalked fingertips.
6. Combine jumping with other locomotor skills —run, jump, run, and leap.
7. Skip rope (see pages 440 to 451 for suggestions).
8. Jump from various heights—from a box, bench, or other apparatus. This should be combined with a roll to allow for a gradual dissipation of force.

Hopping

Hopping is the transfer of weight from a foot to the same foot. In the upward phase, the toe leaves the floor last; on the way down, the toe contacts the floor first, then the weight is gradually shifted to the ball and heel of the foot (fig. 5.21).

Application of the Principles of Movement

Force. Since the hop is performed on one leg, the body should lean slightly in the direction of the jumping leg, allowing the center of gravity to shift slightly away from the midline of the body. For maximum height, the angle of takeoff should be as close to vertical as possible. Additional height may be gained by simultaneously moving the arms upward.

Common Faults in Hopping

1. Taking off and landing with stiff knees and ankles.
2. Taking off with the trunk bent too far forward, sideward, or backward.
3. Taking off on one foot and landing on the other foot or both feet.
4. Landing on the heel or flat-footed.
5. Bending the trunk too far forward, producing an exaggerated forward movement upon landing.

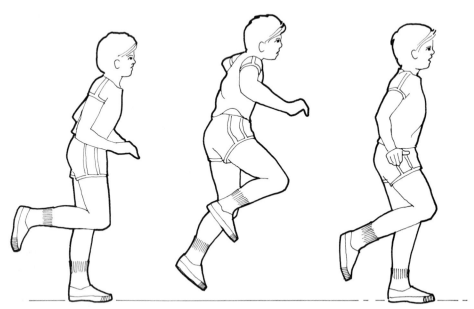

Figure 5.21 Hopping

Figure 5.22 Skipping

Hopping Activities

1. Hop in place. The first hop should just clear the floor, and each succeeding hop should gradually increase in height.
2. Hop forward, sideward, and backward.
3. Hop in place and make a quarter turn on each hop.
4. Hop in place to a 4/4 rhythm. Do different positions in the air on ascent, such as right leg forward, arms sideward or overhead.
5. Hop several times on one foot, then switch to the other foot without losing rhythm.
6. Combine hopping with other locomotor skills —run, hop, skip.
7. Hop over small equipment, such as beanbags or ropes.
8. Hop in time with a partner.

Skipping

A skip is a combination of a long step and a short hop, alternating the lead foot after each hop (fig. 5.22).

Application of the Principles of Movement

As the skipping movement is a combination of a step and a hop, the same mechanical principles that apply to these skills also apply to the skip. The following additional principles are important.

Balance. Since the base of support is narrow and alternately shifts from foot to foot, the arms should be extended sideward to help maintain balance.

Force. Since the extension of the leg on the hop part of the skip produces the upward movement, the angle of takeoff should be nearly vertical. An exaggerated forward lean on the hop will cause too much forward movement, and also will make it difficult for the child to freely swing his opposite leg forward.

Common Faults in Skipping

1. Inability to hop on both feet.
2. Landing flat-footed rather than on the toes.
3. Failing to swing the arms in opposition to leg movements.
4. Leaning too far forward or backward.

5

Skipping Activities

1. Skip forward or backward in a circle.
2. Skip with a partner with the hands crossed in a skating position.
3. Skip four long steps forward, then four short steps backward.
4. Skip four steps beginning with the right foot, then four steps beginning with the left foot.
5. Skip diagonally right for three steps (right-left-right) and bring feet together on the fourth count. Repeat to left.
6. Combine a skip with other locomotor skills—run, skip, walk.
7. Skip and change directions on the step phase of the movement.

Sliding

A slide is a combination of a step and a short leap and can be performed in a forward, sideward, or backward direction; when the direction is forward or backward, the slide is called a *gallop*. The movement is performed by stepping with one foot, then sliding with the other foot. The weight is transferred from the leading foot to the closing or back foot. Once the sliding or galloping action begins, the same foot will always be the lead foot (fig. 5.23).

Application of the Principles of Movement

Sliding employs many of the mechanical principles listed under walking, running, and leaping. Of these, the following are important for the proper execution of the slide.

Balance. The center of gravity should be kept within the base of support. When moving to the side, the body should not lean too far, or the center of gravity will fall outside of the body. Similarly, when moving forward, the angle of takeoff for the leap should be close to vertical.

Sliding

a. Step   b. Short hop and slide   c. Step

Figure 5.23

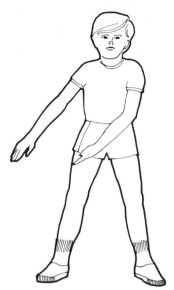

Figure 5.24a Swinging

Figure 5.24b Swaying

Force. Forward or sideward momentum is generated by the forceful action of the leap. In dance and sport activities, control rather than height is normally desired. Therefore, a child should learn to control or adjust the force he can generate by the extension of his back leg movement.

Common Faults in Sliding

1. Sliding on the heels rather than on the balls of the feet and the toes.
2. Leaning too far over toward the lead foot.
3. Landing on the heels rather than on the toes.
4. Keeping the legs too stiff; both knees should be bent.
5. Failing to shift the weight to the lead foot, then to the back foot.
6. Holding the arms too rigid or not moving them in opposition to foot action.

Sliding Activities

1. In a circle or line formation, slide forward, backward, and sideward.
2. Slide four steps to the right, make a half turn, then slide four steps to the left.
3. With partners slide four steps right, then four steps left.

4. Slide and vary the height of the leap.
5. Slide with the left foot forward, stop, then change to the right foot forward.
6. Slide in different directions.
7. Combine the slide with other locomotor movements—run, slide, skip.

Nonlocomotor Movements

Nonlocomotor, or axial, movements—swinging and swaying, bending and stretching, rising and falling, twisting and turning, striking and dodging, and pushing and pulling—are performed from a relatively stable base of support. These movements are usually performed while standing, kneeling, sitting, or lying; however, they may be combined with locomotor skills.

Swinging and Swaying

Swinging (fig. 5.24a) is a pendular movement with the axis of support above the moving parts, such as an arm swinging from the shoulder in a downward and backward movement or a leg swinging from side to side. Swaying (fig. 5.24b) is the same type of movement, but with the support below the moving parts.

5

Application of the Principles of Movement

The following principles apply to the swinging movements of parts of the body while the body as a whole remains stationary while standing or sitting.

In movements of the arm, the hand will have greater speed when the elbow is kept straight. Similarly, the foot has greater speed when the knee is straight.

The momentum of any part of a supported body can be transferred to the rest of the body. For example, swinging the arm sideward and upward will move the whole body in those directions. This transfer can take place only when the body is in contact with a supporting surface.

The movement of a pendulum is caused by the force of gravity. As the pendulum swings downward, its speed increases, and as it swings upward, its speed decreases, until it stops at the top of the swing. The speed of pendular movement is not increased by body weight; it is increased only by the application of additional muscular force.

Common Faults in Swinging and Swaying

1. Lack of flexibility—inability to swing or sway through the full range of movement.
2. Inability to distinguish between a swing and a sway.
3. Movements are rigid rather than graceful and continuous.

Swinging and Swaying Activities

1. Swing arms forward and backward and from side to side.
2. Sway arms overhead, forward and backward and sideward.
3. Repeat (1) with legs.
4. Allow children to experiment with this movement. Ask them how many parts of the body can swing or sway from standing or sitting positions.
5. Swing or sway parts of body in pantomime. Tell the children to sway like a tree, swing like a windshield wiper, and so on. Change tempo with each pantomime movement.

6. Swing arms or legs with moderate speed, then shift to slower or faster speeds.
7. Stand on a box, step, or other apparatus and swing the leg.
8. Grasp chinning bar and swing body forward and backward. Flex arm and repeat.
9. Swing on a rope and release it at different points on the forward and backward swing. Note that the top of the backswing is the best point to release a rope.
10. Combine swinging and swaying with other locomotor skills such as a jump or slide.

Bending and Stretching

Bending (fig. 5.25a) is flexing any or all parts of the body; stretching (fig. 5.25b) is extending the body.

Application of the Principles of Movement

Flexibility, defined as the elasticity or range of motion about a joint, is increased by gradually increasing the amount of force when bending and stretching a muscle.

Common Faults in Bending and Stretching

1. Inability to bend or stretch to the full range of a movement.

Bending and Stretching Activities

1. Bend and stretch different parts of body— arms, legs, trunk.
2. Imitate things that bend or stretch—tree, snake, dog, ostrich, giraffe, and so on.
3. Sit or lie in different positions and explore various bending and stretching movements.
4. Bend and stretch to music.
5. Stretch one arm slowly and bend it back rapidly; reverse movement. Do the same with other parts of the body.
6. Bend one part of the body (arms) while stretching another (legs).
7. Stand on a box or step with toes touching near the edge. Keep legs straight, bend forward and down, trying to extend the fingers beyond the toes.

Figure 5.25a Bending

8. Bend and stretch different parts of the body with varying speeds. Stretch arm up slowly, then bend it back to the original position slowly. Repeat with other parts of the body.
9. Combine bending and stretching with other locomotor or nonlocomotor movements—bend and stretch, swing, jump.

Rising and Falling

Rising is the slow movement of the body or any parts of it to a higher level (fig. 5.26a, page 88). Falling is the controlled gradual relaxation by the body or any parts of it while moving to a lower level (fig. 5.26b).

Application of the Principles of Movement

When Landing in a Downward Movement. There should be a gradual loss of force; this is accomplished by landing on the balls of the feet and immediately shifting the force to the ankles, knees, and hips. Regain balance by keeping the center of gravity over the base of support when landing; to do this, keep the weight evenly dis-

Figure 5.25b Stretching

tributed on both feet or over as many parts of the body as possible.

When Landing in a Forward Movement. There should be a gradual loss of forward momentum; do this by continuing a forward falling movement to a roll or slide. Regain balance by landing with the weight of the body forward. If the force of the fall is broken by the hands, make sure the elbows, wrists, and fingers are slightly bent to absorb the shock.

When Falling on Parts of the Body. When a child lands on a part of his body, such as his knee, the remaining momentum should be received on the padded part of the body in order to protect more vulnerable parts. For example, after landing on his knee, the child should immediately attempt to fall sideward onto the thigh, then onto the side of the arm.

Figure 5.26a Rising

Common Faults in Rising and Falling

1. Dropping to the floor rather than gradually descending through a slow relaxation of the muscles.
2. Rising rapidly off the floor rather than gradually and gracefully.
3. Using the arms to stop the fall. The hands should touch floor, but they should relax, along with the arms and shoulder muscles.

Rising and Falling Activities

1. Have the children gradually relax their muscles and "drop" from an erect standing position to a front lying, back lying, or side lying position.
2. Have the children relax their muscles and lower their bodies from an erect standing position one-half or three-quarters toward the floor, then rise back to the standing position.
3. Assume various positions on the floor— crouched, sitting on feet, etc.—and rise to a standing position.
4. Have partners hold hands and rise and fall to floor.

Figure 5.26b Falling

5. Combine rising and falling with other locomotor and nonlocomotor movements— rise, fall, jump, land, and roll.
6. See pages 395-402 for a description of safety rolls.

Twisting and Turning

Twisting is the rotation of the body or any part of it while maintaining a stable base of support (fig. 5.27a). Turning is a partial or total rotation of the body, thus shifting the base of support (fig. 5.27b).

Application of the Principles of Movement

Balance. Balance is dependent upon the size of the base of support, as well as the position of the center of gravity. In turning and twisting movements, the body weight should be kept as low as possible to assure a stable support position for the next move. This is particularly important in individual and team games where a quick change of direction is required.

Figure 5.27a Twisting

Figure 5.27b Turning

Momentum. In rotary movements of the body, speed is increased by shortening the radius of the moving parts. Thus, the arms and/or legs should be drawn in close to the body to increase the speed of a turn. Examples are drawing the arms in while pirouetting on ice skates or pulling a basketball in as one pivots.

Common Faults in Twisting and Turning

1. Losing the balance while twisting parts of the body.
2. Inability to judge and perform a full turn.

Twisting and Turning Activities

1. Turn the body a quarter, half, or full turn to the right, then to the left.
2. Turn the body to music.
3. Turn to pantomime movements—tops, doors, washing machine.
4. Let children experiment to see how many parts of the body they can twist, as well as the number of combinations they can make.
5. Twist to pantomime movements—trees and wind.

6. Combine twisting and turning with other locomotor skills—walk, stop, and turn on one foot (pivot).
7. Face partner and pivot toward or away from each other.
8. Begin turn with the arms outstretched, then quickly draw in the arms as the turn is made. Repeat with legs or legs and arms.

Striking and Dodging

Striking (fig. 5.28a, page 90) is a percussive-type movement directed toward an object or person, real or imaginary. Dodging (fig. 5.28b) is a quick shifting of one or all parts of the body away from a stationary or moving object.

Application of the Principles of Movement

Those Applying to Striking. When an object is struck—hitting a ball, punching a bag, chopping wood—the force must be great enough to overcome the mass of the object, as well as restraining forces such as wind or friction.

The force exerted by the body is transferred to the external object in proportion to the counterforce of the body against the ground (all actions have equal and opposite reactions).

The direction an object moves when struck is determined by the direction in which the force is applied. If the force is applied in line with the center of gravity of a freely moving object, the object will travel in a straight line. If the force is not applied in line with the center of gravity, the object will travel in a rotating motion.

The greater the speed of the striking implement, such as a bat, at the moment of contact, the greater the velocity of the struck object, the ball. Similarly, the greater the velocity of the approaching object, the greater its velocity in the opposite direction after it is struck (again, equal and opposite actions).

Those Applying to Dodging. Since dodging requires a quick shift in position, the center of gravity just before the shift should be low and close to the center of the base of support.

Common Faults in Striking and Dodging

Striking

1. Striking an object while standing with too narrow a base of support or too high a center of gravity.
2. Striking an object, such as a volleyball, with relaxed fingers or while holding the striking implement with a loose grip.
3. Failing to rotate the body backward before striking the object.
4. Striking an object too far above or below its center of gravity.
5. Failing to follow through after the object has been struck.

Dodging

1. Failing to lower the body after stopping in order to prepare for a quick movement in one or more directions.
2. Making rigid and inflexible movements, producing a loss of momentum.
3. Moving only in one direction. This will occur with children who favor one side of the body.

Figure 5.28a Striking

Figure 5.28b Dodging

Figure 5.29a Pushing

Striking and Dodging Activities

Striking. See the games section, Part IV, for a description of skills and practice activities.

Dodging

1. Run, stop, and move right, then left.
2. Run to a partner, stop, and change direction.
3. Run around obstacles—beanbags, balls, chairs.
4. Bounce or dribble a ball, stop, and change direction on command.
5. Bounce or dribble a ball around obstacles.
6. Play relay or tag games involving dodging movements (see Chapters 10 and 11).
7. Combine dodging with other locomotor skills —slide, stop, dodge, run.

Pushing and Pulling

Pushing (fig. 5.29a) is directing a force or object away from the base of support, such as pushing a door open or pushing against an imaginary object with one foot. Pulling (fig. 5.29b) is directing a force or object toward the body, such as pulling a wagon.

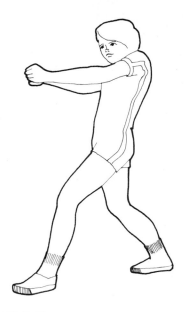

Figure 5.29b Pulling

Application of the Principles of Movement

The important consideration when pushing or pulling an object is to apply the force efficiently. Whenever possible, the force should be applied in the direction the object is expected to move.

The strong muscles should be brought into action in all movements requiring excessive force to push or pull an object. A heavy object should be lifted (pushed) with the knees flexed and the back straight; force thus is applied upward, using the strong leg and back muscles.

Common Faults in Pushing and Pulling

1. Failing to maintain balance throughout the action.
2. Making rigid or inflexible movements rather than smooth, extended thrusts.
3. Lifting or pulling objects with an improper body position, such as lifting a bench with the legs straight and the back bent forward.

Pushing and Pulling Activities

1. Push and pull in pantomime—push a box or wheelbarrow, pull a cart, row a boat.
2. Push and pull objects of various weights and sizes. Begin with small objects and gradually increase weight and size.

a   b   c

Figure 5.30 Two-hand side throw

3. Push objects with the hands, feet, and back.
4. Do partner activities—from a standing position, one partner assumes a good base of support and the other attempts to pull him forward. Experiment with different parts of the body in various positions. For example, have both partners face each other on the floor and push their legs or arms against each other. From back-to-back position, one partner can pull the other over his head.
5. Rope climbing (see Chapter 23).

Basic Game, Dance, and Gymnastic Skills

There are two types of basic skills involved in games, dance, and gymnastic activities—structured and unstructured skills. Structured skills, such as an overhand throw, a headstand, or a schottische step, are performed in a standardized way. Unstructured skills, such as pantomiming a mechanical object or interpreting a feeling, have no common standard or form. An unstructured skill is simply a movement response to a verbal challenge.

Both types of skill are described here. Also included are references to primary and intermediate activities contained in later chapters.

Game Skills

The basic game skills of throwing, catching, kicking, dribbling, and striking represent the foundation of all major individual and team sport activities. These skills should be taught to primary children in a systematic manner through a variety of running, tag, and simple team game activities. As children progress to the intermediate grades, the skills are organized in a sequential way within each major sport. Thus the following skills should be acquired by boys and girls before they enter the fourth grade.

Throwing

Primary children normally begin with a two-hand side throw, then progress to a one-hand underhand throw, and finally tackle a one-hand overhand throw.

Two-Hand Side Throw

The child stands with her left foot forward and her weight evenly distributed on both feet. The ball should be held in front of the body with the elbows slightly bent and the fingers spread around the sides of the ball (fig. 5.30a). She then swings her arms back to the right side until the ball is opposite her right hip, and shifts her weight to her right foot. At this point, her right hand is behind the ball, her left elbow is bent, and her left hand is on the front of the ball (fig. 5.30b). She then swings her arms forward simultaneously as her body weight shifts to her left foot (fig. 5.30c). Note that the ball should leave both hands at the moment of release.

Common Faults

1. Failing to spread the legs far enough apart to provide a good base of support.
2. Failing to rotate the body toward the right as the ball is shifted back.
3. Keeping the arms bent on the forward swing, thus reducing the ball's speed.

One-Hand Underhand Throw

The child faces the target with her legs slightly apart and her weight evenly distributed on both feet. She holds the ball in front of her body with both hands slightly under the ball (fig. 5.31a). Her right hand swings down and back as her body twists to the right and her weight shifts to her right foot (fig. 5.31b). Her right arm swings forward and, at the same time, she steps forward onto her left foot. The ball is released off the fingertips (fig. 5.31c).

Common Faults

1. Failing to rotate toward the right.
2. Failing to extend the arm far enough in the initial backward swing.
3. Keeping the arm bent through the forward swing.
4. Failing to follow through after the ball is released.

One-Hand Underhand Throw

a   b   c

Figure 5.31 One-hand underhand throw

a   b   c

Figure 5.32 One-hand Overhand Throw

One-Hand Overhand Throw

The player begins with her left foot forward and her body weight evenly distributed over both feet. She holds the ball with both hands in front of her body (fig. 5.32a). In the first part of the backswing, she raises her upper arm, lifts her forearm above her head, and flexes her wrist so the hand points backward. At this point, her left side faces the direction of the throw and her left arm is extended forward. Her weight is on the rear foot (fig. 5.32b). In a simultaneous movement, her upper arm is lifted up and forward and her left arm moves down and back as her weight shifts to the front foot. The ball is released off the fingertips when the arm is about shoulder-high. The follow-through should be in a downward direction, ending with the palm of the throwing hand toward the ground (fig. 5.32c).

Common Faults

1. Failing to rotate the trunk toward the right.
2. Holding the ball too close to the palm of the hand.
3. Failing to lead the throw with the elbow.
4. Failing to keep the elbow away from the body in the forward throwing action.
5. Failing to follow through after the ball is released.

Application of the Principles of Movement

The following mechanical principles apply to all three basic throwing skills.

Momentum. The momentum of any part of the body can be transferred to the ball. The application of this principle is to rotate the body toward the side, while shifting the weight to the back foot. The throwing arm should also be brought back as far as possible. If the forward swinging action is smooth, maximum force can be transferred to the ball as it leaves the hands.

Speed. Greater speed can be gained by increasing the distance over which the force is applied. This is particularly important in the one-hand underhand and overhand throws. The straighter the arm in the forward throwing movement, the greater the force that is generated and the greater the speed of the ball.

Catching

A ball can be caught with one or two hands and from virtually all angles. In the primary grades, however, two main catches, the two-hand underhand catch and the two-hand overhand catch, should be stressed.

The two-hand underhand catch should be used when the ball approaches below the waist. The player should stand with his feet about shoulder-width apart, his elbows bent, and his fingers pointing down (fig. 5.33a). As the ball approaches, the player should step forward, extend his arms, and bring his hands close together. The ball should be caught with the tips of the fingers and thumbs (fig. 5.33b). The baby fingers should be close together when the ball is caught. As the ball is caught, the hands should recoil toward the body to soften the force.

a

b

Figure 5.33 Two-hand underhand catch

a

b

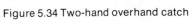
Figure 5.34 Two-hand overhand catch

If the ball approaches above the waist, the two-hand overhand catch should be used. In this skill, the elbows are bent and held high, and the fingers and thumbs are spread (fig. 5.34a). As the ball approaches, the arms extend forward and up. The ball should be caught with the tips of the fingers and thumbs; the thumbs are now close together (fig. 5.34b). As the ball is caught, the hands recoil toward the body to deaden the force of the oncoming ball.

Application of the Principles of Movement

Center of Gravity. The body should be kept in line with the ball, with the legs comfortably spread or in a stride position. This provides a firm base of support, as the center of gravity is close to the center of the body. With the underhand catch, a slightly crouched position lowers the center of gravity, providing an even firmer base of support.

Absorption of Force. To absorb the impact of the oncoming ball, the force should be spread over either as large an area as possible or as long a distance as possible, or both. Catching the ball with the arms extended and the fingers spread and cupped, then recoiling the arms toward the body, provides the greatest surface and distance to absorb the force.

Kicking

The majority of kicking games played in the primary grades involve kicking a stationary or moving ball with the top or side of the instep. Just before the ball is kicked, the nonkicking foot should be even with the ball, the head and trunk should be leaning forward slightly and the kicking leg should be well back, with the knee slightly bent (fig. 5.35b). The eyes should be focused on the ball, and the arms should be extended sideways. The kicking leg is then brought downward and forward, and the top of the instep contacts the ball. The kicking leg continues forward and slightly upward (fig. 5.35a).

a   b   c

Figure 5.35 Kicking.

Application of the Principles of Movement

Acceleration. A ball that is kicked will move in the direction of the force, and the resulting change of speed will be directly proportional to the force acting upon it. It is important that the force applied by the kicking foot be directly behind the ball and moving in the direction in which the ball is intended to move.

Production of Force. To repeat, the total effective force of a movement is the sum of all the forces produced by the muscle groups applied in the same direction and in a proper sequence. To gain maximum force, therefore, each movement must be made in succession—the run, the backward leg swing, the forward kicking movement—and immediately after the preceding movement has made its greatest contribution to the force and movement.

Increasing Linear Velocity. Kicking a ball involves the conversion of angular velocity to linear velocity. Linear velocity can be increased by taking more steps prior to the kick or by extending the lower leg more to create a longer lever and thus more force when the ball is contacted.

Common Faults

1. Kicking the ball with the toes.
2. Leaning too far back prior to and through the kicking movement.
3. Contacting the ball too soon or too late.
4. Failing to follow through in the direction of the ball.

Dribbling

There are a variety of primary games that involve either a controlled bouncing or dribbling action by the hands or a similar controlled dribbling skill by the feet.

5

a

b

Figure 5.36 Dribbling with the hand

a

b

Figure 5.37 Dribbling with the feet

When dribbling with the hands, the body should be leaning forward slightly, with the knees bent and the weight evenly distributed over both feet. The wrist of the dribbling hand should be flexed, with the fingers cupped and spread (fig. 5.36a). The forearm extends downward and the ball is "pushed" toward the ground (fig. 5.36b). As the ball rebounds, the fingers, wrist, and arm should "ride" back with it.

Common Faults

1. Slapping the ball with the palm of the hand.
2. Failing to keep a steady, rhythmical bouncing action.

To dribble the ball with the feet, move it with short, controlled pushes by either foot (fig. 5.37). The body should be bent slightly forward, with the head over the ball.

Common Faults

1. Leaning too far back while dribbling.
2. Kicking rather than pushing the ball.
3. Using the toe rather than the instep to move the ball.

Application of the Principles of Movement

The following principle applies to dribbling with either the hands or the feet.

Inertia. An object has its greatest inertia when it is not moving. Once dribbling has begun, it should be continued by easy, sequential pushing actions. Each time the ball comes to rest, more force must be applied to overcome the initial inertia.

Figure 5.38

Striking

There are two basic types of striking skills that are used in individual, partner, and group games for primary children. These striking skills are hitting a ball with the hand or fist, and hitting an object with a bat or other implement.

When striking a ball with the hand or fist, the player should stand in line with the oncoming ball. The feet should be in a stride position, with the weight on the back foot. If the ball is hit with an underhand striking action (fig. 5.38), the striking arm should be extended straight back, then forcefully moved forward to contact the ball when it is opposite the front foot. The hand of the striking arm must be held firm as the ball is contacted. There should also be a forceful follow-through in the direction of the hit. If the ball is hit with an overhand striking action, the elbows should be bent slightly, the fingers spread apart, and the thumbs facing each other. As the ball drops, the body and arms extend upward and slightly forward, and the ball is hit with "stiff" fingers. The follow-through should be in an upward and forward motion in the direction of the ball.

When striking the ball with a bat, the player should stand with his feet parallel and about shoulder-width apart (fig. 5.39a). His left side should be toward the pitcher. He should grip the bat where it feels comfortable and then shift it to the back of his head and about shoulder high. His arms should be bent at the elbows and held away from his body. As the ball leaves the pitcher's hand, the batter shifts his weight to his rear foot, then swings the bat forward as he shifts his weight to his front foot (fig. 5.39b). He must keep a firm grip on the bat as the ball is hit. After the ball is hit, the bat continues to swing around the left shoulder.

Common Faults

1. Holding the bat on the shoulder and keeping the elbows too close to the side.
2. Failing to maintain a firm grip through the forward swing and follow-through.
3. Swinging the bat up and under the ball.

Application of the Principles of Movement

Stability. In all striking skills, the legs should be comfortably spread to provide a wide, stable base of support from which to hit the ball. Standing with the knees slightly bent also lowers the center of gravity, further increasing stability.

Action-Reaction. For every action there is an equal and opposite reaction. When a player begins to swing his bat toward the oncoming ball, he is building up force. If he maintains a firm grip at the moment of contact, the ball will recoil with an equal force.

Production of Force. Hitting a ball is basically the transfer of rotary force to linear force. More force can be gained by increasing the distance of the backswing and by cocking the wrist at the top of the backswing. Additional force is also gained by extending the arms as the bat is moved toward the ball.

Direction of Force. The direction in which an object moves is determined by the direction in which the force is applied. If the force is applied in line with the ball's center of gravity, the ball will travel in a straight line. But if the bat hits the ball above or below the center of gravity, the ball will travel in a rotary motion, losing distance and speed.

Game activities stressing these basic skills are contained in the following chapters:

Chapter 10: "Running, Tag, and Simple Team Games"
Chapter 11: "Relay Activities"

a

b

Figure 5.39 Batting

Skills for Intermediate Grades

The basic game skills described in this section for primary children are the foundation for a wide variety of new skills that are learned in grades four through six. Through the activities provided in Chapters 10, 11, 12, and 27, intermediate children develop more style and form in the basic game skills. In the following chapters, a suggested sequence for introducing new skills for each sport is provided, along with a description of the skills, practice activities, and lead-up games:

Rhythmic and Dance Skills

Rhythmic and dance skills for elementary school children can be described under the broad categories of rhythmic skills, folk dance skills, and creative dance.

Rhythmic Skills

The fundamental difference in the rhythmical ability of primary and intermediate children is the progressive ease of moving in time or in harmony with a rhythmical accompaniment. Following are the basic rhythmic skills that primary and intermediate children should acquire; each is described in Chapter 24, "Rhythmic and Movement Activities."

1. Moving in time to a rhythmic beat
2. Changing movement patterns in harmony with the musical accompaniment
3. Varying the speed of a movement according to the tempo of the musical accompaniment
4. Changing or emphasizing the force of movement according to the varying intensity of a musical accompaniment

Folk Dance Skills

All singing games and traditional folk dances involve one or more of the locomotor and nonlocomotor skills described on pages 76-92. The dance activities contained in Chapter 25 "Traditional and Contemporary Dances," begin with primary singing games, which normally involve a walk, run, skip, or gallop step performed in a simple dance pattern or movement. The intermediate folk and square dance activities that follow involve more complex locomotor and nonlocomotor movements and more style and finesse in the movement patterns.

Creative Dance

It is extremely difficult to classify the skills used in creative dance activities. The pantomime movements of primary children are essentially combinations of locomotor and nonlocomotor skills. However, since these movements are creative or interpretive, there are no common standards involved. The movement skills described early in this chapter under the categories of body awareness, qualities, space awareness, and relationships are also used as a medium of expression in creative dance. Chapter 26, "Creative Dance Activities," illustrates how a variety of creative dance activities can be developed for primary and intermediate children.

Gymnastic Skills

The basic skills of traditional gymnastic activities are classified as balance, vaulting, climbing, and agility skills. These skills are organized within each category according to their difficulty. Chapter 21, "Stunts, Tumbling, and Movement Skills," includes the basic stunts and tumbling skills that are appropriate for primary and intermediate grades and describes how the movement skills of body awareness, qualities, space awareness, and relationships can be integrated with these structured skills. Chapters 22 and 23 follow a similar pattern, combining the structured and movement skills used with small equipment and large apparatus.

Physical Education Curriculum

The physical education curriculum includes all of the organized and directed experiences within both the instructional program and the extraclass program. Chapter 6 includes basic information about planning a comprehensive program for each elementary grade. Equipment and supplies, tournaments, and the development of safe, instructional playing areas are discussed in Chapter 7. Chapter 8 examines methods of teaching physical education and provides information about lesson planning, routine procedures, and class organization. Evaluation, grading, and reporting pupil progress are discussed in Chapter 9.

The Physical Education Curriculum

6

The Instructional Program

The Extraclass Program

The contemporary definition of an elementary school curriculum would include all the experiences of children for which the school accepts responsibility. In physical education, this would encompass all the learning experiences that relate to the physical activities provided within the regular instructional period and out of class. How the school or teacher organizes the physical education curriculum can take several forms. But the fundamental purpose of such an organization is to provide an effective means of choosing activities, teaching strategies, and experiences that best meet the goals of the program.

The elementary physical education curriculum is divided into two types of programs. The *instructional program,* of course, is the central core within which children acquire knowledge and skills relating to human movement. The *extraclass program* is a series of structured and unstructured activities in which children apply the skills and concepts learned in the instructional program.

This chapter is organized around these two programs. First, the types of activities that are included in a well-balanced instructional program are described. Next is a section telling how to construct a yearly program and instructional units for primary and intermediate grades. A discussion of the extraclass program concludes the chapter.

The Instructional Program

The instructional program is more than the physical activities that are taught to the class. Rather, it is the total experience of activities, methods, and teaching strategies.

The activities themselves serve two very basic functions. First, through the activities children learn the basic movement skills and concepts and the more complex skills involved in games, dance, and other organized activities. Mastering these skills, in turn, helps the child maintain an optimum level of physical fitness, move his body easily and efficiently, and express himself creatively.

And second, the physical activities provide a medium within which the child learns many intangible, yet important, lessons of life. He learns, for example, to share his experiences, to give and take, and to control his emotions under a variety of cooperative and competitive situations.

Types of Activities

Prior to the introduction of movement education concepts and skills to the elementary school physical education program, activities were arranged according to three levels of contribution, as shown in the accompanying pyramid. The foundation of all movement was the main components of physical fitness—strength, endurance, power, flexibility. The next level included the fundamental locomotor and nonlocomotor movements—walking, running, falling, dodging, and so on. The highest level included the specialized skills involved in individual and team

games, folk and creative dance, stunts, tumbling, and other gymnastic activities.

Physical activities are no longer seen in such a simplistic organization and progression. Instead, the activities are arranged according to the following diagram.

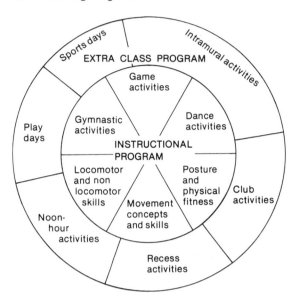

Generally speaking, primary children need to spend time in such areas as locomotor and nonlocomotor skills and low-organization games, dance, and gymnastic activities. As children progress through the intermediate grades, more time is devoted to individual and team sports, folk dance, and gymnastic activities. The concepts and skills of the movement education approach have become an integral part of games, dance, and gymnastic activities rather than being treated as a separate activity area. Parts IV, V, and VI describe the concepts and skills of games, dance, and gymnastic activities and illustrate how movement concepts and skills can be effectively integrated within these activities.

Following are brief descriptions of activities included in the instructional program and references to detailed discussion about them elsewhere in the book.

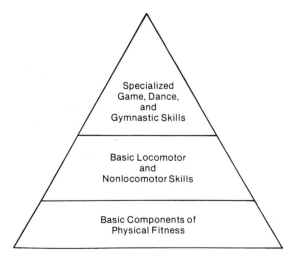

Posture and Physical Fitness

Posture and physical fitness activities include methods of assessing and improving fitness and posture. Special activities such as circuit training, obstacle courses, and yoga exercises are provided in Chapter 4, "Posture and Physical Fitness" (pages 46-65).

Locomotor and Nonlocomotor Skills

Activities involving locomotor and nonlocomotor skills stress such fundamentals as walking, running, skipping, and dodging. Chapter 5, "Basic Skills and Movement Fundamentals," (pages 76-92) describes each of these movements, including the basic mechanical and movement principles involved.

Movement Concepts and Skills

The movement concepts and skills that are integrated into the game, dance, and gymnastic activities in this book are grouped under the elements of body awareness, qualities, space awareness, and relationships. These elements are the basis of the unstructured movements that are used to describe what the body can do, how it moves, where it moves, and the relationship of the body to the floor, apparatus, or other performers.

The basic movement skills are described in Chapter 5, "Basic Skills and Movement Fundamentals" (70-76). There is also an extensive application of these movement concepts and skills in Part V, "Gymnastic and Movement Activities"; Chapter 24, "Rhythmic and Movement Activities"; and Chapter 26, "Creative Dance Activities." And within Part IV, "Game and Movement Activities," there are numerous examples of the application of the concepts and skills of movement education to individual, partner, and group games.

Game Activities

Game activities have always constituted a major portion of the physical activities for children in both primary and intermediate grades. The basic game skills for primary grades are described in Chapter 5, "Basic Skills and Movement Funda-

mentals" (pages 92-100). Chapter 10, "Running, Tag, and Simple Team Games," has a variety of low-organization games that enhance these skills. Chapters 11, "Relay Activities," and 12, "Individual and Partner Games," also contain numerous activities that contribute to the development of basic game skills and concepts. These chapters also include activities appropriate for boys and girls in grades four through six.

The more organized individual and team sports that are taught in the intermediate grades are arranged into separate chapters, 13 to 20. Each includes a suggested sequence for presenting skills, descriptions of the main skills, and a variety of practice activities and lead-up games. All of these chapters are organized on the basis of progressing from simple to more complex activities. However, each chapter also includes suggestions for incorporating the problem-solving method, or what is becoming known as the *inventive* or *creative games approach*. The approach includes many of the movement concepts and skills. A teacher can therefore emphasize the structured games approach or adopt a more exploratory method. Which route she takes will depend on the age of the children and their background in game type activities.

Gymnastic Activities

Gymnastic activities for elementary school children commonly include three basic types of self-testing skills and movement patterns. The first category, stunts and tumbling (Chapter 21), includes basic animal walks and balance and tumbling skills. The second category includes a wide variety of skills and movement patterns performed on or with small equipment, including beanbags, hoops, individual ropes, and wands (Chapter 22). The third type of gymnastic activities involves skills and movement patterns performed on or over large apparatus (Chapter 23). The apparatus include the vaulting box, climbing rope, trampoline, and a new series of agility apparatus designed primarily for elementary school children.

6

Within each of these three chapters all skills are organized from the simple to the more complex, whenever possible. Each chapter also includes numerous illustrations and suggestions for the sequential introduction of movement concepts and skills.

Dance Activities

Dance activities for primary and intermediate children include basic rhythmic skills, singing games and folk dances, and creative or interpretive movement. Chapter 24, "Rhythmic and Movement Activities," describes how the basic rhythmic skills can be taught to children in the primary and intermediate grades. Chapter 25, "Traditional and Contemporary Dances," includes the more popular singing games for early primary children and a selection of folk and square dances for the late primary and intermediate grades. And Chapter 26, "Creative Dance Activities," provides basic approaches for teaching creative dance.

The accompanying chart lists the types of activities included in each chapter in Parts IV, V, and VI. This chart can be used as a basic reference when planning a yearly program or individual instructional units, which will be described next.

Games, Gymnastics, and Dance Activities

Activities	Chapter	K	1	Primary Program 2	3	Pages	Intermediate 4	5	6	Pages
Games										
Basic Game Skills	5	x	x	x	x	92-100				
Running, Tag, and Simple Team Games	10	x	x	x	x	177-87	x	x	x	187-97
Relay Activities	11	x	x	x	x	200-05	x	x	x	200-05
Individual and Partner Games	12	x	x	x	x	209-11	x	x	x	211-18
Classroom Games	27	x	x	x	x	567-74	x	x	x	567-74
Soccer Activities	13						x	x	x	219-48
Hockey	14						x	x	x	249-62
Football	15						x	x	x	263-79
Volleyball	16						x	x	x	280-97
Basketball	17						x	x	x	298-324
Softball	18						x	x	x	325-50
Track and Field	19						x	x	x	351-73
Swimming	20				x	375	x	x	x	374-78

Games, Gymnastics, and Dance Activities—*Continued*

Activities	Chapter	K	1	Primary Program 2	3	Pages	Intermediate 4	5	6	Pages
Gymnastics										
Stunts & Tumbling Skills	21	x	x	x	x	386-401	x	x	x	402-23
Movement Skills	21	x	x	x	x	423-32	x	x	x	423-32
Pyramid Building	21						x	x	x	420-21
Beanbag Activities	22	x	x	x	x	435-39	x	x	x	435-39
Individual and Long Rope Activities	22	x	x	x	x	440-50	x	x	x	440-50
Hoop Activities	22	x	x	x	x	453-55	x	x	x	453-55
Wand Activities	22	x	x	x	x	457-63	x	x	x	457-63
Chair Activities	22		x	x	x	464-66	x	x	x	464-66
Indian Clubs, Traffic Cones	22	x	x	x	x	466-68	x	x	x	466-68
Balance Beam and Benches	23	x	x	x	x	470-78	x	x	x	470-78
Climbing Ropes	23	x	x	x	x	478-84	x	x	x	478-84
Springboard, Vaulting Box	23		x	x	x	484-90	x	x	x	484-90
Horizontal Bar, Ladder, Stall Bars	23	x	x	x	x	490-98	x	x	x	490-98
Agility Apparatus	23	x	x	x	x	498-500	x	x	x	498-500
Outdoor Apparatus	23	x	x	x	x	500-03	x	x	x	500-03
Dance										
Elements of Rhythm	24	x	x	x	x	507-08	x	x	x	507-08
Rhythm Activities	24	x	x	x	x	509-20	x	x	x	509-20
Singing Games	25	x	x	x		521-34				
Folk Dance	25						x	x	x	535-48
Creative Dance	26	x	x	x	x	550-60	x	x	x	550-60

Games, Gymnastics, and Dance Activities—*Continued*

Activities	Chapter	Primary Program				Pages	Intermediate			Pages
		K	1	2	3		4	5	6	
Related Activities										
Classroom Activities	27	x	x	x	x	567-74	x	x	x	567-74
Yoga Exercises	27	x	x	x	x	578, 58-65	x	x	x	578, 58-65
Isometric Exercises	27						x	x	x	575-77
Gymnastic and Movement Skills	27	x	x	x	x	578-79	x	x	x	578-79
Rhythmic and Dance Activities	27					580-81	x	x	x	580-81
Posture and Physical Fitness	4	x	x	x	x	37-45	x	x	x	37-45
Jogging	4			x	x	45	x	x	x	45
Circuit Training	4				x	46-48	x	x	x	46-48
Obstacle Course	4		x		x	48	x	x	x	48
Conditioning Exercises	4	x	x	x	x	49-57	x	x	x	49-57

Developing a One-Year Program

In the majority of elementary schools in this country, the classroom teacher is mainly responsible for planning the yearly physical education program. Her task is to translate the goals expressed by school officials, parents, and the teacher herself into a broad-based activity program that will meet the needs and interests of the children.

If every class was assigned thirty to forty-five minutes a day for physical education. . . . If the interests and abilities of each class were equal, or at least similar. . . . And, if all facilities, equipment, and supplies were available for any activity that is selected . . . then a basic program with specific percentages of time allocated for specific activities would be suggested for each class. This ideal situation simply does not exist in elementary schools in this country. Therefore, the following suggestions provide a framework upon which the classroom teacher can develop her own program.

Step 1: Establish the basic goals of the program. The basic goals of an elementary school physical education program discussed in Chapter 1 can be used as a starting point for the classroom teacher. Of course, these goals may be modified or others may be added to reflect the philosophy of the local school district or the wishes of parents and school officials. However, these goals should provide a basis for selecting appropriate activities and roughly allocating time. The goals are

1. to enhance physical growth and development
2. to develop and maintain maximum physical fitness
3. to develop useful physical skills
4. to develop in socially useful ways
5. to develop wholesome recreational skills
6. to develop intellectual competencies
7. to develop creative talents
8. to develop the child's self-image

We know, however, that certain physical activities accomplish some of these objectives more effectively than others. For example, the activities listed under games on the chart on pages 108-10 can help develop useful physical skills, wholesome physical recreation, and social traits such as team loyalty and sportsmanship. However, it is questionable whether games are as effective as gymnastic activities in developing and maintaining an optimum level of physical fitness or in developing basic movement concepts and skills. Furthermore, neither games nor gymnastic activities are as effective as dance activities in accomplishing certain social, creative, and physical skills.

Step 2: Select general activity areas. This step is perhaps the most difficult for inexperienced teachers. A primary teacher may teach a few animal walk skills, one or two movement skills, and a simple team game within a single lesson. This pattern is appropriate throughout the primary grades. However, the difficulty lies in allocating percentages of time to each sub-activity within the game, dance, and gymnastic activities. Most elementary teachers follow the plan suggested in the Primary and Intermediate Physical Activities diagrams.

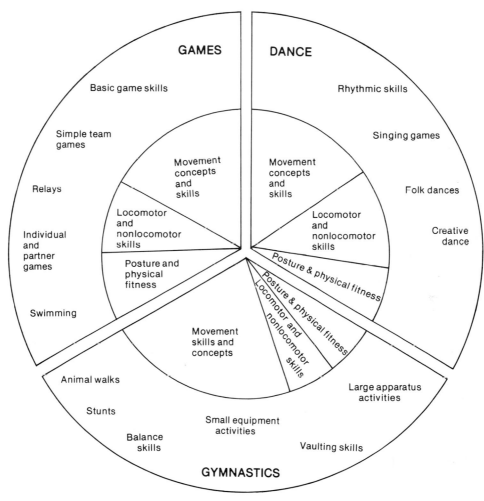

PRIMARY PHYSICAL ACTIVITIES

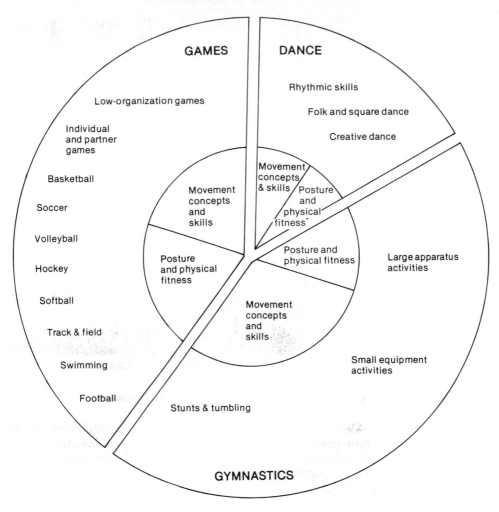

It is very difficult for the classroom teacher who is planning a physical education program to allocate exact percentages of time to each of the six activity areas discussed earlier. Classes vary according to the students backgrounds, their current needs and interests, and available time and facilities, among other things. Of equal importance is the interrelationship of activity areas. To teach gymnastic activities no longer is simply to teach isolated stunts or balance activities, but to teach these activities along with one or more movement concepts or skills. Likewise, the components of physical fitness or a particular locomotor skill may not be directly taught or emphasized in a single gymnastic lesson or unit,

but nevertheless, they are enhanced through the gymnastic activity.

In the Primary Physical Activities diagram, equal time is allocated to game, dance, and gymnastic activities. And within each of these major areas, emphasis is placed on developing movement skills, and locomotor and nonlocomotor movements, and posture and physical fitness. The exact amount of time the teacher will devote to the main activity areas and the concepts and skills within the inner circle will be based on the characteristics and needs of her class.

The Intermediate Physical Activities diagram shows the changing characteristics and needs of children in the intermediate grades. Games and gymnastics are each allocated about 40 percent of the instructional time, and dance activities, the remaining 20 percent. The time and emphasis given to posture and physical fitness, locomotor and nonlocomotor skills, and movement concepts and skills are reduced throughout these grades (note the smaller inner circle). Also, as children progress through the intermediate grades, more time is devoted to individual and team sports and less to gymnastic activities. The percentage of time spent on dance activities should stay about the same throughout these grades.

The General Outline of a Yearly Program shown here illustrates how a teacher can plan a tentative outline of activities. The table on pages 108-10 will provide a quick reference for detailed descriptions of each type of activity for primary and intermediate grades.

General Outline of a Yearly Program

Note: A few minutes of each session throughout the year should be spent on physical fitness activities (see Chapter 4).

	Fall	Winter	Spring
	Kindergarten	*Kindergarten*	*Kindergarten*
Games	Throwing and catching skills. Individual and partner games. Locomotor skills.	Throwing and catching skills. Simple games. Movement skills. Classroom games.	Kicking skills. Individual and partner games. Tag activities. Locomotor skills.
Gymnastics	Animal walks and simple stunts. Movement skills. Small equipment. Outdoor apparatus.	Animal walks and simple stunts. Movement skills. Small equipment.	Simple stunts. Movement skills. Small equipment. Outdoor apparatus.
Dance	Singing games. Locomotor and nonlocomotor skills. Creative dance.	Singing games. Locomotor and nonlocomotor skills. Creative dance.	Singing games. Locomotor and nonlocomotor skills. Rhythmic skills. Pantomime activities.
	Grade One	*Grade One*	*Grade One*
Games	Throwing and catching skills. Individual and partner games. Classroom games.	Throwing, catching, and hitting games. Individual, partner, and simple team games. Classroom games.	Kicking games. Individual and partner games. Simple team games. Relay and tag games.
Gymnastics	Animal walks and simple stunts. Movement skills. Small equipment. Outdoor apparatus.	Simple stunts. Movement skills. Small equipment. Large apparatus.	Movement skills. Small equipment. Large apparatus. Outdoor apparatus.
Dance	Singing games. Movement skills. Pantomime activities.	Singing games. Movement skills. Rhythmic skills. Creative dance.	Singing games. Rhythmic activities. Creative dance.

	Fall	Winter	Spring
	Grade Two	*Grade Two*	*Grade Two*
Games	Throwing, catching, and kicking skills. Individual, partner, and simple team games. Classroom games.	Throwing, bouncing, and catching games. Simple team games. Relay activities.	Kicking, dribbling, and hitting games. Individual, partner, and simple team games. Relay and tag games.
Gymnastics	Simple stunts and tumbling skills. Movement skills. Small equipment. Large apparatus.	Simple stunts and tumbling skills. Movement skills. Small equipment. Large apparatus.	Movement skills. Small Equipment. Large apparatus. Outdoor apparatus.
Dance	Folk dance activities. Rhythmic skills. Creative dance.	Folk dance activities. Rhythmic skills. Creative dance.	Folk dance. Rhythmic skills.
	Grade Three	*Grade Three*	*Grade Three*
Games	Kicking and dribbling skills. Individual, partner, and simple team games. Running and tag games.	Throwing, dribbling, and catching games. Individual, partner, and simple team games. Relay activities.	Throwing, catching, and hitting skills. Simple team games. Running and tag games. Track and field activities.
Gymnastics	Stunts and tumbling skills. Movement skills. Small equipment. Large apparatus.	Stunts and tumbling skills. Movement skills. Small equipment. Large apparatus.	Movement skills. Small Equipment. Outdoor apparatus.
Dance	Rhythmic skills.	Folk dance. Rhythmic skills. Creative dance.	Folk dance. Rhythmic skills.
	Fall	**Winter**	**Spring**
	Grade 4	*Grade 4*	*Grade 4*
Games	Simple team games. Soccer activities. Volleyball activities.	Individual and partner games. Basketball activities. Classroom games.	Relay and tag activities. Softball activities. Track and field activities.
Gymnastics	Stunts, tumbling, and movement skills. Small equipment. Large apparatus.	Stunts, tumbling, and movement skills. Small equipment. Large apparatus.	Outdoor apparatus. Obstacle course.
Dance	Rhythmic skills.	Folk dance. Creative dance.	Rhythmic skills. Folk dance.

General Outline of a Yearly Program—*continued*

	Fall	Winter	Spring
	Grade 5	*Grade 5*	*Grade 5*
Games	Individual and partner games. Flag football activities. Volleyball activities.	Individual and partner games. Basketball activities. Floor hockey activities.	Field hockey activities. Track and field activities. Swimming activities.
Gymnastics	Stunts, tumbling, and movement skills. Small equipment: ropes, skipping, wand, and chair activities.	Stunts, tumbling, and movement skills. Pyramid building. Small equipment. Large apparatus.	Stunts and tumbling. Pyramid building. Large apparatus. Outdoor apparatus. Obstacle course.
Dance	Rhythmic skills.	Rhythmic skills. Folk Dance.	Folk and square dance.
	Fall	**Winter**	**Spring**
	Grade 6	*Grade 6*	*Grade 6*
Games	Soccer activities. Individual and partner games. Flag football.	Individual and partner games. Basketball activities. Volleyball activities.	Individual and partner games. Field hockey activities. Track and field activities.
Gymnastics	Stunts, tumbling, and movement skills. Large apparatus. Outdoor apparatus	Stunts, tumbling, and movement skills. Pyramid building. Small equipment. Large apparatus.	Outdoor apparatus. Obstacle course.
Dance	Rhythmic skills.	Folk and square dance activities. Rhythmic skills.	Folk and square dance.

Developing an Instructional Unit

Once the teacher has decided on the type and amount of activities she will include in the yearly physical education program, she must plan smaller units of instruction. She must consider the time available, interest and ability levels, and equipment and facilities available in deciding on a teaching unit. There are three basic types of teaching units that can be used in the primary and intermediate grades—the multiple teaching unit, the modified teaching unit, and the solid teaching unit. The teacher should select the unit that most readily meets her class's needs and is in harmony with her basic teaching approach.

Multiple Teaching Unit

The multiple teaching unit is actually three units taught concurrently throughout the year. In other words, games, dance, and gymnastic ac-

tivities would be taught on alternate days for an indefinite period. To illustrate, kindergarten activities (page 116) might include games on Monday, gymnastics on Tuesday, dance on Wednesday, and singing games (representing dance) on Thursday to start the second rotation. In this case, the rotation system has been modified by having similar activities two days in a row.

Advantages of this approach are its variety of activities and its flexibility; therefore, it can be used in kindergarten and first-grade classes to cope with the short attention spans of five- and six-year-olds. The facilities and equipment available may determine whether this method is adopted. Whatever the reasons for selecting the multiple unit, the teacher should make sure that games, dance, and gymnastic activities are given the appropriate amount of emphasis suggested for the primary grades.

6

Sample Weekly Plan for Kindergarten (Multiple Unit)

Monday	Tuesday	Wednesday	Thursday	Friday
Game Skills	*Floor Stunts*	*Rhythmic Activities*	*Singing Games*	*Classroom Games*
Bouncing practice activities— 1. bounce and catch 2. bounce several times 3. bounce to partner	Camel walk, elevator, tightrope walk	Pantomime animal walks, such as bears, lions, dogs, and horses	"London Bridge"	"Ringmaster"

Modified Teaching Unit

The modified teaching unit is a block of time allocated primarily for the instruction of one type of activity. For example, dance might be emphasized 90 percent of the time during a three- or four-week period, while the remaining 10 percent could be devoted to games and gymnastic activities. In the example below let us assume a third-grade class has a thirty-minute physical education period every day in the gymnasium. During the first week of the unit, dance activities would be taught on Monday, Tuesday, Thursday, and Friday. Wednesday is set aside for gymnastics or outdoor games.

This method provides both continuity and variety. For example, "Paw Paw Patch" is introduced on Monday and repeated on Tuesday so that the basic skills and dance patterns are learned. Later in the Tuesday lesson, "Bleking" is introduced. To provide variety, Wednesday is set aside for vigorous running and tag games which could be played in the gymnasium or outdoors. The remaining two days would be devoted to dance activities. This pattern is continued throughout the second and third weeks.

Dance Unit (Grade 3)

Week	Monday	Tuesday	Wednesday	Thursday	Friday
1st week	Introduce "Paw Paw Patch"	Review "Paw Paw Patch" Introduce "Bleking"	Games: Stunts Relay, Pinch-oh.	Review "Bleking" "Skip to My Lou"	Review "Paw Paw Patch," "Bleking," "Skip to My Lou"
2nd week	Review "Skip to My Lou" Introduce "Pease Porridge Hot"	Review "Pease Porridge Hot," "Skip to My Lou"	Gymnastics— stunts, balance beam, rope skipping	Review "Bleking," "Pease Porridge Hot"	Review "Skip to My Lou" Introduce "Heel and Toe"
3rd week	Review "Heel and Toe" Introduce "Shoo Fly"	Review "Heel and Toe" "Shoo Fly"	Review Games or Stunts	Review "Paw Paw Patch," "Bleking," "Skip to My Lou"	Review "Pease Porridge Hot," "Skip to My Lou," and "Heel and Toe"

Not only does the modified block, unlike the multiple unit, provide continuity in learning skills, but it also has certain desirable instructional features. It permits the teacher to plan one type of activity for an extended period, rather than three different types each week. Furthermore, it is much easier to plan a one-year program using the modified unit than the multiple approach.

Solid Teaching Unit

A solid teaching unit is an extended period of instruction—from one to several weeks—devoted exclusively to one type of activity. Its value lies in its continuity, as there is no disruption in the type of skill development. Perhaps the solid unit has its greatest application in team teaching, where the most qualified teacher is used to maximum effectiveness. However, fifth and sixth grade teachers who are responsible for their own physical education programs may find this type of unit applicable in teaching those activities that are of great interest to their students.

To illustrate this method, a solid four-week unit of softball has been organized for a sixth-grade class. Note that the physical education period is forty minutes long on Monday, Wednesday, and Friday, but only fifteen minutes long on Tuesday and Thursday. New skills are explained and demonstrated, drills are practiced, and lead-up games are played during the longer periods. The shorter periods are just long enough for a short drill and possibly a lead-up game.

It is suggested that the first week be planned in detail. After four or five days of instruction the teacher may note that certain skills will require additional concentration, or that the students are ready for more advanced skills and lead-up games. The remaining three weeks should be planned around the skill level and interests of the class.

It is possible to use both the modified and solid units during the year. Early fall and spring activities are particularly adaptable to the solid unit, while the modified unit may be the only feasible approach for activities requiring use of indoor facilities.

The final stage in the process of developing a physical education program is the development of daily lesson plans. This is discussed in Chapter 8, "Teaching Strategies and Techniques" (pages 154-56).

The Extraclass Program

The extraclass program includes such activities as sports competition between classes, all-school track meets, and limited competition with other schools. The extraclass program should be supplemental to the instructional program.

Softball Unit for Grade Six Using the Solid Block Approach

	Monday (40 min.)	Tuesday (15 min.)	Wednesday (40 min.)	Thursday (15 min.)	Friday (40 min.)
First week	Explain: Underhand throw (pitching) Practice: Zigzag passing Lead-up: Center ball	Practice: Throwing Lead-up: Shuttle throw	Explain: Bunting Practice: Swing at four Lead-up: Twenty-one softball	Review: Shuttle throw and Twenty-one	Explain: Grounders Practice: Zigzag passing Lead-up: Bat ball

Note: Continue the above pattern in second, third, and fourth weeks.

6

Figure 6.1

Furthermore, to be truly intramural in principle, it should be a voluntary program with a major emphasis on participation and student leadership and minor emphasis on winning. These principles are contained in a platform statement issued by the National Conference on Physical Education for Children of Elementary School Age. The following points are guidelines for the development of any extraclass physical program (Athletic Institute 1951):

1. First, as a foundation, all children should have a broad, varied, and graded physical education under competent instruction through all grades. In many of the activities in this program the competitive element is an important factor. The element of competition provides enjoyment and, under good leadership, leads to desirable social and emotional as well as physical growth.

2. Based upon a sound, comprehensive instructional program in grades five through eight, children should have opportunity to play in supervised intramural games and contests with others who are of corresponding maturity and ability within their own school. In grades below the fifth, the competitive elements found in the usual activities will satisfy the needs of children.

3. As a further opportunity to play with others beyond the confines of their own school or neighborhood, play or sports day programs may be planned with emphasis on constructive social, emotional, and health outcomes. Teams may be formed of

participants coming from more than a single school or agency, thus making playing together important.

In order to develop a comprehensive program of extraclass activities, teachers should understand the methods of organizing for competition, when to offer activities, and the types of activities that children enjoy playing in the intramural program. These topics are discussed next.

Intramural Program

A contemporary intramural program for elementary school children should include competition between classes or other equal competitive groups. The purpose of the intramural program should be to provide a way for every child who wishes to participate in a sport or club activity of his choice. The program obviously needs strong, enthusiastic support and guidance by the teacher. However, once the program has been organized, the children should assume the major responsibility for running virtually all aspects of it. The following information will provide the basic material for developing a comprehensive intramural program (see also the film "Participation for All," Appendix A).

Figure 6.2

Time Schedules for Participation

The time that is scheduled for intramural activities usually depends on the nature of the school population and the available facilities. Before school can be an effective time, particularly in districts where many parents work or when children arrive early by bus. The most popular time, of course, is the noon hour; this provides an opportunity for virtually all children to participate. There is, however, a general trend to hold more intramural activities after school. In urban areas where many parents work and there are limited community recreational facilities, the school playground or gymnasium is now being used for many after-school intramural and club activities. The success of these programs depends upon effective supervision by teachers, parents, and older students.

Types of Intramural Activities

The intramural activities that children enjoy generally are the activities they have learned in the regular instructional program. Since participation is voluntary, children should be allowed to choose their activities. The following team and individual games have proved very popular in intramural programs throughout the country:

Team Activities

Cross-country meet	Floor hockey
Soccer	Goodminton
Basketball	Line soccer
Bucketball	Indoor soccer
Volleyball	Flag football
Two-pitch softball	Yards
Track and field meet	Scoopball
Field hockey	California kickball

Individual and Dual Activities

Paddle tennis	Shuffleboard
Modified golf	Table tennis
Ring tennis	Four square
Handball	Horseshoes
Curling	Hand wrestling
Badminton	Punt, pass, and kick
Foul shooting	Frisbee
Tetherball	Beanbag bowling

Club Activities

Club activities should be considered as part of the intramural program. Teachers may find a group of children who are interested in continuing an activity learned in the instructional program but which does not lend itself to competition, such as yoga or folk dance. Other activities that cannot be offered in the regular instructional program, such as skiing or canoeing, can also be organized as a club activity.

The basic responsibility of the teaching staff is to provide the initial organization. Obviously, if a teacher is interested in sponsoring a skiing or canoeing club, the children will gain by the teacher's efforts and talents. However, club activities can and should reach out into the community for parents and other interested citizens to assist in activities that are beyond the financial, facility, and staff limitations of the school.

Interschool Activities

Perhaps one of the most controversial issues in the contemporary elementary physical education program is the desirability of interschool, or extramural, competition. Medical authorities and professional organizations oppose highly organized sports below the ninth grade from a general health point of view, including physical and psychological reasons (AAHPER 1968). However, they agree that from an *educational* point of view, minimal competition between schools is acceptable and, under proper supervision, even a desirable experience for children of upper elementary school age. These activities, however, should not drain the resources required in the instructional or intramural program.

Various organizations and experts in the area of study have proposed guidelines for interschool activities in the elementary school. The following points should be considered when developing an interschool program:

1. Interschool leagues or events should not interfere with the ongoing instructional or intramural program.

2. Boys and girls should have equal access to the interschool program.
3. Adverse parent or community pressure should not be allowed to interfere with the philosophy and general management of the interschool program.
4. All forms of competition should be minimized, with emphasis placed on participation rather than winning. Play days and sports days should be given higher priority than organized leagues between schools.
5. Adequate facilities, equipment, and supervision must be available.
6. Interschool activities should usually take place after school. Evening and weekend competition between schools should not be permitted.
7. The health, safety, and general welfare of boys and girls competing in interschool events should be stringently protected. This means medical examinations prior to competition, safe transportation to and from events, and safe facilities and equipment.

On the basis of these points, play days and sports days have become the most popular form of interschool activities.

Play Days
A play day involves children from two or more schools playing together on the same teams. Consider, for example, a basketball play day involving four schools. Player number one from each school is assigned to team A. Player number two from each school is assigned to Team B, player number three to team C, and player number four to team D. Player five for each school goes to Team A, player 6 to Team B, and so on until all children are assigned to a team. Schools loose their identity in this type of competitive event.

Sports Days
Sports days are similar to play days except that the teams represent their own schools. Each school enters one basketball team in a round-robin tournament, with one school eventually declared the winner.

Play days are more compatible with the goals of an interschool program than sports days. However, if a sports day is organized among two or more schools, it is important that players from participating schools possess relatively equal playing ability.

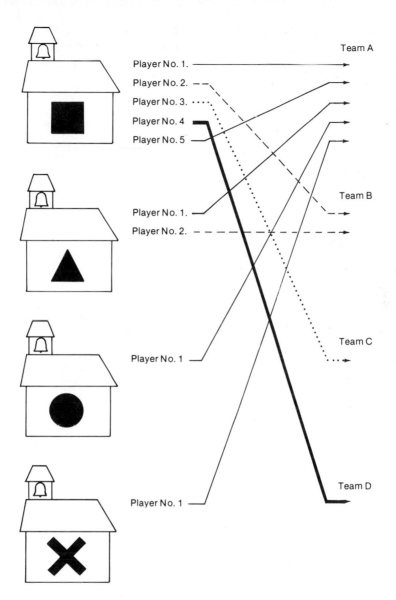

Player No. 1. ——————→ Team A

Player No. 2. - - - -

Player No. 3. · · · · ·

Player No. 4

Player No. 5

Player No. 1. ——————

Player No. 2. - - - - Team B

Player No. 1 Team C

Player No. 1 Team D

PLAY DAYS

Organizing for Physical Education

The quality of any physical education program depends primarily on the interest and competence of the teacher and the time and facilities available. Although these components will vary from school to school, some organizational problems are common to all schools. This chapter discusses the effective use of teachers in the physical education program and problems concerning equipment, supplies, and the safety of the instructional area.

Responsibility for Physical Education

The Playground, Gymnasium, and Classroom

Basic Equipment and Supplies

Types of Tournaments

Accidents and Preventive Safeguards

Responsibility for Physical Education

Several methods are used in assigning the responsibility for teaching physical education. The most ideal method is to employ a trained physical education specialist to handle virtually all phases of the physical education program. Another is to employ rotating specialists or consultants to assist classroom teachers in such areas as program development, equipment and facility planning, and general instruction. The third, and certainly most common, approach is to assign all responsibility for physical education to the classroom teacher. This becomes "team teaching" when classroom teachers pool their talents to provide a well-rounded physical education program.

Full-Time Physical Education Teachers

Employing a full-time physical education teacher in the elementary school has been the exception rather than the rule until the past few

124

years. In recent years, however, more school districts have hired physical education specialists, particularly in the upper grades. Underlying this trend is the recognition of the value of a well-rounded physical education program and the subsequent need for a specialist to develop individual programs for children with perceptual-motor or low-fitness problems, as well as to provide enriched programs for all children in such areas as dance, gymnastics, and individual and team sports.

Consulting Specialists

Because of the increased demands on the classroom teacher in all areas of the curriculum, administrators have attempted to alleviate their teaching load by employing consultants or teaching specialists. This is particularly the case in larger school systems, where music, speech, and physical education teaching specialists provide classroom teachers with up-to-date materials, methods, and techniques, and conduct classroom demonstrations and in-service sessions. The responsibility for these subject areas, however, still rests with the classroom teacher.

A classic example of how a teaching specialist is used in a large school is the Blair Elementary School near Spokane, Washington. This is the largest elementary school in the state of Washington with nearly twelve hundred students from kindergarten through grade eight. Recognizing the need for qualified physical education instructors, the administration hired a teaching specialist to assist classroom teachers.

Since it was virtually impossible for the specialist to meet with every teacher on a daily basis, a modified approach was taken. During the first three months of the school year, the specialist and each teacher developed instruction units and daily lesson plans. This procedure gave the specialist an opportunity to evaluate the teacher's ability to use her physical education guide, as well as her general competence in handling the physical education program. At the end of the three-month experimental period, a policy was established by the school administration requiring any teacher needing help to submit a lesson plan three days before the lesson. This not only motivated the teacher to develop lesson plans, but it also assisted the specialist in his own preparation for the classroom teacher. Within several months he was able to put many teachers "on their own."

Generally speaking, the mutually developed program provided the assistance the teachers needed to develop their own programs. With additional "free" time, the specialist was able to enrich the program by providing in-service sessions for specific grades in such activities as basketball skills, gymnastics, and track and field activities.

Self-Contained Classroom

Although administrators and teachers alike recognize the need for physical education specialists, the fact remains that elementary schools are predominantly self-contained, meaning that a classroom teacher, regardless of grade level, must be able to teach as many as eight or nine subjects. The majority of classroom teachers have had approximately one general course in physical education during college. Obviously, this preparation is inadequate, indicating a definite need for in-service workshops, better teaching guides, additional audiovisual aids, and summer school courses. These should provide assistance in content, organization, methods, and evaluative devices for all levels in the elementary school.

To say the current situation is hopeless or to consider physical education as a period of free play does disservice both to the intelligence of the classroom teacher and the needs of growing children. Research, educational philosophy, and automation in its broadest meaning indicate the need for a daily physical education program (President's Council on Youth Fitness 1961). The program must include a variety of activities to enhance normal growth and development and to provide opportunities that will foster emotional growth, social adjustment, and permanent leisure-time pursuits.

There are numerous examples of how school districts, large and small alike, have attempted to provide physical education programs without the assistance of physical education specialists. In Holt, Michigan, for example, the school board had no official physical education policy in its four elementary schools, yet a program was initiated. According to the director of elementary education, teachers were encouraged to attend workshops, summer sessions, and other in-service sessions. Their efforts led to the writing of a guide for kindergarten through grade six which covered physical education, health, and safety. Since most schools in the district were equipped with all-purpose rooms, each teacher was scheduled for one forty-five minute physical education period each week in such a facility. In addition, all teachers could devote thirty minutes a day to classroom or outdoor activities. As a follow-up, the administration hired adults to supervise noon-hour activities on the playing field and indoors during inclement weather.

Team Teaching

Team teaching is the organization of teachers and students into instructional groups which permit maximum utilization of staff abilities and enhance optimum growth of students. Team teaching may range from two teachers exchanging classrooms for one subject to the pooling of all teachers into a unified effort. The latter may involve regrouping of children, major curriculum changes, and extensive use of outside experts. Obviously, some form of team effort in handling physical education in the elementary school is worthy of consideration. The self-contained classroom structure, particularly for the intermediate grades, is not flexible enough to permit or encourage utilization of the special abilities of all teachers.

Since there are many forms of team teaching, it is difficult to present a list of advantages that will apply to every situation. However, it can be said that even the simplest form of team teaching

1. provides a means whereby the most effective use of teacher skill and talent is utilized

2. encourages more complete and detailed lesson preparation and presentation
3. provides an opportunity for students to be exposed to a larger number of capable teachers
4. provides an opportunity for more flexible grouping of students
5. provides a means of in-service experiences for all teachers
6. provides an opportunity for teachers to investigate the effectiveness of new methods, materials, and techniques
7. provides an opportunity for teachers to experience greater personal and professional satisfaction. (Cunningham 1960)

The simplest form of team teaching is for teachers to exchange classes for an assigned subject. When there are limited facilities, such as one gymnasium, and when two or more teachers are willing to share their talents, team teaching can be established. For example, a fourth-grade teacher who is extremely well qualified in music may exchange classrooms with a fifth-grade teacher who is equally competent in physical education. In this situation, both the teachers and the students benefit.

Another type of team teaching is two or more teachers pooling their talents to instruct several classes in one subject area. Applied to physical education, this would mean dividing two or more classrooms into groups based upon such criteria as skill performance or physical fitness levels, or a classification index based upon age, height, and weight.

The writer studied such a program in the Eastern Elementary School near San Juan, California. The school was experimenting with this type of team teaching in physical education, using a classification index as a means of grouping children from grades three to six. Four teachers formed the instructional staff for the team approach. In their planning sessions, it was found that one teacher was strong in gymnastics, one in dance, and one in track and field. The fourth teacher, not too strong in any area, was assigned games as an area of emphasis. Since the climate permitted outdoor activities virtually year-round, and since there were sufficient teaching stations in the playground area, a half-hour in the afternoon was set aside for physical education for grades three through six. The children were assigned to one of four groups based upon the classification index.

A three-week instructional schedule for the four groups was then established. The gymnastics teacher was assigned group one for a three-week block of stunts and tumbling activities in the gymnasium. Each of the other teachers was assigned one of the remaining groups for a similar period, emphasizing her own specialty. At the end of the three-week period, each student group rotated to a different instructor, who taught her specialty to the new group.

This type of team effort encourages the teacher to develop more detailed lesson plans. Throughout the rotation system, better understanding of student performance was obtained, as well as a greater effort by the equated groups of students. With a limited area of preparation, each teacher found time to experiment with new methods and techniques of learning. And because of the equalizing classification system, students could compete realistically for the same goals, and found more satisfaction and enjoyment in physical activities.

The Playground, Gymnasium, and Classroom

Another important consideration in the success of the physical education program is the adequacy of indoor and outdoor facilities. If playing space is inadequate, teaching procedures are ineffective, activity offerings are limited, and optimum growth and development of children are usually restricted. Important considerations relating to facility placement, size, and safety precautions will be discussed next.

Playground

The size of the school facility, including the gymnasium and outdoor space, is dependent first, of course, upon the number of children in the school. National standards recommend a minimum of five acres for any elementary school, plus one acre for every 100 pupils (Athletic Institute 1974). Hence, a school with 200 children would require seven acres. Beyond this minimum standard, the dimensions of a school site depend upon such factors as climate, economic conditions, and the attitude of the school and community toward physical education.

The primary consideration, however, of any play area is safety. School playgrounds in urban areas should be surrounded by heavy wire fences; entrances should have double fences rather than gates. If the playground is used by both primary and intermediate children, separate areas should be designated for age groups. If space is limited, a fence around the kindergarten-primary area may be called for. Part of the playground should be set aside for permanent equipment such as climbing cubes, horizontal ladders, obstacle courses, and adventure playground areas. This apparatus should be permanently anchored in cement casings. The area immediately under and around each apparatus should be loose dirt, sawdust, or sand. A portion of the playground, preferably close to the school, should be blacktop and large

Figure 7.1

enough for such activities as running and tag games. The remaining playground area should be grass turf, when water supply permits. Other types of surfaces used are oil-treated dirt, mixed sand, dirt and sawdust, and asphalt.

Following are basic recommendations for the playground:

1. Remove any physical hazard.
2. Restrict children to specific play areas.

Figure 7.2

3. Choose equipment on the basis of proven safety and practical value.
4. Provide adequate room within each area for additional equipment.
5. Establish a list of safety rules and make sure each child follows them.
6. Teach children to think in terms of safety for themselves and their classmates.
7. Inspect all equipment regularly.
8. Provide competent supervision within the playground area during regular class time, recesses, and the noon hour.

Creative Playgrounds

Teachers who are serious about helping children become self-directing individuals capable of expressing themselves creatively not only must practice creative teaching strategies; they must also see that the physical environment stimulates the creative process. In many schools, boxlike gymnasiums and flat, unobstructive playing fields constitute the physical education facilities. Playground equipment normally includes swings, slides, and unattractive steel climbing apparatus encased in concrete and surrounded by asphalt, cement, or sand. Although these apparatus may be easy to

Figure 7.3

keep tidy, they are unimaginative and lack educational value.

Basic Criteria for Creative Playgrounds

The following ten criteria (Ledermann and Trachsel 1968) for creative playgrounds will provide a guideline for evaluating existing play ground facilities and for constructing new ones. Several illustrations of commercial equipment, as well as "homemade" and "natural" equipment, show how schools in urban and rural areas can utilize available, inexpensive equipment. An extensive list of references is also provided in the appendixes.

1. Playgrounds must always be designed and equipped with their function for play foremost in mind.

   The playground should not be designed purely from the landscape gardener's aesthetic conception or the educator's concern for children's play habits and needs. It must serve the play characteristics of children and, at the same time, be aesthetic in the selection and arrangement of apparatus, pathways, and shrubs and greenery.

2. Architects, landscape designers, and educators must work together to produce good solutions to playground problems.

   There is a tendency for the architect, the landscape designer, and the educator to visualize the creative playground from their own points of view. The architect tends to inject his bias toward artistic creations; the landscape gardener may be more concerned with tree and flower arrangements than a child's play activities; and the educator is often tempted to see the creative playground as an extension of the classroom. All three specialists must recognize the contributions of the others, so that each plan is seen as a cooperative effort.

3. The playground is not meant for passive entertainment. It must encourage active, spontaneous, and creative play.

   The creative playground should not be a simple collection of commercial equipment, old cars, or concrete tunnels arranged in parallel rows. The apparatus, whether natural or commercial, should be selected and arranged to stimulate the child's imagination and enhance continuous exploration.

Figure 7.4

Figure 7.5

7

Figure 7.6

Figure 7.7

Figure 7.8

4. Half-finished components and materials for play are more valuable than mechanical equipment.

Most playgrounds are dominated by inflexible apparatus such as slides, swings, and a variety of rotary type equipment. It is not suggested that slides and swings be removed but that consideration be given to including more creative and, if possible, natural equipment such as large roots or trees or other materials that are available in the local area.

5. Playground design and equipment must conform to the typical games of the age group for which the playground is intended.

In the majority of cases, creative playgrounds are first seen as an addition to the primary school playground area. Children from age five to eight thoroughly enjoy playing on or around a creative playground. Intermediate children may appear to be more sophisticated; however, experience shows that children of this age level are equally interested in using creative equipment. Thus plans should consider the full age range in the elementary school.

6. The playground must offer a variety of possibilities for play.

A set 'of swings, a slide, and possibly a climbing tube or an unobstructed playing area do not constitute an adequate play area. Swinging for hours is similar to an adult playing a slot machine for hours. Neither activity is inherently creative. The playground should be arranged to stimulate creative movements both on apparatus and on the play surface.

7. The playground design must reflect the functions and movements of different games.

This involves the total play area of the school. For example, an elementary school playground has to service both primary and intermediate children. Consequently, the creative playground area should be away from the main ball game areas. If the school is near an area with trees, a ravine, or any type of natural area, the creative playground should be put near this site. Of course safety must be considered; natural areas that are potentially hazardous should not be considered as desirable locations.

8. The games of fantasy should not be overlooked.

Some children enjoy playing by themselves. Therefore, the creative playground, particularly for primary children, should provide small individual areas on or near apparatus where the child can absorb himself in fantasy or other forms of individual self-expression.

9. Architects and landscape designers themselves should "play" a little while designing the creative playground.

The specialists should observe children at play and attempt to visualize the potential area through "the eyes of a child." The designer who does this would not build a square sandbox, place a slide in the middle of an area with slopes and contours, or place equipment in straight lines. Relevance, too, is important. A creative playground near a coast should be representative of the area, with "ships" and "trees"—natural or man-made—in the general play area. Similar themes for the South and Midwest should be present in the creative playground.

10. Interested groups of people should cooperate in designing, equipping, and maintaining a playground.

The majority of creative playgrounds that have been constructed in Canada and the United States are the results of cooperative parent-teacher groups that wished to do something for local school children. Initially such projects

Figure 7.9

were undertaken because of the lack of tax money to construct this type of outdoor facility. This cooperative action has given the parents an understanding of the value and purpose of such playgrounds, and has also significantly reduced the amount of vandalism, as parents and children alike consider these jointly built facilities community property, and not just for use during school hours.

Gymnasium

The location, size, and special features of the gymnasium should be determined by the philosophy and activities of the physical education program. All too often, however, incorrect planning results in inadequate court dimensions, low ceilings, and, in many cases, avoidable hazards or obstructions. To help eliminate mistakes in the planning and construction of future elementary school gymnasiums, a guide to planning facilities has been developed by national leaders in the field of health and physical education. Included in this guide, *Planning Facilities for Athletics, Physical Education and Recreation* (Athletic Institute 1974), are standard recommendations for floor construction, playing space, storage facilities, and numerous other aspects of a well-planned gymnasium. It is advisable when planning new facilities to use this publication as a basic reference for nationally acceptable standards of gymnasium construction.

There are, however, basic recommendations relating to floor dimensions, placement of equipment, and general safety that apply to any gymnasium or multipurpose room that is used for physical education. The following suggestions will assist teachers in organizing an indoor facility for maximum use and optimum safety:

1. Maintain gymnasium temperature between sixty and sixty-five degrees.
2. Paint permanent boundary lines on the floor for activities held most often. Use different colored lines for each—black for basketball, red for volleyball, and green for a large center circle.

3. Provide adequate safety margins for all games. The standard basketball dimensions for elementary school children are seventy-four by forty-two feet. If the facility is only seventy by forty feet, the actual court dimensions should be sixty-seven by thirty-seven to provide a minimum three-foot safety zone around the court.
4. Remove all equipment that is not being used during the physical education class.
5. Request that any hazardous fixtures, such as floor level heating ducts and lighting fixtures, be covered with protective screens.
6. Establish a standard procedure for obtaining and returning equipment to the storage room.

Classroom

In many elementary schools throughout the country the only available space indoors for physical education is the classroom. Granted, this is inadequate; however, with some minor furniture adjustments the classroom can be used for many different physical activities (see Chapter 27). It is possible to shift moveable desks and tables to provide one area of the classroom that is free of obstructions. Since most lighting and window fixtures in the classroom are not screened, do not permit activities that will in any way create a potentially hazardous situation. Adjustable and moveable bars may be placed in doorways, mats can be used for tumbling activities, and short four-by-four beams and chairs can be used for balance activities.

Basic Equipment and Supplies

Physical education equipment refers to the more permanent apparatus such as balance beams and outdoor play apparatus. Generally speaking, these materials will last from five to twenty years, even with repeated use. Supplies, on the other hand, are expendable items such as balls, whistles, and records. These items will last one to two years. Each teacher should be able to list the proper equipment for her grade level and, where budgets are limited, to suggest how to make various types of equipment. (See Appendix B for diagrams of inexpensive equipment. See Appendix C for a list of commercial manufacturers and distributors of equipment and supplies.)

The type of physical education program, the geographic area, and economic conditions, among other things, will determine the type of equipment a school will buy. The following lists of suggestions will assist in ordering the proper type and size of equipment and supplies.

Recommended Playground Equipment

Climbing apparatus: climbing cubes, Big Toy apparatus, etc.

Horizontal bar: "chinning" or "turning bar" at three levels—forty-eight, fifty-four, and sixty-four inches—all five feet wide

Monkey rings

Horizontal ladder: 6½ feet high, length optional

Slide: eight feet high, with safety platform

Balance beam: eight to twelve feet long, three levels—eighteen, twenty-four, or forty-eight inches

Tether ball standards: minimum of three

Basketball standards: minimum of two; eight feet high

Volleyball standards: minimum of two

Softball backboards: minimum of two

Soccer goalposts: minimum of two

Creative playground apparatus (see Chapter 23)

Sandbox: six by ten feet, with cover

Track and field equipment: long jump pit, high jump pit and standards, hurdles

Optional and Homemade Equipment

Automobile tires suspended on rope or chain, with bottom of line twelve to fourteen inches off ground

Moveable barrows and kegs

Moveable planks eight to twelve feet long, with planed edges

Sawhorses of different heights (see Appendix B)

Concrete sewer pipes arranged in units of three or four

Obstacle courses, permanent or portable; type and construction should complement the climate and geographic area (see Chapter 4)

Recommended Indoor Equipment

Tumbling mats: minimum of four; light synthetic material; sizes are optional, although four by six feet mats are easy to handle and store

Individual mats: eighteen by thirty-six by three-fourths inches; minimum of forty, or one per child

Record player (three speeds)

Dance drum

Balance beam: one foot to four feet high, depending on general use, and approximately twelve feet long (see Appendix B)

Balance benches: reversible for optional use, plus hook attachment on one end (see Appendix B)

Horizontal bar (see Appendix B)

Scooters: twelve by twelve inches with four casters (see Appendix B)

Volleyball net and standards with adjustable heights

Basketball standards with rims eight feet from floor

Climbing ropes: fifteen to twenty feet high; 1½ to 2 inches in diameter

Vaulting box (see Appendix B)

Set of jumping boxes (see Appendix B)

Springboard or mini-tramp

Sawhorses: minimum of six (see Appendix B)

Portable agility apparatus (see Chapter 23)

Hockey nets: two

Optional equipment: trampoline and spotting apparatus, pegboards, parallel bars

Recommended Supplies for Gymnasium and Playground

The number of items listed here is a suggested minimum based on a maximum of thirty children using the supplies during one physical education period. If two or more classes meet at the same time, double or triple the number.

Supplies	Minimum Number
Long skipping ropes: ⅝ inch sash, nylon or plastic; 13, 14, and 15 feet	2 of each length
Individual skipping ropes: ⅜ inch sash, nylon or plastic; ten each of 6, 7, 7½, and 8 feet	1 set or 40 ropes
Utility balls	6 each size
Soccer balls (rubber cover)	10 to 15
Volleyballs (rubber cover)	10 to 15
Softballs	10 to 15
Softball mats	10 to 12
Beanbags (six by six inches)	30
Wands: ten each at 3, 3½, 4 and 4½ feet	1 set of 40 wands
Indian clubs or bowling pins	24 to 30
Measuring tape (50 feet)	1
Ball inflater with gauge	1
Rhythm drums	1
Records (see Part VI)	
Colored arm bands	2 sets of 15
Whistles	10 to 12
Stopwatch	6
Hoops	30
Jacks	60
Softball bases	4 sets
Softball catcher's mask, mitt, and body protector	2 each
Softball batting tee	2
Footballs (junior size)	6 to 8
Basketballs (junior size)	10 to 15
Plastic tape (1, 1½, and 2 inches in assorted colors)	2 rolls of each
Clipboards	4
Braids (cloth)	30
Blocks (4 inches by 4 inches by one foot)	30
Deck tennis rings	10 to 15
Paddles (paddle tennis)	24
Dance supplies (castanets, tambourines, bells, etc.)	4 of each
Sponge balls (assorted colors)	40
Fleece balls	40
Traffic cones	10 to 15
Lummi sticks	40
Scoops	15 to 30
Tinikling poles	12 to 16
Tote bags	10 to 15

Types of Tournaments

There should be opportunities within both the instructional and extraclass programs for children, particularly those in the intermediate grades, to test their abilities in organized competition. Such competition, however, should be well organized and, wherever possible, provide for maximum participation by all children.

There are numerous ways teams or individuals can compete. The type of tournament that is selected will depend upon the activity, the space available, the time, and the number of competitors. An Olympic meet plan is the only feasible type of tournament for track, swimming, and gymnastic activities. Single- or double-elimination and round-robin tournaments may be used for a variety of team and individual sports. Ladder tournaments are very useful for individual activities which can be played during instruction time, the noon hour, or after school. Careful consideration should be given to the strengths and weaknesses of each type of tournament on the basis of available time, space, and number of competitors.

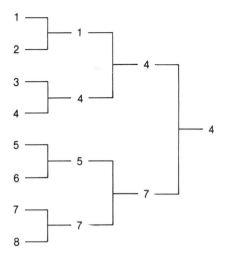

TOURNAMENT A
(For even number of teams)
Round 1   Round 2   Round 3

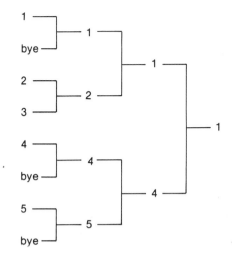

TOURNAMENT B
(For odd number of teams)
Round 1   Round 2   Round 3

Olympic Meet Plan

The Olympic meet tournament is used for contests that include a number of separate events, such as track and field activities. The winners of each event are awarded points, with an aggregate individual and team champion determined on the basis of points. In keeping with the idea of wide participation, first- to sixth- or seventh-place winners are awarded points. In an all-school track meet, for instance, the first six places in a fifty-yard dash might be awarded ten, nine, eight, seven, six, and five points, respectively. To encourage participation, relay and tug-of-war teams might be awarded a higher number of points than individual events.

Single Elimination

The elimination tournament is the easiest type to organize and the quickest way to declare a winner. Its use, therefore, will depend upon a large

number of teams, limited facilities, and minimum number of days to complete the tournament. Two examples of a single-elimination tournament are shown.

In the first round of tournament A, the odd-numbered teams played the even numbered, with teams 2, 3, 6, and 8 eliminated from competition. In the second round, team 4 beat team 1 and team 7 beat team 5. Teams 4 and 7 competed in the last round, and team 4 won the tournament. In tournament B three teams were given a "bye" in the first round, because there were an odd number of teams.

The single-elimination tournament does not require any byes when there are an even number of teams, providing they equal any power of two (2, 4, 8, 16, etc.). With an odd number of teams, it is necessary to give one or more teams a bye in the first round; the number of byes required for specific numbers of teams is shown in the following chart:

Number of Teams	Number of Byes	Number of Teams	Number of Byes	Number of Teams	Number of Byes
3	1	11	5	19	13
5	3	13	3	21	11
7	1	15	1	23	9
9	7	17	15	25	7

7

Round Robin

In a round-robin tournament each team plays every other team in the league. If time and facilities permit, this is the most desirable type of competition for team and individual sports. The winner is the player or team that wins the most games. Following is the procedure for organizing a round-robin tournament:

1. Determine the number of games to be played by applying the formula
   $[n(n-1)] \div 2$ (n equals the number of teams). For example, six teams would require $[6(6-1)] \div 2$, or 15, games.
2. Give each team a number and arrange in two columns.
   Round No. 1.
   1 plays 6
   2 plays 5
   3 plays 4
3. Keep team number 1 constant and rotate all other teams one place in a counterclockwise direction until fifteen games have been scheduled.

Round No. I	Round No. II	Round No. III	Round No. IV	Round No. V
1 vs 6	1 vs 5	1 vs 4	1 vs 3	1 vs 2
2 vs 5	6 vs 4	5 vs 3	4 vs 2	3 vs 6
3 vs 4	2 vs 3	6 vs 2	5 vs 6	4 vs 5

4. With an odd number of teams, use bye in place of a number and follow the same procedure. The example below is for five teams, with each bye indicating the team will not play.

1 vs bye	1 vs 5	1 vs 4	1 vs 3	1 vs 2
2 vs 5	bye vs 4	5 vs 3	4 vs 2	3 vs bye
3 vs 4	2 vs 3	bye vs 2	5 vs bye	4 vs 5

Ladder Tournament

A ladder tournament is a continuous competition limited only by the space and time available. Each player or team is placed (arbitrarily, by chance, or by the results of prior competition) on a ladder, as shown in the accompanying chart. The object is to climb to the top of the ladder and remain there until the end of the tournament. This type of competition is primarily used in individual activities during the instructional period, the noon hour, or after school. Its weakness is that only a limited number of stu-

dents can participate. Its main advantage is that students, once oriented to the rules, can run their own tournaments.

The following procedure is suggested for organizing a ladder tournament:

1. Construct a ladder chart on which names can be written (in grease pencil) or placed (tagged names or cards).
2. Place all players on the ladder. The simplest procedure is to draw names from a hat and record them from the top of the ladder down.

Free Throw Tournament
Bill
Mary
Jim
Susan
Jane
Don
Mike
Jack

3. Establish rules and post them near the tournament chart. Rules should include the following:
   a. A player may challenge only the players one rung or two above his name.
   b. The winner of a game remains on the higher rung, if originally there, or exchanges positions if originally on a lower rung.
   c. Once a challenge has been made, a deadline must be set by which the game must be played or cancelled (within two or three days).
   d. Set a completion date for the tournament.
   e. Other rules will depend upon the nature of the tournament, as well as what the teacher and class would like included. Allow players to add any legitimate rule.

Accidents and Preventive Safeguards

In virtually every school situation the teacher acts *in loco parentis,* in place of the parent. Whether in the classroom, on the playground, or on a class trip, the teacher is responsible for her pupils' welfare and safety. The teacher of physical activities must plan and supervise in ways that are not negligent. Since teachers can be held legally liable for acts of negligence, an understanding of this problem and its implication for the physical education program is extremely important.

Negligence

The National Education Association has defined negligence as any act—or its absence—that falls below the standard established by law for the protection of others against unreasonable risk or harm. Negligence, therefore, may be (1) an act which a reasonable person would have realized involved an unreasonable risk of injury to others or (2) failure to do an act which is necessary for the protection or assistance of another and which one is under duty to do. According to this definition, teachers can be held liable if their behavior is proved negligent in the following circumstances:

1. If a pupil is injured on school premises (playground, buildings, or equipment) that are judged defective.

   Safety standards for all facilities and equipment are usually set by the school district, and they must be maintained. Consequently, for the protection of the children, any facility or piece of equipment that does not meet these standards (excessive damage to a field, such as large rocks showing; extensive holes caused by flooding; or broken gymnastic equipment) should be reported and *not used* until competent authorities have certified it meets all safety requirements.

2. If an injury occurs while the teacher has left an assigned instructional or supervisory group for any period of time.

   In virtually every teaching situation in the public schools, only a qualified teacher—usually defined as one holding a teacher's credential and under contract with a school district—can assume responsibility for the pupils' instruction and safety. Classroom teachers, therefore, should seek clarification about delegated authority to student teachers and paraprofessional assistants (part-time helpers, parents, etc.). Certainly, a teacher who leaves a student in charge while she leaves the instructional area, regardless of the reason or duration of time, is negligent.

3. If a pupil is injured while attempting to perform an exercise or movement that is beyond his ability.

   This is probably the most vulnerable area for a teacher, particularly within gymnastics, where there are stunts that are potentially hazardous. If a child has been taught according to a normal progression of skill and has been given adequate instruction in form and safety, an accident probably will not occur. If an accident does happen, the teacher is usually not considered liable if adequate teaching has been provided and safety precautions taken.

   The important point is that teachers should follow the recommended programs and provide adequate instruction and safety for all participants. The gymnastic program recommended in this book adheres to the principle that each child should progress according to his demonstrated ability, not according to some arbitrary standard set for all participants.

4. If a pupil is injured as the direct result of another pupil's negligence.

   The teacher should be able to foresee and prevent malicious conduct by any child under her care. The class must adhere to a standard of conduct that includes respect and consideration for the safety of every class member. This is usually stated by the teacher (and better yet, agreed upon by the pupils) in the form of "rules of conduct" which the children must follow. When one child's malicious behavior causes injury to another, the "case" against the teacher would depend upon an evaluation of the teacher's ability, the situation, and a thorough investigation of the incident.

Accidents and Preventive Safeguards

An accident is an unforeseen event that occurs without the will or design of the person whose act caused it; it is an event that occurs without fault, carelessness, or lack of proper circumspection for the person affected, or that could not have been avoided under the existing circumstances (Bucher, 1963). An accident, therefore, excludes negligence. If the following basic standards are followed, optimum safety will be guaranteed:

1. Maintain playground and gymnasium equipment in proper working order. Repair defective equipment immediately or remove it from the play area.
2. Introduce activities that are appropriate to the child's skill level. Follow educationally acceptable textbooks or physical education guides, and never require a child to perform a stunt or skill beyond his capability.
3. Provide continuous supervision for any scheduled physical education activity. Recess and noon-hour activities also must be adequately supervised according to a desirable pupil-teacher ratio. This ratio should be stated in a written policy agreed to by the school board, principal, and teachers.

4. Provide safe instructional play areas. The size of the area should meet the standards established by national, state, or local authorities and be free of physical hazards and known nuisances. When it is virtually impossible to remove potential hazards, safety rules should be established and followed.
5. Provide competent, periodic health and physical examinations to determine whether the child should participate in regular or remedial physical education activities.* Also establish adequate follow-up procedures for allowing children to return to physical activities after illness, and provisions for detected physical deficiencies.
6. Employ only certified personnel for teaching or supervising physical education activities.

Physical education by its very nature is susceptible to accidents. And, because activity is vital to the normal growth and development of the child, teachers should not eliminate vigorous activities from their program out of fear of accidents. They should, however, use wisdom and prudence in the selection, instruction, and supervision of the physical education program.

*The interpretation of "competent" should be made by the principal or superintendent. Generally speaking, a competent health and physical examination is one that is given by a licensed medical practitioner.

Teaching Strategies and Techniques

8

Contemporary teaching in the elementary school is emphasizing concept development, rather than the simple acquisition of facts and knowledge. Accompanying this emphasis is an effort to individualize and personalize the learning process in order to respond to individual differences and to provide a learning atmosphere that will enhance positive relationships. The teacher's role in this type of educational process is to help the child achieve his full intellectual, physical, and creative potential. This goal can be reached only through an informal learning atmosphere where the responsibility for learning is shared by the teacher and the child.

A child learns new skills and concepts when he is capable of exploring alternatives. This means he must have a goal, some uncertainty as to how to reach it, and the ability and motivation to attempt to reach it. The essential duties of the teacher of physical education, as with all subjects, are to provide learning tasks that are within each child's reach and to give continuous encouragement and assistance throughout the learning process.

The many skills and movement concepts of physical education cannot be learned through one approach, however. Each new learning situation must be tailored to the varying degrees of interest and skill found in a class of twenty-five or more young learners. There is no ideal style of teaching, no single set of concepts or learning principles, no one best method that will guarantee success. The teacher should draw from the areas discussed in this chapter and develop her own teaching style or approach.

Concept development, how children learn motor skills, and how various teaching methods and techniques can be used to teach physical activities are discussed in the first part of this chapter. Then, how to plan and present a lesson will be discussed, along with a few important routine procedures.

Concept Development in Physical Education

In physical education, as in all subject areas, a concept can be defined as the meaning a person attaches to something he has experienced. Elementary school children's conceptual understanding of things, principles, and values varies according to their experiences and abilities. For example, a first grader's concept of balance is based upon his limited experience of holding a balance position or moving in various ways without losing his balance. He gains a deeper understanding of the concept, and increased skill, with continued experience in balance activities and a teacher's or parent's assistance in helping him understand why and how he can maintain balance.

A sixth grader who has experienced a wide variety of balance stunts and movements and has received continuing explanation from his teacher will develop a much higher level of conceptual understanding about static and dynamic forms of balance. The child who learns the principles of gravity—a wider base of support and lowering the center of gravity—while he performs a headstand not only will improve his skill, but will also increase his conceptual understanding of balance.

The important consideration for teachers is that we cannot *teach* concepts. The child must *formulate* concepts through his perception of his experiences and his own unique cognitive processes. In physical education, we too often have taught skills and knowledge without trying to help the child develop a conceptual understanding of his movement patterns. And since we cannot directly teach a concept, we must create a learning environment that allows the child to experience, to clarify, and to build his own conceptual understanding of how and why his body moves in a particular way.

The acquisition of concepts is important because concepts provide the young learner with the basis for understanding the world around him, for making decisions, and for responding or acting in a particular way. There is no established list of concepts in physical education that should be acquired by primary or intermediate children. Throughout this book, however, the teacher will find important concepts relating to safety, balance, and force, and to a wide variety of game, dance, and gymnastic skills and movement patterns. It is important that she constantly attempt to help each child understand these essential concepts. Such an understanding may well lead to a desire by the young learner to participate in physical activities throughout his life.

Individualized Learning

Individualized learning is based on the premise that teaching should be adapted to the unique abilities and special needs of each learner. This places the learner, not the subject, at the center of the curriculum and teaching. It must be understood that a teacher who provides individual assistance to one or more children in a class of thirty or more is applying a *technique,* and is in no way teaching an individualized instructional program.

Individualized learning occurs only when there is a sequential plan for every child, including a diagnosis of the child's potential ability and a teaching prescription to develop that potential. True individualization is possible when there is a ratio of one teacher to one child. However, for groups of two or more children with varying degrees of ability, it is rare that a true individualized instructional program is ever achieved.

Figure 8.1

When we use the term individualized instruction in physical education, we are really talking about a form of differential instruction. Such a program usually takes two approaches. The first is to *vary the time* it takes the children to achieve a specific movement task. For example, we can ask three children with varying levels of ability to walk across a narrow balance beam, allowing each child to complete the task in his own time. However, when the task is a structured one, such as a specified walking movement, and the child does not possess the ability to accomplish it regardless of the time given him, we have a nice example of an exercise in futility.

The second approach used to individualize a physical education program is to *vary the task,* and, if necessary, the time. Allowing each child to cross the length of the balance beam in any way possible would be varying the task. If a teacher can vary the task, she has a very real possibility of providing an individualized program.

There are several ways that primary and intermediate teachers can individualize parts of the physical education program. Virtually all of the following approaches and techniques allow the task to be varied for each individual while he is a member of a larger group or the whole class. These approaches also allow each child to progress at his own rate and ability, and to feel at ease and successful and that he is an equal and participating member of the class.

Movement Education

Movement education meets the criteria for individualized learning in two fundamental ways. First, there are no standardized skills. Rather, there are four categories of movement that describe what the body is capable of doing, how the body can move, where it can move, and its relationship to apparatus or other performers. Each child attempts to answer a movement challenge according to his ability and interest. Second, there is an infinite number of ways that each child can *vary the task* and the teacher can *vary the time* it takes to complete the task. This approach was introduced in Chapter 5 (pp. 70-75) and is applied in a sequential way in Part V, "Gymnastic and Movement Activities." A further application is found in Chapter 26, "Creative Dance Activities."

Inventive Games

The inventive games approach, introduced in Chapter 10 (pp. 173-77) is an effective way of individualizing the teaching of partner, team, and individual games. By changing the number of players, playing space, rules, skills, or equipment, the task is automatically varied. The inventive, or creative, games approach is incorporated into each chapter of Part IV, the games section of this book.

Task or Challenge Cards

Task or challenge cards are another enjoyable way of individualizing games, dance, and gymnastic activities. The value of this technique is that the teacher can prepare a series of tasks, varying from simple to complex movement challenges, to adapt to the differences in ability that exist within a class of thirty or more. The follow-

```
┌─────────────────────────────────────┐
│                                       │
│                                       │
│           Inventive Games             │
│         (Partner Activities)          │
│  Make up a game with your partner     │
│  that includes one ball, a bounce,    │
│  and a catch.                         │
│                                       │
│                                       │
└─────────────────────────────────────┘
```

```
┌─────────────────────────────────────┐
│                                       │
│                                       │
│             Gymnastics                │
│        (Individual Sequences)         │
│  Make up a sequence that includes     │
│  a stretch, a curl, and a change      │
│  of direction.                        │
│                                       │
│                                       │
└─────────────────────────────────────┘
```

```
┌─────────────────────────────────────┐
│                                       │
│                                       │
│                Dance                  │
│     (Rhythmic Activities: Group Work) │
│  In your group of four, develop a     │
│  routine that includes clapping,      │
│  walking, hopping, and two changes    │
│  in direction. (Music: "Pluma Blanca")│
│                                       │
│                                       │
└─────────────────────────────────────┘
```

ing examples illustrate how this technique can be applied to game, dance, and gymnastic activities:

There are several examples of the application of tasks or challenges in later chapters. Refer specifically to Chapter 22 (pp. 434-35) and Chapter 24 (pp. 512-13) for additional ideas.

Theory and Principles of Learning

A theory of learning is a theoretical assumption of how an organism learns. In physical education, the theory must provide a reasonable basis for understanding motor learning and a list of principles of learning that can be applied to the teaching and learning of physical activities. Brief descriptions of two major theories of learning follow; they provide a framework for understanding motor learning and the important principles that should be considered in teaching physical education. It is impossible to include an extensive coverage of each theory here. Such treatment can be found in the selected references listed in Appendix A.

Stimulus-Response Theory

The Stimulus-Response Theory developed by Thorndike in 1906 was an attempt to describe how a person learns and adjusts to his world. His hypothesis was that learning is the strengthening of the connection—called a "bond"—between a stimulus and a response. Accordingly, his conception of learning was that a person is acted upon and then initiates an act in response. In brief, his "laws" of learning, which are still highly influential in teaching today, are:

1. The Law of Readiness: Learning depends upon readiness to act, which, in turn, facilitates the response.
2. The Law of Effect: Learning is facilitated or retarded according to the degree of satisfaction or annoyance that accompanies the act.
3. The Law of Exercise: The more often a connection between bonds is repeated, the more firmly the connection (pairing of bonds) becomes fixed (learned).

Thorndike modified his laws in later years on the basis of additional findings. He found that greater effects result from satisfaction than displeasure. The obvious implications of this for providing rewards rather than punishment have greatly affected the nature of teaching.

Principles of teaching physical education based on the Stimulus-Response Theory appear to be helpful, but incomplete. They are helpful in recognizing the importance of repeating motor skills and the need to make the learning task satisfying to the learner. This theory has at least partial application to learning such skills as throwing, kicking, swimming, and gymnastic movements. But since the theory fails to recognize the fundamental concept (from a Gestalt viewpoint) that a learner is a purposeful and holistic organism capable of thinking, it is limited in providing a basis for understanding other types of learning and behavior. For example, the theory falls immeasurably short when used to explain social behavior, individual and team strategy, or creative movement in dance or gymnastics.

Field Theory

The Field Theory, developed by Wertheimer and others, assumes that the learner has a personality and reacts as a whole from the very beginning. It maintains that the human organism possesses a certain order from the beginning. All attributes are considered as integral and indivisible parts of the whole personality; they may be differentiated but cannot be separated from the organization of the whole being (Knapp, 1967). Learning proceeds from the comprehension of the whole to the identification of the smaller parts. Therefore, learning is not considered to be an additive process, as it is with the Stimulus-Response Theory, but consists of a continuous reorganization of new learnings with previous ones, resulting in new insights.

This theory stresses that the fundamental importance that any learning experience has on the learner depends upon his unique perception of the experience in relation to his previous experiences, abilities, and personal desires. From this point of view, learning is an individualized process, with the teacher serving as a guider of the learning experience.

Principles of Learning Motor Skills

Continuous experimentation has produced principles of learning that provide a reasonable guideline for teachers as they organize learning experiences and select teaching methods and techniques. Some of the following principles are derived from the Stimulus-Response Theory, while others are the direct application of the Field Theory. Thus the principles represent an eclectic point of view. Since knowledge of the learning process is still incomplete, these principles should be used only as guidelines. The teacher should apply her own common sense to every learning situation.

Principle of Interest

Any skill, whether it be climbing a rope or throwing a softball, will be acquired more efficiently if the child has a motive for learning it. His attitude toward learning the skill will determine for the most part the amount and kind of learning.

It is inherent in this principle that the teacher foster in the child a desire to learn motor skills. Learning will generally take place if the child experiences immediate satisfaction, if he sees the necessity of building a strong, healthy body, or if he values the skill as something he can use during his leisure time. It is also possible that learning can occur out of fear or because of some extrinsic reward, such as a star or check put beside his name.

Implications for Physical Education

1. Select activities that are appropriate to the child's interests, needs, and capacities.
2. Stress the intrinsic value of the activity.
3. Present activities in such a way that each child achieves some degree of success.

Principle of Practice

Research in motor learning strongly suggests that practice is necessary for the acquisition of a motor skill. The child must practice correctly, however, and until the skill becomes overlearned or automatic. Once a child has learned to swim, several months may elapse without practice, yet he will still be able to swim. In general, the more the skill is overlearned, the longer the time before it is lost. But if practice is done badly, it will not lead to improvement, and might even lead to regression (Arnold, 1968).

Implications for Physical Education

1. Select skills that are appropriate to the group's interests and maturation level.
2. Stress proper form while the skill is being learned. After the skill has been learned, stress other factors, such as speed and distance.
3. Repeat drill activities after several months to insure retention.

Principle of Distributed Practice

A motor skill is learned more effectively with distributed practice periods than with massed practice periods. The length of the practice period, as well as the time between practices, depends upon the difficulty of the skill, the child's ability, and his background. However, as a general rule, a short period of intense effort and attention is better than a halfhearted longer period (Knapp 1967).

This principle generally applies to all age levels and virtually all skills. But there are certainly times, depending on the interest of the children and the amount of effort required, when the practice period might be longer or shorter than normally considered wise. For example, if children are permitted to practice a forward roll until they become dizzy and fatigued, the practice period is too long and too strenuous, regardless of student interest. Self-testing activities for any age group should have a variation so that one part of the body is not overworked.

A teacher working with fifth- and sixth-grade children in an activity such as volleyball lead-up games may find that the students remain interested and enthusiastic for ten or fifteen minutes or even longer. So long as interest is high and skill development is fostered, it is not only permissible, but desirable, to extend the practice period. On the other hand, when the children are indifferent and are not attaining the skill, a change in the lead-up activity or a shorter practice period is suggested.

Implications for Physical Education

1. Adjust the length of the practice period and the spacing of rest periods of the class and to the material being taught.
2. Change an activity whenever the children show fatigue, boredom, and poor skill development.

Principle of Skill Specificity

The ability of a child to acquire a particular skill depends upon his unique characteristics. He may excel in one skill but be awkward in others that require about the same maturity and physical effort (Cratty 1967). A nine-year-old boy may be able to throw, catch, and hit a softball with ease and accuracy, but still show a subpar performance in volleyball activities, which require about the same effort and physical attributes.

This principle also applies to children who have reached the same psychological and physiological maturity level. After a single demonstration of a skill, one child may be able to perform it in its entirety, while another child may need more demonstration and practice to perform even a part of the skill. This is seen in such sports as swimming, basketball, and track and field.

Implications for Physical Education

1. Provide varied activities at all grade levels.
2. Allow for individual differences in standards of performance of a skill.
3. Allow for variations in the speed at which children acquire the same skill.
4. Develop standards based upon the individual's level and rate of development rather than the class average.

Principle of Whole-Part Learning

According to Knapp, material is learned in the *whole method* by going through it completely again and again. In the *part method,* the material is divided into portions, which are practiced, and eventually the parts are joined as a whole. In physical education, and within any skill area, it is difficult to define what is whole and what is a part of the skill or game. Recognizing this difficulty, the available evidence indicates that the whole method is superior to the part method in teaching motor skills (Knapp, 1967).

A teacher applying this principle must decide whether to teach a movement in its entirety or break it down into parts. The choice depends first upon the complexity of the skill and second upon the learner's amount and speed of skill development. For example, a teacher demonstrates to her third-grade class a one-foot hop-skipping skill using a single rope. The children then attempt to do the skill in its entirety; this is practice through the whole method.

But if only a few children learn the skill after repeated attempts, it would be better to break down the skill into simpler movements. The children could do a one-foot hop over a long rope turned by two people, then attempt the one-foot hop with a single rope, using a half swing. Finally, with a full turn of the rope, the hopping movement could be integrated into the rhythmic turning of the rope.

Implications for Physical Education

1. Use the whole method whenever the skill represents a single functional movement.
2. It may be desirable to break down more complex skills into smaller parts. Complexity depends upon the skill as well as the learner's ability.
3. Generally, the rate and amount of learning will indicate the effectiveness of the method used.

Principle of Transfer

Transfer in physical education can be defined as the effect that practice of one motor task has upon the learning or performance of a second, closely related task (Cratty 1967). Underlying this principle is the assumption that a learner will take advantage of what a new situation has in common with his previous experience, such as applying the knowledge of an underhand throwing motion in learning to serve a volleyball. Although it has been contended that transfer particularly will occur between identical skills or movements, there is no conclusive evidence to support this. This evidence instead seems to support the principle of specificity discussed earlier.

Implications for Physical Education

Proponents of the movement education approach, including its originator, Rudolph Laban, have said that it has a strong carry-over to other skill learning, but there is no evidence to indicate a common motor skill factor. Current research indicates that transfer depends upon the degree of resemblance between the skills.

There are, however, many other reasons for incorporating the movement education approach. One important one is that a carry-over does occur with movement education in the form of a positive attitude toward other activities.

Principle of Skill Improvement

A child does not always learn every physical skill in the same way. There are too many factors affecting the learning curve, including the complexity of the skill, the child's motivation and physical ability, and the adequacy of instruction.

Generally speaking, however, the initial phase of learning is usually quite rapid. This may be due to the child's enthusiasm for a new activity and the fact that he learns the easy parts first, utilizing previously acquired skills. But progress slows down gradually, even as practice continues, to a period of almost no overt improvement. There are numerous explanations for these learning "plateaus," such as lack of motivation, failure to learn a prerequisite skill, and improper instruction. With proper analysis and correction an increase in skill attainment should result.

Implications for Physical Education

1. Teachers should recognize children's individual differences in the learning curve for the same activity.
2. After a new skill is introduced, allow sufficient practice time for mastery.
3. Be aware of physiological limitations that hinder or prevent additional improvement.

Older concepts of teaching methods were based upon the premise that the teacher was the sole authority of what was correct and desirable for children. Children were expected to learn, regardless of their limitations and interests or the inadequacies of the learning situation. Contemporary education has replaced these concepts with principles of learning that are based upon tested thinking and experimentation.

All principles of learning are applicable to physical education. Those stated in this chapter, however, are extremely important for selecting physical activities, choosing appropriate methods, and understanding how motor skills are learned. When these principles are considered in relation to the goals of the physical education program and the characteristics of the learner, the scope and direction of the program and the way it should be taught should become abundantly clear.

Figure 8.2

Methods of Teaching

An *approach to teaching* can be defined as a comprehensive way of utilizing both content and method. A *teacher-directed* approach is not simply the direct method of instruction (described in this section); it emphasizes this, but it also includes other methods and a unique arrangement and emphasis of content. Similarly, such terms as *individualized, student-oriented, movement exploration,* and *movement education* refer to approaches because they too involve a unique arrangement of content and special use of one or more instruction methods and techniques.

A *method,* as distinguished from an approach or technique, is a general way of guiding and controlling learning experiences (Davis and Wallis 1961). There are, in turn, various ways of classifying methods, such as *lecture, tutorial,* or *problem-solving.* And each of these can be subdivided into more specific methods. This procedure, however, often leads to confusion rather than clarification. Recognizing the limitations of any definition, then, the following classification, based upon the amount of freedom or choice given to students in a particular learning task, will provide a basis for understanding and applying one or more "methods" of instruction in teaching physical education.

Direct Method	Limitation Method	Indirect Method

←————— Toward teacher control of — — — — — — — — — — Toward student choice of —————→
movement and use of equip- movement and use of equip-
ment or apparatus ment or apparatus

Direct Method

A teaching method is direct when the choice of the activity and how it is to be performed is entirely the teacher's (Bilborough and Jones 1969). The teacher arranges the class in lines or a circle, chooses the activity, such as practicing a basketball chest pass, and prescribes how and where each child is to practice the movement. Use of the direct method is illustrated here in teaching the forward roll (fig. 8.3).

1. Class Organization: The class can be arranged in parallel lines facing a mat or scattered, with each child working within his own area, as illustrated. The essential aspect is that all children will watch a demonstration and then practice the skill.
2. Choice of Activity: In this example, all children are restricted to practicing the forward roll. The choice is the teacher's.

Although student participation in choosing the activity and how it should be practiced is limited in the direct method, there are situations when this method is extremely useful and educationally defensible. It is the most effective and efficient way, for example, to teach a specific movement skill, safety procedure, or the rules of a game. And when the general level of skill is low, such as for heading in soccer or performing a headstand in gymnastics, the direct method is appropriate to use to illustrate, clarify, and practice various aspects of a skill or movement. In addition, this method can be used when class discipline is low to regain control and direction.

Figure 8.3

Indirect Method

The indirect method allows the children, individually or collectively, to choose the activity and decide how they wish to use their time. Obviously, there must be some reference to a particular activity or age level. To allow six- or seven-year-olds complete freedom of choice in a well-equipped gymnasium without prior instruction in skill and safety would be unfair to students and teacher.

However, when children have been taught a basic movement "vocabulary," as well as to progress according to their own ability, the indirect method has value. Once children have developed the ability to work independently and have respect for the safety and interests of other children, they should be given freedom to develop leadership, creative movements, and group cooperation without the direct assistance of the teacher. The indirect method can thus be used in game, dance, and gymnastic activities to develop and foster these skills and characteristics.

Limitation Method

The limitation method is actually a compromise between the direct and indirect methods of instruction. It simply means that the choice of the activity or how it is performed is limited by the teacher in some way. For example, when teaching a forward roll, the teacher might limit the choice by indicating that the forward roll was to be practiced on the floor or on mats. But by posing a challenge, such as "practice the forward roll and see how many variations in leg positions you can make," some freedom of interpretation still is provided. This freedom is a basic characteristic of the limitation method. Figure 8.4 illustrates this freedom of interpretation as the children answer another challenge.

Since the limitation method possesses the best aspects of both the direct and indirect methods of teaching, it has the greatest application and value in virtually all areas of the physical education program. For example, when

Figure 8.4 "Can you balance on three parts of your body?"

teaching dance, a primary teacher might use the direct method initially to teach a skip or gallop step. Once the step has been learned, she might apply the limitation method by providing musical accompaniment and allowing the children to move in any direction and create individual or dual patterns. The single limitation would be that all use a skip movement.

A few of the more obvious advantages of this method are

1. It allows the teacher to give some direction without restricting the free or creative expressions of the children.
2. It allows for physical differences and varying interests of the children.
3. Through a careful choice of activities it allows the teacher to develop all aspects of movement rather than what might become a "one-sided" development if left solely to each child.
4. Analysis and correction of movements by the teacher is simplified because one type of movement is to be practiced.

There is a problem that virtually all teachers must overcome when using the limitation method—shifting from *directing* children to perform a movement to *guiding* them through suggestions and challenging questions. Although each teacher will develop her own style

of asking questions, the following phrases and words have proved quite successful:

> Can you make a . . .?
> Can you discover a new . . .?
> Can you add to this by . . .?
> Can you find another way of . . .?
> Can you add a different way to . . .?
> Can you vary your . . .?
> Can you improve on the . . .?
> Could you move from . . .?
> Could you shift . . .?
> Could you change . . .?
> Try to add on to . . . .
> Try to vary . . . .
> How many different ways . . .?
> Are you able to . . .?
> See if you can . . . .
> Attempt to do . . . .
> Is it possible to . . .?
> Discover a new way to . . . .

Avoid the words "I want you to do . . .." The key words should stimulate a creative interpretation of a task or challenge. Once you have posed the question, it is usually necessary to give some command to start. Probably the most common, and informal, beginning is "off" or "away you go." Children react extremely well to this type of comment. Other expressions are "and begin" or "start."

The direct, limitation, and indirect methods of instruction should not be considered as separate entities, even within a single lesson. The selection and emphasis of any method should depend upon how a particular movement skill or understanding can best be learned by the children. Also to be considered are the teacher's philosophy and ability, the facilities, and the ability grouping of students.

Techniques of Teaching

A method has been defined as a general way of guiding and controlling the learning experiences of children. A *technique* can be defined two ways. In a restricted sense, it is a small part of a method. For example, a demonstration by the teacher of a throwing or kicking skill is clearly a part of the direct teaching method. A carefully worded question or a unique movement challenge is one technique of the limitation method.

But there are other types of techniques, such as variations in voice inflections, ways of using equipment and apparatus, and unique applications of audiovisual materials, that do not belong to any particular method, but are used in varying ways and degrees by each teacher. It is the emphasis that the teacher gives to such techniques that produces her "style" of teaching. Hence, there is no set number of techniques that one must master to be an effective teacher. It takes the teacher years to develop her style of teaching, and she retains or discards each technique on the basis of its efficiency in the learning process.

Creating an Effective Learning Atmosphere

The atmosphere for a physical education lesson should be the same as for any other classroom situation—a setting where all children are actively engaged in learning skills and the teacher assumes the role of guider or helper. The atmosphere should be friendly, and there should be a minimum amount of noise. Children should be able to work in the gymnasium and hear the teacher's voice at any time. A teacher who consistently has to raise her voice to be heard will find she is competing with, rather than controlling, the noise of her class.

Because classroom teachers are responsible for their own physical education programs in most elementary schools, they rarely have time to change clothes for gym period, except for tennis shoes. In fact, it is no longer considered to be vitally important anyway. "Spotting" by the teacher is used to a limited degree, since each child is taught to progress at his own rate and to be concerned with his own and others' safety. And, although teachers can demonstrate skills, it is preferable from both practical and educational points of view for children (who normally possess greater skill than the classroom teacher) to demonstrate. Of course, teachers

who wish to change into gym clothes may do so, particularly those who are assigned to physical education for a large percentage of their time.

Teaching Motor Skills

There are many ways to teach motor skills, but the technique that is best is usually the one that works. To learn any skill a child must have the inherent ability, a clear understanding of the movements involved, a reason for learning it, and an opportunity to repeat the skill until it is learned. Generally speaking, a skill is learned through a process of explaining, demonstrating, discovering, and perfecting. But this in no way means there is a simple progression from demonstration of a skill to practice and analysis; each child will acquire a skill in his own way. However, to help children learn *standardized* skills, which are those that are performed in much the same way by all children, we usually follow a pattern—explaining and demonstrating, then allowing time for individual practice and analysis.

Following are basic suggestions to assist the teacher in developing her own effective techniques:

1. Arrange the class so that every student has a clear view of the demonstration. Eliminate unnecessary interference, such as equipment, poor lighting, and excessive noise.
2. Explain the skill clearly and concisely. Allow time for the class to digest each important part of the skill.
3. Pause repeatedly during the explanation and check to see if the class understands; when necessary, repeat parts of the demonstration.
4. Speak in a vocabulary that is appropriate to the group.
5. Provide an accurate demonstration of the skill. If the teacher cannot demonstrate it, use a pupil or visual aids.
6. Do the skill at a slower speed than it is normally performed.
7. Repeat the demonstration several times, including explanations of one or more key parts.
8. Keep the demonstration short and to the point.

9. Be patient and sympathetic; a child acquires skills according to his own readiness and capacity.
10. If a child is not learning a skill in its entirety, break it down into simpler parts.
11. Give encouragement and praise, rather than scorn and punishment, regardless of how small or large the task.

Effective Use of Teaching Formations

Basic formations that teachers can use in organizing physical education activities are the line, circle, and shuttle. These patterns are used to divide classes into smaller groups for relays, team games, and drill exercises. Once learned, the patterns can be formed quickly and in an orderly manner at a simple command by the teacher. They will save valuable practice and play time, eliminate confusion, and minimize the potential for accidents.

In many cases, the selection of a formation is determined by the activity itself. Running and tag games require a specific formation, and many folk dances begin with the children in a circle or line. Activities such as warm-up exercises, apparatus activities, and low-organization games can be performed from a variety of formations. Two principles, however, apply to all formations. First, each squad should be aligned so that all members can see the performer. Second, the activities of one squad should not interfere with those of another. These principles should be remembered when selecting the following formations:

Formation	Explanation	Uses
Circle	Children may form a circle by following the teacher as she walks around in a circle. Other methods include all joining hands and forming a circle, or having the class take positions on a circle printed on the floor or play area.	-simple games -warm-up exercises -circle relays -teaching simple stunts -teaching basic dance steps -teaching throwing and kicking skills -marching -mimetics
Line	Place one child for each line desired equidistant apart, then signal the class to line up behind these children. The first child in each line may move out in front of his line or shift to the side as illustrated.	-relays -simple games -marching -teaching stunts on floor or mats -roll taking -teaching basic skills
Fan	The fan formation is used for small group activities. First, arrange children in a line facing their leader, then have them join hands and form a half-circle.	-throwing and kicking drills -relays -mimetics -simple floor stunts -teaching dance skills

Formation	Explanation	Uses
Shuttle 1 X 6 X 4 X 3 X 5 X 6 X	Arrange children in two, three, or more equal lines, then separate lines the distance required for the activity. Player 1 performs his skill, then shifts to the rear of the opposite line; player 2 performs and shifts to the rear of the opposite line, etc.	-throwing and kicking drills -relays -tumbling activities from opposite ends of mat -activities requiring close observation by teacher
Zigzag 1 X X 2 3 X X 4 5 X X 6	Arrange class or squads into two equal lines, with partners facing each other. Player 1 passes to 2, 2 passes to 3, 3 passes to 4, until the last player is reached.	-throwing, catching, and kicking skills
Scattered X X X X X X X X X X X	Allow children to find a spot in the play area. Have each child reach out with his arms to see if he can touch another person. Require the children who can touch others to shift until they are free of obstructions.	-warm-up exercises -mimetics -tag games -simple floor stunts -creative activities

Effective Grouping Procedures

Grouping children in physical education classes is arranging them in squads according to their age, height, ability, or some other criterion. The type of grouping technique a teacher selects will depend upon the activity and the performance levels of her class. For example, a third-grade teacher who wishes to organize her class into four teams for a relay could arrange them into teams of two boys and two girls by numbering the children from one to four or by having four captains choose their own teams. Since the latter is a common method for organizing equal teams, as well as fostering leadership and team loyalty, it will be explained in detail.

The teacher or the class selects four captains. To preclude favoritism, sex preferences, and emotional-social problems stemming from the order in which children are selected, the captains should meet with the teacher away from the class to select teams in private. As shown in the chart, squad leader A is awarded first choice; B, second; C, third; and D, fourth. At this point, tell each squad leader that if his first choice is a boy, the next choice must be a girl; alternate boy and girl until the last member is chosen. Let us assume captain D selected a boy in round one, and that captain D also has the next selection, which must be a girl.

Other methods of organizing children into squads should be used throughout the year to provide opportunities for children to work with different groups, as both leaders and followers. The method chosen will depend upon the activity, the space, and the age of the children. Following are some methods:

1. Skill tests or observation of skill ability.
2. Numbering off in twos, fives, or whatever other number of teams is desired.

8

	Squad Leaders			
Round No.	A	B	C	D
1	1st	2nd	3rd	4th
2	8th	7th	6th	5th
3	9th	10th	11th	12th
4	16th	15th	14th	13th
5	17th	etc.		

3. Arranging the class in a circle, then dividing it into the desired number of squads.
4. Selecting teams on the basis of birth dates. For example:
Team 1: children born between January and March
Team 2: children born between April and June
Team 3: children born between July and September
Team 4: children born between October and December
5. Administering a classification test such as McCloy's Index, which places the heavier and older children in one group and the lighter and younger children in another group. The formula, 10 times age plus weight, may be used for ages fifteen and below.

Once children can effectively move into squads (or teams, groups, section places, or units), such groupings can be highly profitable to both the students and the teacher. From the teacher's point of view, the children can be organized quickly according to a particular criterion selected either by the teacher or jointly with the class.

The duties of the elected or assigned leader should include the following:

1. Maintaining order and general control of the squad
2. Checking routine procedures such as attendance, uniforms, and tardiness
3. Assisting the teacher in daily planning and lesson organizing
4. Setting an example of leadership

The inherent value of squads from a purely organizational standpoint cannot be overemphasized. However, we should provide maximum opportunity for every child to experience a leadership role. We recognize that some stu-

dents seem to develop this ability in the early primary grades, while others need encouragement and subtly planned experiences as leaders. Consequently, squad leaders should be considered temporary so that each child is given an opportunity to test his ability as the squad captain. There will always be moments of frustration when young children are given leadership roles, so both teachers and children must develop tolerance, understanding, and patience.

Use of Time Before a Lesson Starts

The normal procedure in physical education programs is for children to change into physical education uniforms or at least into tennis shoes, and to begin the lesson when everyone is present. The following procedure does not remove any of the teacher's responsibilities before the lesson; it does, however, contribute to maximum utilization of every minute in the gymnasium or on the playing field, and encourages children to develop self-discipline and respect for their own safety and that of every other class member. The following procedure has been adopted in numerous schools and has proved to be extremely effective. Although the type of activity and the time available vary from class to class, this procedure can be applied to every physical education lesson, whether in the gymnasium or on the playing field.

Figure 8.5

Procedure

The fundamental purpose of this procedure is to allow each child to use the free time before the lesson begins constructively. Thus, the basic procedure is simply to provide the children who enter the gymnasium or go out on the playing field early an opportunity to practice any skill or movement pattern while waiting for the lesson to begin.

This procedure is slightly different for various types of instructional units, of course. In a game-type lesson, have a variety of balls available when the children enter the instructional area. A few instructions could be given, such as "practice bouncing and catching by yourself or with a partner as soon as you come into the gymnasium." In a gymnastic unit, place a variety of small equipment—hoops, beanbags, skipping ropes—on the floor. As the children enter the gymnasium, they are instructed to choose equipment and practice any skill they learned in the previous lesson or to explore any movement they want. But practice with large apparatus, such as climbing ropes, vaulting box, or springboard, should be avoided during the free practice time. Free practice activities prior to a dance lesson could involve ball or other small equipment activities, rather than practice of a specific dance step or movement pattern.

It must be emphasized that this procedure cannot be initiated until the class as a whole has demonstrated its understanding and ability to work independently without the teacher determining the skill to practice. Primary children who have not been taught with a teacher-directed type of program will usually adapt to this procedure within a few lessons. But older children, particularly those in the upper elementary grades who are accustomed to moving from a well-established squad or line formation only when permitted to do so by the teacher, may have difficulty adjusting to such a procedure. The time and patience that will be required by the teacher will be worth it.

A few further suggestions will show how this procedure can be used effectively even in the first few lessons. As soon as the children have been instructed how and where to change their clothing, use one or more of the following ideas while they are changing:

1. Balls: Indicate to the children that as soon as they have changed they may choose a ball and practice bouncing it (or throwing and catching it, jumping over it, or playing catch with a partner).
2. Beanbags: Same as above.
3. Hoop: Place on the floor and practice jumping over it, jumping in and out of it, or hopping around it.
4. As skills are taught, select one or two to be practiced during this free practice time.

Since children in the intermediate grades have acquired many gymnastic skills, the teacher need only to require that the children practice one or more of them as they enter the gymnasium. Some examples are

1. Balance stunts: Practice a handstand, cartwheel, one-foot balance, and so on.
2. Balls: Require bouncing and change of direction (bounce, throw into air, and make a full turn of body before bouncing again).
3. Partners: Do not suggest free practice with partners until the class has demonstrated its ability to work independently in this type of atmosphere.

Structure of a Lesson

Part One	Part Two	Part Three
Introductory Activity	*Skill Development*	*Group or Final Activity*
Stress vigorous warm-up activities.	**Games:** Stress acquisition of skills and concepts through individual and partner activities.	**Games:** Stress group games.
Standard for all types of physical education lessons.	**Gymnastics:** Stress acquisition of stunts and movement skills and concepts through individual, partner, and small equipment activities.	**Gymnastics:** Stress application of previously learned skills to large apparatus.
	Dance: Stress acquisition of skills and movement ideas and concepts through individual and partner activities.	**Dance:** Stress group activities.

Planning and Presenting a Lesson

A physical education lesson plan should be considered a flexible guideline that includes a brief summary of objectives, activities, methods, and organizational procedures. Although each teacher will eventually develop her own abbreviated lesson plan outline, the following basic structure can be used when teaching game, dance, and gymnastic activities.

The first part of a game, dance, or gymnastic lesson is the introductory activity, lasting about three to five minutes. This activity should be vigorous and somewhat related to the main focus of the lesson.

The second part introduces one or more skills or movement concepts and sets the focus and direction of the lesson. In a game lesson, for example, previously learned skills are reviewed and one or more new skills or concepts are introduced. Similarly, in gymnastic lessons, movement skills are introduced through individual, partner, and small equipment activities. A similar pattern is followed in a folk or creative dance lesson, with this part used to set the focus and direction of the lesson.

The third part of a game or dance lesson normally involves a group activity. For example, in dance a schottische step might have been introduced in part two, using individual and part-

ner activities. Then, in part three, groups of four or more might do a schottische dance. The third part of a gymnastics lesson is used to apply movement skills and concepts to large apparatus.

The accompanying sample lesson plan illustrates how a third-grade teacher has planned a thirty-minute games lesson. Approximately ten minutes are spent in changing clothes and free practice activities, leaving twenty minutes of instructional time.

The amount of detail that a teacher records on her lesson plan will depend, of course, upon her professional background and experience. Generally speaking, beginning teachers tend to write down more detail. Abbreviated notes under each of the main parts of the lesson will usually suffice for the more experienced teacher.

Variations in Lesson Plans

The previous lesson plan was based on a thirty-minute physical education period. But in many schools, particularly for the primary grades, the period may last only ten to twenty minutes. It is virtually impossible to cover the three main parts of a lesson in such a short period, so the lesson can begin on one day and continue onto the next. The previous lesson will be used to illustrate such a modification. The first two parts of the lesson are covered in the fifteen-minute instructional period on Monday. On Tuesday, the

Lesson Emphasis: Chest pass
Materials: 30 balls, 15 hoops, box of beanbags

Free Practice Activities
Instruct children to get balls and practice dribbling or catching with a partner.

Introductory Activities (5 minutes)
Circle formation. Begin running in place. Shift to conditioning exercises, stressing arm and shoulder girdle exercises.

Skill Development (7 to 10 minutes)
Keep circle formation.
—Explain and demonstrate chest pass.
—Move to center of circle and pass to each child. Check skill level.
Arrange in partners with a ball.
—partner passing, 10 feet apart
—vary distance
—one stationary; one on move

Group Activities (7 to 10 minutes)
Arrange in groups of six.
Game: "Keep Away"
Inventive Game: Make up a game that includes the following:
1. Use only a chest pass.
2. Every player must be moving.
3. Must use two hoops in the game.
If time remains, change (3) hoops to three beanbags.

Notes and References

Place four bags of balls in four corners of gymnasium.

Kirchner pages 49-57

Kirchner, 189
Kirchner, 173

---

teacher starts with a five minute warm-up, then moves directly to part three of the lesson. This type of procedure can be followed throughout an instructional unit without any major loss in the continuity of learning.

Changing Lesson Emphasis as Unit Develops

When a new unit of instruction is introduced, more time is usually needed during the first and second parts of the lesson to introduce and practice skills and movement concepts. This means that less time is available for the third part of the lesson. If the instructional period is thirty to forty minutes long, the transition normally occurs in the instructional unit as shown.

Regardless of the time available during the first five or six lessons, a considerable amount of it must be devoted to skill development, until the children acquire sufficient skill and movement understanding. Then more time gradually can be spent on group activities. There is, of course, no rigid rule to follow in allocating time that should be devoted to parts two and three of the lesson as the unit develops. The best guideline is the

15 minutes

Monday	*Introductory activities* (5 minutes)	*Skill development* Cover part two of previous lesson (10 minutes)	*Group activities* Leave until Tuesday
Tuesday	Introductory activities (5 minutes)	Leave out	Cover part three of previous lesson

		Length of physical education period		
	Part One:	Part Two: Skill Development		Part Three:
First Part of Unit	Introductory Activities			Group or Final Activity
		Devote more time to this part during the initial stages and gradually decrease as skill and movement ideas are developed.		
Latter Part of Unit	Devote approximately three to five minutes to this activity throughout the unit.			Devote less time to this section during early part of the unit and gradually increase time as skill and movement ideas develop.

children's progress. If the skill level appears to be quite low, continue to emphasize part two. If there is marked improvement, increase the difficulty of individual and partner activities and give more time and emphasis to group activities.

Routine Procedures

The success of any physical education program will depend to a large extent upon the simple routine procedures a class follows in going to, participating in, and returning from a physical education activity. Primary teachers usually are not confronted with the problems of showering; however, they are concerned with problems relating to changing clothes, class excuses, and class control. At the intermediate level, where classes may be segregated, the teacher must solve problems of changing clothes, showering, and individual excuses.

Physical Education Apparel

Elementary school children usually are not required to wear special uniforms for physical education. The time required to change in relation to the time available for physical education, particularly for five-, six-, and seven-year-olds,

does not justify a complete change. However, tennis shoes should be worn for games and some dance activities. And in gymnastic activities the teacher should seriously consider letting the children participate in bare feet, if the floor is clean and free of hazards. Bare feet assist in balancing activities and encourage freedom of movement. However, this should be a gradual process to allow the children to get used to running, balancing, jumping, and landing on their bare feet. If the children enjoy participating in gymnastic activities with bare feet and there are no adverse effects (plantar warts or excessive bruising), continue the practice.

Roll Call

Since physical education periods are usually all too short anyway, don't lose time in the routine procedure of checking attendance. In most cases, roll call is not necessary in the primary grades. And the classroom teacher, regardless of grade, who is responsible for her own physical education program will know if any child is absent. However, when the use of specialist teachers or team teaching requires a roll-call procedure, the following methods can be used:

1. A line formation based upon alphabetical list in the roll book

2. Line formation based upon the tallest to the shortest child, with each child assigned a number
3. Squads, with one member assigned to take roll

Class Excuses

Excuses for physical education range from permanent waivers because of chronic health conditions to temporary waivers because of colds or other illnesses. It is imperative that the principal, the school nurse, and the teacher establish policies covering problems encountered in this area. The following situations should be included in the policies:

1. A temporary excuse should be authorized by the school nurse.
2. The school nurse should authorize children to return to physical activity after any illness.
3. Children with physical handicaps should be encouraged to participate in physical education classes. The amount and type of participation, of course, should be indicated by the parents and or family physician.
4. On the recommendation of the teacher, a child may be excused from participation in a physical education class because of a detectable illness or injury.

8

The Process of Evaluation

9

Evaluating Student Progress

Grading and Reporting Pupil Progress

Evaluating Program Progress

Evaluation is essential to all phases of the physical education program. A teacher who assesses the effectiveness of her program of activities or her methods and techniques is able to detect strengths and weaknesses and make appropriate changes. Children's test results can be sent to parents and other interested members of the community. Such communication helps others to understand the scope of the program and often leads to needed facilities and equipment.

Teachers must first consider the very practical uses of testing within such areas as physical fitness, skill development, knowledge, and social adjustment. Perhaps the most common use of testing is for grading purposes; this is not, however, the most important. The more salient value of testing is to determine the child's level of performance in order to establish realistic goals for him. Furthermore, when testing is used continually throughout the school year, additional changes can be made to meet the child's needs and potential.

Numerous other practical values for a testing program could be mentioned. However, the writer would be remiss not to stress the importance of testing as a motivational device. When a child can see his test results and realize his possibilities for improvement, greater personal effort and satisfaction usually result. Once a child sees how far he can throw a ball, he will usually set a higher goal and continue to practice so long as he improves.

The important point to keep in mind when measuring a pupil's performance is to judge his score in relation to his *own* performance, not in relation to the class norms. The latter are useful as guidelines; they are not established goals for all children.

Evaluating Student Progress

Both subjective and objective measuring devices that are used to evaluate student progress in physical education must be judged upon their ability to measure accurately the extent to which the objectives of the program are being realized. As previously stated, these objectives include health and physical development, motor skill development, knowledge, and social adjustment. Factors involved in these objectives can be measured, to some degree, by subjective judgment or objective tests. Most teachers rely heavily upon subjective ratings of student progress in such areas as movement concepts and skills and social development. However, within all grade levels, there are aspects of the child's performance that can be measured by objective tests.

Health and Physical Development

Continuous concern for each child's health and physical development is the responsibility of teachers and school health officials. Physical education provides a special avenue to detect possible anomalies and to refer children with them to more competent authorities. A teacher who understands posture, nutrition, and physical fitness can correct or prevent problems, in certain situations. It is also the teacher's responsibility to detect early signs of illness and to refer these problems to the school nurse or physician.

In most school districts, physical examinations are required annually or at other scheduled times throughout the elementary school program. The results should be made known to the classroom teacher, particularly for children who require special treatment in the physical education program because of rheumatic fever, birth anomalies, etc. There are other evaluations that the teacher can make which will help her plan for the growth and development needs of each child.

Several of the more important evaluative techniques are described in the following pages of this book:

1. Age, height, and weight: pages 36-37
2. Posture: simple plumb line test, pages 37-39
3. Physical fitness: description of standardized test batteries for elementary school children, pages 41-42
4. Perceptual-motor screening tests: pages 575-80

Skill Development

There are two basic types of motor skills that should be measured. First are the fundamental or basic skills, including locomotor skills—walking, running, skipping—and nonlocomotor skills—dodging, pushing, pulling. Descriptions of these skills are found in Chapter 5. The second type are the specific sport, dance, and gymnastic skills. Examples of how each type can be measured follow.

Fundamental Skills

In the accompanying table (page 160) the teacher has subjectively rated the child's performance of fundamental skills at the beginning of the school year as "good," "fair," or "poor." Under "correction indicated," she has made comments that will help her plan activities to correct the child's weaknesses. This type of evaluation sheet can also be developed for specific sports skills and gymnastic activities. It is especially useful in explaining the child's level of performance to parents and in pointing out corrective measures that can be undertaken at home.

Game Skills

There are very few standardized tests that can be used to measure specific game skills of elementary school children, so teachers often must rely on their own test batteries. Each test, whether standardized or homemade should have the following characteristics:

1. Each item in the test battery should accurately measure one important skill (for example, an underhand catch).

Table 9-1   Subjective Rating for Fundamental Skills

Name: Jim Adams
Date: September, 1978

Performance in Fundamental Skills

Name of Skill	Good	Fair	Poor	Correction Indicated
		Rating		
Walking			X	Toes inward
Running			X	Toes inward
Skipping	X			
Leaping	X			
Jumping		X		
Sliding			X	Changes lead foot
Hopping	X			
Swinging and swaying		X		
Rising and falling		X		
Pushing and pulling		X		
Bending and stretching		X		
Striking and dodging		X		

2. The test battery should be inexpensive and easy to administer and should yield scores that can be added up to produce a total score.

3. Each test item should accurately represent the skills and movements of the activity it intends to measure. A dribbling test item in basketball or soccer should include such factors as speed, change of direction, and ball control.

4. Each item in the battery should be able to distinguish between low and high levels of ability. If all children score eight or ten points out of a possible ten on an accuracy test—throwing at a large target from ten feet away—the test would be of little value. The results would indicate the distance was too short or the target too large.

The following teacher-made test for throwing and catching skills is an example of a simple, inexpensive, and easy-to-administer test battery. Each test item could be modified to meet the skill levels of several grades. The first four tests measure form and accuracy, while the fifth measures distance.

Test No. 1. Underhand catch: The teacher stands twenty feet away from the child and throws him ten balls, which he must catch with an underhand catch. One point is awarded for each successful catch.

Test No. 2. Overhand Catch: Repeat Test No. 1, but require an overhand catch.

Test No. 3. One-hand Underhand Throw: The child stands fifteen feet away from a wastepaper basket and attempts to throw ten softballs into it. The underhand throw must be used. One point is awarded for each successful throw.

Test No. 4. Two-hand Chest Throw: Repeat Test No. 3, but with a two-hand chest throw.

Test No. 5. Throw for Distance: The child throws a softball three times. The total score is divided by three and recorded in the appropriate column of the chart.

Other examples of teacher-made skill tests are found in Part IV, the games section, on the pages listed. Other examples can be found in the suggested readings in Appendix A. Teachers should use these sample test batteries as guidelines in developing their own tests.

A teacher-made skill test should be devised so that the individual scores can be added into one composite score. This provides a means of ranking children, as well as indicating where additional emphasis should be placed in the selection of practice activities and lead-up games.

Rhythmic and Creative Dance Skills

There is a similar problem in evaluating gymnastic and dance skills. The structured locomotor and nonlocomotor skills can be checked easily by the classroom teacher; the checklist on page 160 is an example. However, performing these skills in rhythmic activities and folk dance involves style, grace, and creativity—all of which the teacher must evaluate subjectively. The creative dance activities described in Chapter 26 also must be evaluated on a subjective basis.

Gymnastic and Movement Skills

Evaluation of a student's progress in gymnastic activities, as in dance, is relatively easy when teaching standardized skills, but difficult when teaching movement concepts and skills. In the first instance, all skills are performed the same way, thus providing a standard performance. And since these skills are arranged from simple to complex, evaluation becomes an assessment of how many skills are performed and how well.

Evaluation of the child's progress using a cumulative number of stunts should be made on the basis of individual achievement, with room for individual choice of stunts, rather than having the same expectations for all children. There are simply too many variations in skill and maturity to demand the same of all children.

There is a major difference in the way children should be evaluated when teaching movement concepts and skills. The essential purpose of these skills is to help the child use his body in a variety of ways on and off apparatus; each movement task should produce different shapes

Figure 9.1

Table 9-2   Objective Skill Test

Name of Student	Throwing and Catching Skills					Total	Grade
	Test No. 1 Underhand Catch	Test No. 2 Overhand Catch	Test No. 3 One-Hand Underhand Throw	Test No. 4 Chest Throw	Test No. 5 Throw for Distance		
1. John Smith	7	5	6	5	38'	61	B
2. Mary Able	6	4	5	5	26'	46	C
3.							
4.							

and movement patterns for each child. Thus there is no common standard by which to judge progress. It is an individualized matter and must be evaluated on that basis. Nevertheless, the teacher must still observe and evaluate each child's progress according to some criteria, however subjective and personal they may be.

The evaluation can be made jointly by the teacher and the child. Each child learns to progress at his own rate and according to his potential ability. Evaluation by the teacher thus is assessing whether the child is sufficiently challenged and is continually improving his ability to produce more difficult shapes and movements. Progress, as the teacher will come to see in this approach to teaching gymnastic activities, is as much concerned with the quality of movement as with the individuality and variety of the movements the child performs.

Knowledge

One of the objectives of physical education is to acquire knowledge and understanding of physical activities and their contribution to physical and mental health. When children know the team positions, rules, and strategy of a game, there is less chance of misunderstandings and fighting. Furthermore, knowing the rules of a team sport, the verses in a singing game, or the parts to a complex gymnastic skill enhances motor learning.

In the primary grades, verbal questions are used to teach simple rules and verses in singing games and to stimulate creative thought through interpretive movements. Written tests can be used in the upper grades in all phases of the physical education program. The choice of true or false, multiple choice, or short-answer tests depends on the teacher and the capabilities of her students. Regardless of the type of test chosen, care should be taken to pose questions that are clear and appropriate to the physical activity.

Social Development

The traits represented in the term "social adjustment" do not lend themselves readily to either subjective or objective measurement. For example, "the ability to get along with others," "team loyalty," and "sportsmanship" cannot be measured accurately by a rating scale, an anecdotal record, or even an expert's judgment. Nevertheless, these are extremely important qualities that we profess to develop within the physical education program. Consequently, there should be some attempt, however meager, to evaluate the development of these qualities. Some of the more practical techniques and tests are described.

Teacher Observation

Probably the most commonly used technique to assess individual social growth is the daily observation a teacher makes while the children are playing in a structured situation or during free-play activities. Behavioral problems such as cheating and poor sportsmanship may be noted by the teacher. The manner in which she copes with adjustment problems vary from a change in the method of instruction to a complete change in activities.

Figure 9.2

Interview

A personal interview between the teacher and the child or parent is another technique used to gain a better understanding of the general behavior of a child. Usually, specific adjustment problems are discussed with the child or, when appropriate, the parent, to determine the reasons behind certain behavioral problems. The teacher should take care, however, not to lecture but to win the child's confidence and to develop genuine concern for the child. When a child has respect for and trust in the teacher, there is a good chance that he, in turn, will be able to understand his problem and make appropriate changes.

Sociogram

The sociogram is a technique used to study the relationships within a group. By posing such key questions as "With whom would you like to practice catching skills during recess?" or "Who would you like to have on your team?" it is possible to identify children who appear to be well adjusted within the group and those who are isolated and rejected. To obtain the best results from this technique it is wise to keep the following procedures in mind when asking students such questions (Kozman, Cassidy, and Jackson 1967):

1. Make sure the situation for which students are asked to make choices is a real one.
2. Make use of the choices to group students according to their preferences.
3. Make sure that the atmosphere is informal and friendly.
4. Let the students understand that their answers will be confidential.
5. Give no cues to the students about how to choose.

The results of the sociogram can be very helpful in identifying children who need assistance. By drawing circles on a sheet to represent each child and lines to each child as the answers dictate, it becomes quite clear who are the popular children and the rejected children in a particular social group. By a simple regrouping, the shy and retiring child can be brought into a more favorable group without making the reasons for such a change obvious. Furthermore, undesirable group situations can also indicate possible variations in methods of class organization, selection of team captains, and the type of group activities.

Grading and Reporting Pupil Progress

The purpose of grading in physical education is identical to that in all other subjects to report the child's progress. Although the majority of elementary school report cards require only an S, or U, or P, or F, additional information relating to skill performance, physical fitness, and social adjustment should be available in the form of a cumulative record. When the parent asks, "How is my child doing in physical education?" and the answer is, "He is well adjusted in his group" or "He is doing fairly well in physical skills," very little insight has been gained and the parent may come away with an unfavorable impression of the program.

To overcome the weakness of the P or F grading and reporting system, many schools now require a cumulative record in physical education (see Chapter 4). This is particularly true in districts where children are given physical fitness tests in the fall and spring. After the spring test has been given, the physical fitness scores are reported to parents or passed on to the next grade to assist the new teacher in setting reasonable limits for the child. Additional information about skill performance in rhythmic, game, and gymnastic activities should be recorded within the cumulative record. The child's grade should then be based on his improvement rather than how he ranks with others in his class.

Evaluating Program Progress

The physical education program in its broadest meaning includes all the organized experiences, the facilities, and the teachers involved in teaching and supervisory roles. Evaluative techniques to measure all these factors are simply not available. Even if they were, the time element alone would prohibit extensive assessments. There are, however, periodic evaluations that teachers should make about the effectiveness of the content and methods used and the allocation of time and space for physical education.

Participation

Since the time available for physical education is usually quite short, each lesson must be planned carefully to encourage maximum participation. The teacher should, therefore, assess

1. The time children take to change and enter the gymnasium.
2. The amount of time devoted to explaining and demonstrating skills. Most teachers spend too much time explaining and allow too little time for actual practice.
3. The time available for each child to practice each skill or movement.

Effective Routine Procedures

Many unnecessary problems and wasted time can be avoided when children know what is expected of them in the gymnasium. Simple routine procedures should therefore be established and followed from the first lesson. These should include

1. arrangement of apparatus—who should be responsible
2. rotation procedure—moving from one piece of equipment or apparatus to another
3. carrying and putting away equipment and apparatus

Providing Sufficient Challenge to Children

When teachers are continually confronted with disciplinary problems, the reason could be lack of challenge in the tasks given. The teacher should constantly observe the amount of con-

centration and effort the children are giving to the task. If she notices general boredom and excessive noise, the work may be either too easy or too hard. In either case, a change is indicated.

Individual Observation and Guidance

In any learning situation, each child needs some guidance and encouragement, regardless of ability. Too often the outstanding performer is selected for demonstrations and praise, while it is the low achiever who really needs attention and encouragement. Hence, consideration should be given to

1. observing, correcting, and encouraging as many children as possible
2. selecting many different children for demonstrations
3. recording important and successful techniques that will assist in future lessons

Keeping Up-to-Date

Every teacher should appraise her teaching to determine how she can improve her effectiveness in the classroom and gymnasium. Since the physical education program is undergoing extensive changes, both in content and methods of instruction, teachers should assess whether they are as up-to-date in this area as they are in other subjects. Consideration should be given to the following areas:

1. New developments in movement education, movement exploration, and creative games
2. New textbooks in the general field of physical education and specialized texts in game, dance, and gymnastic activities
3. New developments in audiovisual materials for physical education (films, filmstrips, and videotapes)
4. New developments in equipment and apparatus, particularly the new agility apparatus
5. Related research in perceptual-motor development and physical education
6. New program developments, particularly the programs supported by federal and state funds

Information and general assistance in these areas can be secured from state and local district supervisors of physical education. In addition, numerous national organizations, such as the American Alliance of Health, Physical Education and Recreation (AAHPER), the Office of Education, and the Athletic Institute will provide information on request.

Facilities and Equipment

The majority of school districts have established policies for the allocation of funds for physical education. Normally, each school receives an annual equipment and supplies grant based upon the number of children in the school. Teachers should refer to the list of suggested equipment and supplies in Chapter 7 as a basic guideline. It is extremely valuable for each school district to establish its own recommended list so teachers have a reasonable idea of the quantity and quality of equipment they can expect to receive.

Following are other questions that the teacher should ask herself:

1. Are the facilities and equipment maintained in safe working order?
2. Is there equipment in the gymnasium or outdoor playing area that is not recommended for use in the elementary school program? Serious consideration should be given to such apparatus as merry-go-rounds, swings with steel or wooden seats, and such gymnastic equipment as the trampoline and mini-tramp. The latter two pieces of equipment are desirable for upper elementary, provided there are competent teachers to teach skills on them.
3. What kinds of improvised equipment and supplies can be secured with limited funds? Appendix B tells teachers how to construct inexpensive equipment.

Program

Evaluation should be an ongoing process of assessing whether goals are being achieved. Adequate program evaluation primarily involves the day-to-day assessment of each lesson in order to make modifications in activities and methods of instruction. Contemporary programs also include student evaluation of the program. Although the children cannot always see the value and reason for all activities, they can provide valuable assistance with respect to their needs and interests. Provision should be made for children to participate actively in program evaluation. When children are respected for their contributions, they, in turn, will generally provide the effort and enthusiasm to make the program a success.

Game and Movement Activities

Game activities constitute a major portion of the elementary school physical education program. As children progress through the elementary grades, game activities are given more time and emphasis, and gymnastics and dance, less. Consequently, the teacher should clearly understand the organization of games so that she can select and emphasize the appropriate skills, practice activities and games without unnecessary repetition.

The first three chapters of Part IV include simple team games, relays, tag activities, and individual and partner games. Although these activities are given major emphasis in the primary grades, many of the games in these chapters are also appropriate for and thoroughly enjoyed by upper elementary school children.

Chapters 13 through 19 are primarily designed for boys and girls in the intermediate grades. However, primary teachers should also refer to these chapters for more advanced practice activities and lead-up games that can be modified to meet the skill and ability of younger children. The chapter on swimming has been included because of a growing recognition of the importance of teaching young children basic water safety and swimming skills.

Within each chapter of this section the writer has attempted to illustrate how a variety of approaches can be used to teach game activities. There are situations in every grade when skills, rules, and games should be presented in a more structured and direct way. At other times, however, application of problem-solving methods, through creative or inventive games, is appropriate. These chapters show how each approach can be used separately and how the structured and problem-solving methods and techniques can be blended into a single lesson or unit of instruction.

Running, Tag, and Simple Team Games

10

Basic Considerations

Teaching Game Activities

Incorporating the Inventive Games Approach

Games for Kindergarten to Grade Two

Games for Grades Three and Four

Games for Grades Five and Six

This chapter provides a vast and culturally rich reservoir of running, tag and simple team games. The purpose and emphasis of these activities vary from grade to grade. For primary children, particularly those from kindergarten to grade two, these games provide an important and enjoyable means of acquiring the fundamental skills and movement patterns of all major team sports. And if these activities are taught in a progressive manner, with a generous application of exploratory teaching methods, such characteristics as sportsmanship, leadership, and creativity can also be developed in a natural way.

The purpose of these activities remains the same as children reach the third and fourth grades. However, this is an important transitional period. These children still enjoy running and tag games, but they also are beginning to show a much keener interest in learning the more complex team games such as basketball and volleyball. And by the time children reach the fifth and sixth grades, the transition is almost complete. The major emphasis of their games program is developing knowledge and skills of the major individual and team sports. The running, tag, and simple team games provided in this chapter still have a place in the upper intermediate grades, however. They are vigorous and enjoyable activities for a classroom break, recess, or warm-up during regular instructional classes.

Basic Considerations

Teaching game-type activities to elementary school children in large instructional areas such as the gymnasium or playground can present unnecessary obstacles. The following suggestions relating to arrangement of the instructional space, class control, and safety will help overcome most of the obstacles. (Also see the film "Teaching Games to Primary Children" on page 602 in Appendix A.)

Arranging the Instructional Space

Most schools have one or more large playground areas that are suitable for running and simple tag games, but usually they are too large to handle a class in a normal conversational manner. To overcome this problem, assign one or two children to mark off the instructional area just before the class is taken outside; traffic cones or milk cartons are excellent markers.

Use a similar technique in a large gymnasium. Do not use equipment such as metal volleyball posts that can cause injury if knocked over.

Many of the running and simple team games described in this chapter require a lot of beanbags, balls, milk cartons, and other equipment. To ensure maximum use of instructional and playing time, place the equipment in cardboard boxes or nylon sacks and put them in the corners of the instructional area. Team leaders or monitors can do this job extremely well.

Class Management and Control

The following procedures for controlling the class can be used by teachers of any grade. Each teacher, of course, will modify the amount of freedom she will give according to her class's maturity and cooperation.

1. Divide the class into four groups. For primary children use "Sections 1, 2, 3, and 4." Intermediate children usually prefer to be "Teams 1, 2, 3, and 4," or to go by the names of popular teams such as Bears and Rams.
2. Select section leaders or team captains and rotate these positions each week to give every child a chance to be a leader.
3. Choose a place for each group to sit whenever you call "section places"—normally the middle of the instructional area. This is extremely important for good class control. Repeat the procedure until the children move to their places quickly and efficiently.
4. Follow normal and reasonable safety procedures, paying particular attention to the following:
   a. Tennis shoes should be worn during game activities, although bare feet could be allowed if the floor is free of splinters and other hazards.
   b. Goal lines should be drawn a reasonable distance from the end or side walls—three

Figure 10.1

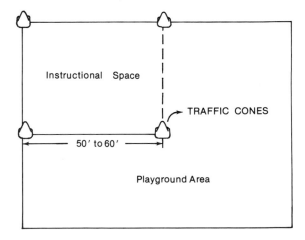

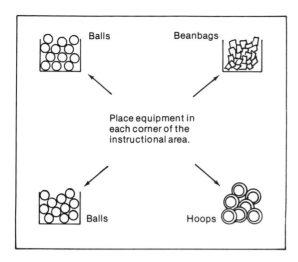

Balls

Beanbags

Place equipment in each corner of the instructional area.

Balls

Hoops

to five feet for moderately active games and six to ten feet for vigorously active games.

c. Require that glasses, if possible, and other personal items such as chains and baggy sweaters be removed.

Teaching Game Activities

It is very difficult to recommend a standard approach to teaching running and simple team games. Teachers must adapt to differences in children's maturity, their skill levels, the time allotment, and the supplies available. As a general guideline, however, all game activities can be effectively taught to any grade level by progressing from *individual* to *partner* to *group* activities.

This basic progression allows a child first to practice a skill or movement pattern by himself. The next step is partner activities. Many more challenges and variations can now be introduced, and partner activities can also provide important lessons in sharing, give and take, and other forms of cooperative behavior. The last phase in this progression is group activities. The games described later in this chapter provide a variety of ways for children to practice skills they have learned during individual and partner activities. The accompanying lesson illustrates this basic progression.

LESSON "X" Bouncing and Catching

	Teaching Suggestions
Level: Grade 1 Equipment: Any available inflated balls Length of lesson: Approximately 20 minutes	
Introductory Activities (5 to 6 minutes) From his section place, have each child get a ball, find a space, and place the ball on the floor. Then have the child 1. run in different directions around the ball 2. run, jump over ball 3. run, jump over ball, change direction, and repeat	By having the balls placed in a scattered formation, you are essentially ready for the next part of the lesson.

Skill Development (6 to 7 minutes)

Each child has a ball and is standing in his own space. Demonstrate how to bounce with one hand. Have the children practice. Pose such questions as

1. "Can you bounce the ball with two hands?"
2. "Can you bounce the ball with one hand?"
3. "Can you bounce the ball with your other hand?"
4. "See if you can find another way to bounce the ball."
5. "See if you can bounce the ball very low, then very high."

Have children join with partners, putting one ball away. Tell them to stand about six feet apart and bounce the ball back and forth to their partners. As they practice, introduce bounce with right, left, and both hands; bounce to the side; and bounce to a partner who is moving.

Demonstrations should be very brief, stressing one or two main points. After children have practiced the basic bounce, pose questions that permit them to explore and test their abilities.

A brief demonstration by two children will illustrate distance between players, as well as the correct skill to practice.

Group Activities (7 to 8 minutes)

Refer to Running, Tag, and Simple Team Games and choose a game that emphasizes BOUNCING and CATCHING.

    Game: "Teacher and Class," page 180

    Divide playing area into quadrants and play four separate games.

The Running, Tag, and Simple Team Games (pp. 177-87) are arranged in approximate order of difficulty. Select one that will emphasize bouncing and catching and that is appropriate to your class's general skill level.

If a first-grade teacher has only ten or fifteen minutes for physical activities each day, a modification of the illustrated lesson can be adopted. On the first day, cover the first and second parts of the lesson. Begin the second day with "Teacher and Class." It is the progression from individual to group activities that is important, not simply covering every part of a lesson in a set period of time.

As children progress through the third grade, running, tag, and simple team games are used more for a "change of pace" from classroom activities or as recess and noon-hour activities. Therefore, the suggested progression may not be followed as closely. However, this suggested progression should again be followed with the introduction of team games in later chapters as children acquire more complex skills and game strategies.

Incorporating the Inventive Games Approach

The evolution occurring within the elementary school curriculum is essentially a movement from teacher-directed activities toward a learning environment in which the teacher is a vitally important guider of children who learn by example, practice, and the joy of discovery. We have witnessed in gymnastics and dance the gradual adoption of the movement education approach, which fosters exploration, experimentation, and discovery—key elements in the creative learning process. This approach also allows the child to develop according to his own intellectual and physical ability and readiness. In essence, the style of teaching exemplified in movement education is parallel to the current practices in other areas of the elementary school curriculum.

Running, tag, and simple team games have traditionally been organized and taught on the premise that skills, rules, and strategies should be learned in an orderly and progressive manner. It would seem imperative that any new approach should still use the common terms, such as throw, catch, and kick, and that the skills and

Figure 10.2

knowledge of the games should still be acquired. The approach that follows can develop these important skills and strategies while contributing to the child's needs and interests and the development of his creative processes. This approach can be called an *inventive* or *creative games* approach, but it is essentially the use of the *discovery method* in the medium of games.

The structure within which a creative game can be played has four elements (p. 175). The first element is the number of players, here a choice among one player, partners, or a group. The second element is the area assigned or available for the game. Next is the equipment that is available or is chosen by the players. And comprising the fourth element are the rules and skills. Within this structure, teachers and children can develop an infinite number and variety of games. Some of these games lead to the acquisition of standard sports skills, while others contribute to fun and the enhancement of creative abilities.

Games for kindergarten and grade one should be predominantly creative in nature. Beyond the first grade, however, children are exposed to more formal games. They enjoy learning the proper form of a specific sports skill and practicing drills or playing lead-up games that will increase their proficiency. For these reasons, it is important that teachers not abandon specialized sports skills, drills, and lead-up games because they are considered old-fashioned.

A structured program at any grade level can, and should, incorporate the creative games approach within a unit or a specific lesson. This blending of methods neither confuses nor restricts the learner. On the contrary, it enriches the learning environment and stimulates the creative process, and it helps the child acquire specific motor skills or more complex strategies involving perceptual, cognitive, and motor abilities.

Primary Program

There are several ways to organize and teach creative games to primary school children. The approach suggested here begins with game skills suitable for this age level, then gradually allows the children to invent or modify games within the limitations imposed by the teacher.

The procedure should be adapted to the ability, maturity, and interest of the class. And the emphasis that the teacher gives to the creative games approach obviously will depend on her philosophy and the nature of her program. However, a major emphasis on creative activity is suggested for all primary games programs. (See film "Teaching Games to Primary Children" in Appendix A, page 602.)

The two sample lessons that follow show how creative games can be incorporated into more formal programs. The lesson plan for creative games is structured similarly to plans for other activity areas. Generally, the lesson should begin with an introductory activity involving all the children in vigorous activities that have some relationship to the main theme of the lesson. The next part is theme development—the basic idea of the lesson. Part three, the final activity, should incorporate the main skills practiced in the previous parts of the lesson into a game situation. This format will vary, of course, according to the children's ages, interests, and prior experiences in creative-type games.

Example Lesson Plan No. 1 (Grades 1-2)

Main Emphasis: Bouncing a Ball

Part One—Introductory Activity:
If children are used to moving around the floor freely without bumping into each other, have them begin running in different directions. Then have them change speeds, slide backwards, then to the right, then to the left. If children are used to warming up by running around the floor and then doing a series of calisthenics, it is not necessary to change the format. After finishing the warm-up, move to the second part of the lesson.

Part Two—Theme Development (Bouncing a Ball):
Each child should have a ball; any type of utility ball can be used. If the balls are different sizes, give the bigger ones to children who are less proficient in ball-handling skills. Ask the children to take their balls and find spaces on the floor. When they are properly spaced around the floor, pose the following:

1. "Try to stay in your space and bounce the ball very low, then very high." Do not specify one or two hands—let them experiment.
2. "Can you bounce the ball with one hand?" Allow time to practice, then ask, "Can you bounce it with the other hand?"
3. Ask questions that relate to the following skills:
   a. Bounce in different directions (forward, backward, sideways).
   b. Bounce on the floor, then against the wall.
   c. Bounce around small equipment (beanbags, bowling pins, ropes).

Teaching Suggestions:

1. Allow sufficient time to practice.
2. Pick out different ways of performing each task and let the other children watch.
3. Praise the children constantly while they are practicing.
4. Ask the children if they can think of another way of bouncing. A child may suggest that they try sitting down or kneeling while bouncing. Have the class try its own challenges.

Part Three—Final Activity:
Create a game involving the skill that has been practiced.

Table 10-1 lists four areas where limitations can be imposed for the games created. As a general guideline, begin at the top and add more complex challenges as the lessons progress. In this first lesson you could challenge the children to make up a game

1. with a partner
2. in their own space
3. using one ball
4. and requiring a bounce

Teaching Suggestions:

1. Give the children time to think up a game and to practice.
2. Have a few children demonstrate the games they have created.
3. If time permits, make up a new game and add (1) beanbags, (2) a chair, or (3) a hoop.

Example Lesson Plan No. 2 (Grades 1-2)

(Continuation from Lesson No. 1)
Main Emphasis: Bouncing and Catching

Part One—Introductory Activity:
Repeat previous introductory activity. Add other warm-up activities as desired.

Part Two—Theme Development (bouncing and catching):
Have children select balls of different sizes than in previous lesson and find spaces. Ask them to

1. Bounce the ball in different directions.
2. Bounce the ball very hard against the floor and see if they can catch it before it touches the ground again.
3. Bounce the ball, turn around, and then catch the ball.
4. Bounce the ball, jump up, and catch it before it touches the floor.
5. Make up a game to play by themselves (usually they will ask to play with a partner) which involves a bounce and a catch. If you have beanbags, hoops, or other small equipment, let each child choose one piece to use in his game.

Teaching Suggestions:

1. Allow sufficient time after each challenge for the children to think up a game and to practice.
2. While the children are practicing, move around the floor and note their skill levels. This careful observation should be used as a basis for planning future lessons.

Part Three—Final Activity:
Refer to Table 10-1 and note how progression in skill and game strategies can be planned.

Table 10-1 Structure of Creative Games

Game Skills	Areas Where Limitations Can Be Imposed			
	Number of Players	Playing Space	Equipment	Skills and Rules
1. Locomotor and nonlocomotor skills —walk —run —skip —slide —jump —hop —dodge —turn	from individual activities to partners to group activities	from limited space to use of general space	from use of simple equipment to use of more varied and complex equipment	from single skills and rules to more complex skills and rules
2. Controlling ball with hands —bounce —throw —catch				
3. Controlling ball with feet —kick —pass —dribble —trap				
4. Projecting ball with hand or equipment —striking ball with hand, hitting ball with bat, racquet, or stick				

Following from the first lesson, ask the children to make up a game

1. with a partner
2. in their own space
3. using a ball
4. and requiring a bounce and a catch

Teaching Suggestions:

1. After the children have had time to create and practice their games, select a few for demonstration to the class.
2. Try other variations, such as
   a. in partners
   b. in their own space
   c. using two balls and a hoop
   d. and involving a catch
3. Allow children to make up games with their own imposed limitations.
4. Keep a creative games notebook. Children will create many exciting games that are worth remembering, so record the best ones for posterity. Next year you could use some of these games to illustrate and motivate children to develop similar ones. This project could also be incorporated into the language arts program by having each child or the whole class make up an illustrated creative games notebook.

Intermediate Program

Incorporating the creative games approach in the intermediate grades presents some problems for both the teacher and the children. (See film "Teaching Games to Intermediate Children," Appendix A, page 602.) Running, tag, and simple team games are normally selected from a book and taught according to specific rules and regulations. In essence, these are structured activities, taught by the direct-teaching method. It is possible, however, to add another dimension to these activities by injecting the creative games approach.

The four areas of limitation in Table 10-1 (p. 175) can be used with intermediate children with equal success. Since most children of this age range know and enjoy running, tag, and simple team games, this would be the logical place to introduce creative or student-designed games. The first example that follows illustrates how a teacher can begin with a familiar game and transform it into a very different and, in most cases, more enjoyable activity. The second ex-

ample shows how to use the Table 10-1 format to develop a framework for more creative student-designed games.

Example No. 1: This is a fourth-grade class. It is the middle of the afternoon and the class is apathetic. The teacher decides to take the children outside for a "ten-minute game." After a brief discussion they decide to play dodge ball using two balls. The game is played for a few minutes, then the teacher asks the class to stop and listen.

The teacher has four elements through which she can introduce a change. They are

1. the number of players: class divided into equal groups
2. the playing space: a large circle
3. the skills and rules: throwing and hitting below the waist
4. the equipment: two inflated balls

She decides to pose a challenge by varying the skills and rules. She says, "Start the game over. However, children in the middle must keep both hands on their knees at all times, and the circle players can only roll the ball." After a few minutes of play she stops the game again and poses another challenge: "In the game you have just played, I changed the rules. Can you think of another rule change that you would like to try?" Several suggestions are made and the teacher chooses Mary Ann's: "Mrs. Brown, since the players inside were put out too quickly, how about all circle players rolling only with their left hand?" (Left-handed players must use their right hand.)

The process of introducing creative or inventive games has begun. The main tools are the four elements by which the teacher or the children can impose limitations. As the teacher learns to use the challenge method, she will give more freedom of choice to the children. And, with practice, the children will appreciate the freedom to modify or create games of their own.

Example No. 2: Let us assume that a fifth-grade teacher has experimented with modified tag and simple team games and has noted a positive change in her class's cooperation and enthusiasm. The following suggestions could be tried as part of a regular games lesson or as a ten-minute break:

1. Arrange the class in partners (imposing a limitation on the number of players), give partners a ball and a hoop (limiting the equipment), and tell them to find their own space in the playground area (limiting the playing space). Pose the question "Can you make up a game with your partner that includes a bounce, a pass, and your hoop (limiting the skills and rules)?" Figure 10.3 illustrates such a game.

2. Join two sets of partners together and pose this question: "With four players, two balls, and two hoops, can you make up a new game that involves all the equipment, a bounce pass, and a dribble?"

3. Now join two groups of four and pose this challenge: "See if you can make up a game using two hoops and one ball."

These examples illustrate how the creative games approach can be used to modify existing games or to provide a basis for children to invent their own. Children adapt to this method of

Figure 10.3

teaching with ease and enthusiasm in a very short time. This approach will be used in later chapters, along with more structured methods and techniques, to teach individual skills, rules, and game strategies.

Games for Kindergarten to Grade Two

Since children in kindergarten and first and second grades show great differences in growth and maturity, the running, tag, and simple team games described on the following pages have been arranged according to their difficulty. The first few activities are geared to the individualistic and creative natures of five- and six-year-olds. Then, as children learn to play, share, and cooperate, they should be exposed to simple team games that involve the basic throwing, catching, and kicking skills.

Toward the end of the first grade and during the second grade, running and tag games become a little more complicated, and simple team games become more structured and require more skill and team play. Because there is such a spread of interests and abilities in each of these grades, teachers should try any game they feel may be appropriate for their classes.

Running, Tag, and Simple Team Games: K-2		
Name of Game	Level	Page
Ringmaster	K	178
Tommy Tucker's Land	K	178
Brownies and Fairies	K-1	178
Old Mother Witch	K-1	178
Gardener and Scamp	K-1	179
Simple Tag	K-1	179
Slap Jack	K-1	179
Birds and Cats	K-1	179
Do As I Do	K-1	180
Mousetrap	K-1	180
Eyeglasses	K-1	180
Teacher and Class	K-1	180
Tunnel Ball	K-1	180
Touch the Ball	K-1	181
Duck on the Rock	K-1	181
Beanbag Basket	K-1	181
Circle Roll Ball	K-1	181
Drop the Handkerchief	1	182
Wild Horse Roundup	1	182
North Winds and South Winds	1-2	182
Animal Tag	1-2	182

Ringmaster (K)

Skills: Locomotor skills
Playing area: Playground, gymnasium, or classroom
Equipment: None
Players: Class
Formation: Single circle with one child in center

One child is selected to be "ringmaster" and starts in the center of the circle. The ringmaster moves around inside the circle, pretending to crack his whip and calling out the names of animals. Circle players imitate the animals called. If the ringmaster calls out, "All join the parade," the children may imitate any animal they wish.

Tommy Tucker's Land (K)

Skills: Running, dodging, and tagging
Playing area: Playground, gymnasium, or classroom
Equipment: Eight or ten beanbags for each game
Players: Six to ten players
Formation: Ten-to-fifteen-foot square with beanbags scattered inside the square

One child is chosen to be "Tommy Tucker" and stands in the center of the square. As Tommy Tucker guards his treasures, the other players sing

> "I'm on Tommy Tucker's land,
> Picking up gold and silver."

As they sing, they try to pick up as many beanbags as they can without being tagged by Tommy. If a child is tagged, he must return the treasures and leave the game. The game is completed when all the beanbags have been taken or when there is only one player left.

Variations
If the game is too slow, add another Tommy Tucker.

Brownies and Fairies (K-1)

Skills: Running, dodging, and tagging
Playing area: Playground, gymnasium, or classroom
Equipment: None
Players: Class
Formation: Two lines drawn about thirty feet apart with team lined up along each line

Divide the class into two groups, "brownies" and "fairies." The fairies turn their backs to the brownies. The brownies creep up to the fairies as quietly as possible. When they get close, the teacher calls out, "Brownies are here!" The fairies then try to tag the brownies before they can run back over their own line.

Old Mother Witch (K-1)

Skills: Locomotor skills, dodging, and tagging
Playing area: Playground or gymnasium
Equipment: None
Players: Class
Formation: Scattered around a small circle

One player is selected to be the "old witch" and stands in the middle of a circle drawn near one end of the playing area. A line is drawn across the other end; this is the "safe line." Children approach the circle and begin to tease the Old Witch by chanting

> "Old mother witch
> Fell in a ditch,
> Picked up a penny,
> And thought she was rich."

At the end of the verse the witch asks, "Whose children are you?" and the children answer with any name they wish. When a child says, "Yours," the witch begins chasing the player and tries to tag him before he can cross the "safe line." If the child is caught, he becomes the Old Witch.

Variations

Assign only one child to answer "yours." Before each new game is started, tell the children, including the old witch, that they must move back using a different locomotor skill, such as hopping or skipping.

Gardener and Scamp (K-1)

Skills: Locomotor skills, dodging, and tagging
Playing area: Playground, gymnasium, or classroom
Equipment: None
Players: Class or eight to ten per game
Formation: Circle

One child is chosen to be the "scamp" and stands in the middle of the circle. A second player is chosen to be the "gardener" and stands outside the circle. The gardener and the scamp act out the following:

> GARDENER: "Who let you into my garden?"
> SCAMP: "No one."
> GARDENER: "I'll chase you out."
> SCAMP: "Try and catch me."

The scamp leaves the circle, with the gardener following the scamp's exact path through the circle. The scamp may perform any stunt he wishes, such as crawling on all fours, and the gardener must copy him. The scamp must make it back into the circle through the same place he left before the gardener tags him. If the gardener fails to perform all the stunts demonstrated by the scamp, the scamp wins. Change both players after every turn.

Simple Tag (K-1)

Skills: Locomotor skills, dodging, and tagging
Playing area: Playground or gymnasium
Equipment: None
Players: Class
Formation: Scattered

One child is chosen to be "it." All players are scattered within a designated playing area. "It" tries to tag another player. When a player is tagged, he must call out, "I'm it," and the game continues.

Variations

A simple tag game may be changed in the following ways:

1. Vary the locomotor skill, such as requiring all to hop or skip, or require animal walking movements, such as "crab walk," bear walk," and so on.

2. Tagger must tag a particular part of the body, such as the side, back or leg.
3. Any player is safe when he assumes a particular position such as balancing on one foot, crouching, or standing back to back with another child.
4. Add one or more taggers.

Slap Jack (K-1)

Skills: Running and tagging
Playing area: Playground or gymnasium
Equipment: None
Players: Class
Formation: Circle with eight to ten players.

One child is chosen to be "it" and stands outside the circle of players. Circle players face the center, holding hands together, palms up, behind their backs. "It" walks around the circle and slaps a player on the hands. This player chases "it" around the circle and tries to tag him before he returns to the empty space. If "it" is caught before he reaches the empty space, he remains "it." If he is not caught, the chaser becomes "it" and the game continues.

Birds and Cats (K-1)

Skills: Running and tagging
Playing area: Playground, gymnasium, or classroom
Equipment: None
Players: Class
Formation: Circle

One child is chosen to be the "cat" and stands in the center of the circle. Circle players are "birds." Circle players hold hands and walk in the circle singing

> "Little birds are we,
> We live up in the tree,
> The old grey cat is coming,
> But can't catch ME."

On the word "me," circle players stoop. The cat tries to tag any player before he has stooped. The circle player who is caught becomes the cat and the old cat takes his place in the circle.

Do as I Do (K-1)

Skills: Locomotor or other "inventive movements"
Playing area: Playground, gymnasium, or classroom
Equipment: None
Players: Class
Formation: Line or circle.

One child is chosen to start the game. When he says, "Do as I do," he must make a movement, such as hopping, running, or an animal walk, and all must follow his movement. After each child has had one or two turns, choose a new leader and repeat the game.

Mousetrap (K-1)

Skills: Running and dodging
Playing area: Playground and gymnasium
Equipment: None
Players: Class
Formation: Circle

Five children are chosen to be the "mice," while the remaining children form a large circle called the "trap." The teacher starts the game with the mice outside the circle and the circle players holding hands. When she says, "Open trap," the circle players raise their hands as high as their heads and hold them in this position. The teacher then calls, "Run, little mice, run!" and the mice run freely in and out of the circle. When she says, "Snap," the circle players lower their joined hands. Any mice caught inside the circle must join the circle players. Continue until all mice are caught. Choose new mice and repeat the game.

Eyeglasses (K-1; from Korea)

Skills: Running, jumping, and tagging
Playing area: Playground or gymnasium
Equipment: None
Players: Class
Formation: Draw a pattern in the shape of eyeglasses and allow players to stand anywhere inside the area.

One child is chosen to be "it" and stands outside the "glasses." Other children scatter inside the area. "It" tries to tag any player inside the area or to get him to step over the line. The tagger may jump across the playing area but may not step inside. Players may move anywhere

within the boundaries of the "glasses." If a player is tagged or steps on or over the line, he becomes "it." If one of the circles becomes empty, the tagger can jump into and conquer it. When this occurs, the teacher chooses another tagger.

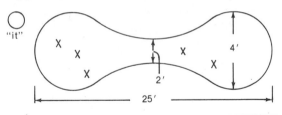

Teacher and Class (K-1)

Skills: Rolling, bouncing, throwing, and catching
Playing area: Playground, gymnasium or classroom
Equipment: Utility ball (six, nine, or thirteen inches)
Players: Six to twelve players
Formation: Large semicircle with approximately five feet between each player

Children stand in a semicircle with about five feet between each player. The teacher or "leader" stands six to ten feet away, facing the group, and bounces the ball to the player at the head of the line, who catches it and repeats bounce pass to the leader. Continue this pattern to the last player. After the last player has had a turn, the leader goes to the end of the line and the first person in the line becomes the new leader.

Teaching suggestions

1. Increase the distance between the leader and the circle players as the skill level increases.
2. Use various sizes of balls.
3. Change rules according to the skills you wish to emphasize.

Tunnel Ball (K-1)

Skills: Rolling and catching
Playing area: Playground, gymnasium
Equipment: Utility ball (nine or thirteen inches)
Players: Ten to twelve players
Formation: Circle with children facing the center and one player standing in the middle

Children form a circle with each player in a "stride" position (legs apart). One child is chosen to be "it" and stands in the center of the circle with the ball. He attempts to roll the ball between the legs of any circle player or between any two players. Circle players may use their hands to stop the ball; however, they cannot move their feet. If a circle player allows the ball to roll out of the circle, he becomes "it."

Variations
For an element of surprise, have all circle players turn around. The ball must be rolled through the legs.

Touch the Ball (K-1)

Skills: Throwing and catching
Playing area: Playground, gymnasium, or classroom
Equipment: Large rubber ball
Players: Six to ten players
Formation: Circle

Children form a circle, with the person chosen to be "it" in the center. Circle players throw the ball to other players and "it" tries to tag the ball. If he touches the ball, the player who threw it becomes "it."

Variations
Change the type of throw (one hand, from the side). Increase the distance between players.

Duck on the Rock (K-1)

Skills: Throwing
Playing area: Playground or gymnasium
Equipment: One milk carton for each game and one beanbag for each player
Players: Five to six players
Formation: Arrange children in a line ten feet from the milk carton

Place a beanbag ("duck") on top of a milk carton ("rock"). One player, the "guard," stands three feet to one side of the duck. The guard cannot stand in front of the duck. The first player throws his beanbag and tries to knock the duck off the rock. If he succeeds (including knocking the rock over), he runs to retrieve his beanbag and returns to his place behind the line. The guard must try to stand the rock up, place the duck on top, and tag the thrower before he retrieves his beanbag and runs back. If tagged, the thrower and guard change positions. Any thrower who is unsuccessful in knocking the duck off must leave his beanbag on the ground until another player knocks the duck off. When this occurs, all players whose beanbags are on the ground run and attempt to retrieve them and return to their positions. The guard may tag any of these players.

Teaching suggestions
If the guard is too successful, move him four or five feet away from the rock.

Beanbag Basket (K-1)

Skills: Throwing
Playing area: Playground, gymnasium, or classroom
Equipment: Three beanbags and one wastebasket for each team
Players: Five to six on each team
Formation: File formation behind a starting line, with about five to six feet between each team and a wastebasket five feet in front of each team

Each child is given three consecutive throws at the basket. After each player completes his third throw, he collects the bags and gives them to the next player and then goes to the rear of the line. The player or team with the highest number of baskets wins.

Teaching suggestions
As skill improves, use smaller baskets or increase the throwing distance.

Circle Roll Ball (K-1)

Skills: Rolling and catching
Playing area: Playground or gymnasium
Equipment: One utility ball and three milk cartons or bowling pins
Players: Six to eight per group
Formation: Circle, with milk cartons in middle

One player in the circle rolls the ball at the milk cartons. If he knocks one or more down, he sets them back up. If the ball is still in the middle or out of reach of any circle player, the person who is setting cartons back up rolls the ball to any circle player. As the game continues, stress that the only player who can enter the circle to fetch a ball is the child who last rolled it. He, in turn, must roll the ball to any circle player.

Variations
Introduce a second ball after the children understand the basic rules. Play the same game from a square or two opposing line formations. Change the positions and pattern of the milk cartons.

Drop the Handkerchief (1)

Skills: Locomotor skills
Playing area: Playground, gymnasium, or classroom
Equipment: Handkerchief
Players: Eight to ten players
Formation: Circle

One child is chosen to be "it" and stands outside the circle of players. "It" runs (or does any other locomotor skill) around the outside of the circle and drops the handkerchief behind a student. (You might add, ". . . and calls out the circle player's name.") The student behind whom the handkerchief is dropped must pick it up and run around the circle in the opposite direction. The player who reaches the open place last becomes "it."

Variations
Change the locomotor skill with each game. After a person has been chosen to be "it," he cannot be chosen again until all players have had a turn.

Wild Horse Roundup (1)

Skills: Running and tagging
Playing area: Playground or gymnasium
Equipment: None
Players: Class
Formation: Large circle or square called the "range" and a small circle beside the range called the "corral"

Four children are chosen to be the "cowboys" and start inside the "range." All other players are the "wild horses" and scatter outside the range. When the teacher calls, "Wild horses!" the horses must enter and stay in the range and avoid being caught by the cowboys. When a horse is tagged, he is taken to the corral. The last horse caught becomes the new "foreman" and chooses three new cowboys to begin the game again.

Variation
Play the same game in partners.

North Winds and South Winds (1-2; from Sweden)

Skills: Running and tagging
Playing area: Playground or gymnasium
Equipment: Two blue ribbons and one yellow ribbon (colors are optional)
Players: Class
Formation: Large rectangular area and scattered formation

This is essentially a "tag" game with the delightful addition of a player who can *free* any tagged player. Two players are chosen to represent the "north wind" and are marked with blue ribbons. One child is chosen to represent the "south wind" and is marked with a yellow ribbon. All other children are scattered in the rectangular playing area. The two north wind players, representing "cold" and "danger," try to tag as many players as possible. When a player is tagged by a north wind player, he must squat down on all fours and become stiff and motionless. The south wind player tries to free as many tagged players as possible by touching them and shouting, "Free!" As soon as a player is touched, he is free and continues to take part in the game. The teacher sets a time limit and the number of players that constitute the end of the game. For example, the games might last two minutes, and if there are fewer than three tagged players, the south wind wins. But if more than three tagged players remain, the north wind wins.

Animal Tag (1-2)

Skills: Locomotor skills, animal movements, and tagging
Playing area: Playground or gymnasium
Equipment: None
Players: Class
Formation: Two parallel lines about thirty to forty feet apart

Place half the class behind each line. Players behind one line decide upon an animal they wish to imitate. They tell the teacher the name of the animal. They then move to within five or six feet of the opposing line and begin to imitate the animal. The opposing team members try to guess the name of the animal, raising their hands. When the teacher hears the correct name, she calls, "Chase," and the animals try to run back across their own line before being tagged. Change sides and the type of animals after each game.

Uncle Sam (1-2)

Skills: Running and tagging
Playing area: Playground or gymnasium
Equipment: None
Players: Class
Formation: Two lines drawn thirty to forty feet apart, with the children placed along one line and the other line called the "river"

One player is chosen to be "Uncle Sam" and stands in the center of the play area. Other players stand behind the line and call, "Uncle Sam, may we cross your river?" Uncle Sam says, "Yes, if you have on—blue" (or whatever color). All children wearing blue must run to the opposite side. Uncle Sam tries to tag as many as he can before they cross the opposite line. Those caught must help Uncle Sam. The last person to be caught wins the game.

Midnight (1-2)

Skills: Running and tagging
Playing area: Playground or gymnasium
Equipment: None
Players: Class
Formation: Draw two lines twenty-five to thirty feet apart, with the class placed behind one, called the "home" line. In the middle of the other line draw a five-foot square; this is the "fox's den"

One player is chosen to be the "fox." He stands in his den. The "chickens" approach the fox's den and ask, "What time is it?" The fox can give any time for an answer. When the fox answers, "Midnight," he tries to tag as many chickens as he can before they cross the home line. Any chicken tagged must go to the fox's den and help him catch the remaining chickens.

Red Rover (1-2)

Skills: Running and tagging
Playing area: Playground and gymnasium
Equipment: None
Players: Class
Formation: Three parallel lines drawn twenty feet apart, with children placed on one end line facing the centerline

One player is chosen to be "it" and stands on the centerline. All other players stand on one end line. "It" calls, "Red Rover, let Jim and Mary and Joe and Sue (four or five players) go." These

players run to the opposite end line, while "it" attempts to tag as many as possible before they reach the line. Allow "it" three or four turns, then choose a new "it." The player who catches the most wins the game.

Posture Tag (1-2)

Skills: Running, balancing, and tagging
Playing area: Playground or gymnasium
Equipment: Two beanbags
Players: Class
Formation: Scattered

One player is chosen to be "it" and another to be the runner. The runner and "it" have beanbags on their heads and cannot hold them on. "It" chases the runner and tries to tag him. The runner may transfer his beanbag to any player's head, and that player then becomes the new runner.

Squirrel in the Tree (1-2)

Skills: Running
Playing area: Playground or gymnasium
Equipment: None
Players: Class
Formation: Scattered in groups of three

Arrange class in groups of three, scattered about the play area. Two join hands to form a "hollow tree" and the third player, the "squirrel," stands in the middle. Two or three extra squirrels should be placed randomly throughout the play area. On a signal from the teacher, all the squirrels must find new trees. After four turns, have children return to original positions and repeat game.

Back-to-Back Tag (1-2)

Skills: Running and tagging
Playing area: Playground or gymnasium
Equipment: None
Players: Class
Formation: Scattered

This game is played the same way as simple tag except that when any two players stand back to back, they are safe. As soon as back-to-back players feel they are safe, they separate to find new partners. Any player tagged becomes "it" and the game continues.

10

Jet Pilot (1-2)

Skills: Running and turning
Playing area: Playground or gymnasium
Equipment: None
Players: Class
Formation: Two lines drawn across the ends of the playing area, with one line the "takeoff" line and the other the "turning" line

All players line up behind the takeoff line. One child is chosen to be the "captain" and calls out, "Pilots, take off!" All pilots run to the turning line, then back across the takeoff line. The first pilot back across the takeoff line becomes the new captain and the game continues.

Red Light (1-2)

Skills: Running and stopping
Playing area: Playground or gymnasium
Equipment: None
Players: Class
Formation: Two lines drawn across the ends of the playing area

One player is chosen to be "it" and stands on one line with his back to the opposite line. All other players stand on the opposite line. As "it" begins to count to ten, all players begin to run toward his line. At any time before he reaches ten, "it" may call out, "Red light," and turn around. If he sees anyone moving, he sends him back to the opposite line. The game continues until the first player crosses over the line. That player becomes "it" and the game starts over.

Fire Engine (1-2)

Skills: Running, dodging, and tagging
Playing area: Playground or gymnasium
Equipment: None
Players: Class
Formation: Two lines drawn across the ends of the playing area and one across the center

One child is chosen to be the "fire chief" and stands on the centerline. All others stand on one of the end lines and are given a number between one and five, which represents the "alarm number." The fire chief begins to call out the numbers and after any of them may yell, "Fire!" All the children with this number then must run to the opposite line before being tagged. The first to cross the opposite line becomes the new fire chief.

Variations
Call, "General alarm," which signals that all must run. Clap hands instead of calling the number.

Queen Bee (1-2)

Skills: Locomotor skills
Playing area: Playground or gymnasium
Equipment: Beanbags (or colored paper squares) for each child
Players: Class
Formation: Scattered

Choose three children to be "queen bees." All other children place a beanbag (a "flower") on the floor and stand beside it. Have them scatter the beanbags evenly throughout the playing area. On a signal from the teacher, the queen bees "fly" around the "garden," tapping "bees" on the shoulder. The tapped bees follow the queen bees. When the teacher says, "Fly home," all the "bees" and the three "queen bees" run to any available "flower." The three remaining players become the new queen bees.

Call Ball (1-2)

Skills: Throwing and catching
Playing area: Playground or gymnasium
Equipment: One ball for every five or six players
Players: Five to six players
Formation: Circle, with one player standing in the center

The center player tosses the ball into the air and calls out the name of a circle player. That player must catch the ball before it bounces. If the circle player is successful, he becomes the next thrower.

Variations
If skill level is very low, allow one bounce before attempting to catch the ball.

Hot Ball (1-2)

Skills: Kicking
Playing area: Playground or gymnasium
Equipment: One ball for every six to eight children
Players: Six to eight players
Formation: Circle

One child is chosen to start the game. He pretends to set a fire under the ball, then kicks it and says, ''The ball's hot.'' Circle players try to kick the ball away from them to keep from getting ''burned.'' If the ball goes out of the circle, the person who last touched it becomes ''it'' and pretends to set the ball on fire again.

Variations
Play the same game with the hands. Or allow circle players to use only the left or right foot to kick the ball.

Indian Club Bowl (1-2)

Skills: Rolling
Playing area: Playground or gymnasium
Equipment: One ball and one Indian club or milk carton for each team
Players: Five or six on each team
Formation: Indian club placed about twelve inches in front of each line

The first player on each team rolls the ball and tries to knock over the club. The last player retrieves the ball. The first player then runs to the retriever's position and the old retriever goes to the back of the line. Continue the game, awarding one point for each club that is knocked over.

Variations
Change distance according to level of skill. Add one or more Indian clubs. For fun, bowl backwards between legs.

Ball Stand (1-2)

Skills: Running, stopping, and throwing
Playing area: Playground or gymnasium
Equipment: Utility ball
Players: Class
Formation: Circle, with one player standing in the center holding the ball

The center player places the ball on the ground and calls a circle player's name. This player runs to the ball while all the other players run as far away from the ball as possible. When the player picks up the ball he calls, ''Stand,'' and all players must stop immediately. The player now tries to throw the ball and hit a player. Players must keep their feet on the ground, although they are allowed to bend, twist, or duck to avoid being hit. If a player is hit, he becomes the center player and the game is repeated.

Cat and Rat (2)

Skills: Running, dodging, and tagging
Playing area: Playground or gymnasium
Equipment: None
Players: All
Formation: Circle

One child is chosen to be the ''cat'' and stands in the center of the circle. Another child is chosen to be the ''rat'' and stands outside the circle. Circle players hold hands and try to prevent the cat from tagging the rat by moving their arms up and down. Both the cat and rat may move in and out of the circle. When the rat is caught, start a new game with a new cat and rat.

Crows and Cranes (2)

Skills: Running, dodging, and tagging
Playing area: Playground or gymnasium
Equipment: None
Players: Class
Formation: One line drawn at each end of the playing area and two lines drawn about three feet apart in the center

Divide class in half and call one group ''crows,'' the other ''cranes.'' Each team lines up on its center line, facing the other. When the teacher calls ''Crrr—ows,'' the crows turn and run toward their goal line and the cranes try to tag them before they cross it. If a player is tagged, he joins the opposite team. The game continues until last player is caught.

Teaching suggestions
Draw out the beginning of both words to keep the children in suspense as long as possible.

Hill Dill (2)

Skills: Running and dodging
Playing area: Playground or gymnasium
Equipment: None
Players: Class
Formation: One line drawn at each end of the playing area

One child is chosen to be ''it'' and stands between the two parallel lines. All other children line up on one end line. When the center player calls, ''Hill dill, come over the hill,'' all players try to run to the other end line without being tagged. Any player that is caught helps "it" catch players until the last player is caught. The last child caught becomes "it" in the next game.

Two Deep (2)

Skills: Running and stopping
Playing area: Playground or gymnasium
Equipment: None
Players: Ten to fifteen
Formation: Circle

One child is chosen to be "it" and one child the runner. Players forming the circle should stand about two feet apart facing into the circle. On a signal from the teacher, "it" chases the runner around the outside of the circle. The runner may stop in front of any circle player at any time to save himself. Whoever he stops in front of then becomes the new runner.

Two Square (2)

Skills: Bouncing and hitting
Playing area: Playground or gymnasium
Equipment: Utility ball (nine or thirteen inches)
Players: Two to eight
Formation: Two five-foot squares drawn side by side, with one player in each

One player stands in each square while the remaining players stand just outside the squares. Player in one square bounce-serves the ball into the other square. (It may be wise to let players throw the ball at first instead of bounce-serving it. As skill increases, require a bounce-serve). After the ball bounces in the opposing player's square, that player returns it by batting it upward with one or both hands back into the server's square. Continue play until one of the following violations occurs:

1. The ball lands out of the square (liners are good).
2. The ball is hit with the fist.
3. The player holds the ball (catches it).
4. The ball is hit downward.

When a violation occurs, the player committing it leaves the game and the next waiting player takes his place.

Simple Dodge Ball (2)

Skills: Throwing and retrieving
Playing area: Playground or gymnasium
Equipment: Volleyball or utility ball
Players: Class
Formation: Circle

Divide players into two teams; one team remains in circle formation, while the other stands in the center. On signal, players in the outside circle try to hit inside players below the waist with the ball. To avoid being hit, the inside players may move anywhere within the circle. Outside players may enter the circle to retrieve the ball; however, they may not throw at an opponent while inside the circle. Any player hit below the waist joins the outside circle. The last person remaining in the circle is the winner.

Teaching suggestions

1. To start, allow any player hit by a bouncing ball to be eliminated. Later, allow only a "fly" hit to count. (A fly hit is one in which the ball travels directly from the thrower to a circle player.)
2. Use two or more balls.

Boundary Ball (2)

Skills: Kicking and trapping
Playing area: Playground or gymnasium
Equipment: Two soccer balls
Players: Ten to fifteen players on each team
Formation: Three lines drawn with twenty to thirty feet between each, and each team scattered on each side of the centerline

Each team is given a ball and kicks it toward the opponent's goal line. Players on both teams may move about freely, but only in their own half of the playing area, trying to prevent the opponents' ball from crossing the goal line. Players cannot touch the ball with their hands. One point is scored each time the ball crosses the opponents' goal line.

Teaching suggestions
Allow only left foot or right foot kicking.

Three Down (2)

Skills: Rolling a ball
Playing area: Playground or gymnasium
Equipment: Two balls and four clubs or milk cartons per group
Players: Six to eight players per game
Formation: Circle

Four clubs are arranged in a square about three feet apart in the middle of the circle. Two players are pinsetters. Circle players roll the two balls at the clubs, attempting to knock them down, while the pinsetters keep setting up the clubs. When three clubs are down, the circle players call, "Three down." The pinsetters then choose two new pinsetters and the game continues.

Snowball (2)

Skills: Running, throwing, and dodging
Playing area: Playground or gymnasium
Equipment: Ten to twelve yarn or fleece balls
Players: Class
Formation: Two end lines and one centerline, with each team scattered along its side of the centerline

Divide the class into two equal teams and give each team an equal number of balls (about five or six each). On signal, players attempt to hit opposing players with the balls. Any player who is hit must move to the sideline. Sideline players may retrieve balls and throw them to teammates, but they may not throw them at opponents. The game ends when one player remains.

Games for Grades Three and Four

Children in grades three and four are at a transitional stage when it comes to game activities. While they still thoroughly enjoy running, tag, and simple team games, particularly if they are rough and involve team spirit and competition, children in these grades are becoming interested in team games. If skill level and student interest are extremely high, do not hesitate to draw from the lead-up games in Chapters 13 through 18. Page references are included in the accompanying chart.

Running, Tag, and Simple Team Games: 3-4

Name of Game	Level	Page
Partner Tag	3	187
Chinese Wall	3	188
Fly Trap	3	188
Loose Caboose	3-4	188
Crab Tag	3-4	188
Dumbbell Tag	3-4	188
Commando	3-4	189
Up the Field	3-4	189
Jump the Shot	3-4	189
Ball Race	3-4	189
Keep Away	3-4	189
Circle Ball	3-4	190
Progressive Dodge Ball	3-4	190
Place Kickball	3-4	190
Battle Ball	3-4	190
Crab Soccer	3-4	190
Swing at Five	3-4	191
Bat Ball	3-4	191
Guard Ball	3-4	191
Long Ball	4	191
High Ball	4	192
Shower Ball	4	192
Bounce Net Ball	4	192
Bombardment	4	192
Additional Lead-up Games		
Basketball	3-4	319
Soccer	3-4	241
Football	3-4	273
Hockey	3-4	258
Volleyball	3-4	292
Softball	3-4	343

Partner Tag (3)

Skills: Running and Tagging
Playing area: Playground or gymnasium
Equipment: None
Players: Class
Formation: Partners scattered around the play area

One child is chosen to be "it" and another to be the "chaser." Other children select partners and link elbows. The chaser tries to tag "it," who may run anywhere in the play area. Whenever "it" links elbows with a player, he is safe, but the partner of the player "it" links onto them becomes the new "it." If the chaser tags "it," they change positions and the game continues.

Chinese Wall (3)

Skills: Running, dodging, and tagging
Playing area: Playground or gymnasium
Equipment: None
Players: Class
Formation: Two end lines and two parallel lines drawn about ten feet apart across the middle of the playing area, with the space between the two centerlines called the "wall"

Two children are chosen as "defenders" and must remain inside the wall. All other players line up on one end line. On signal, everyone tries to cross the wall to the opposite end line without being tagged by the defenders. Anyone caught becomes another defender. The game continues until only two runners remain; these players become the new defenders and the game starts again.

Fly Trap (3)

Skills: Running, stretching, and stopping
Playing area: Playground or gymnasium
Equipment: None
Players: Class
Formation: Scattered

Have half of the class sit cross-legged in a scattered formation. These children are the "trappers." The other half are the "flies." On signal, the flies run in any direction they wish but they must stay within the playing area. When the teacher calls, "Freeze," the flies must come to an immediate stop. The trappers, still seated, try to touch the flies. Any trapper who can touch a fly changes position and the game continues.

Variation
If there is sufficient room, require the trappers to keep only one foot on the floor as they stretch toward the fly. Change locomotor skill.

Loose Caboose (3-4)

Skills: Running, dodging, and tagging
Playing area: Playground or gymnasium
Equipment: None
Players: Class
Formation: Scattered

Arrange class into groups of three. The three players form a line, holding onto the waist of the player in front. The first player is the "engine,"

the second the "baggage car," and the last the "caboose." Choose two players to be "loose cabooses." On signal, each train tries to prevent a loose caboose from attaching onto its own caboose. When this occurs, the engine becomes a new loose caboose, and each player moves up one place on the train. If a train pulls apart trying to avoid a loose caboose, this constitutes being caught.

Crab Tag (3-4)

Skills: Running and tagging
Playing area: Playground or gymnasium
Equipment: None
Players: Class
Formation: Scattered

This game is played the same way as simple tag, except that a player in a crab-walk position (see p. 388) is safe.

Teaching suggestions
Change the "safe" position to a seal walk or an elephant walk, or to a continuous exercise movement, such as push-ups. This could become a "fun" approach to the warm-up period.

Dumbbell Tag (3-4)

Skills: Running and tagging
Playing area: Playground or gymnasium
Equipment: "Dumbbell" (beanbag or towel)
Players: Class
Formation: Scattered

One player is selected to be the runner and is given the "dumbbell." Another player is selected to be "it." To start the game, "it" begins to chase the runner with the dumbbell. The runner may give the dumbbell to any player at any time, and that player must take it. If "it" tags the player who has the dumbbell, that player becomes "it." The new "it" must count to three before chasing anyone; during this time, the "old it" takes the dumbbell and gives it to anyone in the class, who then becomes the new runner.

Commando (3-4)

Skills: Running, dodging, and tagging
Playing area: Playground or gymnasium
Equipment: None
Players: Eight to ten in each circle
Formation: Circle

One player is selected to be "it" and stands in the middle of the circle. Circle players join hands. On the signal, "it" tries to break through the circle by crawling under or over the joined hands or by breaking the link. If "it" breaks through, the two circle players chase him and the one who tags him becomes the new "it."

Up the Field (3-4)

Skills: Throwing and catching
Playing area: Playground
Equipment: Utility ball (6½-8½ inches)
Players: Class
Formation: Large rectangle (100 by 50 feet), with line drawn across the center and the end lines as goal lines

Divide class into two teams and arrange each team in a scattered formation on its own half of the playing area. Players must stay on their own side of the field. The ball is given to a player who is standing on his own goal line. The object is to throw the ball over the opponent's goal line. Each team is allowed three passes before the ball must cross the centerline. To score, the ball must be in the air as it crosses the opponent's goal line and it cannot have been touched by any defending player.

Jump the Shot (3-4)

Skills: Jumping
Playing area: Playground or gymnasium
Equipment: Rope
Players: Eight to ten per game
Formation: Circle

One player holds the rope in the middle of the circle. He begins to swing the rope by one end in a circle, keeping it about one foot off the ground. Circle players try to jump the rope as it approaches. If hit, they are charged with one shot. The game continues for a designated period. The winner is the player with the least number of shots charged against him, and he becomes the "turner" in the next game.

Variations
Vary the length and speed of the rope according to level of skill. Have circle players join hands with a partner. Have circle players bounce a ball (start with two-hand bounce) as the rope is turned.

Ball Race (3-4)

Skills: Dribbling (with hands or feet)
Playing area: Playground or gymnasium
Equipment: One soccer ball for each team
Players: Six to eight on each team
Formation: File formation behind a starting line, with about five to six feet between each team, and a two-foot circle drawn about ten feet in front of each team

Lead players dribble the ball around the circle and back to their starting lines. The first child back is the winner.

Teaching suggestions
Place the circles far enough apart to prevent interference between players.

Keep Away (3-4)

Skills: Passing, catching, and guarding
Playing area: Playground or gymnasium
Equipment: One utility ball or basketball
Players: Eight to ten on each of two teams
Formation: Scattered formation within a designated playing area

The teacher gives the ball to a player on one team, who then passes it to a teammate. The opposing players attempt to intercept the ball or break up the pass. If they are successful, they pass the ball to each other. Fouls are called whenever a defensive player grabs or holds onto an offensive player.

Teaching suggestions
Do not let players run with the ball. Players who are waiting their turns must be kept out of the playing area. If adequate space is available, divide the class into four teams and play two games at once. If the teams are large and there is a limited playing area, rotate in fours or fives every few minutes.

Circle Ball (3-4)

Skills: Passing and catching
Playing area: Playground or gymnasium
Equipment: Basketball or utility ball
Players: Ten to fifteen in each circle
Formation: Single circle with six to eight feet between each player

The ball is passed from player to player around the circle. Once the ball is started, introduce a second ball to be passed in the same direction.

Teaching suggestions
Use a stopwatch to time speed. Change direction frequently to keep the children's interest.

Progressive Dodge Ball (3-4)

Skills: Throwing and dodging
Playing area: Playground
Equipment: Ball
Players: Class
Formation: Three parallel twenty-foot squares designated as A, B, and C

This game is played in three periods of three to five minutes each. Teams rotate playing areas (A, B, and C) after each period. On the signal, a player in one section tries to hit players, with the ball (below the waist) in either of the other two sections. No player is eliminated, so a player who is hit should try to get the ball as soon as he is hit and throw it at an opponent. Scores are made by hitting players on another team. The teacher or leader keeps the score for each team, and the team with highest score after three periods wins. Players may not cross boundary lines.

Place Kickball (3-4)

Skills: Running, kicking, and catching
Playing area: Playground
Equipment: Utility or soccer ball
Players: Ten to twelve on each team
Formation: Softball diamond with thirty feet between bases, and one team in the field and one in a line formation behind home base

Place the fielding team in the playing area outside the baselines. Each player on the kicking team is given one stationary kick from the home plate. If the kick is fair (inside the boundary lines), the kicker tries to run around the bases before a member of the fielding team can get the ball and beat him to home plate. The kicker is out if a fly ball is caught.

Teaching suggestions
After the stationary kick is learned, introduce a "dribble and kick." Draw a line ten to fifteen feet behind the home base and require the kicker to dribble to the base and then kick the ball. The second time "up to bat," require that the kick be made with the opposite foot. If only a few players make it around the bases, have players run to first base and back.

Battle Ball (3-4)

Skills: Kicking and Trapping
Playing area: Playground
Equipment: A slightly deflated soccer ball
Players: Ten to twelve on each team
Formation: Two parallel lines twenty feet apart, with one team on each line and the players holding hands

Side A tries to kick the soccer ball over side B's goal line. Side B tries to stop the ball and kick it back over side A's line, and so on. The team that kicks the ball over the opponent's line receives two points. The first side to reach a score decided by the teacher wins the game. If a player touches the ball with his hands, his team loses a point. And if the ball is kicked too high—over the heads of the other team—one point is deducted.

Teaching suggestions
Have players pass the ball from teammate to teammate before kicking it toward the opponent's line. Allow children to use their hands to prevent the ball from hitting their faces.

Crab Soccer (3-4)

Skills: Kicking
Playing area: Playground or gymnasium
Equipment: Utility or soccer ball
Players: Fifteen to seventeen on each team
Formation: Playing area divided into two equal sections, with one team in each section and goals placed on end lines

Players from both teams may start from any position within the playing area and may move anywhere in the court area. All players except one goalie for each team must remain in a crab-walk position (p. 388). The goalies may use their hands; however, all other players must move the ball with their feet. A foul occurs when a player catches the ball or strikes it with his hands. The teacher should stop the game when a foul occurs and give the ball to the nearest opponent. Award one point for each goal scored.

Teaching suggestions
Practice the crab walk first. After the game is well understood, require striking with hands only or allow a combination of hands and feet.

Swing at Five (3-4)

Skills: Throwing, catching, and fielding
Playing area: Playground
Equipment: One bat, one softball, and four bases
Players: Nine to twelve on each team
Formation: Softball diamond with thirty feet between each base, one team in the field, and one team in a line formation behind a restraining line drawn ten feet back and to the right of home plate

The game is similar to softball except the batter is given five pitches. All foul balls count as swings. A ball landing in the infield scores one point, while a ball landing in the outfield scores two points. Players do not run around the bases. The pitcher must use the underhand throw. Alternate the pitcher. Waiting batters should stand at least ten feet away from the batter.

Bat Ball (3-4)

Skills: Batting, running, and throwing
Playing area: Playground
Equipment: Softball, bat, and two bases
Players: Nine on each team
Formation: Softball diamond with thirty to thirty-five feet between each base, one team in the field, and the other in a file formation behind a restraining line drawn ten feet back and to the right of home plate

One team is in the field and the other at bat. Players on the team at bat try to hit the ball into the field and run to first base and back home in one complete trip. The batter may not stop on base. If he makes a complete trip without being put out, he scores one run. The batter is out if (a) fielder catches a fly ball or (b) a fielder touches the runner with the ball before he reaches home. When the team at bat has three outs, it goes into the field and the team in the field comes to bat. The winner is the team with the most points at the end of the playing period. (Teams must have same number of times at bat.)

Teaching suggestions
Alternate pitchers and catchers. Alternate boy and girl in the batting order. Try two outs if one team stays up too long. Vary the distance between bases according to the level of skill.

Guard Ball (3-4)

Skills: Throwing, catching, and guarding
Playing area: Playground or gymnasium
Equipment: Utility ball (8½ inches)
Players: Class
Formation: Scattered

Divide a large rectangle (thirty by ninety feet) into three equal sections, A, B, and C. Place half the class (Team 1) in section B and split the other half (Team 2) equally into sections A and C. Players on Team 2, using a roll or a bounce pass, try to pass the ball to teammates in the opposite section. The ball must be passed below head level. Players on team 1 attempt to block the passes with their hands. Award one point for each successful pass. Rotate teams every two or three minutes.

Long Ball (4)

Skills: Running, pitching, catching, and batting
Playing area: Playground
Equipment: Softball, bat, and two bases
Players: Nine on each team
Formation: Softball diamond with thirty to thirty-five feet between each base, one team in the field, and the other in a file formation behind a restraining line drawn ten feet back and to the right of home plate

Players are divided into two teams (number each player). Each team selects a pitcher and a catcher; other players are fielders or batters. When a ball is hit, the batter runs to first base and, if possible, returns home. The runner may stop on first base, and any number of runners may be on base at the same time. Runners may not steal home. Any hit is good; there are no fouls in this game. Batter is out when he strikes out, is touched with the ball off base, steals home, throws the bat, or a fly ball is caught. One point is awarded for each run to the base and back.

Teaching suggestions
Alternate pitchers and catchers. Keep children away from batters. Move pitcher closer as skill indicates.

10

High Ball (4)

Skills: Throwing, catching, and volleying
Playing area: Playground
Equipment: Volleyball, net, and court
Players: Ten to fifteen players on each team
Formation: Drop the volleyball net down to about six feet or string a rope between two standards. Place one team on each side of the net in a scattered formation.

A player on one team throws the ball over the net, and any player on the other team must catch it before it hits the ground and return it over the net. When a player drops the ball, the other team gets a point.

Teaching suggestions
Add the following rule: As soon as a player catches the ball, he must throw it to one of his teammates, who, in turn, must hit it over the net. Keep children in their assigned areas; allow no wandering.

Shower Ball (4)

Skills: Volleying and catching
Playing area: Playground
Equipment: Volleyball, net, and court
Players: Ten to twelve on each team
Formation: Drop a volleyball net down to about six feet or string a rope between two standards. Place one team on each side of the net in a scattered formation.

Action is started by one player hitting the ball over the net. Any player on the opposite team attempts to catch the ball. The player who catches it is allowed one step and then must hit the ball back over the net. The serving team scores one point if the receiving team does not catch the ball. The receiving team gets a point if it catches the ball before it bounces.

Teaching suggestions
As skill improves, have each child throw the ball up and then hit it over the net.

Bounce Net Ball (4)

Skills: Volleying
Playing area: Playground or gymnasium
Equipment: Volleyball, net, and volleyball court
Players: Six to nine on each team
Formation: Drop the volleyball net down to about six feet or string a rope between two standards. Place one team on each side of the net in rows or in scattered formation.

Play is started by one player hitting the ball over the net. The ball must bounce before being returned. Any number of players can hit the ball any number of times; however, it must bounce once between each player. The team that loses the point starts the ball the next time. Fouls occur when the ball is (a) thrown, (b) caught and held, (c) allowed to bounce more than once, or (d) out of bounds. When a team commits a foul, the opposite team gets one point.

Teaching suggestions
Instead of allowing one bounce between players, make them hit the ball directly from a volley pass.

Bombardment (4)

Skills: Running, throwing, catching, and guarding
Playing area: Playground or gymnasium
Equipment: Twelve to twenty milk cartons or Indian clubs, 10 balls
Players: Class
Formation: Scattered

Divide the playing area in half and draw a four-foot restraining line next to each team's end line. Place equal numbers of milk cartons or Indian clubs in these four-foot sections. Each team starts with five balls and tries to knock down the cartons or clubs in the opponent's goal area. Players may use their hands or legs to prevent the cartons or clubs from being knocked over. All players must stay in their own half of the playing area. Defending players must also stay in front of the four-foot restraining line. The team that knocks down all of its opponent's milk cartons or Indian clubs first wins. If the game is played in time periods, the team with the most pins knocked down wins.

Games for Grades Five and Six

Running, tag, and simple team games become less important as children reach grades five and six. Their dominant interest, of course, is team games. However, there are times when boys and girls of this age enjoy a vigorous running game or a simple team game such as California Kickball or Ricochet. Teachers should also review the games listed in the previous pages as possible additions to their programs.

Hip Tag (5-6)

Skills: Running and tagging
Playing area: Playground or gymnasium
Equipment: Towel
Players: Class
Formation: Scattered

One player is selected to be "it" and is given a towel to tag other players. On signal, "it" tries to tag other players. He must hit below the waist. Any player tagged may assist "it" by holding other players and calling, "It." The last one tagged is the winner.

Chain Tag (5-6)

Skills: Running and tagging
Playing area: Playground or gymnasium
Equipment: None
Players: Class
Formation: Scattered

One player is chosen to be "it" and tries to tag another player. The first player tagged joins hands with "it" and helps tag other players. Both use their free hands. Each player tagged joins hands with the one who tagged him. Continue the game until last person is tagged. No tag is fair if the line is broken.

Circle Tug-of-War (5-6)

Skills: Pulling and pushing
Playing area: Playground or gymnasium
Equipment: Six to eight Indian clubs
Players: Twelve to fifteen
Formation: Circle

Scatter the Indian clubs inside the circle reasonably close together. All players join hands. On signal, each player pushes or pulls and tries to make other players knock down the clubs. Any player who knocks down a club is eliminated from the game. And, when two circle players break or lose their grip, both are eliminated.

Gold Rush (5-6)

Skills: Running, dodging, and tagging
Playing area: Playground or gymnasium
Equipment: Eight beanbags
Players: Class
Formation: Arrange playing area as shown in diagram. Place four beanbags ("bags of gold") in each "bank." Players should wear identifying singlets or arm bands.

Divide the class into two equal groups and arrange in scattered formation on each side of centerline. On signal, players try to run through the opponent's side and steal "bags of gold" (one per try). If a player returns to his home bank by running around the outside of the playing area, he cannot be tagged. But if he crosses

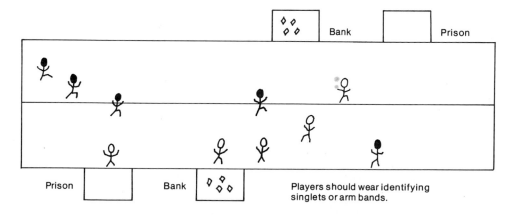

Players should wear identifying singlets or arm bands.

through the opponent's playing area with the bag of gold, he can be tagged. Tagged players go to the opposing team's jail. When there are prisoners in jail, players on their team must attempt to rescue all of them before they can try to steal the gold. The same rules apply when returning home with a teammate.

Borden Ball (5-6)

Skills: Throwing and catching
Playing area: Playground or gymnasium
Equipment: Football and two posts or traffic cones
Players: Class divided into two equal teams
Formation: Playing area divided into two equal sections, with one team in each

Place one goalie from each team in an eight-foot goal area in the center of each end line (use two posts or traffic cones for goal posts). Other players take any position they wish in the playing area. The object is to throw the ball through the opponent's goal. The game is started with a jump ball between two opposing players. The ball may be thrown in any direction, but it may not be hit or kicked. A player may not hold the ball for longer than three seconds. He may take a maximum of three steps. On penalties the ball is given to the nearest opponent. Members of the team that does not have possession of the ball may check the player with the ball, but they may not touch, hold, or push him. One point is awarded for each goal. After a point is scored, at halftime, or at any official stopping of play, start play with a jump ball at the center. If the ball goes over the sidelines, a player on the opposing team throws it into the field of play.

Goodminton (5-6; from Canada)

In terms of antiquity, goodminton, like Canada, is very young; the game is not more than twenty-five years old. It is a combination of badminton and volleyball. Because of the inexpensive equipment, the simple and flexible rules, and the fun of this game, it shows every promise of becoming popular in any country.

Skills: Batting
Playing area: Playground or gymnasium
Equipment: Volleyball net (or rope), bats (see diagram in Appendix B), badminton bird (used ones are quite suitable) or yarn ball (covered with tape or cloth)
Players: Six or fewer on each team

The referee tosses a coin for court or service; the winner of the toss chooses either to serve first or to pick his court. The server has only one serve to get the bird over the net, and the bird must clear the net on each serve. The server continues to serve so long as his team wins points. After the first serve has been taken by each team, and after each succeeding "side out," the team receiving the serve rotates one position clockwise. (The front row players move to the right, the back row players to the left, and the left back moves to the left forward position.) Teams change sides after each game.

Playing the bird:
The bird may be batted in any direction, but scooping, lifting, and any form of holding are not permitted. The bird, except on service, may be recovered from the net, provided the player avoids touching the net. The bird may be batted only three times by one team before being

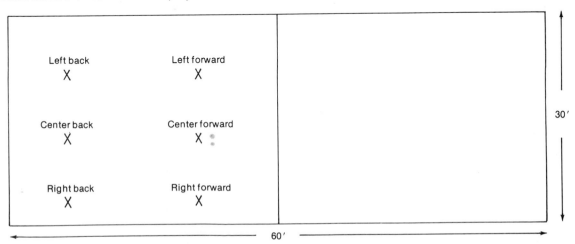

Goodminton—positions and court dimensions

Figure 10.4

returned over the net. A player may not hit the bird twice in succession, but he may give it the first and third hits.

Points and service:

If any player on the serving team commits any of the following acts, it shall be "side out." If any player on the receiving team commits any of the acts, the serving team is awarded a point. The illegal acts: Serving illegally; catching or holding the bird; touching the net with any part of the body or bat (if two opponents touch the net simultaneously, the bird shall be re-served); reaching over the net; playing out of position; touching the floor on the opposite side of the centerline; allowing hands or bats over the centerline; "spiking" or "killing" the bird when playing a back position.

Scoring:

The serving team earns a point if the receiving team fails to return the bird legally over the net into the serving team's court. A game is won when either team has a two-point lead with fifteen or more points. Teams change sides at the end of a game. Two out of three games constitutes a match.

Substitution:

Any number of players may be substituted, but only when the bird is declared dead.

California Kickball (5-6)

Skills: Running, throwing, catching, and kicking
Playing area: Playground or gymnasium
Equipment: Utility ball or old volleyball
Players: Nine per team
Formation: Arrange the playing area the same as in a softball game. Modify the length of bases and other rules according to space and other conditions.

The game is played like softball with the following modifications: (a) Use a utility ball or old volleyball; (b) the ball is rolled and the "batter" kicks it; (c) the batter must run whether the ball goes fair or foul; (d) first base is the only base that the fielding team can touch to get a batter out—on all other bases the fielder must tag the runner or throw the ball and hit him to get him out; (e) any number on the batting team may get on a base and stay, running when they think it is safe to try for another base; (f) on any hit balls, if the fielding team throws the ball to the pitcher, any runner who is between bases must go back to the last base; (g) any runner caught between bases on a caught fly ball is automatically out; (h) change teams after three to six outs, or when everyone on the batting team has had a turn at bat.

Figure 10.5

Long Ball (5-6; from Denmark)

Skills: Hitting, catching, running, and rolling
Playing area: Gymnasium or playground
Equipment: One ball
Players: Class
Formation: As in diagram

Players on Team A are scattered behind the centerline. Players on Team B stand along the end line between two Indian clubs. The first player on Team B hits a volleyball over the centerline. When a player on Team A catches the ball, all his teammates line up behind him. The ball is then rolled back between the legs of all the players. The last player in the line picks up the ball and runs to the front of the line, holding the ball over his head. Meanwhile, as soon as the first player on Team B had served the ball, he started to run around the Indian clubs. A run is scored when the player runs around both clubs. The runner on Team B must stop, however, when the Team A player reaches the front of his line and has the ball held overhead. Continue until every player on Team B has had a turn. Teams change positions and repeat game. The team with the highest score wins the game.

Variation
Allow players on Team B to throw the ball.

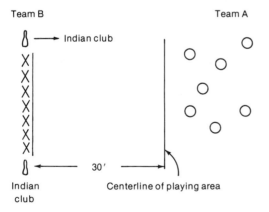

Ricochet (5-6)

Skills: Throwing
Playing area: Gymnasium
Equipment: One large utility ball (twenty-four inches) and approximately twenty small play balls (six inches)
Players: Class
Formation: Two end lines approximately three feet from each wall and a line drawn across the center of the playing area

Divide the class in half and arrange students along the end lines, facing each other. Give ten play balls to each team and place the large utility ball in the center of the playing area. On signal, both teams begin throwing the small balls at the large utility ball, attempting to force it over the opponent's goal line. Players may retrieve the play balls from their own half of the playing area, however, they must go back over their own end line before they attempt another throw. The team that forces the ball over its opponent's goal line wins the game.

Quadrant Dodge Ball (5-6)

Skills: Throwing, dodging, and catching
Playing area: Gymnasium
Equipment: Two utility balls (8½ inches) or volleyballs
Players: Class
Formation: Square divided into four quadrants, as shown in diagram

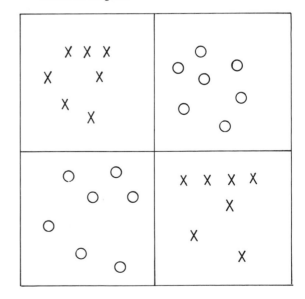

Divide class into two equal teams and put half of each team in diagonally opposite quadrants. Give each team a ball. Any player may move freely from his quadrant into his team's other quadrant. On signal, each team tries to hit members of the opposing team below the waist. Only direct hits count. Play continues for a set period of time, and the team with the most hits wins.

European Handball (5-6)

Skills: Throwing, running, catching, and checking
Playing area: See diagram
Equipment: Four goalposts or four upright markers (six feet), utility ball or volleyball
Players: Six on each team
Formation: As shown in diagram

The object of the game is to throw the ball through the goalposts. The game begins with a jump ball between two opposing forward players. Once the ball is tapped out of the center circle, any player may attempt to retrieve it. A player who has possession of the ball may take three steps, then he must throw it to another player or attempt to throw it through the goalposts. A player may check an opponent in the same way as in basketball. If a defensive player fouls his opponent, the opponent is given a free throw at the point of infraction. All defensive players must stay ten yards away until the throw is taken. If the ball goes over the sidelines or end lines, the nonoffending team throws the ball back into play (one- or two-hand throw, according to age and ability). The goalie must stay within the crease (the semicircle around the goalposts); however, no other player may enter this area. One point is awarded for each goal that is scored from outside the crease area.

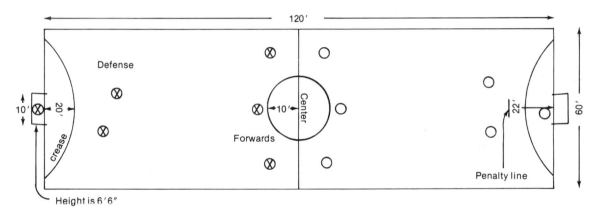

Relay Activities

General Considerations

Relay Formations

Applying the Inventive Games Approach

Relay Activities

Relay activities can be played in the gymnasium or on the playground. They require a minimum of class organization, skill development, and playing facilities. Generally speaking, relays develop such skills as running, jumping, dodging, and stopping. And indirectly they help develop more advanced skills, such as throwing and kicking, and improve speed, reaction time, and coordination.

However, teachers should carefully consider their use of relays. They can be overused. Another negative aspect of relays is the general lack of activity by the majority of children. Both of these criticisms can be met by careful planning and the use of more exploratory teaching techniques.

General Considerations

The teacher should establish a procedure for presenting relay activities applicable to the grade level and facilities available. The following suggestions should help:

1. Divide the class into as many equal teams as space and equipment permit.
2. Appoint team leaders and give them specific responsibilities.
3. Arrange the teams in the correct formation before explaining the rules.
4. Tell the children the name of the relay.
5. Explain the basic rules and have several pupils demonstrate the relay.
6. Start the relay with a definite signal, such as a whistle, verbal command, or loud drum beat.
7. Always pick a certain number of winners and give them credit for their success.

8. Encourage student participation in rule changes and modifications of the relay.
9. Establish a few basic safety rules. These should include the following:
   a. Put the turning line a minimum of eight feet from any wall or obstruction.
   b. Traffic patterns should be clearly understood and followed by every player. For example, have the children run forward, turn around with the right side toward the turning post, then run back around the right side of the team.
   c. Allow adequate space between each competing team.
10. Have the students help judge turning points and winners, particularly when you cannot watch every line.
11. Whenever possible, place the slower and less skilled players in the middle of the team. If given the opportunity, children usually will place their slowest runners at the beginning, hoping to make up for lost time with faster runners at the end. This places a lot of pressure on the slower players, causing unnecessary anguish.

Relay Formations

There are four basic formations used to organize players for relays. Although the file formation is most often used in elementary schools, line, circle, and shuttle relays are also appropriate. The formation a teacher selects depends on the type of relay, the space available, and the skill required of the children.

Line Formation: A number of teams are selected and players are arranged one behind the other as shown in the diagram. Each player runs to the turning line and back.

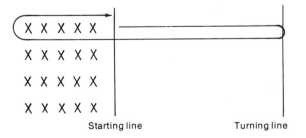

Starting line · · · · · · · · · · · · Turning line

Variations include (1) running through obstacles (chairs or beanbags) to the turning line; (2) running around an obstacle at the turning line; and (3) running to the turning line and stopping, usually to throw something back to the next player.

Teaching suggestion
To prevent cheating, require the returning player to run around his team and back to the front of the line.

File Formation: This formation is quite similar to the line formation except that players face one or more players positioned in front.

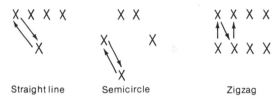

Straight line   Semicircle   Zigzag

Shuttle Formation: The shuttle formation is basically a line formation with half of each team placed behind an opposite line. As soon as player number one reaches player number two, player number two moves forward and player number one walks back to the end of this line. Each player then moves forward one place.

Circle Formation: Players are placed equidistant apart on a circle.

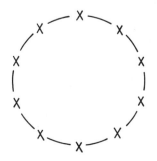

11

Teaching suggestions

1. Use available painted circles or draw them with chalk inside or a (stick on the ground). Tie the chalk or stick on the end of string to make circles.
2. Provide adequate space between each circle.

Applying the Inventive Games Approach

In the previous chapter the inventive games approach was described as the application of the problem-solving method in order to change a game or create a new one. This approach can be quite effective with relay activities, too. When children are permitted to inject their own ideas, they usually show increased enthusiasm, cooperation, and team loyalty. Improved skill development and cardiorespiratory fitness often accompany this type of program.

The following examples illustrate how to apply this process to structured relays and how to develop new types of relays. Refer to the four areas where limitations can be applied (p. 175) when changing the structure of a relay. These areas are the number of players, the playing space, the amount and type of equipment, and the skills and rules.

Let us use the Circle Post Relay to illustrate the use of the inventive games approach. The teacher begins the process after the class has completed one relay. In the next race, the teacher imposes any of the following limitations:

1. Join a partner and repeat the relay (changing the number of players).
2. Join a partner in piggyback position and repeat the relay (changing skills and rules).
3. Add two or more posts spaced five feet apart and behind the first turning post. Players must circle all posts (changing skills, rules, playing space, and equipment).

If the class has had previous experience with this approach, try one of the following ideas:

1. Repeat the original relay, but add these directions: "You must now move on three parts of your body." This allows each child or team to choose a way of traveling.
2. Give each team two hoops and ask them to think up a way to use the hoops in the relay. Let each team demonstrate and, if time permits, try all the ideas.

Relay Activities

It is very difficult to arrange relay activities according to grade level. Most of the relays that follow can be enjoyed by children in grades one through six. Teachers should vary the running distance or limit the number and type of obstacles to meet the abilities of their classes. Most are running-type relays.

Locomotor Skill Relay

Formation: Line
Equipment: None
Players: Four to six on each team.

Draw a turning line twenty to forty feet away from the starting line; the distance depends on the children's age and ability. Each player performs any specified locomotor movement—run, walk, hop, leap, slide, or gallop—to the turning line and back.

Leapfrog Relay

Formation: Line
Equipment: None
Players: Four to six on each team

Place teams in a line formation with enough space between players so that each player can reach the player's hips in front of him. Player number one bends over, places his hands on his knees, and tucks his head. Player number two places his hands on number one's hips, jumps over him, and assumes the same position as number one. Each succeeding player moves forward and continues action until the last player reaches the front of the line.

Teaching suggestions
Make sure all keep their heads tucked until players have leaped over them. Vary relay by having players crawl under each other's legs.

Rescue Relay   3

Formation: Line
Equipment: None
Players: Four to six on each team

Each team stands in a line formation behind the starting line. The captain stands behind a second line drawn twenty feet in front of the starting line. On signal, the captain runs to the first member of his team, grasps his hand, and runs back with the player to his turning line. The player whom the captain brought over returns to the starting line and brings the next player back. Continue the relay until the last child has been brought over the captain's line.

Teaching suggestions
Vary the way players are brought back, such as, holding both hands, locking elbows back to back, and piggyback.

Shuttle Relay   4

Formation: Half of each team behind each of two restraining lines, spaced approximately twenty feet apart
Equipment: None
Players: Four to six on each team

Place half of each team behind each of the two restraining lines. Put players one, three, and five on one side, and players two, four, and six on the other side. Player number one runs across around the left side of his team and tags number two. Number two runs back around opposite side and tags number three, and so on, until all have had a turn.

Zigzag Relay 🔔 5

Formation: Line formation with players six to eight feet apart
Equipment: None
Players: Eight to twelve on each team

Player number one runs in and out of his teammates in a zigzag pattern to the last player on the team, circles him, then repeats the movement back to his original position. Player

number two starts zigzagging backward around player number one, and continues the zigzag pattern up the line, then back to his original position. The first team back in the original position wins the relay.

Animal Walk Relay

Formation: Line
Equipment: None
Players: Four to six on each team

This is a basic line relay, but the movement is an imitation of a specific animal walk. Some of the most enjoyable animal walks for relays are described on the following pages:

> Crab walk, page 388
> Lame puppy walk, page 388
> 5 Seal walk, page 389
> Rabbit jump, 388
> Kangaroo hop, page 389
> Wicket walk, page 387

Stunt Relay

Formation: Line
Equipment: None
Players: Six to eight on each team

Teams stand behind the starting line. A turning line is drawn about thirty to forty feet away. On signal, the first player runs to the turning line and performs a stunt on his way back. Some of the most popular stunts are

1. turning around four or more times
2. picking up a ball and bouncing it a number of times
3. performing a balance stunt

Teaching suggestions
The teacher may require the stunt to be performed from different positions—a front lying or a sitting position.

Skipping Rope Relay

Formation: Line
Equipment: One skipping rope for each team
Players: five to six on each team

Teams line up behind the starting line, with the first player holding a skipping rope. Draw a turning line about twenty feet away. On signal, the first player skips to the turning line and back. Continue until every player has had a turn.

11

Teaching suggestions

Skip backwards. Or have each player stop on the turning line and do ten, fifteen, or twenty stationary skips before returning to the starting line.

Circle Post Relay

Formation: Line
Equipment: Posts, pins, or chairs
Players: Four to six on each team

Arrange each team behind the starting line and draw a turning line twenty feet in front of the starting line. Place a chair or pin on the turning line directly in front of each team. Player number one runs forward, makes a full circle around the post, moving left, then runs back around his own team and tags player number two. Continue until each player has circled the post.

Stick and Ball Relay

Formation: Line
Equipment: One stick and one ball for each team
Players: Four to six on each team

Draw a turning line about twenty to fifty feet in front of the starting line. The first player holds the stick in contact with the ball and guides it while running to the turning line and back. Continue until every player has had a turn.

Obstacle Relay

Formation: Line
Equipment: Utility or soccer balls, chairs
Players: Four to six on each team

Place chairs (or Indian clubs) six to ten feet apart and directly in front of each team. The first player runs "in and out" around the chairs and back around his team to the starting position. Continue until every player has had a turn.

Teaching suggestions

If sufficient chairs, clubs, beanbags, wands, are available, create a variety of obstacles to go around, under, or through.

Figure 11.1 Kneeling relay on scooter

Scooter Relay

Formation: Line
Equipment: Twelve to twenty four scooters
Players: Variable

Scooters provide an additional reservoir of file relays. Since this may be a new activity to many teachers, possible relay positions are listed.

> two-hand relay (hands on scooter)
> one-hand relay (one hand on scooter)
> one-hand, one-foot relay
> two-hand, one-foot relay
> sitting relay using feet to propel
> kneeling relay using hands to propel
> lying relay using hands to propel
> two-feet relay propelling with hands
> seat and feet relay propelling with hands

Partner Relays

Partner relays are the same as previous relays except that they are performed with partners. It is important to match partners according to size. Partners should exchange positions after each turn.

Wheelbarrow Relay

Formation: Partners in line formation
Equipment: None
Players: Eight to ten on each team

Divide each team into pairs of equal height and weight. On the signal, one partner places his hands on the floor and raises his legs to other partner's hips. The standing partner holds his partner's feet close to his sides and they walk to the turning line twenty to twenty-five feet away. When both have crossed the turning line, they exchange positions and return to the starting line.

Teaching suggestions
Instruct the standing partner not to push the "walking" partner, but only to hold his feet and walk. Increase distance as strength increases.

Two-Legged Relay

Formation: Partners in a line formation
Equipment: None
Players: Eight to ten on each team

Each team lines up in pairs. Partners grasp each other around the waist with their inside arms and raise their inside legs off the floor. On the signal, each pair hops to the turning line twenty to thirty feet away. Once behind the line, they change positions and hop on the other foot. As soon as they are ready, they return to the starting line and the next pair repeats the action.

Back-to-Back Relay

Formation: Partners in a line formation
Equipment: None
Players: Eight to ten on each team

Each team lines up in pairs. The first pair stands back to back and links elbows. One player faces the turning line, and the other faces his team. The front player is the carrier and his elbows are inside his partner's. On the signal, the front player leans forward and lifts his partner off the ground and carries him to the turning line about twenty to thirty feet away. Once they cross the turning line, they change positions and return to the starting line. The relay continues until the last pair has crossed the finish line.

Siamese Twins

Formation: Partners in line formation
Equipment: One four-foot stick for each team
Players: Eight to ten on each team

Each team lines up in pairs. The first two players stand back to back, straddle the stick, and grasp it between their legs with both hands in front. One player faces the turning line about twenty to thirty feet away, and the other faces his team. On the signal, the partners run to the turning line, the front player running forward and his partner running backward. Once they cross the line, they reverse positions and return to the starting line. The relay continues until the last couple has crossed the finish line.

Piggyback Relay

Formation: Line formation
Equipment: None
Players: Four to six on each team

The first player piggybacks the second player to the turning line about twenty to thirty feet away. The second player runs back to the starting line and piggybacks the third player to the turning line. The relay continues until all players have crossed the turning line.

Paul Revere

Formation: Shuttle
Equipment: None
Players: Four to six on each team

Draw two parallel lines about thirty to forty feet apart. Each team chooses one "rider" and the remaining players count off. The even-numbered players line up behind one line and odd-numbered players line up behind the other line, directly opposite their teammates. On signal, the rider mounts the back of player number one, who carries him to the other line. The rider must change mounts to player number two without touching the ground. Player number two carries the rider back to player number three, and so on until all mounts have carried the rider. If the rider falls off, he must mount at the point where he fell off. If he falls while changing mounts, he must get back on his original mount before changing to his new one.

Group Relays

Group relays are thoroughly enjoyed by upper elementary children. They require a lot more teamwork, strength, and timing than individual and partner relays. Allow the children to practice the skill or movement pattern involved in the relay, then make a run before the competition begins.

Skin-the-Snake Relay

Formation: Line formation
Equipment: None
Players: Four to six on each team

Each player extends his left hand back between his legs and grasps the right hand of the player behind him. On the signal, every member of the file except the last player starts moving backward. The last player lies down on his back, still holding onto the player in front. The second rear player, after passing over the last player, lies down, still maintaining his grasp with both his hands. Continue this pattern until everyone is lying down. As soon as all are lying on their backs, the one at the rear stands and moves forward, pulling the second player to his feet. Continue this until everyone is standing up. The first team up wins.

Caterpillar Race

Formation: Line
Equipment: None
Players: Five to six on each team.

Each player bends forward and grasps the ankles of the player in front. On the signal, the team moves forward toward the turning line about twenty to thirty feet away. The lead player may use his hands in any manner, but all other players must keep their hands on the ankles of the player in front. If a player releases his grip, he must regrasp the player's ankles before his team can continue. The first team to cross the turning line wins.

Chariot Race

Formation: Line
Equipment: None
Players: Nine to twelve players on each team

Players on each team run in groups of three. The first player stands erect, the second bends forward and holds the first player's hips, and the third player rides on the second player's back. On the signal, the three players on each team run to the turning line about 20 feet away and back to the starting line. If a rider falls off or if the second player releases his grip, the group must stop and reform before continuing the race. As soon as each chariot has crossed the starting line, the next chariot starts. The relay continues until everyone has had a turn.

Row-a-Boat Relay

Formation: Shuttle
Equipment: None
Players: Six to eight on each team

Each team lines up behind the starting line and counts off. Even-numbered players face odd-numbered players. The first player sits down and places his feet on the starting line. Player number two sits down facing player number one, and they join hands. Player number three sits down behind player number one and puts his arms around number one's waist and his feet on either side of number one. Player number four does the same with player number two, and so on until all players are seated. On the signal, each team tries to row to the turning line without loosing their grips. Player number five acts as the coxswain and gives all directions. The first team to completely cross the turning line, about fifteen to twenty feet away, wins the relay.

Sports Skill Relays

In most intermediate physical education programs, sports skill relays are taught as part of a team sport, such as soccer, volleyball, or basketball. However, primary children, particularly second and third graders, should also participate in sport skill relays to develop the basic skills of team and individual sports. Primary teachers should modify the following relays to meet their classes level of skill.

Sports Skills	Name of Relay	Page
Soccer Skills	Line Dribbling	239
	Shuttle Dribbling	239
Volleyball Skills	Shuttle Volleying	289
	Zigzag Volleying	289
	Wall Volleying	297
Basketball Skills	Circle Passing	314
	Line Dribble	316
	Wall Passing	314
Softball Skills	Overtake	341
	Softball Throw Relay	342
Track & Field Skills	Call Race	370

11

Individual and Partner Games

12

There are several games for elementary school children that can be played by one, two (singles), three, or four (doubles) players. These games have usually been played before school, during recess, and after school. However, with the trend toward more individualized teaching, individual and partner games are becoming more popular during the regular instructional period. When taught in the regular class period, all children have an opportunity to learn the basic skills and rules of these activities. In addition, the basic fundamentals of the more advanced games, such as handball and paddle tennis, can be introduced systematically. Finally, the inventive games approach can be easily applied to these activities.

Teaching Individual and Partner Games

Although many of the games listed on the following pages are very familiar to elementary school children, others may be new. If adequate space, equipment, and supplies are available, a game can be explained and demonstrated, and then the entire class can play it. In most instances, however, teachers do not have enough equipment for this type of lesson format. The following organization and method of instruction deal with this problem. (See films "Teaching Games to Primary Children" and "Teaching Games to Intermediate Children" in Appendix A, page 602.)

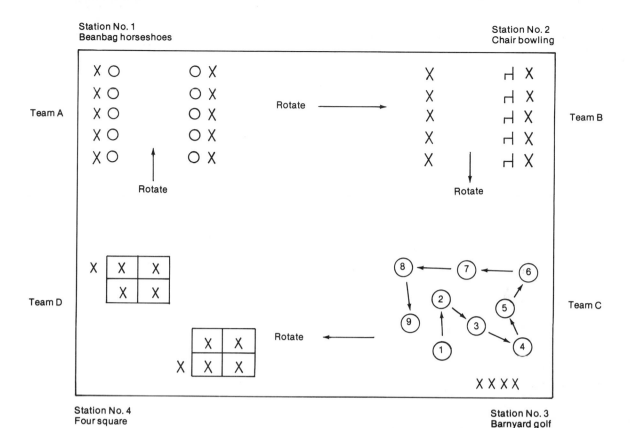

Station No. 1
Beanbag horseshoes

Station No. 2
Chair bowling

Team A

Rotate

Team B

Rotate

Rotate

Team D

Team C

Rotate

Station No. 4
Four square

Station No. 3
Barnyard golf

Station Work

To illustrate the station work technique, let us assume that a third-grade class knows how to play Chair Bowling and Four Square. The teacher wishes to introduce Beanbag Horseshoes and Barnyard Golf in the next lesson. During the first few minutes of this lesson the teacher assigns each team to its station, as illustrated in the diagram. Brief demonstration of Beanbag Horseshoes and Barnyard Golf are given before each team is allowed to play its assigned game. Each game is played for a few minutes. The teacher then asks the class to stop, return the equipment to its original position, and rotate to the next station. This procedure is continued until all the teams have played all four games. If time does not permit the class to complete the rotation, pick it up in the next lesson.

Figure 12.1

Applying the Inventive Games Approach

The problem-solving method described in Chapters 10 and 11 can also be applied to individual and partner games. If children are familiar with this approach, a question such as "With your

12

partner can you make up a new hopscotch game?" or "Can you change the Alphabet Game (page 211) to a game that includes numbers?" should be sufficient direction for the children to undertake the challenge.

Individual and Partner Games

Individual and partner games are so enjoyable that they belong to virtually every grade level. The difference is the children's skill and finesse as they mature and develop more speed and coordination. The following games have been organized on the basis of grade, but the children's interest and, to a much lesser degree, the relative order of difficulty also have been considered.

Name of Game	Grade Level	Skills	Page
American Hopscotch	1-4	throwing, hopping	209
French Hopscotch	1-4	throwing, hopping	209
Italian Hopscotch	1-4	throwing, hopping	210
Chair Bowling	1-6	rolling	210
Marbles	1-6	shooting	210
Jacks	1-4	throwing, catching, balancing	210
Beanbag Horseshoes	2-6	throwing	211
Tetherball	2-6	hitting	211
Barnyard Golf	2-6	throwing	211
Alphabet Game	3-6	vaulting	211
Four Square	3-6	bouncing and catching	212
Paddleball	3-6	serving, running, hitting	212
Deck Tennis	3-6	running, throwing, catching	213
Sidewalk Tennis	3-6	serving, running, hitting	214
Shuffleboard	4-6	shooting	214
Shufflecurl	4-6	shooting	215
Orienteering	4-6	running	215
One-Wall Handball	5-6	serving, hitting, running	217
Paddle Tennis	5-6	serving, hitting, running	217

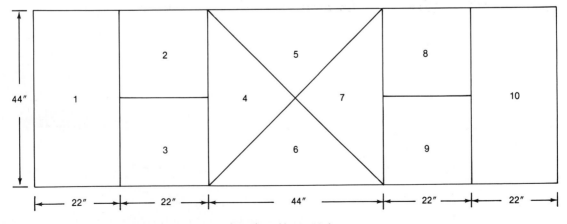

American Hopscotch

American Hopscotch (1-4)

Formation: Pattern shown in diagram (see page 208)
Equipment: Beanbags, buttons, beads, or other small objects
Players: Two to four players

Arrange teams in a line formation with player number one facing area one. Player number one stands on one foot outside area one, holding a "puck" (beanbag, button, etc.) in her hand. She tosses the puck into area one, then hops over this area lands with her left foot in area two and her right foot in area three. (Landing with the feet in adjacent areas is known as spread eagle. She then hops and lands on one foot in area

Figure 12.2

four, then hops and lands with left foot in area five and right foot in area six. She continues this pattern, hopping and landing with one foot in single spaces and with both feet in adjacent areas. Two hops are permitted in area ten in order to turn around and get ready for the return. Upon landing in areas two and three, the player leans forward, picks up the puck and hops out.

Player number one now tosses the puck into area two and repeats the pattern. She must, however, modify her hopping to avoid landing in area two. On the return, she must land on one foot in area three, pick up the puck, hop over to area two, then to area one, and hop out. Player number one continues this pattern through area ten and back. A player is out if she steps on a line, tosses the puck onto a line or into the wrong area, changes feet on single hops, or touches her hand or other foot during any hopping or retrieving movement. When a child commits an error, she goes to the back of the line.

French Hopscotch (1-4)

Formation: Pattern shown in diagram
Equipment: Beanbags, beads, buttons, or other small objects
Players: Six to eight on each team

The game follows the same basic rules as American Hopscotch with the player hopping on one foot in single squares and landing with both feet in adjacent squares. When a player lands with one foot in area seven and the other in area eight, he must jump up, turn around in the air, and land in the same areas.

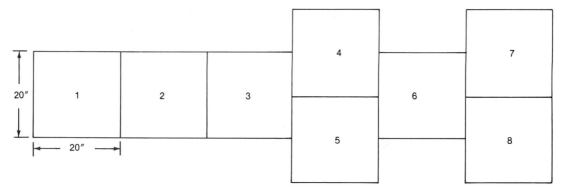

French Hopscotch

12

Italian Hopscotch (1-4)

Formation: Pattern shown in diagram
Equipment: Beanbags, buttons, beads, or other small objects
Players: Two to four players

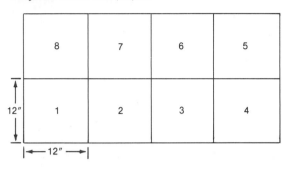

Arrange teams in a line formation with player number one facing square one. Player number one stands on one foot outside square one, holding a "puck" (beanbag, etc.) in his hand. He throws the puck into square one and then hops into this area. Still standing on one foot, he kicks the puck into square two, then hops into that square. He continues this pattern to square eight. When he reaches square eight, he places both feet on the ground, picks up the puck, and hops backwards through all squares to the starting position. A player is out if he steps on a line, if his puck stops on a line, if he puts both feet down in any square except eight, or if he changes feet. When a child commits an error, he goes to the back of the line.

Chair Bowling (1-6)

Formation: Two parallel lines drawn approximately fifteen to thirty feet apart, depending on the level of skill, with chairs placed on one line
Equipment: One chair, one ball (sponge ball, tennis ball, or softball), pencil, and score sheet for each couple
Players: Two per game

One partner stands behind one line with a ball. The other partner stands directly opposite, behind the chair. The chair's backrest should face the bowler. The score sheet and pencil should be placed on the seat of the chair. The bowler rolls three balls, then changes places with his partner. Award five points for each ball that rolls through the legs of the chair. The game may be played to any score, selected on the basis of skill and available time.

Marbles (1-6)

Formation: Circle five to six feet in diameter
Equipment: Marbles of various sizes
Players: Two to four

Each player places one or two marbles in the center of the circle. The playing order is determined by each player throwing his shooting marble—called the taw—toward a line six to ten feet away. The player whose marble is closest to the line shoots first; the player whose marble is next closest shoots second, and so on. A player may shoot from anywhere outside the circle, trying to knock the marbles out of the circle. His taw must remain inside the circle. If successful, he continues from where his taw has stopped. After each player has had a turn, he removes his taw from the circle. At the end of the game all marbles should be returned to their owners, but the author still remembers his boyhood days when he would go home with more marbles than he started with and sometimes with fewer.

Jacks (1-4)

Formation: Circle on a hard surface
Equipment: Six jacks and a small rubber ball
Players: Two to four players

The first player tosses the jacks on the ground. He then throws the ball into the air, picks up one jack, and tries to catch the ball before it lands. If successful, the player holds the jack in his other hand and continues playing until he picks up all jacks. If unsuccessful, the next player takes his turn. If a player has picked up all the jacks one at a time, he repeats the game, picking up two at a time. Continue with three at a time, and so on.

Variations
Pigs in the Pen: Jacks are brushed into the other hand, held in cupped position.

Eggs in the Basket: Jacks are picked up and transferred to the opposite hand before the ball is caught.

Lazy Susan: The ball is allowed to bounce twice before the jacks are picked up.

Beanbag Horseshoes (2-6)

Formation: Two hoops or old bicycle tires placed about twenty to thirty feet apart, depending upon the level of skill
Equipment: Three beanbags and two hoops per game
Players: Two or four players

Player number one stands behind his hoop. He attempts to throw each beanbag into the middle of player number two's hoop. Award five points if the beanbag lands in the center and three points if it lands on the rim. Player number two then takes his turn. The first player to score fifteen points wins.

Tetherball (2-6)

Formation: Court area drawn as shown in diagram
Equipment: Tetherball, pole, and rope
Players: Two players per game

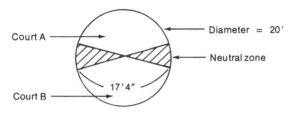

Court A — Diameter = 20'

Neutral zone

17'4"

Court B

One player stands in each court. A player starts the game by throwing the ball into the air and hitting it with his hand or fist in any direction he chooses. The opposing player may not strike the ball until it passes him on the second swing around the pole. He must strike it in the opposite direction. The player who winds the ball around the pole first is the winner. A foul line may be drawn on the pole five feet above the ground. In this case, the players must wind the ball around the pole above the foul line. Fouls occur when a player

1. hits the ball with any part of his body other than his hands
2. touches the pole
3. catches the ball
4. hits the rope
5. plays the ball while standing outside the playing area
6. steps into the neutral zone
7. throws the ball
8. winds the ball below the five-foot foul mark

The penalty for fouls is to forfeit the game to the opponent.

Barnyard Golf (2-6)

Formation: Nine hoops or old bicycle tires (or circles drawn on blacktop) scattered and numbered as "holes"
Equipment: One beanbag for each player, nine hoops
Players: Four players for each game

Allow each group of four to arrange its own "golf course," scattering the hoops in the space that has been allocated. Player number one begins from behind the starting line and attempts to throw his beanbag into the first hoop. If it lands inside or on the rim, he is awarded one point. He then picks his beanbag up and moves to the side of the first hoop and throws his beanbag into the second hoop. As soon as player number one starts his second throw, player number two may begin his first throw. The game continues until every player has completed the course. The player with the most points wins the game.

Variations

This version is more similar to golf. Player number one attempts to throw his beanbag into the first hoop. If he fails, he fetches it and tries again. He cannot advance to the next "hole" until his beanbag lands in the hoop. This pattern is continued around the course. The winner is the player with the lowest score.

Alphabet Game (3-6)

Formation: Pattern drawn as shown in the diagram on dirt, gravel, or blacktop surface, with the size of the squares adjusted according to level of ability

	Z		|→ 2' ←|
Y	P	G	O
F	X	R	C
L	J	T	N
S	Q	B	H
W	E	M	D
K	I	V	U
		A	

Equipment: One wand for each game
Players: Two per game

Player number one begins in square A. With the aid of his wand, he moves from squares A to Z, in alphabetical order, without touching any lines. As soon as player A touches a line, he is out and player B takes his turn. The winner is the player who has progressed to the highest letter in the alphabet.

Four Square (3-6)

Formation: Sixteen-foot square divided into four four-foot squares, designated as squares A, B, C, and D
Equipment: Large utility ball
Players: Five to seven players per group

One player stands in each square. Player D starts the game by bouncing the ball, then hitting it with one or both hands so that it bounces into one of the other three squares. The player who receives the ball must hit it after one bounce to any of the other squares. The game proceeds until one player fails to return the ball properly or a foul is committed. When this happens, the offending player is eliminated and goes to the end of the waiting line. All players move one square toward D; the waiting player always moves to square A.

Basic rules

1. The ball must arc before landing; it cannot be struck downward.
2. Service always begins from square D.
3. A player may go anywhere to return a fair ball, even out of his own court.
4. The ball may not be held.

Fouls occur when

1. a ball hits any line
2. a ball is struck with closed fists
3. a ball hits a player who is standing in his own square

Paddleball (3-6)

Formation: Draw a court outline as shown in diagram using any available wall and floor space. Use chalk or plastic tape to mark court dimensions.
Equipment: Tennis or sponge ball and bats
Players: Singles (two players), doubles (four players), and triples (three players)

Singles: The server may stand anywhere between the wall and the serving line. He bounces the ball, then hits it toward the front wall. The ball must hit the wall above the two-foot line and land behind the serving line but inside the court. He is allowed one serve. The receiver waits until the ball has bounced once, then he hits it back to the wall. After the serve, all returned balls by either player must hit above the two-foot line, but they may land anywhere inside the full court area (sixteen by twenty-six feet). The players alternate hitting the ball. If the server hits the ball above the line and back over the serving line, and the receiver fails to return the ball, the server receives one point. He continues

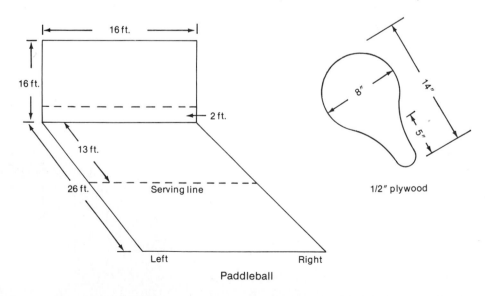

Paddleball

serving until he faults or misses the ball. Any player may go outside the court to return a ball. Game may be played to eleven, fifteen, or twenty-one points.

Doubles: The game is played according to singles rules with a few modifications. On the serve, the server's teammate should stand outside the court to prevent any hindrance to the opponents who are trying to return the service. When the server loses his serve, his teammate takes a turn. Each team, therefore, has two serves in succession. On the serve, either opponent may return the ball. Thereafter, players on each team must alternate hitting the ball. For example team one includes players A and B, and team two, players C and D. Player A serves and player C returns. Then player B must return the next ball and, if the rally continues, player D must hit the next fair ball.

Triples: This game is played according to singles rules, with the following modifications. The server represents one team and, therefore, is playing against the other two players as a team. When the server loses his service, he moves to the right back court. The right back court player shifts to the left, and the left back court player becomes the new server. The latter player is now playing against the "new team." After the serve, the server will hit every other ball. For example, the server hits, then player A of the opposing team, then the server, then player B. Each player keeps his own score.

Deck Tennis (3-6)

Formation: Court drawn as shown or any existing volleyball or badminton court
Equipment: Deck tennis ring, which can be purchased through local sports stores or made from two-inch rope or plastic tubing (see Appendix B)
Players: Singles (two players) or doubles (four players)

Singles: The server must stand outside the baseline and on the right half of the court. He must deliver the ring in a forehand fashion and with the ring rising to an arc before it begins to descend into the opponent's right court. The server must serve into alternate courts each time. The receiver must catch the ring with one hand and immediately return it. The server scores a point if the receiver fails to return the ring or commits one of the following fouls:

1. Catching the ring with both hands
2. Changing the ring to his other hand before returning it
3. Holding the ring too long before returning it (count three seconds)
4. Stepping over the net line
5. Failing to make the ring arc before it begins to descend into the opponent's court

If the server faults or misses the return throw, his opponent then serves. However, no point is scored by the opponent. Game may be played to eleven, fifteen, or twenty-one points.

Doubles: The game is played according to singles rules, with some modifications. Each team has two serves in succession. After the receiver has returned the server's toss, any player may return a toss. For example, player A from team one serves, and player C of team two catches the ring and returns it to player A. It is legal for player A to catch the ring and return it.

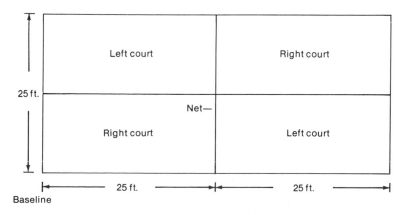
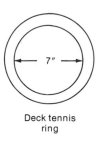

Deck tennis ring

Sidewalk Tennis (3-6)

Formation: Draw a court outline as shown in the diagram. A regular sidewalk can be used for this game, with four squares making a court.

Equipment: Tennis ball, sponge ball, or other small rubber ball

Players: Singles (two players) or doubles (four players)

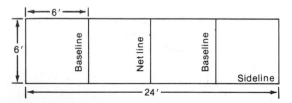

The server, standing behind the baseline, bounces the ball and then hits it with an underhand hit over the net line. The ball must land in the opponent's court. The receiver must let the ball bounce once and then hit it with an open palm. The ball must pass over the net line. After the receiver has returned the first serve, players may return the ball while it is in the air ("on the volley") or on the first bounce. The server scores one point if the receiver fails to return the ball or commits one of the following fouls:

1. Hitting the ball with any part of the body other than the open palm
2. When returning a serve, hitting the ball while it is in the air and before it bounces once

   If the server commits any of the following fouls, there is a change in servers:

1. Stepping over the baseline when serving
2. Serving the ball with a side or overhand serve

Games may be played to eleven, fifteen, or twenty-one points. If the score is tied at ten, fourteen, or twenty, a player must make two consecutive points to win the game.

Variations

1. Doubles game: The same rules apply, with partners alternating on serves and returns. When a teammate loses his serve, it goes to an opponent.
2. Place a rope or net across the net line.
3. Hit the ball with a paddle.
4. Use a large utility ball. If this is too difficult, increase the size of the court.

Shuffleboard (4-6)

Formation: Draw a court outline as shown in the diagram. Shuffleboard must be played on a smooth, flat surface; a gymnasium floor is ideal, but a blacktop or cement surface is adequate.

Equipment: Two or four cues (forked sticks) and eight disks

Players: Singles (two players) or doubles (four players)

Singles: Each player is given four disks (player A's are red; B's are black). Player A begins the game by pushing one of his disks with his cue from the right-hand side of the Ten Off area, trying to get his disk into scoring position at the opposite end of the court. Player B then pushes one of his disks, trying either to get it into scoring position or to knock player A's disk out of scoring position. Both players shoot from the same Ten Off area. The players take turns hitting their remaining disks until all eight have been played. Disks that land between the dead lines are taken off the playing surface.

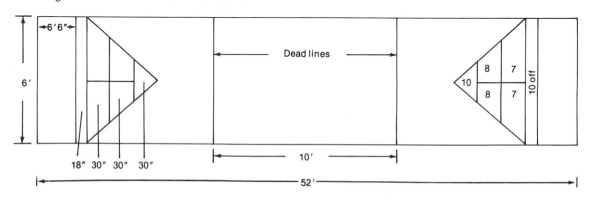

After the last disk is played, the players walk to the opposite end and count their scores. If a disk lands in the Ten Off zone, ten points are deducted from the player's score. Any disk that touches a line is not counted. Player B starts the second round at the opposite end of the court and the process is repeated. Games may be played to 50, 75, or 100 points.

Doubles: Two opponents play from each end and remain there throughout the game. The red player plays first at each end. At the beginning of the second round, the black player plays first at each end. Continue the rotation.

Shufflecurl (4-6)

Formation: Draw a court outline as shown in the diagram. Chalk lines are adequate.
Equipment: Shuffleboard cues and disks
Players: Singles (two players) or doubles (four players)

The rules are the same as in shuffleboard, but the object is to slide the disks as close to the center of the circle as possible. Players in this game also try to knock the opponent's disks out of scoring position. When each player has used his four disks by sliding them to the opposite circle one "end" has been completed. Two "ends" make one round, and a game may be five, ten, or any other number of rounds. To score, award one point for each disk that a player has placed closer to the center of the circle than the closest disk of his opponent. (In the diagram, the player with the black disks would score three points.)

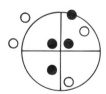

Orienteering (4-6)

True or official orienteering is competitive way finding across country on foot, using a map and a compass (Schaanning 1965). Both Norway and Sweden claim to have originated this sport, and its beginnings can be traced to World War II, when many Scandinavians were initiated to orienteering through the Resistance movement. Accurate navigation often meant the difference between life or death, since a compass was needed to find supplies, avoid enemy camps, and seek out hidden installations.

Figure 12.3

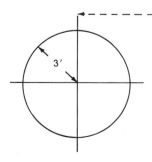

30′ or vary distance according to skill level and available space

3′

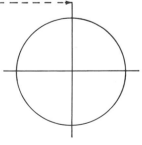

Today orienteering is a wholesome outdoor activity and a lifesaving skill for the ever-increasing number of people who are taking up camping and other outdoor recreational activities. Orienteering is taught in many Scandinavian schools, and the writer believes this sport has a place in many elementary and secondary schools in North America. Several schools in Canada and the United States already have incorporated orienteering in their programs.

Since authentic maps and compasses are expensive, another type of orienteering—called score orienteering—will be described for use in elementary school programs. It is extremely popular with boys and girls in the intermediate grades as well.

Score orienteering: Each player is given a hand-drawn map of the area, including all necessary landmarks—buildings, statues, trees, paths, and so on. The diagram here shows a school and the immediate major landmarks. Each player is also given a ''word description chart.'' Note in the accompanying chart that each description is simple, and that the farthest sites are awarded the highest points. Players leave the starting point at a designated time and, with the aid of their maps and charts, try to find the various landmarks or checkpoints.

General procedure and instructions: Each student writes his name on his chart and leaves everything else blank. Four or five runners leave the starting point at the same time; to avoid congestion, allow thirty seconds between groups. The teacher marks the starting time on each chart, and the runners have ten minutes (or whatever time the teacher sets) to go to as many check points as possible and return to the recorder's desk. The teacher has placed a code

Figure 12.4

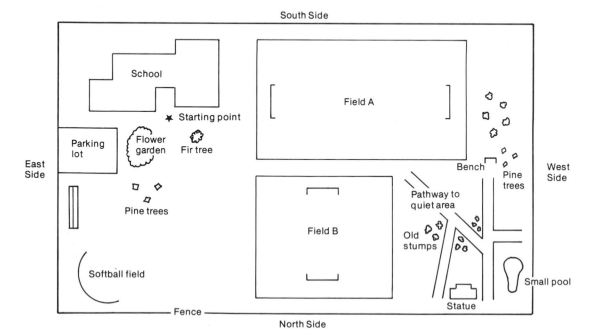

Word Description Chart

Time Allowed: 10 minutes

Name: John Smith

Start Time:
Finish Time:
Penalty Points: (at 5 points a minute)

No.	Description of Landmark (Checkpoint)	Value	Insert Code Letter
1.	On the east end of softball backstop	15	T
2.	On the north side of flower garden	10	B
3.	On the south goalpost of field B	5	C
4.	On the northwest side of an old stump	10	F
5.	At the northeast end of the softball stands	15	R
6.	On the bench near three pine trees	15	U
7.	On the southwest side of field A	10	A
8.	On the west corner of statue	25	Y

Total points_____
Penalty points_____
Final score_____

letter on each landmark or checkpoint before the orienteering lesson and when a runner arrives at the checkpoint, he places that code letter in the appropriate space on the recording sheet. Runners may choose their own order of reaching checkpoints. A runner is penalized five points for each minute he exceeds the ten-minute time limit.

Teaching suggestions

Competitions can be developed on the basis of one type of landmark, such as trees, flowers, or buildings. If a school is near a park or wilderness area, the possibilities are almost unlimited. Also, the addition of compasses and authentic maps of the area open the door to an enjoyable and constructive recreational pursuit. Finally, if a teacher is not skillful at reading a compass or a geographical map, she will find many people in the community, such as scout leaders and surveyors, more than willing to donate their services.

One-Wall Handball (5-6)

Formation: Same court size as in paddleball (page 212), but two-foot wall line is not used
Equipment: Tennis ball, sponge rubber ball, or Oregon size regulation handball
Players: Two, three, or four

This game is played according to paddleball rules, with the following modifications: On the serve, the ball may hit anywhere on the front wall

(two-foot line not used), and then it goes back over the serving line. The receiver may hit the ball "on the fly" (before it bounces) or after the bounce. All players must hit the ball with one hand; two-hand hits are not permitted. Players may not catch the ball and then hit it.

Paddle Tennis (5-6)

Formation: Court outline as shown in diagram (page 218) or existing badminton court
Equipment: Paddles (see diagram under paddleball), tennis or sponge rubber ball
Players: Singles (two players) or doubles (four players)

Singles: The server must stand behind the baseline and on the right-hand side of the court. He must bounce the ball and then hit it over the net into the opponent's right fore court. The receiver must hit the ball back after it has bounced once. After the receiver returns the serve, the ball may be hit "on the volley" or after one bounce. In singles, the ball must land inside the small court. Simple scoring may be used, with each player serving until he loses by fault or fails to return a ball. The score may be eleven, fifteen, or twenty-one points.

Paddle tennis also may be played and scored according to proper tennis rules. A player serves for one full game, then his opponent serves, and they alternate until a set (six games) is completed. A single game is scored fifteen points (first point), thirty points

12

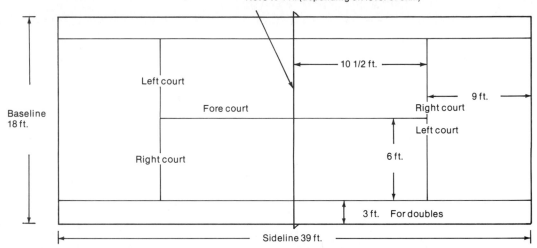

Net 3 to 4 ft. (depending on level of skill)

Baseline 18 ft.

Left court

Fore court

Right court

10 1/2 ft.

Right court

9 ft.

Left court

6 ft.

3 ft. For doubles

Sideline 39 ft.

(second point), forty points (third point), and *game* (fourth point). If both players have forty points, this is called *deuce.* When this occurs, one player must score two successive points to win. The next point after deuce is called *advantage,* and the next is game. If the server has the advantage, it is called *advantage-in.* If the receiver has the advantage, it is called *advantage-out.*

Doubles: The game is played according to singles rules with the following modifications: One player serves the full game. On each point, however, he alternates, serving from right to left side and vice versa. Service changes after each game. After the receiver returns the service, the ball may be hit by either member of the team. An additional three-foot alley is used for doubles.

Soccer Activities

13

Emphasis and Skill Presentation

Teaching Procedures

Description of Skills

Practice Activities

Lead-Up Games

Soccer: Rules and Regulations

Evaluative Techniques

Of all the major sports played in the United States and Canada, soccer has shown the most rapid increase in participation in recent years. It requires a great deal of skill in kicking, running and dribbling. However, since it is an inexpensive sport—only a ball and two goalposts are needed—and involves total body movement, it is an excellent activity for upper elementary children. Furthermore, only a few basic skills and rules need to be learned to enjoy the game.

This chapter provides sufficient information to develop a major soccer unit. The central purpose is to give the children an opportunity to acquire the basic soccer skills, rules, and playing strategies through as many enjoyable game-like situations as possible. Modification of practice activities and lead-up games, coupled with the application of inventive games approach, should be the rule rather than the exception when teaching soccer.

Emphasis and Skill Presentation

Children have usually learned to kick a stationary or moving ball by the end of grade three. Their ability to stop the ball is normally limited to a very basic foot or shin trap. They understand dribbling but are not very proficient at it as they tend to use their toes and to "kick and chase."

As outlined in the accompanying chart, a systematic presentation of the basic soccer skills and rules should begin in grade four. These children should learn to kick and pass with either foot, to trap with the side of the foot, and to increase their control while dribbling the ball. A few of the basic rules relating to type of kicks, handling the ball, and checking should also be introduced in this grade. Lead-up games such as Circle Soccer and Soccer Dodgeball should be emphasized, rather than playing a modified version of soccer or the official game.

Throughout grade five the emphasis should be on improving passing, trapping, and dribbling skills. When these basic skills have been acquired, the children should be introduced to a few of the more specialized kicking skills, the side-of-leg trap, and to heading the ball. More advanced lead-up games such as Forwards and Backs and Seven-Man Soccer with more specific rules and playing positions are also indicated.

Previously learned skills should be refined and a few of the more advanced skills and rules of the official game should be learned in grade six. Although these children should play seven- and eleven-person soccer, their skill level still calls for a lot of individual and small group practice and lead-up activities. It is important during regular instruction periods to balance the time spent on these two types of activities with the regulation soccer game. Seven-Man Soccer, which uses half the field, is also more desirable than the official eleven-person game for the intramural program as it allows more children to participate.

Suggested Sequence of Presenting Soccer Skills and Rules

Skills and Rules	Grade Level			
	Grade 3	Grade 4	Grade 5	Grade 6
Kicking				
Instep kick	Acquired or introduce	Pass with either foot	Increase distance and accuracy	Increase distance and accuracy
Inside-of-foot kick	Introduce	Pass with either foot	Increase distance and accuracy	Increase distance and accuracy
Outside-of-foot kick		Introduce	Increase distance and accuracy	Increase distance and accuracy
Punting			Introduce	Increase distance and accuracy
Volley kick				Introduce
Rules: Kickoff		Introduce		
Free kick			Introduce	
Corner kick		Introduce		
Goal kick		Introduce		
Penalty kick			Introduce	

Skills and Rules	Grade Level			
	Grade 3	Grade 4	Grade 5	Grade 6
Trapping				
Foot trap	Acquired or introduce	Refinement	Refinement	Refinement
Side-of-foot trap		Introduce	Refinement	Refinement
Shin trap	Acquired or introduce	Refinement	Refinement	Refinement
Leg trap			Introduce	Refinement
Body trap				Introduce
Rules: Handling the ball		Introduce		
Dribbling				
Inside of feet	Acquired or introduce	Increase accuracy and speed	Increase accuracy and speed	Increase accuracy and speed
Outside of feet		Introduce	Increase accuracy and speed	Increase accuracy and speed
Heading				
Stationary heading			Introduce	Refinement
With feet off ground				Introduce
Throw-in				
From behind head		Introduce	Increase distance and accuracy	Increase distance and accuracy
Rules: Throw-in rule		Introduce		
Tackling				
With feet and shoulders		Introduce	Refinement	Refinement
Rules: Charging		Introduce		
Other Rules				
Team positions		Introduce		
Goal keeper privileges			Introduce	
Offside rule			Introduce	

Teaching Procedures

The general instructional procedures discussed in previous chapters also apply to teaching soccer activities. Of particular importance are the development of a unit of instruction discussed on pages 115-17 and the illustrated lessons on pages 152-56. In addition, the inventive games approach (pp. 173-76) can be applied successfully to the teaching of soccer and all other team game activities.

Developing a Soccer Unit

Since each teaching situation varies according to the length of the unit and lesson and the available facilities and equipment, the suggested approach that follows should be considered as only a basic guideline. Soccer is a relatively new sport to many teachers and children, so this outline should be modified to meet each situation.

Step One: Decide on the length of the unit. Since a class may have from one to five physical education lessons a

13

week, the units should be expressed in terms of the number of lessons.

Step Two: Assess the class's level of ability. The evaluative techniques in the latter part of this chapter (p. 247) can be used. Having the class play one or two lead-up games will also provide an overview of its ability.

Step Three: List sequentially the skills, rules, and playing strategies that will be emphasized (p. 220).

Step Four: Choose the appropriate practice activities and lead-up games. The practice activities (p. 236), listed by skill, are organized into individual, partner, and group activities. The lead-up games (p. 241) are arranged in order of difficulty.

Structure of a Lesson

The following approach is a basic guideline for planning and teaching a lesson. Each lesson should include a vigorous introductory activity that has some relationship to the general theme of the lesson. The second part of the lesson should be devoted to acquiring and practicing one or more skills. And finally, the third part stresses a group activity that applies the skills and knowledge learned earlier.

INTRODUCTORY ACTIVITIES	SKILL DEVELOPMENT	GROUP ACTIVITIES
Vigorous running, dodging, and conditioning exercises	Demonstrations Individual practice Partner and practice activities Exploratory activities	Lead-up games Inventive games Modified or official game of soccer

Each soccer lesson should begin with running, dodging, and general conditioning activities to increase the children's cardiorespiratory endurance and to prepare them for the next part of the lesson.

During the first few lessons, the second part should be given a considerable amount of time in order to introduce and practice skills and playing strategies. After a skill is explained and demonstrated, each child should have an opportunity to practice it without excessive pressure and to test and explore other ways of performing a movement pattern. Once the child understands the skill and can perform it, he should

practice with a partner. Since most classes are now mixed, partner activities are an excellent way to cope with varying levels of ability and to mix boys and girls subtly.

Partner activities also provide a springboard for introducing inventive games. For example, in a lesson that emphasizes passing and trapping, partners can be challenged to "make up a game with your partner that involves a pass and a trap ... and a hoop" (or any other piece of small equipment). Refer to pages 173-77 for more ideas. The more structured practice activities (pp. 236-41) that are used in this part of the lesson can be presented initially in a more formal or direct manner. After the class has practiced the activity, the teacher can introduce variations by presenting simple challenges to each group. For example, if the class is practicing Keep Away, a challenge such as "See if you can play the same game but add a hoop" (or three beanbags) gives each group a chance to create a new version of the game.

During the third part of the lesson, lead-up games (pp. 241-44) provide a low-key means of practicing skills in a gamelike situation. Playing space should be used to maximum capacity. Divide the playing field into halves or quarters so that two or four games can be played. The inventive games approach also works extremely well with lead-up games. Limit these games in some small way at first; later, challenge each group to design its own game or to choose any equipment it wants. This will open the door to many new and exciting soccer-type games.

As the soccer unit progresses, more time should be devoted to the third part of the lesson and less to the second part. Group activities should include a wide variety of lead-up games, inventive games, and, to a lesser degree, modified or official soccer. The more competitive aspects of soccer and other team games should be reserved for the junior and senior high school physical education program.

The following suggestions can also help in developing a safe and effective program of activities:

1. Limit the playing field to a small, manageable instructional area. Mark off a 100-foot-square

section of the field with traffic cones or milk cartons (p. 170) for the demonstrations and practice activities. Enlarge the area as needed.

2. Soccer requires a great deal of endurance, particularly of the heart and lungs and the leg muscles. Increase running and other endurance activities gradually, and systematically. Watch for overfatigued children and switch them to less demanding positions.

3. Although soccer rules do not allow any players except the goalie to use their hands, adjustments should be made for the children's safety. They should be taught to protect their faces against oncoming balls, and, in addition, girls should be instructed to fold their arms across their chests to prevent injury.

4. Many soccer activities can and should be performed in the gymnasium. The children can control the ball better within the confines of the gymnasium if it is slightly deflated.

5. One of the cardinal principles of good teaching is total participation by all children. Whenever possible, keep each team small and divide up the playing area so two or more games can be played.

Description of Skills

Soccer is basically a kicking and running game; however, when played correctly, skills such as dribbling, trapping, heading, and throwing are also necessary for maximum success and enjoyment. Each of these skills is described, along with the more common faults to observe and correct.

Kicking

In soccer, the ball may be kicked from a stationary, running, or volley (while in the air) position with either foot. There are certain fundamentals that should be stressed in every practice and game situation. First, the player should keep his eye on the ball as it approaches him or as he approaches the ball. Second, the player should kick the ball with his instep (top side of the foot), never with his toes. Finally, after the ball has been kicked, the player

Figure 13.1 Kicking

should follow through with his kicking foot for a short distance in the direction of the kick. Each of these fundamentals applies to the following five basic kicking skills.

Instep Kick   The instep kick is the most common skill in soccer. It is used for passing and for shooting at the goal. Just before the ball is kicked, the nonkicking foot should be even with the ball, the head and trunk should be leaning forward slightly, and the kicking leg should be well back, with the knee slightly bent (fig. 13.2a). The eyes should be focused on the ball and the arms extended sideways. As the kicking leg moves downward and forward, the knee moves forward and over the ball. The ankle also extends downward to allow the top of the instep to contact the ball (fig. 13.2b). Continue forward and upward with the kicking leg (fig. 13.2c).

Figure 13.2a Kicking leg back   Figure 13.2b Contact with instep   Fiqure 13.2c Follow-through

If the kicker wishes to make a low pass, the instep should contact the center of the ball (fig. 13.3a). Sometimes the player wishes to make a high loft pass over a defender's head. To perform this type of kick the instep must contact the ball just below the center (fig. 13.3b).

Common Faults

1. Too much back lean prior to kicking the ball
2. Kicking with the toes
3. Lack of follow-through

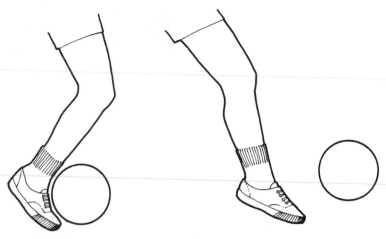

Figure 13.3a Low pass

Figure 13.3b Loft pass

Kicking with Inside of Foot

The inside-of-foot kick (fig. 13.4) is a slight variation of the instep kick, used for short, accurate passes or for shooting at the goal. The body is bent slightly forward, with the weight evenly distributed on both feet. The ball should be about six inches in front of the feet. Shift the weight to the nonkicking foot and swing the kicking foot outward, with knee slightly bent. Swing the foot down and toward the ball, contacting it with the inside of the foot. Follow through with the kicking foot crossing in front of the opposite leg.

Figure 13.4 Contact with inside of foot

13

Common Faults

1. Failing to turn the kicking foot outward
2. Kicking with the toes
3. Contacting the ball too low

Kicking with Outside of Foot   This type of kick is a pushing or jabbing action with the outer part of the foot, used for short passes, dribbling, or to avoid an oncoming opponent. The nonkicking foot is six to eight inches behind and slightly to the side of the ball. Bend the knee of the kicking leg and swing that leg across the other leg (fig. 13.5a). Swing the kicking foot downward and back across the opposite leg, contacting the ball with the outer and forward side of the foot. Follow through until the knee is nearly extended (fig. 13.5b).

Figure 13.5a Swing knee downward and across other leg

Figure 13.5b Knee extended in follow-through

Common Faults

1. Too much backward lean prior to kicking the ball
2. Contacting the ball too soon or too late
3. Failing to follow through

Volley Kick   The volley is a kick that is performed when the ball is in flight. This is a difficult kick, so elementary school children should not be expected to do it with a high degree of accuracy. However, because this kick is a time-saver and because it generates much force, children will attempt to perform it. The player should stand with his nonkicking foot in front and his weight evenly distributed on both feet. His head and body face the ball and his body is tilted forward slightly (fig. 13.6a). As the ball approaches, the player shifts his weight to his nonkicking foot and raises his kicking leg, with the knee slightly bent and the toes pointing down. He contacts the ball with the top of the instep and follows through in a forward and upward direction (fig. 13.6b).

Figure 13.6a Body tilted forward slightly

Figure 13.6b Follow through forward and upward

Common Faults

1. Contacting the ball too late
2. Failing to follow through

Punting   The goalkeeper is the only player who is allowed to use a punting kick. The ball is held about chest high (fig. 13.7a). The kicking leg is swung forward and upward (fig. 13.7b). The ball is dropped and is contacted on the instep as the leg moves in a forward and upward direction (fig. 13.7c). Follow through into an extended leg position (fig. 13.7d).

a. Hold ball chest high.   b. Swing kicking leg forward.   c. Contact ball with top of foot.   d. Follow through to an extended leg position

Figure 13.7

Common Faults

1. Throwing the ball downward rather than dropping it
2. Contacting the ball too late, causing a high upward lift

Trapping   Trapping is stopping the ball while it is moving through the air or rolling on the ground. Any part of the body except the hands and arms may be used to trap a ball. The type of trap a player uses depends upon the flight of the ball, the position of opponents, and the amount of time the trapper has. Upper elementary school children should be able to perform the following five trapping skills.

Foot Trap   The foot trap is used to trap a rolling or bouncing ball. As the ball approaches, the player raises her foot about eight inches off the ground with her toes up to form a "V" between the ground and the sole of the foot (fig. 13.8a). When the ball makes contact with the sole, the foot should relax to let the ball lose its recoil action and remain beneath the foot (fig. 13.8b).

Figure 13.8a   Figure 13.8b

Side-of-Foot Trap   The side-of-foot trap is used in the same manner as the front foot trap, the main difference being the direction from which the ball approaches. The player raises her leg slightly, with the inside of the foot toward the ball. As the ball strikes, her foot relaxes to absorb the force of the ball, allowing it to drop rather than to recoil forward (fig. 13.9).

Figure 13.9 The foot gives slightly

Leg Trap The leg trap is used when the ball is approaching from a high volley or a low bounce. As the ball approaches, the player shifts her weight to the foot nearest the oncoming ball. Her trapping leg is bent at almost a right angle and her foot is well off the ground. When the ball makes contact, the leg should give a little to prevent the ball from rebounding too far forward (fig. 13.10)

Figure 13.10 The leg gives slightly when the ball makes contact.

Shin Trap The shin trap is one of the easiest trapping skills and is used in much the same way as the foot trap. As the ball rolls toward the player, she flexes both knees, bends her trunk forward slightly, and extends her arms to the side. At the moment of contact, her legs extend slightly and her weight shifts to her nonkicking foot in preparation for the next move.

Figure 13.11 Legs extend slightly at contact

Body Trap The body trap is used when the ball is descending from a high volley or when a player wants to prevent a high-rising ball from getting past him. To perform this type of trap, the player brings his extended arms forward but does not touch the ball with his hands or arms. The arm position helps to create a "hollow" chest or pocket for the ball (fig. 13.12). However, the player's chest is held

Figure 13.12 Arm position creates a hollow chest or pocket.

in a normal position up to the moment the ball makes contact. Upon contact, the player relaxes his chest muscles, thus creating a pocket for the ball to stop and drop directly below. Girls should fold their arms across their chests when attempting this trapping skill (fig. 13.13).

Figure 13.13

13

Common Faults

The following faults apply to all types of trapping skills:
1. Failing to keep the eyes on the oncoming ball
2. Failing to move into position to trap the oncoming ball
3. Failing to give as the ball makes contact with the body

Dribbling

Dribbling in soccer is moving the ball with short pushes by either foot. These pushes permit the player to control the ball whether she is dribbling forward or sideward. Dribbling with the inside of the foot is quite easy; however, good ball control also requires use of the outside of either foot. Dribbling backwards is bad practice as it only helps the opponent.

Figure 13.14 Dribbling

The body should be bent forward slightly when dribbling, with the head over the ball. Gently push or "persuade" the ball and keep head up high enough to be able to make an offensive move and to watch oncoming opponents (fig. 13.15).

Common Faults

1. Holding the body too erect or leaning too far back while dribbling
2. Kicking rather than pushing the ball
3. Using the toes rather than the instep or the outside of the feet
4. Keeping the head down and not watching opponents while dribbling

Figure 13.15 Push or "persuade"
the ball while dribbling.

Heading

Heading the soccer ball is actually hitting or bunting it with the front or side of the forehead. The player drops her head back as the ball approaches, raises her arms, and shifts her weight to her back foot (fig. 13.17a). She then shifts her body weight forward and upward and brings her head forward to meet the ball (fig. 13.17b). The ball must be contacted with the front or side of the forehead and with a continuous forward movement of the body in the direction of the intended flight of the ball (fig. 13.17c). The key to good heading lies in correctly judging the speed and the height of the oncoming ball.

Figure 13.16

a   b   c
Figure 13.17
a. Head drops back in preparation   b. Contact with forehead
                                        c. Continuous forward movement

13

Common Faults

1. Closing the eyes before the ball contacts the head
2. Failing to drop the head back in preparation for the forward thrust of the head and neck
3. Contacting the ball on the top of the head
4. Trying to hit the ball solely by moving the head, rather than using the whole body with the head as the point of contact

Throw-in Whenever the ball goes over the sidelines, it is put back into play by a throw-in. The ball must be thrown from behind the head with both hands. Part of both feet must remain on the ground until the ball leaves the player's hands, although, any position of the feet is permissible. Begin with one foot in front of the other or with the feet parallel (fig. 13.18a). Bring the ball back to the top of the shoulders and arch back (fig. 13.18b). Shift the body weight forward and upward and bring the ball over the head, extending the arms toward the direction of the throw. Release the ball and follow through with hands and arms (fig. 13.18c).

Figure 13.18a One foot in front of the other

Figure 13.18b Ball starts from behind head

Figure 13.18c Release and drag back foot

Common Faults

1. Failing to bring the ball back far enough
2. Throwing the ball with one hand like a baseball pass
3. Taking both feet off the ground before the ball has been released

Tackling   In soccer, the players of the team that has possession of the ball are known as the *offensive* or *attacking team.* Any defensive player may legally tackle a player who has possession of the ball, but only from the front or side and with the feet or shoulders. Using the hands or tackling from behind is clearly against the rules. When tackling, the defensive player should watch the ball and her opponent's feet for clues to the direction she may take (fig. 13.19a). The body weight should also be evenly distributed on both feet in order to shift right or left. The tackle should be made when the opponent is slightly off balance (fig. 13.19b).

Figure 13.19a Watch feet for clues.

Figure 13.19b Tackle when opponent is off balance.

Important points to remember in tackling an opponent are

1. to be quick and decisive when you approach an opponent who has possession of the ball
2. to tackle the opponent when she is in control of the ball but is slightly off balance, usually when she pushes the ball forward a little
3. to be ready to pass the ball as soon as you gain possession

13

Practice Activities

The following practice activities are organized by skill. Where possible, the activities begin with individual movements, progress to partner activities, and then to group drills.

Kicking and Trapping Activities

The majority of practice activities relating to kicking and trapping skills involves two or more players. However, the few individual activities that follow give each child an opportunity to get used to the bounce of the ball and to control the ball with his feet. Partner and small group activities provide more realistic ball-handling situations including one or more skills.

Individual Activities

Throw, Bounce, and Trap

Each child has a ball (any inflated ball can be used) and finds his own space in the playing area. Have the child throw his ball into the air, allow it to bounce once, and then try to trap it with one foot. Add other limitations, such as trapping with the left foot, the side of the leg, or the shins.

Wall Kicking

Arrange children in a line formation along available wall surface. Each players stands about six feet away from the wall, kicks the ball to the wall, and retrieves his own rebound with a foot or shin trap.

Variations
1. Allow each child to kick the ball as it rebounds back to him (no trap required).
2. Start several yards back from the ball, run up and kick it, and trap the rebound.
3. Start several yards back, dribble to a line, kick the ball to the wall, and trap the rebound.
4. Place a target on the wall (a circle or square) and repeat previous activities.
5. Repeat previous activities with the opposite foot.

Partner Activities

Passing and Trapping

Partners have one ball between them and find a space in the playing area. They should stand about ten to fifteen feet apart. One player passes to the other, who traps the ball and returns the pass.

Variations
1. Change the type of pass and trap.
2. Repeat above with one player stationary and the receiving player on the move.
3. Repeat above with both players on the move.

Wall Passing and Trapping

This is essentially the same drill as Wall Kicking listed under Individual Activities. One player kicks the ball to the wall and his partner traps it and returns the kick. All other variations can be adapted to partner activities.

Target Shooting

Partners have one ball and two traffic cones (or milk cartons). Arrange partners and equipment as shown in the diagram. One partner kicks the ball through the goals between the cones and the other partner traps the ball and repeats the kicking skill.

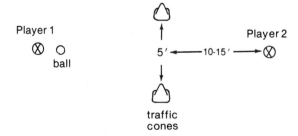

Variations
1. Change the type of kicking and trapping skills.
2. Change the angle of shooting.
3. Change the distance between goals.
4. Change the distance away from goals.

Teaching Suggestions

This is an opportune time to introduce the problem-solving method. For example, after several variations of the previous activity have been practiced, pose a question such as "Can you change the position of your traffic cones and make up a drill that involves an inside-of-foot pass and a shin trap?" If children have had experience with the inventive games approach, a challenge such as "Using the two cones and a ball, create your own passing and trapping drill" will produce a wide variety of responses.

Group Activities

Several simple games and relay activities described in previous chapters may be adapted for practicing soccer skills. They include Keep Away (p. 189) and Crab Soccer (p. 190).

Zigzag Kicking

Formation

Divide the class into squads of six to ten players. Arrange the squads in two lines about fifteen feet apart, with partners facing.

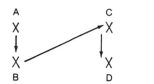

Basic Drill

Player A kicks the ball to player B. B may use his hands or feet, depending on the level of trapping skill, to stop the ball. B places the ball on the ground and kicks it to C. Continue pattern to player F or allow players to continue the pattern back to player A.

Variations

1. A rolls the ball to B, who kicks it to C. C kicks the ball to D, and so on, until F, or back to player A.
2. A bounces the ball to B, who kicks it to C. This time C stops the ball, picks it up, and bounces it to D. Continue pattern.
3. Repeat number 2 with the opposite foot.

Circle Kicking

Formation

Divide the class into three or four squads of eight to twelve players. Arrange each squad in a large circle with at least fifteen feet between players.

Basic Drill

Player A turns, faces B, and kicks the ball to him. B traps the ball (or he may stop it with his hands), turns, and kicks the ball to C. Continue pattern until A receives the ball.

Variations

1. All children remain facing the center of the circle. A, using the inside of the left foot, kicks to B. B traps the ball with his right foot, then kicks it to C with his left foot.
2. Repeat number 1 in the opposite direction, trapping with the left foot and kicking with the right.
3. Place one child in the center. Center player kicks to A. A traps the ball and kicks it back to the center player, who traps it and kicks to B. Continue pattern.

Kicking for Distance

Formation

Divide the class into two squads. One squad lines up to kick, while the other scatters in the field to retrieve the ball. The field can be marked with lines every five yards or the retrievers can simply mark the kick. The class also can be divided into four squads with two teams playing in each half of the field.

Basic Drill

Each child on the kicking squad is given three or four kicks, depending upon the number of balls available. Mark where the ball lands, not where it rolls. After each player on the kicking squad has had a turn, change squad positions.

Variations

The kicking squad may vary the type of kick—a stationary kick, a punt, or a kick while the ball is rolling forward.

13

Goal Kicking

Formation

Divide the class into four squads and arrange them in semicircles on each side of the goalposts.

Basic Drill

Player on team A kicks the ball through the goal, and any player on the opposite team traps the ball and returns the kick. Do not allow any player to move more than two yards from his position to retrieve the ball. If the ball goes through the retrieving team, allow the player who was closest to the ball as it passed by to retrieve it.

Variations

1. Vary the type of kick—a stationary kick, kicking a moving ball, using the inside and outside of the instep. (Move closer to the goal when practicing this type of kick.)
2. Place a player in the center of the goalpost to practice goaltending (guarding the goal).
3. Practice volley kicking. Players on team A must throw the ball over the goalposts. Any player on team B may attempt to kick the ball through the goalposts before it lands.

Dribbling Activities

The same procedure used to teach passing and trapping can be followed when teaching dribbling skills. Begin with individual activities, add small equipment, then move on to partner activities, and finally to group activities.

Individual Activities

Individual Dribbling

Each child has a ball (any inflated ball) and finds his own space in the playing area. Allow children to dribble anywhere within the playing area so long as they do not bump into other players.

Figure 13.20 Dribble and stop

Variations

1. Dribble and stop on whistle or voice command (fig. 13.20).
2. Dribble in different directions on voice command (right, forward, left, right).
3. Dribble with the outside of the foot.
4. Give each player two or more pieces of small equipment (beanbags, hoops) and have him dribble around them.
5. Add other skills, such as dribbling, stopping, trapping, and then shooting at the wall.

Partner Activities

Follow the Leader

This is an excellent activity to teach ball control and keeping an eye on another player. Each player has a ball. One partner dribbles in any direction and her partner must follow.

Variations

1. Same as previous, but with partners side by side.
2. Same as the original drill, but add one or more obstacles to dribble around.

Figure 13.21 Follow the leader

Dribble and Pass

Begin this drill with partners dribbling and passing a ball back and forth.

Variations
1. Add two or more obstacles to dribble around.
2. Repeat earlier drills dribbling with outside of feet.
3. Add other skills such as dribble, pass, and trap.

Group Activities

Line Dribbling

Formation
Divide the class into squads of four or five players, and give each squad a ball. Arrange the squads in a file formation behind a restraining line. Draw a second line approximately twenty feet away.

Basic Drill
Each player dribbles the ball to the second line, stops the ball on the line, turns around, and dribbles back to and all the way around his squad. He stops the ball opposite the next player, who repeats the action. The first player then goes to the back of the line. By requiring the players to go around the squad, they develop better control of the ball.

Variations
1. Dribble around a pin or chair.
2. Dribble and stop. Start the first child from each squad at the same time. As they dribble, blow your whistle and require each child to stop the ball as soon as he can. Another variation is to blow the whistle and say, "Left," "Right," "Back," or "Forward." The child must stop the ball, then dribble it in the direction you have designated.

Shuttle Dribbling

Formation
Divide the class into squads of six to eight players. Place half of each team behind one line and the other half behind a second line thirty feet away.

Basic Drill
Player A dribbles the ball over to the second line and stops it in front of B. B repeats to C, while A moves to the back of B's line. Continue pattern.

Variations
1. Player A must go around B's team, then back to B.
2. Dribble to a centerline, stop the ball, and then pass to the next player.

Heading and Throw-in Activities

Heading and throw-in skills are normally practiced together in partner or group activities. However, if a wall is available, a few individual activities can be practiced.

Individual Activities

Throw and Head

Each player has a ball and stands about five or six feet away from the wall. Practice the throw-in, then do a throw-in and head the rebound back to the wall. Repeat the throw-in, then turn sideways and attempt to head the ball back to the wall.

13

Figure 13.22 Throw and head with
partners

Partner Activities

Throw and Head

Partners face each other about eight to twelve
feet apart. One partner, using a throw-in pass,
throws the ball high into the air so that it
descends just in front of his partner. That
partner then attempts to head the ball forward
and downward toward the first partner's feet.
Repeat several times, then change positions.

Variations
1. Tie a rope between two posts; the height may
   vary from four to six feet. Repeat the original
   activity, but with the throw-in going over the
   rope and the headed ball returning under the
   rope.
2. Place a hoop on the floor between the players.
   Repeat the original drill, requiring the headed
   ball to hit the center of the hoop.

Group Activities

Around the Square

Formation
Divide the class into squads of four players.
Arrange the squads into squares with ten feet
between players. Letter each player, A, B, C, and
D around the square.

Basic Drill
Player A, using a regulation throw-in, throws the
ball to B. B attempts to head the ball to C. C
catches it and throws to D, and D heads it to A,
and so on.

Variations
Start with A throwing to B. Now B heads it to C
and C attempts to head the ball to D. D heads it
to A, and so on.

Goal Heading

Formation
Divide the class into as many squads as you have
goals. (Wire backstops or any substitute goal
area will work for this drill.) Arrange squads in a
line ten feet in front of and parallel to the goal.
Player A in each squad moves fifteen feet in front
of his team beyond the goal, turns, and faces the
second player in the line.

Basic Drill
Player A throws to player B, who attempts to
head the ball through the goal. B chases his own
ball, throws it to A, then returns to the end of the
line.

Variations
Make two lines facing the goal, with A standing
on the goal line and the front players of the two
lines standing ten feet away. A throws the ball up
and between the first two players. Both attempt
to head the ball back to A.

Tackling Activities

Tackling is normally practiced in combination with another skill, and two or more players are involved.

Partner Activities

Partner Keep Away

One player is given a ball and tries to keep it from his partner by dribbling, dodging, stopping, and pivoting away from his partner. As soon as the defensive partner touches the ball, the players exchange positions and repeat the drill.

Variations
Partners begin about twenty feet apart, facing each other. On a signal from the teacher, each approaches the other, the player with the ball trying to dribble past his opponent and the defensive player attempting to gain possession of the ball.

Group Activities

Shuttle Dribble and Tackle

This is a basic shuttle relay formation, with the following modifications. Player number one dribbles the ball toward the other line while player number two at the same time moves out to tackle player number one. Player number one tries to reach the opposite line without being tackled, and player number two attempts to touch the ball. Allow about twenty seconds of play, then blow the whistle and start the next two players.

```
5   3   1                    30'              2   4   6
X   X   X   <----------------------------->  X   X   X
```

One Versus Two Players

Two players attempt to keep the ball away from the third player. If player number three touches the ball, the opposing player who last touched it changes position with him.

Variations
1. Add a goal behind the defensive player and require the two offensive players to move in and attempt to score.
2. Repeat the previous activities and change the combination to one of the following:
   a. One defensive player versus three offensive players
   b. Two defensive players versus two offensive players
   c. Two defensive players versus three offensive players

Lead-up Games

The lead-up games described in this section are arranged according to level of difficulty. Slight modifications can make any of them suitable for any upper elementary school grade, however.

Several games described in other chapters can be adapted to a soccer-type activity. See California Kickball, (page 195, and Keep Away, page 189).

Lead-up Game	Grade	Page
Circle Soccer	4	242
Soccer Dodge Ball	4-5	242
Boundary Ball	4-5	242
Circle Soccer Tag	4-5	242
Sideline Soccer	4-5	242
Pin Soccer	5-6	243
Forwards and Backs	5-6	243
Punt Back	5-6	244
Seven-Man Soccer	5-6	244
Soccer: Basic Rules	5-6	245

13

Circle Soccer (4)

Formation: Form a large circle with two feet between each player. Draw a line through the center of the circle, thus creating two teams.
Equipment: One soccer ball
Players: Eight to ten on each team
Skills: Kicking and trapping

The captain of one team puts the ball into play by kicking it toward the opponents. The players on each team attempt to kick the ball past the opposing players, below their shoulders. They also must try to prevent the ball from going out of the circle on their own side. Every player must remain at his place in the circle while the ball is in play. Only the captain may move out of the circle. One point is awarded for each time the ball is kicked out of the circle.

Soccer Dodge Ball (4-5)

Formation: Half the players form a large circle while the other half scatter inside.
Equipment: One soccer ball
Players: Half of class on each team
Skills: Kicking and trapping

The circle players attempt to hit the players inside by kicking the ball at them. Inside players cannot use their hands to stop the ball, except for a pass that may strike the face. When a player is hit below the waist, he must join the circle. The winners are the last three players remaining inside the circle.

Boundary Ball (4-5)

Formation: Divide the playing area into halves. Players are scattered on their own side of the centerline.
Equipment: Two soccer balls
Players: Ten to fifteen players on each team
Skills: Kicking and trapping

Each team is given a ball, which it kicks toward the opponent's goal line. Players may move about freely in their own half of the field to prevent the opponent's ball from crossing the goal. However, they cannot touch the ball with their hands. One point is scored each time a ball crosses a goal line.

Circle Soccer Tag (4-5)

Formation: Large circle with approximately two feet between players and one child in the center.
Equipment: One soccer ball
Players: Twenty or fewer
Skills: Kicking, passing, trapping, and heading

Circle players try to keep the center player ("it") from touching the ball (Keep Away). If the ball goes outside the circle, "it" is replaced by the person who missed the ball. If "it" touches the ball, he is replaced by the last person to kick the ball. No score is kept.

Teaching suggestions
If a player misses the ball, have him retrieve it, return to his position, and proceed to pass the ball. Stress accurate passing and trapping.

Sideline Soccer (4-5)

Formation: Playing area and teams arranged according to diagram
Equipment: Soccer ball, four markers, and four goalposts or (traffic cones or milk cartons)
Players: Ten to fifteen players on each team
Skills: Passing, trapping, heading, and tackling

Five players from each team line up inside the playing area as shown in the diagram. The remaining players line up outside the court. A kickoff by the center player starts the game and restarts it after each point is scored. Once the game is started, inside players may move anywhere within the court. Sideline players must stay behind the line but may shift sideward to the next player. Sideline players are allowed to trap and to pass to court players, but only court players may score. If a ball goes over the

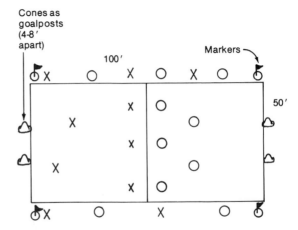

Cones as goalposts (4-8' apart)

sidelines or end lines, the ball is given to the nearest sideline opponent of the team that last touched the ball. The same procedure is followed for any other violation, such as touching the ball with hands or sideline players entering the court area. One point is awarded for each goal. Rotate sideline and field players every two minutes.

Pin Soccer (5-6)

Formation: Playing area and teams arranged according to diagram
Equipment: Five or six Indian clubs (or milk cartons), two soccer balls
Players: Six to eight on each team
Skills: Kicking and trapping

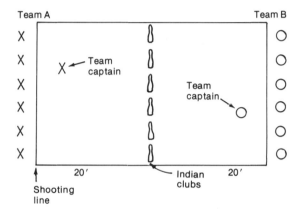

A captain is chosen for each team. He remains in his own half of the playing area. One ball is given to a player on each team who kicks the ball from behind the shooting line and tries to knock over one or more Indian clubs. The team gets a point for every Indian club knocked over. The team captain retrieves all balls and resets any clubs knocked over by his teammates.

Variations

1. Increase the number of balls.
2. After a player has scored, make him the team captain.
3. Increase the distance between end lines as skill increases.
4. Vary the type of kick and trap.

Forwards and Backs (5-6)

Formation: Playing area and teams arranged according to diagram
Equipment: One ball
Players: Ten to twelve players on each team
Skills: Passing, dribbling, and trapping

The center forward of Team A starts the game with a kickoff. The Team A forwards then try to kick the ball over the opponent's goal line. Players on Team B try to gain possession of the ball and kick it over their opponent's goal line. Forwards may not cross back over their own center zone line, and backs may not cross the center zone line. Only forwards can score a goal. Each goal counts one point. If the ball goes over the end line or sideline, it is thrown in by the nearest player on the opposite team.

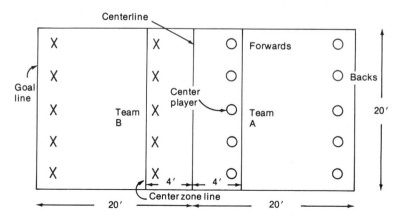

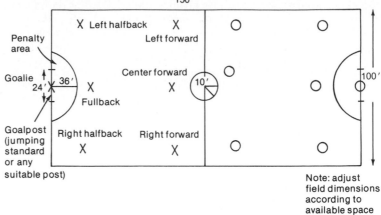

150'

X Left halfback   X

Penalty area

Left forward

Goalie

24'   36'

Center forward

X   X

10'

100'

Fullback

Goalpost (jumping standard or any suitable post)

Right halfback   Right forward

X   X

Note: adjust field dimensions according to available space

Punt Back (5-6)

Formation: Players on each team in a scattered position on their own half of the field
Equipment: One soccer ball
Players: Four to twenty
Skills: Trapping and kicking

A captain is chosen for each team. The ball is placed in the middle of the field and the captain of the kicking team kicks the ball to start the game. Once the game has started, opposing teams must stay at least fifteen feet apart. Any member of the receiving team may trap the ball. The player who traps the ball must kick it toward his opponent's goal. If a player kicks the ball over the opponent's goal, his team receives one point. The team that did not score starts the ball from the center of the field. Any player who contacts another player while the latter is attempting to kick the ball commits a foul. A free kick is then awarded to the other team.

Teaching suggestions
Use only one soccer ball at the start; two or more may be added later.

Seven-Man Soccer (5-6)

Formation: Playing area and teams arranged according to diagram
Equipment: Soccer ball and colored arm bands or pinnies to identify teams
Players: Seven on each team
Skills: All soccer skills, as this is essentially a miniature version of soccer

See the official rules of soccer in the following section. Since there are seven players on each team, this is an ideal game to accommodate an average-sized physical education class. The playing field is normally divided in half to allow two games to be played at the same time. Modify any rule to cope with local conditions.

Variations
There is a very strong tendency for young players to "follow the ball" rather than to play their positions. Too often the fullback and halfbacks are "caught" too far in front of their forwards. To prevent this, play the same game as Seven-Man Soccer but after the kick-off require:

1. forwards to remain in their opponent's half of the field
2. backs to remain in their own half of the playing field

Soccer: Rules and Regulations

By the time children reach the fifth grade they should have learned the majority of skills necessary to play soccer. This does not imply, however, that time should not be devoted to practice activities and lead-up games. With some basic modifications, the game of soccer should be played in its entirety periodically during an instructional unit. Children thus will understand that practice sessions and lead-up activities are designed to improve the speed and accuracy of the required skills.

I. Field of play:
Length of field—not more than 120 yards and not less than 110 yards
Width of field—not more than 75 yards and not less than 65 yards

II. Names of players and line-up positions (positions the players take at the start of the game, after a goal is scored, and after halftime):
A. Left wing (outside left)
B. Inside left
C. Center forward
D. Inside right
E. Right wing (outside right)
F. Left halfback
G. Center halfback
H. Right halfback
I. Left fullback
J. Right fullback
K. Goalie

III. Penalty kick: If a defensive player other than the goalie touches the ball in the eighteen-by-forty-four-yard penalty area, a penalty kick is awarded to the offensive team. This kick is taken from the twelve-yard penalty mark by any member of the offensive team. The goalie must stand on the line between the goalposts, and all other players must stand outside the penalty area until the ball has been kicked. After the kick has been taken, any player from either team may enter the penalty area.

IV. Free kicks: There are two types of free kicks, the direct free kick and the indirect free kick.
A. Direct free kick: This is a kick from which a goal may be scored directly. In other words, the ball can be kicked from where an infraction occurred and travel directly through the goal. This kick is awarded to a team when any opposing player commits any of the following infractions outside the penalty area (a kick inside the penalty area is a penalty kick, taken from the penalty mark):
1. Kicking an opponent
2. Charging in a violent and dangerous manner
3. Tripping an opponent
4. Handling the ball (The goalkeeper may handle the ball only when he is inside the penalty area. If he handles the ball when he is outside the penalty area, a direct free kick is awarded to the opposing team.)

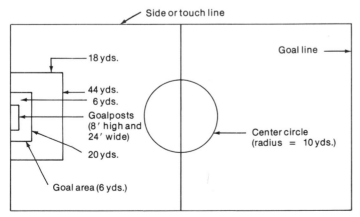

Side or touch line
Goal line
18 yds.
44 yds.
6 yds.
Goalposts (8' high and 24' wide)
20 yds.
Goal area (6 yds.)
Center circle (radius = 10 yds.)

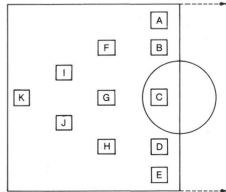

13

5. Pushing with the hands or arms
   When such an infraction occurs, the ball is placed on the spot where it happened. Any player on the team awarded the kick may take the kick. He lines up three or four yards behind the ball and players from both teams may stand anywhere in front of him, providing they are at least ten yards away. The whistle sounds, the ball is kicked, and play resumes.

B. Indirect free kick: This is a kick from which a goal cannot be scored, unless the ball is touched by another player before it enters the goal. (The goalie does not count as another player.) This kick is awarded to a team when any opposing player commits any of the following infractions:
   1. A player kicks the ball a second consecutive time after a kickoff, a free kick, a goal kick, or a corner kick.
   2. A ball is not kicked forward from a penalty kick.
   3. The goalie carries the ball more than four steps. He must bounce the ball on the ground before he takes one or more steps.
   4. Ungentlemanly conduct—improper language, unnecessary arguing, and so on.
   5. Offside.
   6. Obstruction other than holding.

V. Throw-in: When the ball is pitched, headed, or legally forced over the touch line by a player, the opposing team is awarded a throw-in. The ball is put back into play from behind the touch line at the point at which the ball went out. The player who makes the throw-in must have both hands on the ball and throw it from behind his head. He must also have part of both feet in contact with the ground until he has released the ball. If the ball is not thrown in properly, the opposing team is awarded the second throw-in.

VI. Corner kick: When the ball is kicked, headed, or legally forced over the goal line by a defensive player, the opposing team is awarded a corner kick. The ball is placed on the corner of the field—where the sideline meets the goal line—on the side the ball went out. Usually a wing player kicks the ball into play. All other players may stand anywhere on the field, providing they are at least ten yards away from the ball.

VII. Goal kick: When the ball is kicked, headed, or legally forced over the goal line by a player on the attacking team, a goal kick is awarded to the defensive team. The ball is placed in the goal area on the side nearest to where the ball crossed the line. Any defensive player may kick the ball back into play; however, it must cross the penalty line to be in play. If it does not, the kick is taken over. The offensive team remains outside the penalty area until the ball has crossed the penalty line.

VIII. Offside: A player is offside if he is nearer his opponent's goal line than the ball at the moment the ball is played. He is not offside, however, if (1) he is in his own half of the field; (2) there are two opponents nearer their goal than he is at the moment the ball is played; or (3) he received a ball directly from a corner kick, a throw-in, or a goal kick.

A. Example of offside: The right winger is offside because he did not have two defensive players in front of him at the moment the ball was kicked.

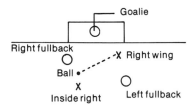

B. Not offside: In this case, "at the moment" the inside right kicked the ball, the right winger had two defensive players in front of him. Now the right winger may dribble in and attempt a shot at the goal.

IX. Scoring: One point is awarded to the attacking team if any player kicks, heads, or legally causes the ball to cross over the goal line between the goalposts and under the crossbar. A ball accidentally kicked through the goal by a defensive player, therefore, would count for the attacking team.

Evaluative Techniques

Although there are a number of standardized tests to measure soccer skills, these generally are designed for secondary and college level students. These tests, however, can be modified to meet the ability of upper elementary children. The following test battery is an example of a "teacher-made" test that can be administered without elaborate equipment and in a short period of time. Keep scores from year to year in order to develop appropriate norms for your school.

			Soccer Skill Test			
Name	Kick and Trap total score	Dribbling	Shooting	Subjective evaluation	Total score	Grade
1 2 3 4 5		Rank all total scores for the class, then convert ——→ to letter grades or to ratings (Superior, Good, etc.).				

Test No. 1   **Kick and trap**

Draw a line five feet from the wall. The ball is placed on the line. Each player attempts to kick the ball and hit the front wall as many times as possible within thirty seconds. All kicks must be taken from behind the five-foot line. If a player loses control of the ball, he may retrieve it with his feet and continue kicking. Award one point for each successful hit. Allow two trials and record the highest score.

Test No. 2   Dribbling

Arrange four chairs as shown in the diagram. Place a ball on the starting line. Each player starts behind the starting line with both hands resting on his knees. On the "go" signal, he dribbles the ball around the chairs in a zigzag pattern. One point is awarded for each time he passes a chair as he moves forward and as he returns to the starting line. Allow thirty seconds for the test. Two trials are also allowed, and the highest score is recorded.

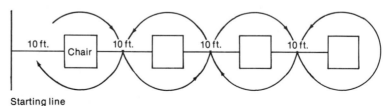

Starting line

Test No. 3   Shooting

Arrange the field markings in front of the goalposts as shown in the diagram. A player may use the right or left approach. The player starts to dribble the ball in the approach area and must continue moving into the shooting zone. While he is in the shooting zone, he must attempt to kick the ball through the goalposts. Ten trials are given, with five points awarded for each successful goal.

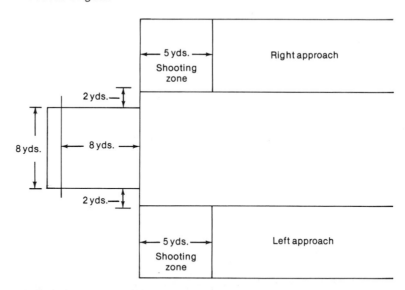

Test No. 4   Subjective evaluation

Establish criteria that represent the skills and playing ability required in soccer. For example, using such skills as passing, dribbling, team play, and defensive ability, the teacher would award each player a total score from zero to fifty points. Three players can be used as judges, with the average score recorded.

Field and Floor Hockey Activities

14

Emphasis and Skill Presentation

Teaching Procedures

Description of Skills

Practice Activities

Lead-up Games

Field Hockey: Rules and Regulations

Floor Hockey: Rules and Regulations

Evaluative Techniques

When we think of hockey for upper elementary school children we often visualize a vigorous and noisy intramural floor hockey game with little concern for skill and playing strategies. We also tend to think of it as a "boys versus boys" and "girls versus girls" activity.

In this chapter the author has arranged the basic skills that are common to both floor and field hockey into one unit of instruction. More emphasis is devoted to field hockey activities since this sport has become very popular with children of this age level. Field hockey also provides an enjoyable medium for boys and girls to learn to play together on more equal terms. Finally, the larger number of children required to play this game is in harmony with the philosophy of the elementary school physical education program.

Emphasis and Skill Presentation

Many of the basic skills and simple playing strategies of hockey have been introduced in grades three and four through street hockey and organized floor hockey during school hours. Although field hockey is similar to these two games, it has several unique skills and rules that should be learned correctly and in an organized manner in grades four, five, and six.

During the fourth grade, the main emphasis should be on learning the correct way to dribble, pass, and shoot a ball or puck. These children should also learn how to stop a ball and a few basic rules of the game. The major portion of any unit of instruction should be devoted to practice activities and lead-up games.

The basic dribbling, passing, and shooting skills should still be emphasized through grades five and six. Teachers should expect a general increase in the accuracy, speed, and control of these skills. New skills such as the scoop shot, tackling, dodging, and the roll-in should be introduced in grade five or six. More time should also be devoted to seven-person hockey, as well as sufficient time to play eleven-person field hockey. The latter is important in order to give each child an opportunity to understand and appreciate the importance of good ball control and positional play.

Suggested Sequence of Presenting Hockey Skills and Rules

Skills and Rules	Grade Level Grade 4	Grade 5	Grade 6
Dribbling	Introduce		
Rules		Increase speed and accuracy	Increase speed and accuracy
Dribbling with face of blade	Introduce	Refinement	Refinement
Driving	Introduce		
Left drive		Increase distance and accuracy	Increase distance and accuracy
Scoop shot		Introduce	Increase accuracy
Rules: Hit with face of blade		Introduce	
Fielding	Introduce		
Rules		Increase accuracy	Increase accuracy
Tackling		Introduce	Increase accuracy
Rules			
Fouls		Introduce	
Dodging		Introduce	Increase accuracy
Rules			
Offside		Introduce	
Face-off	Introduce	Increase accuracy	Increase accuracy
Rules			
Player positions and three hits		Introduce	
Roll-in		Introduce	Increase distance and accuracy
Rules			
Roll-in		Introduce	

Teaching Procedures

Throughout this chapter numerous references are made to various sections in Chapter 13, "Soccer Activities." The reason for this is that both soccer and field hockey may be relatively new to many elementary school children and the same approach can be used to teach both activities. In addition, many practice activities and lead-up games described in Chapter 13 can be easily adapted to field hockey skills. Teachers should also adapt the information in pages 221-22 in organizing and planning a hockey unit.

The following suggestions will assist teachers in coping with several problems that are unique to hockey:

1. Hockey can be a dangerous sport if children are not taught proper stick handling and legal checking methods. Since boys and girls may play this activity together, it is especially important that the proper skills be taught and enforced.
2. Since there may not be enough sticks for every member of the class, station work (pp. 207-08) and a rotation system should be used.
3. Hockey, like soccer, requires a high level of strength and endurance. Teachers should plan practice activities and lead-up games so the children gradually build up their cardiorespiratory endurance. Station work can be used to alternate vigorous running drills with less tiring shooting activities.

Description of Skills

Field and floor hockey skills are classified as dribbling, passing or driving, and fielding skills. The following skills should be taught to elementary school children in a systematic and progressive way. Special attention must be given to proper stick handling, reinforcing it throughout every lesson.

Grip

The basic hockey grip is fundamental to all shooting, dribbling, and fielding skills. To begin, grasp the stick in the middle with the right hand and hold the stick parallel to the ground. The toe of the blade should be sticking up and the side of the blade facing left. Grasp the top of the stick with the left hand, with the thumb pointing down to the blade. Lower the stick to the ground and turn the blade so that it faces outward. Keep the same grip with the left hand and reposition the right hand to about six to twelve inches below the left hand. The result is that the hands grip the handle from opposite sides (figs. 14.1 and 14.2). The player will

Figure 14.1 Left palm faces body and right palm faces forward.

Figure 14.2

14

want to experiment to find the most suitable distance between her hands.

The player should carry her stick ahead and to the right of her feet, with her body leaning forward slightly and her head over the ball.

Dribbling

Dribbling in hockey is a controlled means of propelling the ball along the ground with the hockey stick. The ball should be dribbled slightly to the right of the feet by making short taps with the flat side of the blade (fig. 14.3). The movement should come from the shoulder rather than the wrists. In open field play and when the opponent is not near, the ball may be tapped ten to fifteen feet ahead, followed by short running steps, then another tap of the ball. The flat side of the blade should always be to the ball, and the blade should be close to the ground. For more controlled dribbling—two to three feet per hit—the hands should be spread farther apart in order to quickly rotate the blade directly behind the ball.

a   b   c

Figure 14.3 Dribble slightly to the right and make short taps with the flat side of the blade.

Common Faults:

1. Ball constantly moving to the left of the dribbler because the left arm is not being turned so that the flat side of the stick angles toward the right
2. Holding the arms too close to the body and hitting the ball with wrist action
3. Failing to look up and around while dribbling

Driving   Driving is forcefully hitting the ball along the ground. The left drive is the most common driving stroke, used for long and medium passes, shots on goal, and free and corner hits. As the player moves into position to hit the ball (the ball should be about twelve inches in front of the left foot), his right hand moves close to his left hand, his left shoulder points into the direction of the drive, and his head is over the ball. His arms swing back, keeping the stick below shoulder level (fig. 14.4a). He then brings his arms forward and downward and contacts the ball just off his left foot (fig. 14.4b). The follow-through should be low and in the direction of the hit.

Figure 14.4a Stick below shoulder height

Figure 14.4b Swing through the ball

Common Faults

1. Holding the stick with a loose grip
2. Holding the hands too far apart
3. Failing to point the left shoulder in the direction of the hit
4. Hitting the ball too soon or too late

Scoop Shot The scoop shot is used to lift the ball slightly off the ground in order to dodge an opponent, to pass, or to shoot the ball into the corner of the goal. The player leans forward with her right foot in front and her stick tilted back as it is placed under the ball (fig. 14.5b). She then makes a strong lifting and shovel-like action with her right arm (fig. 14.5c).

Figure 14.5a Approaching the ball

Figure 14.5b Contact under the ball

Figure 14.5c Strong shovel-like action

Fielding Fielding a hockey ball or puck (figs. 14.6 and 14.7) is very similar to fielding a grounder in softball. The face of the stick should be at right angles to the direction of the oncoming ball. As the ball

Figure 14.6 Apply the same principles as catching a ball.

Figure 14.7 For aerial stops, the hand can act only as a rebound surface.

contacts the stick, the player should loosen her grip slightly to absorb the impact of the ball. She should also contact the ball as far away from her body as possible to allow the force to be absorbed over the greatest distance.

Common Faults

1. Failing to get in line with the ball
2. Tilting the stick backward causing the ball to bounce over the stick
3. Failing to relax the grip as the ball makes contact with the face of the stick

Tackling

A tackle is a legal means of taking the ball or puck away from an opponent. The defensive player should move in toward her opponent with her eyes on the ball, her body well forward, with her weight evenly distributed over both feet. The blade of the stick should be held close to the ground (fig. 14.8a). The tackle should be made when the ball is farthest from the opponent's stick. At this moment, the defensive player should place the face of her blade on the ball and perpendicular to the ground (fig. 14.8b). As soon as the defensive player has possession of the ball, she should immediately pass it to another player or quickly dribble it away from her opponent.

Figure 14.8a Approach with blade close to the ground.

Figure 14.8b Blade is on the ball and perpendicular to the ground.

Common Faults

1. Taking the eyes off the ball as the opponent approaches
2. Swinging the stick forward
3. Failure to pass or dribble when possession of the ball is gained.

Dodging   A dodge is an evasive movement that an offensive player uses to move the ball past his opponent. It is essentially a controlled pass to oneself. In the diagram, the dribbler pushes the ball to the right, then runs around the other side to pick up his own pass. The most important part of this movement is the timing. The ball must be pushed late enough to prevent the opponent from backing up to gain possession of the ball.

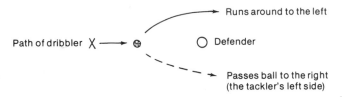

Path of dribbler X ⟶ ⊕   ◯ Defender

Runs around to the left

Passes ball to the right
(the tackler's left side)

Common Faults

1. Slowing down just before making a move and a pass
2. Keeping the ball too far in front, allowing the defensive player to tackle and gain possession of the ball

Face-off (Bully)   The face-off or "bully" used to start the game, after a goal is scored, and when the ball is prevented from further play by two opposing players. The face-off is taken between two opposing players, who stand on either side of the ball with their left sides facing their opponent's goal line. Both players start with the blades of their sticks on the ground and on their own side of the ball (fig. 14.9). Both players then lift and touch their sticks over the ball, then touch the ground. They do this three times, then each tries to gain possession of the ball.

Figure 14.9 Stick is on player's own
side of the ball.

Roll-in

A roll-in is a means of putting the ball back into play after it has been sent over the sideline. The roll-in is an underarm rolling action. The player must keep her feet and stick behind the sideline until the ball has been rolled into play.

Figure 14.10 Roll-in

Practice Activities

The following practice activities are, in many respects, modifications of soccer drills and relay activities. A few hockey-type activities have also been included in this section. Since hockey, particularly field hockey, may be a completely new game to many children, these practice activities are extremely important in developing basic skills.

Dribbling Activities

One of the most important skills to learn is dribbling the ball using the flat surface of the blade. The following activities should help children learn to move the ball in a variety of directions by shifting their bodies and the blade surface in the direction they want the ball to go.

Individual Activities

Free Dribbling

Give the children an opportunity to see how well they can move the ball anywhere in the field. Begin with a walking speed, then increase to a jog, and finally go to a run. After several minutes of practice have each child attempt one of the following:

1. Dribble forward, shift left, shift right, and repeat.
2. Repeat above, but stop and control ball before shifting to a new direction.

Dribble around Obstacles

Set up one obstacle (milk carton, tin can, or traffic cone) and dribble around it. Dribble around the right side, then the left side. Dribble around either side, stop the ball, turn around, and return around the opposite side. Add two or more obstacles and repeat.

Partner Activities

Modify the partner activities suggested for soccer (pp. 238-39) to dribbling with a stick.

Group Activities

Modify the group activities suggested for soccer (p. 239) to dribbling with a stick.

Passing and Fielding Activities

The partner activities suggested for soccer (pp. 236-37) can be used when partners practice passing and fielding a hockey ball or puck. Teachers should also note the suggestions about applying the problem-solving method on page 237. This approach can work extremely well with this type of activity.

Group Activities

The following group relays can be adapted to passing and fielding a hockey ball:

1. Zigzag passing, page 237
2. Circle passing, page 237
3. Goal shooting, page 238

Push Pass

Formation
Arrange three players according to the diagram.

Player No. 2 ⊗

⊗ Player No. 1

⊗   Player No. 3

Basic Drill
Player number one passes to player number two. Player number two returns to player number one, who then passes to player number three. Three returns the ball to one and the sequence begins again.

Variations
1. Pass from player one to two to three to one and continue in the same pattern.
2. Repeat above with every player moving one position to the left. Player one dribbles to two's position and passes to two, who has shifted to three's position.

Dodging and Tackling

The partner and group activities suggested for soccer can be adapted to practicing dodging and tackling skills used in hockey activities. (See page 244)

Lead-up Games

The lead-up games described in this section are arranged according to their difficulty. Modify the rules to meet the class's general level of ability. Also modify any game to accommodate play on indoor or outdoor surfaces.

Lead-up Game	Grade	Page
Mass Field Hockey	4-5	258
Line Field Hockey	4-6	259
Zone Field Hockey	5-6	259
Substitute field hockey ball and sticks in the following games described in previous chapters:		
Sideline Hockey	4-5	242
Pin Hockey	5-6	243
Seven-Man Hockey	5-6	244

Mass Field Hockey (4-5)

Formation: Any available field. Place markers on the corners of the area to be used and draw a line across the middle.
Equipment: Four markers, one ball (perforated plastic ball or tennis ball), and one stick for each player
Players: Half of the class on each team
Skills: Running, dribbling, passing, and driving

The game begins with each team lining up behind its own goal line. The ball is placed in the middle of the field. On signal, each team tries to gain possession of the ball. A goal is scored when the ball crosses the opponent's goal line. A free hit is awarded for any foul or violation (see field hockey rules later in chapter) and is taken at the point where the foul occurred. If a ball passes over the sideline, a roll-in is taken by the nonoffending team.

Line Field Hockey (4-6)

Formation: Arrange playing area as shown in diagram. Players are numbered from one to the last player.
Equipment: One stick for each player and one ball for each game
Players: Six to eight players on each team
Skills: Shooting, passing, and stopping

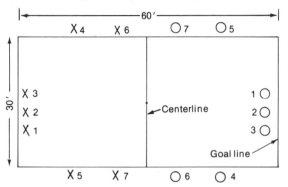

The ball is placed in the middle of the field. On signal, player number one from each team runs out and tries to gain possession of the ball. Once the ball is in possession, a player may pass to any side player or try to shoot the ball over his opponent's goal line. No other player on his team may enter the field of play or score a goal. After each goal, rotate players and start the game again.

Variations

1. Allow two players to come out each time.
2. Shorten the distance between goals as skill improves.

Zone Field Hockey (5-6)

Formation: Playing area arranged as in diagram
Equipment: One stick for each player and one ball for each game
Players: Ten to twelve on each team
Skills: All hockey skills

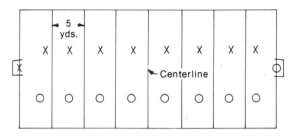

The game starts with a face-off between two opposing players at the center of the field. All players must remain in their own five-yard zone. The game is played like regular field hockey. After each goal is scored, the player in the zone closest to the centerline becomes the new goalie, and all other players move forward into the next zone.

Field Hockey: Rules and Regulations

The following basic rules of field hockey are essentially a modification of regulation field hockey. By dividing a playing field in half, two games with seven players on a team can be played (one goalie, one fullback, two halfbacks, and three forwards). Since the game is similar to soccer, it is wise to introduce it after the class has been exposed to a unit of soccer.

Note: The playing positions for field hockey are the same as for soccer (p. 245). Also, the same field dimensions can be used for both games. The semicircle (or penalty area) is the only difference in the general layout of the field.

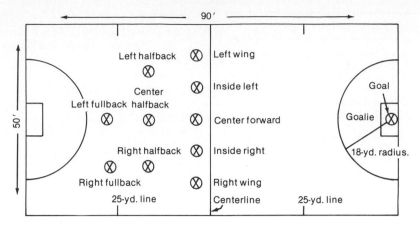

Field diagram labels:
- 90' (top width)
- 50' (left height)
- Left halfback
- Center
- Left fullback / halfback
- Left wing
- Inside left
- Goal
- Goalie
- 18-yd. radius.
- Center forward
- Right halfback
- Inside right
- Right fullback
- Right wing
- 25-yd. line
- Centerline
- 25-yd. line

I. Field of play and players: Field approximately ninety by fifty yards

II. Time: Two periods of thirty minutes (divide your available time in two). Teams change ends at halftime.

III. Face-off (or "bully"): This is taken at the center of the field at the start of the game, after each goal, and after halftime. After the third hit of the sticks, one of the two players must hit the ball and put it into play. During the face-off, all other players must stand on their own side of the face-off line until the ball is played.

IV. Ball rolls over sideline: When a ball is forced over a sideline, a roll-in is awarded to the opposing team.

V. Ball sent over end line:
   A. If by the attacking team, the defending team is awarded a free hit fifteen yards from the end line opposite the spot where the ball crossed.
   B. If by the defending team, the attacking team is awarded a corner hit. The hit must be taken from a point on the end line within five yards from the corner of the field.

VI. Fouls committed outside of the penalty area (the semicircles in front of goals): A free hit is awarded to the opposing team. All players must be five yards away from the player taking the hit. Fouls are
   A. using any part of the stick except the *flat surface of the blade*
   B. raising the stick above the shoulder
   C. using any part of body to propel the ball, although hand may be used to stop the ball
   D. hitting another player, or hooking, slashing, or interfering with opponent's stick
   E. being offside, which means that an offensive player who is in his opponent's half of the field and does not have possession of the ball must have three opponents between him and the goal line.

VII. Fouls committed inside the penalty area:
   A. If by the attacking team, the defending team is awarded a free hit from anywhere inside the semicircle.
   B. If by the defending team, any player on the attacking team is given a free hit on a spot five yards in front of the center of the goal. All other players, except the goalie, must remain behind the 25-yard line until the penalty hit is taken.

Floor Hockey: Rules and Regulations

I. Formation: The playing area is the entire gymnasium floor or a suitable hard-surfaced playing ground. Goalposts (jump standards or cardboard boxes are adequate) should be placed six feet apart and away from the wall to allow for play behind the net.

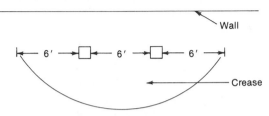

II. Equipment: Floor hockey sticks, forty inches long with rounded and padded ends, or wands, and regulation pucks or a deck tennis ring. If the latter is used, wrap it with plastic electrical tape for additional strength and to reduce floor friction.

III. Players: Six on each team—one goalkeeper, two defensemen, and three forwards

IV. Skills: Running, dribbling, and shooting

V. Face-off: The game begins with a face-off in the middle of the floor. Two players face each other, with their left sides facing their opponent's goal. Each places the tip of his wand or the blade of his stick on the floor alongside the puck. Each then lifts his wand from the floor and taps his opponent's wand. This is repeated three times. After the third tap the puck may be played by either player.
Face-offs are taken
A. to start the game
B. after every goal
C. after a "held puck" (two players immobilizing the movement of the puck)
D. after the puck slides under the bleachers or leaves the playing area
E. after an accident or illegal play
When the puck is immobilized in the area behind the goal, or after a violation occurs near the crease, the face-off is taken in the foul circle in front of the crease. During the face-off, all players must stay at least five feet away from the face-off players.

VI. Goals: a goal is scored when the puck passes completely over the goal line through the goalposts, providing it has been flipped from a point outside of the crease. A player must have both hands on the stick when involved in any play.

VII. Goalie: The goalkeeper is the only player who is allowed to handle the puck. He may pick it up to clear it but must throw it to the side or behind. He is not allowed to throw it forward. If he does, a face-off is taken five yards in front of and to the side of the goal. The goalkeeper is allowed to go down on one knee but may not sit or lie on the floor. In addition, he must keep his stick upright, never flat on the floor.

VIII. Time: The length of a game will depend upon the available time. Teachers can set a certain number of minutes for three periods to allow teams to change ends. All rules relating to substitutions and serious infractions should be made by each teacher to cope with local conditions.

IX. Free flip: A free flip is awarded for any of the following infractions:
A. Carrying: Lifting the puck and carrying it. The puck must slide along the floor.
B. Slashing: Striking another player, his stick, or the puck.
C. Charging: Body checking is allowed so long as both players are playing the puck. All other forms of charging will result in a free flip.
D. Kicking: The puck may be stopped by the foot, but in no case may it be kicked in any direction.
E. High sticking: Passing the stick above the level of the shoulder.
F. Crease shooting: Shooting at the goal when the player or his stick is in the crease.
G. Third man: A third player entering the play when two players are fighting for possession of the puck.
H. Boarding: Holding a player against the walls or other boundaries.
I. Goalkeeper infractions: See Section VII. All opponents must be at least five yards away from the player taking a free flip or behind the goal line if the penalty occurs within five yards of the goal. A goal may be scored directly from a free flip.

14

Evaluative Techniques

There are very few standardized hockey tests for elementary school children, so the teacher must develop her own. Since this is a relatively new activity, several of the basic skills can easily be developed into objective test items. And most classroom teachers can also make reasonably accurate subjective ratings of the child's general playing ability.

If a teacher wishes to develop a simple test battery, tests No. 2, 3, and 4 in the previous chapter on soccer activities can be modified for a basic test battery for hockey. Other items should be added according to the teacher's discretion.

Flag or Touch Football Activities

15

Emphasis and Skill Presentation

Teaching Procedures

Description of Skills

Practice Activities

Lead-up Games

Touch Football: Rules and Regulations

Evaluative Techniques

When football is suggested as an appropriate activity for elementary school children, parents and teachers usually think of the competitive game involving expensive equipment, elaborate coaching, and the problems associated with a contact sport. These points are valid and should be taken into consideration. However, this does not mean that modified games involving many of the skills of football should not be taught to children in the upper intermediate grades. Appropriate football skills and rules can be taught through modified games such as Field Ball, flag football, and touch football. None of the practice activities or lead-up games suggested in this chapter involves tackling or any other form of body contact. Thus, the nature of these activities, coupled with such instructional techniques as station work and inventive games, provides an opportunity for boys and girls to participate in a cooperative and enjoyable way.

This chapter has been arranged to assist teachers in developing an instructional unit that takes into consideration such factors as mixed-sex classes, variable levels of instruction, and the equipment available. It is strongly suggested that flag rather than touch football be emphasized in the regular instructional period. Flag football is the same as touch football, except that two flags located on the seat of each player are removed. Pulling off these flags avoids disputes over whether a player was actually touched with two hands, and it is a safer game.

Emphasis and Skill Presentation

The problems of teaching football skills are very similar to those found in teaching basketball and softball. Many boys, even ten- and eleven-year-olds, can throw a spiral pass, punt a ball, and elucidate the advantages of a single- or double-wing formation. Other children may not have even thrown or kicked a football. Equal opportunities for girls also must be considered. Girls do enjoy throwing and catching a football and playing many of the lead-up games described in this chapter. However, cultural patterns have generally denied girls an opportunity to play football and, consequently, their understanding and skill are much less developed than the boys'.

Although there are major differences in the level of skill within each grade, the following suggested sequence of presenting skills will provide a basic guideline for most elementary school situations.

Basic throwing and catching skills have normally been learned in the primary grades, so the main task for fourth graders is to learn to throw and catch an oblong-type ball. They should also be introduced to punting.

The major skills and playing strategies should be taught in the fifth and sixth grades. Children in these grades should learn the various stances and how to throw a ball to a moving receiver. They should also learn other ways of passing the ball and a few simple play patterns.

Suggested Sequence of Presenting Football Skills and Rules

Skills and Rules	Grade Level Grade 4	Grade 5	Grade 6
Passing			
Forward pass	Introduce	Increase accuracy and distance	Increase accuracy and distance
Lateral pass		Introduce	Increase accuracy
Centering	Introduce	Increase accuracy	Increase accuracy
Rules: Passing and receiving	Introduce		
Scoring	Introduce		
Catching			
Pass receiving	Introduce	Refinement	Refinement
Receiving a kicked ball	Introduce	Refinement	Refinement
Stance			
Three-point stance		Introduce	Refinement
Four-point stance		Introduce	Refinement
Rules: Line of scrimmage		Introduce	
Punting		Introduce	Refinement
Rules: Kickoff	Introduce		
Safety		Introduce	
Blocking		Introduce	Refinement
Rules: Use of hands and shoulders		Introduce	
Other Rules			
Downs		Introduce	
Position and plays		Introduce	

Teaching Procedures

Teaching flag or touch football activities presents a few major problems for most upper elementary school classes. As stated earlier, football has been mainly a boy's activity. Even with mixed classes, girls were usually given other games to play while the boys enjoyed touch or flag football. But most girls enjoy football activities and, therefore, should participate in many practice activities and lead-up games, with a few modifications to cope with differences in skill levels and previous football experience.

Inadequate numbers of footballs are also often a major problem for teachers planning partner and small group practice activities.

The following suggestions are intended to assist the teacher in developing an integrated and meaningful football unit.

Station Work

Station work is basically organizing the field into stations where specific skills are practiced by small groups. Each group practices the skill assigned to a station for several minutes, then rotates to the next station. In the accompanying example, boys and girls may be mixed at each station, or they may be separated if their skill

varies widely or they definitely prefer to work with their own sex. If only a few footballs are available, use them at stations No. 3 and 5 and use a soccer or utility ball for the other stations.

In addition, the following considerations and safety procedures should be included in a football instruction unit:

1. Use junior-size footballs.
2. Play flag rather than touch football. If commercial flags are not available, strips of cloth may be used.
3. All positions should be rotated frequently to permit each player to experience and enjoy the skills required for each position.
4. If there is a marked difference in the skill level between boys and girls, separate games may be warranted.

Inventive Games Approach

It has been stated in previous chapters that the inventive games approach can be used to teach skills, as well as to nurture children's creative abilities. This approach can be applied to football, too. If two boys and two girls are assigned a drill such as "center, throw, and catch," the boys will normally show more skill and thus will dominate the practice session. However, a chal-

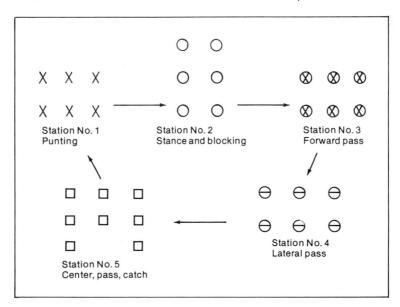

lenge such as, "In groups of four, make up a drill in which the ball must be alternately passed from a boy to a girl," encourages cooperative planning and copes with the problem of one sex dominating.

Adding small equipment such as milk cartons or traffic cones can also break down the rigidity of many football drills and make the practice activity less competitive and more enjoyable. The teacher could add, ". . . in some way use four milk cartons in your drill," to the earlier challenge. Passing is still emphasized in the drill, but the additional equipment adds to the challenge and encourages everyone in the group to suggest ways of incorporating it.

Description of Skills

Touch or flag football requires the same skills as the competitive game, with the exception of tackling and blocking. For elementary school children the emphasis should be on passing, catching, and kicking skills, team positions, and simple play formations.

Passing

Three types of passes are used in touch football. The forward pass is similar to the baseball throw; however, it requires a different hand grip and release so that the ball spirals. Lateral passing is a sideward throw of the ball and is an effective technique virtually anywhere in the field of play. Hiking or centering the ball is a throw used solely by the center to start each play from the line of scrimmage.

Forward Pass

Figure 15.1

In executing a forward pass, the player should stand with the opposite foot to his throwing arm forward and pointing in the direction of the throw. His weight is evenly distributed on both feet, and he holds the ball with both hands. The fingers of his throwing hand grip the lace behind the center of the ball, and the other hand holds the front and side of the ball (fig. 15.1). The ball is shifted back past the ear and the body rotated away from the throw. The elbow of the throwing arm should be kept high (fig. 15.2a). Young children with proportionately smaller hands find this difficult and tend to drop the elbow in order to hold the ball in this position. The ball is then rotated toward the target, the forearm and wrist are thrust forward, and the wrist is dropped to allow the ball to roll off the fingers (fig. 15.2c). This "roll-off" gives the ball the spiral action.

  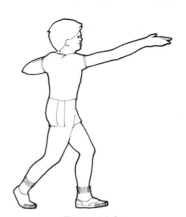

Figure 15.2a

Figure 15.2b

Figure 15.2c

Common Faults

1. Holding the ball too close to the palm of the hand
2. Releasing the ball too soon
3. Failing to snap the wrist just before the ball is released off the fingertips

Lateral Pass

The lateral pass is basically a sideways throw of the ball. The ball is shifted from a one-arm carry to two hands. Once the ball is firmly held in both hands, shift it to the opposite side of the intended throw (fig. 15.3a). Then bring the ball across the body and release it about waist-high (fig. 15.3b).

Figure 15.3a Shift ball to opposite side.

Figure 15.3b Release ball about waist-high.

Common Faults

1. Releasing the ball too soon
2. Releasing the ball with too much force, causing it to rebound out of the receiver's hand

15

Centering or Hiking the Ball

Once the ball is placed into position for the next play, it cannot be removed from the ground until a pass, or hike, is made by the center player. The center positions his body in a wide stride position, with his knees bent and his body weight well forward over his shoulders and arms. He then grasps the ball in the same way as a forward pass (fig. 15.4). On the signal from the quarterback, the center extends his arms and hands backward through his legs and releases the ball off his fingertips.

Figure 15.4 Hiking or centering the ball

Common Faults

1. Lifting the ball off the ground before the quarterback has called the signal.
2. Passing the ball backward too low or too high for the receiver

Catching

A ball thrown from a hike or a lateral pass is normally caught with an underhand catch. But a forward pass is usually caught while on the run, requiring balance, timing, and a cradling action of the hands. This skill requires an accurate pass and lots of practice on the part of the receiver.

At the moment the receiver is ready to catch the ball, he should be turned slightly toward the passer, with his hands held forward and upward. His elbows should be slightly flexed and his fingers spread (fig. 15.5a). He reaches for the ball (fig. 15.5b) and immediately pulls it toward his body, then shifts it to a carrying position. The ball should be carried with one hand under and around the front end of the ball. The other end of the ball is held close to the body by the inside of the forearm and elbow.

Figure 15.5a Elbows flexed and fingers spread

Figure 15.5b Cradling action of hands

Common Faults

1. Failing to judge and reach the position to catch the ball
2. Failing to reach for the ball
3. Holding the ball too far away from the body while running with it

Stance   The type of starting position a player takes depends upon whether he is in an offensive or defensive situation and whether he is playing on the line or in the backfield. The following stances are typical positions for defensive or offensive playing situations.

Three-Point Stance   Assume a wide crouched and stride position with the knees slightly bent, the seat down, the left arm forward, and the hand touching the ground (fig. 15.6). The body weight should be well forward, and the head should be up and the eyes focused straight ahead.

Figure 15.6 Offensive position: three-point stance

Four-Point Stance   Assume a wide crouched and stride position with the knees slightly bent, the seat down, both arms forward, and the hands touching the ground (fig. 15.7). The body weight should be well forward.

Figure 15.7 Defensive position: four-point stance

Common Faults

1. Failing to lean forward over the hands
2. Looking or pointing in the direction of the move

Punting

In touch football, the ball may be punted or kicked from a stationary or "placekick" position. Punting a football is very similar to punting a soccer ball, with the football contacted on the top side of the instep and with a more pronounced follow-through of the kicking leg. Since tennis shoes are usually worn in physical education class, the placekick should be performed with the top of the foot and not the toe. This means the ball should slant toward the kicker.

The player stands with his right foot slightly forward and his weight evenly distributed over both feet. He holds the ball with his right hand on the right side near the front of the ball. His left hand holds the left side of the ball (fig. 15.8a). He steps right, then left, and simultaneously drops the ball as he brings his kicking leg forward (fig. 15.8b). The ball should be contacted with the top and slightly outer side of the foot (fig. 15.8c). He then continues the forward and upward movement of his kicking leg (fig. 15.8d). His arms should extend sideways to assist balance.

a. Hold ball in front.　　b. Drop ball.　　c. Contact ball on top and outer side of foot.　　d. Follow through.

Figure 15.8

Common Faults

1. Throwing rather than dropping the ball from the hands
2. Kicking the ball with the toe
3. Failing to straighten the leg and to follow through sufficiently

Blocking   A player in flag or touch football may block by simply placing his body in the way of an opponent. The blocker must stay in contact with the ground and must not use his hands.

Figure 15.9 Act as an obstruction.

Common Faults

1. Using fists and shoulders to stop an opponent
2. Failing to move into an effective blocking position

Practice Activities

Football normally requires two or more players in practice situations. Begin with partner activities; if there is a limited supply of footballs, use soccer or utility balls.

Partner Activities

Normally two or more football skills are practiced in the same drill. The following partner activities can be adapted to each grade level:

1. Partners pass and catch.
2. One partner runs and tries to catch the other's pass.
3. One partner centers, then runs forward to catch the other's pass.
4. Both run and pass back and forth, using a lateral pass.

5. Inventive drills. Make up drills involving passing and catching. Later, add small equipment.
6. Partners punt and catch.
7. One partner runs with (or without) the ball and the other partner tries to block, as in basketball.
8. Repeat above with one partner trying to tag the other.

Group Activities

Several relays described in other chapters can be used to practice football skills. Refer to the following:

Activity	Page	Used for	Change to Football
Zigzag Relay	201	Volleyball	Substitute a football
Shuttle Volleying	289	Volleyball	Substitute a football

Blocking Practice

Formation
Arrange the field and players as shown in the diagram.

```
    X          X  Offense  X        X          X
  ⊢ 8 ft. ⊣   _____   _____   _____   _____

    O          O  Defense  O        O          O
```

Basic Drill
One player is designated as the offense, the other as defense. Both assume a football stance position. On the signal "hike," the offensive player attempts to get past the defensive player. The offensive player must stay within the eight-foot line and may feint, dodge, or do any movement to get around the defensive player. Neither player is allowed to use his hands or cause body contact.

Variations
Repeat the drill with a ball.

Pass and Defend

Formation
Arrange field and players as shown in the diagram.

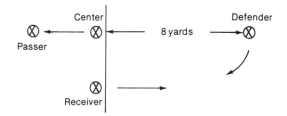

Basic Drill
The center snaps the ball to the passer. As soon as the passer has the ball, the receiver runs forward and tries to catch the pass. The defender moves at the same time and tries to prevent the receiver from catching the pass or to intercept it. If the skill level is high enough, allow the receiver and defender to move at the moment the snap is made.

Lead-up Games

The lead-up games described in this section may be played by boys and girls together or separately, depending upon the children's ability. If their skill and experience vary widely, girls and boys will normally be much happier playing separate games. This is particularly true with fifth and sixth grade children.

Lead-up Game	Grade	Page
One-Down Football	4-6	274
Punt and Catch	4-6	274
Punt Back	4-6	275
Field Ball	5-6	275

The following games described in other chapters can also be adapted to touch football activities:

Activity	Page
Soccer Dodge Ball	242
Boundary Ball	242
Sideline Soccer	242
California Kickball	195
European Handball	197
Borden Ball	194

One-Down Football (4-6)

Formation: Field and team positions arranged as in diagram
Equipment: One football
Players: Eight on each team
Skills: Throwing, catching, and tagging

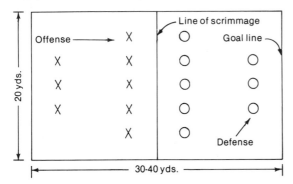

To start the game, both teams line up on opposite sides of the centerline. One team is designated as the offense and is given one down to score a touchdown. After the hike, the ball may be run or passed any number of times in any direction from any position on the field. The defensive team attempts to tag the ball carrier below the waist with two hands. If a player is tagged before he reaches the opponent's goal line, the ball is downed and the other team takes its down at this point. If a ball is intercepted, the game continues with the defensive team becoming the offensive team.

Teaching suggestions

1. When introducing this game, have all players play "man-to-man," that is, linemen checking linemen and backs checking backs. Later, variations can be made to meet the wishes of the defensive team.
2. Play same game using only the lateral pass.

Punt and Catch (4-6)

Formation: Field and team positions arranged as shown in diagram
Equipment: One football
Players: Eight or nine on each team
Skills: Punting and catching

A player from one team punts the ball over the neutral zone into his opponent's area. The opponent who is closest to the ball tries to catch it. If successful, he punts the ball back and the game continues. If an opponent misses a catch (it must be in the air), the kicking side is awarded one point. If the ball does not pass out of the neutral zone, the captain of the opposite team may enter the zone to retrieve it. No score is awarded if the ball lands outside the playing area.

Teaching suggestions

1. Rotate the lines on each team after a number of points have been scored or at set intervals.
2. Play the same game using a forward pass.

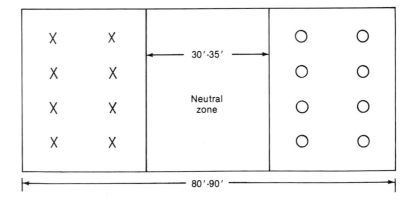

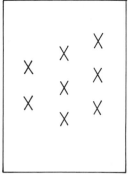

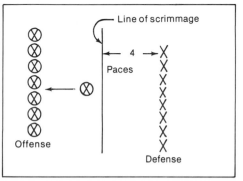

Field Ball

Receiving position for kickoff

Offensive and defensive lineup positions

Punt Back (4-6)

Formation: Half of a regular playing field, with each team scattered on its own side of the field
Equipment: One football for each game
Players: Eight to ten on each team
Skills: Punting and catching

The object of this game is to punt the ball over the opponent's goal line. One player begins the game by punting the ball from his own twenty-five-yard line. Once the game is started, opposing players must stay at least ten yards apart. If the ball is caught by a player on the opposite team and he calls "mark" and remains motionless for two seconds, he has two options. First, he may take five steps and then punt the ball, or second, he may pass it to any teammate. All players on his team, however, may be checked (as in basketball) as they try to catch the pass. If a player catches the ball, he must kick it from the point of the catch. If the catcher moves his feet while he is catching the ball or fails to call "mark," he is allowed only three steps before kicking the ball. If the ball is not caught, the player who secures the ball must punt it from the point where it was stopped.

A ball that goes over the sideline is punted back from the point where it went over the line. A ball that is caught in the air behind the goal line does not count as a point; it is put back into play by a punt from the goal line. One point is awarded for a successful punt over the goal line provided it is not caught. The ball is put into play again at the twenty-five-yard line.

Variations

Use a placekick or a forward pass instead of a punt.

Field Ball (5-6)

Formation: Arrange field and team positions as shown in the diagram. The length and width of the field are optional.
Equipment: One football
Players: Eight on each team
Skills: Kicking, passing, catching, and running

The game is started with one team kicking the ball into the opponent's half of the field. The kicking team may not advance until the ball has been caught or recovered. (Balls kicked out-of-bounds are kicked again.) The receiving team starts its advance by either running with the ball or passing it. Any number of passes are permitted in any direction and from any position on the field. Opponents must tag the ball carrier with two hands below the waist. When this occurs, the opponents take over the down.

Note the offensive and defensive lineups in the diagram. The offensive team has one down to score a touchdown (6 points). Any play that starts from a kickoff return or a run back from an intercepted pass is not counted as a down. Players may not block, trip, hold, or push an opponent. If the offensive team fouls, the ball is awarded to the defensive team. If the defensive team fouls, the ball is advanced eight paces from where the foul took place. The ball may not, however, be placed closer than five paces from the goal line.

Teaching suggestions

1. Determine your own length of a playing half.
2. Restrict the game to one type of pass, such as a forward pass or a lateral pass.
3. Play the same game with a soccer ball.

Touch Football: Rules and Regulations

It is recommended that upper elementary school children play seven-person touch or flag football. Commercial flags may be purchased from local sports stores, or you may improvise your own. (Flags are sometimes called tags.)

I. Field layout and lineups:

II. To start game: The game is started with a kickoff (punt or placekick) from the goal line. The ball must be kicked past the centerline and must land within the field of play. If the first ball is kicked out-of-bounds, it is kicked again. If the second kick goes out-of-bounds, the other team starts play at its twenty-yard line. The kickoff team may recover the ball only after the other team touches and fumbles it.

III. Offensive play:
   A. Once a player who is returning the kickoff is touched, the ball is placed on the spot where he was tagged. The line drawn through this spot is known as the *scrimmage line.* In all cases the ball must be placed five paces in from the sideline.
   B. The offensive team has four downs to move the ball into the next twenty-yard zone or to score a touchdown. Always start a new series of downs whenever a team crosses a zone line.
   C. The offensive team must have at least three players on the scrimmage line when a play begins. The center player must pass the ball backward through his legs. A backfield player who receives the ball may hand off or throw a lateral or forward pass from behind the line of scrimmage. Any player except the center

Field layout:

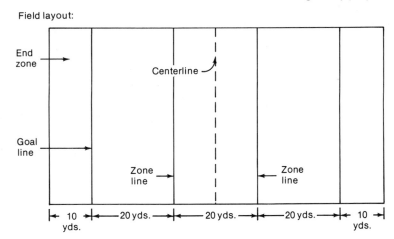

Offensive and defensive lineup positions:

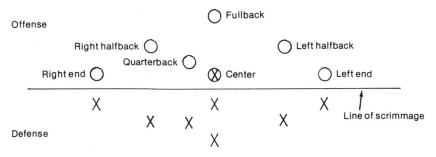

may receive the forward pass. The offensive team may punt on any down, providing it calls for a punt formation. When this occurs, neither team may cross the scrimmage line until the punt receiver has caught the ball.

IV. Defensive play:
   A. The defending team must remain behind the scrimmage line until the ball has left the opposing center's hands. A special rule applies to a punt, as previously described.
   B. A defensive player may stop the ball carrier if he places two hands on or below his opponent's waist.

V. Blocking: A player may block only by placing his body in the way of an opponent. Neither team is allowed to use hands or any form of body contact.

VI. Scoring: Points are awarded for the following:
   A. Touchdown: Six points. Following the touchdown, one play or down is given to the scoring team from the three-yard line, and one more point is awarded if the team crosses the goal line.
   B. Safety: Two points. The defensive team is awarded two points if the team in possession of the ball is tagged behind its own goal line. Immediately following the safety the ball is put into play by the team scored against by a kickoff from behind the goal line.

VII. Touchback: A touchback occurs when a defensive player intercepts a ball behind his own goal line and does not run it out or when the ball is kicked over the goal line by the offensive team. The ball is taken to the twenty-yard line and given to the defending team.

VIII. Penalties: Award five yards to the non-offending team for the following infractions:
   A. Pushing, holding, or tripping
   B. Unsportsmanlike conduct
   C. Interfering with the pass receiver
   D. Offside

IX. Length of game: Two eight-minute periods

Evaluative Techniques

There are a few standardized tests that are designed to measure the basic football skills. The majority of these tests, however, are designed for high school or college level players, so they must be modified for elementary school-age players. The "teacher-made" test battery that follows can be administered without elaborate equipment and in a short period of time. Use students to assist in testing, and keep scores from year to year in order to develop appropriate norms for your school.

Touch Football Skill Test						
Name	Accuracy Pass (total points)	Punting (total points)	Ball Carrying (total points)	Subjective Evaluation (50 points)	Total Score	Grade
1 2 3 4		Rank all total scores for the class, then convert to letter grades or ratings (superior, good, etc.) ⟶				

Test No. 1   **Accuracy pass**

Place a target on the wall as shown in the diagram. Each player is given ten consecutive throws from behind the starting line. He must use a forward pass. Score six, four, and two points for hits within each respective circle. If the ball hits a line, award the higher score. Record the total score.

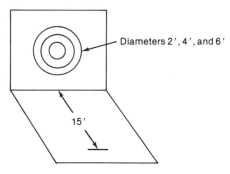

Diameters 2′, 4′, and 6′

15′

Test No. 2   **Punting**

Place lines on the field as shown in the diagram. Stakes can be used as a substitute for gypsum lines. Each player must punt a regulation-size football from behind the starting line. Mark where the ball lands with a stick or small object. Allow a total of three kicks and record the highest score. Yards are equivalent to points.

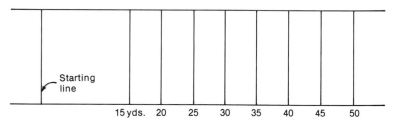

Starting line

15 yds.   20   25   30   35   40   45   50

Test No. 3   **Ball carrying**

Arrange four chairs as shown in the diagram. Place a ball on the starting line. Each player stands behind the starting line with both hands resting on his knees. On signal, he picks up the football, places it in his left hand and runs around the left side of the first chair. He continues the zigzag running pattern, changing the ball to his opposite hand as he passes each chair. Allow thirty seconds for the test. One point is awarded for each chair he passes correctly. Two trials are allowed, with the highest score recorded.

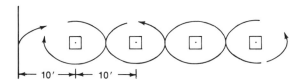

|← 10′ →|← 10′ →|

Test No. 4   **Subjective evaluation**
Establish criteria that represent the skills and playing ability required in touch football, such as passing, feinting, kicking, and defensive ability. The teacher or a group of three players awards each player a total score ranging from zero to fifty points. When three players are judging, take an average of their scores.

Volleyball Activities

16

Emphasis and Skill Presentation

Teaching Procedures

Description of Skills

Practice Activities

Lead-up Games

Volleyball: Rules and Regulations

Evaluative Techniques

Volleyball was originated by William G. Morgan in 1895 while he was teaching at the YMCA in Holyoke, Massachusetts. Although the rules, number of players, and size of the ball have changed since that first game, volleyball can be classified as an American contribution to the world of sports. Today, it is played by more than fifty million people in more than sixty countries each year. This phenomenal growth in such a short time is probably due to the game's simplicity, enjoyment, and contributions to physical fitness.

Because volleyball can be adapted to the available facilities and varying levels of proficiency, it is a particularly good activity for the upper elementary school physical education program.

Emphasis and Skill Presentation

One of the most difficult tasks in teaching physical education is to determine whether the children are already familiar with the activity you wish to teach and whether they have the potential to develop the required skills. Volleyball is no exception. Some children already understand the rules of the game and have acquired a few of the basic skills. Others may not have seen a volleyball game or even have hit the ball correctly. With these factors in mind, the suggested sequence of presenting skills and rules that follows should be considered as a basic guideline.

Prior to grade four most children have learned to hit a utility ball from a bounce (Two Square and Four Square) or to hit a balloon or beachball with a two-hand overhand hit. The main skills of volleyball, however, are normally taught from grades four through six. In grade four, as indicated in the accompanying chart, the overhand pass and underhand serve should be introduced with a utility ball or beachball. Once the skill level is high enough, a regulation volleyball should be used. Serving distances, as well as the height of the net, should also be adjusted to each class's ability.

Suggested Sequence of Presenting Volleyball Skills and Rules

Skills and Rules	Grade Level		
	Grade 4	Grade 5	Grade 6
Volleying			
Overhand pass	Introduce	Refinement	Refinement
Forearm pass (bumping)		Introduce	Introduce
Rules: Number of hits	Introduce		
Rotation	Introduce		
Line violations	Introduce		
Personal fouls		Introduce	
Serving			
Underhand serve	Introduce	Refinement	Refinement
Overhand serve			Introduce
Rules: Serving positions		Introduce	
Side out and points		Introduce	
Setup		Introduce	Refinement
Spike			Introduce
Block			Introduce
Recovery from net			Introduce
Other rules			
All other official rules			Introduce

16

The major emphasis throughout grade five should be on developing the accuracy and power of the pass and the serve. These children are also ready to learn the forearm or bump pass and how to set up the ball to their teammates. Although children in this grade enjoy playing regulation volleyball, it should be played on a limited basis. Such games as Modified Volleyball and Sideline Volleyball are more appropriate as they contribute to skill development yet allow for greater participation and success by every player.

Sixth-grade children still need a lot of practice in the underhand serve and in volleying with both the overhand and underhand pass. The lead-up games later in this chapter provide this opportunity and should be extensively used in any unit of instruction. These children should have an opportunity, however, to learn and practice the overhand serve and spiking, blocking, and net recovery skills and to apply them in a regulation game.

Teaching Procedures

A general format for planning a unit of instruction has been discussed extensively in previous chapters. Teachers should review pages 115-17 prior to developing a volleyball unit. In addition, the sample lesson plans described on pages 152-56 and the suggestions about incorporating the creative games approach on page 173 can be applied to volleyball activities.

The following suggestions may help the teacher with some of the problems that are unique to teaching volleyball activities.

1. When there is only one instructional area, such as a gymnasium, choose or modify activities to be played on smaller courts (divide the volleyball court in half) and require fewer players (six or less on a team).

2. During the initial stages of a volleyball unit, use lightweight utility balls (8½ inches) or heavy balloons. Young children, particularly those in grade four, normally lack sufficient arm and wrist strength to hit a heavy ball. Lighter balls are also slower, giving the child a little more time to get into position.

3. Adjust the height of the net to the ability of the class. As a general guideline, the net should be six feet high for fourth graders and seven feet high for fifth and sixth graders. Ropes with a few ribbons spaced every few feet can be used as a substitute net.

4. Require the ball to be rolled to the server in all lead-up games or any type of modified volleyball activity that involves two teams on opposite sides of the net. Experienced teachers can verify the amount of time this simple procedure will save.

Description of Skills

There are two basic skills in volleyball, serving and passing or volleying a ball. Each of these skills, however, can be modified, such as the two-hand underhand volley requiring use of the forearms. Basic skills for intermediate grades are described and illustrated in this section.

Passing or Volleying

The ball may be passed or volleyed to another player or over the net by an underhand or overhand hit. Both hands must be used in the overhand pass, while the forearms are normally used in the underhand pass. Children should be taught to watch the ball, not their hands or opponents. The body weight should be evenly distributed on both feet before the ball reaches the player. Finally, stress follow-through with the hands and arms after the ball has been hit.

Two-Hand Overhand Pass

The two-hand overhand pass is the most important volleyball skill for elementary school children to learn. It is virtually the prerequisite to playing volleyball; therefore, it requires a great deal of practice and constant correction by the teacher. The knees should be slightly bent, the back straight, and the elbows bent and sideward. The fingers should be spread apart slightly, with the thumbs facing each other. As the ball approaches, the player should be able to see it through the "window" created by his thumbs and fingers (fig. 16.1a). As the ball drops, the player extends his body upward and slightly forward (fig. 16.1b) and hits the ball with "stiff" fingers. He should not allow his fingers to relax, as this leads to catching the ball and throwing it. He follows through in upward and forward direction (fig. 16.1c).

a
Figure 16.1a Look through the "window."

b
Figure 16.1b Move upward and forward.

c
Figure 16.1c Follow-through.

16

Common Faults

1. Contacting the ball with the body erect
2. Contacting the ball below the shoulders, usually with the palms
3. Hitting the ball forward rather than upward and slightly forward
4. Relaxing the fingers, wrist, and arms as the ball is hit

Forearm Hit (Bumping)

The forearm bounce pass, also known as *bumping* or the *two-hand dig,* should be used when the ball must be hit below the waist or when a player's back is toward the net. As the ball approaches, the back should be kept straight and the knees bent slightly. The arms are lowered in preparation for the underhand hit (fig. 16.2a). At the moment of contact the arms should be relaxed to allow the ball to rebound rather than to be hit vigorously (fig. 16.2b). As the ball is hit, the whole body moves slightly in the direction of the ball.

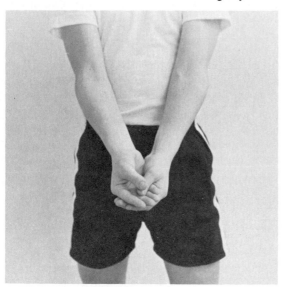

Figure 16.2a Arms straight, with one hand on top of the other

Figure 16.2b Contact with arms straight and relaxed

Common Faults

1. Failing to bend the knees prior to contacting the ball
2. Swinging at the ball
3. Hitting the ball off one arm
4. Hitting the ball with the arms directed upward

Serving   It is permissible to serve the ball from either an underhand or overhand position. The hand may be open or closed. Boys and girls in the intermediate grades are capable of developing a high level of skill in both serves. Begin with the underhand serve and, after sufficient skill has been developed, introduce the overhand "float" serve.

Underhand Serve   The underhand serve is performed with the left foot (right foot for left-handed players) slightly in front of the right foot. The weight is on the rear foot and the body is bent forward slightly (fig. 16.3a). Hold the ball with the palm of the left hand in a "ready" position in front of the right knee. The right arm is extended backward and upward. Swing the right arm down and forward and, at the same time, begin to shift the weight to the front foot. The ball should be hit "out of the left hand" with the heel of the right hand (fig. 16.3b) or the side of the fist (fig. 16.3c). Continue the follow-through action of the right arm and step forward with the right foot.

Figure 16.3a Begin with weight on the rear foot.

Figure 16.3b Contact the ball with the heel of the hand . . .

Figure 16.3c . . . or the side of the fist

Common Faults

1. Holding the ball too far to the left, causing the right arm to swing across the body forcing the ball to move sideways
2. Contacting the ball with the fingertips
3. Contacting the underside of the ball, causing it to rise straight up rather than over the net
4. Failing to follow through

Overhand Serve   The overhand serve should be learned only after a player has mastered the underhand serve. The advantages of the overhand or "float" serve are that it can be placed accurately and it has an element of deception caused by its floating, wobbling action.

16

The server should stand with her left foot (right for left-handed players) in front and her left side turned slightly toward the net. Her right hand is held in a ready position just above her right foot. She tosses the ball up with her left hand two or three feet above her right shoulder (fig. 16.4a). As the toss is made, she shifts her weight to her back foot. As the ball begins to descend, she shifts her weight to the front foot, snaps her striking arm forward, and contacts the ball about a foot above her head (fig. 16.4b). The contact should be made near the center of the ball with the fingertips or a clenched fist. Her wrist should remain rigid as contact is made (fig. 16.4c). She continues the follow-through in the direction of the ball.

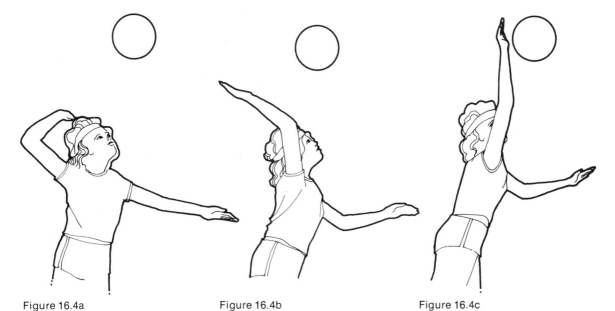

Figure 16.4a   Figure 16.4b   Figure 16.4c

Common Faults

1. Contacting the ball with the forearm, wrist, and fingers too relaxed
2. Contacting the ball as it descends below shoulder height
3. Contacting the ball too far to the left of the body

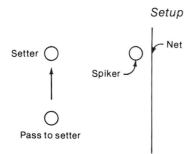

Setup

The setup is a two-hand overhand hit, normally the second hit in the series of three that is allowed each team. This overhand hit is used to pass the ball about fifteen feet above the receiver (spiker) and approximately one foot away from the net. Since the ball will move in the direction the body is facing, it is extremely important for the setter to get into position under the ball and facing the intended receiver just before the pass is made.

Common Faults

1. Failing to get into proper position prior to passing the ball
2. Failing to raise the ball high enough so that it drops or floats down to the spiker.

Spike   A spike is a ball that is hit downward as it goes into the opponent's court. It is the most effective offensive skill and, of course, is the most difficult one to learn. The spiker may take several running steps toward the net before she jumps into the air. As she jumps, she flings both arms up and twists her trunk slightly to the left. Her left arm continues to an extended position above her head and her right elbow bends to allow the wrist and hand to get into a cocked position (fig. 16.5a). Simultaneously, she draws her left arm down, whips her right arm forward and downward, and contacts the top of the ball with the heel of her hand moving downward (fig. 16.5b). The spiker should land facing the net (fig. 16.5c).

Figure 16.5a   Figure 16.5b   Figure 16.5c

Common Faults

1. Jumping too late to reach the spike position.
2. Hitting the ball upward
3. Touching the net on the downward movement

Blocking   The two-hand block is the best defense against an oncoming spiked ball. The blocker should face the net and jump up at the same time the spiker does. Both arms should swing upward to bring the hands to about six inches above the net; the palms face the opponent. The ball should rebound off the blocker's hands back over the net.

Common Faults

1. Failing to jump at the same time as the spiker
2. Hitting the ball rather than allowing it to rebound back into the opponent's court

Practice Activities

The following practice activities are designed to allow students to practice one or more volleyball skills in an enjoyable, gamelike situation. Each skill should begin with individual activities so that the child develops a basic understanding of the skill and can explore the limits of his ability. Partner activities should follow, stressing ball control and positional play. Finally, group activities involving three or more players provide a gamelike experience while concentrating on one or two basic skills. There is ample opportunity in each type of activity for teachers to inject the inventive games approach, by modifying existing drills or creating student-designed practice activities.

Passing Activities

The most important contribution of passing or volleying activities is to teach the young performer the importance of getting into the proper position to pass or receive a hit and executing the skill with reasonable accuracy and control. Simple drills and practice activities that allow children to hit the ball repetitively from any position and in any manner simply to keep the ball moving will not develop good volleyball skills. There should always be a conscious concern on the part of the teacher and performer to execute each skill correctly and with the highest level of performance.

Individual Activities

Individual Volleying

Arrange players in a scattered formation. This drill requires one ball for each child; however, any type of inflated ball can be used. Begin with each player throwing the ball into the air and catching it close to his forehead after one bounce. He should be in a semicrouched position. Gradually introduce the following individual variations:

1. Throw the ball up, perform an overhand volley on the returning ball, then catch it.
2. Throw . . . set . . . set . . . catch.
3. Throw . . . set . . . set . . . continue.
4. Throw . . . set . . . allow one bounce . . . set . . . catch.
5. Throw . . . kneel and set . . . stand and set . . . catch.
6. Repeat (1) to (3) while sitting.
7. Arrange the class in a line formation around the gymnasium and approximately six feet away from the wall. Then have the children
   a. throw the ball against the wall, set, and catch
   b. throw against the wall, set, set, and catch
   c. throw against the wall and continuously set the ball back to the wall
   d. throw against the wall, allow one bounce, set, and catch

Partner Activities

Arrange partners in a scattered formation with about ten feet between each.

1. One partner throws a high pass and the other catches it. Stress moving into position to receive the ball.
2. Player number one throws to number two. Two sets back to one, who catches the ball.
3. Player number one throws to number two. They continue to set to each other.
4. Player one throws to two. As soon as one has thrown, he moves to a new position. Two then sets to one, then moves to his new position. Continue pattern.

Arrange partners around the gymnasium and about ten feet away from the wall.

1. Player number one throws against the wall and player number two sets the ball above player one. One catches. Partners change positions and repeat.
2. Player number one throws against the wall, player number two sets back to wall. Continue drill alternating sets.
3. Repeat (2), but require a bounce before the return set is attempted.

Arrange partners on opposite sides of a net or rope.

1. Player number one throws over the net and player number two sets back over the net to player one, who catches the ball.
2. Repeat (1) but continue setting back and forth.

Group Activities

The following basic relay formations have been adapted to volleyball activities. Adjust distances to meet the class's ability.

Shuttle Volleyball

Formation
Divide class into three or four squads. Arrange squads in a shuttle formation with about six feet between players.

Basic Drill
The first player throws the ball to the second player, who volleys it back to the third player, who has taken the first player's position. Each player goes to the end of his line after he has volleyed the ball. Reverse the direction of the throw after everyone has had a turn.

Variations
1. Same formation with net between lines.
2. Volley with one or two hands.
3. As proficiency develops, increase the distance between the lines.
4. Bounce the ball rather than making a direct throw.

Circle Volleying

Formation
Divide class into three or four squads. Arrange squads into circle formation with about five feet between each player.

Basic Drill
The first player throws the ball up and toward the next player, who volleys it back to the first player. The first player then throws to the third person and so on until every circle player has volleyed the ball back to the first player.

Variations
1. As proficiency increases, have the first player throw to the second player, the second player volleys to the third, the third volley to the fourth, and so on around the circle.
2. Keep It Up. After the first player has started the drill, allow anyone to hit the ball and see how long the squad can keep it up.

Zigzag Volleying

Formation
Divide the class into three or four squads of six to eight players. Arrange squads in a zigzag formation with about ten feet between each line.

Basic Drill
The first player throws the ball across to the second player, who volleys the ball back to the third player. Continue the zigzag volleying pattern until the last player receives the ball.

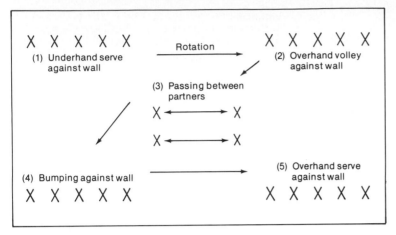

X X X X X   Rotation   X X X X X
(1) Underhand serve   (2) Overhand volley
    against wall   against wall

                (3) Passing between
                    partners
              X ⟷ X
              X ⟷ X

(4) Bumping against wall   →   (5) Overhand serve
                                     against wall
X X X X X   X X X X X

Circuit Volleyball

Formation
Divide the class into five teams and arrange as shown in the above diagram.

Basic Drill
On "go" command each team practices its respective skill for a set period of time (ranging from one to several minutes). At the end of each practice period each team places the ball on the floor and rotates to the next station. Continue rotation.

Serving Activities

Children in the intermediate grades should be able to perform a reasonably accurate underhand serve from the end line over the net before moving on to an overhand serve. Fourth and fifth graders should spend a major portion of their practice time on the underhand serve. Introduce the overhand serve late in grade five and allow proportionately more time for this skill during the sixth grade.

Individual Activities

Arrange the class in a line formation around the gymnasium and about ten feet from the wall.

1. Serve to the wall and catch the rebound.
2. Combine serve and set. Serve to the wall, set the rebound back to the wall, catch and repeat.

Partner Activities

Arrange partners on opposite sides of the net. Adjust the distance to the class's level of ability.

1. Have partners free serve back and forth.
2. Move partners closer together. Player number one serves to player number two, who sets the ball back to player one. Change positions and repeat.
3. One partner serves to the wall, the other catches the ball and repeats the serve.
4. One partner serves and the other sets back to the wall. Continue setting until one partner misses a return.

Group Activities

If enough space is available, shuttle and zigzag formations can be used equally as well as the following activities to practice serving skills.

Baseline Serving

Formation
Divide class into two squads, with each evenly distributed along its baseline. One player from each team is assigned to the retriever position. Use as many balls as you have available.

Basic Drill
Any child on the baseline may begin by serving the ball over the net. The ball is then served back by the child who retrieves it. No serving order need be kept. The retriever's job is to catch and pass the ball back to anyone on his team. Note: Start with one ball, then bring in the remaining balls one at a time.

Alley Serving

Formation
Divide class into two squads, with the first player on each team behind the baseline. Divide the playing area on both sides of the net into three equal sections and place one retriever in each section as shown in the diagram. The retrievers return balls to the appropriate lines. Retrievers rotate after everyone has had a serve.

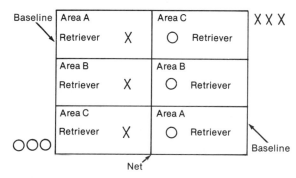

Basic Drill
Each player has three serves. He attempts to serve one ball into each of the three areas. The sections are perpendicular to the net.

Variations
1. Have players serve into one area only.
2. Adjust the serving line to meet the skill of your students.

Setup, Spike, and Blocking Activities

The following drills should be used only after the class has shown reasonable proficiency in setting up the ball. Adjust the height of the net according to the class's ability.

Drill No. 1

Arrange the practice area as shown in the diagram.

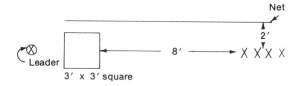

The leader tosses the ball to the first player, who tries to return a high arc set into the square. Each player is given three turns, then goes to the back of the line. The leader rotates after every player has had a turn.

Variations
1. The leader throws, the first player returns a set and then goes to the back of line, and the leader returns a set to the second player in the line.
2. Add a retriever on the opposite side of the net. The leader throws, the first player returns a high set, and the leader spikes the ball over the net.

Drill No. 2

Arrange the practice area as shown in the diagram.

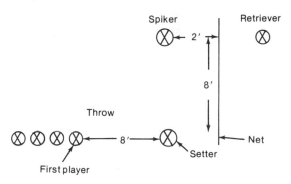

The first player throws a high arc pass to the setter, who sets up the ball for the spiker. The spiker attempts to spike the ball into the opposite court. After each play, the retriever goes to the back of the line and all other players move up to the next position.

Variations
1. The first player throws the ball up to himself, then volleys it to the setter. The drill continues as previously described.
2. Add a blocker opposite the spiker and continue to use the receiver.

16

Lead-up Games

The lead-up games described in this section are extremely popular with upper elementary school children. Grade four requires the greatest number of modifications to the rules and court dimensions in order to provide a game that is within these children's general level of ability. The following lead-up games described in previous chapters can be adapted to volleyball with minor changes in the rules and playing strategies. They are Shower Ball, page 192; and the Bounce Net Ball, page 192.

Lead-up Game	Grade	Page
King Ball	4	292
Bound Ball	4-5	292
Mass Volleyball	4-5	292
Newcomb	4-5	293
Keep It Up	5-6	293
Modified Volleyball	5-6	293
Volleyball Keep Away	5-6	294
Four-Way Volleyball	5-6	294
Sideline Volleyball	5-6	294

King Ball (4)

Formation: Volleyball court with players arranged in rows
Equipment: Volleyball, net or ropes
Players: Nine to twelve on each team
Skills: Throwing and catching

Prior to starting the game, each team secretly chooses a "king," two "ministers," and a scorekeeper. All other players are members of the king's court. The success of this game depends on keeping the identity of the king and his two ministers secret. The game involves throwing the ball back and forth over the net. If the king catches the ball before it bounces, his team scores 100 points; his ministers, 50 points; and members of the court, 10 points. If any player throws the ball below the net or out-of-bounds, it must be thrown again by the same team. The first team to reach 1,000 points wins the game.

Teaching suggestions
Caution scorekeepers not to announce any score until 1,000 points have been reached. Otherwise, the individual scores will reveal the identities of the king and the ministers.

Bound Ball (4-5)

Formation: Volleyball court with a line drawn across the center. No net is used. Players line up in two rows as in a regular volleyball game.
Equipment: Volleyball
Players: Six players on each team
Skills: Serving and volleying

The server stands anywhere behind the end line. He must bounce the ball once and then hit it over the centerline. The ball must bounce once before an opposing player is allowed to return it over the line. Each team is allowed three hits; however, the ball must bounce between each hit. No player is allowed to hit the ball twice in succession. If the ball hits the centerline, it is considered dead and the play is retaken. Balls hitting boundary lines are considered to be still in play. If the nonserving team fails to return the ball within three bounces, the serving team is awarded one point. If the serving team fails to get the serve over the centerline or fails to return a played ball, no point is scored and the ball is given to the other team. Game continues to fifteen points.

Mass Volleyball (4-5)

Formation: Players of each team arranged in equal rows on each side of the net
Equipment: Volleyball court, net, volleyball or large utility ball
Players: Nine to twelve on each team
Skills: Serving and volleying

Any player may serve the ball from anywhere in his court. Teams volley the ball back and forth across the net. Anyone may hit the ball as many times as he wishes; however, only three players may touch the ball before it is returned over the net. Change the serve after a team fails to return the ball. The serving team scores one point whenever opponents commit one of the following fouls: (1) A team fails to return the ball; (2) a player catches the ball; (3) the ball goes out-of-bounds; (4) the ball touches the floor; or (5) a player touches the net. A game may be played to any number of points (eleven or fifteen is desirable).

Newcomb (4-5)

Formation: Volleyball court with teams arranged in equal rows on each side of net
Equipment: Volleyball court, net, volleyball or large utility ball
Players: Nine on each team
Skills: Serving and volleying

Server serves the ball over the net (a second hit from another player is permitted). The other team tries to return the ball after the serve, with any number of players allowed to hit the ball. The server continues until his team loses the ball. Only the serving team scores. A predetermined time limit or score is set.

Fouls are (1) hitting the ball out-of-bounds; (2) holding the ball; (3) touching the net; (4) walking with the ball; (5) throwing the ball out-of-bounds; or (6) letting the ball hit the floor.

Teaching suggestions
If skill level is too low, allow players to catch the ball, then hit it. Also, adjust the position of the serving line to the level of skill.

Keep It Up (5-6)

Formation: Squads arranged in circle formation with or without a player in the middle
Equipment: One volleyball for each circle
Players: Six to eight on each team
Skills: Volleying

Each circle tries to keep its ball up in the air the longest by volleying it from player to player. The ball may be hit to any player in the circle. The team that keeps the ball up the longest wins.

Teaching suggestions
1. Hit the ball up rather than at a player.
2. Simplify the game by allowing one bounce between each hit.
3. Place a player in the middle of the circle.
4. As skill improves, allow only one type of hit—two-hand underhand or one-hand underhand.

Modified Volleyball (5-6)

Formation: Teams arranged as in diagram
Equipment: One volleyball per game
Players: Nine to twelve on each team
Skills: Serving, volleying, and rotating

The server must stand behind the end line and serve the ball over the net. If the level of skill is too low, allow any player on the front line to assist in getting the ball over the net. The opposing team attempts to get the ball back over the net before it touches the ground. The ball can be volleyed by as many players on each team as is necessary to return the ball over the net. All other volleyball rules and scoring apply to this game.

Variations
1. Allow the server two tries to get the ball over the net.
2. Use only one type of hit.

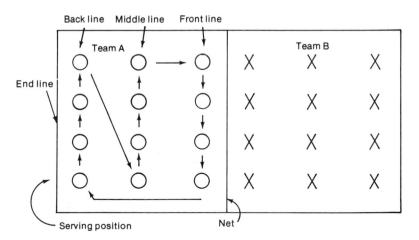

Volleyball Keep Away (5-6)

Formation: Teams arranged in a scattered formation within a designated play area
Equipment: Volleyball or large utility ball
Players: Any number on each team
Skills: Volleying

By volleying the ball from one team member to another, the team with the ball tries to keep the ball away from the other team. Members of the other team try to intercept the ball. It can be intercepted only when it is dropping (on the downward arc). After the ball has been intercepted, the team in possession volleys the ball. The team volleying the ball the highest number of times wins. A time limit also may be used.

Four-Way Volleyball (5-6)

Formation: Volleyball court and teams arranged according to the diagram
Equipment: Two nets (or ropes) and one volleyball
Players: Six to nine on each of four teams
Skills: Serving, volleying, blocking, and rotation

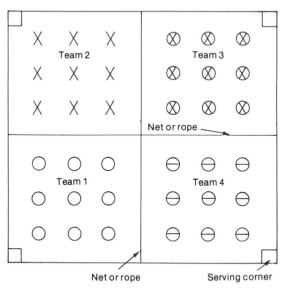

There are four separate teams in this game. Players in courts one and two may serve only into courts three and four. Similarly, players in courts three and four may serve only into courts one and two. However, after the serve a team may hit the ball into any of the other three courts. When a fair serve is made and the ball touches the floor or fails to get out of the

receiver's court within the allotted three hits, the serving team scores one point and continues serving as in regular volleyball. However, when a receiving team hits the ball into another court fairly, this team becomes the serving team the moment the ball leaves its court. If the new receiving team fails to pass the ball out of its court, the new serving team is awarded one point. All other regular volleyball rules apply.

Sideline Volleyball (5-6)

Formation: Volleyball court and teams arranged according to diagram
Equipment: One volleyball or utility ball for each game
Players: Twelve on each team
Skills: Serving, volleying, and rotation

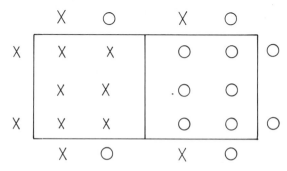

This game is played like regular volleyball but with the addition of active sideline players. The sideline players must stay in their assigned positions. They cannot enter the court area, but they are permitted to pass any loose balls from either team, providing they have not touched the ground. Sideline players cannot pass to each other. A hit made by a sideline player is a free hit for his team and does not count as one of the team's hits. Rotate the court and sideline players after six points are scored and continue the game to fifteen points.

Variations

1. Count sideline hits.
2. Restrict sideline hits to one type of volley.

Volleyball: Rules and Regulations

Although there are fewer skills to learn in volleyball than the other major sports, it is one of the more difficult games for boys and girls in grades four through six. The difficulty, in most cases, is the result of inadequate arm and shoulder girdle strength and inaccuracy in serving and volleying. Nevertheless, fifth and sixth graders should be exposed to the complete game of volleyball early in the instructional unit. Modify the rules to meet the level of skill, available facilities, and the number of children. Consider modifying the length of the game, the number of players, the height of the net, and the size of the playing court.

   I. Field of play:

   II. Recommended net heights:
      Grade four—six feet
      Grade five—seven feet
      Grade six—seven feet

   III. Positions and rotation pattern (after opponents lose their serve):

   IV. To start the game: The right back player starts the game by serving the ball from anywhere behind the end line. (It is wise to begin the service from the right-hand corner; later allow children to serve from various positions along the end line.) The server must serve with both feet behind the line. He is allowed only one serve, unless the ball hits the top of the net; then he is given another serve. But if the server has already made one point and his next serve hits the top of the net, he loses his serve. The server continues to serve until his team loses the ball. Before serving, the server must call out his score, his opponent's score, and then "service."

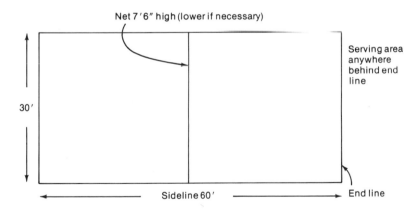

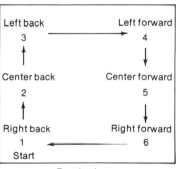

For six players

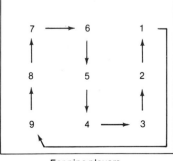

For nine players.

V. To return the ball: After the ball has been served, players on both sides must abide by the following rules:
  A. Any player who receives the ball is allowed one volley (hit). He may hit the ball back over the net or to another teammate.
  B. The ball may not be volleyed (hit) more than three times by a team before it is sent over the net.
  C. If the ball hits the net on the return volley and falls into the opponent's court, it is a fair ball.
  D. If the ball hits the net on the return volley and falls back into the court from which it was sent, it may be played before it hits the ground, provided (1) it is not volleyed by the player who hit it into the net and (2) it was not volleyed by more than two players before it hit the net.

VI. To play: The server hits the ball over the net. If the opposing team fails to return it over the net, one point is awarded to the serving team. However, if the ball is returned to the serving team and it fails to return again, the serving team loses the serve. No point is awarded on the loss of serve. Player rotation should be made only by the team receiving the serve.

VII. Violations: If any of the following violations is committed by the serving team, the serve is lost. This is called *side out*. If one is committed by the receiving team, the serving team is awarded one point.
  A. Failing to make a fair or legal serve.
  B. Allowing the ball to hit the court surface.
  C. Returning the ball in any way other than by hitting it. Balls may not be caught and thrown over the net.
  D. Volleying the ball more than three times before it goes over the net.
  E. Letting the ball touch the floor outside the court lines. Note: A ball may be played from outside the court area if it has not touched the ground.
  F. Failing to return the ball over the net.
  G. Failing to rotate in the proper order.

VIII. Scoring:
  A. Only the serving team can score.
  B. Eleven, fifteen, or twenty-one points constitutes a game. A team must win by two points; thus, if the score is ten all in an eleven-point game, one team must score two successive points to win.

Evaluative Techniques

There are numerous methods of measuring volleyball skills and knowledge (Campbell and Tucker 1967). The majority of tests used by classroom teachers are of an objective nature and usually are modifications of existing standardized test batteries. Teachers should be encouraged to develop their own test batteries and keep scores of each test in order to develop appropriate norms for their teaching situations.

The following test battery is an example of a "teacher-made" test that can be administered by the children in a short period of time.

	Volleyball Skill Test				
Name	Wall Volley total score	Service over net (50 pts.)	Subjective Evaluation (50 pts.)	Total Score	Grade
1 2 3 4	Rank all total scores ⟶ for the class, then convert to letter grades or ratings (superior, good, etc.)				

Test No. 1 **Wall volley**

Draw a line on the wall six feet up from the floor and a second line on the floor three feet from the wall. Each player must stand behind this line, toss the ball in the air, and begin to volley it against the wall and above the six-foot line. One point is awarded for each hit above the line. Score the number of hits made in twenty seconds. If a player drops the ball within this period, he may pick it up and continue volleying. Allow two trials and record the highest score.

Test No. 2 **Serving over the net**

Each player is given ten consecutive serves, with each successful serve awarded five points. This test can be modified by dividing the opposite court into zones, with each given a different point value. For example, make three equal zones running perpendicular to the net; the zone farthest away from the server would equal five points; the next one, three points; and the nearest zone, one point.

Test No. 3 **Subjective evaluation of playing ability**

Establish criteria that represent the skills and playing ability required in volleyball. For example, using such factors as positional play, alertness, volleying ability, and team play, the teacher would award each player a score from zero to fifty points. Three players can be used as judges, with the average score recorded.

Basketball Activities

17

Emphasis and Skill
Presentation

Teaching Procedures

Description of Skills

Practice Activities

Lead-up Games

Basketball: Rules and
Regulations

Evaluative Techniques

Basketball, like volleyball, originated in the United States and has since become a sport that is played in nearly every country in the world. There is no single reason for its popularity as both a participant and spectator sport. Children, youth, and adults enjoy the game because it is fun, challenging, and contributes to many important components of physical fitness. Since the game can be modified to meet court size limitations and varying levels of skill, it should be considered as a basic activity for the upper elementary school physical education program. This chapter has been organized to provide a format for teaching basketball skills and knowledge to these children.

Emphasis and Skill Presentation

Many basketball skills have been learned in earlier grades or out of school. The many backyard basketball courts not only attest to the popularity of the sport, but they also provide the opportunity for elementary school children to learn basketball skills from their older brothers and

Skills and Rules	Grade Level			
	Grade 3	Grade 4	Grade 5	Grade 6
Passing				
Chest pass	Acquired or introduce	Increase distance and accuracy	Increase distance and accuracy	Increase distance and accuracy
Bounce pass	Acquired or introduce	With one hand	To a moving target	Refinement
Baseball pass	Acquired or introduce	Increase distance and accuracy	Increase distance and accuracy	Increase distance and accuracy
Overhead pass			Introduce	Refinement
Rule: Held ball			Introduce	
Catching				
From below the waist	Acquired or introduce	Increase distance and proficiency	Catching while moving	Refinement
From above the waist	Acquired or introduce	Increase distance and proficiency	Catching while moving	Refinement
Rules: Line violations		Introduce		
Out-of-bounds		Introduce		
Dribbling				
While standing and moving	Acquired or introduce	Forward and backward	Dribble and weave	Dribble and change pace
		With either hand	Dribble and pivot	Refinement
Rule: Traveling		Introduce		
Shooting				
Two-hand chest	Acquired or introduce	Increase distance and accuracy	Increase distance and accuracy	Increase distance and accuracy
One-hand push		Introduce	Increase distance and accuracy	Increase distance and accuracy
Lay-up		Introduce	With either hand	Refinement
Free throw			Introduce	Refinement
One-hand jump				Introduce
Rules: Scoring		Introduce		
Key positions			Introduce	
Related Skills				
Pivoting			Introduce	Refinement
Feinting			Introduce	Refinement
Guarding			Introduce	Refinement
Rebounding				Introduce
Rules: Personal fouls			Introduce	

17

sisters and parents. Consequently, there is a wide variation in the level of basketball skill in virtually every intermediate grade in the elementary school. With these considerations in mind, the following suggested sequence of presenting skills and rules is provided as a basic guide.

By the time they have reached grade four, most children have learned several of the basic skills involved in passing, catching, dribbling, and shooting. However, the acquisition of these skills prior to grade four should not result in a conscious extension of the basketball program down to the primary grades. Rather, the primary grades should continue to emphasize low-or-ganization games, with some of the specialized skills of basketball and other sports being acquired in the process.

Children in grade four should continue to practice the basic passing, catching, dribbling, and shooting skills to improve their accuracy and proficiency. They should also be introduced to a few new shooting skills and several main rules of basketball.

The fifth and sixth grade program places more emphasis on using both hands, pivoting and weaving, and general playing ability. It is a period of refining playing skills and team strategies.

Teaching Procedures

Teaching the skills and team strategies of basketball to upper elementary children presents several problems. A main one, as stated earlier, is that the skill level and playing ability of these children vary widely. Some children have played on out-of-school teams or have their own backyard hoops, while others have not had any experience with the game. The challenge to the teacher is to cope with these major differences in the design and presentation of an instructional unit.

Developing a Basketball Unit

The general instructional procedures discussed in previous chapters also apply to basketball activities. Of particular importance is the process of developing units of instruction on pages 115-17 and the illustrated lessons on pages 152-56. In addition, the inventive games approach described on pages 176-77 can be applied to the teaching of basketball activities.

Since the length of the unit and the lesson, as well as the facilities and equipment available, will vary in each teaching situation, the following suggested approach should be considered as a basic guideline. Modify it to cope with your individual situation.

Step One: Decide on the length of your basketball unit. Express this in number of lessons rather than weeks.

Step Two: Assess the general level of ability of your class (see evaluative techniques on pages 323-24).

Step Three: Select the skills and rules you wish to emphasize in your unit (see the suggested sequence of presenting skills and rules on page 249).

Step Four: Choose the appropriate practice activities (pp. 314-19) and lead-up games (pp. 319-23).

Structure of a Lesson

The detailed explanation of how to plan a lesson described in Chapter 13, "Soccer Activities," (page 221) should be followed when preparing and presenting basketball activities. It should be noted that the suggested procedure of moving from individual to partner to group activities can be adapted successfully to each basketball lesson.

Description of Skills

Basketball skills can be broadly classified as passing, catching, dribbling, shooting, guarding, and feinting. Each skill, in turn, can be subdivided, such as the chest pass, two-hand overhead pass, and the baseball pass. Each of these skills is described in this section, accompanied by a list of the more common faults.

Figure 17.1

Passing   Passing is transferring the ball from one player to another from a stationary position or while in motion. A player may pass the ball with one or both hands and from a variety of positions. The basic fundamentals of all passes are to (1) be accurate, avoiding "wild throws"; (2) follow through with every pass; and (3) shift the ball as quickly as possible from a receiving position to a passing position.

Two-Hand Chest Pass   The two-hand chest pass or push is one of the most useful and effective passes in basketball. Since its main advantage is ease and speed of delivery, it is the most often used pass, particularly for short distances. The player stands with both feet together and holds the ball chest-high. His fingers should be spread around the center of the ball, and his thumbs should be close together (fig. 17.2a). As he takes one step forward, he extends his arms and releases the ball in a "pushing" action off his fingertips (figs. 17.2b and c).

Figure 17.2a

Figure 17.2b

Figure 17.2c

Common Faults

1. Holding the ball with the palms touching its surface
2. Holding the elbows too far away from the body
3. Pushing more with one hand than the other
4. Failing to release the ball with a quick wrist snap in a downward and outward direction

Two-Hand Bounce Pass

The two-hand bounce pass is performed like the two-hand chest pass except that the ball is bounced on the floor and then rebounds to the receiver (fig. 17.3). The main advantage of this pass is that it permits a player to pass the ball past an opponent before the latter can bend down and block the pass.

Figure 17.3 Two-hand bounce pass

Baseball Pass

The baseball pass is used when a player wishes to throw the ball a long distance. Care must be exercised in using this pass, particularly with beginners, as it may lead to inaccurate passing. The player begins the pass with one foot slightly forward and her weight evenly distributed on both feet. She holds the ball in front of her body, with her elbows bent and her fingers spread around the sides of the ball. She then brings her arms back and transfers the ball to her right hand when it is above her shoulder and behind her ear (fig. 17.4a). The body weight should shift to the right foot when the hands shift backward. She then extends her right arm forward, rotates her body toward the left, and shifts her weight to her forward foot (fig. 17.4b). She releases the ball with a final snap of the wrists and fingers (fig. 17.4c).

Figure 17.4a

Figure 17.4b

Figure 17.4c

17

Common Faults

1. Throwing the ball with a side arm action, causing a sideward spin of the ball
2. Failing to finish with a final wrist and finger snap
3. Releasing the ball too late, causing the ball to hit the floor in front of the receiver

Two-Hand Overhead Pass

The two-hand overhead pass is extremely effective when a player wishes to throw the ball to a teammate above the reach of an opponent. In addition, when the ball is held overhead, it is very easy to "fake" or pretend to pass, thus putting the opponent off guard before the ball actually is released.

Start the pass with the feet together and the knees slightly bent. Hold the ball above the head with the hands on the side of the ball (fig. 17.5). Then shift the arms forward and release the ball with a wrist and finger snap. Hold the arms above the head momentarily before starting the next move.

Figure 17.5

Common Faults

1. Using only arm action
2. Holding the ball too far back or too far in front of the body, which gives the defensive player a better chance to get the ball

Catching   There are two basic catching skills in basketball. The overhand
catch (fig. 17.6a) is used if the ball is caught above the waist. The
fingers should be pointed up for this catch. The underhand catch
(fig. 17.6b) is used to catch a ball below the waist. The fingers are
pointing down. In both types of catches the receiver should reach
out and catch the ball on his fingertips, then gradually relax his
arms to reduce the speed of the oncoming ball. However, young
children often do not have adequate strength to catch the
basketball in this manner, so allow them to catch the ball with
their palms, then quickly shift to a fingertip grip.

Figure 17.6a Overhand catch   Figure 17.6b Underhand catch

Common Faults

1. Standing and waiting for a pass rather than shifting to meet the
   ball
2. Failing to relax the arms to provide "give" as a fast-moving ball
   is caught

17

Dribbling   Dribbling is controlled bouncing in any direction and at varying speeds. The basic fundamentals to stress in teaching this skill are: (1) Do not slap the ball downward—push it toward the floor; (2) learn to dribble with both hands; and (3) when a player is not being checked, he should bring the ball in front of his body and raise the height of the dribble in order to increase his running speed.

The dribbler's body should lean forward slightly, his knees should be partially flexed, and his head up. The wrist of his dribbling hand should be relaxed, with the fingers cupped and spaced apart (fig. 17.7). He should "push" the ball toward the floor off his fingertips. As the ball rebounds, his fingers, wrist, and arm should "ride" back with the ball.

When a player is being checked, he must place his body between his opponent and the ball. When dribbling, he must learn to keep his eye on his opponent to watch for sudden moves and to shift the ball to a more advantageous position. Also, when a player is being checked, he should keep the ball close to his body and lower the bounce to between his waist and his knees.

Figure 17.7

Common Faults

1. Slapping the ball with the palm of the hand
2. Watching the ball while dribbling
3. Dribbling the ball on the same side as the approaching opponent

Shooting   It is quite obvious that all the skills of basketball are important; none, however, is as important as shooting. When teaching the following basic shooting skills, stress these fundamental principles: (1) Watch the target and not the ball and (2) follow through after every shot.

If elementary school-age children are to learn shooting skills correctly and efficiently, the height of the basket rim should be lowered from the official ten feet to a height that allows the children to shoot without undue strain. The appropriate height for upper elementary school children should be between eight and nine feet, depending upon the children's age and ability.

Two-Hand Set Shot   This shot is the same as the one-hand set shot (description follows), except that two hands are used. Begin the shot with one foot slightly in front of the other and the weight evenly distributed on both feet. Hold the ball between spread fingers in front of the chest, with the elbows close to the sides (fig. 17.8a). Bend the knees slightly to aid in the upward motion, then simultaneously straighten the knees and extend the body forward and upward, pushing the ball toward the basket. Release the ball with a slight snap of the wrists and fingers. Continue the follow-through with the arms and palms extended toward the basket (fig. 17.8 b).

Figure 17.8a

Figure 17.8b

17

Common Faults

1. Lowering the arms in a "preparatory" move, then raising them to shoot. Lowering the ball gives the opponent an opportunity to get the ball or stop the shot.
2. Pushing more with one hand than the other.
3. Failing to follow through after releasing the ball.

One-hand Set Shot
The one-hand set shot is performed by placing the same foot as the shooting hand slightly in front of the body. The ball is held with both hands opposite the chin and above the lead foot (fig. 17.9a). The back should be straight and knees partially bent. In a simultaneous action, the player straightens her knees, releases her nonshooting hand, and extends her shooting arm forward and upward, and pushes the ball toward the basket (fig. 17.9c). The ball is released with a slight snap of the wrist and fingers.

Figure 17.9a

Figure 17.9b

Figure 17.9c

Common Faults

1. Placing opposite foot forward
2. Failing to extend the wrist and fingers

Jump Shot   The jump shot has the same arm, wrist, and fingertip action as the one-hand set shot (fig. 17.10a). The player starts with a two-foot jump into the air, lets go of the ball with the nonshooting hand, and continues the arm action toward the basket (fig. 17.10b).

Figure 17.10a   Figure 17.10b

Lay-up Shot   The lay-up, which involves dribbling, leaping, and the ability to judge distance, can be learned by boys and girls in the intermediate grades. In fact, most children are more successful at this skill than other shooting skills, such as the one- or two-hand set shot. The reason is the short distance between the hand when the ball is released and the rim of the basket.

The player should approach the basket at a forty-five degree angle (fig. 17.11a). Just prior to shooting, she shifts her weight to her inside foot and raises the ball as far as possible with both hands. She releases her nonshooting hand as her shooting arm carries the ball up (fig. 17.11b). She releases it off her fingertips (fig. 17.11c). The ball should bounce against the backboard about eighteen inches above the hoop, then drop into the hoop.

Figure 17.11a   Figure 17.11b   Figure 17.11c

Common Faults

1. Dribbling, then stopping before executing the upward phase of the skill
2. Taking off too soon and from the wrong foot
3. Throwing the ball rather than extending the arm and "pushing" the ball against the backboard

Free Throw (Two-Hand Underhand)

Although any shot may be taken from the free-throw line, the two-hand underhand shot is normally the easiest to perform. Since this is an "unguarded" shot, it is recommended only for the free throw.

The player stands with her back straight, her knees slightly bent, her arms straight, and her weight equally distributed on both feet. She holds the ball with the fingertips of both hands and slightly under the ball (fig. 17.12a). In a simultaneous action, she swings her arms forward and upward and straightens her knees (fig. 17.12b). It is important to keep the back straight throughout this movement and to release the ball off the tips of the fingers.

Figure 17.12a   Figure 17.12b

Common Faults

1. Bending too far forward and not keeping the back straight
2. Releasing the ball too soon, causing a low arc as the ball moves toward the basket

17

a   b

Figure 17.13 The Pivot

Pivoting   Footwork in basketball involves stopping, starting, pivoting, and turning in all directions and at varying speeds. When teaching the pivot and turn (fig. 17.13), stress the importance of gaining body control before attempting the pivot or turn. Also, teach pupils not to change the pivot foot once it is declared; otherwise, traveling will be charged. Finally, emphasize the need to maintain fingertip control of the ball for quick release after the pivot is made.

Prior to performing a pivot, the weight should be evenly distributed on both feet. The ball should be held firmly with the fingertips of both hands. The elbows should be out to protect the ball. As soon as one foot becomes the pivot foot, it must remain on the floor. The player may turn in any direction on his pivot foot; however, he may not drag it away from the original pivot spot. The opposite foot is permitted to step in any direction.

Defensive Skills
It is essential that elementary children first learn to move the ball by dribbling and passing, and then learn the basic skills of defense. It is important to stress the fact that legally stopping an opponent from scoring is just as important as scoring itself. The following basic defense techniques should be emphasized, particularly in the fifth and sixth grades:

1. Never cross the feet when checking an opponent—use a sliding step.
2. Keep the buttocks low and the back upright.
3. When checking, keep one hand up at all times.
4. Do not reach across for a ball; move the body to a position in front of the offensive player and then attempt to take the ball.
5. Always try to get the body in front of the offensive player.
6. Check with one hand toward the ball and the other hand toward the opponent.

Figure 17.14

Practice Activities

The following practice activities will assist in developing passing, shooting, dribbling, and pivoting skills. Modify any of them to meet limitations of the playing area and variations in the children's level of skill and interest.

All activities described in this section are designed to give each student the maximum amount of practice. If there are not enough basketballs, use soccer balls, volleyballs, or utility balls. Also, it is important for the teacher to circulate among students during practice activities in order to correct errors or to provide encourgagement and praise where needed.

Many of the low-organization games and relays described in Chapters 10 and 11 can be modified and used as passing, catching, and other basketball skills.

Passing and Catching Activities

Passing and catching activities are normally practiced together.

Partner Passing

Formation
Partners scattered around playing area. Partners stand about ten to fifteen feet apart, depending on skill

Basic Drill
Each player remains in a stationary position. After a few minutes of practice, have one player remain stationary and the other move around him. After a few more minutes of practice, have both players move, pass, and catch.

Wall Passing

Formation
Line formation around available wall surface. Players should stand approximately five feet from the wall and gradually move back as their skill increases. This wall drill can be used to practice all types of passing and catching skills.

Variations
1. Put lines or targets on the wall to increase accuracy.
2. Add timing contests—for example, the number of hits in ten seconds.

Pig in the Middle

Formation
Arrange three players in a line with approximately six feet between each. The two outside players are the end players, while the middle player is designated as the "pig."

Basic Drill
Do not allow the end players to move to the right or left. They attempt to pass the ball to each other without the middle player (the pig) touching the ball. If the pig touches the ball, he replaces the person who threw it. The ball may not be thrown above the reach of the middle player and he must always advance toward the ball.

Variations
Allow the end player who is receiving the ball to move into an open space.

Circle Passing

Formation
Divide the class into squads of five to six players. Arrange the children in circles with approximately six feet between them.

Basic Drill

The first player turns toward the second player and passes the ball to him; the second player catches the ball, turns toward the third and passes to him, and so on. If the ball is dropped, it is retrieved by the receiver, who returns to his place in the circle and continues the drill.

Variations

1. Five against one: One player goes to the center of the circle. The five outside players pass the ball to each other, always skipping a person, while the center player tries to intercept the pass. When the center player intercepts a pass, he switches positions with the player who threw the ball.
2. One player goes to the center of the circle with the ball and passes to each player in the circle.
3. Double passing: This is similar to (2), with the addition of one more ball. Require the center player to make a bounce pass, while the circle players make direct passes.

Dribbling Activities

Dribbling activities normally begin with each player practicing the skill alone, then shift to partner activities, and finally to group activities.

Figure 17.15 One-Knee dribble activity

One-Knee Dribble

Formation
Scattered

Basic Drill
All players kneel on one knee and begin bouncing the ball with the same hand as the kneeling knee. This drill will eliminate unnecessary arm action. Players should keep their eyes on the teacher and "feel" for the ball.

Variations

1. Dribble the ball, with the elbow of the opposite arm at the side.
2. Move the ball backward and forward.
3. Move the ball around the front of the opposite leg and change hands.
4. Move the ball under the leg to the other hand (fig. 17.16).
5. Bounce the ball in rhythm set by the teacher.
6. Play follow the leader while kneeling. This makes everyone look at the leader and not the ball.
7. Repeat above drills standing.

Figure 17.16

Figure 17.17 Movement Drill

Movement Drill

Formation
Scattered, with each player in possession of a ball.

Basic Drill
The teacher or a leader stands in front of the group, then dribbles to the right, left, forward, or any other direction. All players move in the same direction as the leader, but with a mirror image, bouncing the ball with the appropriate hand.

Variation
The leader may use hand directions instead of actually shifting positions.

Line Dribble

Formation
Divide class into three or four squads of about eight to ten players. Arrange each squad in a line formation and place one pin (or chair) twenty feet in front of each line.

Basic Drill
The first player dribbles around the pin and back around his squad and passes the ball to the next player. The first player goes to the end of the line and the second player continues the relay.

Weave Dribble

Formation
Divide the class into three to five squads of about six to eight players. Arrange each squad in a straight line formation with about ten feet between each player.

Basic Drill
The first player dribbles around the second player, back and around the opposite side of each successive player until he is back in his original position. Everyone moves up one position and the first player goes to rear of the line.

Variation
Use chairs or pins instead of players for obstacles.

Whistle Dribble

Formation
Divide class into three or four squads of about six to eight players. Line the squads up at one end of the floor. The teacher stands in the center of the playing area.

Basic Drill
When you blow the whistle, the first player from each squad dribbles forward. When you blow the whistle again, all players must stop immediately and hold the ball ready for the next move. As soon as any player reaches a line parallel to you, he turns and dribbles back to his team.

1. Use hand signals rather than the whistle for stopping and starting; this encourages the "head-up" dribble. A hand over the head means dribble; a hand straight down means stop.
2. Extend arms sideward (right or left) as a signal to pivot right or left. The signals then would be hand over head (dribble forward), hand down (stop), arm out to right (pivot right, then back and ready for next command).

Shooting Activities

A variety of shooting skills can be used in the following activities. Other skills, such as passing, dribbling, and guarding, can be added to most of these simple practice activities.

Basket Shooting

Formation

Divide the class into as many squads as you have baskets. Arrange each squad in a file formation behind the free throw line. One player remains on the end line behind the basket.

Basic Drill

The first player behind the free throw line dribbles forward, and the player on the end line comes forward to guard the basket. The player with the ball must attempt a shot, and then both players try to recover the rebound. Whoever retrieves it passes it on to the next player. The two rebound players exchange positions, the player who took the shot moving behind the end line and the guarding player going to the end of the line of children behind the free throw line.

Variations

1. Have two offensive players team up and try to get by the guard and shoot.
2. Do the same with two guards and two offensive players.
3. Repeat with two guards and three offensive players.

Dribble and Shoot

Formation

This drill should follow three stages, with the last stage arranged as shown in the diagram.

Basic Drill

1. Each player stands three to four feet away from the basket, takes one step with the left foot (if shooting with the right hand) and shoots.
2. Same as (1), but begin with the right foot.
3. Place chairs in a line at approximately a forty-five degree angle. Chairs should be about three to four feet apart. Players now dribble around the chairs and shoot.

Set Shot Shooting

Formation

Arrange six to eight players in a semicircle near a basket. One player, the leader, is stationed under the basket with a ball.

Basic Drill

The leader passes the ball to the first player in the semicircle, who attempts a set shot. The leader recovers each ball and passes it to each player in sequence. Adjust the distance from the basket according to the group's level of skill.

Variations

Use two or more balls and have the leader return the balls to any player.

Lay-up Shooting

Formation
Arrange two lines of players at a forty-five degree angle to the basket. The first player in each line should be about twenty feet away from the basket.

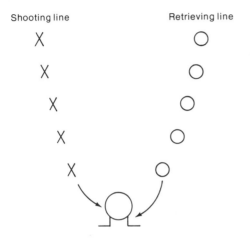

Shooting line   Retrieving line

Basic Drill
The first player in the shooting line dribbles toward the basket and attempts a lay-up shot, then goes to the end of the retrieving line. The first player in the retrieving line leaves his line at the same time as the shooting player to retrieve the ball and pass it to the next player in the shooting line. The retriever then goes to the end of the shooting line. Continue the drill to the last shooting player; then reverse lines and repeat drill.

Offensive and Defensive Activities

One on One

Formation
Partners facing each other scattered around the gymnasium

Basic Drill
Without a ball, one player attempts to run past the other. The defensive player must move his body into position to stop the offensive player. He may not use his arms and feet to stop the player or lean into him. Players are not allowed to touch each other.

Variations
1. Repeat drill with a ball.
2. Repeat (1) and dribble toward a basket.
3. The following combinations can be used in a variety of ways. Begin each with passing only, then add dribbling, and finally add a target. (Improvise according to available backboards.)

Two on one	Three on one
Two on two	Three on three
Two on three	

Pivot and Pass

Formation
Circle with six to eight players standing about ten feet apart

Basic Drill
Each player faces the center of the circle. A player on each side of the circle is given a ball. On signal, each player with a ball keeps his left foot on the ground and pivots a quarter-turn away from the center of the circle, then steps forward on his right foot and passes to the next player. Continue the drill around the circle, and then reverse directions and repeat.

Pass, Post, and Shoot

Formation
Arrange players as shown in the diagram.

   Defensive player

   Post player

   Offensive player

Basic Drill

The post player remains stationary throughout the drill. The ball is given to the offensive player, who tries to maneuver past the defensive player and take a shot at the basket. The ball may be passed back and forth between the offensive player and the post player until the offensive player is ready to move toward the basket and attempt a shot. Allow about thirty seconds to complete the drill, and then blow the whistle and rotate players to next position.

Teaching Suggestions

Set up two drills on each side of the key. If facilities and equipment are limited, draw circles on the wall and place traffic cones or other markers on the floor and restrict players to their assigned areas.

Lead-up Games

The lead-up games described in this section are designed to give children practice in playing games that require one or more basketball skills. Each game can be modified to meet the class's ability and the available facilities and equipment. Whenever possible, divide the playing area into two, three, or four sections to allow two or more games to be played at the same time.

continues until one team makes a basket. The general rules of basketball are followed; however, modify any rule as desired.

Variations

1. Play the same game, but use two tires suspended from the ceiling or walls as goals.
2. Play the same game, but require one type of locomotor movement such as jumping, hopping, or sliding.

Lead-up Game	Grade	Page
Bucket Ball	4-6	319
Guard Ball	4-6	319
Keep Away	4-6	320
Sideline Basketball	4-6	320
Five Passes	4-6	320
Twenty-One	4-6	320
Basketball Snatch Ball	5-6	321
In and Out Basketball	5-6	321
Captain Ball	5-6	321

Guard Ball (4-6)

Formation: Draw two lines approximately ten to fifteen feet apart, and arrange three teams as shown in the diagram.
Equipment: Three or four balls
Players: Five on each of three teams
Skills: Passing, catching, and guarding

Players on teams A and B must stay behind their own lines, and players on team C must stay between the lines. On the signal, players on teams A and B try to pass the balls back and forth to each other. All passes must be below head height of the opposing player. Players on team C attempt to intercept the passes. If a pass is intercepted, player C returns the ball to the passer and stays in position while the game continues. Play the game for one minute and count the number of successful passes. Rotate teams after each game.

Bucket Ball (4-6)

Formation: Draw a rectangle approximately thirty by forty feet or divide the gymnasium into two playing courts.
Equipment: Two wastepaper baskets and one ball for each game
Players: Six to eight on each team
Skills: Passing, catching, dribbling, shooting, and guarding

Place the wastepaper baskets on the floor at the center of the end lines. If desired, a player may stand on a chair and hold the basket. Players on team A pair off with players on team B, and each checks the other. The game begins with a jump ball between two opposing players. The game

Keep Away (4-6)

Formation: Two teams arranged in a scattered formation within a designated play area
Equipment: One basketball
Players: Eight to ten on each team
Skills: Passing, catching, pivoting, and dribbling

On the signal, the teacher gives the ball to one of the teams, which passes it among themselves, trying to keep it away from the other team. Players on the opposing team check as in regular basketball. If teams are large and space is limited, rotate in fours or fives every few minutes.

Teaching suggestions
Keep observing students out of the playing area. Players may be allowed only two dribbles.

Sideline Basketball (4-6)

Formation: Five players from each team play in the court area, while the remaining players from both teams are placed alternately along the sidelines and end lines. Leave equal spaces between line players.
Equipment: One basketball for each game
Players: Ten to twelve per team
Skills: Catching, passing, shooting, dribbling, and pivoting

Basketball rules are followed, except that the ball may be passed to a sideline player. Sideline players cannot enter the court, dribble, or pass to another sideline player. Start the game with a jump ball in the center of playing area. The team that gains possession is designated as the offensive team. If the defensive team intercepts the ball, it must pass to one of its sideline players before it becomes the offensive team. Stepping over the sideline gives the ball to opponents on their sideline. Players on the sidelines rotate with players on the floor. Field goals score two points and free throws one point.

Teaching suggestions
Assign numbers before the game and use these in the rotation sequence. More players may be used on the court.

Five Passes (4-6)

Formation: Two teams arranged in a scattered formation on one side of the playing court or within a designated playing area
Equipment: One basketball
Players: Four or five on a team
Skills: Passing and catching

Play is started with a jump ball between any two opposing players. Basketball rules are followed with respect to traveling, fouling, and ball handling. Passes must be counted out loud by the passer. One point is awarded whenever a team completes five passes in a row. The ball cannot be passed back to the person from whom it was received, and no dribbling is allowed. Whenever a series of passes is interrupted by an interception or a fumble, a new count is started by the team that gains possession of the ball. A free throw from one teammate to another is awarded to the team that did not commit the foul.

Teaching suggestions
Call fouls closely. Encourage quick passes. After a point, the ball may be awarded to the other team or a jump ball may be used. By using half a court, two games can be played simultaneously.

Twenty-One (4-6)

Formation: Players of each group arranged in a scattered formation around one basket
Equipment: One basket and one ball for each group
Players: Six or seven players
Skills: Shooting and catching

The object of this game is for any player to score twenty-one points by a combination of field shots and free throws. Player number one shoots from the free throw line, while the other players stand wherever they wish in the playing area. Player number one continues shooting from the free throw line until he misses, with each successful basket counting one point. When number one misses, any player who can get possession of the ball may try for a field goal; if he's successful, it counts two points. If the try for a field goal fails, any player who can get the ball may try for a field goal. This procedure is continued until a field goal is made. After a field goal is made, the ball is given to the number two player, who takes his turn at the free throw line. Continue until one player has twenty-one points.

Basketball Snatch Ball (5-6)

Formation: Divide the class into two equal groups and place one team on each sideline. Place two balls in the center of the court.
Equipment: Two basketballs
Players: Ten to fifteen per team
Skills: Catching, shooting, and dribbling

Players are numbered consecutively and must stand in this order on the sideline of the basketball court. When the teacher calls a number, that player from each team runs to one of the balls, picks it up, dribbles it to the basket on his right, and shoots until he makes a basket. When he succeeds, he dribbles back and replaces the ball. The first player to make a basket and return the ball scores one point for his team.

Teaching suggestions

Players may run by pairs, with two players from each team having the same number. In this case, the ball must be passed between the players three times before and after the shot is made.

In and Out Basketball (5-6)

Formation: Two teams play in half of the basketball court, and a third "waiting" team stands on the sideline.
Equipment: Two basketballs
Players: Six teams of five players each
Skills: Shooting, catching, dribbling, and pivoting

Regular basketball rules apply with the following modifications: (1) Three teams play in half the court; (2) two teams play, while the third team remains on the sidelines; (3) when a field goal or free throw is made, the third team takes the loser's place; and (4) each player is allowed only two dribbles.

Teaching suggestions

Keep third-team players off the playing floor. Use this game to explain rules and strategy, as well as skills. If goals are not being scored, use a time limit instead. If there is enough room, have passing or dribbling drills for the inactive team.

Captain Ball (5-6)

Formation: Playing area arranged according to the diagram below.

Note: Two games can be played in each half of a typical elementary school gymnasium.

The captain and three forward players of Team A must keep one foot inside their hoops. Four guards from Team A may roam anywhere in Team B's side of the playing area; however, they cannot enter the circle of any opposing player. The object of this game is for the guards to get the ball to any of their forward players. The forward players, in turn, try to get the ball to their captain. Start the game with a jump ball between two opposing guards. Award two points each time the captain receives the ball from one of his forwards.

Fouls occur when

1. a guard steps into an opposing player's circle, steps over the centerline or boundary line, or throws the ball directly to the captain (ball is given to the nearest forward player on opposing team)
2. a forward steps out of his circle, holds the ball longer then five seconds, or commits unnecessary rough play (ball is given to the nearest guard on the opposing team)

Variations

1. Add more circle or guard players. Even numbers makes the game more difficult.
2. Require only one type of pass.
3. Add any rule or modification as desired.

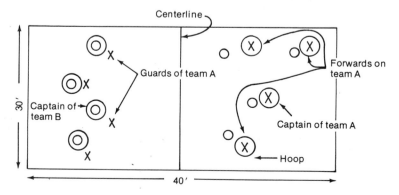

17

Basketball: Rules and Regulations

Basketball is probably the most popular team sport in the upper elementary grades, particularly with boys. Although skill development, especially ball handling and shooting skills, necessitates that the majority of the time be spent on drills and lead-up games, the full game should be played several times during a unit of instruction. Modify the rules, such as lowering the height of the basket and limiting the number of dribbles, to encourage the development of specific skills. Care should be taken, however, not to play the full game too often, perhaps neglecting needed skill development.

I. Field of play:

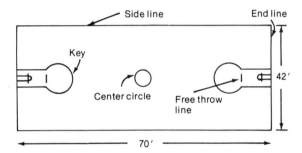

II. Positions:

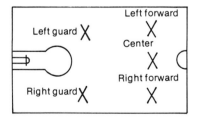

III. To start game: The game is started at the center circle. The referee tosses the ball in the air between the two opposing centers, who attempt to tap it to one of their teammates. This jump ball is also used (a) when the ball is held by two opposing players (jump to be taken at the nearest key or center circle); (b) when the ball goes out of bounds and the referee is uncertain which team caused it to go out; and (c) to start the second half of the game.

IV. After a successful free throw: The ball is put into play at the end of the court by the defending team.

V. After a ball goes out of bounds: The ball is put into play from behind the line and immediately in front of the place where it went out. Any player from the team that did not cause it to go out may put it into play.

VI. Game time: The game is divided into four quarters of six minutes each.

VII. Points: Two points are awarded for every field goal, and one point for every successful free throw.

VIII. Substitution: One or all substitutes may enter the game whenever the ball is not in play (out of bounds, before a jump ball, etc.).

IX. Violations: A violation is charged against a player if he
   A. travels—takes more than one step with the ball without dribbling
   B. double dribbles—dribbles the ball, stops, then dribbles again without another player handling the ball, or palms the ball, that is, does not clearly dribble, or dribbles with two hands
   C. steps on or over a boundary line while he has possession of the ball
   D. kicks the ball
   E. stays longer than three seconds in the key area under the offensive basket, in which case play is stopped and the referee awards a throw from the sideline to the other team near the point where the infraction occurred

X. Fouls: A foul is charged against a player if he
   A. kicks, trips, or pushes another player
   B. holds or charges another player
   C. commits unsportsmanlike conduct

XI. The penalty: Play is stopped and the referee awards one or two free throws to the nonoffending team from the free throw line. The number of free throws awarded is based upon the following:

A. One free throw is awarded to a player who is fouled while participating in an activity other than shooting. If the free throw is successful, the defending team puts the ball into play from behind the end line. If the free throw is unsuccessful, the ball continues in play.

B. Two free throws are awarded to a player who is fouled when he is shooting. If the second free throw is successful, the defending team puts the ball into play from behind the end line. If the second free throw is unsuccessful, the ball continues in play.

Evaluative Techniques

There are several tests that can be used to measure the basic skills of passing, dribbling, and shooting. The following test items are reliable and quite easy to administer. Modify any of them to meet your own teaching situation and add additional ones if desired. Also keep scores from each year in order to build appropriate norms for your school.

Basketball Skill Test

Name	Passing (total pts)	Dribbling (total pts)	Shooting (50 pts)	Subjective Evaluation (50 pts)	Total Score	Grade
1.						
2.	Rank all total scores for the class then convert to letter grades →					→
3.						

Test No. 1   **Passing**

Place a target on the wall as shown in the diagram.

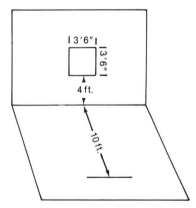

The player must stand and pass from behind the ten-foot line. He has thirty seconds to hit the target as many times as possible. If a player drops the ball within the time period, he may pick it up, return to the ten-foot line, and continue adding to his cumulative score. One point is scored for each pass that lands on the target area. Allow two trials and record the highest score.

Test No. 2   **Dribbling**

Arrange four chairs as shown in the diagram.

Basketball test no. 2

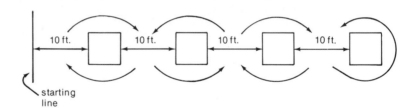

10 ft.   10 ft.   10 ft.   10 ft.

starting
line

A ball is placed on the starting line. Each player must stand behind the starting line, with both hands resting on his knees. On the "go" signal, he picks up the ball and dribbles around the chairs in a zigzag pattern. One point is awarded each time he passes a chair. Allow twenty seconds for the test. Two trials are also allowed, with the highest score recorded.

Test No. 3   **Shooting**

Draw a line at a forty-five degree angle and thirty feet away from the basket. Each student attempts ten lay-up shots. He must begin dribbling from the thirty-foot line and attempt a shot when he reaches the basket. Award five points for each successful basket. Other shooting tests, such as free throws or one- or two-hand sets, may be substituted for the lay-up test.

Test No. 4   **Subjective evaluation**

Establish criteria that represent the skills and playing ability required in basketball. For example, using shooting ability, dribbling, defensive skill, and passing, the teacher would award each player a total point score from zero to fifty points. Three players can be used as judges, with the average score recorded.

Softball Activities

18

Emphasis and Skill Presentation

Teaching Procedures

Description of Skills

Practice Activities

Lead-up Games

Softball: Rules and Regulations

Evaluative Techniques

Softball is an extremely popular recreational activity throughout the United States and in many other countries. Its popularity is probably due in part to the game's relative ease and safety. In addition, softball requires only a minimum amount of protective equipment and a smaller playing field than is required for baseball.

If softball is to be played as a competitive recreational game, every participant must know the rules and be reasonably proficient in the basic throwing, catching, and batting skills. Furthermore, every child should be given an opportunity to play all positions. Assigning only the more proficient players to the catcher, pitcher, and first base positions is educationally unsound.

This chapter has been organized to provide a basic approach to teaching softball to upper elementary school children. Although the lead-up games should be emphasized more than regulation softball during the instructional period, the official game or a modified version should be played occasionally to provide an opportunity for the class to understand the skills and playing strategies and, of course, for the teacher to test their abilities as batters and fielders.

Emphasis and Skill Presentation

The problems of selecting and teaching softball skills and rules are very similar to those found in teaching basketball activities. Through television, organized leagues, and "sandlot" games, most children of this age level are already acquainted with many of the skills and rules of softball. Thus, there will be a very wide variation in the development of softball skills in virtually every grade and within each class. The following suggested sequence of presenting skills and rules, therefore, should be used as a basic guideline.

The skills chart indicates that children normally have been introduced to most throwing, catching, and batting skills by the third grade. The emphasis prior to grade four, however, has been on acquiring these skills through enjoyable lead-up games rather than regulation softball.

Several changes should occur in the fourth grade. More care and attention should be given to increasing the distance and accuracy of throwing skills. The pitching rule should be introduced, and all boys and girls in this grade should have an opportunity to play this position. More consistency in batting should be expected, as well as reasonable skill in fungo hitting.

The fifth- and sixth-grade programs should be seen as continuous periods of refining the basic softball skills. More experienced players will also develop a reasonable level of skill in the sidearm throw and bunting. Major improvement in general positional play should also be shown by most of these children. And it is not uncommon for sixth graders to be able to steal a base, sacrifice, or make a double play.

Suggested Sequence of Presenting Softball Skills and Rules

| Skills and Rules | Grade Level | | | |
	Grade 3	Grade 4	Grade 5	Grade 6
Throwing				
Overhand throw	Acquired or introduce	Increase distance and accuracy	Increase distance and accuracy	Increase distance and accuracy
Underhand throw	Acquired or introduce	Increase speed and accuracy	Increase speed and accuracy	Increase speed and accuracy
Pitching	Acquired or introduce	Increase speed and accuracy	Increase speed and accuracy	Increase speed and accuracy
Sidearm throw			Introduce	Increase speed and accuracy
Rules: Safe and Out	Acquired or introduce			
Fair and foul ball	Acquired or introduce			
Strike zone	Acquired or introduce			
Pitching rule		Introduce		

Skills and Rules	Grade Level			
	Grade 3	*Grade 4*	*Grade 5*	*Grade 6*
Catching and fielding				
Catching low and high throws	Acquired or introduce	Refinement	Refinement	Refinement
Catching fly balls	Acquired or introduce	Refinement	Refinement	Refinement
Fielding grounders	Acquired or introduce	Refinement	Refinement	Refinement
Rules: Fielding positions	Acquired or introduce			
Foul tip		Introduce		
Bunt rule		Introduce		
Batting				
Batting	Acquired or introduce	Increase distance and accuracy	Increase distance and accuracy	Increase distance and accuracy
Fungo hitting		Introduce	Increase distance and accuracy	Increase distance and accuracy
Bunting				Introduce
Rules: Balls and strikes	Acquired or introduce			
Base running				
To first base	Acquired or introduce	Increase speed	Increase speed	Increase speed
Around bases		Introduce	Increase speed	Increase speed
Rules: Touching base	Acquired or introduce			
Off base on caught fly		Introduce		
Related skills				
Positional play			Introduce	Refinement
Stealing bases			Introduce	Refinement
Double play				Introduce
Sacrifice				Introduce

Teaching Procedures

There is a very close similarity between the approaches used to teach softball and basketball. Many elementary school children have played modified versions of softball such as scrub and two-man softball; their skill and general understanding of the game are well beyond the beginner stage. But children who have not had this advantage are far behind in skill development and general playing ability. Since the teaching approach suggested for soccer can apply equally to softball, review pages 221-22 to see how a unit of instruction and individual lessons can be developed.

The inventive games approach suggested in previous chapters can also be applied with equal success to softball activities. Presenting challenges such as "Make up a four-person drill emphasizing grounding and a sidearm throw" provides freedom for a group to develop an activity that is challenging and enjoyable yet con-

18

centrates on one or two important skills. You can also cope with problems associated with sex and peer performances through this problem-solving approach.

The following suggestions apply more specifically to problems associated with teaching softball activities:

1. One of the more chronic problems is that softball is too inactive for most of the players. To help overcome this problem
   a. rotate positions as often as possible
   b. use a batting tee if pitching and batting abilities are generally low
   c. select lead-up games that require smaller playing areas and fewer players
   d. modify the official game, such as two outs before changing positions or all players hitting before changing sides, or shorten the distance between bases
2. There are several safety precautions that should be considered during every instructional and recreational period involving softball activities.
   a. All waiting batters should stay behind a designated safety line.
   b. Every player should be taught how to release the bat after hitting the ball. Stringent enforcement of this rule is extremely important for the safety of all players.
   c. Proper-fitting face masks should be provided for the catcher.
   d. Sliding should be prohibited since it can cause unnecessary injury and tear street clothes.
   e. All bases should be made of soft material.
3. An umpire should be used in the more complex lead-up games and in every modified or regulation softball game. Establish a procedure for rotating the umpire as the teams change positions.
4. Modify every game to cope with the class's general level of ability and interest.

Description of Skills

Softball skills for elementary school children can be classified as hitting and fielding skills. All throwing and catching skills are appropriate for this age range. As for batting skills, most children have little difficulty in learning to hit a ball with a full swing, although bunting and fungo batting will present some problems, particularly for fourth graders.

Throwing

The major part of all fielding and defensive play depends upon how fast and how accurately a player can throw the ball. Although the skill and style of performance will vary from child to child, each is capable of throwing an overhand, sidearm, and underhand toss or pitch with relative ease and accuracy.

Gripping the Ball

There are two basic ways to grip a softball. If the hand is large enough, the ball can be held between the thumb and first two fingers, with the third and fourth fingers just resting against the side of the ball. Elementary school children's smaller hands make it necessary for them to grip the ball with the thumb, and all four fingers spread around the side and bottom of the ball (fig. 18.1a). However, only the top surface of the fingers should touch the ball. A good check for the young thrower is to be able to see daylight between the ball and his hands (fig. 18.1b).

Figure 18.1a Thumb and four-finger grip

Figure 18.1b See daylight

Overhand Throw

This is the basic throw for all players except the pitcher. The upper arm of the throwing arm is raised shoulder-high, then the forearm is lifted above the head and the wrist flexes so the hand points backward (fig. 18.2a). At that point, the left side faces the direction of the throw and the left arm is extended forward. The weight is on the rear foot. In a simultaneous movement, the upper right arm is lifted upward and forward and the left arm moves down and back as the weight shifts to the front foot (fig. 18.2b). The ball is released off the fingertips when the arm is about shoulder-high. The follow-through should be in a downward direction, ending with the palm of the throwing hand facing the ground (fig. 18.2c).

Figure 18.2a Forearm above the shoulder

Figure 18.2b Arm raised upward and forward

Figure 18.2c Follow-through

Common Faults

1. Holding the ball too close to the palm of the hand
2. Failing to lead the throw with the elbow
3. Failing to follow through in a downward direction

18

Sidearm Throw   The sidearm throw is used when the ball has to be thrown a short distance and in a hurry; thus it is the most effective throw for infielders. The general body action of this throw is similar to the overhand throw, except that the upper throwing arm is extended diagonally out and down from the shoulder and the forearm is extended straight up from the elbow (fig. 18.3a). As the arm swings forward, the forearm drops down and swings parallel to the ground (fig. 18.3b and c). As the ball is released, the arm continues across and around the body.

Figure 18.3a   Figure 18.3b   Figure 18.3c

Common Faults

1. Failing to extend the upper arm diagonally out
2. Swinging the throwing arm forward and downward
3. Failing to follow through across the body

Underhand Toss   The underhand toss is used for short, quick throws, most often around the infield area. The player extends his upper arm and forearm backward as his weight shifts to his rear foot. On the forward movement, he swings his arm down and forward and shifts his weight to the front foot (fig. 18.4). As the ball is released, the player follows through with his upper arm and hand in the direction of the throw.

Figure 18.4 Forward pendulum action of the arm

Common Faults

1. Failing to shift the weight to the back foot
2. Releasing the ball too soon or too late
3. Failing to follow through in the direction of the throw

18

Pitching   The pitcher stands with her feet parallel, holding the ball in front of her with both hands and facing the batter. She moves both hands forward until her arms are extended to about waist-high (fig. 18.5a). She then releases her right hand from the ball as she brings her throwing arm down and back. At the top of the backswing, her body should be slightly twisted toward her pitching arm and her weight should be on her left foot (fig. 18.5b). In a simultaneous action, she swings her left arm forward and close to the body, rotates her shoulders toward the right, and steps forward on the opposite foot (fig. 18.5c). As the ball is released off the fingertips, she follows through with the pitching arm.

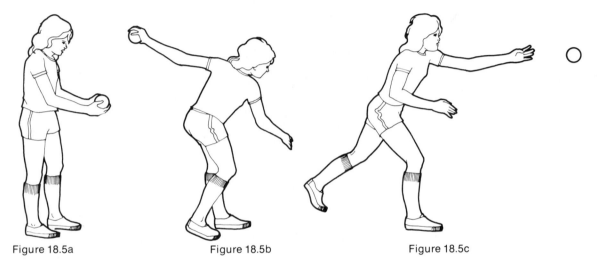

Figure 18.5a   Figure 18.5b   Figure 18.5c

Common Faults

1. Failing to extend the throwing arm back and up prior to pitching
2. Failing to rotate the shoulders toward the left on the forward swing of the throwing arm
3. Releasing the ball too soon or too late

Catching and Fielding   Good fielding ability requires the player to be able to catch a high fly ball and a variety of throws and to stop a ball hit along the ground. In all types of fielding it is important to be in a ready position, with the feet spread apart comfortably and the weight on both feet. The trunk leans forward slightly and the knees are flexed. The hands should be in front of the body and about knee-high. The eyes should be on the ball (fig. 18.6).

Figure 18.6

Catching   If the ball approaches below the waist, the fingers should be pointing with the little fingers together (fig. 18.7a). When the ball approaches above the waist, the thumbs should be together and the fingers pointing upward (fig. 18.7b). As the ball is caught, the hands should recoil toward the body to deaden or soften the force of the oncoming ball.

Figure 18.7a Catching below the waist

Figure 18.7b Catching above the waist

18

Common Faults

1. Failing to get into line with the ball
2. Failing to reach out to catch the ball
3. Failing to "give" or recoil with the ball

Fielding Grounders   The first important move in grounding a ball is to shift the body toward the direction of the oncoming ball. As the fielder moves toward the ball, she shifts her weight forward, holding her arms low and in front of her body (fig. 18.8a). Just before grounding the ball, she stops, with her right foot slightly in front of her left foot, her knees bent, and her trunk well forward (fig. 18.8b). She should contact the ball just inside her front foot with her left hand, then cover or trap it with her throwing hand (fig. 18.8c). The eyes should be kept on the ball until it is firmly held. Once the ball is caught, the fielder begins to straighten up and takes a step in the direction of the throw.

Figure 18.8a

Figure 18.8b

Figure 18.8c

Fielding a ground ball requires good fielding position and split-second timing to catch the ball on a good bounce. Because of these factors, plus the use of poor and uneven playing fields, the "sure-stop" grounding skill should be used, particularly by outfielders. This is similar to the regular grounding skill, except that the fielder turns toward the right and lowers one knee to the ground. The thigh and lower leg provide a good rebound surface for a ball that is missed (fig. 18.9).

Figure 18.9 "Sure-stop" grounding

Common Faults

1. Failing to keep the eyes on ball until it is caught
2. Failing to get in line with the ball
3. Failing to "give" with the fingers, hands, and arm as the ball is caught

Batting   There are three basic ways of hitting a ball in softball. The first, and most important, is hitting a pitched ball with maximum force and follow-through. *Bunting* is a form of hitting a pitched ball; however, there are basic differences in grip, force, and follow-through. *Fungo batting* is simply throwing the ball up with one hand, regrasping the bat, and hitting the ball before it hits the ground.

The bat may be gripped in one of three positions, depending upon the batter's strength and the type of hit he wishes to make. In the long grip (fig. 18.10a), the hands are placed close to the bottom of the bat. For the medium grip (fig. 18.10b), the hands are moved up about one to two inches. And, for the choke grip (fig. 18.10c), the hands are about three to four inches away from the knob of the bat. In each grip, the bat is held with the hands together and the fingers and thumbs wrapped around the handle. For right-handed batters, the right hand grips the handle above the left hand.

Figure 18.10a Long grip

Figure 18.10b Medium grip

Figure 18.10c Choke grip

Batting   The batter should stand with his feet parallel and about shoulder-width apart. The left side of the body faces the pitcher. The bat should be held back of the head and about shoulder-high. The arms should be bent at the elbows and held away from the body (fig. 18.11a). As the ball leaves the pitcher's hand, the batter shifts his weight to the rear foot. He then swings the bat forward as his weight shifts to the lead foot (fig. 18.11c). After the ball is contacted, the batter continues to swing the bat around in a wide arc, ending over the left shoulder.

Figure 18.11a

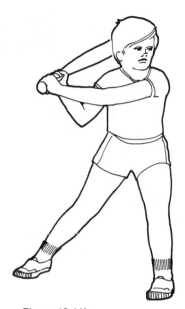

Figure 18.11b

Figure 18.11c

Common Faults

1. Holding the bat on the shoulder and keeping the elbows too close to the sides
2. Swinging the bat up and under the ball
3. Contacting the ball with a relaxed grip

18

Bunting   In bunting, the bat is placed in the way of the oncoming pitch, then allowed to "give" as the ball contacts the bat. As the ball moves toward the strike zone, the batter draws his rear foot forward and squares his body to the pitcher. At the same time, he slides his top hand up the bat, keeping the hand cupped and the fingers resting just behind the hitting surface (fig. 18.12). When the ball is hit, the bat should be angled in the direction of the intended bunt.

Figure 18.12

Common Faults

1. Moving into the bunting stance too soon
2. Failing to "give" as the ball contacts the bat
3. Failing to direct the ball to the right field position

Fungo Batting   Fungo batting is useful for hitting the ball during fielding practice and in many lead-up games. Start with the feet parallel and comfortably spread apart, with the weight evenly distributed on both feet. Suspend the bat over the right shoulder while holding the ball in the left hand (fig. 18.13a). Simultaneously toss the ball up and swing the bat down and forward, grasping it with both hands (fig. 18.13b). Continue forward, transferring the weight to the front foot and twisting the body toward the left. Hit the ball approximately in front of the left foot (fig. 18.13c) and follow through with a swing around the left shoulder.

Figure 18.13a   Figure 18.13b   Figure 18.13c

Common Faults

1. Throwing the ball too far in front of the body
2. Hitting the ball too far in front of the body

Base Running   As soon as a ball is hit, the batter should drop his bat and run as fast as possible to and through the first base. The base runner touches the foul line side of the bag with either foot. If he decides to try to run to second base, he should begin to curve to the right a few feet before reaching first base, touch the inside corner of the bag and continue running to second base.

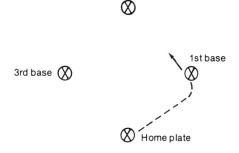

Common Faults

1. Failing to run on every hit
2. Failing to run "through" first base

Practice Activities

One of the most common complaints by elementary school teachers is the insufficient number of balls and bats for practice activities. This can be overcome by using a station system and rotating groups. The illustration below shows several partner and group activities involving a variety of skills going on simultaneously. Each group rotates to the next station after a set period of time. If the groups do not have time to rotate through all the stations in one lesson, simply continue in the next one.

The majority of practice activities for softball involves partners or small groups. Each of the following drills and practice activities should be modified to cope with the available space, time, and equipment.

Throwing and Catching Activities

Perhaps the most common type of softball practice activity involves two players. Some of the most useful partner activities are described.

Partner Activities

1. Have the partners throw and catch. Have both partners remain stationary, varying the distances; then have one remain stationary while the other moves, practicing grounders.
2. Have the pitcher and catcher alternate positions.
3. Practice hitting a target. Set up a target on a wall or the ground for pitching or accurate throwing practice.

The inventive games approach can be used quite effectively in partner activities to increase skill and to provide an avenue for unique and enjoyable practice activities. The following example should provide a general idea:

Situation: Divide the class into partners. Give the partners a ball and one piece of small equipment (bat, hoop, traffic cone).

Challenge: "Can you make up a game (or drill) with your partner that includes a sidearm throw, a grounder, and one piece of small equipment?" Allow the class several minutes to make up their games, then select one or two partner groups and have them demonstrate their games.

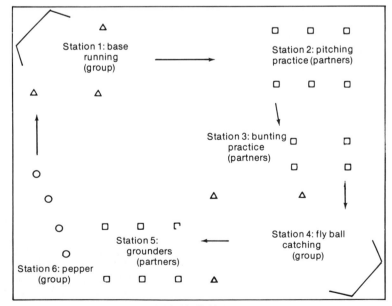

Available field space

Activity	Page	Used for	Change to softball
Zigzag volleyball	289	Volleyball	X
Shuttle volleying	289	Volleyball	X

Group Activities

Several relays described in previous chapters can be adapted for practicing softball skills.

Overtake the Base

Formation

Divide the class into squads of eight to ten players. Arrange the squads around the bases, with player A at the pitcher's line, B on home plate, C on first base, D on second, and E on third. The remaining players form a line near home plate.

Basic Drill

When the whistle blows, player A throws to B, B throws to C, and on around the diamond to home plate. At the same time as A throws the ball, F takes off for first base and continues around the bases, attempting to reach home plate before the ball. Two rules apply: (1) The base runner must touch all bases and (2) the players rotate after each run. A takes B's position, B goes to C, F takes A's. Everyone shifts one place to the right, with the player on third—E—going to the back of the line.

Variations

1. Make two diamonds, with the smaller one for runners and the larger one for throwers.
2. Add one or more fielders.

Fly Ball Catching

Formation

Place one batter at home plate and scatter the remaining players in the field.

Basic Drill

The batter, using fungo batting, hits fly balls into the field. When a fielder catches a fly ball, he becomes the batter.

Variations

1. Place all fielders in a large semicircle and require the batter to hit two balls to each player in turn. Rotate after the last player has received his second fly.
2. Add a pitcher and a catcher.

Throw for Distance

Formation

Arrange field as illustrated.

Throw for distance

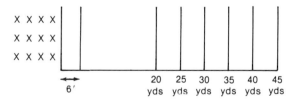

Basic Drill

The throw must be made from within two restraining lines. After a reasonable warm-up, the player throws the ball as far as possible from behind the restraining line. He may take one or more steps, providing he remains within the lines. The player with the longest throw or the team with the most total yardage wins.

Softball Throw Relay

Formation
Arrange teams in equal lines behind a starting line, with approximately six feet between each team. Draw a throwing line ten feet in front of the starting line. Place a catcher for each team on a third line twenty-five feet in front of the throwing line.

Number of players
Twenty to thirty

Equipment
Balls and chalk or stick to draw lines

Skills
Throwing and catching

Basic Drill
A player on each team runs to the throwing line to receive the ball thrown by the catcher, then throws it back to the catcher. The thrower returns to the starting line and tags the next player, who continues the relay.

Teaching Suggestions
1. Have the children use various throwing skills —underhand, overhand, left-handed, and right-handed.
2. Alternate catchers each time a team wins; the first person in line becomes the catcher.
3. Keep the children behind the starting line until it is their turn to throw.

Batting Activities

The success of any softball game centers on each player's ability to hit the ball. But too often, batting practice is one player hitting the ball to ten or more very inactive fielders. The following partner activities are very effective in developing batting skills:

1. One player hits the ball off a tee to his partner. Use a traffic cone mounted on a cardboard box as a substitute tee.
2. One player fungo hits to his partner.
3. Add a third player. One player pitches, another bats, and the third player fields the ball. Rotate after three hits.
4. Practice close-range bunting. One player pitches, while the batter attempts to bunt the ball back.

Group Activities

The following group activities should be modified to meet the class's level of ability.

Swing at Four

Formation
Divide the class into two or three squads of ten to twelve players. Arrange squads in infield positions, with spare players in a line behind home plate.

Basic Drill
The pitcher throws four balls to each batter, who attempts to hit them into the infield. Infield players retrieve the ball and throw it to first base. The first baseman returns the ball to the pitcher. Rotate players after each player has had four hits. The batter takes the third baseman's position and everyone shifts one place to the left. The catcher goes to the back of the "waiting" line, and the pitcher becomes the catcher.

Variations
Add outfielders and allow batters to hit anywhere.

Pepper

Formation
Divide the class into groups of five or six. Place five players in a line, with about ten feet between each player. One player, the "leader," stands with his bat about twenty feet in front of the line.

Basic Drill
The first player in the line pitches the ball to the leader, who hits it to the next player in line. The second player fields the ball and pitches it back to the leader. Continue the drill to the last player, then rotate the leader.

Variations
If a line player misses the ball, he goes to the end of the line. If a batter misses a fair pitch, he changes places with the player at the end of the line.

Lead-up Games

The following lead-up games are designed to provide maximum participation and practice in one or more softball skills. As a general guideline, use these games extensively in grades four and five and proportionately less in the sixth grade. Playing the official game of softball can be a challenging and enjoyable experience for upper elementary school children. This is true, however, only when the majority of players have developed adequate throwing, catching, and batting skills. These lead-up games can be played in smaller areas and require fewer players than the regulation game.

Six-Player Softball (4-5)

Formation: Playing field and players arranged as illustrated in diagram
Equipment: Three bases, one bat, and one softball
Players: Six on each team
Skills: Throwing, catching, and hitting

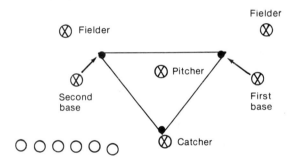

This game is similar to softball, but with the following modifications: (1) A game has six complete innings; (2) there are four outs in each inning; (3) a batter is out after two strikes; (4) a foul ball counts half a strike; and (5) a base-on ball is given after three balls rather than four. All players rotate one field position after each inning.

Danish Rounders (4-5)

Formation: Playing field and players arranged as illustrated in diagram
Equipment: Tennis ball or five-inch utility ball
Players: Ten on each team
Skills: Throwing, catching, and base running

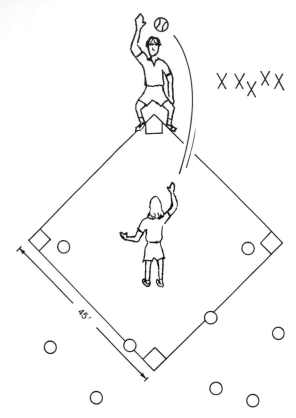

The pitcher throws an underhand pitch slightly above the batter's head, and the batter tries to hit the ball with his hand. Whether he hits the ball or not, he must run to first base, and farther, if possible. The fielding team tries to return the ball to the pitcher, who tries to touch his base with it before the batter reaches first base. If the ball touches the pitcher's base before the runner reaches first base, he is out. Any number of batting players may be on any base at the same time, and on any strike or hit they may remain on base or run to the next one. But when the pitcher downs the ball, any base runner who is off base is out. Also, a caught fly automatically puts out the batter and any player who is running between bases. Play continues until every member of the batting team has had a turn at bat; then the teams change positions. A point is scored when a player makes it to home plate.

Flies and Grounders (4-6)

Formation: One batter and five other players scattered in the playing area
Equipment: One bat and ball for each group
Players: Six players in each group
Skills: Throwing, batting, and fielding

The batter fungo hits the ball into the field. The player in a position to catch the ball calls "Mine" and attempts to catch it. He receives five points for catching a fly ball, three points for a ball caught after one bounce, and one point for a grounder. The first player to reach fifteen points becomes the new batter.

Variations
Use a batting tee rather than fungo hitting.

One Old Cat (4-6)

Formation: Divide players into two teams of nine each, with one team in the field and one at bat
Equipment: Softball and bat, two bases (first and home)
Players: Nine on each team
Skills: Throwing, catching, and batting

The first player on the batting team hits the ball into the field and tries to run to first base and home in one complete trip. He may not stop on the base. If he makes a complete trip without being put out, he scores one run for his team. The runner is out if (a) a fielder catches a fly ball, or (b) a fielder touches the runner with the ball before he reaches home. When the team at bat makes three outs, it goes into the field and the team in the field comes to bat. The team with the most scores at the end of the playing period wins. (Teams must have the same number of times at bat.)

Teaching suggestions

1. Have waiting batter stand behind a restraining line.
2. Alternate pitchers and catchers. Alternate boy and girl in batting order.
3. Try two outs if one team stays up too long.
4. Vary the distance to base according to the level of skill.

Long Ball (4-6)

Formation: Divide class into equal teams. The fielding team consists of a pitcher and a catcher, with the remaining players scattered in the field.
Equipment: Softball, bat, and two bases (home and first)
Players: Nine on each team
Skills: Throwing, catching, and hitting

Each team selects a pitcher and a catcher. Other players are fielders or batters. When a batter hits the ball, he runs to the base, and, if possible, returns home, scoring a point. Any hit is good and there are no fouls. The base runner may stop on first base, and any number of runners may be on base at the same time. Runners may not steal home. The batter is out when he strikes out, is touched off base, steals a base, throws the bat, or a fly ball is caught. One point is awarded for each run.

Teaching suggestions

1. Alternate pitchers and catchers.
2. Draw a line behind the batter's box for other children to wait behind.
3. Move the pitcher closer if skill indicates.

Tee Ball (4-6)

Formation: Regulation softball
Equipment: Softball, bases, and tee (commercial tee or traffic cone mounted on a cardboard box)
Players: Nine on each team
Skills: All softball skills except pitching and stealing bases

This game is played in the same way as softball, with the following modifications:

1. The batter is allowed one hit off the tee.
2. Since there is no pitcher, no one is permitted to steal a base. A runner must stay on the base until the ball is hit by his teammate.

Cricket Softball (4-6)

Formation: Playing field arranged as illustrated
Equipment: One softball, two bats, four Indian clubs, and two bases
Players: Ten players arranged in partners
Skills: Batting, throwing, catching, and fielding

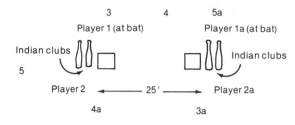

The object of this game is for each set of partners to score runs by hitting the ball and running to opposite bases before the Indian clubs (or milk cartons) can be knocked down by any fielder. The game begins with players 1 and 1a at bat. Players 2 and 2a are pitchers and stand beside each base. All other players are fielders. There are no boundaries. The batter must begin with the butt end of the bat touching the base. Player 2 throws the ball at the Indian clubs and the batter protects them by hitting the ball. If the pitcher knocks over a club, an out is called. When this occurs, players 1 and 1a become fielders and players 2 and 2a become the new batters. If 1a hits the ball, he exchanges positions with his partner. The fielders try to recover the ball and knock over the Indian clubs by rolling or throwing the ball at them before the runners can change places. A run is scored if the fielders cannot knock down the Indian clubs before the runners exchange positions. As long as the clubs remain standing, the batters may exchange bases any number of times, scoring a run for each exchange. Pitchers must alternate throwing after each successful run. A caught fly is an out for the batting team. After an out players 2 and 2a become the new batters and players 3 and 3a become the new pitchers.

18

Twenty-one Softball (4-6)

Formation: Arrange teams as in regular softball
Equipment: One bat, one ball, and four bases
Players: Nine to ten on each team
Skills: Throwing, catching, and hitting

Play according to regular softball rules, with the following exceptions: The batter gets three swings to hit the ball. When he hits the ball, he runs the bases in order until he is put out. A runner safe at first scores one point; a runner safe at second, two points; safe at third, three points; and safe at home, four points. Teams exchange places after three outs. The first team to score twenty-one points wins.

Teaching suggestions

1. Teach fielders to throw to the base ahead of the runner to put him out.
2. Keep waiting batters ten to fifteen feet away from batter's box.
3. Change pitcher and catcher each time the teams change positions.
4. Use fungo hitting instead of a pitcher.
5. Change scoring to eleven or fifteen points rather than twenty-one.

Overtake the Ball (4-6)

Formation: Class arranged in large circle with ten to twenty feet between each player
Equipment: One softball per team
Players: Ten to sixteen per team
Skills: Throwing and catching

The players stand in a circle and count off by twos. The ones are members of one team and the twos, the other. Each team selects a captain, who stands in the center of the circle. Both captains have a ball. On signal, each captain tosses his ball to any team member, who tosses it back to the captain. The captain tosses it to the next team member (in a clockwise direction), who also tosses it back to the captain. The ball is tossed in this manner clockwise around the circle by both teams until each ball has been thrown to all members of the team and is back in the captain's hands. One team "overtakes" the other when its ball passes that of the other team as the balls are tossed around the circle. The team that tosses the ball completely around the circle first scores one point. When a team overtakes and finishes first, it scores two points. The first team to score five points wins the game.

Teaching suggestions

1. Explain and enforce response to the signal used to start the tosses. Use the same signal for each start.
2. Play the game with various kinds of balls and different throws and passes.
3. Vary the distance according to the level of skill.

Roll at the Bat (4-6)

Formation: Outdoor playing area with fielders in a scattered formation facing the batter
Equipment: One bat and one softball
Players: Four to nine for each game
Skills: Fungo hitting, catching, and throwing

One player is chosen to be the first batter and fungo hits the ball anywhere into the field of play. If a player catches a fly ball, he rolls it back and tries to hit the bat, which has been placed on the ground. The length of the bat must face each "roller." If the ball is not caught, it is thrown back to the batter again. A fielder becomes the new batter when (a) he successfully rolls a ball back and hits the bat, (b) he catches two fly balls, or (c) he successfully retrieves three grounders. All players start at zero when a new batter takes a turn.

Beatball Softball (5-6)

Formation: Teams arranged as in regular softball
Equipment: Bat, softball, and four bases
Players: Nine on each team
Skills: Throwing, catching, and hitting

Play according to regular softball rules, with the following exceptions: Any fielder who gets the ball must throw it to the first baseman, who must touch the base with the ball in his hand, then throw from first to second, second to third, and third to home. If the ball gets home ahead of the runner, he is out. If the runner beats the ball home, he scores a run for his team. After three outs the teams exchange places.

Teaching suggestions

1. Teach the fielders to throw around the runner when he is running the bases.
2. Rotate the fielders so they learn to play all positions.
3. Use fungo hitting instead of a pitcher.
4. Move bases closer together for the girls or play boys' and girls' games on separate diamonds.

Scrub (5-6)

Formation: Playing field with a home base, pitcher, and first base
Equipment: One ball, one bat, and three bases—home, first, and pitching
Players: Seven to twelve for each game
Skills: All softball skills

One player (the "scrub") takes his place at bat. All other players are numbered; the catcher is one; pitcher, two; first base, three; and fielders, four and up. The batter hits a pitched ball and must run to first base and back. He is out if he is tagged at first or home, strikes out, slings his bat, or hits a fly ball that is caught. If he gets home, he bats again. The batter is allowed only three times at bat; then he becomes the last fielder. If the batter is put out, every player moves up one position.

Variations
If a player catches a fly ball, he exchanges positions with the batter. Two players may be up at the same time. In this situation, the first batter is permitted to stop on first base and be hit home by the other batter.

Five Hundred (5-6)

Formation: Outdoor playing area with fielders in a scattered formation facing the batter
Equipment: One softball and one bat
Players: Four to nine players for each game
Skills: Fungo batting, throwing, catching, and fielding

One player is chosen to be the first batter. The object of the game is for each fielder to try to be the first to reach 500 points. Points are scored as follows: 100 for catching a ball on the fly; 75 for a ball caught on the first bounce; and 50 for fielding a grounder. The same number of points is deducted from a player's score if he commits an error. As soon as a player has reached 500 or more points, he exchanges positions with the batter.

Softball: Rules and Regulations

Although the skill development will vary for each grade and class, the complete game of softball should be played periodically throughout a softball unit. By playing the game according to the basic rules, children learn to appreciate the value of practice and team play. Modifications might include shortening the length between bases, allowing the less proficient to pitch to the less proficient, and reducing the number of strikes to two. While children are playing the full game, the teacher should note their major weaknesses so she can select appropriate drills and lead-up games that can be used to improve these deficiencies.

I. Field of play and positions:
II. Batting order: Players are permitted to hit in any order; however, it is wise to have players bat according to their positions. Once an order is established, it cannot be changed, even if players change their positions.

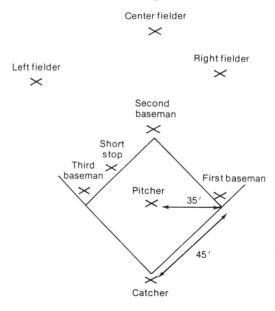

18

III. The batter advances to first base when he
    A. hits a fair ball and reaches base before the ball does
    B. is walked (receives four called balls)
    C. is hit by a pitched ball
    D. is interfered with by the catcher when batting

IV. The batter is out when he
    A. has three strikes
    B. is thrown out at first
    C. is tagged before reaching first base
    D. hits a fair or foul ball that is caught on the fly
    E. hits the third strike and the ball is caught by the catcher
    F. bunts a foul on the third strike
    G. throws the bat more than ten feet
    H. steps on home plate when batting
    I. interferes with the catcher when he is catching a fly or putting out a runner coming home
    J. fouls any ball to the catcher that rises above the batter's head and is caught

V. The base runner when traveling the bases
    A. may advance to the next base after a fly is caught
    B. must advance to the next base when forced to do so by another base runner
    C. may advance one base on an overthrow at first or third base
    D. may advance two bases when overthrows are in the field of play
    E. may attempt to steal a base as soon as the ball leaves the pitcher's hand
    F. may advance to the next base on a fair hit that is not caught on the fly

VI. The base runner is out when he
    A. leaves the base before the ball leaves the pitcher's hand
    B. is forced to run to the next base and does not arrive before the fielder touches the base with the ball in his possession
    C. leaves the base before a fly ball is caught and a fielder tags him or that base before he returns
    D. is hit by a batted ball when off base
    E. intentionally interferes with a member of the fielding team
    F. is tagged when off base
    G. fails to touch a base and the fielder tags him or the base before he returns
    H. passes another base runner
    I. touches a base that is occupied by another base runner

VII. The pitcher
    A. must stand with both feet on the rubber, face the batter, and hold the ball in front with both hands
    B. is allowed one step forward and must deliver the ball while taking that step
    C. must deliver the ball with an underhand throw
    D. cannot fake or make any motion toward the plate without delivering the ball
    E. cannot deliberately roll or bounce the ball
    F. cannot deliver the ball until the batter is ready

VIII. If there is an illegal pitch, the batter is entitled to take a base.

IX. The game is five to seven innings, as agreed by both teams. When there is not sufficient time to complete the game, the score reverts to the even innings score (the score after both squads have been up to bat the same number of times).

X. One point is scored each time a batter touches home base after touching each base sequentially.

Evaluative Techniques

There are several tests that can be used to measure the basic softball skills. The following tests are quite reliable and can be administered with student help in a short period of time. Modify any test item to meet your own teaching situation and add items if desired. Also, keep scores from year to year in order to build appropriate norms for your school.

Softball Skill Test

Name	Accuracy throw (total points)	Distance throw (total points)	Fielding (total points)	Subjective Evaluation (50 points)	Total	Grade
1						
2	Rank all total scores for the class					
3	then convert to letter grades or change				→	
4	to ratings (superior, good, etc.)					

Test No. 1 **Accuracy throw**

Place a target on the wall as shown in the diagram. Use a regulation softball.

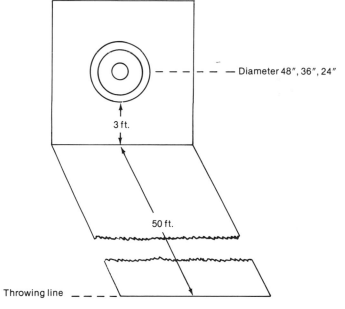

Diameter 48", 36", 24"

3 ft.

50 ft.

Throwing line

A player is given ten consecutive throws from behind the throwing line. He must use the overhand throw. Score six, four, and two for hits within each respective circle. If a ball hits a line, award the higher value. Allow only one trial and record the total score.

Test No. 2   Distance throw

Place lines on the field as shown. Stakes can be used as a substitute for white gypsum lines. Use a regulation softball.

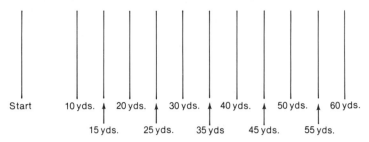

Test No. 3   Fielding

Place lines on a field as shown. Stakes or other "corner" markers can be substituted for lines.

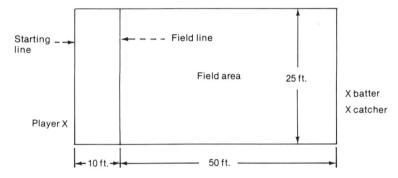

The teacher (or a student who is proficient at fungo batting) bats a grounder into the field area. As soon as the ball is batted, the player runs from the starting line, picks up the ball inside the field area and throws it to the catcher. Ten trials are given, with five points awarded for each successfully fielded ball. Since it is difficult to hit grounders with reasonable consistency, use your discretion to allow retrials on any ball you feel was unfair to the contestant. Also, if batting skill is too poor, substitute a throw for the fungo batting.

Test No. 4   Subjective evaluation

Establish criteria that represent the skills and playing ability required in softball. Since it is difficult to construct a fair and reliable test for batting, include this skill as part of your subjective evaluation. Consider other skills such as base running, catching, and team play. Award a total point score (zero to fifty points) and use three players as judges. Take an average of the three ratings.

Track and Field Activities

19

Upper elementary school children have a keen interest in track and field activities. They can participate in these events according to their ability and motivation. Furthermore, track-and-field activities are relatively easy to teach, require little expense, and provide vigorous competitive experience for all children. The inherent values of this activity, coupled with the feasibility of modifying facilities, make it one that should be considered a basic requirement in the elementary school physical education program.

This chapter describes the basic track and field events and presents methods of organizing and teaching these activities. Special attention has been given to developing improvised equipment and to planning track meets.

Emphasis and Skill Presentation

Skill development in any of the official track and field events is dependent upon the performer's potential or inherent ability and the amount and type of previous training. Taking these factors into consideration, the suggested sequence of skills shown in the accompanying chart is provided as a rough guideline. In this type of activity, improvement in individual events is not simply the accumulation of new skills; it is the sequential addition of skills plus improvement in form and general conditioning.

The fourth grade is an important starting point for many track and field skills. Correct starting positions, sprints, and distance running should be introduced to children in this grade. They also should develop reasonable skill in the

Suggested Sequence of Presenting Track and Field Skills and Rules

Skills and Rules	Grade Level			
	Grade 3	Grade 4	Grade 5	Grade 6
Starting				
For distance runs		Introduce	Refinement	Refinement
For sprints		Introduce	Refinement	Refinement
Rules: False start		Introduce		
Running				
Sprints	30- to 40-yd. dashes	40- to 60-yd. dashes	50- to 80-yd. dashes	50- to 100-yd. dashes
Relay running			Introduce	Refinement
Hurdling			Introduce	Refinement
Distance running		500- to 600-yd. run	Increase distance and speed	Increase distance and speed
Rules: Lane position			Introduce	
Passing rule			Introduce	
High jumping				
Scissors method	Introduce	Increase height and form	Increase height and form	Increase height and form
Straddle method			Introduce	Increase height and form
Rules: Number of jumps		Introduce		
Broad jump				
Standing long jump	Introduce	Increase distance and form	Increase distance and form	Increase distance and form
Long jump		Introduce	Increase distance and form	Increase distance and form
Rules: Foot fault		Introduce		
Triple jump				
Rules: Foot fault				Introduce
Shot put				
Rules: Foot fault			Introduce	Increase distance and form
Other rules				
General track meet rules		Introduce		

standing and running long jump, as well as the high jump using the scissors method.

Most of the remaining track and field skills are introduced in grade five. These youngsters are interested in and capable of learning baton passing, hurdling, high jumping using the straddle method, and putting the shot. There is a major increase in skill and performance levels in both track and field events. Children in grade six learn the triple jump and continue to improve their form and performance in other events.

Expected Proficiencies

Since proficiency in track and field events is measured in time or distance, the accompanying chart provides a rough estimate of what can be expected of elementary school children. If teachers are introducing track and field activities similar to those listed in the chart, it is wise to establish school records. Use the suggested high and low records shown in the chart as a guide in establishing "expected" records within your school.

Proficiency Levels for Track and Field

Minimum to Optimum Records

Event	Grade 4		Grade 5		Grade 6		Grade 7	
	Low	High	Low	High	Low	High	Low	High
50-yd. dash (boys)	10.0	6.0	9.5	6.0	9.0	6.0	8.9	5.8
50-yd. dash (girls)	10.0	6.0	10.0	6.0	10.0	5.9	10.2	6.0
220-yd. run (boys)	42.0	31.0	40.0	32.5	38.0	30.5	37.0	30.0
150-yd. run (boys)	27.0	22.0	25.0	19.1	23.0	18.2	22.5	18.0
150-yd. run (girls)	28.0	23.0	26.0	21.0	25.0	20.0	24.0	19.5
High jump (boys)	2'11"	3'4"	3'0"	3'10"	3'6"	4'2"	3'8"	4'6"
High jump (girls)	2'10"	3'2"	3'0"	3'4"	3'0"	3'6"	3'3"	4'0"
Standing long jump (boys)	4'0"	6'4"	4'8"	6'8"	4'10"	6'11"	4'5"	8'9"
Standing long jump (girls)	3'9"	5'9"	3'11"	6'4"	4'2"	6'10"	3'9"	7'6"
Running long jump (boys)	11'0"	12'2"	12'0"	13'2"	13'0"	14'2"	13'6"	15'0"
Running long jump (girls)	10'0"	11'0"	11'0"	12'0"	12'0"	13'6"	12'6"	14'0"
Softball throw (boys)	35'	175'	70'	205'	76'	207'	88'	245'
Softball throw (girls)	21'	167'	32'	141'	37'	159'	36'	150'

Teaching Procedures

Several important factors must be considered when planning a track and field unit. Although it is important for all children to experience the enjoyment and challenge of all the events, they should be allowed to concentrate on a few events that they enjoy and do well. This means the teacher should introduce the children early to as many track and field events as possible. Each child can then select a certain number of events for more extensive practice.

A second major consideration is how to cope with available space and equipment. Since there is never enough equipment for all children to practice the same event at the same time, station work should be used. The accompanying drawing of a track and field circuit provides a basic guideline.

It is important to put each event in a relatively permanent place on the field. Jumping pits are normally located in the corners of the field. A temporary track can be made by placing traffic cones or milk cartons in an oval pattern. Placing the shot put circles inside the oval provides a safe, restrictive area for this event. Sprints and hurdles can be located near each other for dual instruction purposes.

Once the general layout is established, the teacher can divide her class into squads and assign each to a station. Give brief demonstrations at each station, then allow time for practice before the squads are rotated to the next station. Rotation should be from a track event to a field event.

The following general considerations and safety procedures should be included in every track and field unit of instruction:

1. All facilities and equipment should be checked before the class begins. In particular, look for broken glass or other hazardous materials in jumping pits and field areas.

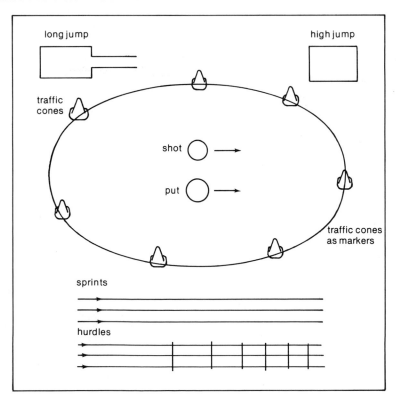

2. Each lesson should begin with a comprehensive warm-up or conditioning period involving running, jogging, and conditioning exercises designed to increase strength, endurance, and flexibility.

3. Whenever possible, provide instruction to mixed groups rather than separating boys and girls. The difference in performance levels of boys and girls at this age is more often due to motivation and prior experience than to inherent physiological differences.

Description of Skills

There are two basic types of events in track and field. The first is the running events, which include sprints, hurdles, and longer endurance runs. The second type is field events, including the high jump, the long jump, and the shot put. These skills should be taught to all students, regardless of their inherent ability. Once the children have been exposed to these skills, allow them to select and concentrate on those events that are best suited to their potential capabilities.

Starting

The starting position for running events is determined by the length of the race. For short races, such as twenty- and thirty-yard dashes, the "kneeling start" or "sprint start" is best. For longer races, the "standing start" is more acceptable.

Standing Start

In the standing start (fig. 19.1) one foot is close to the starting line and the other foot is slightly to the rear. The head is up, the trunk is bent forward, the knees are slightly flexed, and the weight is on the front foot. The opposite arm to the lead foot is held forward with the elbow flexed, while the other arm is down and slightly back.

Figure 19.1 Body leans forward slightly.

Sprint Start   The sprint start is important to the success of any beginning sprinter. The form and techniques of this skill are quite easy to master, even for fourth graders.

On the "On your mark" command the runner kneels and places the toe of her front foot about six to twelve inches behind the starting line (fig. 19.2a). The front foot is normally the opposite foot to the "kicking foot." She extends her arms straight down, with the weight on the fingertips. (If children do not have adequate arm and shoulder girdle strength, allow them to support their weight on their knuckles.) The runner squeezes her fingers together to make a "bridge" with the thumb. On "Set" she raises her lower knee and buttocks until her back is straight and parallel to the ground (fig. 19.2b). Her weight should be evenly distributed between her hands and her front foot. Her head is not raised as she should be looking at a spot on the ground a few feet in front of the starting line. On "Go" she drives forward with her lead leg and, at the same instant, brings her rear leg forward (fig. 19.2c).

Figure 19.2a "On your mark"   Figure 19.2b "Set"   Figure 19.2c "Go"

Running   There are several types of running positions, each with its own body lean, arm action, and foot contact. The elementary school track program, however, involves only two types, sprinting form and distance running form. In the sprinting form (fig. 19.3), the runner's body leans well forward and contact is made with the ball or front of the foot. The arms are bent at the elbows and swing vigorously from the shoulders. In distance running (fig. 19.4), the body is more erect and the weight is taken on the heel, then rocked forward. The elbows are bent slightly and the arm action is less vigorous than in sprinting.

Figure 19.3 Sprinting form

Figure 19.4 Distance running form

Relay Running   Many teachers have observed that fast runners lose relay races to slower competitors simply because of poor passing techniques. It is quite possible to teach upper elementary children the correct "upswing" method of passing in a short period of time. This method is perhaps the easiest for the beginner to master.

The runner who is to receive the baton draws her right hand straight back toward the approaching runner. She holds her fingers together, pointing to the side, while she points her thumb toward her body. This forms a "V" into which the approaching runner places the baton (fig. 19.5). The approaching runner brings the baton up into the receiving runner's hand (fig. 19.6). As soon as the front runner receives the baton, she should bring it forward into her left hand in preparation for the next pass.

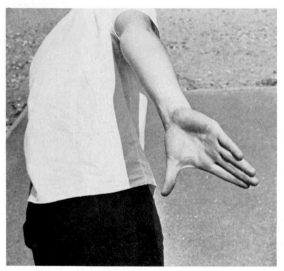

Figure 19.5 Form a "V".

Figure 19.6 Upward into the hand

When students are ready to practice baton passing at full speed, it is important that they establish their own check marks—when they should start to run. As a general rule, have the runner place a mark on the ground five yards back of his starting point.

The incoming runner starts fifty yards back of the passing zone and runs as fast as possible. When he passes the check mark, the outgoing runner turns and runs as fast as possible. When the outgoing runner reaches the passing zone, he puts his hand back for the baton. He must be inside the passing zone before he receives the baton or his team is disqualified. If the incoming runner cannot catch up to the outgoing runner, the check mark should be moved closer to the outgoing runner's starting point. If the incoming runner runs past the outgoing runner, the check mark should be moved farther back from the outgoing runner's starting point.

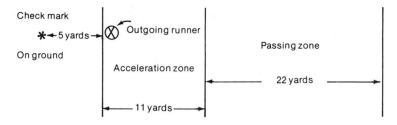

Check mark

* ←5 yards→ ⊗ Outgoing runner

On ground

Acceleration zone

Passing zone

22 yards

11 yards

Standing Long Jump

The performer stands with his toes just behind the starting line, his feet comfortably spread, his knees bent, and his trunk well forward (fig. 19.7a). After several preliminary swings with the arms, he swings his arms forward and upward vigorously and extends his legs. As soon as his feet leave the ground, he begins to flex his knees, keeping his arms forward (fig. 19.7b). He lands with his feet parallel and his trunk and arms extended in a forward direction (fig. 19.7c).

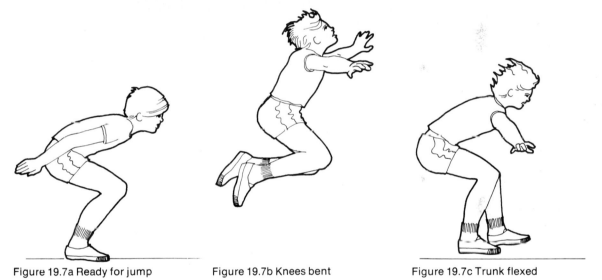

Figure 19.7a Ready for jump   Figure 19.7b Knees bent   Figure 19.7c Trunk flexed

19

Long Jump   A successful long jumper must be able to combine jumping and speed. Elementary school children have sufficient speed for this event and can execute the approach flight and landing relatively well. The performer begins several yards back from the takeoff board, runs forward, and places her takeoff foot on the board (fig. 19.8a). As soon as she leaves the board, she brings her rear leg and both arms forward and upward (fig. 19.8b). Her heels contact the ground and she immediately thrusts both arms back (fig. 19.8c), forcing her body well forward.

a   b   c   d

Figure 19.8

An effective technique to help the students gain height in the jump is to suspend a hat from a crossbar or on the end of a rope attached to a stick (fig. 19.9). The height of the hat should be adjusted so that the student must jump to maximum height in order to put the hat on his head. The distance from the takeoff point will vary, but it should be a little more than half of the total jump.

Figure 19.9

Hurdles   Elementary school children can run the hurdles with speed and efficiency. The main reason they usually do not learn the proper form is because the hurdles are set too high and too far apart.

When the runner is approximately seven feet away from the hurdle, she lifts her lead leg and extends it forward (fig. 19.10a). The opposite arm to this leg should also be extended forward. She continues to move her lead leg forward and upward until it clears the hurdle (fig. 19.10c). The rear leg then starts forward, with the toes turned up. Note the important forward body lean as the runner prepares for the next stage. She draws her lead leg down and thrusts her trailing leg forward. Note throughout this whole movement, that the shoulders should be parallel to the finish line.

Figure 19.10a Lift lead leg.

Figure 19.10b Good body lean.

Figure 19.10c Thrust trailing leg down.

The following stages should be followed when introducing hurdles:

1. Begin by having the children sprint about twenty-five yards.
2. Place an obstacle (a cane or an old broom handle) on the ground approximately halfway or between thirty to forty-five feet from the starting line. Again, the children sprint the full length; however, they should make no attempt to hurdle the obstacle.

19

3. Place a second obstacle on the ground so that it is midway between the third and fourth strides. The teacher can check whether runners are taking the correct three strides between hurdles by observing to see if they are taking very short steps (usually five) or if they land on a different foot after each hurdle (usually four steps). In order to assist the runner in developing the three-step sequence between hurdles, set up numerous courses (see diagram) so that each runner can select the one that fits his step pattern.

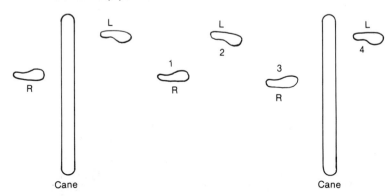

4. The obstacles should now be raised nine to twelve inches. Use shoe boxes, bricks, small stands, or adjustable hurdles. Let the children practice and then gradually raise the hurdle height to thirty inches. When the obstacle approaches twenty-four inches, the children should be taught what to do with the trailing leg. Have them walk down beside the hurdle. As they approach it, have them step in front and slightly to the side of the hurdle with their lead leg and then take the trailing leg over the hurdle. The thigh of the trailing leg should be parallel to the top of the hurdle; then it should be brought through quickly into the next stride. Once the correct technique is acquired, the children should jog down beside the hurdles doing the same drill. Finally, have them run from the starting position and hurdle in the center of each hurdle.

Teaching Suggestions

1. The takeoff must be between five and seven feet from the hurdle. The actual distance will depend upon the child's size and strength. This seems like a long way when you stand and look at it, but it is very easy to negotiate the hurdle from this distance when in motion.
2. Bring the knee of the lead leg up quickly toward the hurdle.
3. Lean forward into the hurdle to acquire good balance.
4. Bring the lead leg down quickly.
5. Snap the trailing leg through quickly into the next running stride.
6. Always lean forward on the hurdle, never backward.

Recommended Competitive Hurdles

The chart indicates the recommended hurdle height, the distance between hurdles, and the length of a race for various age levels.

	Height of hurdles (inches)	Number of hurdles	Start to first hurdle	Between hurdles	Last hurdle to finish line	Total distance
11 and under *BOYS*	30	6	33'4"	22'3"	35'5"	60 yards
GIRLS	30	6	33'4"	22'3"	35'5"	60 yards
13 and under *BOYS*	30	8	39'4" (12 m)	26'3" (8 m)	39'4" (12 m)	87½ yards (80 metres)
GIRLS	30	6	36'4"	24'3"	22'5"	60 yards
15 and under *BOYS*	36	10	14 yds.	9 yds.	15 yds.	110 yards
GIRLS	30	8	39'4" (12 m)	26'3" (8 m)	39'4" (12 m)	87½ yards (80 metres)

High Jump   Two types of jumping styles are described here. The "scissors style" is the easier of the two and should be learned first. The "straddle roll," or "western roll," although more difficult to learn, is the better of the two in terms of heights that can be reached. Regardless of which method is taught, it is imperative that a good landing surface be provided. Children will not learn to jump correctly if they are afraid to land in the pit. Although foam rubber is more acceptable, shavings or an improvised rubber tube pit provide a satisfactory landing surface.

A very inexpensive jumping pit can be constructed by using discarded automobile tire inner tubes. Place tubes on the ground, as shown in Appendix B, and tie them together. Then place a tumbling mat on top of the tubes. This provides a safe and comfortable landing surface that can be used both indoors and outdoors.

Scissors method The jumper approaches from the left at a slight angle to the bar— fifteen to twenty degrees (fig. 19.11a). He takes a few steps, plants his right or "takeoff" foot, then swings his left foot high into the air. The left leg continues over the bar (fig. 19.11b), followed by the right in a scissors action. At the same time, the arms swing forward and upward, assisting the upward lift of the body (fig. 19.11c). The right foot should land first, followed by the left, completing the scissors action.

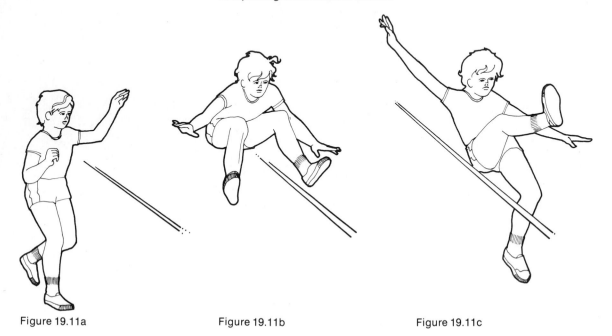

Figure 19.11a   Figure 19.11b   Figure 19.11c

Straddle Method　　　It is important that proper technique be stressed while introducing this method of jumping. Poor technique will lead to little or no improvement and a disillusioned jumper. The jumper approaches from the left side at approximately forty-five degrees to the bar. He takes a few steps, plants his left or "takeoff" foot, swings his right leg forward and upward and raises his arms (fig. 19.12a). He continues the upward and forward movement, extending his body and lifting his leg upward (fig. 19.12b). At the height of the jump, his body should be parallel to the bar (fig. 19.12c). He continues "rolling" movement over the bar, landing on his hands and "takeoff" foot (fig. 19.12d).

a　　　　　　　b　　　　　　　c　　　　　　　d

Figure 19.12

Hop, Step, and Jump (Triple Jump)

This event has proved to be a very popular event among boys and girls alike. The appeal seems to be both the distance that is traveled and the immediate improvement once the proper techniques are learned. The runner starts thirty to forty yards back to gain maximum speed at the takeoff mark. The first stage is a hop on the right foot from the takeoff board (fig. 19.13a). To maintain forward speed, the hop is kept low. The left leg drives forward and the jumper lands on his right foot (fig. 19.13b). He continues forward with a thrust of the left leg, lands on the heel of his left foot, and rocks forward toward the toe (fig. 19.13c). He continues the forward action by pushing off from his left foot and landing on both feet in the pit (fig. 19.13d).

a. Hop right.   b. Land right.   c. Step left.   d. Jump.

Figure 19.13

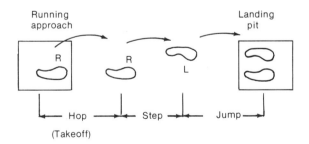

Shot Put   The six-pound shot put event has proved to be an extremely safe and enjoyable activity for boys and girls in the upper elementary school. Too often, however, this event is neglected in the upper elementary school track and field program. Various reasons are given for this, but most of the arguments prove invalid upon close investigation.

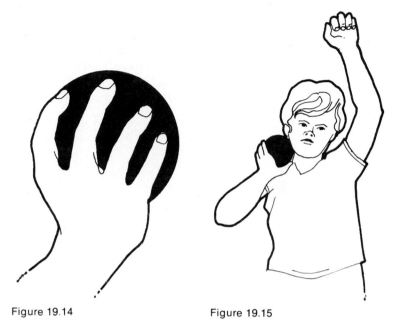

Figure 19.14   Figure 19.15

The performer should stand near the back of the circle with his weight on his right leg. He holds the shot in a "cradled" position on the side of his neck. He extends his left arm upward for balance (fig. 19.16a). He then lowers his trunk over his right leg and raises his left leg upward and toward the front of the circle (fig. 19.16b). In a simultaneous action, he drives his right leg toward the front of the circle and shifts his left leg in the same direction. Throughout this shifting movement, the body should be kept low (fig. 19.16c). At the end of this shifting movement, he begins to extend his right leg upward, rotates his trunk toward the front, and extends his right arm forward and upward. The shot is released with a final push off the fingertips (fig. 19.16d). The body continues to move around to the left side.

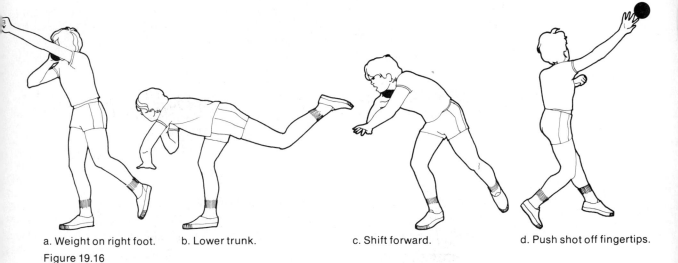

a. Weight on right foot.   b. Lower trunk.   c. Shift forward.   d. Push shot off fingertips.

Figure 19.16

To construct a throwing area for shot putting, take a piece of rope approximately five feet long and tape the ends. Drive two nails through the rope exactly 3½ feet apart. Hold one nail stationary and scribe an arc with the other end.

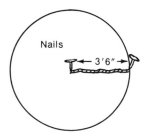

Nails   3'6"

Practice Activities

Track and field skills require a great deal of individual attention by the teacher and extensive practice by the student. The following practice activities should be used throughout the track and field unit to supplement individualized instruction and to encourage the competitive spirit among all members of the class. Several relays described in previous chapters are also suitable for track and field. They are the Circle Post Relay, page 202; the Zigzag Relay, page 237; the Rescue Relay, page 201; and the Obstacle Relay, page, 202.

Continuous Running

Basic Drill

A set distance is established. For example, the children could be asked to run one mile on the track or to run from the school to a point one mile away. Each child runs as far as he can, then walks the rest of the mile. With practice, the children should gradually increase the distance they run. Enjoyable courses can be set up on the school ground or in a nearby park or wilderness area.

Interval Training

Basic Drill

This is the most commonly used training method among track and field athletes. This form of training has three components: (1) the distance covered on each interval; (2) the recovery period between intervals; and (3) the number of repetitions performed. The following example will illustrate this form of training:

A group of children are training for a 440-yard race. The best time for the group is seventy seconds. Since the length of the interval is 220 yards, the time is reduced to thirty-five seconds expected for each 220-yard run. Each child would attempt to run the first 220 yards within thirty-five seconds, rest or walk for three minutes, then attempt to run the next 220 yards within thirty-five seconds. This procedure is continued to the end of the fifth 220-yard run.

When a runner can complete the five 220-yard runs in the time allotment, the training can be increased in three different ways. These are to (1) reduce the running time, (2) reduce the recovery period, or (3) require more repetitions (increase to six or seven 220-yard runs).

(1) Distance covered for each interval=220 yards

(2) Recovery period between intervals=3 minutes (rest or walk)

(3) Number of repetitions (220 yards) performed=5 repetitions

Walk, Jog, Run

Formation

Make a small track out of pins or any other type of markers.

Basic Drill

Teach the children the difference between walking, jogging, and running. A jog is about half speed and a run is full speed. To start, students are allowed to walk at their own speed around the markers. The first blow of the whistle means that everyone jogs. The second blow means that everyone runs at top speed. The third blow means that everyone jogs, and the fourth blow means everyone walks. Continue this sequence.

Teaching Suggestions

At the beginning of the unit, allow more time between the walk and jog phases and short periods at top speed. Gradually increase the time at full speed.

Start and Pass

Formation
Arrange class into a line formation, with six to eight on each team. Put half the team behind each of two starting lines twenty-five feet apart.

Basic Drill
This is essentially a starting drill. The teacher should use the following commands: "Take your marks," "Set," and "Go," or blow a whistle. On the whistle, two runners on each team behind opposite lines make fast starts and run until they pass each other. At the passing point each player slows down to a walk and goes to the rear of the line.

Teaching Suggestions
1. Each player runs all the way over the opposite line, then slows down to a walk back to the rear of the line.
2. Use standing and kneeling starts.

Call Race

Formation
Arrange two teams of five to ten runners on a starting line. Draw a turning line thirty feet in front of the starting line.

Basic Drill
Line up each team along the starting line. Number the players on each team. The teacher calls out any number, such as "four." Both number four players run to the turning line and back across the starting line. Continue calling numbers at random until all runners have had a turn.

Teaching Suggestions
Call out "Take your mark," "Set," and then the number. Only players whose numbers were called should run. The remaining players stand up and wait. This is an excellent starting drill.

Number of Jumps

Formation:
Arrange class in a long line formation, with the children's toes touching the starting line. Draw a finish line twenty to thirty feet in front of the starting line.

Basic Drill
This is a standing broad jump activity. Each child begins on the starting line and jumps as far as possible. His subsequent jumps start from where his heels touched. The object is to see who can make it across the finish line in the fewest number of jumps.

Teaching Suggestions
Use partners to mark landing positions and to count jumps.

Over the Rope

Formation
Arrange teams of five to eight in a line formation facing a mat.

Basic Drill
This high jumping activity can be used outside on grass or indoors on mats. Two players hold a long skipping rope at various heights while the remainder of the squad practices the scissors or western roll over the rope.

Baton Passing

Formation
The class is divided into groups of four to eight runners placed in a single line approximately four feet apart.

		Pass with left		Take with right and pass with left					
	X Baton →		X →		X →		X →		X
Basic drill:	X Baton	X	X	X	X	X	X	X
	X Baton	X	X	X	X	X	X	X
	X Baton	X	X	X	X	X	X	X

Basic Drill

From a stationary position the children start passing the baton from the end of each line. The runner passes with his left hand to the runner in front, who takes the baton in his right hand. He immediately brings it forward into his left hand in preparation for the next pass. The baton should be brought up into the receiving runner's right hand. When the baton reaches the front of the line, everyone turns around and the drill is repeated.

After the students have the feel of passing the baton in a stationary position, have them do it in a slow jog. Therefore, the distance between runners will have to be increased. Repeat the drill, gradually increasing the speed and the distance between runners.

Hash Running

Formation
See accompanying diagram.

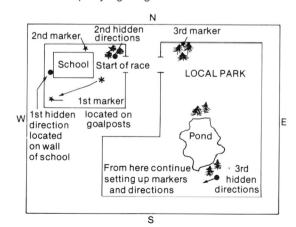

Basic Drill

Hash running is a team race in which markers are located along the route, hidden directions are located near the markers, and a total team effort is required in order to finish the race in the shortest period of time. The following example provides a basic format that can be used in any rural or urban school.

Before the class arrives for physical education, set up your "hash course." In the sample course the starting position is in front of the school. Each team (the size is optional) starts here (stagger the starting times) and is told it will find the first marker—a red ribbon placed on a goalpost—within fifty yards of the starting position. As soon as the marker is found by any member of the team, he calls to his teammates and they all come to the marker. They know that the first hidden directions will be somewhere within fifty yards (keep this distance constant) of the marker. The teammates move in different directions until one finds the directions, located on the school wall. As soon as a player finds the directions, he calls his team together. This pattern is continued throughout the course. The team that returns in the shortest time wins the race.

Some Considerations

1. Since the majority of physical education periods are approximately thirty minutes, begin with three to four markers, then increase the number and difficulty as experience dictates.
2. Make a rule that markers must be located before the directions. Some children may find directions first.

19

3. Although teams are staggered, one team may catch up to another, and thus vital information may be "given away." Encourage teams to make up diversionary signals if this occurs.
4. If you have taught orienteering and compass directions (chapter 12), use these skills in hash running.

5. Since schools in urban areas have problems with traffic and restrictive park areas, take care in planning hash courses to ensure the children's safety and the protection of public gardens.

Track and Field Meet: Rules and Regulations

The organization and general rules and regulations of any elementary school track and field meet will depend upon the children's general interest, the available time, and the facilities. The following information, although not complete, will assist in developing the facilities, meet rules, and order of events for most elementary school track meets.

I. Track dimensions: The 220-yard running track illustrated can be constructed on most outdoor playing areas.

II. High jump pit: The pit should be twelve feet long and ten feet wide. Sawdust or shavings should be used to fill the pit, which should be boarded with straw bales. (Also see the improvised pit constructed of rubber tubes in Appendix B.)

III. Long jump pit: The runway to the pit should be approximately thirty yards long, with an eight-inch takeoff mark five feet from the pit. The pit itself should be ten feet wide and twenty feet long. It should be filled with fine sand.

IV. Order and number of events: Each school, of course, may vary the length of dashes

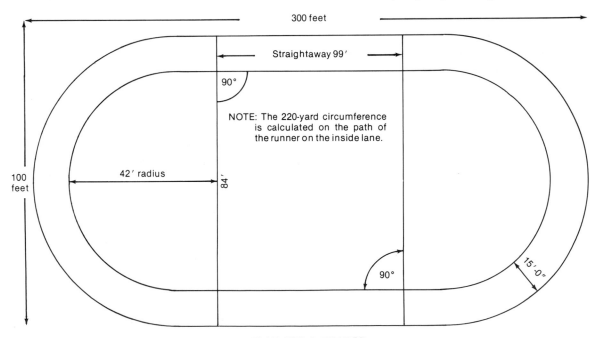

PLAN FOR A 220-YARD
RUNNING TRACK

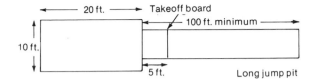

20 ft. ⟶ Takeoff board
⟵ 100 ft. minimum ⟶
10 ft.
5 ft.   Long jump pit

and include additional events. The following order of events should provide a format for scheduling:

A. 50-yard dash
B. Shot put
C. Standing long jump
D. Long jump
E. 220-yard relay
F. High jump
G. 220-yard run
H. Triple jump
 I. Softball throw
J. Hurdles
K. Obstacle race
L. Tug-of-war

V. Track and field officials: The following jobs should be allocated to teachers or dependable students:
A. Meet director
B. Starters, same for all track events
C. Finish judges—head finish judge and first-, second-, and third-place judges, and additional place judges, if desired
D. Field judges—one judge and one helper for the high jump, standing long jump, and running long jump

E. Announcer and head recorder with assistants for running messages and obtaining results of the events

VI. Meet requirements: Each school should establish its own eligibility requirements for the following situations:
A. Number of events each participant may enter. For example, perhaps each child could enter two track events and one field event.
B. Classification of participants. There are several methods that can be used to classify participants, such as age, grade, or a classification index.
C. Number of places and point awards. For example, the first four places could be recorded with five, four, three, and two points respectively.

There are many other questions that need to be answered if the track meet is to be successful. Give some thought to type of awards, methods of keeping school records, and required practice before a participant is eligible for the track and field meet. Once you and the students agree on the basic rules and regulations of the track meet, take time to explain them to the students, and post rules in the classroom and gymnasium.

Evaluative Techniques

Although performance in track and field events would appear to be easy to evaluate, quite the contrary is true. Each event is scored on the basis of either distance or time. The problem lies in placing a value on improvement rather than merely awarding an arbitrary number of points for the student's ranking in each event. This is further complicated by the philosophy underlying a track and field unit. At this age level, boys and girls should be free from excessive competitive pressure and should not have to judge themselves against the standards set by the exceptional athlete.

The solution is to allow each student to select a certain number of events and then record his initial and final scores. This approach to evaluating performance and improvement thus becomes a personal assessment. A child who is a low achiever can set a realistic goal for himself without worrying about who is the best in each event. Similarly, the outstanding performer can set a high standard, which motivates him to work at his maximum capacity.

Swimming Activities

20

Purpose and Emphasis

Content of Program

Methods of Teaching

Sample Instructional Programs

Portable Pools

One of the most important safety and recreational skills a child should learn is swimming. For decades, swimming has been given high priority by national, state, and local educational leaders. However, the lack of facilities and qualified teachers and a host of restrictive administrative policies have prevented aquatics from becoming an integral part of the physical education program in the vast majority of elementary schools.

But increased leisure time and the unprecedented growth in water sports have created a pressing need for children to learn to swim at the earliest possible age. The major increase in public and private swimming facilities and the development of relatively inexpensive portable pools have made it possible now for school children to learn to swim in an in-school aquatics program or through a variety of cooperative programs with such agencies as local recreation commissions and the YMCA.

These trends and developments make it imperative for elementary school teachers to understand which skills should be included in an elementary school swimming program, as well as how such a program can be implemented within their schools. A basic outline of an aquatics program is provided in the following sections as a format for developing individual or local school programs. A few sample programs are also described to illustrate how some programs operate through cooperative effort. An extensive aquatics bibliography is also provided at the back of this book.

Figure 20.1

Purpose and Emphasis

The fundamental purpose of an elementary school aquatics program should be to teach beginning swimmers the basic survival skills and a variety of recreational swimming skills for leisure use. Such a program should begin at the earliest possible age. Since many pools are too deep for early primary children, it is recommended that the aquatics program begin in the third grade. With limited facilities and staff, the nonswimmers should be given priority. This is in no way prejudicial to other children but is in harmony with the fundamental purpose of the aquatics program.

Content of Program

There are several nationally recognized swimming programs that provide basic skills for various levels of swimming ability. Teachers should check such programs as the Red Cross Water Safety Program or the YMCA Aquatics Program for a detailed list of swimming and water-safety skills that should be taught to beginning swimmers. These programs include the following knowledges and skills:

1. Safety rules
   general safety rules relating to where to swim, use of equipment, and artificial respiration
   personal safety rules relating to each person's level of skill
   safety rules relating to recreational sports such as fishing, hunting and boating
2. Adjustment to the water
   understanding relative temperature of body and pool and adjustment factor of body
   chlorine and chemical agents in water
   pool regulations and courtesy
   entering the water
   breath control
   eye and ear adjustment to water
3. Buoyancy
   buoyancy and recovering balance
   floating positions and recovery
   survival techniques
4. Propulsion through the water
   use of arms and legs
   combining arm and leg action
   combining arm and leg action and breathing
   moving under water
5. Skill in playing a variety of recreational games individually, in partners, and in groups

Beyond the beginning swimmer level are normally the intermediate and advanced swimmer stages, each with similar but more difficult skills, knowledges, and endurance levels. Teachers should review the standardized programs for a list of appropriate skills in each category and adjust the programs to cope with the class's ability. Standardized programs should not be followed blindly; they should be considered as guidelines that can be adjusted to a variety of local conditions.

Methods of Teaching

Many aquatics programs that are taught in elementary schools are cooperative efforts, with local recreational personnel assigned to the teaching responsibilities. Generally speaking, the majority of the existing Red Cross and YMCA programs adhere to a rather traditional method of instruction. There is evidence, however, that more exploratory methods similar to those being used in the movement education and creative

20

games programs in elementary schools are being adopted by recreational swim programs. If an elementary school enters into a contractual agreement with an outside agency, teachers and recreation specialists should hold discussions to explain their teaching philosophies and methods. In essence, there should be a great deal of similarity in the methods and techniques used by the classroom teacher and recreational specialist and in how each copes with individualization, motivation, and evaluation of a child's progress.

Sample Instructional Programs

Under ideal conditions, the classroom teacher or physical education specialist should teach swimming as an integral part of the physical education program. This, of course, means that the teacher must be a qualified swimming instructor and that the school must have its own pool or at least have access to a nearby public or private swimming facility. At present, the majority of elementary school teachers are not qualified to teach swimming. However, teachers can become qualified through instructional pro-

Figure 20 2

grams offered through universities and local recreational institutions.

Furthermore, the major increase in swimming facilities in virtually every community has made it at least possible for a much larger number of schools to develop some form of cooperative aquatics program. With these factors in mind, the following programs are provided to illustrate the types of cooperative instructional programs that have been developed in a variety of geographical areas.

New Trier Swimming Program

The New Trier swimming program in Winnetka, Illinois, is an example of school-sponsored programs taught by senior high school students under the direction of a teacher (Gabrielsen, Spears, and Gabrielsen 1968). The main purpose of the program is to teach elementary school children how to swim. It is conducted every Saturday morning during the school year and five days a week throughout summer vacation. Children are taught by high school students under the supervision of the high school swimming director. The instructional program is divided into eight units, ranging from beginning skills to the more advanced skills of racing, diving, and synchronized swimming. Children may enter the program at any time during the school year and take as many lessons as they wish. When they have learned the skills of one unit, they move on to the next level. This is an excellent example of how a well-organized program can cope with individual differences in ability and can provide for continuous progress.

The success of this program is measured, in part, by the number of children who have learned to swim or have improved their swimming skills. Since the inception of the program in 1937, 90 percent of each incoming high school freshman class of approximately 950 students had taken swimming lessons during their elementary school days. Of these, there are seldom more than ten students who cannot swim at least forty yards.

Coquitlam Cooperative Program

The program in Coquitlam, British Columbia, is a typical example of a cooperative program between a school district and a local recreation agency. The school district contracts with the local park and recreation department to provide swimming lessons for all fifth-grade children. Since there are no swimming facilities in the elementary schools, the instructional program is offered in adjacent park swimming pools during May and June. A large percentage of these pools are shallow-water, family-type pools which are ideal for the beginning swimmer. Because of these facilities, two of the schools within the district are able to offer swimming lessons to all children from kindergarten to grade seven. As budget and staff become available, other schools will offer the same program.

Until 1972, the local park and recreation department followed the Red Cross Water Safety Program's swimming classification system, lesson format, and examination procedures. However, the department became dissatisfied with the program's formal approach, particularly the emphasis on the final test for each pupil. In too many instances children who "failed" would be fearful and disappointed rather than feeling any sense of accomplishment. The department's aquatic staff discussed the program with school personnel and observed physical education classes in schools that emphasized more crea-

tive and exploratory approaches to teaching physical education. Workshops and seminars were held to plan an experimental program during May and June of 1972. The main purpose and direction of this program are contained in the following statements which were presented to school authorities and parents (Coquitlam Park and Recreation Department 1972):

To provide a positive learning situation for your child the Aquatics Program will: 1. Utilize Continuous Evaluation to measure your child's progress. 2. Have No Test Days. Children progress at different rates and therefore should be spared any high pressure comparisons with their peers. Your child will be moved to more advanced skills as his ability allows. 3. Give No Badges to children as they complete Red Cross Requirements. In the place of badges will be progress cards. However, as a parent, you may present your child's progress card at any Coquitlam pool and obtain a badge which you may give to your child if you believe he will benefit from it.

The experimental program that followed had many of the characteristics of the regular physical education program. Each swimming instructor attempted to create an informal learning environment. Children were taught in small groups, often through the creative games approach. Instructors experimented freely with a variety of techniques and such learning aids as balls, hoops, masks, and other floating devices. The results were most impressive. The children acquired a high level of proficiency in the begin-

---

Coquitlam Cooperative Program

a

b

c

Figure 20.3

ning water safety and survival skills. In comparison with previous years, this new approach produced a remarkably high success record. When one considers the positive attitude developed through this approach, its advantages are greatly increased.

Portable Pools

One of the most significant developments in the aquatics field during the past few years is the construction of relatively low-cost "portable pools." Several school districts have experi-

Figure 20.4 Portable pool

mented with various types of portable pools as an inexpensive approach to teaching beginning swimming to a large number of school children. In 1968 the Seattle Public Schools offered an experimental swimming program to several schools using a portable pool measuring sixteen by twenty-four feet by thirty inches. It proved to be a successful program, with administrators and classroom teachers indicating virtually no serious problems relating to scheduling, maintenance, and general safety and sanitation standards.

A similar program was initiated in the Federal Way School District near Seattle in 1969. Since the school authorities wanted to offer a year-round beginning swimming program to fifth-grade children, a portable pool measuring sixteen by twenty-four feet by thirty inches was covered with an inexpensive bubble top. The pool is used during the school day for instructional purposes, after school for recreation, and during the summer by the King County Park Department. This cooperative aquatics program has proven to be so successful that the State Board of Health has unanimously approved the use of water safety teaching stations (portable pools) for all elementary schools and park recreation programs in the State of Washington.

Gymnastic and Movement Activities

Part V has been organized to meet the conditions existing in the majority of elementary schools. Many classroom teachers are still teaching gymnastic activities through a reasonably structured approach. At the same time, however, they are attempting to apply movement education concepts and skills into various parts of their gymnastic programs.

The three chapters in this section attempt to bridge the gap between the structured and movement education approaches to teaching gymnastic activities. Chapter 21 provides the basic stunts and tumbling activities. At the end of this chapter the concepts and skills of movement education are introduced in a systematic fashion. Numerous examples show how to incorporate these new movement skills and ideas into stunt and tumbling lessons or units of instruction. Similarly, Chapters 22 and 23 present the structured skills that are performed with small equipment and large apparatus while providing additional suggestions for applying movement concepts and skills.

Stunts, Tumbling, and Movement Skills

21

Basic Considerations

Teaching Stunts, Tumbling, and Movement Skills

Stunts and Tumbling Activities for Kindergarten to Grade Three

Stunts, Tumbling, and Pyramid Activities for Grades Four to Six

Movement Concepts and Skills

Probably the most familiar gymnastic activities to elementary school children are stunts and tumbling. For generations, children have learned to mimic animal walks, to balance on their heads, hands, and other parts of their bodies, and to perform a variety of agile tumbling skills. The purposes of these activities have remained the same. Children learn to move their bodies safely and gracefully. They improve their strength, agility, balance, and other important aspects of physical fitness. And they learn the importance of safety and perseverance when attempting a difficult stunt or tumbling skill.

One of the most recent and exciting additions to this program has been the introduction of movement concepts and skills developed in the movement education approach. These unstructured skills, coupled with the use of exploratory teaching methods and techniques, have provided an effective way for every child, regardless of physical ability or prior gymnastic experience, to experience success and enjoyment.

This chapter has been organized to cope with the varying programs and conditions that exist in elementary schools. The basic teaching procedures are presented first. The next two sections illustrate a variety of stunts and tumbling skills that are appropriate for primary and intermediate children. It is almost impossible to arrange skills by grade level since children vary in their physical ability and previous stunt and tumbling experiences. Therefore, this chapter's grouping according to primary or intermediate levels is a very rough guideline.

The last section of this chapter describes movement concepts and skills, and shows how they can be incorporated into a stunts and tumbling program. It is an extremely important section. Once children learn this new movement vocabulary, they can enrich their own experiences in stunts and tumbling activities. And, just as important, these skills provide a means of exploring and testing each child's physical and creative abilities with a wide variety of small equipment and large apparatus, such as vaulting boxes, climbing ropes, and the new, specially designed agility apparatus.

Basic Considerations

Each elementary school grade presents unique organization and teaching problems. The children's age and maturity will dictate the amount of material that can be covered within the allocated time in the gymnasium or activity room. The number of mats available may very well become the reason for organizing a class in a particular way. And the teacher's own ability and confidence in handling this type of physical activity may become the central reasons for organizing a class in a certain fashion and for selecting particular activities. Regardless of such individual conditions, the following general teaching suggestions apply to all grade levels:

1. Children should be taught to listen to your normal conversational voice for all directions and commands. Once they learn to move and listen to your voice, there is no need to rely upon a loud whistle.
2. Teach children standard procedures for (a) changing their clothes and entering the gymnasium, (b) using their free time before the lesson begins, and (c) lining up in a specific way or place before the lesson begins or at any time you want to speak to all of the class.
3. Try to provide maximum participation and movement for each child during the instructional period. If a limited number of mats and other equipment means that the children must wait in long lines, the program should be changed. Techniques such as station work, task cards, and rotation procedures can be adapted to any grade level.

4. Establish a stunts and tumbling program that is based upon the children's individual abilities and progress. Do not establish a set number of skills for every child to accomplish. Some children simply are physically incapable of performing certain stunts. This obviously means that a wide variety of activities should be presented to each grade level.
5. Establish and consistently maintain a basic list of safety rules and regulations. These should include the following:
   a. If children are permitted to wear street clothes during this activity, do not allow bulky sweaters, watches, and other jewelry.
   b. Children should not be allowed to practice any stunt or tumbling activity unless the teacher is in the gymnasium.
   c. When a spotter is called for in a stunt, children should be taught the proper spotting techniques. Once the techniques are learned, children should be permitted to perform stunts with the assistance of the required number of spotters.

Purposes and Techniques of Spotting

Spotting in stunts and tumbling or other gymnastic movements is defined as providing assistance in the performance of a skill. Spotting is both a teaching technique and a safety device. The teaching aspect is accomplished by the teacher or a classmate holding the performer or positioning himself in a way to assist the performer. The spotter helps the performer maintain his balance, or gently pushes or lifts him at the strategic moment, helping him to get the "feel" of the movement before he attempts it on his own. The safety aspect of spotting is the positioning of one or two helpers near the performer to provide additional support and to prevent a loss of balance, a fall, or an accident.

It is difficult to say which stunts and gymnastic skills require the use of spotters. Furthermore, the teacher and the child must judge when to remove close spotting so the child can attempt the skill on his own. As a general guideline for elementary school children, be overcautious until you are completely sure that the performer can execute the skill with relative ease.

The following suggestions may also help you to a safe procedure and environment for teaching the more difficult and challenging stunts and tumbling and gymnastic skills:

1. Analyze each stunt's points of difficulty and teach spotters the correct positions and movements.
2. Teach spotters to stay close to the performer but not to hamper his movement.
3. Use the strongest and most reliable children for the most difficult stunts.
4. Teach children not to "over spot." Instruct spotters to help only when the performer needs the extra lift or push so he does not come to rely too much on the assistance.

Teaching Stunts, Tumbling, and Movement Skills

There are several approaches to teaching stunts, tumbling, and movement skills. The approach that a teacher decides to use will depend upon such factors as the children's age, the time and equipment available, and the emphasis the teacher wishes to give to various stunts, tumbling skills, and movement skills. Thus, a standard lesson plan suitable for any grade level would be of little value. The reader should review "Planning and Presenting a Lesson" on pages 154-56 for a detailed presentation of the process of developing lessons and units of instruction.

The accompanying chart will provide the teacher with a basic framework for the selection of appropriate activities. Stunts and tumbling skills are organized according to primary (kindergarten to grade three) and intermediate (grades four to six) skills. The movement concepts and skills described in the last part of this chapter are appropriate for both levels.

As a general guideline, begin each lesson with some type of vigorous warm-up activity such as running, jumping, and landing followed by exercises designed to increase the child's general strength and fitness (see Chapter 4, pages 44-66). Circuit training and vigorous tag and team games are also appropriate warm-up activities. The rest of the lesson should include a mixture of balance and tumbling stunts and movement skills and concepts rather than concentrating solely on one type of skill. If the gymnasium is equipped with small equipment and large apparatus, stunts and tumbling activities involving them should not be taught as separate units or lessons but integrated into a broad gymnastic unit. Depending on the time available, each lesson should include a warm-up period, followed by stunts, tumbling, and movement skill activities, and finishing with small equipment and large apparatus activities.

When there is not enough time to complete a lesson, it is quite acceptable to teach stunts, tumbling, and movement skills on the first day and then begin with a short warm-up period the next day and move directly to small equipment and large apparatus activities. This procedure can be followed throughout a series of lessons. The essential point is to provide every child with an opportunity to experience and enjoy all the available gymnastic equipment and apparatus.

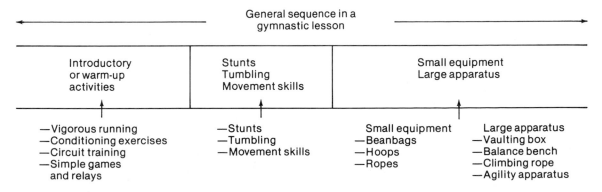

General sequence in a gymnastic lesson

Introductory or warm-up activities	Stunts Tumbling Movement skills	Small equipment Large apparatus	
—Vigorous running —Conditioning exercises —Circuit training —Simple games and relays	—Stunts —Tumbling —Movement skills	Small equipment —Beanbags —Hoops —Ropes	Large apparatus —Vaulting box —Balance bench —Climbing rope —Agility apparatus

Stunts and Tumbling Activities for Kindergarten to Grade Three

The primary stunts and tumbling activities contained in this section (figs. 21.1 to 21.33) include numerous animal movements, balance stunts, simple partner activities, and several tumbling and safety skills. These activities are the foundations upon which the more advanced stunts and tumbling skills are built. As the reader will note in the last section of this chapter, there is a very close relationship between the activities described here and many movement skills. Each complements the other in a very natural way.

The suggested levels are only rough guidelines. Begin with the skills suggested for a particular grade. If the class's skill level is high, move on to more advanced skills. As children progress to the third grade, they will be ready for more challenging skills. In this case refer to the next section on stunts and tumbling for intermediate grades.

Wicket Walk

Figure 21.1 Bend forward and grasp the legs just above the ankles. Take short steps without releasing the grip.

Variations:
1. Walk backward, sideward, and in a circle.
2. Place hands on opposite ankles and repeat.
3. Keep legs straight and repeat.

Camel Walk

Figure 21.2 Place one foot in front of the other, bend over from the waist, and lock hands behind back to represent the camel's hump. Walk slowly, raising the head and chest with each step.

Tightrope Walk

Figure 21.3 Draw a line on the floor. Stand with arms extended sideward, head up, and both feet on the line. Walk forward placing the toe, then the heel on the floor.

Variations:
1. Change position of arms.
2. Walk backward.
3. Half knee-bend and repeat.

Bouncing Ball

Figure 21.4 Stand erect with arms at the sides and feet approximately shoulder-width apart. Take short jumps and gradually lower the body. Continue jumping and lowering the body until the hands touch the floor. This should simulate a ball coming to rest. Repeat action upward until the standing position is again reached.

Lame Puppy Walk

Figure 21.5 Begin with both hands and one foot on the floor. Keep the head up and walk or run "on all threes" like a lame puppy.

Variations:
1. Move in different directions—sideways, backward, and so on.
2. Change the position of the hands—farther apart, facing inward like a monkey, and so on.
3. Do a Double Lame Puppy Walk, with one hand and one foot off the floor.

Crab Walk

Figure 21.6 Start with the hands and feet on the ground. The back should be fairly straight to keep the seat off the ground. Walk forward by lifting the left hand and right leg up and forward. Walk backward repeating the same action.

Rabbit Jump

Figure 21.7 Begin in a squat position with the body weight over the toes. Leap forward and land on the hands and then the feet to simulate a rabbit hop.

Measuring Worm

Figure 21.8 Begin in a squat position with the arms shoulder-width apart and the hands on the floor. Without moving the feet, take short steps with the hands until the legs and back are straight. Now, without moving the arms, take short steps with the feet until the toes touch the back of the hands.

Seal Walk

Figure 21.9 Begin in a prone position with the belly down, the body and legs straight, and the toes pointed. Keep the arms straight to support the body and move the right hand forward. Shift the left hand forward and drag the legs, simulating the walking action of a seal.

Variations:
1. Use elbows instead of hands.
2. Crawl holding one leg in the air.

Knee Walk

Figure 21.10 Start with the hands and knees on the mat. Reach back and grasp the feet or ankles. Shift the weight to the left side and take a short step with the right knee. Continue movement with short steps forward.

Kangaroo Hop

Figure 21.11 Begin in a squat position with the arms folded across the chest and the body weight over the toes. Jump up and forward, land on the toes, and gradually lower the body to the starting position.

Knee Jump

Figure 21.12 Stand with the feet about shoulder-width apart, the knees slightly bent, and the arms raised forward and sideways. Jump up, pull the knees up to the chest, wrap the hands around the lower legs, release grip, and land on the toes. Landing should be made with the knees bent.

Turk Stand

Figure 21.13 Begin in a cross-legged sitting position, with the arms folded across the chest and the body leaning forward slightly. Without releasing the grip, lean forward and extend the legs to a standing position. Return to the cross-legged sitting position.

Heel Slap

Figure 21.14 Stand with the feet about shoulder-width apart. Jump up, slap heels, and return to starting position.

Variations:
1. Jump and make a half or full turn in the air.
2. Jump, slap heels, and clap hands over head.
3. Jump and slap heels twice.

Single Leg Balance

Figure 21.15 Stand on one leg with the knee slightly bent, lower the trunk, and raise the arms and other leg until they are parallel to the floor.

Variations:
1. Extend the elevated leg to the side.
2. Place the arms in different directions—pointing forward or downward or holding against the sides.

Leapfrog

Figure 21.16 One partner squats, keeping her head down. The other partner assumes a semicrouched position about two feet behind, with his hands resting on his partner's shoulders. Back partner spreads his legs and leaps over his partner. Continue sequence for several jumps.

Wheelbarrow

Figure 21.17 One partner lies on the floor, spreads his legs, and extends his arms. The other partner stands between the extended legs and grasps her partner's lower legs. The lead partner takes short steps with his hands while the other player follows with short walking steps.

Rocking Chair

Figure 21.18 One partner lies on the floor on her back with her knees bent and her arms extended upward. The other partner stands at her feet, bends forward, and grasps her hands. One partner rocks back, pulling the other up and forward until they have changed positions.

Chinese Get-up

Figure 21.19 Partners sit back to back with their elbows locked, knees bent and together, and feet flat on the floor. Both rise off the floor by pushing against each other and, if necessary, taking short backward steps.

Wring the Dishrag

Figure 21.20 Partners face each other and join hands. With hands joined each partner raises one arm (right for one partner and left for the other), and they turn back to back. Repeat with the other arms to return to the original position.

Twister

Figure 21.21a Partners stand back-to-back with legs apart and left hand on left knee. Each partner reaches through his legs with his right hand and grasps his partner's hand.

Figure 21.21b Keeping the hand grip, one partner swings to the right and lifts his left leg over his partner's back. Return to the original position by reversing the movement.

Elephant Walk

Figure 21.22 One partner sits on the floor with her legs extended sideward while the upper partner bends down and places his hands between his partner's legs (his feet are opposite the sitting partner's shoulders). The lower partner wraps her legs around the upper partner's trunk and places her hands over his seat. The lower partner rises off floor and the upper partner takes short "elephantlike" steps while the lower partner holds on.

Rooster Fight

Figure 21.23 Stand on one leg with the arms folded across the chest. On "go" command, attempt to push opponent off balance; do not hit. As soon as one player touches the floor with his free foot, the other partner is declared the winner.

Crab Fight

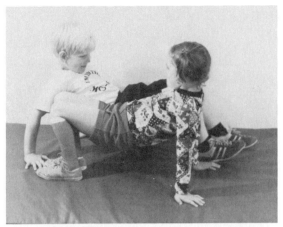

Figure 21.24 Partners assume a crab walk position with hands and feet on the mat and seats off the mat. On "go" signal, each attempts to push the other off balance. As soon as one player touches the mat with his seat or falls over, the other is declared the winner.

Tip-up

Figure 21.25 a Squat with the arms straight, hands resting on the mat, and the knees outside the elbows. The fingers should be pointing forward and spread apart for balance.

Figure 21.25 b Lean forward slowly, pressing the inside of the thighs against the elbows. As the feet rise off the ground, lower the head until it touches the mat. Return to the starting position.

Variations:
Shift forward and keep the feet and head off the mat.

Head Stand

a   b   c

Figure 21.26

a. Prior to raising the feet off the mat, form a triangle with the hands and forehead.

b. Push off the mat with the toes of both feet, flex the knees, and raise the body to a halfway position.

c. Once the body is in a stable, balanced position, continue raising the legs until the body forms a straight line. Note: Too much arch in the back will tend to cause the body to fall forward.

Spotting:
Stand on the left side of the performer. As she lifts her legs grasp the thigh of the left leg with both hands. Once she is in the head stand position, gradually release the hands, but keep them a few inches away and ready for support.

Figure 21.27a

Figure 21.27b

Tumbling and Safety Skills

The first safety skills to learn in gymnastics are moving skills. Primary children should learn to run in different directions, change speed, stop, start, and listen for commands or challenges given by the teacher. This means the children must learn to move quietly while constantly looking, moving to open spaces, and stopping whenever the teacher wishes to give additional directions. If this is not learned early in the gymnastic program, the teacher will have trouble controlling her class and teaching all future skills.

The following ideas will help in developing good verbal control by the teacher and safe, effective moving and stopping skills:

1. Have the children run sideward, then backward, changing verbal commands as the children move.
2. Have them move with other locomotor skills, such as skipping or sliding, while you call out the skills.
3. On your command, have the students run as high as possible, then low to the ground.
4. Have the children run. When you say "Stop," each child stops and places both hands on the floor. *This is an important movement* since each child must lower his body close to the floor, thereby controlling his stopping action and putting him in a position to attempt a rolling action.

A child's safety in gymnastics, as in any other sport or in daily activities, depends upon his ability to land and roll. In gymnastics, each child must be able to run, jump, land, and roll on a mat or on the floor without hurting himself or colliding with others. Gradually he will learn to jump from various heights and from different directions and to land and roll with ease and efficiency. The rolls in figures 21.28 to 21.33 should be learned in a systematic progression. Since these skills are the prerequisites for all future lessons, direct teaching and constant repetition are clearly indicated.

Log Roll

a

b

Figure 21.28

a. This is the easiest roll to perform. Lie on the back with the arms extended over the head and the hands locked together.

b. Keep the body in a straight line and roll to the side and then around to the starting position.

Side Roll

a

b

Figure 21.29

a. Begin in a back lying position. The roll should be performed with the elbows, knees and nose "hidden" or tucked in.

b. It is important to explain to young children that hiding these parts of the body helps them to roll in a ball-like fashion and to protect vulnerable parts.

a

b

Figure 21.30 After the children have mastered this skill, see if they can combine the Log Roll with the Side Roll.

c

c. Children should also learn to roll toward either side, stop halfway through, and change directions.

c

c

Backward Diagonal Roll

a

b

Figure 21.31

a. This is one of the most important safety rolls. It is a means of rolling backward with a gradual dissipation of speed, thus preventing injury as well as providing an effective and graceful means of shifting from one movement to another.

b. The roll is performed by rolling backward and bringing both legs *to the side of one ear*.

Forward Roll

a

b

Figure 21.32

a. Most children have already learned this skill before the first grade and can usually demonstrate many variations involving different leg and arm positions. Begin in a squat position with the head up, the arms extended forward slightly and the fingers pointing straight ahead.

b. Push off from the toes, raise the seat, and tuck the chin to the chest.

c

Spotting:
Kneel on the performer's right side and face in the direction of the backward roll. Place the left hand under her neck and hold the right hand ready to assist the performer in her backward movement.

c. This takes the weight off the neck and allows the child to roll off the shoulder. It is an appropriate skill for children who are not strong enough to perform the backward roll.

c

Spotting:
Kneel on the right side of the performer, place the right hand under her neck and the left hand on the back of the right thigh. When indicated, lift with the right hand and push forward with the left hand against the thigh.

c. Continue forward movement, landing on the base of the neck and the top of the shoulders. Push off with the hands and continue forward motion to a crouch or standing position.

Backward Roll

a

b

Figure 21.33

a. This is the most difficult roll to perform as it requires the weight to be taken on the arms as the child rolls back. Begin in a squat position with the body weight evenly distributed on the fingers and toes. The back should be toward the mat. Push off with the hands and roll backward, keeping the knees to the chest and the chin down.

b. Continue backward roll until the body weight is well over the shoulders. At this point, push off with the hands.

Incorporating Rolling Skills

Since children have learned to run in different directions without colliding, it is time to incorporate a rolling skill into their movement patterns. This can be accomplished in the following stages:

Step one: Scatter all available mats on the floor. Assign four to six children around each mat as illustrated.

Number each child in each group. On your command of "Number one," child number one in each group approaches the mat from any direction, bends down, touches the floor, and performs a roll across the mat. He then gets up, moves to a new position and repeats his movement. Next, call "Number two." Child number two must wait for an open space across the mat before he attempts to bend and perform a roll. When number one and number two develop the ability to wait and then roll, call "Number three," who joins in the process. Continue

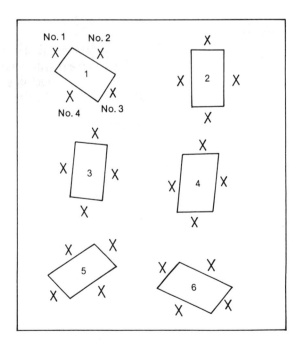

c

c. . . . and land on the knees and toes.

Spotting:
Kneel on the left side of the performer, and place the right hand on her left shoulder. As she rolls onto her shoulders, place the left hand on her lower back. When indicated, lift up with the right hand and push up and forward with the left hand.

Figure 21.34

to the last performer. It is important at this stage to encourage children to keep moving to new positions, then to bend and roll across the mat.

Step two: Join two groups but do not shift the mats. (fig. 21.35). Start each group on its own mat. When all the children are moving, call out "Number one." Number one from each group then shifts to the other mat and joins that group. Once he is on the other mat, he may elect to stay there or shift back and forth as space dictates. Continue calling numbers two, three, and four with a few seconds between each.

Figure 21.35

Step three: Join three groups and continue the process (fig. 21.36).

Step four: When three or four mats are being used by all the children, stop the class. Have half the class stand on the side of the gymnasium while the other children scatter on the floor. On command, the children on the floor run, stop, bend, and roll across any mat. Allow time for practice, then rotate the groups.

Step five: Allow all children to run, bend, and roll. Then have them run, jump, land, and roll.

Stunts, Tumbling, and Pyramid Activities for Grades Four to Six

The stunts and tumbling program for intermediate children is essentially a continuation of the primary program. As children progress to the more advanced balance and agility stunts, more strength and control are required. More spotters also are needed because of difficulty and potential hazards in the improper performance of several balance and tumbling movements. The spotters should be given adequate training to ensure a safe performance.

Pyramid building has been included in the latter part of this section (pp. 420-23). These activities require strength, balance, and teamwork and are thoroughly enjoyed by children of this age level.

It is recognized that many of the stunts and tumbling activities suggested here (figs. 21.37 to 21.72) are structured or formal gymnastic movements. Therefore, it may appear to be a contradiction to suggest that the unstructured movement skills described on pages 423-32 be incorporated with these highly structured stunts and tumbling skills. But when a child learns such movement skills as "weight bearing," "transfer of weight," "direction and pathways," and the various qualities of movement, he can enrich all the structured stunts and tumbling skills. Several examples will be provided to show how formal stunts can be joined with one or more movement skills.

Figure 21.36

Activity	Type	Page
Stunts		
Bear Dance	agility	403
Knee Dip	balance	403
Rolling the Log	agility	404
V-Sit	balance	404
The Bridge	balance	405
Knee and Shoulder Stand	balance	406
Side Stand	balance	406
Knee Stand	balance	407
Pig Walk	agility	407
Shoulder Wrestling	agility	407
Elbow Wrestling	agility	407
Leg Wrestling	agility	408
Going Down	agility	408
Push War	agility	408
Seal Slap	agility	409
Hand Stand	balance	409
L-Support	balance	410
Walking down the Wall	balance	410
Back Layout	balance	411
Forearm Head Stand	balance	411
Elbow Balance	balance	411

Bear Dance

Figure 21.37 Squat on the left foot, extend the right leg forward. Arms may be extended from the sides or folded across the chest. Simultaneously jump forward, draw the right leg back, and extend the left leg forward.

Knee Dip

Figure 21.38 Stand on the left foot, bend the right leg back and up, grasping the foot with the right hand. Gradually bend the left leg until the right knee touches the floor. Return to the starting position without releasing the grip.

Rolling the Log

a

Figure 21.39

a. Begin in a front leaning position.

b

b. Keeping the right hand on the floor and the legs and back straight, swing the left arm up and over the turning body.

V-Sit

Figure 21.40 Sit with the knees bent, the feet flat on the floor, and the hands grasping the inner sides of the ankles. Still grasping the ankles, extend the knees and balance on the seat.

c

c. The left hand returns to the floor. Then swing the right arm up and toward the left side, turning the body back to the original position.

The Bridge

Figure 21.41a Sit on the edge of the mat holding the elbows high and the palms of hands facing up. Lower the back and place the palms on the mat.

Figure 21.41b Move the heels close to the seat, then arch the body.

Knee and Shoulder Stand

Figure 21.42 The base partner lies on his back with his knees bent and his arms up. The top performer stands facing her partner and places her hands on her partner's knees as she brings her shoulders forward. The base partner places his hands on the top performer's shoulders. As soon as the top performer's shoulders are held in a fixed position, she begins to raise her legs until they are in a vertical position.

Side Stand

Figure 21.43 Base partner assumes a wide kneeling position with his weight evenly distributed on his arms and legs. Top performer stands on the side and curls his arm around his partner's trunk. The palms of both hands face up. The top performer leans across his partner and gradually raises his knees to a partially bent position above his partner's back. Then he extends his legs fully.

Knee Stand

Figure 21.44 Base partner stands with his legs about shoulder-width apart, bends forward, and places his head between his partner's legs. Top partner places his hands on base partner's shoulders and base partner grasps upper partner's thighs. Base partner begins to stand up, while top partner places his feet on base partner's thighs, releases his hands from his partner's shoulders, and begins to arch forward.

Pig Walk

Figure 21.45 One partner assumes a partial pushup position with his legs apart and his seat up. The lower partner faces the opposite direction and shifts backward until his arms are opposite his partner's ankles. The lower partner then wraps his legs around his partner's trunk and grasps his partner's ankles. The upper partner takes short "piglike" steps.

Shoulder Wrestling

Figure 21.46 Partners kneel side by side with their hands locked behind their backs and their shoulders touching. On signal, and without losing contact with their shoulders, partners attempt to push each other off balance.

Elbow Wrestling

Figure 21.47 Partners kneel with their right elbows on the mat and holding hands. Their left forearms should be in contact with the mat. On signal, and without taking their elbows off the mat, partners attempt to push each other's hands to the mat.

Leg Wrestling

Figure 21.48 Partners lie on their backs facing opposite directions. On the "go" signal, both raise their inside legs so that their knees are crossed. From this position, each partner tries to force his opponent's leg down to the mat.

Going Down

Figure 21.49 Players sit side by side with their arms linked. On the "go" signal, each player tries to force the other to roll backward. Players are not allowed to touch the floor with their free hands.

Push War

Figure 21.50 Draw three lines twenty to thirty feet apart. Players stand at the center line and place their hands on each other's shoulders. On the "go" signal, each player attempts to push his opponent back over the end lines.

Seal Slap

Figure 21.51a Begin in a front lying position with the toes on the mat and the hands directly under the shoulders.

Figure 21.51b Simultaneously push off from the hands and toes, clap the hands in the air, and return to the starting position.

Handstand

Figure 21.52 Begin this stunt with the arms approximately shoulder-width apart, hands on the mat and the fingers slightly bent (this aids in maintaining balance). Both feet should also be on the mat in the starting position with the right knee drawn up and close to the chest. With the body weight well forward on the arms, kick the right leg up and follow with the left. Continue the upward movement of the legs, ending with the legs, body, and arms in a nearly straight line. The head should be well forward to assist in maintaining balance.

Spotting:
Use the same spotting technique described for the head stand (p. 394). An alternate is to stand just in front of the spot where the performer's hands will be placed. The spotter's left leg should be extended back to provide a firmly balanced position. As the performer shifts her legs upward, the spotter should brace the performer's right shoulder against his own right leg and catch her legs as they come up.

L-Support

Figure 21.53 Sit on the floor with the legs together and pointing straight ahead. The hands are resting on the floor below the shoulders. Keep the shoulders slightly forward of the hips, press down, and raise the hips and legs off the floor.

Walking down the Wall

a   b   c

Figure 21.54

a. Stand facing away from the wall with the feet about two feet away from the wall, the elbows high, and the palms facing up and toward the wall.

b. Arch the head and shoulders back and place the hands on the wall.

c. Walk the hands down the wall and touch the head to the mat. This movement should be performed without moving the feet; however, most children will have to move their feet a little farther away from the wall as they reach the lower phase of the arched position.

Back Layout

Figure 21.55 The base partner lies on his back, extends his arms up, and bends both knees. The soles of his feet should face his partner's back. The top partner rests the small of her back against her partner's feet and slowly extends back as her partner straightens his legs. The base partner can give support to the top partner by holding her arms just above the wrists.

Spotting:
Stand near the top of the base performer's right shoulder and assist in placing the feet and maintaining balance when indicated.

Forearm Head Stand

Figure 21.56 Kneel with the elbows, hands and forehead on the mat. Gradually begin to raise upward until the legs are fully extended and the toes are pointed.

Spotting:
Use the same spotting technique described for the head stand (p. 394).

Elbow Balance

Figure 21.57 Begin this stunt in a partially front lying position with the elbows bent and touching the sides of the body, and the fingers pointing toward the feet. Keep the elbows close to the sides and shift the trunk slightly downward and forward as the legs are raised.

Tumbling Activities

Forward Roll Variations

There are many different approaches, arm and leg positions, and combinations that add to the difficulty of the basic forward roll. Following are some of the more popular movement patterns:

1. Do a one-foot takeoff.
2. Run to a two-foot takeoff.
3. Roll with the legs in a straddle position.
4. Roll while grasping the toes or ankles.
5. Roll with crossed arms or crossed legs.
6. Perform two or more rolls in succession.
7. Combine a forward roll with other rolls and balance stunts.

Backward Roll Variations

The backward roll, described on page 400, requires sufficient arm and shoulder-girdle strength to keep the weight off the neck as the body shifts backward. Once this roll can be performed with relative ease, the following variations can be attempted:

1. Backward Extension: (Figure 21.58)
2. Roll with legs in a straddle position, crossed, or one in front of the other.
3. Perform one or more backward rolls in succession.
4. Combine the backward roll with other rolls and balance stunts.

Spotting:
Use the same spotting technique described for the backward roll (page 401).

Backward Roll Variations

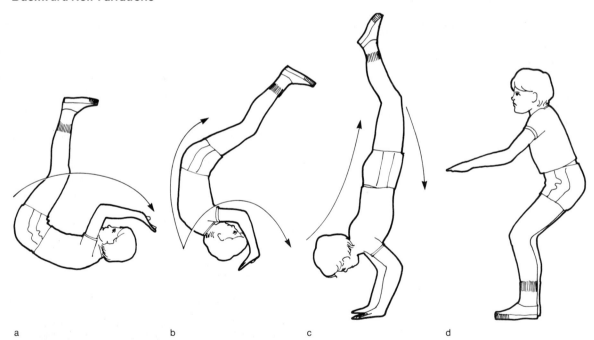

a   b   c   d

Figure 21.58 Backward extension

a. This roll starts with the same backward rolling action as the backward roll.

b. As soon as the hands begin to press against the mat, the legs begin to extend upward.

c. At the moment the legs are vertical, vigorously push off from the hands and snap the feet downward toward the mat . . .

d. . . . Landing in a partially crouched position.

Egg Roll

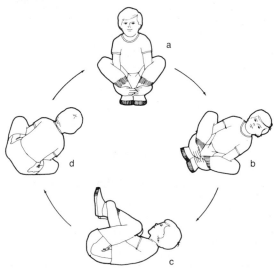

Figure 21.59 Begin in a squat position. Place the arms on the inside of the knees, then stretch the hands around the lower legs and overlap them over the feet. Roll sideways on the shoulder to the back to the shoulder and then back to a sitting position. Continue the action around the circle to the starting position.

Judo Roll

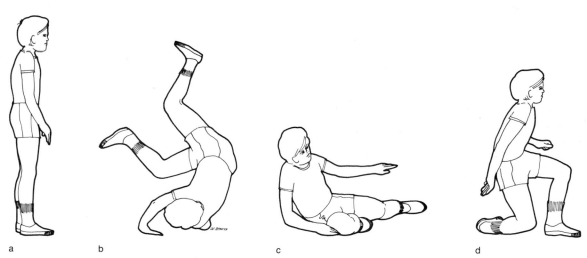

a   b   c   d

Figure 21.60 Start this roll from a standing position. Bend forward, extend the left arm and turn the head toward the right side. As the body moves forward and downward, swing the left arm toward the right and contact the mat with the top of the left shoulder. Continue the forward rolling action over the back and side, then move forward and upward.

Triple Roll

Figure 21.61a This is a continuous Log Roll involving three performers. As the center performer begins to roll to his right, the outside performer begins to thrust himself upward, over, and toward the center performer's former position.

Figure 21.61b The new center performer stands and rolls toward the other side. As soon as he starts his roll, the other outside performer thrusts himself up, over, and toward the center position. This action is then continued for several rotations. The important aspects of this triple stunt are the timing of each performer and the quick recovery of the outside performer.

Jump Through

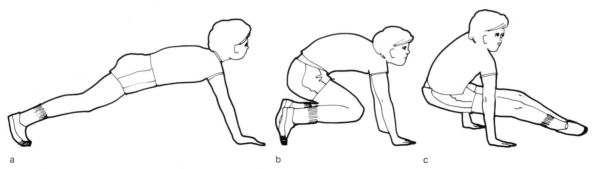

a   b   c

Figure 21.62

a. Begin in a front leaning support position with the hands about shoulder-width apart.

b. In one continuous movement, shift the legs forward between the arms . . .

c. . . . to a back leaning support position.

Variations:
1. Walk through. Same as above but walk through the movement.
2. Side shift. Same as the walk through, except that as the performer moves forward, he tilts slightly to one side, raises the opposite arm off the floor, and brings his legs through.

Upswing

a   b   c

Figure 21.63

a. Kneel with arms extended sideward and backward.

b. Swing arms forward and upward vigorously and at the same time push off from the feet.

c. Finish in a partially crouched position.

Kip

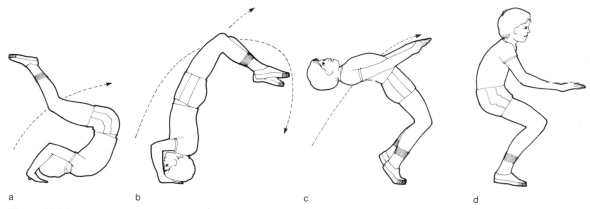

a   b   c   d

Figure 21.64

a. Begin in a back lying position with the arms at the sides and the legs extended. From this position, raise the legs, and rock back until the knees are above the head. Note: The fingers should be pointing toward the body.

b. Vigorously thrust the legs forward and upward and push off with both hands.

c. Continue raising trunk forward and upward.

d. And land in a partially crouched position.

Spotting:
Kneel on the right knee of the performer's left side. Extend the left leg slightly to the side for balance. Grasp the performer's upper left arm with your right hand and his wrist with your left hand. Assist the performer in his forward and upward movement when indicated.

Cartwheel

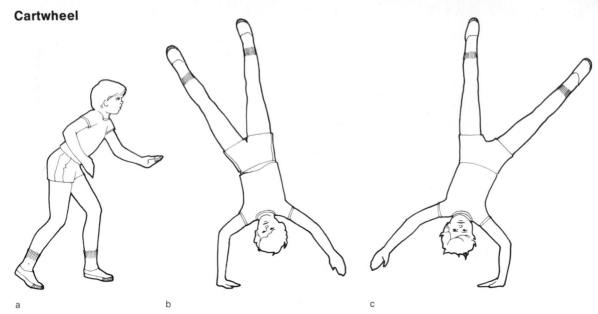

a   b   c

Figure 21.65

a. Begin with the back straight, the arms extended sideward, and the legs approximately shoulder-width apart.

b. Bend toward the left, placing the left hand, then the right on the mat and, at the same time, raising the right, then the left leg up and over toward the opposite side.

c. Note: In the middle of this stunt, the legs and arms should be fully extended and the body in a straight line.

Spotting:
Stand on the performer's right side opposite the spot where his hands will be placed. Cross the right arm over the left, then place both hands on the performer's hips as he pushes off from his right foot. Aid the performer in his sideward motion and vertical balance position when indicated.

Handspring over Partner

Figure 21.66 This is a lead-up stunt to the Handspring. One partner kneels on the mat, places his hands well apart, and tucks his head toward his chest. The standing partner places his hands opposite the trunk of the kneeling partner, keeping his arm straight, and raises one leg off the mat. Still keeping his arms straight, he kicks upward with his free leg, pushes off with his back leg, and rolls over the kneeling partner.

Knee Handspring

Figure 21.67 The knee handspring can also serve as a lead-up stunt to the Handspring. One partner lies on his back with his knees bent and together and his arms extended forward. The standing partner places his hands on his partner's knees, lowers his body forward, and raises one leg slightly off the mat. The top partner then swings top leg up, pushes off his lower leg, and continues the forward movement, placing his shoulders against the lower partner's hands. The lower partner keeps his arms extended to assist the top partner's forward motion.

Handspring

a   b   c

Figure 21.68

a. Begin in a standing position. Run forward, skip on the left foot, place the right foot on the mat and then the hands, with the arms extended.

b. Continue the upward and forward thrust of the right leg, followed by the left leg.

c. When the body is in front of the head, push off from the hands and land on both feet with the knees partially bent.

Spotting:
Sit in a straddle position near the end of the rolled mat. As the performer places his hands on the mat, place your left hand under his left shoulder and your right hand under his upper left arm, then forward over it. As the performer shifts forward and upward, lift with the left hand and guide the forward action with the right hand. A second spotter may be required on the other side of the mat.

Round-off

a   b   c

Figure 21.69

a. The first part of the round-off is the same as the cartwheel.

b. As soon as both feet are off the ground, bring them together, then make a half turn toward the left (counterclockwise).

c. Bend at the hips, and land on both feet facing the opposite direction.

Spotting:
Stand on the left side of the performer and opposite the spot where his hands will be placed. As the performer places his right hand on the mat, place your left hand under his right shoulder. Lift as he pushes off from his hands when indicated.

Forward Drop

Figure 21.70 Stand with the arms extended over the head. In a simultaneous action, shift the weight to the right leg, begin to fall forward, and slowly raise the extended left leg back and up. Land with the hands and arms gradually absorbing the downward momentum.

Variations:
Dead Man Fall: This stunt is similar except that the arms begin at the sides of the body and both feet remain in contact with the mat throughout the movement.

Neck Spring

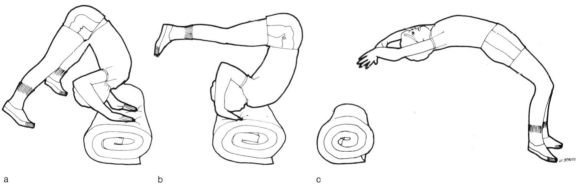

a   b   c

Figure 21.71

a. This stunt should be taught from a stationary position over a rolled mat. Once the performer can execute the kipping action, he should be allowed to attempt the skill with a running approach to the rolled mat.

b. Run toward the rolled mat, take off with both feet, place the hands on the mat, bend the arms, and place the back of head on the mat.

c. Roll forward, dropping the legs, then extend the legs forward and upward vigorously and push off the hands.

Spotting:
Sit in a straddle position near the end of the rolled mat. As the performer places his hand and the back of his head on the mat, grasp his upper left arm with your right hand and his wrist with your left hand. Assist the performer in his forward and upward movement when indicated.

Head Spring

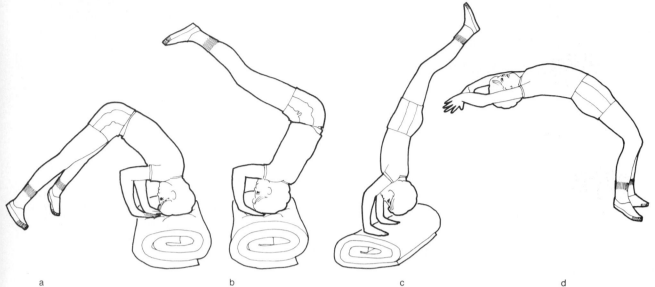

a   b   c   d

Figure 21.72 This stunt is similar to the Neck Spring and should also be taught from a stationary position over a rolled mat. Once the performer can execute a kipping action, he should be allowed to attempt the Head Spring with a running approach.

a. Run toward the rolled mat, take off with both feet, place the hands, then the top of the head on the rolled mat.

b. Keep the head and hands on the mat and bring the extended legs forward until an "overbalanced" position is reached.

c. Then extend the legs up and forward vigorously and push off with the hands.

d. Land on both feet, swing the arms forward, and bend the knees to regain a forward balanced position.

Spotting:
Use the same spotting technique described for the Forward Handspring (p. 417).

Pyramid Building

A human pyramid is usually considered to be a group of students forming a pyramidlike structure with one child at the top and the others gradually tapering to the sides. This is known as a *true pyramid;* however, there are other kinds of pyramids that have high points somewhere within the pyramid or even at the ends. The block illustrations may be used as basic guides in constructing pyramids with two, three, or more students.

The first stage of pyramid building is to learn or create individual poses that can be used for the center, side, or end positions. Many balance stunts, such as the Head Stand and the V-Sit, can be used for these positions. Other poses such as the Attention, the Dog, and the Inclined Stand can be added to these basic poses (figs. 21.73-21.75). It is also important to allow the class to design its own individual positions.

Figure 21.73 The Attention

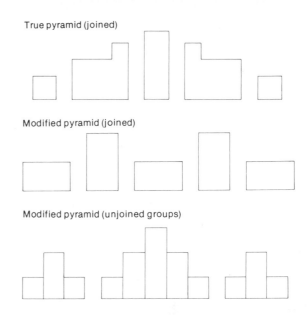

True pyramid (joined)

Modified pyramid (joined)

Modified pyramid (unjoined groups)

Figure 21.74 The Dog

Figure 21.75 The Inclined Stand

The next stage in pyramid building is the development of dual stunts (figs. 21.76-21.78). Again, many of the dual balance stunts described in the previous section can become the nucleus of a pyramid. Require the heaviest and strongest students to form the base of the pyramid and lighter students to be on top.

Figure 21.77 Base Stand

Figure 21.76 Handstand Arch

Figure 21.78 Double Incline

Figure 21.79 Stride Stand

Figure 21.80 High Center Pyramid

Once the dual stunts are learned, combine these positions. A symmetrical six-person pyramid can be formed with two facing Base Stands and one individual pose such as the Dog Stand on each end facing toward the center. Beyond this point, the teacher and students can use their imaginations to design and construct an unlimited variety of pyramids. Examples are shown in Figure 21.79 and 21.80.

Since pyramid building involves teamwork and timing, a standard procedure or set of whistle cues should be developed by the teacher. The first blow of the whistle could mean that all stand at attention and face one direction. The second blow could signal that all participants are to move into the ready or primary position. A third blow might be necessary in two- and three-person high pyramids for the upper participants to shift into the final position. A similar procedure should be followed to dismount.

Movement Concepts and Skills

The stunts and tumbling skills described in the previous two sections are classified as structured skills or movement patterns. Each skill is performed in a particular way. There can be variations in the approach or the position of the hands or legs, but the skill cannot be changed from its basic form. In order to overcome the structured limitations of formal stunts and tumbling activities, many of the movement concepts and skills developed in the movement education approach are being incorporated into stunts and tumbling and into activities with small equipment and large apparatus. These new movement concepts and skills allow the child to perform a movement according to his own level of physical and creative ability. (See film "Introducing the Elements of Movement Education," Appendix A.)

However, the problems of introducing these unstructured movement concepts and skills to stunts and tumbling, small equipment activities, and large apparatus activities are similar to the problems encountered in introducing the problem-solving method in games programs. Introducing the new movement concepts and skills to primary children, particularly those in the first two grades, is relatively easy. Primary children do not have a wide background of stunts and tumbling skills. Also, many of their skills are imitative movements rather than the complex balance and agility skills taught in later grades. And primary children are normally taught through more informal methods both in the classroom and in the gymnasium. As a consequence, primary teachers will have little difficulty incorporating movement concepts and skills into their stunts and tumbling program. Once the teacher understands this new movement vocabulary, she will usually give more emphasis to movement concepts and skills and less to structured stunts activities.

As with the problem-solving method, introducing the new movement concepts and skills is more difficult for intermediate teachers. By the time boys and girls have reached the fourth or fifth grade they have been taught many stunts and tumbling skills. Furthermore, these skills were normally taught through a process of explanation, demonstration, and practice. It would be difficult and unwise to change this process completely and adopt a new movement vocabulary and a new way of learning. A more profitable approach is for the intermediate teacher to acquire an understanding of the basic movement concepts and skills described in this section and then to introduce them gradually into the regular stunts and tumbling activities. If the class is receptive to these ideas and demonstrates the ability to work independently and safely, greater emphasis can be given to the movement concepts and skills.

The general movement education concepts of body awareness, qualities, space awareness, and relationships will be described on the following pages. Wherever possible, suggestions for teaching these movement skills will be offered, along with ideas for relating or incorporating them into the stunts and tumbling activities of the primary or intermediate program.

Body Awareness (What the Body Can Do)

The concept of body awareness describes the ways in which the body or its parts can be controlled, balanced upon, or moved from one position to another. Skills involved in body awareness fall into the following three groups.

Balancing or "Weight Bearing"

A child is capable of balancing or "taking the weight" on different parts of his body. He can balance on one foot, on his head, or on all "threes" such as in the Lame Puppy Walk. In order to help the child learn what parts of his body he can balance upon, it is necessary to present a challenge in the form of a movement problem and then let him answer the challenge in his own way. The question should begin with such phrases as "See if you can . . .", "How many ways . . .", "Can you . . .", or "Try to discover . . .", rather than a direct command such as "I want you to . . . ." The following questions show how to use the problem-solving method to assist the child in finding his own way of balancing on one or more parts of his body:

1. "Can you show me the one-leg balance?" Children may have already learned this balance stunt, so they should be capable of performing it.
2. "See if you can balance on your seat." This is still somewhat structured, yet the question allows each child to put his arms and legs in any position he wishes. A series of similar questions directing the child to balance on other parts—side, back, stomach—could follow.

Figure 21.81

3. Present a series of questions involving two or more parts of the body—"Can you balance on one foot and two other parts of your body?" "See if you can balance on three (or four) different parts of your body." "Can you find another way of balancing on three parts of your body?"

The main task here is to help the children become aware of the many different ways in which they can balance their bodies. The move-ment challenges began with a familiar stunt (the one-leg balance), then shifted to specific parts of the body. The final challenge mentioned only a certain number of "points of contact," thus providing more freedom for the child to discover other ways that his body or its parts can be balanced.

Transfer of Weight

Transfer of weight is the ability to shift from one balanced position to another. Therefore, this skill can be developed as a logical extension of balancing on different parts of the body. The following questions illustrate how this progression can occur:

1. From one known skill to another. "Can you show me the Measuring Worm stunt, then change to a Head Stand?" (This is shifting from one three-point balance to another three-point balance.)
2. From a known part to three unknown parts. "See if you can balance on your seat, then shift to balancing on three different parts of your body." (From a one-point balance to a three-point balance.)
3. From unknown parts to unknown parts. "Can you show me a three-point balance, then shift to a new three-point balance?"

Transfer of Weight

a

b

c

Figure 21.82

Figure 21.83 Can you make a curled shape? ...

Figure 21.84 See if you can show me a stretched shape ...

Shapes

Shapes are the third movement skill of body awareness. The human body can make stretched, curled, wide, narrow, and twisted shapes. The task is similar to balancing or weight bearing in that questions must be presented to help the child discover what shapes he can perform.

Stretch and curl shapes should involve the whole body first, then progress to individual parts. Questions should encourage the children to make shapes from the following starting positions:

1. For curled shapes (fig. 21.83)
   a. from a sitting position
   b. from a standing position
   c. while in flight
   d. from a front, back, or side lying position
   e. from a curled position to another curled position
2. For stretched shapes (fig. 21.84)
   a. from a standing position
   b. while in flight
   c. from a sitting position
   d. from a front, back, or side lying position
   e. from a stretched position to another stretched position

Progression should be from a stationary position into a curled or stretched shape. A teacher can begin with questions directed at curled shapes (from a-e), then try the same with stretched shapes (a-e), or switch from one to the other.

Following are sample questions:

"Can you curl up and make a very small ball-like shape?"

"Can you make a stretched shape from a standing position?"

"See if you can repeat your stretched shape or find a new one and then change into a curled shape."

"See if you can start with the Turk Stand and when you are low to the ground roll to a very curled-up shape."

Allow sufficient time for experimentation. During this time look for unusual shapes and provide encouragement and praise wherever necessary. Choose one or two shapes and let the children show the rest of the class; don't always choose the same children.

Once the class has a general understanding of stretch and curl, introduce wide and narrow and twisted shapes in a similar way. Wide and narrow shapes, like curl and stretch shapes, are contrasting. A wide shape (fig. 21.85) requires the legs or arms or both to be away from the trunk in some way. In contrast, a narrow shape is characterized by its thinness, which means the arms or legs must be close together or in line with the trunk.

Figure 21.85 Wide shapes

Figure 21.86 Twisting—body stabilized

A twisted shape can be performed in two ways. The first is by holding one part of the body in a fixed or stabilized position, such as on the floor, and then turning the body or any part of it away from the fixed base. In figure 21.86 the body is fixed or stabilized as the feet restrict the degree of twisting. A twisted shape can also be made when the body is in flight. In this case, as illustrated in figure 21.87, one part of the body is held in a fixed position while the other part turns away from the *fixed* part, producing a twisted shape. Although it could be argued that the latter is a *turn,* (usually defined as rotation of the body and loss of a fixed contact), with younger children the synonymous use of *twist* and *turn* is quite acceptable. The refinement in meaning can be made later.

At this stage in the introduction of movement skills and concepts, children should have learned the meaning of balance and shape. They should also be able to develop simple sequences involving a variety of shapes and balance skills.

Figure 21.87 Twisting—body in flight

Qualities (How the Body Moves)

The concept of qualities describes how the body moves from one position to another. It includes the movement skills relating to speed, force, and flow.

Speed

Speed is the ability to move quickly or slowly from one position to another (fig. 21.88).

Figure 21.88

Force

Force is the effort involved in a single movement or throughout a series of related movements. A child may leap high into the air, demonstrating a strong and forceful movement of the leg muscles (fig. 21.89). In contrast, a gentle shift from a high stretch to a low curl illustrates a light or gentle movement.

Figure 21.89

Flow

 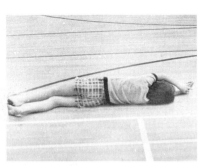  

a. A smooth transition ...

b. ... from one position ...

c. ... to another position ...

d. ... and to another position.

Figure 21.90

Flow

Flow is the smooth transition or linking of one movement pattern to another (fig. 21.90).

These aspects of qualities can be integrated into previously learned stunts, tumbling and safety skills, and the three components of body awareness. The following examples show a few of the many applications of speed, force, and flow to a single skill or a sequence of skills:

1. To stunts: Ask the class to perform the Measuring Worm stunt. After one or two practices, ask the class to perform part of the stunt very slowly and part very quickly (fig. 21.91).

Figure 21.91

2. To tumbling skills: Pose a challenge such as "See if you can move slowly from a Log Roll to a Side Roll, then quickly from a Side Roll back to a Log Roll."
3. To shapes: Ask the class to make up a sequence of stretched, curled, and wide shapes. After each child knows his sequence, pose the following suggestion: "As you practice your sequence, try very hard to make each movement link smoothly to the next with no sudden stops or jerky movements between each skill." The stress here is on flow, or the ease and efficiency of moving from one shape or position to another.

Space Awareness (Where the Body Moves)

The third main concept, space awareness, includes movement skills relating to use of general or limited space, direction, and levels of movement.

General or Limited Space

All the space in a gymnasium that can be used by a child constitutes his *general space* (fig. 21.92). In contrast, *limited* or *personal space* is the immediate area a child can use around him to perform a movement or series of movements. When a child is challenged to perform a series of different balance positions while remaining inside his hoop, he is using his personal or limited space (fig. 21.93).

Figure 21.92 General Space

Figure 21.93 Limited Space

Figure 21.94 Directional movements

DIRECTION
Direction is the ability to move safely and purposely in a variety of pathways, such as forward, backward, or sideways, and to trace out pathways such as over, under, around, and through.

Levels
Levels concerns the ability to perform a movement or series of movements that requires the body to be low to the ground, as when performing series of rolls (fig. 21.95), at a medium level, as in moving on all fours (fig. 21.96), or at a high level, as when performing a cartwheel or a leap from the floor (fig. 21.97).

Many of these aspects of space awareness have been stressed in teaching stunts and tumbling and, to a lesser degree, when teaching the movement skills of body awareness and qualities. For example, when each of the tumbling skills was introduced, each child began on his own mat. This was his personal or limited space. Gradually, his space was expanded to two mats, then to three, and finally to all the mats available in the general space of the gymnasium. Each child was also asked to move to an open space on the mat. His rolling movement may have been forward, sideways, or diagonal.

Relationships
The fourth main concept of movement education is the relationship of the individual or group to other performers or objects.

Figure 21.95 Low level

Figure 21.96 Medium level

Figure 21.97 High level

Partner Relationships
Movements with a partner can involve matching shapes or movements (fig. 21.98), contrasting shapes or movements (fig. 21.99), or one child acting as the leader while the other acts as the follower through a sequence of movements.

There are many useful and enjoyable applications of partner activities to a stunts and tumbling program. All of the partner activities described under the stunts sections for primary and intermediate children are essentially dual balance stunts or tandem-type agility walks. With "matching," "contrasting," and "following" challenges, partner-type activities can be greatly enriched. Following are examples of the many ways that partners can develop structured and unstructured movement sequences:

1. Matching movements using structured skills: "See if you can make up a sequence (or routine) with your partner that begins with a Head Stand, includes a roll and ends with both in a balancing position (fig. 21.100)."
2. Contrasting movements using unstructured skills: "One partner makes a stretched shape and the other partner makes a contrasting curled shape. Next, the first partner makes another stretched shape and his partner

Figure 21.98 Matching shapes

Figure 21.99 Contrasting shapes

Partner Relationships

a. ... that begin with a headstand ...   b. ... includes a roll ...   c. ... and ends in a balance position.
Figure 21.100

makes a contrasting curled shape." Repeat again with two new stretched and curled shapes. Allow time to practice the contrasting shapes in a smooth sequence.

3. Follow the leader: One partner leads and the other must copy each movement. Challenges can be "Make a shape, change direction, make another shape, change direction," and so on. "Develop a sequence of balancing and rolling with one following the other." Or, "Make up a sequence with your partner that includes a change of direction and a change in speed."

Equipment Relationships

This is the ability to perform a movement in a manipulative way, such as rolling with a hoop (fig. 21.101), or in a nonmanipulative manner, such as leaping over a hoop (fig. 21.102). Numerous examples of these types of relationships will be described in the next two chapters.

This introduction to the four movement concepts has simply opened the door to a new range of movement skills. Each of the skills within body awareness, qualities, space awareness, and relationships are unstructured and thus allow each child to perform each movement in his own unique way. Since these new movement skills can be mixed with stunts or tumbling skills, they enrich a child's movement experience.

The next two chapters deal with a wide variety of small equipment and large apparatus. Structured skills such as individual rope skipping, vaulting over boxes, and balancing on a beam will be presented. But the children have developed a basic understanding of the four movement concepts, they will be able to apply movement skills to each piece of equipment and to the large apparatus in a very exciting and creative way.

Figure 21.101 In a manipulative way

Figure 21.102 In a nonmanipulative way

Stunts and Movement Skills with Small Equipment

22

Teaching Procedures

Beanbag Activities

Individual and Long Rope Activities

Hoop Activities

Wand Activities

Chair Activities

Indian Club, Milk Carton, and Traffic Cone Activities

This chapter should be considered as a logical extension of stunts and tumbling activities. Adding a variety of small equipment to the gymnastic program provides an opportunity for each child to develop strength, balance, and coordination. Each piece of equipment included in this chapter can be used in a structured manner, such as teaching basic rope-skipping skills. And when the movement concepts and skills described in the previous chapter are applied, many additional uses can be found for the equipment. By presenting movement challenges or tasks, the equipment may be used in a manipulative manner or as an obstacle to maneuver around or over. (See film "Using Small Equipment in Movement Education," Appendix A.)

The material in this chapter has been organized to provide both primary and intermediate teachers with sufficient information to teach a wide variety of structured skills or to combine these skills with movement concepts and skills in an interesting and challenging way.

Teaching Procedures

The addition of small equipment activities to a gymnastic lesson presents several organizational and instructional problems. The following suggestions relating to routine procedures, teaching techniques, and lesson development will provide a basic framework for incorporating small equipment into a primary or intermediate program.

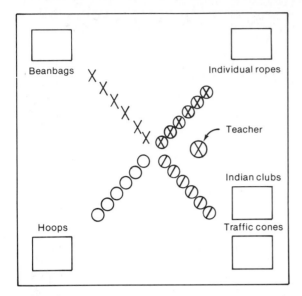

Beanbags
Individual ropes
Teacher
Indian clubs
Hoops
Traffic cones

Routine Procedures

Perhaps the most frustrating aspect of using small equipment is getting it out and putting it away in an orderly manner. One of the most successful and efficient ways of handling equipment is to have each type of equipment that is going to be used in a lesson placed in boxes or containers near the instructional area. The teacher can then give instructions about who will be using what type of equipment and where their working areas will be. When the equipment is not being used, it is returned to the appropriate container. Suggestions relating to carrying and placing equipment such as wands and hoops are given in the sections on each type of equipment.

Using Small Equipment

It was stated in the previous chapter that small equipment should be used to provide additional challenges to stunts, tumbling skills, and movement skills (see lesson outline on page 385). Since each class and grade level varies according to the time and equipment available and the students' background of skill, no standard application of this equipment can be recommended.

Each of this chapter's sections includes a suggested list of structured skills and a list of ideas and challenges to develop movement concepts and skills.

Task or Challenge Cards

Task or challenge cards are an interesting and enjoyable way of presenting challenges to primary and intermediate children. Since the movement skills and the problem-solving method may be relatively new approaches to many classroom teachers, task cards allow them to prepare challenges before the lesson. The task cards here contain movement questions. Each group is given a card and assigned an area of the gymnasium. As soon as each child has read the task, he begins to make up his sequence using the assigned equipment. The teacher can make up a series of cards for individual work, partner activities, or larger group tasks.

Many variations can be made to this general idea, such as allowing the child to select his own card or asking the class members to make up their own challenges. One enjoyable variation is to write movement skills on separate cards and then give each group three or four cards. Their task, as illustrated, is to rearrange the cards individually or as a group and then practice the sequence. Primary and intermediate children thoroughly enjoy making up their own sequences. This approach also gives the teacher an idea of the class's general understanding of movement concepts and skills and a clear indication of the level of physical and creative ability.

Hoops	*Beanbags*
Make up a sequence of stretch and shapes while in contact with your hoop.	Place the beanbag on the floor and see how many ways you can cross the beanbag.

Individual Ropes	*Wands*
Make up a routine that includes a hop, two-foot basic, and a rocker step.	Make up a sequence with your wand that includes balance, shapes, and a change of direction.

Balance

Diagonal roll

Quick

Twisted

Their answer:
Balance on three parts,
quickly roll backwards
to a twisted shape.

Beanbag Activities

Beanbags are the most common type of small equipment, being available to virtually every classroom teacher. The beanbag should be at least six inches square for the activities suggested in this program. Cloth covers rather than smooth plastic or nylon ones are preferred for homemade beanbags.

Although the beanbag traditionally has been used by primary teachers for simple games and manipulative activities, there are many applications at the intermediate level. The more familiar, structured beanbag activities are presented first to illustrate the contemporary use of the beanbag in the gymnastic program. Following that is a section on how the beanbag can be used as an obstacle or focus point in developing movement concepts and skills.

Figure 22.1

Structured Activities

Individual Activities
The beanbag can be used to increase the difficulty of many previously acquired stunts and tumbling skills, as well as with many new balance and stunt activities. The following examples illustrate the beanbag's versatility.

1. Previous stunts and tumbling skills:
   a. Wicket Walk (page 387), beanbag behind neck.
   b. Tightrope Walk (page 387), place beanbag on head.
   c. Bouncing Ball (page 387), place beanbag on head.
   d. Single Leg Balance (page 390), place beanbag on head or arm.
   e. Forward Roll (page 398) and Side Roll (page 396), tuck beanbag under chin.
   f. Knee Dip (page 403), place beanbag on head.
   g. L-Support (page 410), place beanbag between knees.

2. Throwing and catching skills: The wide surface and lack of rebound property make the beanbag a valuable tool in helping young children to learn how to throw and catch. Following are a few examples of how primary teachers can use the beanbag to develop hand-eye coordination:
   a. Toss the beanbag into the air and catch it with both hands, then with the left hand and then with the right.
   b. Toss the beanbag into the air, change direction, or perform a hand movement (clap hands, touch the floor), and then catch the beanbag.
   c. Place targets on floor (hoops, milk cartons) and throw the beanbag into the target. Change throwing skill and distance.
   d. Move, throw and catch. Have the children use a variety of locomotor skills (running, skipping, and so on) and throw and catch beanbags as they move about the instructional area.

Figure 22.2 Balance the beanbag on your head

Figure 22.3 . . . on your foot

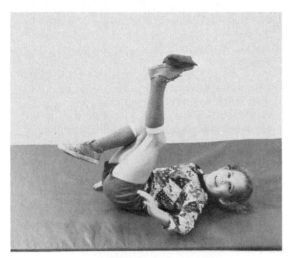

Figure 22.4 . . . on your feet

3. Balance the beanbag on different parts of the body (figs. 22.2 to 22.4): Designate specific parts of the body—head, elbow, and so on. Change body position and continue. For example, "Put beanbag on your back and balance on one foot."
4. Move the beanbag with different parts of the body: Ask the class to propel the beanbags with their knees and catch them; then designate other parts of the body, such as the head, foot, elbow, and shoulder.

Partner Activities:

Many of the previous individual skills can be performed with two performers, and several new partner-type activities can be presented. Several examples follow.

1. Throwing and catching:
   a. Throw the beanbag back and forth, changing the type of throw, distance, and position and angle of throw.
   b. Throw and catch with two beanbags.
   c. Throw and catch with one or both performers on the move.
2. Pass and catch the beanbag with different parts of the body: Propel with the feet and catch with the hands or feet. Propel with the head and catch with the stomach or another part of the body.

Figure 22.5

Figure 22.6

Applying Movement Skills to Beanbag Activities

The individual and partner activities that have been described indicate the value and potential of beanbag activities in developing throwing, catching, balancing, and agility skills. If children have been taught through the problem-solving method and have acquired a basic understanding of movement concepts and skills, the next step is to use beanbag activities in a much more creative and challenging way. The following examples illustrate how the beanbag can be used as an obstacle to balance on or with and to maneuver on or over. By posing tasks or challenges using movement skills, children discover through their own exploration the various ways their bodies or parts of them can manipulate and control small obstacles such as beanbags.

Although the same challenge can be presented to primary and intermediate children, the movement response should be quite different. As children progress through the grades, they acquire more skill and movement understanding, which are revealed in the complexity and quality of their movement patterns. Following are examples of the type of questions that should be asked and the type of responses that can be expected from primary and intermediate children. Each teacher, however, should present challenges according to her class's previous gymnastic background and receptiveness to this exploratory approach.

1. *Direction and speed:* Scatter beanbags around the floor area and pose these challenge activities illustrating how the beanbag acts as an obstacle or focus point in the development of directional movements and the quality of speed.
   a. "Move around as many beanbags as possible, but do not jump over any."
   b. "Run in any direction and when you come to a beanbag, run completely around it, then on to another beanbag."
   c. "Move in any direction and when you approach a beanbag, jump over it, land, and then change directions to find another beanbag."
   d. "Can you run in different directions showing a change of speed every time you jump over a beanbag?"

Figure 22.7 . . . on one part of the beanbag.

Figure 22.8 . . . on one part of the beanbag . . .

Figure 22.9 On your seat and . . .

2. *Balance and transfer of weight:*
   a. "How many different parts of your body can you balance the beanbag on?"
   b. "Place the beanbag on the floor. Can you balance with one part of your body on the beanbag (figs. 22.7 and 22.8)?"
   c. "Place the beanbag on your seat and see how many ways you can balance on three different parts of your body (fig. 22.9)."
   d. "Place a beanbag on the floor. How many different ways can you balance over the beanbag (figs. 22.10 and 22.11)?"
   e. "How many different ways can you cross your beanbag (figs. 22.12 and 22.13)?"
3. *Shapes:*
   a. "Can you make a stretched shape with the beanbag on the highest part of your body?"
   b. "See if you can keep the beanbag on one part of your body while you try to make two different curled shapes."
4. *Relationships:* Each partner has a beanbag.
   a. "Place the beanbags on the floor and make up a matching sequence that shows a change of direction and a change of speed."
   b. "Keep the beanbag between your feet and make up a matching sequence that includes moving forward, backward, and sideways."
   c. "Place the beanbags on your heads. One child leads and the other must match her movements (fig. 22.14)."

Figure 22.10 How many different ways can you . . .

Swing

Figure 22.1[...]
the alterna[...]
rebound st[...]
side.

One-Foo[...]

a. Hop left.
Figure 22.20[...]
each turn of t[...]
jump over the[...]
hopping on o[...]
before he tra[...]

slightly forward and away from the body (fig. 22.16). To start the rope turning, swing the arms and shoulders in a circular motion; once the rope begins to follow the circular motion, all further action should be initiated from the wrists and fingers. The jumping action should be a slight push off the toes, just high enough to allow the rope to pass under the feet.

Basic Rope-Skipping Skills

The following rope-skipping skills are listed in approximate order of difficulty. It is helpful to begin each new step without a rope. Once the child can execute the foot movements, let him try with a rope. At this stage, a musical background will help the child to keep up a steady rhythm. Any folk-dance record such as "Shoo Fly" or "Pop Goes the Weasel" with a 4/4 rhythm works very well. All popular tunes with a similar beat will work as well and, in fact, are enjoyed more than folk dance records by upper elementary school children.

Many of the basic steps shown in figures 22.17 to 22.25 can be performed in slow or fast time and with the rope turned forward or backward. With the slow rhythm, the performer jumps over the rope, takes a rebound jump in place as the rope passes over his head, and then performs the original step or shifts to a new movement. The pattern is jump-rebound-jump. If there is musical accompaniment, the performer jumps over the rope on every other beat. With a fast rhythm, the rope is turned twice as fast so the performer executes a step only as the rope passes under his feet. If there is a musical accompaniment, the performer jumps over the rope on every beat.

Two-Foot Basic Step

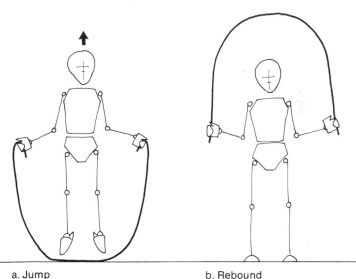
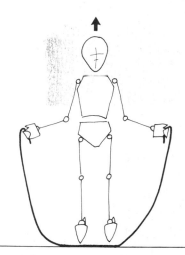

a. Jump   b. Rebound   c. Jump

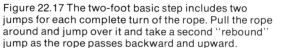

Figure 22.17 The two-foot basic step includes two jumps for each complete turn of the rope. Pull the rope around and jump over it and take a second "rebound" jump as the rope passes backward and upward.

Rocker Step

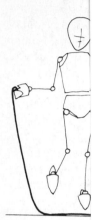

a. Jump right

Figure 22.18 The
the rope with the
same foot (rebou
the left foot (jum
(rebound). Durin
passing overhea

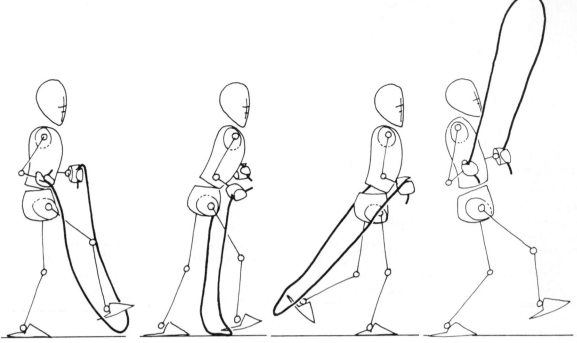

a. Pass rope under front foot.

b. Rock forward.

c. Pass rope under back foot.

d. Rock backward.

Figure 22.21 One leg is always forward and the weight is shifting from the back to the front, or lead, foot. As the rope passes under the front foot, the weight should be transferring forward, allowing the back foot to raise and the rope to pass under it. After the rope passes under the back foot and begins its upward and forward arch, the performer should again "rock" back, transferring the weight to the back foot.

Spread-Legs Step

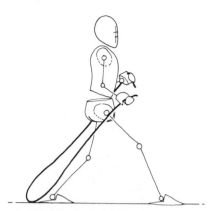 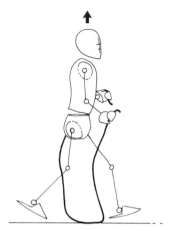

a. Begin in a stride position.

b. Jump and change.

Figure 22.22 Begin this movement in a front stride position with the weight evenly distributed on both feet. Pull the rope around, jump, and as it passes under, change the position of the feet. Continue pattern.

Cross-Leg Step

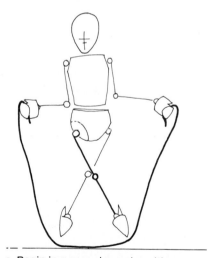 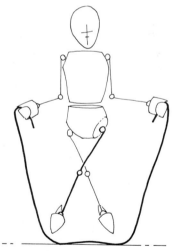

a. Begin in a cross-legged position.

b. Jump and cross left leg over right.

Figure 22.23 Begin with the right leg crossed in front of the left leg and the weight evenly distributed on both feet. Pull the rope around, jump, and as it passes under, cross the left leg over the right. Continue the pattern, alternating the front leg position.

Crossing Arms

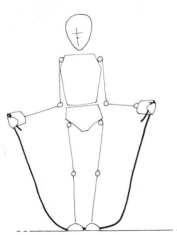

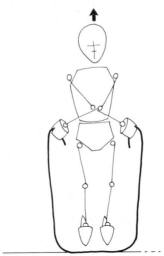

a. From a regular rope-skipping position . . .

b. . . .To cross left over right

Figure 22.24 This action should take place during an ongoing rope-skipping movement. As the rope begins its forward and downward movement, the left arm crosses over the right and the right hand is brought up and under the left armpit. The next jump is made in this position. The performer can continue in the crossed-arm position or alternate the crossed-arm position on each turn of the rope.

Pepper

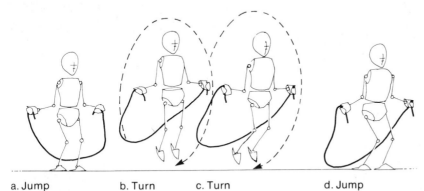

a. Jump   b. Turn   c. Turn   d. Jump

Figure 22.25 The pepper step is two full turns of the rope while the performer's feet are off the ground.

Once the children have learned two or more basic steps, they can begin to create many interesting and enjoyable routines. A few suggestions follow; however, each child should have an opportunity to develop his own routine.

1. Combine a change of speed with the alternate step.
2. Make up a sequence involving three different steps.
3. Make up a sequence involving a hop, an alternate step, and a change of direction.
4. Perform three different steps in a cross-arm position.
5. Move in different directions using hopping, jumping, and rocking step skills.
6. Make up a sequence with the rope turning backward.

Partner Activities

There are several enjoyable partner activities that children can perform with an individual rope. Many variations and routines can be developed from the following basic starting positions.

Enter Front

One partner begins with a two-foot basic step. As the rope comes forward and down, the outside partner enters and places her hands on her partner's waist (fig. 22.26).

Variations:
1. Partners perform mirror images, hopping, jumping, or other basic rope-skipping steps.
2. Outside partner turns her back to her partner and they continue jumping.
3. Outside partner keeps the same jumping cadence as her partner but begins to make a quarter or a half turn, then back to her original position.

Figure 22.26a Begin with a two foot basic . . .

Figure 22.26b . . . partner enters front.

One-In

Partners stand facing each other with the rope held on the same side.

Variations:
1. One partner moves in, then out.
2. One partner moves in, followed by his partner.
3. When both are inside, they make up a sequence of matching steps.

Long Rope Jumping Activities

Rope jumping is performed with one or more children jumping over a rope turned by two other children. Begin with the single rope-skipping skills. After the basic entry and jumping skills have been mastered, introduce the dual activities. To assist in teaching both types of jumping activities, use the suggested list of rope-jumping rhymes on page 449.

There are two ways a rope can be turned for jumping activities:

1. *Front door,* when the rope is turning forward and toward the incoming jumper (fig. 22.27). The children turn the rope toward the jumper (clockwise), and the jumper waits until the rope is moving away from him before he runs in.
2. *Back door,* when the rope is turning backward and away from the jumper. The turners turn the rope away from the jumper (counterclockwise), and the jumper waits until the rope has passed its highest peak and is moving downward before he runs in.

The following progression of rope-jumping activities can be performed by entering through either the front or back door:

1. Run under the rope.
2. Run in, jump once, run out.
3. Run in, jump several times, run out.
4. Run in, jump on one foot, run out.
5. Run in, jump several times on one foot, run out.
6. Run in, jump making quarter, half, three-quarter, or full turns with each jump, run out.
7. Run in, jump on alternate feet, run out.
8. Run in, touch the floor with the hands on every other jump, run out.
9. Run in, take a squat position (on all fours), jump in this position, run out.
10. Run in, jump up and touch toes, land, run out.
11. Run in, turners gradually increase speed to "hot pepper," slow down, run out.
12. Run in, turners gradually raise rope off the ground ("high water").
13. Run in with a ball, bounce the ball several times, run out.
14. Repeat these skills with a partner.
15. Place arm over partner's shoulder, run in, jump several times, run out (fig. 22.28).
16. With partner, run in, stand back to back, jump several times, run out.

Figure 22.27 Front door

Figure 22.28 ... arms over partner's shoulders ...

17. With partner, run in, face partner, hold partner's right leg, jump several times, run out (fig. 22.29).
18. Follow the leader with four or five players and one chosen to be the leader. The leader runs in and performs any skill or stunt, then runs out. Each player must follow and repeat the leader's stunt.

Rope Jumping Rhymes:

Rope-jumping rhymes, like singing games, have been handed down for many generations. These rhymes can be repeated as children perform various rope-jumping activities. Encourage children to use their versions of the following favorites:

Mabel, Mabel

Mabel, Mabel, set the table,
Don't forget the salt, vinegar, pepper....
(Turners turn "pepper" on the last word.)

Fudge, Fudge

Fudge, Fudge, tell the judge,
Mama's got a newborn baby.
Wrap it up in tissue paper,
Send it down the elevator.
Elevator one, splits ... elevator two ... splits, and so on until the jumper misses. (Jumper performs the splits on the word "splits.")

Apple, Apple

Apple, Apple, up in the tree,
Tell me who my lover shall be,
A, B, C, D, E, etc. (Jump to each letter until the jumper reaches his sweetheart's first initial.)

Mama, Mama

Mama, Mama, I am sick,
Send for the doctor, quick, quick, quick.
Mama, Mama, turn around,
Mama, Mama, touch the ground.
Mama, Mama, are you through?
Mama, Mama, spell your name.
(Child performs actions indicated in the verse.)

Figure 22.29 Hold partner's right leg.

Down by the Meadow

Down by the meadow where the green grass grows,
There sits (call the name of jumper) sweet as a rose.
She sang, she sang, she sang, she sang so sweet,
And along came (jumper's sweetheart's name), and
Kissed her on the cheek.
How many kisses did she get?
1, 2, 3, 4, etc.
(Child keeps jumping until she misses.)

All in Together

All in together, this fine weather,
January, February, March, etc.
(Jumper runs in on the month of his birthday.)
All out together, this fine weather,
January, February, March, etc.
(Jumper runs out on the month of his birthday.)

Hokey Pokey

Hokey Pokey went to France,
To teach the ladies how to dance,
First on the heels, then on the toes,
Give a high kick and around you go.
A bow to the captain, a salute to the queen,
And turn your back on the submarine.
(Child performs actions indicated in the rhyme.)

I Love Coffee

I love coffee, I love tea, I love . . . . (name)
I dislike coffee, I dislike tea, I dislike . . . . (name)
So go away from me.

(Child who is jumping calls the name of another
child, who comes in, then goes out.)

Playground Ideas with Long Ropes

Long ropes have traditionally been used for
jumping activities. The following examples illustrate enjoyable uses of one or two long ropes:

1. Jumping over one rope: Two performers hold
   a long rope approximately two feet off the
   ground (vary the height according to the
   ability of the group). Activities may include
   a. high jumping (fig. 22.30)
   b. jumping and making shapes in the air (fig.
   22.31)
   c. jumping and turning in the air
   d. crossing the rope with a cartwheel
   movement (fig. 22.32)
   e. follow-the-leader activities
2. Jumping over two ropes: Two performers hold
   two ropes about two feet off the ground.
   Repeat the same skills (fig. 22.33). Then have
   the rope holders hold one rope low and the
   other high; repeat the skills.

These few examples should provide the
teacher with a starting point. The creative
teacher and class will come up with other ideas,
such as jumping over one rope, then crawling
under the other, or hopping, jumping, or performing some other locomotor movement from
one end to the other.

Figure 22.30 High jumping

Figure 22.31 Making shapes

Figure 22.32 Crossing using the hands

Figure 22.33

Applying Movement Skills to Rope Activities

Several of the basic structured rope-skipping skills that can be performed by an individual or with a partner have been described. The individual rope can also be used in many other interesting and challenging ways. For example, it can become an obstacle to manipulate, as when tying a knot using only the feet (fig. 22.34). And it can become an obstacle to maneuver around or over, such as finding many ways of crossing a rope (fig. 22.35).

It is now possible to apply the problem-solving method and the movement skills described in the previous chapter (pp. 423-32) to individual rope activities. The individual rope thus becomes a means of further challenging the physical and creative abilities of the child. The four movement concepts and the various movement skills become the framework for developing a series of tasks or challenges. Following are some examples:

1. *Balance or weight bearing:* "See if you can hold the rope with both hands and balance on both knees and one elbow." This is a manipulating activity.
2. *Shapes:* "Can you make a twisted shape with your rope?" This is another manipulating activity.

Figure 22.34 . . . tie a knot with your feet . . .

Figure 22.35 How many ways can you cross your rope . . .

Figure 22.36 . . . that involves three changes of direction?

3. *Direction:* "Place the rope on the floor in any pattern you like and make up a sequence that involves three changes in direction (fig. 22.36)." This is a maneuvering activity.
4. *Force and rolling:* "Place the rope on the floor, then move a few steps away from it. See if you can run, leap over the rope, land, and roll."
5. *Relationships and force:* "Make up a sequence with your partner and one rope that has three different pulling actions (fig. 22.37)."
6. *Relationships and shapes:* "Can you make up a sequence of matching shapes with your partner (fig. 22.38)?"

Applying Movement Skills to Rope Activities

a. Make up a sequence . . .   b. . . . that has three . . .   c. . . . different pulling actions.
Figure 22.37

Figure 22.38 Sequence of matching shapes.

Hoop Activities

The introduction of hoop activities will add challenges and variety to any gymnastic program. Hoops are inexpensive, easily stored, and, most important, a very versatile piece of equipment. It is strongly recommended that a class set, plus six to eight extra hoops, be purchased. A mixture of the standard forty-two-inch hoops and the smaller thirty-six-inch hoops is adequate for any elementary grade.

Also, since hoops can be extremely noisy, it is important to establish a strict routine for getting them out of the equipment room, carrying them to instructional areas, and holding them while listening to instructions. Require the children to place their hoops on the floor gently and to sit inside them while listening to instructions.

A few of the more common structured activities will be presented, followed by several suggestions for applying movement skills to hoop activities.

Structured Hoop Activities

The following hoop activities can be presented as a direct challenge. However, variations will occur in the way the children attempt to perform the skills.

Individual Activities

1. Hula hooping: This skill is normally performed around the waist; however, other areas of the body, such as the arm, leg, wrist, and ankles can also be used (fig. 22.40).

Figure 22.39

Figure 22.40

22   Stunts and Skills with Small Equipment   453

Figure 22.41a Hula . . .

Figure 22.41b . . . jumping . . .

2. Hula jumping: The hoop can be used as a jumping rope (fig. 22.41). This is an effective substitute, particularly for primary children.
3. Place the hoop on the floor, then (a) jump over it (fig. 22.42), (b) roll through it (fig. 22.43), or (c) jump across it.
4. Roll the hoop with a reverse spin and as it returns repeat (3).
5. Spin the hoop. While it is spinning, try to run around it or jump over it before it falls.
6. Place the hoop on the floor. Walk around the edge of the hoop or run and jump into the center and then out.

Partner Activities

1. Play catch with one or two hoops.
2. Target throwing with partner: One partner throws the hoop at a designated part of his partner, such as his arm, right leg, or head. Vary the distance according to the level of skill.
3. One partner holds the hoop in a horizontal position while the other tries to run and jump over it or crawl under it (figs. 22.44 and 22.45).
4. One partner rolls the hoop while other partner attempts to crawl through it.

Figure 22.42

Figure 22.43

Figure 22.44 Jump over and ...

Figure 22.45 ... crawl through.

Applying Movement Skills to Hoop Activities

The hoop has become one of the most popular pieces of small equipment to use in conjunction with movement skills. The following challenges illustrate the scope and versatility of this piece of equipment:

1. *Balance or weight bearing:* "Can you balance over the hoop (figs. 22.46 and 22.47)?" "Can you balance with three parts on the hoop?" "See if you can balance on four parts and hold the hoop off the ground." "How many different parts of your body can you balance the hoop on?"

Figure 22.46

Figure 22.47

Figure 22.48 . . . while holding your hoop

2. *Shapes and flow:* "Make up a sequence of three different shapes while holding your hoop. (fig. 22.48)."
3. *Rolling and flow:* "Can you roll while holding onto your hoop (fig. 22.49)."
4. *Direction:* "Place four hoops on the floor in any pattern you wish, then make up a sequence that shows four changes in direction." After the sequence is developed, "Now add a change of speed or level to your sequence."
5. *Relationships and shapes:* "See if you can make up a sequence with your partner with one partner holding the hoop and the other moving from shape to shape (fig. 22.50)."

Figure 22.49a Roll while holding . . .

Figure 22.49b . . . your hoop.

a. . . . with one holding

b. . . . while the other moves

c. . . . from shape to shape

Figure 22.50

Wand Activities

The initial lack of commercial equipment in many elementary schools forced teachers to improvise with what was available or to make their own equipment. The wand is an example of the latter. Discarded broom handles or three-quarters inch to one and one-half inch doweling cut into thirly-six-inch or forty-two-inch lengths are adequate for elementary school children. Wands also present the same noise problem as hoops, so it is wise to establish a similar proce-dure as suggested for hoops.

There are numerous structured stunts that can be performed with a wand. In addition, a wide variety of movement tasks or challenges can be designed to use the wand in a manipula-tive way or as an obstacle to maneuver around or over. The following structured activities should begin in the second or third grade. Move-ment challenges using the wand can begin in the first grade.

Figure 22.51

Structured Wand Activities

The stunts in figures 22.52 to 22.60 are a few of the many individual and partner activities children can perform with wands.

Hand Balance

Figure 22.52 Hold wand with one hand, then place the index finger of the opposite hand under the end of the wand. Release grip and balance the wand on the end of the finger. After practice, try walking forward and backward, and then running.

Foot Balance

Figure 22.53 Place wand near the big toe, raise the foot off the floor, release grip and try to balance the wand on the foot.

Back Touch

Figure 22.54 Begin with the legs straight and the feet approximately shoulder-width apart. Grasp the wand close to one end. Arch back, place the end of the wand on the mat, and continue arching back and down.

Double Foot Balance

Figure 22.55 Begin in a back lying position, hold the wand above the head, and place the feet under the wand. Release hands and extend the legs upward, keeping the wand balanced across the feet.

Jump through Stick

Figure 22.56 Stand with the knees partially bent and the feet about twelve inches apart. Hold the wand with the arms spread apart and the fingers grasping it. The palms face down. Keeping the arms straight, jump up and over the wand and land in front with the knees slightly bent.

Thread the Needle

Figure 22.57a Begin in a back lying position, knees bent and hold the wand in front of the body.

Figure 22.57b Without losing balance or touching the wand, bend the knees, pass the feet up and under the wand, and return to the original position.

Floor Touch

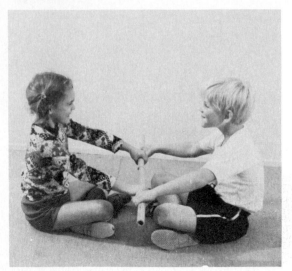

Figure 22.58a Partners sit on the floor in a crossed-leg position. They grasp the wand with their palms facing down and their arms completely extended. The wand must be parallel to the floor.

Figure 22.58b On a signal from the teacher, each child tries to touch the wand to the floor on his right side. Change sides after each contest.

Twist Away

Figure 22.59a Partners stand with their feet about shoulder-width apart, and their knees slightly flexed. They grasp the wand with palms facing down.

Figure 22.59b Each partner attempts to twist to his right. As soon as one partner releases his grip, the other is declared the winner.

Dishrag

Figure 22.60a This is similar to Wring the Dishrag, described on page 391.

Figure 22.60b Both partners must maintain their grips throughout the movement.

Applying Movement Skills to Wand Activities

The wand can be as useful and usable as a hoop or a rope in developing movement concepts and skills. The following examples illustrate how balance, levels, and relationships can be further enhanced by a wand:

1. *Balance or weight bearing:* If the class has had prior experience with a wand, try these: "See how many different parts of your body you can balance the wand on (figs. 22.61 and 22.62)." "Is it possible to balance the wand on your elbow (or knee or stomach, and so on)?"

2. *Transfer of weight and flow:* "Can you hold the wand with both hands and roll along the floor?" "Place the wand on the floor and see how many ways you can cross it using your hands and feet."

3. *Levels and shapes:* "See if you can show me three stretched shapes—one low, one halfway up, and a high stretch—while holding a wand with both hands." "Can you make a twisted shape over your wand? Now under your wand?"

4. *Relationships:* Each partner has a wand. "Make up a sequence of matching (or contrasting) shapes with your partner (fig. 22.63)."

Figure 22.62 . . . on your back

Figure 22.61 . . . on your shoulder

Applying Movement Skills to Wand Activities

a. . . . a sequence of . . .
Figure 22.63

b. . . . matching shapes . . .

c. . . . with your partner.

Figure 22.64

Chair Activities

The use of chairs as gymnastic equipment seems to have followed the same historical course as wands. The lack of equipment, coupled with the combined creative talents of teachers and children, produced numerous creative and challenging individual and dual activities using standard classroom chairs. A few of the most popular activities will be described, and several ideas for using chairs in developing movement skills will be presented.

Structured Chair Activities

The chair exercises and stunts in figures 22.65 to 22.70 contribute to strength, flexibility, balance, and agility. They were created by classroom teachers and children from various grades and schools. To prevent the chair from slipping, place it on a mat or have one child perform the stunt while his partner holds the base of the chair.

Side Balance

Figure 22.65 Lie across the chair, with the left arm extended down and the right arm resting on the right side. Simultaneously raise the right arm and leg.

Human Bridge

Figure 22.66 Sit on the floor, with the arms extended back and the fingers pointing toward the chair. The heels rest on the near edge of the chair. Raise the seat up until the trunk and legs form a straight line. At the top of this movement, the shoulders should be over the hands.

Jump to Seat

Figure 22.67 Stand approximately one foot away from the chair and extend the arms backward and upward. Simultaneously swing the arms forward and upward and push off the toes. Land on the seat of the chair with the knees bent and the arms sideward for balance.

Leg Dip

Figure 22.68 Stand on the chair, bend forward, reach back and grasp the top of the chair. Simultaneously bend the right knee and extend the left leg forward.

Squat and Stretch

Figure 22.69 Begin in a squat position with the arms extended forward, and grasp the lower back legs of the chair. Keeping the hands on the chair, shift forward and upward until the upper trunk touches the back of the chair and the legs are extended.

Over the Hill

Figure 22.70 Begin in a backward sitting position, with the back straight, the knees bent, and the left hand on top of the chair. Raise the left leg to the top of the chair and raise the left hand to allow the leg to continue forward, then downward.

Figure 22.71 How many ways can you balance on it?

Applying Movement Skills to Chair Activities

A chair can become one of the most exciting pieces of small equipment if it is used safely and in a variety of positions. Too often the chair is used only in its normal upright position. However, when children learn to place it with the back or side on the floor, the potential for developing such movement skills as balance, shapes, and levels are greatly enhanced. Following are examples of creative and challenging ways to use this piece of equipment:

1. *Balance and transfer of weight:* "Can you balance with two parts on the seat of the chair and one part on the floor?" "See if you can balance on three parts on the seat of the chair, then shift to a new three parts on the floor." "Place the chair in any position you like and see how many ways you can balance on it (fig. 22.71)."
2. *Shapes and levels:* "Make up a sequence of shapes on or off the chair." "Can you make a shape as you leap off the chair, then land and roll?"
3. *Relationships:* "With your partner and one chair develop a contrasting sequence of shapes." "Do the same with two chairs." "Can you make up a sequence which shows a change of balance and a change in level (fig. 22.72)?"

Indian Club, Milk Carton, and Traffic Cone Activities

The success of any gymnastic program is very closely related to the amount and variety of small equipment that is available to each child. Since most elementary schools lack sets of the previously described equipment, the following "bits and pieces" can serve a very useful purpose. Discarded bowling pins, which can usually be obtained from local bowling alleys, make excellent substitutes for Indian clubs. Plastic-coated milk cartons are also readily available. And traffic cones, which are extensively used in the games program as field markers and goals, are also a valuable addition to the gymnastic program.

a. Make up a sequence . . .

Figure 22.72

b. . . . that shows a change of balance . . .

c. . . . and a change of level

These types of small equipment are basically used as obstacles to maneuver around or over. They are also used in combination with other small equipment such as individual ropes, hoops, and wands to provide more complex and creative challenges. Following are examples of their use:

1. *Direction, speed, and force:* Scatter all available Indian clubs, milk cartons, and traffic cones around the floor area. The following challenges illustrate how this equipment can be used to develop directional movements and a change of speed:

   a. "Run in different directions around the equipment."

   b. "Repeat with a change in speed."

   c. "Run sideways, diagonally, and backward around the equipment."

   d. "Run, jump over any piece of equipment, land, move to a new piece of equipment, and repeat (fig. 22.74)."

   e. "Repeat with a land and roll."

2. *Shape and balance:*

   a. "How many ways can you balance over your equipment?"

   b. "Can you balance with one part on your equipment and one part on the floor?"

Figure 22.73

Figure 22.74

c. "Make three different shapes over your equipment (fig. 22.75)."
d. "Run, jump, and make a shape over your equipment."
3. *Relationships:* Each partner has one piece of equipment.
a. "Make three matching shapes over your equipment."
b. "Develop a matching sequence that includes a balance, a shape, and a change of direction (fig. 22.76)."

The central theme of this chapter has been to provide as many ideas as possible for using small equipment in both structured and exploratory ways. The next chapter will continue this theme with large apparatus.

Figure 22.75 . . . shapes over your equipment.

Indian Club, Milk Carton, and Traffic Cone Activities

a

b

c

Figure 22.76
a. Make up a sequence that includes balance . . .

b. . . . a shape . . .
c. . . . and a change of direction.

Stunts and Movement Skills with Large Apparatus

23

The fundamental purpose of large apparatus in any gymnastic program is to provide an opportunity for the child to test his ability on more challenging apparatus. This chapter continues the central theme of the previous chapter. The structured skills that can be performed on such apparatus as the balance beam, vaulting box, and climbing rope are described and illustrated first. Then there are numerous suggestions for applying movement skills to this apparatus or integrating them with many of the traditional climbing, balancing, and vaulting movements performed on or over large apparatus. (See films "Using Large Apparatus in Movement Education" and "Theme Development in Movement Education," Appendix A.)

Teaching Procedures

Large apparatus is normally used during the latter part of a gymnastic lesson. The following suggestions will assist the teacher in organizing and teaching both structured and movement skills on or with a variety of large apparatus:

1. Children of all ages should learn to carry and arrange apparatus with a concern for their own safety—the position of the body when lifting a heavy piece of equipment—and that of the class.

Figure 23.1

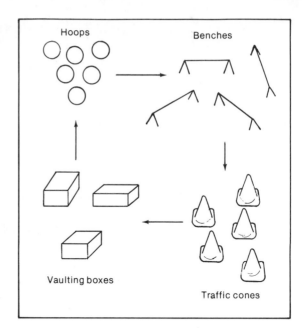

Hoops

Benches

Vaulting boxes

Traffic cones

2. The arrangement of individual and multiple pieces of equipment and apparatus should complement the main theme of the lesson. For example, if the theme is "change of direction" and four benches are to be used, they should be scattered rather than placed in rows. The scattered pattern encourages movements in a variety of directions, while if benches are placed in a row, the children will usually follow one or two classmates around each bench.

3. Since there is never enough large apparatus, adopt station work, using both small equipment and large apparatus, coupled with a rotation system. In the accompanying diagram, the lesson stresses force (jumping and landing) and change of direction. The hoops, benches, traffic cones, and vaulting boxes are arranged to complement this theme. Each group practices at a station for a few minutes and then rotates to the next station. This gives each child an opportunity to use both small and large apparatus during an average lesson.

4. Whenever structured skills require a spotter or spotters, proper instruction should be given to the children prior to and during the time they act as spotters. This is particularly important with vaulting skills over a box or bench.

5. Task or challenge cards described in the previous chapter (pp. 434-35) can be used effectively with large apparatus activities.

Balance Beam and Bench

The balance beam or bench has been used in gymnastic programs for a number of years. However, it has been used in a very limited way, usually flat on the ground with children performing stunts on or across the long axis (fig. 23.2). When the balance beam or bench—now fitted with a hook on one end, as illustrated—is placed at different angles or used in combination with other apparatus, the variety of movements and challenges becomes infinitely greater (fig. 23.3). This applies to teaching structured skills as well as the movement concepts and skills described in the previous two chapters.

A wide variety of structured skills are presented first in their relative order of difficulty, followed by suggestions for applying movement skills to the balance beam or bench.

Figure 23.2

Structured Activities

Activities performed on the balance beam or bench require two types of balance skill. The first is *static balance,* which is the ability to maintain a fixed stationary position. An example is the Foot and Knee Balance (fig. 23.5). The second type is *dynamic balance,* which is maintaining correct body position while moving. Examples of this type of balance are walking forward and backward or the one-foot hop. The majority of primary level balance skills are basically dynamic. As the children's strength and skill increase, the more advanced static balance activities can be introduced. Each of the suggested skills can be made more challenging by varying the angle of the beam or bench.

The skills in figures 23.4 to 23.11 can be performed on the broad surface of the bench or on the narrow beam. Reference will be made to numerous stunts and tumbling skills that can be performed on a beam or bench. To assist in learning, have the children practice all the stunts on the floor, then move to the bench, and finally advance to the narrow surface of a beam. Any fixed line on the floor will serve as an imaginary balance beam or bench.

All locomotor skills such as walking, running, and leaping can be performed on the bench or beam. For variations, perform the movements backward or vary the position of the hands and arms. In addition, the following stunts

Figure 23.3

and animal movements can be performed on the beam or bench:

> Lame Puppy Walk, page 388
> Measuring Worm, page 388
> Seal Walk, page 389
> Single Leg Balance, page 390
> Knee Dip, page 403
> V-Sit, page 404
> "L"-Support, page 410
> Forward Roll, page 398
> Backward Diagonal Roll, page 398
> Cartwheel, page 416

Pick up Eraser

Figure 23.4 Place a small object such as an eraser in the middle of the balance beam. Walk to the object, bend the knees, and extend the right arm down and the left arm back. Pick up the object, stand up, and walk to the end of the beam.

Stunts and Skills with Large Apparatus   471

Foot and Knee Balance

Figure 23.5 Begin with the left foot well in front of the right, the knees bent, and the arms extended sideward. Bend the knees until the right knee rests on the beam. Hold this position for a few seconds, then extend and return to the starting position.

Side Balance

Figure 23.6 Walk to the center of the balance beam and stop, with the left foot in front of the right. Turn the right foot sideways, shift weight to the ball of the foot, and lift the right foot off the beam. Continue shifting sideways, arch the back, and raise the right leg.

Squat on One Leg

Figure 23.7 Stand on the left foot, with the arms extended sideward and the right foot off the beam. Bend the left knee and raise the extended right leg forward and upward. Lower the body until the left knee is fully flexed.

Jackknife

Figure 23.8 Sit on the beam with the legs extended, the heels of both feet resting on the beam, and the hands holding the top edge of the beam. Bend the knees and raise the feet off the beam. Continue the upward movement of the feet, lower the trunk backward, and straighten the legs. After practice, raise the legs without bending the knees.

Swing Turn

a   b   c

Figure 23.9

a. Walk to the center of the beam.

b. Shift weight to the left foot, and swing the right leg forward.

c. Continue swinging the right leg forward, lift up on the ball of the left foot, and make a half-turn, thus facing the opposite direction.

Squat Mount

Figure 23.10a Stand with the feet about shoulder-width apart, the body erect, and the hands resting on the balance beam.

Figure 23.10b Keeping the hands on the beam, jump up and slightly forward and place the feet on the beam.

Front Dismount

Figure 23.11a Begin in a crouched position with the arms straight and the hands grasping the outside edges of the balance beam. Extend the legs back until the head, trunk, and legs are in a straight line.

Figure 23.11b Lift the legs up and sideward, push off with the hands, and land on both feet beside the balance beam.

Figure 23.12

Figure 23.13

Several small equipment activities described in the previous chapter also can be performed on the beam or bench. It may be wise to require students to perform the skill on the bench before they attempt it on the narrower surface of the balance beam.

1. *Beanbag activities*
   Throw and catch to self
   Balance beanbags on different parts of the body

2. *Rope-skipping activities*
   Basic skills, particularly the Two-Foot Basic, One-Foot Hop, and Rocker Step (fig. 23.12)

3. *Hoop activities*
   Hula hooping
   Hula jumping (fig. 23.13)

4. *Wand activities*
   Foot Balance
   Thread the Needle

Figure 23.14

Figure 23.15

Applying Movement Skills to Balance Beam and Bench Activities

Many of the movement tasks presented in Chapters 21 and 22 can be applied to the balance beam or bench. Begin with the beam or bench in a horizontal position, then gradually introduce more creative arrangements of the apparatus as the children's skill, competence, and understanding develop.

Several examples of the application of movement skills to the balance beam or bench are described and illustrated here. This should provide a starting point for the teacher.

One of the teacher's first tasks is to help children use the balance beam or bench in a variety of ways when performing a single movement skill or a sequence of movements. A movement task such as "See if you can make a twisted shape on the balance bench (or beam)" will usually produce something like the shape illustrated in figure 23.14. The parallel arrangement of the benches lacks imagination. Also, the use of the word "on" encourages all children to begin their movements from the same starting position. Questions should be presented in such a way that children begin to see the apparatus in a much wider perspective. Rephrasing the question to "Can you make a series of twisted shapes using various parts of the balance bench?" al-

---

Applying Movement Skills to Balance Beam and Bench Activities

a. ... change from two ...

b. ... to ...

c. ... three points of balance.

Figure 23.16

lows for greater scope, as illustrated in figure 23.15. Thus, when applying movement ideas to the balance beam or bench, think of the apparatus as either a point of contact or an obstacle to move around, across, or over (in flight). The following movement challenges illustrate this application:

1. *Direction and speed:* Move around the benches showing a quick change of direction.
2. *Balance and transfer of weight:* Travel across the benches by changing from two to three to two points of balance (fig. 23.16).
3. *Balance, shape, and direction:* Develop a sequence traveling across the bench including a twisted shape, balancing on the side, and a change of direction.
4. *Flight and rolling:* Begin anywhere on the floor, run, jump onto a bench, leap off, land, and perform a safely roll. The roll may be a sideways, diagonal, or forward roll (fig. 23.17). Repeat and perform a stretch, twisted, or curled shape before landing.
5. *Relationships:* The balance beam or bench can be one of the most effective and versatile apparatus for developing the concept of relationships. The following examples illustrate how matching and contrasting can be integrated with other concepts and skills such as levels, direction, and speed:

Figure 23.17 Flight and rolling

a. "Develop a sequence of matching shapes with your partner on the top surface of your bench." "Repeat with one partner on the bench and the other on the floor (fig. 23.18)." "Repeat with both touching the bench."

Applying Movement Skills to Balance Beam and Bench Activities

a. Matching shapes . . .   b. . . . with one on the floor . . .   c. . . . and one on the bench.

Figure 23.18

b. "With one partner leading and the other following, make up a sequence of balance positions as you move from one end of the bench to the other (fig. 23.19)."

At this stage in the development of movement concepts and skills, the angle of the bench or its combination with other types of apparatus adds to the challenge. These variations provide a greater opportunity for the children to test and expand their physical and creative abilities. A challenge such as "Make up a sequence that shows a change in level," is complemented by the angle of the bench. Also, adding chairs to the same challenge creates new dimensions for partners as they develop a matching sequence.

Climbing Ropes

A variety of climbing, swinging, and movement skills can be performed with a hanging rope. With proper instruction, including strengthening exercises for the arm and shoulder muscles, as well as following a sequential progression of skills, children can develop a high level of skill on the hanging ropes.

Suggestions for safety procedures and conditioning exercises are presented first, followed by a description of the basic climbing skills and ideas for applying movement skills to this apparatus.

Safety Procedures

Many school districts have a policy requiring a mat to be placed under the climbing rope when a child is performing a climbing or swinging skill. But it must be recognized that the mat has very little resilience and thus may be of little value in preventing an injury. The following suggestions and procedures will contribute far more to a child's safety than a mat:

1. Teach the proper hand and foot grip techniques for climbing and descending the rope.
2. Set individual goals rather than an arbitrary standard for every child to accomplish.

Figure 23.19 . . . with one leading and one following.

Figure 23.20

Figure 23.21a

Figure 23.21b

3. Use spotters for difficult stunts, particularly those involving inverted hangs.
4. Establish rigid rules for children who are waiting for their turn.

Suggested Conditioning Exercises

Climbing skills require sufficient arm and shoulder strength to raise and support the full weight of the body. The abdominal muscles also play a very important role in both climbing and descending skills. The following types of exercises will help increase the general strength and endurance of these muscle groups.

1. Floor exercises: Pull-ups, push-ups, Coffee Grinder, Measuring Worm, sit-ups, curl-ups, and V-Sit.
2. Rope exercises:
   a. Lie under the rope with the hands grasping it. Gradually raise the body upward. As strength increases, repeat exercise but keep the body straight throughout the movement (fig. 23.21).
   b. Sitting under the rope with the arms extended over the head and grasping the rope, pull body up. As strength increases, keep the legs extended and parallel to floor.

Figure 23.22a

Figure 23.22b

c. Stand beside the rope, reach up and grasp it, pull body up, and hold position for a number of seconds (fig. 23.22). Variations include holding legs in different positions such as piked, tucked, or straddled.

Structured Skills

Structured rope-climbing skills are illustrated in figures 23.23 to 23.26.

Climbing

Figure 23.23a Grasp the rope with one hand slightly above the other. Pull the body up and loop the rope over the top of the right foot. The left foot is then placed on top of the rope, thus "locking" the foot position.

Figure 23.23b Pull the body up to a new position. Repeat upward movement. Descend by maintaining the locked position of the legs, then moving the hands down in a "hand-under-hand" fashion until the knees are against the chest. Hold the hand grip and slowly lower the legs to an extended position. Continue action to the floor.

Rope Hang

a. Grasp two ropes and . . .

b. . . . pull the body up and over.

c. Continue over to a standing position. Variations include changing leg position to tuck, stride, or vertical.

Figure 23.24

Reverse Hang

Figure 23.25 Grasp the rope and pull the body up and over to a straddle position. Gradually extend the legs upward until the body is in a vertical position.

Swinging

a

b

Figure 23.26 Allow the children to grasp the rope at their own desired heights. Gradually introduce additional body movements and positions while swinging—twist, chin, legs straddle, etc.

Applying Movement Skills to Hanging-Rope Activities

The hanging rope can be used to develop movement skills in three basic ways: (1) movement challenges relating to shapes and weight bearing with a stationary rope; (2) movement challenges while the rope is swinging; and (3) movement challenges with the rope associated with another type of large apparatus.

The following movement tasks illustrate each type of challenge: "Can you balance with one part of your body on the floor and three parts on the rope (fig. 23.27)?" "How many different shapes can you make while holding the rope?" "Can you make different shapes while holding the rope and with both feet off the

Figure 23.27 . . . and three parts on the rope . . .

Figure 23.28 ... different shapes while ...

Figure 23.29 ... both feet are off the ground.

ground (figs. 23.28 and 23.29)?'' ''Repeat previous challenge while the rope is swinging.'' Place one bench near both ends of the rope swing. ''Swing and land on each bench.'' ''Swing, make a half turn and land on the opposite bench.''

Springboard, Beatboard, Mini-Tramp, and Vaulting Box

The springboard and vaulting box are two of the oldest apparatus in the gymnastic program. In this chapter the term ''vaulting box'' will include other similar apparatus, such as the vaulting bench, the jumping box, and the long horse, since they are used in much the same way. Teachers who do not have a vaulting box should refer to the diagrams of inexpensive equipment in Appendix B. The latter can be constructed at a minimum cost by the custodian or an interested parent.

The majority of vaulting stunts are usually performed from the springboard or mini-tramp onto a mat. Once children have developed sufficient skill in using the springboard and control-

Figure 23.30

ling their bodies while in flight, the vaulting box can be added to provide greater challenge and versatility of movements. The approach, takeoff, and landing are essentially the same for all vaulting activities, so children should practice these movements until they become almost automatic. A well-executed and consistent takeoff allows the child to concentrate on height and the execution of a specific vault.

a   b   c

Figure 23.31

Approach and Takeoff

Figure 23.31 illustrates the approach and take-off. Begin the approach several yards back from the takeoff point. Run toward the vaulting box. Continue forward, bringing the feet together, and land on the balls of the feet approximately six to twelve inches away from the end of the board. The knees should be bent slightly at the moment of contact. Push off from the board in an upward and slightly forward direction. Note: Most children will lean too far forward, losing height and control on landing.

Vaulting Stunts from Springboard

The following vaulting stunts can be performed off a springboard, beatboard, or mini-tramp:

1. Jump and tuck.
2. Jump and pike.
3. Jump and straddle.
4. Jump and turn—one-quarter, one-half, or full.
5. Jump and clap hands in front, overhead, or behind the back.

Vaulting Stunts over Box

The standard or structured vaults in figures 23.32 to 23.35 can be performed over a box or long horse with a takeoff from the floor or off a springboard or mini-tramp.

Squat Vault

Figure 23.32 From a two-foot takeoff, reach up and slightly forward, touching the hands on the top of the vaulting box. Simultaneously tuck the knees close to the chest and continue forward and upward. Land with a gradual bending of the knees.

Spotting:
Stand on the opposite side of the vaulting box and to the right of the oncoming performer. As she moves over the box, grasp her right arm above the elbow with both hands. The spotter should prevent or restrict the forward falling action if the performer catches her toes or leaves the box with an exaggerated forward lean.

Straddle Vault

Figure 23.33 From a two-foot takeoff, simultaneously reach forward with extended arms and extend the legs sideward. It is extremely important to gain maximum height to insure foot clearance. Continue forward, bring the legs together, and land with a gradual bending of the knees.

Spotting:
Stand close to the box and directly in front of the oncoming performer. If she catches her toes or has too much forward momentum, place your hands on her shoulders to break the fall. If the performer clears the box and does not have too much forward momentum, step to the side quickly.

Flank Vault

Figure 23.34 From a two-foot takeoff, simultaneously reach forward with both arms and extend the legs toward the right side. As the legs move forward and sideways, release the right hand and continue the forward movement, landing with a gradual bending of the knees.

Spotting:
Use the same spotting technique described for the Straddle Vault.

Head Vault

Figure 23.35 From a two-foot takeoff, place the hands and then the head on top of the box as the body extends upward and over. When the body is in a forward "overbalanced" position, push off from the fingertips and land with a gradual bending of the knees. Note: Most children will tend to push off before they reach the overbalanced position, which causes them to "drop" onto the box rather than gradually arching and landing.

Spotting:
Use the same spotting technique described for the Head Spring (p. 420). It is advisable to use two spotters, one on each side of the performer.

Applying Movement Skills to Springboard and Vaulting Box Activities

The springboard, beatboard, mini-tramp, and vaulting box can be used individually or in combination with other apparatus to provide interesting and challenging movement tasks involving body awareness, qualities, space awareness, and relationships. For example, all the individual shapes performed in flight from the floor can now be applied to the springboard, beatboard, or mini-tramp. These provide additional height and time to execute curled or stretched, wide or narrow, and twisted shapes. In addition, since children have learned safety rolls—sideward, backward, and forward—they should be able to land and roll with grace and ease. The movement tasks shown in figures 23.36 and 23.37 illustrate the additional challenge and increased quality of movements performed from the springboard, beatboard, or mini-tramp. Similar movements can also be performed from the vaulting box.

The vaulting box should also be used as an additional challenge for the development of other movement concepts and skills. Here it is important to present challenges in such a way that all surfaces—particularly the sides and ends—are used when answering movement tasks. The examples that follow illustrate the variable use of the vaulting box:

1. *Shapes and balance:*
   a. "Make a stretched (or wide or twisted) shape on the side, end, and top of the box (fig. 23.38)."
   b. "Can you balance with one part on the apparatus and two parts off?"
   c. "See if you can balance with part of your body on top of the apparatus and part on the side or end of the apparatus."
   d. "Move from one side of the apparatus to the other (fig. 23.39)."
2. *Relationships:*
   a. "Make up a matching (or contrasting) sequence of shapes with one partner on top of the apparatus and the other on the floor."

Figure 23.36

Figure 23.37

a. Make a stretched shape on the side . . .   b. . . . end of and . . .   c. . . . on the top of the box

Figure 23.38

Figure 23.39 Move from one side to the other side of the apparatus.

Figure 23.40

b. "How many different balance positions can you make with your partner on the side or top of the apparatus (fig. 23.40)?"

Figure 23.41a

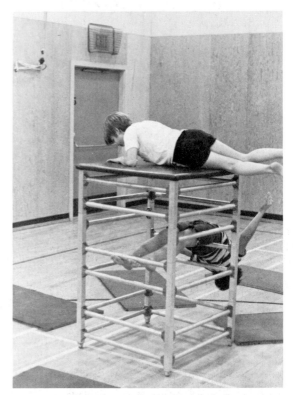

Figure 23.41b

c. "Make up a sequence with your partner on the apparatus and show a change in balance (fig. 23.41)."

Sequences involving body awareness, qualities, space awareness, and relationships can now be designed to include the springboard and vaulting box individually or in combination with other small and large apparatus. The selection and arrangement of the apparatus should complement the movements of the sequence. Excessive rearrangement of apparatus serves little purpose in the development of movement skills, so teachers should caution children if they tend to waste time in arranging apparatus. One arrangement of apparatus should last for several lessons.

Horizontal Bar and Ladder

Many of the skills listed under horizontal bar and horizontal ladder can also be performed on other types of apparatus, including the new agility apparatus and existing outdoor play equipment such as the climbing cube and Swedish gym.

Horizontal Bar (Chinning Bar)

Since stunts performed on the horizontal bar require a great deal of arm and shoulder strength and endurance, teachers should begin with only one or two repetitions of each skill. When a child is able to perform five or six repetitions of a stunt, allow him to progress to the next one. The stunts are illustrated in figures 23.42 to 23.47.

Teaching Suggestions

In comparison with stunts on other indoor apparatus, stunts performed on the horizontal bar are extremely difficult for elementary school children. Thus, a great deal of encouragement must be shown by the teacher. In most cases, the initial disinterest in this apparatus is the result of insufficient arm and shoulder strength rather than an inherent absence of skill. The following suggestions will not make the teacher's task any easier, but they will help prevent unnecessary accidents:

1. Check equipment before allowing children to perform any stunt.
2. Make sure you are in the proper position to spot for safety.
3. Begin with simple stunts and progress to the more difficult.

Hang Like a Monkey

Figure 23.42 Jump up, grasp the bar with the palms forward and the hands about twelve inches apart. Swing the right leg up and over the bar and rest the heel on top. Bring the left leg up and over the right leg and rest the back of the left leg on the top of the right foot.

Roll over Barrow

Figure 23.43 Jump up and take a front support position with the arms straight and the hands on top of the bar (with a front grip). Bend at the waist, drop the head forward, roll over the bar, bring the legs down, and release the grip.

Pull-ups

Figure 23.44a Jump up and grasp the bar with a front (palms facing forward) or reverse (palms facing backward) grip.

Figure 23.44b Pull up with the arms until the chin is even with the bar. Do not allow children to kick with their legs as they swing forward and upward.

Skin the Snake

Figure 23.45 Jump up, grasp the bar with a front grip (palms facing forward), swing the legs forward and upward, and flex the knees. Move both feet under the bar between the hands, then gradually lower the legs to an extended position. Release and drop or return to original position.

Scramble over Fence

Figure 23.46 Begin in a front support position (arms straight and palms down) and swing the left leg up and over the bar to a rest position next to the left hand. Release the left hand, shift the body weight to the left thigh, and grasp the bar on the outside of the left leg. Repeat action with the right side, holding the resting position for a few seconds, and then jump to the ground.

Rocking Chair Swing

Figure 23.47 Jump up and grasp the bar with the palms facing forward and the hands about shoulder-width apart. Draw both legs up and through the bar, drop the knees over it, and rest the back of knees firmly against the bar. Keep the knees bent, release grip, and swing back and forth. Reach up, grasp bar, and return to the starting position.

Horizontal Ladder

Activities performed on the horizontal ladder are similar to chinning bar activities. Both require a great deal of strength and endurance of the arm and shoulder girdle muscles. Therefore, follow the progression of skills in figures 23.48 to 23.54 and do not require *full travels,* that is, all the way across the ladder, until sufficient strength and endurance are developed. As a starting point, require the children to make it one-quarter of the distance. Increase the number of rungs each day until the children can reach the full distance without undue stress.

Teaching Suggestions

The following safety hints require continuous reinforcement. Take a few minutes before the children begin to play or practice stunts on the apparatus to stress the following:

1. Check the apparatus before allowing pupils to perform stunts.
2. Stand close to the performer while he is attempting to do a difficult stunt in order to help him and to prevent accidents.
3. Require each pupil to wait his turn at least five feet away from the apparatus.
4. Allow only two pupils on the ladder at the same time.
5. The second pupil should not begin his stunt until the first child is at least halfway across the ladder.
6. Require pupils to travel in the same direction.
7. All movements require that two parts of the body be in contact with the apparatus.
8. Do not permit children to touch or hinder a child who is performing a stunt.

Swing and Drop

Figure 23.48 Swing forward by raising the legs up and forward. Swing backward by "pulling" the legs down and back. Stop swinging, look down at the landing place, release both hands, and land on the balls of the feet with the knees bent to absorb the fall.

Chinning

Figure 23.49 Allow the children to choose their own grips. Pull body upward until the chin is above the bars. Return to the starting position before releasing the grip and landing on the ground.

Single Rung Traveling

Figure 23.50a Climb up one end of the ladder, rest the feet on the top step, and grasp each side pole with one hand. Reach forward and grasp the second rung with one hand, with the palm facing forward, and the third rung with the other hand.

Figure 23.50b Simultaneously shift the body forward toward the forward hand and release the back hand. Continue forward, grasping the next rung. Repeat the movement with the opposite hand and continue traveling forward to the opposite end.

Double Rung Traveling

Figure 23.51 Begin this movement with both hands on one rung. Swing forward and backward. At the end of the forward swing, release both hands and regrasp the next rung with both hands.

Rung Travel Sideways

Figure 23.52a Begin with the hands on separate rungs and the body facing the side rail.

Figure 23.52b Shift the right hand to the same rung as the left hand, with the palms facing the same direction. Shift the left hand to the next rung, grasping it with palms facing the head. Continue traveling with the body swinging from side to side and the left hand always leading the right.

Side Rail Traveling

Figure 23.53 Travel along one side rail using a hand-over-hand movement.

Double Rail Traveling

Figure 23.54 Grasp both side rails, with the palms of both hands facing in, and swing to a hanging position. Travel forward by sliding one hand forward, then the other. Do not release the grip. Slide the hands the full length of the ladder.

Figure 23.55 Whittle Equipment

Agility Apparatus

One of the most significant contributions to the elementary school gymnasium program has been the development of challenging new agility apparatus. This apparatus has been specifically designed to provide more challenging tasks than the traditional gymnastic apparatus can provide. Generally speaking, this new equipment is higher, wider, and more flexible in its arrangement. Some apparatus is also portable, allowing it to be used in the gymnasium, classroom, or outdoors. Since this apparatus is relatively new to the majority of readers, several of the more popular designs are illustrated.

Whittle Primary Equipment

The Whittle Equipment (fig. 23.55) was developed in England for use in movement education programs. The apparatus consists of two tubular A-frames and a ladder. The ladder can be placed at variable heights by moving the frames closer together. Benches with connecting hooks can also be attached to the ends or sides of the A-frames. This apparatus can be used to develop several structured stunts such as climbing and chinning. Its major contribution, however, is its potential use in developing movement concepts and skills.

Nissen Wall Gym

The Nissen Wall Gym (fig. 23.56) is very similar to the Southampton Cave equipment developed in Great Britain. The apparatus is permanently attached to a wall; however, poles, benches and ropes can be placed at variable heights. Rope climbing, balance, and chinning activities can be performed on this apparatus. The variable levels of the bars and adjustable poles also make this equipment a valuable asset for developing movement skills. One of the main disadvantages of this apparatus is its fixed position. Once erected, it eliminates the potential use of the wall for game skills and other physical activities.

Olympic Apparatus

The Olympic apparatus (fig. 23.57) closely resembles the Whittle Equipment in that it has two A-frames. The set also includes a ladder and a plank. It can be used to develop climbing, balancing, and chinning skills equally as well as the Whittle Equipment. The variable sizes and portability of the A-frames, coupled with the ladder and plank, make the apparatus quite suitable for the development of movement concepts and skills.

Figure 23.56 Nissen Wall Gym

Figure 23.57 Olympic apparatus

Figure 23.58 Agility apparatus

Agility Apparatus

Agility apparatus (figs. 23.58 and 23.59) was designed to develop both structured and movement skills. It consists of a modular turret system that permits two or more interconnecting frames to be stacked in any desired height. A padded top is placed on the top frame. The turret provides a framework or building block to which poles, ladders, planks, beams, or benches can be connected at a variety of levels and angles.

The flexible design allows the apparatus to be used to develop such structured skills as balancing, vaulting, and climbing. And its portability, coupled with the numerous designs that can be created, makes the equipment extremely useful in developing movement concepts and skills. Since it is very light and durable, it can be moved by primary children to the classroom or outdoors with relative ease. The company also provides a teacher's manual that describes a variety of ways to use the apparatus for either the structured or problem-solving approach.

Figure 23.59 Agility apparatus

Figure 23.60 Big toys

Outdoor Apparatus

There has been a major change during the past few years in the type of outdoor apparatus that is being constructed on elementary school playgrounds. New commercial equipment such as Big Toys are replacing the more traditional swings, steel climbing frames, and horizontal

Figure 23.61

Figure 23.62

ladders. This new apparatus has been designed to complement the creative and exploratory natures of young children. The general design provides more levels, angles, and holes for young children to jump off, balance upon, and crawl through. Creative playgrounds described in Chapter 7 (pp. 128-32) are also part of this trend. Natural materials, such as large tree roots and boulders, and discarded building materials or equipment, such as giant sewer pipes and old trucks, are now seen on numerous playgrounds throughout North America.

This new and exciting outdoor apparatus should also be seen as a logical extension of the gymnasium in developing moving concepts and skills. The following examples illustrate how this apparatus can be used as an effective instructional laboratory. The skills learned through the teacher's movement challenges will help the child learn to use the apparatus in a constructive, safe, and creative way.

1. *Balance and weight bearing:*
   a. "Find a place on the apparatus and show me how many different ways you can balance on your spot (figs. 23.61-23.63)."
   b. "Can you move across the apparatus using just three parts of your body?"

Figure 23.63

Outdoor Apparatus

a. ... and show a low

Figure 23.64

b. ... medium ...

c. ... and high position.

Figure 23.65a Matching sequence

Figure 23.65b Matching sequence

2. *Direction and levels:*
   a. "See if you can move across the apparatus and change directions three different times."
   b. "Can you move through the apparatus and show a low, medium, and high position (fig. 23.64)?"
3. *Relationships:*
   a. "One partner leads and the other follows. Make up a sequence involving a transfer of weight and a change of direction."
   b. "Find a spot on the apparatus with your partner. Can you develop a matching sequence including a stretch, curl, and twisted shape (fig. 23.65)?"

Teachers who are hesitant to use the indoor and outdoor apparatus suggested in this chapter should recognize one of the basic characteristics of the movement education approach: If a child is taught through this approach, he will not attempt a movement task on any apparatus until he feels he is mentally and physically ready. If this approach is followed by the teacher, accidents should be a rare occurrence.

Dance and Movement Activities

Part VI has been organized in a slightly different way than the games and gymnastics sections. Chapter 24 describes the basic rhythmic skills that are used in game, gymnastic and in dance activities. This chapter has been placed in this section rather than just before the games section largely on the basis of convenience. Chapter 25 includes the most popular singing games and folk-dance activities for primary and intermediate children. And Chapter 26 describes several approaches that can be used to teach creative dance activities to children in the primary and intermediate grades.

Rhythmic and Movement Activities

24

Understanding the Elements of Rhythm

Teaching Procedures

Rhythmic Activities with Small Equipment

Rhythm is the ability to repeat an action or movement with regularity and in time to a particular rhythmic pattern. It is an essential ingredient of all movement, whether throwing a ball, dodging a player, or dancing a polka. However, rhythm can also be spontaneous, as when a young child makes up his own jumping pattern without any musical background or directions imposed by the teacher. The rhythmic activities described in this chapter are more structured in nature and direction, relating to the performance of a variety of body movements in time to a specific rhythmical accompaniment. When a child understands the basic elements of rhythm, his movement patterns become more efficient and graceful. (See film "Rhythmics in Movement," Appendix A.)

The material in this chapter has been arranged to provide a basic understanding of the elements of rhythm and how they can be combined with a variety of game, dance, and gymnastic movements. Once a child understands the elements of rhythm and can move in time to musical accompaniment, other dance activities can be learned with greater speed and usually with a very positive attitude, particularly by the older elementary school children. The basic approach of gradually moving from individual to partner to group activities is used. This gradual process of joining young children together in a relaxed and creative manner provides the necessary stepping-stone for folk and creative dance activities for upper elementary school boys and girls. Once the teacher has read this chapter, she will also be able to incorporate many of the ideas into future game, dance, and gymnastic units.

Understanding the Elements of Rhythm

There are a few basic elements of rhythm that apply to all forms of movement and dance. All of the following elements are interrelated and all have an effect on dance movements. They can be introduced to children in a meaningful way through the rhythmic activities described later in this chapter.

Underlying Beat

The underlying beat is the steady pulsation that exist in a movement or a musical accompaniment. As a child keeps time, such as tapping his feet to the steady beating of a drum, he is responding to the underlying beat of the music.

Measure

In order to keep time in music, vertical lines are drawn to divide the music into separate spaces. A measure is the space and number of notes between the two lines.

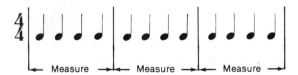

Meter (Time)

Meter indicates the grouping of beats to form the underlying rhythm within a measure. The number sign for each piece of music is known as the *time signature*. These are described as follows:

    4/4 indicates there are four beats in each
        measure.
    2/4 indicates there are two beats in each
        measure.
    3/4 indicates there are three beats in each
        measure.
    6/8 indicates there are six beats in each
        measure.

Accent

The accent is the emphasis given to any one beat in a measure. In most dance meters, the accent is on the first beat; however, it can be placed on any note.

Rhythm Pattern

The rhythm pattern is the grouping of beats or sounds of the song that corresponds to the underlying beat of the music. To illustrate, an even rhythm pattern and an uneven rhythm pattern are described.

1. *Even rhythm:* "Baa, Baa, Black Sheep"
   Rhythm pattern Baa Baa Black Sheep
   Underlying beat 4/4
2. *Uneven rhythm:* Skipping movement
   Rhythm pattern step-hop step-hop
   Underlying beat 2/4

Phrase

In music, a phrase is a group of measures that cling together in a natural way to give a feeling of a complete musical or movement thought or idea. For example, "Baa, Baa, Black Sheep, have you any wool?" represents a complete sentence covering two measures of music.

Tempo

Tempo is the rate of speed of music or movement. The tempo of music can be slow, moderate, or fast, or it may increase gradually from slow to fast according to the purpose and nature of the dance activity.

Intensity

Intensity refers to the quality or force of music or movement. Music or movement can be described as being soft or loud, or light or strong.

Teaching Procedures

The structure of a rhythmics lesson is similar to that of game, dance, and gymnastic lessons. Perhaps the easiest progression is from individual to partner to group activities. Another approach is to move from nonuse of small equipment to the use of hoops, balls, and individual ropes. Also, lessons can be designed to progress from very simple foot movements to more complicated dance steps and movement patterns. The first approach will be described.

Sample Lesson

Progression: Individual to partner to group activities
Music: "Alley Cat" (or any fast popular record with a good beat).

Part One—Introductory Activity: Arrange the class members in a scattered formation sitting on the floor with their legs crossed. This is a good starting position to teach the underlying beat of the music that will be used in the lesson. ("Alley Cat" has four beats per measure.)

Figure 24.1

1. Have the children clap in the following ways (without music):
   a. Clap knees four times, repeating measure (1, 2, 3, 4; 1, 2, 3, 4; etc.).
   b. Clap hands four times, repeating measure.
   c. Clap the floor four times, repeating measure.
   d. Make up combinations of four claps on knees, then four on the floor, and four with the hands.
2. Have the children listen to "Alley Cat" for the 4/4 meter (four beats per measure) and the accent on the first beat.
3. Repeat (a) to (d) with music.
4. Repeat (a) to (d), increasing the speed (faster tempo).

Figure 24.2

Figure 24.3

Additional Ideas: Once the class understands the basic rhythm and can clap to the 4/4 meter, other movements and combinations can be attempted. Some variations follow:

1. Snap fingers.
2. From a standing position, slap different parts of the body.
3. From a standing position, shake one part of the body. Shake the right hand 1, 2, 3, and 4. Add other parts of the body; shake the right hand and the right leg.
4. Move parts of the body to the rhythm of the music. This could include bending, stretching, swinging, or twisting.
5. Perform locomotor movements to the rhythm of the music (figs. 24.2 and 24.3).

Part Two—Movement Training (Partner Activities): In the second part of the lesson partners develop simple matching routines with the movements learned in the first part of the lesson.

1. Have partners start on the floor facing each other. One child begins with four claps on whatever part of his body he chooses; his partner follows. The first performer chooses another part of his body and repeats, with his partner copying him. Continue with two more parts of the body. After the fourth part of the body, ask the partners to work together and perform four clapping movements together on the four parts of their bodies.
2. Join partner clapping: Ask partners to keep facing each other and clap four times on the floor, then four times to each other's hands, then back to four times on the floor (fig. 24.4).

Figure 24.4a Clap four times on the floor . . .

Figure 24.4b . . . then four times to each others hands.

Figure 24.5a ... include a twist ...

Figure 24.5b ... or shift of the body.

As soon as the class understands the idea of matching clapping movements, the number of combinations becomes almost unlimited. Following are some possibilities:

a. Alternative hand clapping—clap the floor, clap one hand, clap two hands.
b. Alternate a hand clap and a finger snap.
c. Include a turn, twist, or shift of the body after each measure (fig. 24.5). This might include four clapping movements followed by four steps around in a circle, then back to four clapping movements.

Part Three–Final Activity (Group Work): Arrange the class into groups of four. Since this may be the first group experience with this type of rhythmic exercise, it is wise to go slow at the start to allow each child to feel comfortable and to be successful with your challenges. The first challenges should be the same as the ones first presented to partners. If they are successful at this, allow the groups to make up their own routines. If not, present a challenge such as "Make

up a routine with each child slapping the floor, then all clapping hands, then slapping the floor again. Next time when you clap hands, place your hands to the side and clap hands with the players on your right and your left." This should be enough to get each group started on its own routine.

The lesson that has been presented concentrated on simple clapping movements to help children move in time to a rhythm. It also demonstrated how to progress to partner and small group activities. Other lessons could be developed with one or more of the basic locomotor and nonlocomotor skills, calisthenics, or combinations of two or more movement skills. A rhythmic lesson emphasizing locomotor skill could include the following main points:

1. *Introductory Activities:* March (brisk walk) to the rhythm of marching music (any marching music can be used), changing directions after each measure. Repeat with a slow run.

24

Figure 24.6a

Figure 24.6b

2. *Movement Training:* March in partners with one following the other, then side by side. Develop other routines involving moving together, away from each other, and in different directions.
3. *Final Activity:* Develop similar routines as in previous part of the lesson.

Task Cards

The application of task or challenge cards was described in previous games and gymnastics chapters (p. 434). In rhythmic activities they can be used with individual, partner, or group activities with equal success. The following example illustrates the type of information that should be written on the card.

Figure 24.7 Make up a bouncing routine . . .

INDIVIDUAL ACTIVITIES

EQUIPMENT: Inflated Ball
Music: "A Familiar Concerto for the Music Lovers"

Task: Make up a bouncing routine that includes four different ways of bouncing and two changes of direction.

It is suggested that six to eight cards with different tasks but the same music be used. Divide the class into small groups. Each child reads the challenge and then proceeds to develop his own routine. Thus, there will be several different types of routines rather than variations of one task. Various levels of ability can be coped with by designing cards ranging from very simple tasks to challenges that require greater skill and creative ability.

The next section describes how rhythmic activities can be applied to a wide variety of small equipment such as balls, individual ropes, and hoops. When there is not enough equipment to supply every child for a particular activity, use task cards and the station work technique. In the accompanying illustration, the

Station 1: Hoops

Station 2: Ropes

Station 3: Balls

Station 4: Lummi sticks

Station #1: Task: Make up a matching sequence with your partner that includes three different twirling movements, a pause in your routine and a change in direction.

Station #2: Task: Make up a matching routine that includes three different steps.

Station #3: Task: Develop a bouncing routine with one partner leading and the other following.

Station #4: Task: Make up a matching routine that includes a change of direction and a change in level.

class is divided into four groups and then subdivided into partners. Each set of partners reads the challenge, then proceeds to develop a matching routine. Any marching record can be used for all stations. Allow four to five minutes for the partners to develop their routines, then put on the record. If time permits, rotate the groups to the next station and repeat the process.

Rhythmic Activities with Small Equipment

Small equipment is used with rhythmic activities in two basic ways. First, the equipment, such as a rope or hoop, can be used as a focal point or obstacle to move in and out of, around, or over. Second, when the equipment, such as a hoop or ball, is held or manipulated, it is used as an extension of the rhythmic movements of the body. Swinging a hoop and bouncing a ball to a rhythm are examples of the latter.

Begin by teaching hand or foot movements without the equipment to allow the children to learn the basic movement and rhythmic patterns. Once these are acquired, introduce the equipment to the routine or movement pattern.

Individual Ropes

The basic rope-skipping skills were described in Chapter 22 (pp. 440-47). Several ideas relating to the development of individual and partner rou-

tines were also presented in this chapter; however, no reference was made to musical accompaniment. The challenges on page 451 can now be presented with musical accompaniment, such as "Maxwell's Silver Hammer," "Next Plane to London," or any current popular tune that has a good beat.

The following examples illustrate the variety of ways an individual rope can be used in rhythmic activities by an individual or by two or more players.

Individual Tasks

Choose a record with a good 4/4 meter for the following individual tasks:

1. "Place the rope on the floor in any pattern desired (straight, curled, or zigzag). Make up a routine of jumping back and forth over your rope (fig. 24.8). Repeat and include a turn."

Figure 24.8

Figure 24.9 Make up a routine that includes a two-foot basic . . .

Figure 24.10 . . . and another new step . . .

2. "Make up a routine that includes a two foot basic skipping step, another new step, and a twirling action of the rope (figs. 24.9 to 24.11)."
3. "Tie the ends of the rope together. Make up a routine that includes bending, stretching, and twisting."

Partner and Group Tasks

1. "Develop a matching routine with your partner and include a Two-Foot Basic, a Swing Step, and a Hop Step. (fig. 24.12)."
2. "Make up a rope-skipping routine with one partner following the other."
3. "Place one rope on the ground and make up a matching routine with your partner (fig. 24.13)."
4. "Have the children place two ropes on the floor and repeat task No. 1 under Individual Tasks (fig. 24.14)."

Figure 24.11 . . . and a twirling action

Figure 24.12 Develop a matching routine with your partner . . .

Figure 24.13 Place one rope on . . .

Figure 24.14a Place two ropes on the floor in any pattern desired and . . .

Figure 24.14b . . . and make up a routine with your partner jumping back and forth over your ropes.

24

5. "In groups of four, make up a matching routine in any pattern you like (fig. 24.15)."

Inflated Balls

Ball bouncing is particularly useful in helping children learn to move to a specific rhythm. Any inflated ball can be used. Slow and fast tunes can be used in all of the following individual and group tasks.

Individual Tasks

Begin bouncing with one hand to the rhythm of the music (choose a slow or fast tune depending upon the class's ability). Add the following challenges:

1. Change hands.
2. Bounce on one knee.

Figure 24.15

3. Bounce the ball around your body.
4. Bounce the ball with another part of your body (elbow, foot, etc.).
5. Bounce the ball and change direction—forward, backward, and sideways.
6. Bounce the ball and change levels—high, medium, and low (fig. 24.15).
7. Bounce, clap hands, bounce, and turn around.
8. Introduce a skipping rope. Place the rope on the floor in a curved or zigzag pattern. Develop tasks that require a bounce and a change of direction around or across the rope.

Partner and Group Tasks

Various partner routines can be developed, such as (1) matching bounces, (2) follow the leader, (3) contrasting routines (one high and one low), and (4) bouncing and exchanging the ball on certain beats of the music.

Group routines involving four or more players can also be developed by most children in the intermediate grades. For example, "Make up a routine with four players that includes four different bounces, a change of direction, and a change in level (fig. 24.17)."

Figure 24.16a Bounce the ball and ...

Figure 24.16b ... change levels.

Figure 24.17a . . . that includes four different bounces . . .

Figure 24.17b . . . a change in direction, and . . .

Hoops

The hoop can be used in two basic ways with rhythmic activities. First, when it is placed on the floor, it becomes an obstacle or focal point to maneuver in and out of, around, or over. Second, when it is held, it can be used to help the child move his body or parts of it to the rhythm of the drum beat or music. Balls can also be used in the same way.

As an Obstacle

Have each child place his hoop flat on the floor. Present challenges such as the following that involve locomotor skills and a change of direction:

1. "Make up a jumping routine moving in and out of your hoop." Later, add other challenges, such as "in and out, around and over."
2. Use two or more hoops on the floor and repeat (1).
3. Introduce ball bouncing with a hoop.

As an Instrument to Maneuver

There are many twirling and movement skills that can be done with a hoop. (An inflated ball can also be used.) The following will provide a basic starting point:

1. "Can you twirl the hoop on your arm to the rhythm of the music ('Summer Place')?" Later, substitute neck, arm, wrist, leg, or foot.
2. "Can you throw and catch the hoop, keeping in time to the rhythm of the music?"
3. "Develop a routine of swinging, jumping, and twisting."
4. In partners: Twirling, throwing, catching, and nonlocomotor skills can be incorporated into a variety of interesting and challenging matching, contrasting, and follow-the-leader routines.
5. Group activities: In a similar fashion, group routines can be created by boys and girls from grades four through six.

a

b

Figure 24.18 Lummi sticks

Rhythm or Lummi Sticks

Rhythm or lummi sticks* are extremely useful in developing eye-hand coordination and the elements of rhythm. The sticks are approximately ten to twelve inches long and can be made from one-inch doweling or old broom handles. The sticks are held between the thumb and fingers near the lower third of the stick (fig. 24.18). The following positions and hitting movements provide the basis for a wide variety of enjoyable individual, partner, and group routines.

*Lummi sticks and records can be purchased from Educational Activities, Inc., Box 392, Freeport, New York, 11520.

Figure 24.19 . . . tap sticks together four times . . .

a. From a standing position develop a routine tapping the sticks in front . . .

b. . . . to the side . . .

c. . . . and, behind the back

Figure 24.20

Individual Tasks

The first tasks presented should give each child an opportunity to learn how to tap the sticks to the rhythm of the music and how to shift from one tapping movement to another. Challenges can include the following simple routines:

1. Sitting cross-legged:
   a. Tap the floor four times, tap the sticks together four times, tap the right on left four times, and so on (fig. 24.19).
   b. Make up a routine tapping the floor in front, to the side, and behind you.

c. Make up a routine that includes tapping, throwing and catching the sticks, and then another tapping movement.
2. From a standing position: Develop a routine tapping the sticks in front, to the side, and behind the back (fig. 24.20).

  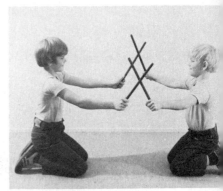

a. Hit sticks on the floor . . .   b. . . . together in front . . .   c. . . . with both arms sideways . . .

Figure 24.21

Partner and Group Tasks

The first partner activities should begin with both players in a cross-legged position facing each other and about two feet apart. This position encourages the players to develop routines using the floor for tapping as well as the partner's sticks. Following are a few sample routines:

1. Hit sticks on the floor, hit both sticks together in front, hit with both arms sideways, hit floor (fig. 24.21).
2. Hit sticks to the floor, each partner hits his own sticks together, exchange right sticks, then exchange left sticks.
3. From a standing position (fig. 24.22). Numerous calisthenic-like and other rhythmic routines can be developed with two players facing each other, standing side by side, or back to back.
4. Group activities can also be developed with sets of three, four, or more children. Once the children have learned the basic tapping skills and have had rhythmic experience with hoops, balls, and skipping ropes, they will develop creative rhythmic routines with lummi sticks quickly and enthusiastically.

The activities presented in this chapter should not be seen as a separate unit of dance. Rather, as was stated earlier, rhythmic activities

Figure 24.22

should be integrated into games, gymnastics, and dance units. This can be done through periodic rhythmic warm-up activities and an occasional complete lesson of rhythmics interspersed within a games or gymnastic unit.

Traditional and Contemporary Dances

25

Singing Games and Folk Dances for Primary Grades

Folk and Square Dances for Intermediate Grades

Glossary of Terms

All structured dances that are performed in the elementary school can be broadly classified as traditional and contemporary dances. This classification includes singing games and traditional dances of past cultures as well as the contemporary dances of the generation. (See film "Creative Folk Dance," Appendix A.)

In this chapter, two general sections have been organized on the basis of ease of use rather than established dance criteria. The first major section includes a wide selection of the more popular singing games and folk dances enjoyed by children in the primary grades. The next section includes appropriate traditional and contemporary dances for intermediate grades. Although grade levels are suggested for each dance, teachers should select dances on the basis of the children's dance background and demonstrated interests. A glossary of terms is included in the final section of this chapter, and information about record companies is provided in Appendix A.

Singing Games and Folk Dances for Primary Grades

Singing games are part of the dance heritage of every country. They are, in essence, the forerunners of the more complicated traditional and contemporary dances. As such, they provide a foundation upon which the more advanced dances can be built. Because of the cultural and historical significance of folk-singing games, primary teachers should take time to provide interesting materials relating to their origin, the customs of the people, and the meaning of various dance movements. There are many ways of presenting this information, such as reading stories and poems about the people, displaying pictures, dolls, and other articles, and showing a film about the country.

Most primary singing games are individual or partner activities; however, both types are performed within a group situation. Since five-, six-, and seven-year-olds are basically individualistic, the singing games presented in the following pages can be performed individually while the children are in a line, circle, or scattered pattern. With practice and maturity, children in the second and third grades progress to more advanced folk dances involving intricate patterns and group participation.

Teaching singing games to children in the primary grades, particularly to five- and six-year-olds, should be an enjoyable experience for teachers and a creative experience for children. The children's uninhibited behavior and joy of movement make singing games an appropriate activity. Once they learn the words, they will provide their own accompaniment and an infinite variety of interesting and creative versions of each singing game.

Since early primary children vary widely in maturity, motor ability, and interests, no single method of teaching will prove successful with this type of activity. Each teacher should experiment with several approaches until she finds the one most suitable to her own style of teaching. Usually this is a combination of methods and techniques rather than one "special" approach. The following suggestions may be helpful:

1. Use musical accompaniment that permits you to work freely with the children, such as commercial records or a tape recording of your own piano accompaniment.
2. Give the name of the folk dance or singing game and its origin, and mention something about the customs of the people. Show motion pictures, slides, or photographs of the people to illustrate.

3. Teach the words of the singing game first. Children should practice singing the song until they have nearly memorized it.
4. Teach the basic steps of the singing game after the children have learned the verses.
5. Combine the basic steps with the words and music.
6. Attempt to create a permissive atmosphere in which children feel free to express their own ideas and movements.

Through singing games, children learn to walk, run, skip, or perform a combination of these basic dance steps to musical accompaniment. And when they can move rhythmically to music, they can create their own singing games. Allow them to develop their own dances to favorite nursery rhymes or songs. For example, "Sing a Song of Sixpence" or "I Saw a Ship a Sailing" have simple phrases and rhythmic melodies which provide the necessary ingredients for new singing games. In addition, children may wish to write their own verses about animals, space ships, or special events, and then try to apply them to musical accompaniment. Finding the appropriate music usually becomes a joint venture for the teacher and class. The supplementary list of singing games and available records will be of some assistance. Children should also be encouraged to create their own music. Perhaps, too, some children may be fortunate enough to have a teacher with a musical background and the talent to write musical accompaniments to fit the verses written by them.

Name of Dance (Arranged in approximate order of difficulty)	Formation	Origin	Page	K	Grade Level		
					1	2	3
1. Baa, Baa, Black Sheep	Circle	English	525	X			
2. Hickory, Dickory, Dock	Circle	English	525	X			
3. Ring around the Rosy	Circle	English	526	X	X		
4. Farmer in the Dell	Circle	English	526	X	X		
5. Sally Go Round the Moon	Circle	American	527	X	X		
6. The Muffin Man	Circle	English	527	X	X		
7. Loobie Loo	Circle	English	528	X	X		
8. Did You Ever See a Lassie	Circle	Scottish	528	X	X		
9. How D'ye Do My Partner	Circle	Swedish	529		X	X	
10. Oats, Peas, Beans, and Barley	Circle	English	529		X	X	
11. Round and round the Village	Circle	English	530		X	X	
12. A Hunting We Will Go	Line	English	530			X	X
13. Jolly Is the Miller	Circle	English	531			X	X
14. Shoo Fly	Circle	American	531			X	X
15. Children's Polka	Circle	German	532			X	X
16. Danish Dance of Greeting	Circle	Danish	532			X	X
17. Paw Paw Patch	Columns	American	533				X
18. Skip to My Lou	Circle	American	533				X
19. Pop Goes the Weasel	Circle	American	534				X
20. Bleking	Circle	Swedish	534				X

Supplementary List of Singing Games and Folk Dances

Name	Formation	Origin	Grade Level K	1	2	3	Record Source
Bluebird	Circle	American	X	X			Folkcraft 1180
Mulberry Bush	Circle	English	X	X			Bowman A-1 Folkcraft 1183
London Bridge	Lines	English	X	X			Bowman 36-A1(2) RCA 45-5056
Little Miss Muffet	Circle	English	X	X			Childhood Rhythms Series 7. No. 703
I Should Like to Go to Shetland	Circle	English	X	X			Folkcraft 1190
Shoemaker's Dance	Circle	Danish		X	X		Folkcraft 1187 RCA 45-6171
Chimes of Dunkirk	Circle	French		X	X		Folkcraft 1185 RCA 45-6176
Thread Follows the Needle	Line	English		X	X		RCA 22760(E-87) Pioneer 3017
Rig-a-Jig-Jig	Circle	American			X	X	Folkcraft 1199
Sing a Song of Sixpence	Circle	English			X	X	Folkcraft 1180 RCA Victor 22760
Carousel	Circle	Swedish			X	X	RCA 45-6179 Pioneer 3004—A
Hansel and Gretel	Circle	German			X	X	Folkcraft 1193 RCA 45-6182
Jingle Bells	Circle	American			X	X	
Jump Jim Joe	Circle	American			X	X	Folkcraft 1180 Bowman, Album 3

Baa, Baa, Black Sheep (K)

Musical Accompaniment
Childhood Rhythms, Series 7, No. 701
Folkcraft 1191

Formation: Single circle, with girls to right of boys and all facing center with hands joined

Skills: Stamp, bow and curtsey, slide, skip, and walk

Song

Baa, baa, black sheep,	*Action*
Have you any wool?	Stamp three times.
Yes sir, yes sir,	Shake fingers.
Three bags full.	Nod head twice.
One for my master,	Hold three fingers up.
One for my dame,	Turn right and bow or curtsey.
And one for the little boy	Turn left and bow or curtsey.
Who lives in the lane.	Turn around.
	Face center and bow or curtsey.

Song
Baa, baa, black sheep,
Have you any wool?
Yes sir, yes sir,
Three bags full.
One for my master,
One for my dame,
And one for the little boy
Who lives in the lane.

Chorus:

Action
Stamp three times.
Shake fingers.
Nod head twice.
Hold three fingers up.
Turn right and bow or curtsey.
Turn left and bow or curtsey.
Turn around.
Face center and bow or curtsey.

Join inside hands and take sixteen steps counterclockwise.

Variation
All join hands and take eight slides to the right, then eight slides left. Raise hands and take four steps into the circle and four steps out. Repeat four in and four out. Drop hands and skip sixteen steps counterclockwise.

Hickory, Dickory, Dock (K)

Musical Accompaniment
Childhood Rhythms, Series 7, No. 702
Square Dance Associates
Album 12, No. 8

Formation: Double circle with inside hands on partner's shoulder and both facing counterclockwise. One child is the "mouse," the other the "clock."

Skills: Running, swaying, and stamping

Song
Hickory, dickory, dock!
The mouse ran up the clock.

The clock struck one,

The mouse ran down,
Hickory, dickory, dock.

Action
Sway toward center of circle.
Sway toward outside. Stamp one foot, then the other.
Mouse runs clockwise around his partner, then stamps feet as above.
Clock claps hands on word "one."
Mouse runs counterclockwise.
Repeat swaying and stamping movements.

Ring around the Rosy (K-1)

Musical Accompaniment
Folkcraft 1199

Formation: Single circle, girls to right of boys, and all facing center with hands joined

Skills: Walking and skipping

Song
Ring around a rosy
A pocket full of posies,
Ashes, ashes,*
All fall down.

Action
With hands joined, walk or skip around the circle.
Drop to a squatting position.

Teaching Suggestions
Use the following verse as a substitute for the one described:
Ring around the rosy,
A pocket full of posies,
One, two, three,
And squat where you be.

*Other words are "hush-a, hush-a," "at-choo, at-choo," or "one, two, three."

Farmer in the Dell (K-1)

Musical Accompaniment
Folkcraft 1182
RCA Victor 41-6152
Bowmar Singing Games, Album II

Formation: Single circle facing center with hands joined. One child, the "farmer," is in the center of the circle.

Skills: Walking and clapping

Song
The farmer in the dell,
The farmer in the dell,
Heigh-ho! the cherry-o,*
The farmer in the dell.
The farmer takes a wife,
The farmer takes a wife,
Heigh-ho! the cherry-o,
The farmer takes a wife.
The wife takes a child, etc.
The child takes a nurse, etc.
The nurse takes a dog, etc.
The dog takes a cat, etc.
The cat takes a rat, etc.
The rat takes the cheese, etc.
The cheese stands alone.

Action
All walk left around the circle, singing verse while the farmer looks about for a wife.
Continue to walk around the circle as the farmer chooses a wife, who joins him at the center of the circle.

Repeat procedure as directed.
Repeat procedure as directed.

Children in the center crowd around the "cheese" and clap their hands over the cheese's head, while circle players stand still, clap hands, and sing verse.

The farmer runs away, etc.
(Repeat for each player as he leaves center of circle.)

Continue walking as the farmer, then wife, etc., leave the center of the circle.
Note: Cheese remains and becomes the new farmer.

Teaching Suggestions
*This song may be sung "derry-o," "dairy-o," or "the dearie-o."

"Sally Go Round the Moon" (K-1)

Musical Accompaniment
Folkraft 1198
RCA Victor 45-5064

Song
Sally, go round the moon,
Sally, go round the stars,
Sally, go round the chimneypots,
On a Sunday afternoon—Boom!
Repeat above.

Formation: Single circle facing center with
    hands joined
Skills: Walking, running, skipping, or sliding

Action
Walk, run, skip, or slide around the circle. On
the word "boom," all jump into the air and clap
hands or perform any movement they wish.
Repeat action in opposite direction.

The Muffin Man (K-1)

Musical Accompaniment
Folkraft 1188
RCA Victor 45-5065

Song
Oh, have you seen the muffin man,
The muffin man, the muffin man,
Oh, have you seen the muffin man,
Who lives across the way.
Oh, yes, we've seen the muffin man
The muffin man, the muffin man
Oh, yes, we've seen the muffin man,
Who lives across the way.

Teaching Suggestions
With large numbers of children start with two
muffin men in the center of the circle. Substitute
"Drury Lane" as an English version.

Formation: Single circle facing center with one
    child (the "muffin man") in the center
Skills: Walk, clap, skaters' position

Pattern
Children join hands and circle to the left using
a walk or a slow skip step.

Children in circle stand facing center and clap
hands while singing "The Muffin Man." The
child in center chooses a partner from circle
and brings him or her back to center (in
skaters' position). This child becomes the new
muffin man while the old partner returns to
circle.

Loobie Loo (K-1)

Musical Accompaniment
Folkraft 1184
RCA Victor 41-6153
Childhood Rhythms
Series 7, No. 706
Bowmar Singing Games
Album 1, No. 1514

Chorus
Here we go Loobie Loo,
Here we go Loobie Light,
Here we go Loobie Loo,
All on a Saturday night.

(Verse No. 1)
I put my right hand in,
I put my right hand out,
I give my hand a shake, shake, shake
And turn myself about.
Repeat chorus after each verse.
I put my left hand in, etc.
I put my both hands in, etc.
I put my right foot in, etc.
I put my left foot in, etc.

I put my elbows in, etc.
I put my shoulders in, etc.
I put my big head in, etc.
I put my whole self in, etc.

Formation: Single circle facing center with
hands joined
Skills: Walking, skipping, sliding, galloping, and
pantomime activities

Pattern
Circle left using eight walking, skipping, or
sliding steps.
Circle right eight steps.
Everyone drops hands and faces the center.

Place right hand toward center of circle.
Turn, place right hand away from circle.
Shake hand.
Turn in place.
Repeat each verse according to the movement
suggested.

Did You Ever See a Lassie (K-1)

Musical Accompaniment
Folkraft 1183
RCA Victor 45-5066
Pioneer 3012-B
Columbia 10008D

Song
Did you ever see a lassie,
("laddie" when boy is in center)
A lassie, a lassie,
Did you ever see a lassie
Go this way and that?

Chorus
Go this way and that way.
Go this way and that way.
Did you ever see a lassie
Go this way and that?

Formation: Single circle facing center with
hands joined. One child is in the center of
the circle.
Skills: Walking and pantomime activities

Action
All join hands and walk eight steps to the left,
swinging joined hands.

All stop, release hands, face the child in center
and imitate her or his movements. Repeat
singing game with a new leader in the center.

Teaching Suggestions
Once the children have learned the basic
movements, have them create impressions such
as birds, animals, and mechanical toys. And
instead of walking, have them walk using
swinging and swaying, stamping, and clapping.

How D'ye Do My Partner (1-2)

Musical Accompaniment
Folkraft 1190
Pioneer 3012
RCA Victor 21685
Bowmar, Album 1. No. 1513 A

Song
How d'ye do my partner,
How d'ye do today?
Will you dance in a circle?
I will show you the way.

Chorus:
Tra,la,la,la,la,
Tra,la,la,la,la,
Tra,la,la,la,la,
Tra,la,la,la,la.
Repeat song.

Formation: Double circle with partners facing. Girls are on the outside circle.

Skills: Bowing, curtseying, skipping

Pattern
Boys bow to partners.
Girls curtsey to partners.
Boy offers hand to partner.
Join inside hands and turn counterclockwise.

With joined hands, skip around the circle. At the end of the chorus, girls move one position forward to new partners.

Oats, Peas, Beans, and Barley (1-2)

Musical Accompaniment
Folkraft 1182
RCA Victor 45-5067
Folk Dancer MH 1110-A
Pioneer 3012

Song
Oats, peas, beans, and barley grow,
Oats, peas, beans, and barley grow,
Do you or I or anyone know
How oats, peas, beans, and barley grow?
First the farmer sows his seed,
Then he stands and takes his ease.
Stamps his foot and claps his hand.
And turns around to view the land.
Waiting for a partner,
Waiting for a partner,
Open the ring and choose one in.
While we all gladly dance and sing.

Song
Tra,la,la,la,la,la,
Tra,la,la,la,la,la,
Tra,la,la,la,la,la,la,
Tra,la,la,la,la,la.

Formation: Single circle facing center with hands joined. One child in the center of the circle is the "farmer."

Skills: Walking and pantomime actions

Pattern
Farmer in center stands while children in circle walk left, taking small steps. Circle players stop, point to the farmer, shrug, turn right, and stamp their feet.

Children in circle stop, face the center, and all dramatize the words of the song.

Children in the circle skip left as the farmer skips around inside the circle and picks a new partner. The farmer and new partner skip around inside the circle.

The two farmers continue to skip inside the circle while the others join hands and circle left. "Old farmer" joins the ring and "new farmer" repeats pattern.

Round and round the Village (1-2)
(Go in and out the Windows)

Musical Accompaniment
Folkraft 1191
Pioneer 3001-B

Song
Go round and round the village,
Go round and round the village,
Go round and round the village,
As we have done before.
Go in and out the windows,
Go in and out the windows,
Go in and out the windows,
As we have done before.
Now go and choose a partner,
Now go and choose a partner,
Now go and choose a partner,
As we have done before.
Now follow me to London,
Now follow me to London,
Now follow me to London,
As we have done before.
Shake hands before you leave me,
Shake hands before you leave me,
Shake hands before you leave me,
As we have done before.

Formation: Single circle with all facing center and hands joined. One or more players are outside the circle.

Skills: Skipping, bowing, and curtseying

Action
Children join hands and hold them high as "it" skips to the right around the outside.

"It" skips in and out under the raised arms ("windows").

"It" skips around the inside of the circle, stops, and bows or curtseys in front of a partner he or she has chosen.

"It" skips around inside the circle, followed by the new partner. Circle players skip in the opposite direction.

The circle players remain in place, clap their hands, and sing while inside players shake hands and bow or curtsey. The chosen player(s) then goes to the outside of the circle while other players return to the circle.

A Hunting We Will Go (2-3)

Musical Accompaniment
Folkraft 1191
RCA Victor 45-5064
Childhood Rhythms,
Series 7 No. 705

Song
Oh, a hunting we will go,
A-hunting we will go,
We'll catch a fox and put him in a box,
And then we'll let him go.

Chorus:
Tra,la,la,la,la,la,la,
Tra,la,la,la,la,la,
Tra,la,la,la,la,la,
la,la,la,la,
Tra,la,la,la,la,la.

Repeat dance with new head couple.

Formation: Two parallel lines facing each other, with girls on one side and boys on the other

Skills: Skipping, casting off

Action
Head couple joins inside hands and skip down between the lines to the foot of the set.

Head couple turns around, changes hands, and skips back to the head of the set.

All other players clap hands while head couple skips down and back.

Head couple skips around the left side of the set, followed by other couples. When the head couple reaches the foot of the line it forms an arch under which all other couples pass. Head couple remains while the second couple becomes the head couple.

Jolly Is the Miller (2-3)

Musical Accompaniment
Folkraft 1192
RCA 45-5067

Song

Jolly is the miller who lives by the mill,
The wheel turns around of its own free will,
One hand in the hopper and
the other in the sack,
The girl steps forward and the boy steps back.

Repeat dance with new partners.

Formation: Partners form a double circle with girls on the inside. One player, the "miller," stands in the center.

Skills: Walking

Action

Couples join inside hands and walk counterclockwise singing the song. During the second line children in the inner circle extend their left arms sideward to form a mill wheel. On the last word of the song ("back"), partners drop hands and children in the inner circle step forward while those in outer circle step backward. The extra player tries to secure a partner during this exchange. The child without a partner goes to the center.

Shoo Fly (2-3)

Musical Accompaniment
Folkraft 1185

Song

Shoo, fly, don't bother me,
Shoo fly, don't bother me,
Shoo, fly, don't bother me,
For I belong to somebody.
Repeat.

Chorus

I feel, I feel,
I feel like a morning star,
I feel, I feel,
I feel like a morning star.

Formation: Single circle with girls at the boys' right. Hands are joined and all are facing the center of the circle.

Skills: Walking, swinging, turning

Action

Walk four steps forward, swinging arms.
Walk four steps backward.

Partners join hands and walk around each other in a clockwise direction. Repeat. On the last "morning star," the boy raises his left hand and turns his partner under his arm. The girl is now on the boy's left. The girl on the boy's right becomes his new partner.

Join hands and repeat dance.

Children's Polka (Kinderpolka) (2-3)

Musical Accompaniment
RCA Victor 45-6179
Folkraft 1187
Pioneer 3004-B

Formation: Single circle with partners facing, both arms extended sideward and hands joined

Skills: Sliding, hopping, and running

Measure	Action
1-2	Take two slides toward center; step lightly three times.
3-4	Take two slides away from center; step lightly three times.
5-8	Repeat action of measures 1-4.
9-10	Slap own knees once, clap own hands once, and clap partner's hands three times.
11-12	Repeat action of measures 9-10.
13	Hop, placing right heel forward, place right elbow in left hand, and shake finger three times.
14	Repeat action of measure 13 with left foot.
15-16	Turn in place with four running steps and step lightly three times.

Teaching Suggestions
To help children learn the dance pattern, count in this manner:
Step, step, tap, tap, tap. Repeat.
Slap, clap, clap, clap, clap. Repeat.
Hop, one, two, three. Repeat.
Turn around now, tap, tap, tap.

Danish Dance of Greeting (2-3)

Musical Accompaniment
Folkraft 1187
RCA Victor 41-6183
Pioneer 3014-B
Burns, Evans, and Wheeler,
Album 1, No. 126 (with words)

Formation: Single circle of couples with all facing center. The girl is on the right side of the boy.

Skills: Clapping, stamping, turning, and running

Song	Action
Clap, clap, bow.	Clap hands twice, turn and bow or curtsey to partner.
Clap, clap, bow.	Clap hands twice and bow or curtsey to child on the other side (neighbor).
Stamp, stamp.	Stamp on the right foot and then on the left.
Turn yourself around.	Turn around in place with four running steps.
Chorus	
Tra,la,la,la,la,etc.	All join hands and circle to the right with sixteen short running steps. Repeat action to the left.
Tra,la,la,la,la,etc.	

Paw Paw Patch (3)

Musical Accompaniment
Folkraft 1181
RCA Victor 45-5066

Formation: Columns of four to six couples with partners facing
Skills: Walking, skipping, casting off

Song

Where, O where is sweet little Sally?
Where, O where is sweet little Sally?
Where, O where is sweet little Sally?
Way down yonder in the paw paw patch.
Come on, boys, let's go find her,
Come on, boys, let's go find her,
Come on, boys, let's go find her,
Way down yonder in the paw paw patch.
Pickin' up paw paws, putting 'em in her pocket,
Pickin' up paw paws, putting 'em in her pocket,
Pickin' up paw paws, putting 'em in her pocket,
Way down yonder in the paw paw patch.

Action

First girl turns right, casts off, circles clockwise, and goes once around the set with sixteen skipping steps.

First girl takes the first boy's left hand and leads line of boys around the set. Boys may join hands. Girls in line clap hands. All finish in place facing the front.

Partners join hands and follow first couple once around to the right. First couple turns away from each other, with the boy going left and the girl going right, and skips to the foot of the line. The rest of the line moves one place forward.

Repeat entire dance with each new "first" girl leading.

Skip to My Lou (3)

Musical Accompaniment
Bowmar Singing Games Album 3, No. 1522-A
Folkraft 1192
Folk Dancers MH 111-A
Pioneer 3003-A

Formation: Single circle with partners side by side and the girl on the boy's right
Skills: Walking, skipping, swinging, and promenade

Song

Verse No. 1
Boys to the center, Skip to my Lou,
Boys to the outside, Skip to my Lou,
Boys to the center, Skip to my Lou.
Skip to my Lou, my darling.

Verse No. 2
Girls to the center, Skip to my Lou,
Girls to outside, Skip to my Lou,
Girls to the center, Skip to my Lou,
Skip to my Lou, my darling.

Verse No. 3
Swing your partner, Skip to my Lou, (three times)
Skip to my Lou, my darling.

Verse No. 4
I've lost my partner now what'll I do, (three times)
Skip to my Lou, my darling.

Verse No. 5
I've got another one, prettier too, (three times)
Skip to my Lou, my darling.

Action

Boys walk four steps forward and four steps backward.

Repeat.

Repeat patterns as described above.

Partners join hands and swing or skip in place.

Release hands. Girls walk forward, boys turn and walk in the opposite direction.

New partners promenade counterclockwise to original position, with the girl on the boy's right.

Repeat dance with new partner.

Pop Goes the Weasel (3)

Musical Accompaniment
World of Fun, M-104-B
Folkraft 1329
RCA Victor 45-6180

Formation: Double circle in sets of four children. Girl is on partner's right. Couples facing clockwise are couples number one, while couples facing counterclockwise are couples number two.

Skills: Walking and skipping

Measure	Action
1-4	Join hands in a circle of four and circle left with eight skipping or sliding steps.
5-6	Walk two steps forward, raising joined hands, then walk two steps backward, lowering hands.
7-8	Number one couples raise their joined hands to form an arch as number two couples pass under. Number two couples continue forward to meet new partners.

Variation	Formation: Three children form a set, with two children joining inside hands. The third child stands in front with his back to the other two, extends his hands back, and holds the outside hands of the other two. All three face counterclockwise in a large circle.

Measure	Action
1-6	All sets skip around in a large circle.
7-8	On "pop" the child in front skips backward under the raised inside hands of the back couple and continues backward, meeting the couple behind him.
9-14	Repeat measures 1-6.
15-16	Repeat measures 7-8.

Bleking (3)

Musical Accompaniment
Pioneer 3016
Folkraft 1188
RCA Victor 45-6169

Formation: Single circle with partners facing. Boys face counterclockwise; girls face clockwise. Partners extend their arms forward at shoulder height and join hands.

Skills: Bleking step

Measure	Action
1-8	Hop on left foot, extend the right heel forward, keeping the right leg straight. As this movement takes place, thrust the right arm forward and pull the left arm back (count one). Continue for seven more counts, changing the lead foot on each count.
9-16	Partners facing, arms extended sideways and hands joined. Boy begins with his right foot, girl with her left foot. Partners begin to turn in place by taking seven step-hops in a clockwise direction and end with a stamp on the last count. As the children turn in place, their arms move in a windmill action up and down with each step-hop.
Repeat measures 1-16.	

Folk and Square Dances for Intermediate Grades

Traditional and contemporary dances are dance patterns of past and present cultures. Generally speaking, when a dance such as Gustaf's Skoal has been handed down for many generations, it is designated as a *traditional folk dance.* On the other hand, a dance that originates within our own generation and is performed to recent or popular music is usually designated as a *contemporary dance.* Examples of the latter are the Patty Cake Dance, the Hitchhiker, and the Twist. Both types of dances, however, express some aspect of the culture from which they originated. The Danish Dance of Greeting and the Sicilian Circle are examples of how dances can be used as a method of greeting or meeting others. Other dances, such as the Sailor's Hornpipe and our American Indian Dance, are part of ceremonial or religious customs.

Obviously there is no "best way" of teaching traditional and contemporary dances. The method that a teacher uses will depend upon such factors as the age of the children, their previous dance experience, and the difficulty of the dance. The following suggestions should be given consideration when developing a basic approach to teaching these dances:

1. Acquire a general background of the people from which the dance originated and their customs for presentation to the class.
2. Present the background information about the dance in relation to the class's interest and maturity. Make it meaningful to the children.
3. Use such audiovisual aids such as costumes, scenery, and folk songs to stimulate interest in and a deeper understanding of the people and customs represented in the dance.
4. Allow the children to hear the music before they learn the dance pattern.
5. Teach the dance by phrases rather than by counts.
6. Use a slower tempo when teaching the steps; after they are learned, increase the tempo to the appropriate speed of the dance.
7. Look for general problems, such as starting off on the wrong foot, and correct these difficulties; later, provide individual assistance.
8. Indicate any change in dance formation just before the beginning of the new phase.
9. Encourage creative expression within the pattern of the dance. Many of the older traditional dances require movements that are uncomfortable or too rigid for children to perform. Creative variations should be encouraged when they do not change the basic theme of the dance.
10. Avoid spending too much time on one dance.

Square Dances

American folk dances include mixers, couples, longways, circles, and square dances that have been developed in this country during the past few hundred years. Of all these American folk dances, square dances have become the most popular with upper elementary school children. There is no single reason for this growth in popularity, although the simplicity of the square-dance steps and the enjoyment of participation could well be two important reasons.

The following suggestions will help teachers present various types of square-dance patterns. A list of basic terms used in square dance is provided in the glossary on page 549.

1. Emphasize fun and enjoyment rather than the perfection of each and every skill.
2. Teach all square-dance movements from a circle formation, with the girls standing to the boys' right side.
3. Select square dances that involve simple patterns, and introduce them at a slower speed.
4. When the dance is being learned, the teacher should call the dance patterns first without music, and then with musical accompaniment. Once the dance is learned, the teacher may continue to call her own dance or use a record with the calls included.

5. The majority of square dancing is done with a shuffle step rather than a run or a hop. Emphasize a smooth and graceful slipping action, landing on the ball of the foot rather than on the heel.

6. The success of square dancing depends, in part, upon keeping the square of four couples symmetrical and the partners parallel. Constantly check to see that children maintain the square and partners do not wander away from each other.

7. Encourage children not only to call their own dances, but, also to create their own sequences of square-dance figures.

Folk and Square Dances for Intermediate Grades

Name of Dance	Type of Dance	Origin	Page	Grade Level		
				4	5	6
1. Cshebogar	Circle	Hungarian	537	X	X	
2. Glowworm Mixer	Circle	American	538	X	X	
3. Little Brown Jug	Circle	American	538	X	X	
4. Grand March	Line	American	539	X	X	X
5. Sicilian Circle	Circle	American	540	X	X	X
6. Virginia Reel	Longways	American	540	X	X	X
7. Solomon Levi	Square	American	541	X	X	X
8. Oh Johnny	Circle	American	541	X	X	X
9. Oh Susanna	Circle	American	542	X	X	
10. Schottische	Circle	Scottish	542	X	X	
11. Badger Gavotte	Circle	American	543	X	X	
12. Norwegian Mountain March	Circle	Norwegian	543	X	X	
13. Heel and Toe Polka	Circle	German	544		X	X
14. Oklahoma Mixer	Circle	American	544		X	X
15. Rye Waltz	Circle	American	545		X	X
16. Red River Valley	Square	American	545		X	X
17. Tinikling	Line	Philippine	546		X	X

Supplementary List of Folk and Square Dances

Name	Formation	Origin	Grade Level			Record Source
			4	5	6	
Greensleeves	Circle	English	X			RCA 45-6175
Seven Jumps	Circle	Danish	X			Folkraft 1163
Gustaf's Skoal	Quadrille	Swedish	X	X		RCA 45-6170
Troika	Threes	Russian	X	X	X	World of Fun 105
Mayim	Circle	Israeli	X	X	X	Folkraft 1108
Hop Morr Anika	Circle	Swedish	X	X	X	RCA 4142
Road to the Isles	Couples	Scottish	X	X	X	Imp. 1005A
Horah	Circle	Israeli	X	X	X	Folkraft 1110
Hinkey Dinkey Parley Vous	Square	French	X	X	X	Folkraft 1023 (with call)
Let's Square Dance	Square	American	X	X	X	RCA 3001 (Album 1 and 2).
Johsey Square Dances	Square	American	X	X	X	MacGregor (Albums 4, 7, 8).
Crested Hen	Threes	Danish		X	X	RCA 6176
Jessie Polka	Couples	American		X	X	Folkraft 1071
Put Your Little Foot	Couples	American		X	X	Folkraft 1165
Manitou	Circle	Canadian		X	X	Lloyd Shaw 6-141
Varsovienne	Circle	American			X	Windsor 7516, Folkraft 1034

Cshebogar (4-5)

Musical Accompaniment
Folkraft 1196
RCA Victor 45-6182
Methodist M-101

Formation: Single circle of couples with hands joined. Couples face the center with the girl on the boy's right side.

Skills: Walking, skipping, sliding, and the Hungarian turn

Measure	Action
1-4	Take eight slide steps to the left.
5-8	Take eight slide steps to the right.
1-4	Take four walking steps to the center, raising your hands high as you go. Take four walking steps backward to place in circle, lowering your hands as you return.
5-8	Face partner and place right hand on his or her waist. Raise left arm, pull away from partner, and skip around him or her. (This is a Hungarian turn.)
1-4	Face partner, join hands with arms held at shoulder height. Slide four steps slowly toward the center of the circle, bending toward the center as you slide. Boys start with left foot and girls with right foot.
5-8	Four step-draw steps outward (step-close-step).
1-4	Two draw steps in and two draw steps out.
5-8	Do the Hungarian turn again.

25

Glowworm Mixer (4-5)

Musical Accompaniment
MacGregor 310-B
Windsor 4613-B

Formation: Players form a double circle and all face counterclockwise. Boy stands on inside circle and holds the girl's left hand in his right.

Skills: Walking, running, do-si-do

Measure	Action
1-4	Promenade counterclockwise with eight walking steps.
5-8	Promenade clockwise with eight walking steps.
9-12	Pass right shoulders, back-to-back, then step back to place (do-si-do).
13-16	Turn to the right, face new partner, and do-si-do with eight running steps.

Little Brown Jug (4-5)

Musical Accompaniment
Columbia 52007
Folkraft 1304A
Imperial 1213

Formation: Double circle with partners facing each other, girls on the outside circle. Hands are joined and raised to shoulder height.

Skills: Sliding and swinging

Measure	Action
1-8	Boy touches his left heel to side, then his left toe next to his right foot. Repeat movement. Take four slide steps to the left. Girls start with outside foot and do the same.
9-16	Repeat measures one through eight with four slides to the right.
17-24	Clap own thighs four times, then own hands together four times.
25-32	Partners clap right hands together four times, then left hands together four times.
33-40	Hook right elbows with partner and skip around in a circle with eight skipping steps.
41-56	Repeat clapping sequence of measures 17 to 24 and 25 to 32.
57-64	Hook left elbows and repeat turns.

Grand March (4-6)

Musical Accompaniment
Any marching record

Formation: Boys line up on one side of the room and girls on the other side. All face the foot of the room. The teacher stands in the center of the end line at the head of the room.

Skills: Walking

Call

Come down the center in twos.

Action

March to meet partners at the foot of the room. As the couples meet, they turn, join hands, and march down the center to the head of the room, where the teacher is standing to give directions.

Two right and two left.

The first couple turns to the right, the second to the left, and so on.

Come down the center in fours.

When the two head couples meet at the foot of the room, they hold hands and walk four abreast down the center.

Four right and four left.

When children reach the front of the room, they divide again, with four going to the right and four going to the left, and so on.

Come down the center in eights.

When the lines of four meet at the front of the room, they join hands to form a line of eight abreast. The lines of eight march to the head of the room and halt.

Note: This process may be reversed, with lines of eight dividing into columns of four. The columns of four march back to the other end of the room, where the two columns merge into one column of fours. The fours divide at the head of the room, and so on, until all are back to the original position of one couple.

Variations

From "Come down the center in fours," separate into twos, then call:

Form arches.

First couple forms an arch and the second couple tunnels under. Third couple forms an arch and the fourth couple tunnels under. Continue this pattern.

Over and under.

First odd couple arches over the last couple in line and then under the next and so on down to the front of the line.

Sicilian Circle (4-6)

Musical Accompaniment
Windsor A7S4A
Folkraft 1115, 1242 (with calls)
Methodist 104

Measure	Call
1-4	Now everybody forward and back.
5-8	Circle four hands around.
1-4	Ladies chain.
5-8	Chain the ladies back again.
1-4	Right and left through.
5-8	Right and left back.
1-4	Forward and back.
5-8	Forward again, pass through.

Formation: Circle of "sets of four" with couple facing couple. The girl should be on the boy's right side.

Skills: Walking, ladies chain, right and left through

Action

Join inside hands with partner. Take four steps forward toward the opposite couple and four steps backward to place.

Join hands and circle left with eight walking steps and finish in original places.

Ladies chain across and back with the two girls changing places. The boy takes the approaching girl's left hand in his left, places his right arm around her waist, and pivots backward to reface the opposite couple.

The girls return to their original positions with the same movement.

Right and left with opposite couple, over and back. Walk forward to opposite couple's place, passing right shoulders, then, keeping side by side as though inside hands were joined, turn half around as a couple (man turns backward while lady turns forward), and reface opposite.

Repeat the same movement, returning to original place.

Forward and back.

All walk forward eight steps, passing opposite by right shoulder, to meet new couple. Repeat dance with new couple.

Virginia Reel (4-6)

Musical Accompaniment
Burns, Album J. No. 558
RCA Victor 45-6180
Folkraft 1249

Measure	Call
1-8	Bow to your partner, go forward and back. Go forward and back again.
9-12	Now forward again with right hand swing, and all the way back.
13-16	Now forward again with left hand swing, and all the way back.
1-4	Now forward again with a two-hand swing, and all the way back.
5-8	Forward again with a do-si-do.
9-16	The head two sashay down the middle and all the way back to the head of the set.
17-24	Cast off, with boys going left and girls going right.
25-32	Form an arch and all pass through.

Formation: Six couples in file formation with partners facing each other. Boys are on the caller's right.

Skills: Walking, skipping, swinging, do-si-do, and cast-off

Action

Players take three skips forward, curtsey or bow, then skip back. Repeat.

Partners hold right hands, turn once around, and then back.

Partners join left hands, turn once around, then back.

Partners join both hands and turn clockwise and back.

All partners do a do-si-do.

Head couple joins hands and slides down the center of the set and back.

All face the caller, with the boys' line skipping left and the girls' line skipping right, ending at the foot of the set.

The head couple meets at the foot of the set, joins hands, and raises them to form an arch. The second couple leads the other couples through the arch and moves to the head of the line to become the new head couple. Repeat dance with each new head couple.

Solomon Levi (4-6)

Musical Accompaniment
MacGregor 007-4A (with calls)

Formation: Square of four couples who are
numbered counterclockwise. Girl is on the
boy's right side.

Skills: Walking, swing, alleande left

Measure	Call	Action
1-4	Everyone swing your honey; swing her high and low.	Swing partner.
5-16	Allemande left with left hand, and around the ring you go. A grand old right and left. Walk on your heel and toe and meet your honey, give her a twirl, and around the ring you go. Sing chorus.	Left hand to corner, walk around corner back to partner. Extend right hand to partner, left to next girl, alternating right and left hands until partners meet. Give partner a swing and promenade.
1-8	Oh Solomon Levi, tra la la la la la Oh Solomon Levi, tra la la la la la	Promenade around set. Repeat dance with couples two, three, and four leading. After couple number four completes its turn, have all four couples separate and repeat dance.

Oh Johnny (4-6)

Musical Accompaniment
MacGregor 652A (with calls)
Folkraft 1037

Formation: Single circle with girls on boys'
right. All join hands.

Skills: Walking, swinging, allemande left, do-si-
do

Measure	Call	Action
1-4	All join hands and circle the ring.	All couples move to the right in walking steps.
5-8	Stop where you are and give your honey a swing.	In closed dance position, swing partners.
9-12	Swing that little gal behind you.	Boy swings girl on his left.
13-16	Now swing your own.	Boy swings girl on his right.
1-4	Allemande left with the corner gal.	Turn to corners, give left hand to corner girl, walk around her, and return to partner.
5-8	Do-si-do your own.	Fold arms and pass right shoulder to right shoulder around partner and back to the corner girl, who becomes new partner.
9-16	Now you all promenade with your sweet corner maid, Singing, "Oh, Johnny, oh, Johnny, oh."	Everyone promenade. Repeat dance.

Oh Susanna (4-5)

Musical Accompaniment
RCA Victor 45-6178
Folkraft 1186

Formation: Partners stand in a single circle, facing center, with hands joined. The girl is on the boy's right side.

Skills: Walking, sliding, do-si-do

Measure	Action
1-16	All take eight sliding steps to the right and eight sliding steps to the left.
1-4	All take four steps to the center and four steps back.
5-8	Repeat measures 1 through 4.
1-4	Release hands. Girls walk four steps toward the center of the circle and four steps back. Boys stand in place and clap hands.
5-8	Boys go to center while girls clap hands.
1-4	Do-si-do with partners.
5-8	Do-si-do with corner girls.
1-8	Everyone promenades around the circle.

Schottische (4-5)

Musical Accompaniment
MacGregor 400A
Folkraft 1101

Formation: Double circle with partners facing counterclockwise. Boys are on the inside circle and hold partners in an open dance position.

Skills: Schottische step

Measure	Action
1-2	Partners start with outside feet (boy's left, girl's right), run forward three steps, and hop on outside foot and extend inside foot forward.
3-4	Begin with inside foot and repeat action.
5-6	All perform four step-hops in place.

Repeat the first six measures as often as desired or substitute the following variations for measures 5 and 6.

Variation One:
Partners drop hands and dance four skip-hops in place, turning away from each other on the first step, and ending in the starting position on the fourth step-hop.

Variation Two:
Boys take four step-hops in place and girls turn under their arms. On the next turn, reverse movements, with the boys turning under the girls' raised arms.

Variation Three:
Partners join hands about waist high and both turn under raised arms, and continue around and back to the starting position.

Badger Gavotte (4-5)

Musical Accompaniment
MacGregor 610 B
Folkraft 1094

Formation: Double circle with couples facing counterclockwise. Partners join hands. Girl is on the boy's right side.

Skills: Sliding, two-step, closed dance position

Measure	Action
1-2	Begin with the outside foot (boy's left, girl's right), walk forward four steps, face partner, join hands, take three sliding steps to the boy's left, and touch the right toe behind the left foot.
3-4	Repeat measures 1 and 2 in the opposite direction.
5-8	Change to a closed dance position and take eight two-steps progressing counterclockwise, with the boys starting with the left foot and the girls with the right foot. Repeat dance until music ends.

Norwegian Mountain March (4-5)

Musical Accompaniment
Folkraft 1177
RCA Victor 45-6173

Formation: Circle in sets of three children, all facing counterclockwise. The "set" is composed of one boy in the center and slightly in front of two side girls. The boy holds the girls' inside hands and the girls join outside hands, forming a triangle.

Skills: Waltzing and turning under

Measure	Call	Action
1-8	Waltz run.	Start on the right foot and take eight running waltz steps (twenty-four steps). All should accent the first step of each measure, and the leader should occasionally glance over his right and left shoulders at his partners.
9-10	Boys under.	Boy moves backward with six running steps under the arch formed by the girls' raised arms.
11-12	Left girl under.	Girl on the boy's left takes six steps to cross in front of and under the boy's raised right arm.
13-14	Right girl turns.	Girl on the boy's right takes six steps to turn under the boy's right arm.
15-16	Boy turns.	Boy turns under his own right arm to original position.
Repeat dance.		

Heel and Toe Polka (5-6)

Musical Accompaniment
Burns, Evans, and Wheeler
Album 2, No. 225
Folkraft 1166
MacGregor 400B

Formation: Double circle, with partners facing counterclockwise. Open dance position with girl on boy's right side.

Skills: Polka step

Measure	*Action*
1-2	Partners touch outside heels forward and bend backward slightly. Touch toes of outside feet backward, bend forward slightly, and take three running steps forward. (Heel and toe, and step, step, step.)
3-4	Repeat 1-2 with inside foot.
5-8	Repeat measures 1-4.
9-16	Partners face each other, the boy places his hands at the girl's waist and the girl places her hands on the boy's shoulders. All polka around the circle in a counterclockwise direction.

Oklahoma Mixer (5-6)

Musical Accompaniment
Folkraft 1035
Methodist World of Fun 102
MacGregor 400

Formation: Double circle of couples, with girl on boy's right. Take the Varsovienne position, with the left foot free.

Skills: Walking, heel-toe, and two-step

Measure	*Action*
1-2	Begin with the left foot and take two two-steps.
3-4	Begin with the left foot and take four walking steps forward.
5-8	Repeat measures 1-4.
9-12	Place the left heel forward and to the left, then the left toe opposite the right foot. Hold left hand, release right. Girls walk to the center of the circle in front of the boys as the boys move to the outside of the circle. The girls finish facing clockwise; the boys, counterclockwise.
13-16	The boy does a right heel and toe and takes three steps in place. The girl does a right heel and toe and walks to the boy behind. Repeat dance with new partner.

Rye Waltz (5-6)

Musical Accompaniment
Folkraft 1103
Imperial 1044

Formation: Double circle with boys in the center facing girls. Partners take an open dance position.

Skills: Sliding and waltz step

Measure	Action
1-4	Boys extend left toe to the side and return to inside of right foot. Repeat point and close. Girls perform the same movement with the right foot. Girls take three slide steps to the boys' left and touch right toe behind left foot.
5-8	Repeat in opposite direction.
9-16	Waltz around the room, with boys using their right shoulders to lead.

Red River Valley (5-6)

Musical Accompaniment
Imperial 1096
MacGregor Album 8 (with calls)

Formation: Square of four couples, who are numbered counterclockwise. Girl is on the boy's right.

Skills: Walking, swinging, do-si-do

Measure	Call	Action
1-4	All join hands in the valley.	Everyone joins hands.
5-8	And circle to the left and to the right.	With joined hands, walk four steps left and back four steps to the right.
1-4	And you swing the girl in the valley.	Boys swing corner girls (girl on boy's left).
5-8	Now swing that Red River Gal.	Boys return to their own partners and swing them.
1-4	Now you lead right down the valley.	Number one and number three couples walk to couples on their right and join hands in a circle.
5-8	And you circle to the left, then to the right.	Walk four steps to the left and back four steps to the right.
9-12	Two ladies star in the valley.	Girls star with right hands (join right hands) in the center of the set and walk once around clockwise.
13-16	Now swing with the Red River Gal.	Boys swing partners.
1-4	Same couples to the left down the valley.	Couples number one and three walk to their left and join hands with new couples.
5-8	And you circle to the left and to the right.	Walk four steps to the left and back four steps to the right.
9-12	Now two gents star in the valley.	Boys star with their right hands and turn once around clockwise.
13-16	And you swing that Red River Gal.	Everyone swings with his partner. Repeat entire dance with two side couples taking the active part. Instead of a star, do-si-do the second time, elbow swing the third, etc.

Figure 25.1

Tinikling (5-6)

Tinikling is a very exciting Philippine folk dance depicting the movements of the long-legged, long-necked tinikling bird, which is similar in appearance to the crane, heron, and flamingo. In the tinikling dance the "bird" moves around two persons who sit on the floor and manipulate two nine-foot-long bamboo poles in an attempt to trap the bird's legs. The poles are placed about two feet apart on two blocks of wood.* The players holding the bamboo poles slide them across the boards and strike them together on count one. On counts two and three, they lift the poles about an inch off the boards, open them about one foot apart and tap them twice against the boards. The musical accompaniment is a 3/4 waltz meter with a distinct "strike, tap, tap" rhythm throughout the dance.

Tinikling Steps

There are several basic tinikling steps that can be performed individually or in combination. Once children learn to perform the following stepping movements, they soon will develop combinations and routines. (See page 548 for suggested records and films.)

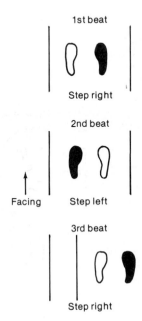

Side Step (fig. 25.2): Two dancers begin in a standing position facing each other and on opposite sides of the poles. Each dancer's left side is closest to his pole. With the 3/4 rhythm, one step is performed outside the poles as they are hit together and two steps inside the poles as they are tapped twice on the blocks.

After the basic side step is learned, the following variations can be attempted:

1. Two dancers are on the same side of one pole, moving together across and back.
2. Join hands while on opposite sides of the poles or together as in (1).

*Bamboo poles or 1-to-1½-inch wooden doweling can be used. Standard two-by-four lumber can be used for the blocks.

a. ... step left

b. ... step right ...

c. ... step left ...

Figure 25.2

Straddle Step (fig. 25.3): The dancer performs two jumps with feet together inside the poles and a straddle jump when the poles are brought together. The rhythm pattern is out-in-in.

Forward and Back: The dancer stands facing the poles. The movement consists of a step forward with the left foot, followed by a step forward on the right foot. As the poles are brought together, the dancer takes a step forward on his left foot to the opposite side. The pattern is re-

Figure 25.3 Straddle jump

25

versed on the next measure, with a step back on the right foot, a step back on the left foot, and a step back to the original position on the right foot (fig. 25.4).

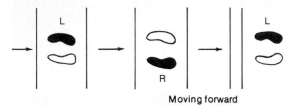

Moving forward

When the class has learned the basic steps and pole movements, the poles can be arranged in a variety of patterns to allow the children to move in different directions. A few examples are shown.

Single file

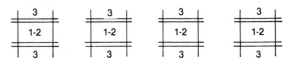

Crossed formation

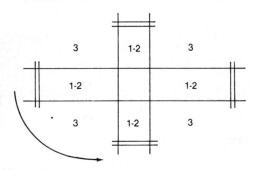

Square formation

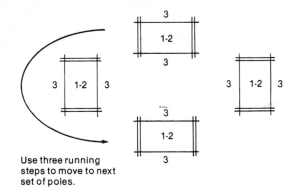

Use three running steps to move to next set of poles.

Figure 25.4 Forward and back

Resource Information

1. *Suggested records*
   a. "Special Folk Dances" (Tinikling," Carino sa, Czardas, Vengorka and Tarantella in 3/4 meter), RCA Victor, EPA-4126
   b. "Alley Cat," ATCA 45-6226
   c. "No Matter What Shape," Liberty Records, 55836
2. *Film*
   "Tinikling—the Bamboo Dance (16 mm)," Martin Moyer Productions, 900 Federal Avenue East, Seattle, Washington

Glossary of Terms

The following words and phrases occur frequently in folk and square dances for children in the intermediate grades:

Active couple(s)
The couple(s) that is designated to start a dance or to whom a part of the dance is addressed.

Advance
To move forward, usually with walking steps.

Allemande left
From a circle or square formation with all dancers facing the center, the boy joins his left hand with the girl on his left and walks around counterclockwise and back to his starting position.

Allemande right
Same as allemande left but toward the opposite direction.

Arch
Two dancers join inside hands and raise arms to form an arch.

Balance
In square dancing the usual movement following a "swing your partner." Partners face each other, join right hands, and step back with weight on the left foot and the right heel touching in front. Both partners may also bow slightly.

Bow and curtsey
The bow, performed by the boys, may be a simple nod of the head or an elaborate and pronounced deep bend of the trunk. The curtsey, performed by the girls, may be a simple nod of the head or an elaborate and pronounced deep bend of the knees and a graceful sideward extension of the dancing costume.

Break
Release hands.

Chain (ladies chain)
In square dancing, the girls move across to the opposite couple, extending their right hands to each other as they pass, then their left hands to the opposite boy. The boy places his right hand behind the girl's back, grasping her right hand, and turns her one full turn counterclockwise.

Clockwise
Moving in the same direction as the hands of a clock.

Corner
When facing the center, the boy's corner is the girl on his left and the girl's corner is the boy on her right.

Counterclockwise
Moving in the opposite direction as the hands of a clock.

Divide or split the ring
Active couples pass through the opposite couples.

Do-si-do
These words mean "back to back" and usually involve two persons who are facing each other. The two dancers walk forward, pass right shoulders and without turning move to the right, passing back to back, and then walk backward to the starting position.

Forward and back
This figure involves dancers facing each other. Both sides advance four steps forward (or three steps and a bow) and take four steps backward.

Grand right and left
This is a weaving pattern and usually follows an allemande left. Face partner and join right hands, pass and give left hand to the next dancer, and continue weaving around set.

Head couple
In square dancing, the couple nearest the music or caller.

Home
The starting place at the beginning of a dance.

Honor
Salute or bow to partner or other dancers.

Opposite
The person or couple directly across the square.

Promenade
This is the skater's position in which partners stand side by side and face the same direction. The girl stands on the boy's right. Partners join left hands about waist high, then join right hands above the left arms.

Sashay
The American term for the French term "chasse." These are sliding steps sideward.

Separate
Partners leave each other and move in opposite directions.

Square
Four couples, with each forming one side of a square.

Star or wheel
Two or more dancers join right hands in the center of the set and walk forward or backward as directed.

Swing
This is a rhythmic rotation of a couple with a walking step, buzz step, two-step, or skip. The swing may be a one-hand, two-hand, elbow, or waist swing.

Varsovienne position
The boy stands slightly behind and to the left of his partner. While both are facing the same direction, the girl raises both hands to about shoulder height and the boy joins his right hand with the girl's right hand and his left hand with the girl's left hand.

Creative Dance Activities

26

The Body

Stimuli

Sound Accompaniment

CREATIVITY, according to Jack Wiener (1969), cannot exist in the abstract, and neither can creative teaching. As teachers, we want children to be able to feel and to express their ideas through movement; we want them to be creative. However, no child can be imaginative or creative without a vocabulary of words, concepts, and ideas. Nor can a child express creative movement without a vocabulary of movement skills and an awareness of various forms of internal and external stimuli.

Our task in enhancing the child's creative process is twofold. First, we should recognize the level of cognitive and motor development of the age group we are teaching. Primary children, for example, have a limited vocabulary and capacity for abstract thinking. Their world of ideas is still very small; they normally demonstrate "being like" or "imitation of" in their first attempts at creative movements. But boys and girls in the intermediate grades have acquired a rich vocabulary, as well as an interest in exploring abstract ideas and the capacity to do it. Their movement vocabulary has also expanded far beyond the basic locomotor skills to personal reservoirs of numerous complex movement skills and motor patterns.

Our second task in enhancing the creative process is to develop an approach or format that can be used to encourage each child to develop his own creative ideas and to express them through movement. This chapter will provide such an approach. It will begin with a discussion of the movements of the body using Laban's movement classification system. Lesson plans are provided to illustrate how creative movements can be built from movements of the body, the efforts or qualities of movement, and the space and directional patterns of each dance movement. The other two sections of this chapter will discuss the use of various types of stimuli and sound accompaniment, which are necessary to the development of creativity.

The elements of creative dance can be grouped under three broad headings. Perhaps the most important is the body itself—what it is capable of doing, how it moves, and its relationship to other objects. These are the body's essential tools for creative movement. They are similar to the manipulative skills of a painter, the vocabulary of a poet, and the vocal control of an opera singer. The second element of creative dance is the individual's reaction to a stimulus. The stimulus, may be a feeling or it may be something from the external world that is communicated to the child's mind through his senses. It may be a picture, word, or story that stimulates the thinking process to produce movement. Sound is a stimulus; however, in a broader sense, it becomes the third element of creative dance. When a child who has a movement vocabulary is stimulated by a poem or picture to express his reaction, sound, in the form of voice, percussion, or other musical accompaniment, enhances the creative process.

The Body

Movements of the body have been classified in dance in a variety of ways. Folk dance, for example, has a series of stylized or standardized steps, such as the schottische, polka, and waltz step. Similarly, ballet and modern dance have unique vocabularies. Only Laban's system of analyzing all movement is comprehensive enough to cover all body movements. His movement classification was used in previous chapters and is used in this chapter as a basic system to describe the movements of the body and as a format for teaching creative dance.

Figure 26.1

All movements performed by a child can be analyzed according to the specific body parts that are involved (body movements or awareness), the effort of the movement (qualities), the space (space awareness) within which a movement takes place, and the relationship of the body to equipment or other performers. This is illustrated in the accompanying table. In gymnastics, as described in Chapters 21, 22, and 23, all movements may be taught according to this classification system. However, since the emphasis in gymnastics is primarily directed toward the efficiency and utility of movement, descriptive terminology such as "swirl," "hasty," and "retreating" are not used. In creative dance the emphasis of movement is directed toward self-expression that is demonstrated through movement. This necessitates the use of additional words that can explain and stimulate creative movements. Several new descriptive words are included under each of the three broad headings that can be used within each creative dance lesson to clarify and stimulate creative movements. The sample lessons provided in the following pages will provide a basic format for teaching creative dance as well as illustrating how these new descriptive words can be used.

Table 26-1

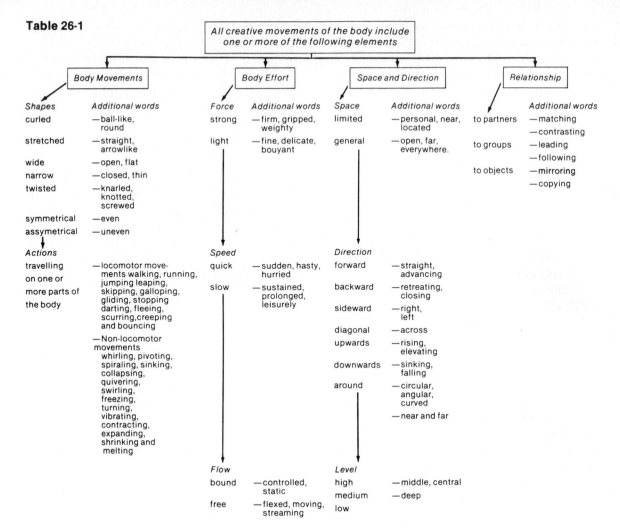

All creative movements of the body include one or more of the following elements

Body Movements		Body Effort		Space and Direction		Relationship	
Shapes	*Additional words*	*Force*	*Additional words*	*Space*	*Additional words*	to partners	*Additional words*
curled	—ball-like, round	strong	—firm, gripped, weighty	limited	—personal, near, located	to groups	—matching
stretched	—straight, arrowlike	light	—fine, delicate, bouyant	general	—open, far, everywhere.	to objects	—contrasting
wide	—open, flat						—leading
narrow	—closed, thin						—following
twisted	—knarled, knotted, screwed						—mirroring
							—copying
symmetrical	—even						
assymetrical	—uneven						
Actions		*Speed*		*Direction*			
travelling	—locomotor movements walking, running, jumping leaping, skipping, galloping, gliding, stopping darting, fleeing, scurring,creeping and bouncing	quick	—sudden, hasty, hurried	forward	—straight, advancing		
on one or more parts of the body		slow	—sustained, prolonged, leisurely	backward	—retreating, closing		
				sideward	—right, left		
				diagonal	—across		
	—Non-locomotor movements whirling, pivoting, spiraling, sinking, collapsing, quivering, swirling, freezing, turning, vibrating, contracting, expanding, shrinking and melting			upwards	—rising, elevating		
				downwards	—sinking, falling		
				around	—circular, angular, curved		
					—near and far		
		Flow		*Level*			
		bound	—controlled, static	high	—middle, central		
		free	—flexed, moving, streaming	medium	—deep		
				low			

Lesson Plans

A lesson plan should be considered a flexible guideline that can be modified to meet many factors. The experienced classroom teacher with an extensive background in teaching creative dance can structure an environment that will produce maximum creative responses from each child. This is a rare talent not possessed by many teachers. Consequently, some basic lesson structure should be followed when beginning to teach creative dance using Laban's basic elements; a suggested format follows.

Suggested Lesson Structure

Main Emphasis: One aspect of the main elements of movement—body movements, effort, space, or relationships—should be chosen as the *main theme* of the lesson. In addition to the main theme, one or more subsidiary themes should be selected from the other three elements.

Part One—Introductory Activity: During this portion of the lesson stress vigorous body activity that relates to the main theme or the subthemes. This part of the lesson is identical to the lesson format suggested in Chapters 21, 22, and 23.

Part Two—Theme Development: This part of the lesson should be devoted to developing the main theme by stimulating the child to explore, discover, and select movements relating to it.

Part Three—Final Activity: In this part of the lesson the child or group of children should develop a sequence of movements from the previous part of the lesson. The sequence may stand alone or develop into a creative dance through the addition of music. The central theme should be emphasized and the sub-theme should play a lesser role.

A teacher cannot anticipate the success of any creative dance lesson. If the class has not had experience in this type of activity and if the classroom teacher is also trying this type of lesson for the first time, each lesson at first will appear to be isolated. Gradually, however, as children build a repertoire of movements and learn to think and move in creative patterns, each lesson will appear to be too short. The teacher, too, will develop greater powers of observation and more effective uses of her voice, percussion instruments, and all other forms of musical accompaniment. The consequence will likely be a central theme beginning with the first lesson and carried on in the second, third, or more lessons. When this occurs, the format will emphasize the latter portion of the lesson to allow the children maximum freedom to create, refine, and express their feelings and ideas through their own creative dance movements.

The sample lessons that follow should be seen as a starting point, not something that should be duplicated each lesson.

Sample Primary Lesson Plan

Perhaps one of the most difficult tasks for a primary teacher is to decide upon the appropriate main themes. There is no standard format for introducing these themes. It depends upon the capabilities of the teacher and the potential creative abilities of her class. The length of time within a lesson or for several lessons that a theme or sub-theme is stressed will depend upon the success and interest of the class. The following sample lesson may assist the teacher in planning her first few lessons. There are several suggested themes at the end that are appropriate for primary children.

Grades: 1-2
Main Theme: Locomotor skills—running and walking
Sub-theme: Change of direction

Part One: Introductory Activity
Music: Bowmar, B1 507 "Rhythm is Fun," Side 1

Begin with the children sitting down near the record player. Explain that when you play the music, they should try to run with "light feet" in any direction and without touching anyone. When the music stops, they should stop and listen to you. Use the expression "Off you go" or a similar informal phrase.

Observe: Are they moving in different directions or simply in a circular fashion around the gymnasium? Are they moving lightly or very heavily on their feet? Are they bumping into each other?

After a few minutes stop the music and say in a normal conversation voice, "Some moved very softly and used all the space. Let's try it again and this time see if you can run lightly and move into all the open spaces. Off you go." Allow time for the children to practice, then stop the music and gather them around the record player.

Part Two: Theme Development
Explain to the children that this time, without music, they are to see if they can walk very lightly and change directions as they walk. "Off you go." As they are walking in various directions, stimulate awareness and change of direction by saying, "Can you move sideways, backward, forward, and turn?"

Observe: Lightness on feet, change of direction, patterns being established.

After a few moments stop the children and then pose the following challenges: "See if you can make up your own 'movement sentence' or sequence which has three different ways of moving—a walk or run and a turn. You may put these movements together any way you like. Ready, away you go."

26

Observe: Different patterns.

Help any child who does not understand.

Wait a few moments, then stop the children and tell them to watch one or two children demonstrate their sequences. Select one or two for demonstration, emphasizing variety, and praise the child or children who have performed for the class. Now tell the whole class to practice the sequences again, but this time to music. Play music and observe.

Part Three: Final Activity
Arrange children in partners. Have each child teach the other his sequence. See if they can perform it together, side by side. If the children are successful in working together, ask them to make up a new sequence they can do side by side or with one following the other. Allow them a few minutes to plan and practice; then, without telling them, simply turn on the music and observe.

Before the end of the lesson, praise the class and point out the main aspects of the lesson—lightness, change of direction, and sequence. This will help the children build a movement vocabulary.

Suggested Themes
The following themes are appropriate for primary children. It should be recognized that the same theme can be presented to grades one to three by varying the words. More sophisticated movements and a more sustained interest in the theme are expected as the children progress through grades two and three.

1. Traveling: All types of locomotor movements —walking, running, and jumping. Begin to use descriptive words such as "swirling," "creeping," and "bouncing."
2. Shapes: Total body shapes—curled, stretched, and twisted. Use the descriptive words shown in the table.
3. Parts of body: Develop themes in which parts of the body are used as a dance form—the hands (clapping, following, shaping), feet (moving, stamping, lightness, and patterns of movement).
4. Effort: Introduce the main differences between strong and light, quick and slow, and static or free-flowing movements.

5. Space: Stress use of all space, moving with awareness of self and others. Simple directions—right and left, forward and backward.
6. Relationships: All creative dance should show a relationship of the individual to others or to objects. Begin with relationships of the individual to the whole group, then to another individual, and then from group to group.

Sample Intermediate Lesson Plan

There are several fundamental considerations when introducing creative dance activities to intermediate children. The vast majority of children in these grades have not been exposed to creative dance. Consequently, they are usually inhibited and negative toward this type of activity. However, on the positive side, their vocabulary is extensive. They know the meaning of and shades of difference between such words as "delicate," "fluent," and "angular." And they can concentrate longer on a subject. Finally, their ability to produce shapes, sequences, and group dances is far beyond that of primary children. These factors indicate that the initial creative dance lessons for "beginners" should start with structure and gradually move to more indirect forms as the children demonstrate their ability and, perhaps, their interest in pursuing more creative challenges.

The following lesson plan is designed for intermediate children with limited experience in creative dance. Additional lesson themes are provided at the conclusion of the lesson.

Grades: 4-5
Main Theme: Body actions—running and body shapes
Sub-theme: Effort—quick and slow and strong and light

Part One: Introductory Activity
Music: Drum

Start by asking the class to find a space anywhere on the floor and sit down. Stress good scatter formation. When they are seated, tell them that when you beat the drum, they are to run quickly about the room. When the drum stops, they should stop and listen for the next challenge. Without telling the children what to do simply say, "Let's repeat." Then begin to vary the speed of your drumbeats and the length of the phrases.

Observe: Are they capable of moving about the room without collisions? Can they vary their speed according to the variations in speed and phrases?

Repeat the running challenge. However, when the drum stops, ask them to assume a very low position. Repeat and each time require a new position, such as high, stretched, V-shaped, twisted, and so on. Repeat the running challenge, but ask them to jump in the air as high as they can at any time while the drum is beating. Tell them to touch the floor with the fingertips of both hands when they land. This ensures good control on landing.

Observe: Height of jumps and control on landing. Notice if any child naturally performs a different type of movement while in the air (twisted, curled, or wide shape).

Following this, have the children find a new space on the floor, sit down, and wait for the next part of the lesson.

Part Two: Theme Development
Without drum: Ask the class to get into low ball-shape positions. When you give the signal, they begin to rise slowly, ending in some form of stretched position, pointing upward, backward, or sideward. Repeat, but this time rise as fast as possible.

With drum: Tell them to rise toward any shape they desire while you beat the drum with a slow, even beat. When you change the beat to a faster tempo, they must begin collapsing to their standing position. Repeat several times.

With drum: Have children rise, turning in a spiral-like fashion as you beat a slow, steady pulse.

Observe and comment: Look for good movements and select one or two children to demonstrate. There may be shyness initially, particularly if the children are experiencing this type of dance lesson for the first time.

Without drum: Repeat similar movements; however, this time ask children to begin in the original position and lift a heavy object in an upward and spiral-like fashion as high as possible. Stress slowness and the strength or force that must be exerted.

Part Three: Final Activity
Up to this point all movements have been performed as an answer to one or more challenges and with or without the use of a drum. No attempt has been made to build up a sequence of movements involving various elements, or with a partner or group. The central theme was taken from body actions emphasizing running and body shapes, with sub-themes emphasizing strong, light, quick, and slow movements.

Without drum: Review the elements you have stressed in the lesson, pointing out running, leaping, shapes, quick-slow, and strong-light. Ask the children to develop a series of movements that includes (1) a run, (2) a twisted shape, and (3) quick and slow. By providing the initial structure, each child, regardless of his inhibitions or "free spirit," has something in common with the class to explore. Allow time to practice.

Observe: While the class is practicing, see how many are working out a sequence with the elements suggested. If the challenge is too difficult, inject more verbal direction, such as, "All right, let's all begin with a run, then a leap, and land on four parts of the body. . . . See if you can continue building your sequence from here."

After the children have had time to practice, have them find a partner to demonstrate their sequences. Allow them time to share their sequences, then suggest they work together and develop a new matching sequence. Indicate they may include and arrange their movements as they see fit.

General Comment
If the class seems to be at ease and enjoying the lesson, have one or two partners demonstrate to the class. Also, experiment with other musical accompaniments such as a popular song or other available records.

Depending upon the class's reaction, plus your own background, plan the next lesson to include a brief review of this lesson and then go on to more challenging questions, always including some form of partner activity. Gradually move toward sequences and dances performed by small groups of three, four, or five children.

Suggested Themes:
Several themes suggested for primary children may also be appropriate for intermediate children. In addition, the following themes are appropriate for grades four through six:

1. Traveling: Combining all forms of locomotor movements, with stress on control, change of pace, direction, and movements.
2. Body actions: Use of individual parts as well as the whole body in leading, matching, contrasting, showing relationships in abstract and concrete ways.
3. Effort: Stress the combination of force, speed, and flow as well as the shades of difference between strong and light or quick and slow.

Stimuli

The previous section provided one way to approach the teaching of creative dance. It would be possible to develop an imaginative creative dance program using Laban's basic elements of body movements, body effort, space, and relationships. These aspects of movement are the paints of the painter or the notes of the musician. How body movements are joined together by the individual, partners, or groups should result both from the teacher's guidance and the children's creativity. Creative movements can be further enhanced by the effective use of a wide variety of meaningful stimuli, such as objects, stories, and paintings. Whatever external stimulus a teacher uses should be within the bounds of the children's understanding and potentially rich in numerous forms of expression. The examples in the chart have proved to be appropriate to elementary school children. The sample lesson also will illustrate how a teacher can approach the class and build several creative dance lessons from one central idea.

| | Grade Level | | | | | | |
Stimuli	K	1	2	3	4	5	6
Balloons	X	X	X				
Animals	X	X	X	X	X		
Pictures	X	X	X	X			
Witches	X	X	X	X			
Weather (snow, wind, etc.)	X	X	X	X	X	X	X
Trees and plants	X	X	X	X	X	X	X
Stories and poems	X	X	X	X	X	X	X
Journeys	X	X	X	X	X	X	X
Marionettes	X	X	X	X	X	X	X
Mechanical objects	X	X	X	X	X	X	X
Rubber bands	X	X	X	X	X	X	X
Clay	X	X	X	X	X	X	X
Wire	X	X	X	X	X	X	X
Sports	X	X	X	X	X	X	X

Figure 26.2

Sample Lesson—Primary

This lesson is written for grades two or three. Its purpose is to stimulate light and heavy movements, with emphasis on the quality rather than the direction of the response. A short discussion should precede this lesson to familiarize children with new words and concepts of clouds as part of nature. This can be done through class discussion or stories and poems about clouds.

Lesson: Clouds and nature
Basic Theme: Interpretive movements
Grade: 2-3
Formation: Multiple (scattered, line, and circle)

Suggested Teaching Procedure

A. Movement introduction:

Arrange children in scattered formation, seated on the floor. The following questions and discussion will provide the stimulus for the interpretive movements.

1. Think of coming to school on a nice warm day when the sky is filled with pretty white clouds. What do the clouds look like?
2. If you could touch a cloud, what do you think it would feel like?
3. If you were a big cloud, what would you do on a nice warm day?

B. Interpretive movements:

1. Let's all move about the room as if we were clouds in the sky.
2. To indicate light movements: Can you run very lightly on the tips of your toes?
3. What else is soft and light and makes you feel like moving as you did?

Introduce musical accompaniment:

tambourine, triangle, or song bells.

4. Can you move your arms and your whole body very softly and lightly while I play the triangle? (Vary the speed but always keep the intensity very soft.)
5. Seated in scattered formation: We have talked about light and soft things and moved so we felt that way. What is very different from softness?
6. What can you think of that is just the opposite of soft, fluffy clouds?
7. Move around the room again, but this time we will be heavy and hard. (Use drum or blocks for accompaniment.)

Possible Responses from Children

A. Movement introduction:

The responses you get to your questions will be tangible objects that are familiar to this age group.

1. Mashed potatoes, cotton candy, or cotton balls.
2. Soft and fluffy like whipped cream or daddy's shaving cream.
3. Sleep, fly around and look at everyone, ride with the wind.

B. Interpretive movement:

1. Running, romping, moving on tiptoes or heavy pronounced steps.
2. Running lightly, swinging or swaying, and so on.
3. Kitten, bunny, feathers.
4. Children may remain in the same spot or shift about the room with light, expressive movements.
5. Stones, big and fat, heavy, rough.
6. Giants, elephants, sledge hammer.
7. Heavy pounding with feet and clenched fists, dragging arms to imitate elephant walk.

Additional Suggestions

Reorganize the class into partners or small groups and pose questions that require a group effort to express the movement. For example, ask partners to interpret two thunderclouds moving toward each other. Continue the lesson, emphasizing soft and heavy movements. For the conclusion, consider discussing the movements or playing a record and allowing the children to interpret the music.

Additional Resource Material

The sample lesson will assist in developing a basic approach to teaching creative or interpretive movements. Numerous other methods and techniques can be used with equal success. Three charts containing possible animal, mechanical, and nature movements are provided as an additional source of creative movements.

The suggested movements can be performed with the musical accompaniment listed. The suggested records and instrumental accompaniments should be considered as illustrative samples. Each teacher, therefore, should develop a similar resource chart and list records that have been successful in creating various types of creative responses.

26

Animal Movements

Animal	Suggested Types of Movement	Musical Accompaniment	
		Record	Instrument
Bear	Heavy, slow walk, running, climbing	Childhood Rhy. Series 5, Re. 501, Bears Bowmar, Rhythm Time #1 and 2	Drum (slow) Wood blocks Claves
Camel	Slow, bouncy walk, carrying object	Childhood Rhy. Series 1, Re. 103, Camels Bowmar, Rhythm Time #1 and 2	Drum (uneven)
Elephant	Heavy, slow, rocking walk, lifting object	Childhood Rhy. Series 1, Re. 103, Elephants Bowmar, Rhythm Time #1 and 2	Drum (slow, heavy)
Frog	Hopping, jumping, bouncing, bending	Childhood Rhy. Series 5, Re. 501, Frogs	Drum (short, quick)
Worm	Curling, bending, stretching		Scraper
Monkey	Fast crawl, bent-knee jumps		Wood block
Rabbit	Jumping, bending, running, sniffing	RCA Rhy. Ser. Vol. 2, 45-5007 Harry and Light of Heart	Wood block
Soldier	Crawling, running, marching	RCA Rhy. Ser. Vol. 2, 45-5007 Soldiers March	Drum Drum rolls
Tall man– short man	Bending and stretching, bent-knee walk, tiptoe walk	Childhood Rhy. Series 2, Re. 201, Fast and Slow	Drum (fast and light, heavy and slow)
Cat	Cautious walking, running, playing, stretching	Cap. 2 Pussy Cat Parade	Wood block Sticks
Chicken	Choppy, quick walk, scratching, pecking, flapping arms	Rhythm Time ES—102	Wood block (short, quick)
Raggedy Andy	Loose, floppy walk, swinging, bending	RCA, Dance a Story LE 106	Drum Tambourine
Giant	Slow, heavy walk and run, exaggerated movements	Childhood Rhy. Series 1, Re. 106, Giants	Drum (heavy and slow) Cymbal
Horse	Galloping, prancing (knees high), walking, carrying rider	Childhood Rhy. Series 1 Re. 102, Horse	Wood block
Butterflies	Light, sustained movements, Use of arms, soft runs and skips	RCA Rhy. Ser. Vol. 2, 45-5005 Waltz	Gong Cymbal

Mechanical Movements

Mechanical Objects	Suggested Types of Movement	Musical Accompaniment	
		Record	*Instrument*
Bulldozer	Pushing, bending, walking, show effort	Rhythm Productions, Adventures in Rhythm Vol. 1 Young People's Records, 10014	Drum Scrapers
Dump truck	Bending and stretching, lifting, locomotion, show effort	Childhood Rhy. Series 2, Re. 201, Up and Down	Drum
Lumber loader	Bending and stretching, lifting, slow and sustained, show effort	Childhood Rhy. Series 1, Re. 104, Elevators	Drum
Washing machine	Twisting, rolling, bouncing	RCA Rhy. Ser. Vol. 2, 45-5004 March from Nut.	Scraper Drum
Ditchdigger	Bend and stretch, push and lift, show effort	Phoebe James Productions, Elementary Rhythms AED 6	Drum
Lawn sprinkler	Twisting, turning, bending, stretching	Childhood Rhy. Series 2, Re. 201, Round and Round	Shakers Maracas
Top	Twisting, turning, running, skipping, walking, falling	Childhood Rhy. Series 1, Re. 104, Top	Scraper Cymbal Gong
Clocks	Locomotion (percussive), swing and sway (stiff)	RCA Rhy. Ser. Vol. 3, Clock	Wood block
Percolator	Rising and falling, jiggling and bobbing (loose and floppy)	Phoebe James Productions, Elementary Rhythms AED 6	Wood block (accelerating beat)
Pop-up toaster	Rising and falling, bending and stretching, hopping, jumping	Childhood Rhy. Series 2, Re. 205, Jumping Jacks	Wood block Drum
Airplanes	Rising and falling, sustained arm movements with running	Childhood Rhy. Series 1, Re. 104, Airplanes	Drum (vibratory beats)
Typewriter	Walking, hopping, jumping, (short, quick) bending, stretching	Phoebe James Productions, Elementary Rhythms AED 6	Wood block Triangle Bell

26

Nature Movements

Object of Nature	Suggested Types of Movement	Musical Accompaniment	
		Record	*Instrument*
Wind	Use of arms, turning and smooth run, bending and stretching while running	Let's Play Kagortman Ser. 2 P.J.	Drum Tambourine
Rain	Rising and falling, bending and stretching, shaking	Garden Varieties AED 4	Drum Maracas
Flowers	Bending and stretching, swinging and swaying	Garden Varieties AED 4	Drum Tambourine
Bees	Swinging and swaying, whipping and slashing with arms and trunk	Garden Varieties AED 4	Drum Tambourine
Sun	Rising and falling, bending and stretching, big and small movements	Garden Varieties AED 4	Gong Cymbal
Clouds	Sustained, smooth movements, tiptoe walks and runs, swinging and swaying	Rhythm Time 104	Cymbal Drum
Shadows	Darting walks and runs, bending and stretching, striking and dodging	Rhythm Time 104	Drum Wood block
Moon	Rising and falling, bending and stretching, sustained locomotion	Rhythm Time 104	Drum
Waves	Rising and falling, skipping, swinging and swaying, dynamic falls	RCA Rhy. Ser. RCA, Dance a Story, L 108 Vol. 2, 45-5006	Drum (loud and soft) Cymbal
Fire	Striking and dodging, jumping, turning, hopping, stretching	Phoebe James Productions, Elementary Rhythms AED 11	Drum (first slow, loud and soft)
Smoke	Rising, turning, swinging, swaying, running, skipping, stretching	Phoebe James Productions, Elementary Rhythms, AED 5	Cymbal Tambourine

Sound Accompaniment

The value of any form of sound accompaniment to a creative movement is judged on how it can further stimulate and enhance a child's imagination and creative movements. Proper selection and application of sound accompaniment is critical to the success of a creative dance program. Some of the more important considerations relating to the teacher's voice, percussion instruments, and other forms of recorded music follow.

Teacher's Voice

All teachers are aware of the importance of their voices in the classroom, the activity room, and the gymnasium. In creative dance, however, the manner and tone of a teacher's speaking voice can become an important stimulus in evoking creative movements. Simply speaking softly to children can create slower and lighter movements. Similarly, speaking sharply in a loud voice or drawing out the words will provide sufficient stimulus for another type of movement response. When a teacher can add other characteristics to her voice such as hissing, clicking, or humming sounds, the mood and action of the dance can be directed in a variety of ways. And the sounds that children make can also provide an equally important stimulus. The reservoir of sounds that the young performer makes should be exploited to the fullest.

Percussion Instruments

There is wide variety of percussion instruments that are most useful in a creative dance program. Instruments such as the drum, tambourine, and cymbals are ideal when teaching children to move in time to the beat and tempo of a musical accompaniment. Perhaps the drum is the most useful to the teacher in the initial stages of teaching creative dance; however, the following percussion instruments are also valuable:

1. Banjo drums
2. Improvised drums—large and small containers such as coffee tins and plastic containers with plastic or cloth covers
3. Tambourine
4. Wood blocks—solid or hollow
5. Rhythm sticks—varying in size from ½-inch by 6 inches to ½-inch by 12 inches
6. Castanets
7. Coconut shells
8. Cymbals
9. Triangle
10. Bells—assorted sizes, individual and on a strip of cloth
11. Shakers—may be made with gravel, beans, or sand

Figure 26.3

Recorded Music

The use of recorded music in any creative dance program needs little elaboration. What a teacher and class select will depend upon the availability of records or tapes. It is suggested that teachers write to the record companies listed in Appendix A for catalogues and attempt to build up a school record library. In addition, the general availability of tape recorders suggests another inexpensive and flexible way of adding musical accompaniment to the dance program. If tape recorders are used, a format should be established for recording taped music and for classifying and storing school tapes.

Related Program Activities

The three chapters in Part VII provide information relating to several important aspects of the elementary school physical education program. Chapter 27 includes a wide variety of game, dance, and gymnastic activities that can be taught within the limitations of the typical classroom. This chapter has been included to meet the many requests from classroom teachers for help in planning activities within the classroom setting. Such requests are based upon the simple fact that many classes are assigned only one or two periods a week in the gymnasium. The activities included in this chapter will not provide a comprehensive program for any particular class, but they will help develop children's physical fitness and motor skills.

Chapter 28 discusses various types of exceptional children and provides suggestions for dealing with each handicap. The last chapter describes how physical education can be correlated in exciting and meaningful ways with other subjects in the elementary school curriculum.

Physical Education Activities for the Classroom

27

Teaching Procedures

Classroom Games

Physical-Fitness Activities

Yoga Activities

Gymnastic and Movement Skills

Rhythmic and Dance Activities

One of the most common complaints of classroom teachers is the lack of time that can be spent in the gymnasium. In many schools, some classes are assigned only one period a week in the gymnasium. This, of course, is totally inadequate for the physical needs of young children. Inclement weather and the lack of outside playing areas may also leave the cafeteria or the classroom as the only available space for physical activity.

The information in this chapter illustrates how many of the activities described in previous chapters can be taught in the regular classroom. A few additional activities that are particularly adaptable to the classroom are also included. (See film "Classroom Physical Education," Appendix A.)

Teaching Procedures

With minor adjustments and the establishment of a few basic rules and safety procedures, the classroom can be used for many physical activities. Whenever a large unobstructed space is required for a physical activity, move the desks and chairs in a safe, quiet, and efficient manner. Designating teams—by rows or any other type of classroom grouping—then creating a contest to see which group finishes first greatly speeds up this procedure.

Classrooms vary, of course, in the amount of free space available, type of furniture, and acceptable noise levels. The following suggestions, however, particularly those relating to safety and noise, should be carefully considered before introducing any physical activity to the classroom.

a. "Get ready to move your desks." b. "Go." c. "Good—it took just 34 seconds this time!"

Figure 27.1

Participation

Provide opportunities for every member of the class to participate in the physical activity. The game activities suggested in the next section present the greatest problem. Break the class into as many separate playing groups as possible—three groups, rather than one, playing charades—or modify the game to increase individual and total class participation.

Safety

It is essential to remove pencils and other materials from the tops of desks and to keep children away from sharp corners and edges. Other safety procedures, such as permitting running only around alternate rows and only when the noise does not seriously disturb adjacent classrooms, must be translated into simple and clearly understood rules.

Noise

Although virtually every classroom differs with respect to acceptable noise levels, a few basic rules can help keep the noise problem under

Figure 27.2 "Clear your desk!"

control. This applies to the noise within the classroom itself as well as the sound that penetrates the walls and ventilation system to other classrooms. In games and contests, modify verbal comments and require hand clapping instead of team or class yells. A lower volume may be called for in dance activities.

Figure 27.3

Classroom Games

Classroom games or what are commonly known as "rainy day activities" are simple games, relays, and contests that can be played within the classroom. Usually these games require little or no adjustment of furniture or elaborate equipment. For purposes of classification, these activities are usually designated as either active or quiet, although the dividing line between the two is rather vague. A very enthusiastic class can turn a quiet game into an active one and vice versa. For ease of selection, however, the more vigorous games will be listed under the active category and the less active under quiet activities.

When to Use Classroom Games

There is no season or time of day that should be set aside for quiet or active classroom games. Their use will depend upon such factors as the weather, the amount of time, and space available, and, perhaps most important, the "mood" of the class. There are times during the day, for example, especially after long periods of mental concentration, when a short classroom game will provide the needed relaxation for both teacher and students. The teacher should judge when and how to present a classroom game.

How to Select the Appropriate Game

In selecting classroom games, first decide on the type—active or quiet—you want to use. Second, check the columns on the right in the accompanying table to see whether the game involves guessing, tagging, imitating, manipulating, or an element of surprise. Finally, check to see whether you have the necessary equipment.

27

Active and Quiet Classroom Games

Name of Game	K	1	2	3	4	5	6	Page	Guessing	Relay	Imitation	Tag	Surprise	Small Manipulation
Active Classroom Games														
Fox and Rabbit	X	X						569					X	X
Beanbag Basket Relay	X	X	X	X				569		X				X
I'm Tall, I'm Small	X	X						569	X		X		X	X
Forty Ways to Get There	X	X	X	X	X			569			X			
Ringmaster	X	X	X	X				569			X			
Follow the Leader	X	X	X	X				569			X			
Go Go Stop	X	X	X	X				570	X				X	
Duck, Duck, Goose	X	X	X	X				570	X			X	X	
A-Tisket, A-Tasket	X	X						570				X	X	
Circle Spot	X	X	X	X	X			570				X	X	
Musical Chairs	X	X	X	X	X	X	X	570				X	X	
Seat Tag			X	X	X	X	X	571				X	X	
Beanbag Pile			X	X	X	X	X	571		X			X	
Vis-a-vis			X	X	X	X	X	571	X				X	
Simon Says		X	X	X	X	X	X	571			X		X	
Poorhouse			X	X	X	X	X	571					X	
Who's Leading			X	X	X	X	X	572					X	
Balloon Base			X	X	X	X	X	572						X
Quiet Classroom Games														
My Ship Is Loaded	X	X	X					572			X		X	
Crumple and Toss		X	X	X				572		X				X
I Saw		X	X	X				572	X		X			X
Hens and Chickens	X	X						572	X		X		X	
Ring, Bell, Ring	X	X						573	X				X	X
Who Moves?	X	X	X					573	X				X	
Hide the Thimble	X	X	X	X				573	X				X	
Crambo		X	X	X				573	X				X	
Clothespin Drop				X	X	X	X	573		X				X
Hat Race		X	X	X	X	X	X	573		X				X
Tic-Tac-Toe				X	X	X	X	574		X			X	X
Rattlesnake and Bumblebee				X	X	X	X	574	X		X		X	
Human Checkers				X	X	X	X	574		X			X	
Puzzled Words				X	X	X	X	574	X				X	X
Spell Act				X	X	X	X	574	X		X			X
Charades						X	X	574	X				X	X

Active Classroom Games

Fox and Rabbit (K-1)

Formation: Single circle or children seated
Equipment: Two beanbags
Players: Class

One beanbag, the "rabbit," is passed around the circle. A second beanbag, the "fox," is started around the circle. When the fox catches the rabbit, the game ends. Start each game with a new player.

Beanbag Basket Relay (K-3)

Formation: Lines facing baskets about six to eight feet in front of first player
Equipment: Beanbags, wastepaper baskets or hoops
Players: Class

Arrange pupils in rows facing the baskets. Draw a line across the front of the rows. On command, the first pupil attempts to throw a beanbag into the basket. One point is awarded for each basket. After shooting, each player retrieves his beanbag, returns it to the next player, and tells the teacher his score. Continue until the last player has had a turn. The team with the highest score wins.

I'm Tall, I'm Small (K-1)

Formation: Single circle with one child in the center
Equipment: None
Players: Class

One child stands in the center of the circle with his eyes closed. Circle players walk slowly around, singing

> I'm tall, I'm very small
> I'm small, I'm very tall
> Sometimes I'm tall
> Sometimes I'm small
> Guess what I am now.

As the children walk and sing "tall," "very tall," "small," or "very small," they stretch up or stoop down depending on the words. At the end of the singing, the teacher signals the circle players to assume a stretching or stooping position. The center player then guesses which position they have taken. If the center player guesses correctly, he remains in the center; if unsuccessful, a new player is selected.

Forty Ways to Get There (K-4)

Formation: Seated
Equipment: None
Players: Class

Each child is given a chance to move across the front of the room in any manner he wishes. Once a child has used a walk, hop, or other movement, no other child may use it. Any novel way of moving is acceptable.

Ringmaster (K-3)

Formation: Single circle with one child in the center
Equipment: None
Players: Class

One child is selected to be the "ringmaster" and stands in the center of the circle. The ringmaster moves about the center of the circle pretending to crack his whip and calls out the names of animals. The circle players imitate the animals. If the ringmaster calls out "All join the parade," the children may imitate any animal they wish.

Follow the Leader (K-3)

Formation: Single lines
Equipment: None
Players: Class

Arrange the class in two or three lines of ten to twelve players. The leader walks and begins to perform any kind of movement, such as hands on head, arms sideward, or leaping from one spot to another. All other players in his line must copy the movement. Anyone who fails to perform the feat goes to the back of the line.

Teaching Suggestions
Play the game in a circle with the leader standing in the center.

27

Go Go Stop (K-3)

Formation: Single line with children facing sideways
Equipment: None
Players: Class

The teacher says "Go, go, go" and all must walk straight ahead. When the teacher says "Stop," all must stop. If a child fails to stop, he must return to the starting line and begin again.

Teaching Suggestions

Use other locomotor movements, such as running, skipping, sliding, or hopping. Turn your back to the students when calling "Go, go, go," then turn around and call "Stop." This will increase the element of surprise.

Duck, Duck, Goose (K-3)

Formation: Single circle with one child standing outside the circle
Equipment: None
Players: Class

One child is selected to be "it" and stands outside the circle. "It" runs around the circle, touches one child and says "Duck," touches another and again says "Duck," and touches a third and says "Goose." The goose chases "it," who tries to run around the circle back to the goose's place before the goose can tag him. If the goose tags "it" before he gets into place, he continues to be "it." If "it" is successful, the goose becomes "it" and the game continues.

A-Tisket, A-Tasket (K-1)

Formation: Circle facing center with one child outside the circle
Equipment: Beanbag
Players: Twelve to twenty players

One player is chosen to be "it" and walks around outside the circle with a beanbag in his hand. While "it" is walking around the outside, the circle players sing

> A-Tisket, A-Tasket,
> A green and yellow basket,
> I sent a letter to my love,
> and on the way I dropped it,
> I dropped it, I dropped it,
> And on the way I dropped it.

When the circle players sing "I dropped it," "it" drops the beanbag immediately behind the circle player and begins to run around the circle. The circle player in front of the beanbag must pick it up and run after "it" and tag him before he returns to the vacant spot. If "it" makes it back before being tagged, he stays in the circle and the chaser becomes "it." If "it" is tagged before reaching the spot, he remains "it."

Circle Spot (K-4)

Formation: Circle with four feet between each player
Equipment: Beanbags
Players: Ten to twenty players

One child is chosen to be "it" and stands in the center of the circle. Circle players stand with at least four feet between them with beanbags on the floor immediately in front of them. On a signal from the teacher, everyone walks, skips, etc. around the circle of beanbags. On the second signal everyone, including "it," tries to place one foot on a beanbag. The extra child becomes "it" and takes his place in the center of the circle.

Musical Chairs (K-6)

Formation: Circle formation with two or three feet between each chair
Equipment: Chairs
Players: Class

Arrange chairs in a circle around the room. There should be one less chair than children. Use a musical accompaniment such as a record, percussion instruments, or clapping as the children march or skip around the chairs. When the music begins, all march around the chairs; when it stops, all try to sit on a chair. The player who remains standing must take a chair from the circle and sit away from the other players. The last player remaining is the winner.

Seat Tag (2-6)

Formation: Seated in rows
Equipment: None
Players: Class

Two players are selected; one is "it" and the other is the "runner." Other players remain seated. "It" begins to chase the runner, who may avoid being tagged by sitting with any player. The player with whom the runner sits immediately becomes the new runner. If the runner is tagged, he becomes "it" and the game continues.

Teaching Suggestions
For safety, stipulate that if the runner touches a desk or chair while he is running, he automatically becomes "it."

Beanbag Pile (2-6)

Formation: Sitting on the floor in rows
Equipment: One beanbag for each member
Players: Five or six in each row

Players are seated in a single line formation with beanbags placed in a pile in front of the first player in each line. On the "go" signal, the first player takes a bag and passes it to the second player. The remaining beanbags are passed back one at a time. The last player lays the first beanbag on the floor. Each succeeding bag must be placed on top of the other, with only the first beanbag touching the floor. The stack must stand without any assistance from the stacker. If the stack falls, it must be restacked. The first team to pile the bags correctly wins the relay.

Vis-a-Vis (2-6)

Formation: Scattered in partners
Equipment: None
Players: Class

One child is chosen to stand among the partners. When the teacher calls "back to back" or "face to face," the children do as directed. When the teacher calls "busy bee," everyone, including the extra child, must find a new partner. The child who fails to get a new partner becomes the extra player.

Teaching Suggestions
After the children have learned the game, allow the extra player to call the directions.

Simon Says (1-6)   4

Formation: Seated in rows, with one player in front of the class
Equipment: None
Players: Class

One player is chosen as leader and comes to the front of the class. The other players remain at their seats. The players at their seats follow the leader's action when he prefaces his instructions with "Simon says." If he says, "Simon says hands on head place," all should follow this movement. But if the leader says, "Hands on hips place," no one should move. Any player who commits an error must pay a forfeit or be dropped from the game.

Teaching Suggestions
Organized teams and count the number of errors to make it a contest.

Poorhouse (3-6)   5

Formation: Semicircle or horseshoe formation
Equipment: None
Players: Class

Players choose partners and sit in chairs placed in a horseshoe pattern. Two chairs representing the "poorhouse" are placed at the open end of the horseshoe. Each couple has a number and must keep their hands joined throughout the game. The game begins with the couple in the poorhouse calling out two numbers. The couples whose numbers are called must change places. During the changeover, the poorhouse couple attempts to reach the chairs vacated by one of the couples.

Who's Leading (2-6) S

Formation: Circle formation
Equipment: None
Players: Class

One player is chosen to be "it" and stands outside the circle with his hands over his eyes. The teacher then selects a player in the circle to be the "leader." The leader starts any motion he chooses (blinking his eyes, waving his arms over his head, etc.). "It" opens his eyes and tries to guess who the leader is. As the game progresses, the leader slyly switches to other movements and it is the task of "it" to find this person. Allow two or three guesses, then change the leader and "it."

Balloon Base (2-6) S

Formation: Desks and chairs moved back against the wall
Equipment: Balloons
Players: Class divied into two teams

A batter starts the game by hitting the balloon with his open hand into the "field." Fielders, with open-hand hitting, attempt to hit the balloon across the home baseline before the batter walks to first base and home. If the fielders catch the ball, the batter is safe. The batter is out if the balloon does not get into the air on the first try. Three outs and the teams exchange position. One point is awarded for each run.

Quiet Classroom Games

My Ship Is Loaded (K-2)

Formation: Seated in a circle
Equipment: Utility ball (nine or thirteen inches)
Players: Class

One child starts rolling a ball to another and says, "My ship is loaded with cars (or any cargo he wishes)." The player who receives the ball repeats what the first child said and adds a new item. He would say, "My ship is loaded with cars and hats," as he rolls the ball to another player. Each player in turn adds a new item. When a child fails to repeat all the "cargo," the ball is given to the player on his right, who starts a new game.

Crumple and Toss (1-3)

Formation: Lines facing baskets with front player about ten feet from the basket
Equipment: Newspapers, wastebaskets or cardboard boxes
Players: Class

Each player is given a piece of newspaper, which he must crumple with one hand. The first player attempts to throw his crumpled paper into the wastebasket. After each child takes his turn, he goes to the back of the line and the next player moves up to the line and takes a turn. The team with the most papers in the basket wins.

I Saw (1-3)

Formation: One child standing and facing others seated at desks
Equipment: None
Players: Class

The child standing is "it" and says, "On my way to school I saw . . ." and pantomimes what he saw. The child who correctly guesses what he saw becomes "it." If no one guesses correctly in five tries, "it" tells what he saw. If the class decides that his imitation was too poor, he must choose a new "it." If the class decides the imitation was a good one and they did not guess it within five tries, "it" continues for another time.

Hens and Chickens (K-1)

Formation: Seated
Equipment: None
Players: Class

One child is chosen to be the "hen" and walks to the cloakroom or hall. While the hen is out of the room, the teacher walks around the room tapping several children, who become "chickens." All the children place their heads on their desks, hiding their faces in their arms. The hen comes in and moves about the room saying "Cluck, cluck." All the children keep their heads down and the chickens answer with "Peep, peep." The hen listens and taps any child she believes is a chicken on the head. If the hen is correct, the chicken must sit up straight; if incorrect, he continues to hide his head. After the hen has selected all the chickens, she or the teacher selects a new hen.

Ring, Bell, Ring (K-1)

Formation: Seated
Equipment: Small bell
Players: Class

One child is chosen to be "it" and closes his eyes while another child hides the bell. The child with the bell holds it so that no sound is heard and runs to another part of the room. The teacher, after seeing that the child with the bell is located and ready, turns to the child with his eyes covered and tells him to call. The child, with his eyes still covered, calls "Ring, bell, ring." The child with the bell rings it a few short times. The first child must guess where the bell is. If he points in the right direction, he becomes the bell ringer. Change the "guesser" after each turn.

Who Moves? (K-2)

Formation: Line formation in front of class
Equipment: None
Players: Class

Five children are selected by the teacher to stand in front of the class. The children who are seated look at the line, then lay their heads on their arms. While the children have their heads down, the teacher changes the positions of two or three children in the line. On a signal from the teacher, the seated children look at the line in front of the class. One child is selected to arrange the line as it was in the first place.

Hide the Thimble (K-3)

Formation: None
Equipment: Small object
Players: Class

The class decides on an object to be hidden, such as an eraser or small toy. The teacher chooses one player to be the "hunter" and sends him out of the room while the class hides the object. As the hunter enters the room and approaches or moves away from the object, the class may hum or clap, loudly or softly, depending upon how close the hunter is to the object. When the hunter finds the object, he chooses another hunter.

Teaching Suggestions
Use various means of "hinting," such as raising or lowering the hands, hissing, and so on.

Crambo (1-3)

Formation: Seated
Equipment: None
Players: Class

One child is chosen to be "it." He starts game by saying, "I am thinking of something (inside or outside the room) that rhymes with rain." Other players ask, "Is it a train?" "Is it a drain?" and so on. The child who guesses correctly has the next turn.

Clothespin Drop (3-6)

Formation: Rows
Equipment: Milk bottle or container and five clothespins for each row
Players: Class

Each row represents a team. Place a milk bottle in front of each row. Players take turns standing erect and above the bottle and dropping the clothespins, one at a time, into the bottle. Each clothespin counts one point.

Hat Race (1-6)

Formation: Rows
Equipment: Ruler and Hat
Players: Class

Every other row participates. All players stand in the aisles with rulers in their right hands. The first player has a hat, which he places on his ruler. On the signal "go," he passes the hat over his right shoulder to the number two player. Number two takes the hat with his ruler and passes it over his shoulder to player number three. The last player in the row walks down the empty aisle to the front of his line. If a player drops the hat, he must pick it up with the ruler; no hands are allowed. Everyone shifts back one position and the relay continues until all players are back in their original positions.

Teaching Suggestions
Try the game sitting down.

Tic-Tac-Toe (3-6)   4

Formation: Seated in rows
Equipment: Chalk
Players: Class

Number each row and draw a tic-tac-toe diagram on the board between the two competing teams (#). Only two teams play at a time. The teacher chooses the starting team. The first player from one team makes an "X" in one of the spaces. The first player from the other team marks an "O" in one of the remaining spaces. Continue alternating until one team gets three marks in a row.

Rattlesnake and Bumblebee (3-6)

Formation: Seated at desks or tables
Equipment: Two small unlike objects
Players: Two equal teams

One player is chosen from each team and sent out of the room. While the two players are out, team captains hide the two articles (Team A hides for Team B and vice versa.) The two players return and begin looking for their articles. Members of either team "buzz" or "hiss" according to how close each player is to his object. Repeat with two new "finders." One point is awarded for the player, and his team, who finds the object first.

Human Checkers (4-6)   6

Formation: Chairs in a row
Equipment: Seven chairs
Players: Six on each team

Place seven chairs in a row. Place three girls on the three chairs at one end and three boys at the other end. The object is to move the girls to the boys' chairs and the boys to the girls' chairs in fifteen moves. Only one move can be made at a time. For example, girl number three moves to the spare chair; on the second move, boy number four jumps girl number three, who is now in the spare position, and so on. Moves are made by sliding into an open chair or "jumping" over one person. Players cannot move backward.

Puzzled Words (4-6)   4

Formation: Groups of five to eight players
Equipment: Pieces of paper
Players: Class

Organize the class into groups of five to eight children. The teacher has previously printed several words on separate pieces of paper. She has cut the words and shuffled them into piles of letters. Each group receives a pile of letters which, after reshuffling, will form a word. On a signal from the teacher, each group tries to put its word together. The first team to assemble its word wins the game.

Teaching Suggestions
After the group puts the word together, allow it to act out the word for the other children to guess.

Spell Act (3-6)   6

Formation: Two teams on opposite sides of the room
Equipment: None
Players: Class

Play this game as a regular spelling match. The letters "A" and "T" must not be spoken, but must be indicated as follows: "A," scratch right ear and raise left hand. "T," scratch left ear and raise right hand.

Charades (5-6)   6

Formation: Small groups
Equipment: None
Players: Class

Five or six groups are selected and allowed sufficient time to work out a charade. A captain is elected from each group. The word or object chosen by a group should have syllables to make it easier to act out. All dramatizations must be in pantomime. One group acts out its charade in front of the class. The captain of the group asks the class to guess the syllable or complete word. If the word has not been guessed within a certain time, the captain tells the class and the next group has its turn.

Teaching Suggestions
Ask the class to decide on a specific category from which all words must be chosen, such as books, cities, famous names, songs.

Figure 27.4a

Figure 27.4b

Physical-Fitness Activities

There are a variety of physical-fitness activities that can be adapted to the classroom with minor adjustments. Several test items within the AAH-PER or the Elementary School Physical Fitness Tests Batteries (p. 42) can be administered in the classroom. If testing can be done in the classroom, gymnasium testing periods can be substantially reduced, leaving more time for game, dance, and gymnastic activities.

Calisthenics

Simple calisthenics, with or without musical accompaniment, may be among the easiest activities to perform in the classroom. Once children appreciate the space limitations, they can do the exercises beside their desks or wherever there is space available in the classroom. Brief circuit-type activities, described on pages 46 to 48, can be designed for the classroom. The ad-

vantages are that the teacher can develop a basic circuit that does not require any mats or other equipment and that all children begin and stop after a set number of minutes. In addition, where there is a noise problem between adjacent classrooms, circuits can be performed in relative silence and without using a whistle or a loud voice to give or change directions.

Isometric Exercises

Isometric exercises are contractions of muscles involving a push, a pull, or a twist against an object that does not move. An isometric muscular contraction, such as grasping the seat of a chair and "pulling" the body upward, requires a high degree of muscular tension without moving the arms or changing the joint angle. Since these exercises require maximum effort to gain strength, it is suggested that only older elementary children do them.

This type of exercise program is very adaptable to the space and equipment limitations of the regular classroom. The exercises in figures 27.5 to 27.8 illustrate the type of exercises that can be performed while seated or near the desk. Each exercise should be performed in a "pushing" action (eight seconds) and a reverse "pulling" action (eight seconds) to gain the maximum benefit. Also, the total series should be repeated three to four times a week.

Many other exercises involving a pushing or pulling action can be designed by the teacher or the class. In addition, individual ropes tied together, wands, or the walls of the classroom can be used to perform numerous isometric exercises.

Figure 27.5 *Arms and Shoulders:* Sit with the back straight and grasp the edge of the chair. Keep the back and arms straight and pull the trunk and shoulders upward. Maintain the same body position and push the trunk and shoulders downward.

Figure 27.6 *Legs, Arms, and Abdominals:* Sit with the back straight and the hands resting on the top of the thighs. Keep the arms straight and push downward with the hands and upward with the legs.

Figure 27.7a *Neck and Arms:* Sit with the back straight and the heels of both hands resting against the forehead. Push with the hands and resist with the forehead.

Figure 27.7b Place hands behind the head and push back with the head and resist with the hands.

Figure 27.8a *Arms, Shoulders, and Back:* Stand with the legs apart and the body twisted toward the left. Join hands. Keeping the left arm bent and the right arm straight, pull with the right arm and resist with the left arm.

Figure 27.8b Reverse sides and repeat.

27

Figure 27.9 Yoga activities

Figure 27.10 Rolling skills

Yoga Activities

The yoga exercises described in Chapter 4 (pp. 58-65) can be performed in virtually any classroom. These exercises have a particular advantage in the classroom—they are performed slowly and quietly.

Elementary children from kindergarten to grade six thoroughly enjoy performing these animal-like movements. The program outlined in Chapter 4 provides a minimum number of yoga exercises for a basic program. Other exercises may be found in the references provided in Appendix A.

Gymnastic and Movement Skills

Gymnastic and movement skills include a large number of activities that can be performed in the classroom with a little planning. Activities such as individual stunts and movement skills (Chapter 21), small equipment and partner activities (Chapter 22), and a few large apparatus skills (Chapter 23) can be adapted to the limited space of the regular classroom. The following examples illustrate the types of skills and equipment that can be used in primary and intermediate classrooms.

Individual Stunts and Movement Skills

The first-grade children in figure 27.10 are practicing rolling skills. Other individual movement skills such as shapes, weight bearing, and simple sequences could also be practiced on the available floor space.

Small Equipment

The children in the fourth grade class shown in figure 27.11 are working on matching sequences using a beanbag. Other small equipment such as hoops, individual ropes, and traffic cones can also be used in the classroom with equal success.

Figure 27.11a

Figure 27.11b

Large Apparatus

The accompanying diagram illustrates how station work and a rotation system enable every child an opportunity to use a variety of small equipment and two available balance benches. Since the area is extremely crowded with equipment, the lesson emphasizes partner activities. The task for every station is to develop a matching sequence with one piece of equipment. In this case, movement is limited to the space immediately around the individual piece of equipment.

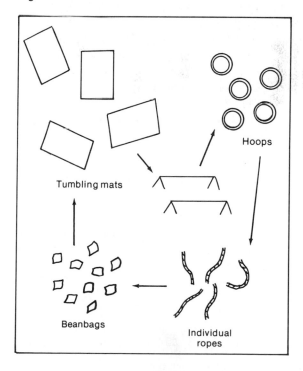

Tumbling mats

Hoops

Beanbags

Individual ropes

Figure 27.12

Figure 27.13

Rhythmic and Dance Activities

The classroom setting has many advantages when teaching rhythmics, singing games, and folk-dance activities. For older children, the familiar environment of the classroom can prove to be a steppingstone for more complex and creative movements in the gymnasium. A few examples and references to previous chapters will assist teachers in developing exciting dance and creative-movement programs for both primary and intermediate grades.

Rhythmic Activities

The rhythmic activities described in Chapter 24 can easily be performed in the classroom. It is suggested that the same progression—moving from individual to partner to group activities—be followed. Small equipment such as beanbags, individual ropes, and rhythm sticks (pp. 518-20) can also be used in the classroom with only minor adjustments. If the noise of a record player or drum is too distracting to adjacent classrooms, limit the accompaniment to light drum beats or encourage the children to move in a rhythmic pattern without musical accompaniment. In fact, the latter will produce some very interesting results.

Figure 27.14

Figure 27.15

Singing Games and Folk Dances

Young children, particularly those in kindergarten and first grade, thoroughly enjoy the singing games described on pages 521-34. The classroom provides an informal atmosphere in which to learn the words of these games and to practice the basic steps and rhythm patterns. Virtually all singing games can be performed in the space available in a regular classroom.

For older children, folk-dance steps, positions, and pathways of movements can be taught in the classroom. If students have had little exposure to folk-dance activities, individual and partner activities involving the basic steps and patterns can be performed in the classroom. This procedure normally breaks the ice for larger group dances that require the larger space of the gymnasium.

Creative Dance

What has been said about the value of an informal classroom atmosphere in teaching folk dance applies more so to creative-dance activi-

ties. Students can begin with very simple and "directed" follow-the-leader or matching movements and then gradually be introduced to more creative tasks. Gradually, more creative challenges involving sound, poetry, or other forms of accompaniment can be introduced to the program. The teacher should review the ideas presented in Chapter 26 to determine what other type of creative-dance activities could be adapted to the classroom.

Comment: Although there are many interesting and exciting physical activities that can be performed in the regular classroom, such activities are inadequate for the child's normal growth and development. It is anticipated that the reader will have the same point of view and will use the classroom only when other facilities are not available.

But there are times when the mood of the class seems to dictate a change of pace before moving on to or shifting to another subject area. A five- or ten-minute break for a quick classroom game, a set of yoga exercises, or a short rhythmic routine may make the contents of this chapter worth reading and remembering.

Exceptional Children

28

Perceptual-Motor Deficiencies

The Slow Learner

Visual and Auditory Handicaps

Obesity

Rheumatic Fever

Asthma

Epilepsy

It is estimated that approximately 12 percent of elementary school children have some kind of physical handicap, such as congenital defects, asthma, and heart disorders. Approximately 85 percent of these exceptional children attend regular schools and are usually taught physical education by classroom teachers. Coping with the special needs of the exceptional child adds a substantial burden to the already busy classroom teacher. Nevertheless, the choice has been the teacher's, as she has fully realized the importance of keeping the handicapped child in a regular classroom setting.

In physical education, as in all other subjects, it is first necessary to distinguish and understand the various types of exceptional children before planned experiences can be provided for them. A few of the more common handicaps will be discussed. Once they are understood, it is possible within the broad range of physical activities and individualized instructional techniques described in this text to provide for the needs of exceptional children.

Perceptual-Motor Deficiencies

In recent years there has been a growing awareness of the importance of perceptual-motor development upon academic achievement, particularly in such areas as reading, writing, and drawing skills. Delacato in 1959 presented a theory known as *neurologic organization* which assumes that every human being progresses sequentially through a series of motor skills. According to this investigator, children with perceptual-motor deficiencies missed specific developmental steps along this continuum.

Another theory proposed by Kephart holds that a child progresses through a sequence of learning stages (1960). His program for slow learners is based upon *levels of generalization* through which a child is taught. Since the ability to read is based upon previously acquired perceptual-motor skills such as directionality and laterality, emphasis is given to these skills for children possessing learning disabilities.

The general conclusion to be drawn from these investigators is that inadequate preschool motor development could lead to serious perceptual-motor problems. A child who does not possess these prerequisite perceptual-motor skills in turn may experience serious difficulties in learning to read, write, and perform other academic skills. Although research evidence is far from conclusive, there is merit in these programs. What is important, therefore, to the classroom teacher is that she know the basic perceptual-motor skills, how to detect serious deficiences, and, finally, how to select activities that develop perceptual-motor abilities. A teacher possessing these competencies will be able to incorporate many of the perceptual-motor skills in her regular instructional program. Children with serious perceptual-motor deficiences would then be channeled into remedial programs handled by trained specialists.

Symptoms of Perceptual-Motor Deficiencies

Perceptual-motor competency is a composite of a number of specific motor skills and movement patterns. The following characteristic symptoms are commonly observed in the primary school, particularly in kindergarten and grade one. Other characteristics such as tactile discrimination, drawing, and other fine muscle movements are not discussed in this section. The reader should refer to the suggested references in Appendix A for more detailed descriptions and classroom implications of these related perceptual-motor skills.

1. *Body image*
   a. Inability to identify and locate body parts, such as the right and left hand, knee, or elbow
   b. Inability to move parts of the body as directed by the teacher, such as "raising the right arm" or "raising the left arm and the left foot"
   c. Inability to imitate movements performed by the teacher or another performer
2. *Balance*
   a. Inability to maintain static balance, such as standing on one foot or standing with the arms folded and the eyes closed
   b. Inability to maintain balance while moving, such as walking forward or backward in a straight line
   c. Inability to maintain balance while in flight, such as a simple run, jump, and land or a jump off a low box or balance bench
3. *Spatial awareness*
   a. Inability to move parts of the body in specified directions, such as crossing the right arm over the left side of the body
   b. Inability to move the body through space, such as moving forward, backward, up, down, and around
   c. Inability to move through space without bumping into objects or other children in the general pathway of movement
4. *Hand-eye and foot-eye coordination*
   a. Inability to throw a ball into the air and catch it after one bounce
   b. Inability to perform basic locomotor skills, such as running, hopping, jumping, or galloping
   c. Inability to kick a stationary or moving ball
   d. Inability to move to rhythm, such as performing rhythmic hand or foot tapping or walking to rhythmic accompaniment

Methods of Assessing Perceptual-Motor Deficiencies

There are several perceptual-motor tests that are widely recommended for assessing perceptual-motor abilities. Since the following tests vary in the type of components measured, as well as evidence of validity, classroom teachers should consult school district specialists in this area to determine the most suitable test.

28

1. *Large Muscle Screening Instrument:* H. A. Lerch et al. *Perceptual-Motor Learning-Theory and Practice,* Palo Alto, Peek Publications, 1974, page 56. A basic screening test covering basic perceptual-motor skills. The textbook also has excellent general coverage of the subject and an extensive list of references and resources.
2. *Perceptual-Motor Rating Scale:* E. Roach and N. C. Kephart, *The Perceptual-Motor Survey,* Columbus, Ohio, C. E. Merril, 1966. The test items and general information provide sufficient materials for the teacher to assess perceptual-motor abilities in a classroom setting.
3. *Six Category Gross-Motor Test:* B. Cratty and M. Martin, *Perceptual-Motor Efficiency in Children,* Philadelphia, Lea and Febiger, 1969, page 183. A three-level general screening test with accompanying research information. This book also includes comprehensive coverage of the subject and additional test batteries.
4. *Dayton Sensory Motor Awareness Survey for Four and Five Year Olds:* Dayton, Ohio, Public Schools. A basic screening test to detect children who may need further assessment and special assistance.

Guidelines for Classroom Teachers

Perceptual-motor skills and movement patterns that appear to be prerequisites to learning such academic skills as reading and drawing apply primarily to preschool and primary children. The following general guidelines will help classroom teachers incorporate and, at times, stress various types of perceptual-motor activities in the regular instructional program:

1. A child who is suspected of possessing serious perceptual-motor deficiencies should be referred to competent specialists.
2. The choice of all physical activities should be commensurate with the child's developmental level.
3. Application of individualized instructional techniques, particularly the limitation method, is imperative in coping with individual differences in levels of ability and rate of development.
4. Every movement task that is presented should allow each child to achieve a measure of success.

5. The primary physical-education program should stress the following types of activities:
a. Balance activities—floor work, with small equipment, and on or over large apparatus
b. Locomotor skills—moving in different directions, changing speed, and moving to a rhythmic accompaniment
c. Body awareness—activities and movement challenges stressing shapes (form) and moving different parts (unilateral and bilateral movements)
d. Manipulative activities—stressing hand-eye and foot-eye coordination (ball handling skills involving throwing, catching, and kicking) and a variety of manipulative skills using beanbags, hoops, and other small equipment

Perceptual-Motor Activities

The accompanying chart provides a quick reference to the numerous perceptual-motor activities contained in this book.

Perceptual-Motor Skills	Game Activities	Gymnastic Activities	Rhythmic Activities
1. *Body Image*		Ch. 21-23	Ch. 26
2. *Balance*		Ch. 21-23	
3. *Spatial awareness*	Ch. 10-11	Ch. 21-23	Ch. 24-26
4. *Hand-eye and foot-eye coordination*	Part IV	Ch. 22	Ch. 24
5. *Locomotor movements*		Ch. 21	Ch. 24-25
6. *Rhythmic movements*			Ch. 25-26

There are several outstanding remedial programs in operation throughout the United States. The following sources provide general information relating to these programs:

1. J. Capon, *Motor-Perceptual Activities for Kindergarten and Primary Grades,* 400 Grand Street, Alameda, California, 94501.
2. Braley et al. *Daily Sensorimotor Training Activities: A Handbook for Teachers and Parents of Pre-school and Primary Children,* Educational Activities, Inc.
3. H. A. Lerch et al. *Perceptual-Motor Learning-Theory and Practice,* Palo Alto, California, 94306.

The Slow Learner

In the majority of cases, a slow learner is classified according to scores on one or more intelligence tests. Generally speaking, children who possess IQs between 70 and 90 are classified as slow learners. These children are usually placed in regular classes, so they become part of the normal problems encountered when planning and teaching physical education. With respect to this type of heterogeneous grouping, the suggestions presented by Ragan are as applicable to physical education as to any other subject (1961). These are the following:

1. Standards of achievement for slow-learning children should be set up in terms of their ability.
2. Short, frequent drill periods are essential for slow learners.
3. Materials should be divided into short, definite learning units.
4. Visual appeal should be used extensively to stimulate interest.
5. Opportunities to succeed in small undertakings.
6. Slow-learning children frequently need help in making adjustments to group living, as well as to school subjects.

Visual and Auditory Handicaps

It is estimated that approximately one in every four school children has some form of visual anomaly and that about 5 percent have some form of impaired hearing. The following visual and auditory handicaps are the most common ailments of elementary children:

1. *Nearsightedness (myopia):* This condition is the result of the anterior-posterior axis of the eye being too long, resulting in the image being focused in the front of the retina. Distant objects will appear blurred, while nearby objects are seen clearly.
2. *Farsightedness (hyperopia):* In this ailment, the anterior-posterior axis of the eyeball is too short. This causes the image to be focused behind the retina. Distant objects can be seen clearly, while nearby objects appear blurred.

3. *Astigmatism:* This condition is normally caused by an irregularity in the curve of the cornea or lens of the eye. When a child attempts to focus, the object will appear blurred.
4. *Hard of hearing:* A child with this condition has a partial sense of hearing and normally functions without a hearing aid.

General Guidelines

1. Consult with the school nurse and parents of children who have auditory or visual handicaps. The teacher's knowledge of each child's deficiency will provide a general guideline for the type of activity and degree of participation appropriate to the child.
2. Refer any child who chronically demonstrates one or more of the following symptoms to the school nurse for further examination:
   a. Excessive squinting.
   b. Constantly leaning toward or moving close for demonstrations.
   c. Inattentiveness and a general lack of interest.
   d. Extremely low level of skill. Visually handicapped generally show poor catching skill even with a large utility ball. Acoustically handicapped children demonstrate chronic improper responses, particularly in game situations
3. Too often, partially sighted and hard-of-hearing children will shy away from vigorous physical activities and thus may tend to be overweight and generally uncoordinated. Whenever possible, provide a little extra encouragement and praise when these children participate in physical activities.

Obesity

Obesity is a condition in which body weight exceeds the standard weight recommended for the individual on the basis of his age and height or frame size. Approximately 20 percent of elementary school children are obese. The primary causes are overeating and lack of vigorous daily activity. Dysfunction of the endocrine glands, which regulate the fat distribution in the body, accounts for a very small percentage of obese children.

General Guidelines

A child who is classified as being obese usually has a very low level of physical fitness, lacks coordination and speed, and reveals emotional and social-adjustment problems. The following guidelines may help the obese child reduce his body weight and help make his participation in physical activities enjoyable and meaningful. These guidelines apply to those children whose obesity is the result of overeating.

1. Contact the school nurse and parents and attempt to establish a weight-reduction program for the obese child. Frequent counseling and encouragement by the teacher can help the child stay on a recommended diet.
2. Do not require obese children to perform balance stunts or movements they are incapable of performing.
3. Use extreme care during endurance activities. Set appropriately lower standards of distance and time for these children.
4. Because of serious social and emotional implications, attempt to guide obese children into less-demanding playing positions or events. In game activities, the goalie and defense positions are less demanding than a center or forward spot. In track and field, the shot put or tug-of-war would be more appropriate than sprints or distance running.
5. Use techniques of team or group selection that do not make the obese child the last to be chosen.

Rheumatic Fever

Two-thirds of all the heart disease among children between the ages of six and twelve is the result of rheumatic fever. The after effects on the heart produce an increased susceptibility to further infections and may result in a diminished efficiency of the heart.

General Guidelines

1. The amount and type of exercise for a child who has had rheumatic fever should be prescribed by a physician.

2. The disease flourishes in the northern parts of the United States, particularly during winter and spring. Teachers should watch for early signs and possible suspicious factors, such as chronic colds, quick fatigue, and "serious" weight losses.
3. The vast majority of children who have had rheumatic fever can eventually participate in physical activities. Once the family doctor gives the child permission to participate in physical activities, the teacher should allow only moderate and brief participation during the first few weeks. As the child demonstrates his capacity to keep up without showing early signs of fatigue, gradually increase the amount and intensity of exercise.

Asthma

The cause of asthma is not known; however, it is considered to be the result of an allergic condition. Basic symptoms are labored breathing and wheezing as the child exhales.

General Guidelines

1. Children with asthmatic conditions should, within the limits of their ability, attempt to increase their level of general fitness and health. Planned developmental programs can help asthmatic children reach this goal.
2. Children with asthma should avoid vigorous and sustained types of activities.
3. Any causative agent (dust on tumbling mats or pollen from flowering trees or plants) should be avoided.

Epilepsy

Epilepsy is a disease of the nervous system which is characterized by seizures or convulsions, loss of balance, and unconsciousness. The "grand mal" produces a true convulsion, loss of balance, and unconsciousness. The attack can last from two to approximately five minutes.

General Guidelines

The successful medical control of epilepsy now permits the majority of children suffering from the disease to attend regular school and participate in most physical activities.

1. A child who suffers from severe epileptic seizures should not be permitted on large apparatus, such as climbing ropes and agility-type equipment.

2. Tolerance and understanding of an epileptic seizure is critically important to the normal growth and development of children who suffer from this disease. Each teacher should explain, within the limits of her class's understanding, the nature of the disease and what should be done when a child has a seizure. The following procedure should be carried out in a very calm, routine manner:
   a. Lay the child down, away from hard or sharp objects.
   b. Do not attempt to restrain the child's movements. The attack must be allowed to run its course.
   c. Place a soft object such as a folded handkerchief or a wrapped newspaper between the back of the teeth when the mouth opens. This prevents the child from biting his tongue or lips.
   d. Immediately after the attack, move the child to a quiet, secluded place until he has regained consciousness. If the child falls asleep, he should be left until he wakes himself.

There are other types of handicaps ranging from orthopedic anomalies to restrictive allergies. The fundamental guideline to follow is to consult first with the parents and competent medical authorities to understand the nature of the disorder. The child should participate in the physical-education program within the limits of his handicap.

Correlating Physical Education with Other Subjects

29

Arithmetic

Language Arts

Social Studies

Health and Science

Art and Music

One of the fundamental themes throughout this book has been that physical education has unique contributions to make to the general goals of elementary education. Through a broad-based program of activities and effective teaching strategies, young children progressively increase their physical attributes and learn the knowledge and skills of a variety of physical activities. And, through the medium of play, both directed and creative, a child also learns about self-control and cooperative behavior.

However, elementary school teachers fully realize that learning in one area, such as arithmetic, can be strengthened by another area, as when adding the number of points in a game played in a physical-education lesson. Contemporary education uses the terms *correlation* and *interrelation* to describe this mutual relationship between subject areas. This interpretation implies a two-way street in which each subject area has a unique place and role in the child's total education. Whenever a concept or skill in one subject area can be fortified or acquired through another subject, the relationship should be consciously planned. The following sections will illustrate the potential contributions that physical education can make to other subjects in the elementary curriculum.

Arithmetic

Classroom teachers from kindergarten to grade six have used physical activity, both in the classroom and in the gymnasium and playing field, to teach a variety of mathematical concepts. If the classroom teacher is also responsible for her own physical-education program, she can decide when the use of a physical activity might help the class or a child learn a particular mathematical concept or skill.

For example, a first-grade teacher has been teaching the concept of adding numbers. Of course, time has been spent in the classroom on number recognition, writing numbers, verbal counting, and manipulation of small objects into groupings. But during the physical-education period a game such as "Red Light" (p. 184), involving counting, or "Squirrel in the Trees" (p. 183), involving grouping into three, would fortify the concept of adding. Numerous other mathematical concepts and skills such as those that follow can be correlated with games, dance, and gymnastic activities.

1. Adding and subtracting numbers (scoring, beats in a measure)
2. Fractions (divide class in half or quarters)
3. Geometric forms (making triangles, circles, and individual shapes)
4. Calculating percentages (average yards gained, batting average)
5. Multiplication and division (divide class into four teams)
6. Conversion to metric system (change track records to metric system)
7. Constructing graphs and charts (physical-fitness profile, intramural scoreboards)

Language Arts

Language-arts in the elementary school is not a single subject. Rather, it is the basis or prerequisite for learning in all areas of education. Through language arts a child learns to communicate—to listen, speak, read, and write. We know that many of these skills are learned in a systematic way during the language-arts period. We also know that many children can learn these skills, or at least reinforce them, in other types of subject areas. The medium of play, whether it is imaginary or real, provides a rich, enjoyable, and stimulating environment in which a child can develop these communication skills.

The list that follows shows the type of language-arts skill that can be applied to a physical-education activity or experience. There are numerous advantages to the physical-education program when these skills are practiced or expressed through games, dance, or gymnasium activities. Rules and regulations are clarified, keener insights into movements involving game skills or dance patterns may develop, and a deeper appreciation of the art of movement may result as the child learns to integrate and communicate his ideas and feelings through speech, writing, and movement. Such applications include

1. listening to and giving directions for a game, dance, or movement skill
2. telling stories or interpreting a dance activity
3. writing about a physical-education experience such as "How I learned to swim" or "How I climbed to the top of the apple tree."
4. reading sports stories
5. writing new games
6. describing movement sequences in written form or in combination with a series of drawings
7. expressing poetry or verse through movement
8. describing a film, picture, or movement performed by another performer

Social Studies

The contemporary social-studies program in the elementary school is similar to language arts in many ways. It is no longer a series of individual subjects such as history, geography, or civics which emphasizes facts and events of past or present cultures. Rather, it is an integrated subject area that attempts to help each child, according to his ability, understand and appreciate the similarities and differences of social groups, of varying customs and morals, and of the values that are held by different people in our own or in other countries.

Physical education has been recognized as a rich environment for teaching and experiencing our own democratic ideals and other people's games, dances, and customs, and for simulating events and customs of past cultures. The following examples represent a vast reservoir of areas within the physical-education program that can be used to help a child appreciate the importance of the interrelationship that exists among the peoples of the world:

1. Pantomime aspects of the child's immediate environment—items in the home, farm animals, and roles such as mother, policeman, or fireman.
2. Study the background of singing games and folk dances. This would include such factors as the historical period and the customs of the people.
3. Study the origin of sports and gymnastic activities. The history of most simple games, such as Drop the Handkerchief, is interesting to children and rich in historical information. Researching the origin of basketball, wrestling, or a piece of gymnastic equipment not only provides an understanding of past cultures, but in addition illustrates how a game or event is changed to meet the different customs, climate, or other conditions of succeeding generations.
4. Write about and discuss different types of physical-education programs. Those of the United States and England or the Soviet Union will illustrate many differences in the political and social environments of the countries.
5. Discuss amateurism and professionalism, particularly in light of the past two or three Olympic games. This will bring out many important questions that youngsters must understand and solve in their lifetimes.

Health and Science

There are many close relationships between science, health, and physical education. The scientific principles of human motion described in Chapter 3 are primary examples. In that case, the laws of motion and gravity can be explained to children as they balance or perform a variety of movement skills. Active health programs that show children how to measure their heart and lung capacities and provide an understanding of the relationship between exercise, diet, and physical health can also be linked to the activities performed in the gymnasium and playing field. The following principles and concepts can be correlated with a variety of physical-education activities and experiences:

1. Understanding the laws and principles of gravity, friction, motion, and pressure as they apply to human movement
2. Understanding the principles of exercise, fatigue, and motivation
3. Understanding the effects of weather—wind, temperature, and humidity—on physical performance
4. Understanding the effects on performance and the limitations caused by obesity, smoking, and physical anomalies
5. Understanding the concepts and principles of sound, pitch, and intensity as illustrated by musical accompaniment in dance and rhythmic activities

Art and Music

Art and music can be linked to physical education in a variety of ways. All three areas are used in one way or another to communicate the child's ideas and feelings about himself or objects in his immediate environment. A teacher who operates in a self-contained classroom can capitalize on the child's interests and abilities in physical activities and relate them to a variety of art forms. Drawing pictures of his gymnastic sequence or painting a picture of a sports hero can motivate the child to draw, paint, or express his ideas in some new artistic manner. Music, too, provides similar possibilities. The following examples illustrate how art, music, and physical education can be joined in mutually interesting activities:

1. Draw a movement sequence performed in a previous gymnastic session. A game, event, or dance skill can also be drawn.

2. Study sculpture, paintings, and other art forms that depict physical movements or activities. R. T. McKenzie's statues, early Greek friezes, and Egyptian paintings are rich in form and information relating to sports, dance, and gymnastic events.

3. Design bulletin boards and gymnasium murals that illustrate events, movements, or health.

4. Design adventure or creative playgrounds requires an understanding of the needs and interests of children, knowledge of the structure and strength of materials, and creativity to draw or illustrate ideas through a variety of materials.

5. Music is an integral aspect of many dance activities in the elementary physical program. If music skills such as beats, measures, tempo, and phrasing are taught in the classroom without reference to movement skills, both the teacher and the child lose. Children can learn rhythm skills when they apply them to a movement and vice versa. The important aspect is to blend these two skill areas into one integrated learning experience.

Figure 29.1 "Design a bulletin board."

Appendixes

A
Bibliography and Audiovisual Materials

B
Inexpensive Equipment

C
Apparatus, Equipment, and Supply Companies

Bibliography and Audiovisual Materials

Appendix

The following bibliography and related audiovisual materials are organized according to general subject areas. Specific written references and films may be located under the following headings:

1. Curriculum and Instruction

2. Facilities, Apparatus, and Equipment

3. Basic Mechanics and Motor Learning

4. Physical Fitness

5. Remedial Programs

6. Games and Sports

7. Stunts, Tumbling, and Gymnastic Activities

8. Dance

9. Movement Education

1. CURRICULUM AND INSTRUCTION

Written Material

American Alliance for Health, Physical Education and Recreation. *Desirable Athletics Competition for Children of Elementary Age.* Washington, D.C.: 1968.

American Alliance for Health, Physical Education and Recreation. *Promising Practices in Elementary School Physical Education.* Washington, D.C.: 1969.

American Association of School Administrators. *Imperatives in Education.* Washington, D.C.: 1966.

Anderson, M. H.; Elliott, M. E.; and LaBerge, J. J. *Play with a Purpose.* 2nd ed. New York: Harper & Row, Publishers, 1972.

Arnold, P. J. *Education Physical Education and Personality Development.* London: Heinemann Educational Books Ltd., 1968.

Boyer, M. H. *The Teaching of Elementary School Physical Education.* New York: J. Lowell Pratt and Co., 1965.

Bruner, J. S. *Towards a Theory of Instruction.* Cambridge: Harvard University Press, Belknap Press, 1966.

Bucher, Charles A. *Administration of School Health and Physical Education Programs.* 3rd ed. St. Louis: C. V. Mosby Co., 1963.

Bucher, C. A. and Reade, E. M. *Physical Education and Health in the Elementary School.* New York: Macmillan Book Co., 1971.

Clarke, H. H. *Application of Measurement to Health and Physical Education.* 4th ed. Englewood Cliffs, New Jersey: Prentice-Hall, Inc., 1967.

Clarke, H. H., and Haar, F. B. *Physical Education for the Elementary School Classroom Teacher.* Englewood Cliffs, New Jersey: Prentice-Hall, Inc., 1964.

Corbin, C. B. *Becoming Physically Educated in the Elementary School.* 2nd ed. Philadelphia: Lea and Febiger, 1976.

Cowell, Charles B., and Hazelton, Helen W. *Curriculum Designs in Physical Education.* Englewood Cliffs, New Jersey: Prentice-Hall, Inc., 1955.

Cunningham, Luvern L. "Team Teaching: Where Do We Stand?" *Administrator's Notebook* vol. 18, no. 8 (April 1960), p. 2.

Dauer, V. P., and Pangrazi, R. P. *Dynamic Physical Education for Elementary School Children.* 5th ed. Minneapolis: Burgess Publishing Co., 1975.

Espenschade, A. "Physical Education in the Elementary Schools." *What Research Says to the Teacher,* no. 27. Washington, D.C.: Department of Classroom Teachers N.E.A., 1963.

Fabricius, H. *Physical Education for the Classroom Teacher.* 2nd ed. Dubuque, Iowa: Wm. C. Brown Company Publishers, 1971.

Fait, H. F. *Experiences in Movement: P.E. for the Elementary Child.* Philadelphia: W. B. Saunders Co., 1976.

Gage, N. L. "Theories of Teaching." In *Theories of Learning and Instruction.* 63rd Yearbook of the National Society for the Study of Education, Part I, edited by E. Hilgard. Chicago: University of Chicago Press, 1964.

Halsey, E. *Inquiry and Invention in Physical Education.* Philadelphia: Lea and Febiger, 1964.

Halsey, E., and Porter, L. *Physical Education for Children.* rev. ed. New York: Holt, Rinehart & Winston, Inc., 1967.

Humphrey, J. H. *Child Learning,* Dubuque, Iowa: Wm. C. Brown Company Publishers, 1965.

Irwin, Leslie W. *The Curriculum in Health and Physical Education.* 3rd ed. Dubuque, Iowa: Wm. C. Brown Company Publishers, 1960.

Jarvis, O. T., and Rice, M. *An Introduction to Teaching in the Elementary School.* Dubuque, Iowa: Wm. C. Brown Company Publishers, 1972.

Jarvis, O. T., and Wootton, L. R. *The Transitional Elementary School and Its Curriculum.* Dubuque, Iowa: Wm. C. Brown Company Publishers, 1966.

Joint Committee of AAHPER and the Society of State Directors for Health, Physical Education and Recreation Education. *Physical Education, An Interpretation for Superintendents, Supervisors, Principals, Directors of Physical Education, Teachers and Parents.* Washington, D.C.: AAHPER, 1951.

Kalakian, L., and Goldman, M. *Introduction to Physical Education.* Boston: Allyn and Bacon, Inc., 1976.

Kirchner, G.; Cunningham, J.; and Warrell, E. *Introduction to Movement Education.* 2nd ed. Dubuque: Wm. C. Brown Company Publishers, 1978.

Kozman, H. C.; Cassidy, R.; and Jackson, C. O. *Methods in Physical Education.* 4th ed. Dubuque, Iowa: Wm. C. Brown Company Publishers, 1967.

Lien, A. J. *Measurement and Evaluation of Learning.* Dubuque, Iowa: Wm. C. Brown Company Publishers, 1967.

MacKenzie, M. M. *Towards a New Curriculum in Physical Education.* New York: McGraw-Hill Book Co., 1969.

Metheny, E. *Movement and Meaning.* New York: McGraw-Hill Book Co., 1968.

Metzger, P. A. *Elementary School Physical Education Readings.* Dubuque, Iowa: Wm. C. Brown Company Publishers, 1972.

Miller, A. C.; Cheffer, T. F.; and V. Whitcomb. *Physical Education: Teaching Human Movement in the Elementary Schools.* rev. ed. Englewood Cliffs, New Jersey: Prentice-Hall Inc., 1974.

Moston, M. *Teaching Physical Education.* Columbus: Charles E. Merrill Publishing Co., 1966.

National Conference on Physical Education for Children of Elementary School Age. *Physical Education For Children of Elementary School Age.* Chicago: The Athletic Institute, Inc., 1951.

Rich, J. M. *Humanistic Foundations in Education.* Worthington, Ohio: Charles A. Jones Publishing Co., 1971.

Schmuck, R. A., and Schmuck, P. A. *A Humanistic Psychology of Education.* Palo Alto, Calif.: National Press Books, 1974.

Siedentop, D. *Physical Education Introductory Analysis.* 2nd ed. Dubuque, Iowa: Wm. C. Brown Company Publishers, 1976.

Shurr, E. *Movement Experiences for Children: Curriculum and Methods for Elementary School Physical Education.* 2nd ed. New York: Appleton-Century-Crofts, 1975.

Van Dalen, Deobold B.; Mitchell, Elmer D.; and Bennett, Bruce L. *A World History of Physical Education.* Englewood Cliffs, New Jersey: Prentice-Hall, Inc., 1953.

Vannier, M., and Foster, M. *Teaching Physical Education in Elementary Schools.* 4th ed. Philadelphia: W. B. Saunders Co., 1973.

Willgoose, C. E. *Evaluation of Health Education and Physical Education.* New York: McGraw-Hill Book Co., 1967.

Willgoose, C. E. *The Curriculum in Physical Education.* Englewood Cliffs, New Jersey: Prentice-Hall, Inc., 1969.

Films

Film: "All the Self There Is"
Details: 16mm, 13½ minutes, color, sound.
Distributor: AAHPER, c/o NEA Sound Studios, 1201 16th Street, N.W., Washington, D.C., 20036.
Description: This film is designed to interpret physical education to teachers, administrators, and parents. It depicts new approaches in physical education and focuses on the importance of sports and activity in developing self-concept and self-confidence.
Purchase Price: $90; rental $15.

Title: "Physical Education for Children,"
Details: 16mm, 21 minutes, color, sound.
Distributor: Canfilm Media, 2450 Victoria Park Avenue, Willowdale, Ontario, Canada. M2J4A2.
Description: "Physical Education For Children" is an interpretive film for teachers and the general public. It illustrates how the basic needs and interests of elementary school-age children are translated into a physical education program. The nature and role of intramural activities and programs for exceptional children are also covered in this film.
Purchase Price: $315.

Title: "Physical Education in Elementary Schools."
Details: 16mm, color, 20 minutes.
Distributor: Stuart Finley, 3428 Mansfield Road, Falls Church, Virginia.
Description: Illustrates physical education from kindergarten through the elementary grades.
Purchase Price: $200.

Title: "They Grow Up So Fast."
Details: 16mm, color, sound, 28 minutes.
Distributor: The Athletic Institute.
Description: Interprets physical education to the public.
Purchase Price: $135.

Title: "Profiles of Elementary Physical Education."
Details: 3 reels, 16mm, color and black and white, 32 minutes.
Distributor: Coronet Films.
Description: Stresses successful methods of teaching physical education to elementary school children.
Purchase Price: $360.

2. FACILITIES, APPARATUS, and EQUIPMENT

Written material

Aaron D., and Winawer, R. P. *Child's Play.* New York: Harper & Row, Publishers, 1965.

Aitken, M. H. *Play Environments for Children: Play, Space, Improvised Equipment and Facilities.* Bellingham, Washington: Educational Designs and Consultants, 1972.

Athletic Institute. *Planning Facilities for Athletics, Physical Education and Recreation.* Washington, D.C.: American Alliance for Health, Physical Education and Recreation, 1974.

Beckwith, J., and Hewes, J. J. *Build Your Own Playground.* Boston: Houghton Mifflin Co., 1974.

Corbin, C. B. *Inexpensive Equipment for Games, Play, and Physical Activity.* Dubuque, Iowa: Wm. C. Brown Company Publishers, 1972.

Cowan, J. C.; Torrance, G. D. and P. E. *Creativity: Its Educational Implications.* New York: John Wiley and Sons, Inc., 1967.

Daltner, R. *Design for Play.* Toronto: Van Nostrand Reinhold Co., 1969.

Gabrielsen, M. Alexander, and Caswell, Miles M. *Sports and Recreation Facilities for School and Community.* Englewood Cliffs, New Jersey: Prentice-Hall, Inc., 1958.

Hurtwood, A. *Planning for Play.* London: Jarrold and Sons Ltd., 1969.

Ledermann, A., and Trachsel, A. *Creative Playgrounds and Recreation Centers.* 2nd ed. New York: Praeger Publishers, 1968.

3. BASIC MECHANICS AND MOTOR LEARNING

Written Material

Abernathy, R., and Waltz, M. "Towards a Discipline: A First Step." *Quest,* 2 April 1964.

Arnold, P. J. *Education, Physical Education and Personality Development.* London: Heinemann Educational Books Ltd., 1968.

Barratt, M., et al. *Foundations for Movement.* 2nd ed. Dubuque, Iowa: Wm. C. Brown Company Publishers, 1968.

Brown, C., and Cassidy, R. *Theory in Physical Education.* Philadelphia: Lea and Febiger, 1963.

Bunn, J. W. *Scientific Principles of Coaching.* Englewood Cliffs, New Jersey: Prentice-Hall, Inc., 1955.

Corbin, C. B. *A Textbook on Motor Development.* Dubuque, Iowa: Wm. C. Brown Company Publishers, 1973.

Cratty, B. J. *Movement Behavior and Motor Learning.* 2nd ed. Philadelphia: Lea and Febiger, 1967.

Davis, E. C., and Wallis, E. L. *Towards Better Teaching in Physical Education.* Englewood Cliffs, New Jersey: Prentice-Hall, Inc., 1961.

Day, R. H. *Perception.* Dubuque, Iowa: Wm. C. Brown Company Publishers, 1966.

Drowatzky, J. N. *Motor Learning: Principles and Practices.* Minneapolis: Burgess Publishing Co., 1975.

Espenschade, A., and Eckhart, H. M. *Motor Development.* Columbus: C. E. Merrill Books Inc., 1967.

Gage, N. L. "Theories of Teaching." *Theories of Learning and Instruction.* 63rd Yearbook of the National Society for the Study of Education, Part I. Edited by E. Hilgard. Chicago: University of Chicago Press, 1964.

Hill, W. *Learning: A Survey of Psychological Interpretations.* San Francisco: Chandler Publishing Co., 1963.

Johnson, G. B. "Motor Learning." *Science and Exercise of Medicine and Sports.* Edited by W. R. Johnson. New York: Harper & Row, Publishers, 1960.

Kephart, N. C. *The Slow Learner in the Classroom.* Columbus: C. E. Merrill Books, Inc., 1960.

Knapp, B. *Skill in Sport.* London: Routledge and Kegan Paul, 1967.

Laban, Rudolf von, and Lawrence, F. C. *Effort.* London: Macdonald and Evans, 1947.

Mathews, Donald K.; Krause, Ronald; and Shaw, Virginia. *The Science of Physical Education for Handicapped Children.* New York: Harper & Row, Publishers, 1962.

Radler, C. H., and Kephart, N. C. *Success Through Play.* New York: Harper & Row, Publishers, 1960.

Rarick, G. L. *Physical Activity and Human Growth and Development.* New York: Academic Press, 1973.

Signer, N. C. *The Psychomotor Domain: Movement Behavior.* Philadelphia: Lea and Febiger, 1972.

Stallings, L. M. *Motor Skills Development and Learning.* Dubuque, Iowa: Wm. C. Brown Company Publishers, 1973.

Thorndike, E. L. *Principles of Teaching.* New York: A. G. Seiler Co., 1906.

Wells, K. F. *Kinesiology.* Philadelphia: W. B. Saunders Company, 1955.

Wissell, J. *Movement Fundamentals.* 2nd ed. Englewood Cliffs, New Jersey: Prentice-Hall, 1961.

4. PHYSICAL FITNESS

Written Materials

Albinson, J. G., and Andrews, G. M. *Child in Sport and Physical Activity.* Baltimore: University Park Press, 1976.

American Alliance for Health, Physical Education, and Recreation. *Youth Fitness Test Manual.* Washington, D.C.: AAHPER, 1976.

Bender, J., and Shea, E. J. *Physical Fitness: Tests and Exercises.* New York: Ronald Press, 1964.

Bureau of Health Education, Physical Education and Recreation. "California Performance Tests." Sacramento, California: California State Department of Education, 1962.

Hunsicker, P. *Physical Fitness: What Research Says to the Teacher,* no. 26. Washington, D.C.: Department of Classroom Teachers, NEA, 1963.

Kraus, Hans, and Hirschland, Ruth P. "Muscular Fitness and Health." *Journal of the American Association for Health, Physical Education and Recreation,* 24 December 1953.

Murtha, Jack. "Physical Fitness Program." Sutter County, California: Sutter County Schools, 1962.

National Conference on Fitness of Children of Elementary School Age. "Children and Fitness: A Program for Elementary Schools." Washington, D.C.: AAHPER, 1959.

"The New York State Physical Fitness Test for Boys and Girls Grades 4-12." Albany, New York: Division of Health, Physical Education and Recreation, Bureau of Physical Education, 1958.

President's Council on Youth Fitness. "Youth Physical Fitness: Suggested Elements of a School-Centered Program." Washington, D.C.: U.S. Government Printing Office, 1961.

Royal Canadian Air Force Exercise Plans for Physical Fitness. rev. U.S. ed. Pocket Books, Inc., 1962.

Sorani, Robert P. *Circuit Training.* Dubuque, Iowa: Wm. C. Brown Company Publishers, 1966.

Wallis, E. L. and Logan, G. A. *Exercise for Children.* Englewood Cliffs, New Jersey: Prentice-Hall, Inc., 1966.

Wallis, E. L., and Logan, G. A. *Figure Movement and Body Conditioning Through Exercise.* Englewood Cliffs, New Jersey: Prentice-Hall, Inc., 1964.

Films

Title: "The Time of Our Lives."
Details: 16 mm, 28 minutes, sound, color.
Distributor: Association Films.
Description: For family audiences, this film is designed to encourage interest in physical fitness and emphasize relaxation.
Purchase Price: $145. Free loan

Title: "Vigorous Physical Fitness Activities."
Details: 16 mm, 13½ minutes, color, black and white.
Distributor: President's Council on Physical Fitness, Washington, D.C.
Description: Shows how to get maximum participation in the physical activity period through proper use of time, equipment, and facilities.
Purchase Price: Color $55; black and white, $30.

Title: "Youth Physical Fitness—A Basic School Program."
Details: 16mm, 13 minutes, color, black and white.
Distributor: President's Council on Physical Fitness, Washington, D.C.
Description: Gives overview of an elementary school physical education program and illustrates techniques of physical fitness testing.
Purchase Price: Color $65; black and white, $30

Title: "Youth Physical Fitness, A Report to the Nation."
Details: 16 mm, 28 minutes, color, sound.
Distributor: Equitable Life Assurance, 1285 Avenue of Americas, New York.
Description: Demonstrates how school and community groups will benefit from a well-rounded physical education program.
Purchase Price: Free loan

Title: "Why Exercise."
Details: 16 mm, color, 14 minutes.
Distributor: Association Films, 3419 Magnolia Boulevard, Burbank, California.
Description: Demonstrates types of activities that develop strength, endurance, and flexibility.
Purchase Price: $152; rental: $54.33.

5. REMEDIAL PROGRAMS

Written Materials

AAHPER. *Approaches to Perceptual-Motor Experiences.* Washington, D.C.: AAHPER, 1970.

AAHPER. *Foundations and Practices in Perceptual-Motor Learning.* Washington, D.C.: AAHPER, 1971.

AAHPER. *Guide for Programs in Recreation and Physical Education for the Mentally Retarded.* Washington, D.C.: AAHPER, 1968.

AAHPER. *Physical Activities for the Mentally Retarded.* Washington, D.C.: AAHPER, 1968.

Adams, R. C.; Daniel, A.; and Rullmar, L. *Games, Sports and Exercise for the Physically Handicapped.* Philadelphia: Lea and Febiger, 1972.

Brasch, R. H. *Achieving Perceptual-Motor Efficiency.* Seattle: Sequin School, Inc., 1967.

Clarke, H. H., and Clarke, D. H. *Developmental and Adapted Physical Education.* Englewood Cliffs, N.J.: Prentice-Hall, Inc., 1963.

Cratty, B. J. *Motor Activity and the Education of Retardates.* Philadelphia: Lea and Febiger, 1969.

Cratty B. J., and Martin, M. M. *Perceptual-Motor Efficiency in Children.* Philadelphia: Lea and Febiger, 1969.

Delacato, C. *The Treatment and Prevention of Reading Problems.* Springfield, Illinois: Charles C. Thomas, 1959.

Fait, H. F. *Special Physical Education.* Philadelphia: W. B. Saunders Co., 1966.

Kephart, N. C. *The Slow Learner in the Classroom.* Columbus: Charles E. Merrill, 1960.

Lerch, H. A.; Becker, J. E.; Ward, B. M.; and Nelson, J. A., *Perceptual-Motor Learning Practices.* Palo Alto, California: Peak Publications, 1974.

Logan, G. A. *Adapted Physical Education.* Dubuque, Iowa: Wm. C. Brown Company Publishers, 1972.

Ragan, W. B. *Teaching America's Children.* New York: Holt, Rinehart, & Winston, Inc., 1961.

Sherrill C. *Adapted Physical Education and Recreation,* Dubuque, Iowa: Wm. C. Brown Company Publishers, 1976.

Films

Title: "If Those Were Your Children."
Details: 16 mm, sound, black and white.
Distributor: Metropolitan Life Insurance Co., 1 Madison Avenue, New York.
Description: A child study with emphasis on the detection of early signs of emotional disturbance in day-to-day behavior patterns.
Purchase Price: Free loan.

6. GAMES AND SPORTS

Written Materials

AAHPER. *How We Do It Game Book.* 3rd ed. Washington, D.C.: American Alliance for Health, Physical Education and Recreation, 1964.

American Red Cross. *Water Safety Instructor's Manual.* Washington, D.C.: American Red Cross, 1968.

Avedon, E. M., and Sutton-Smith, B. *The Study of Games.* New York: John Wiley and Sons, 1971.

Blake, O. William. *Lead-Up Games to Team Sports.* Englewood Cliffs, New Jersey: Prentice-Hall, Inc., 1964.

Boyer, M. H. *The Teaching of Elementary School Physical Education Games and Related Activities.* New York: J. Lowell Pratt & Co., 1965.

Bresnahan, G. W.; Tuttle, W. W.; and Cretzmeyer, F. *Track and Field Athletics.* St. Louis: The C. V. Mosby Co., 1960.

Campbell, W. R., and Tucker, N. M. *An Introduction to Tests and Measurements.* London: G. Bell and Sons, Ltd., 1967.

Cooke, David C. *Better Basketball for Boys.* New York: Dodd, Mead & Co., 1960.

Coquitlam Park and Recreation Department. *Coquitlam Aquatic Program 1972.* Coquitlam, British Columbia, 1972.

Council for National Cooperation in Aquatics. *Water Fun for Everyone.* New York: Associated Press, 1965.

DiClemente, Frank F. *Soccer Illustrated.* New York: A. S. Barnes & Co., Inc., 1955.

Egstrom, G. H., and Schaafsma, F. *Volleyball.* Dubuque, Iowa: Wm. C. Brown Company Publishers, 1968.

Foreman, K. E., and Husted, V. *Track and Field for Girls and Women.* 2nd ed. Dubuque, Iowa: Wm. C. Brown Company Publishers, 1971.

Gabrielsen, M.A.; Spears, B.; and Gabrielsen, B. *Aquatics Handbook.* 2nd ed. Englewood Cliffs, New Jersey: Prentice-Hall, Inc., 1968.

Gomme, A. B., *The Traditional Games of England, Scotland and Ireland.* vol. 2. New York: Dover Publications, 1964.

Hale, P., et al. *Individual Sports: A Textbook For Classroom Teachers.* Dubuque, Iowa: Wm. C. Brown Company Publishers, 1974.

ICHPER. *Book of World Wide Games and Dances.* Washington, D.C.: ICHPER, 1967.

Kneer, M.; Lipinski, D.; and Walsh, J. *How to Improve your Softball.* Chicago: The Athletic Institute, 1963.

Kneer, M. and McCord, C. L. *Softball.* Dubuque, Iowa: Wm. C. Brown Company Publishers, 1966.

Kramp, H., and Sullivan, G. *Swimming for Boys and Girls.* Chicago: Follet Publishing Co., 1966.

Lane, E. C.; Obrecht, D.; and Wienke, P. *Track and Field for Elementary School Children and Junior High Girls.* Chicago: The Athletic Institute, 1964.

Latchaw, Marjorie. *A Pocket Guide of Games and Rhythms for the Elementary School.* Englewood Cliffs, New Jersey: Prentice-Hall, Inc., 1958.

Lawrence, Helen B. and Fox, Grade I. *Basketball for Girls and Women.* New York: McGraw-Hill Book Co., 1954.

Lenel, R. M. *Games in the Primary School.* London: University of London Press Ltd., St. Paul's House, Warwick Lane, E.C. 4, 1970.

Loftus-Tottenham, T. *Your Book of Soccer.* London: Faber and Faber, Ltd., 1958.

Mauldon, E., and Redfern, H. B. *Games Teaching.* London: Macdonald and Evans Ltd., 8 John Street, W.C.I., 1969.

Meyer, Henry O. *Rainy Day Activities.* Modesto, California: Modesto City Schools, 1962.

Mitler, K., ed. *Physical Education Activities.* Dubuque, Iowa: Wm. C. Brown Company Publishers, 1966.

National Collegiate Athletic Association. *Official N.C.A.A. Soccer Guide.* New York: The National Collegiate Athletic Bureau (publishes annually) Soccer Instruction Guide, The Athletic Institute, 1961.

Nelson, R. L. *Soccer for Men.* rev. ed. Dubuque, Iowa: Wm. C. Brown Company Publishers, 1967.

Newell, Pete, and Bennington, John. *Basketball Methods.* New York: The Ronald Press Co., 1962.

Powell, J. T. *Track and Field Fundamentals for Teacher and Coach.* 3rd ed. Champaign, Illinois: Stipes Publishing Co., 1962.

Richardson, Hazel A. *Games for the Elementary School Grades.* Minneapolis: Burgess Publishing Co., 1951.

Robb, G. *Soccer.* London: Weidenfelt and Nicolson, Ltd., 1964.

Schaanning, C. *Hints on Orienteering.* London: B. J. Ward Ltd., 1965.

Smale, R.; Barlee, J.; and Scott, E. J. *Swimming . . . Do It This Way.* London: John Murray Publishers Ltd., 1967.

Stuart, Frances R. *Classroom Activities.* Washington, D.C.: AAHPER, 1963.

Turkington, D. and Kirchner, G. *Volleyball for Intermediate Grades.* Burnaby, British Columbia: Simon Fraser University, 1969.

————. *Basketball for Intermediate Grades.* Burnaby, British Columbia: Simon Fraser University, 1969.

University of the State of New York, State Education Department. *Aquatics, K-12.* Albany, New York, 1966.

Vickers, B. J., and Vincent, W. J. *Swimming.* Dubuque, Iowa: Wm. C. Brown Company Publishers, 1966.

Whiting, H.T.A. *Teaching the Persistent Non-Swimmer.* London: G. Bell and Sons, 1970.

Wiley, Robert C. *Soccer: A Syllabus for Teachers.* Eugene, Oregon: The University of Oregon Cooperative Store, 1962.

Winterbottom, Walter. *Training for Soccer.* London: William Heinemann Ltd., 1960.

Wooden, J. R. *Practical Modern Basketball.* New York: The Ronald Press Co., 1966.

Films

Title: "Teaching Games to Primary Children."
Details: 16 mm, 16 minutes, color, sound.
Distributor: Canfilm Media, 2450 Victoria Park Avenue, Willowdale, Ontario, Canada M2J4A2
Description: This film describes how to plan and organize a primary games program that will develop skills through individual, partner, and group activities. Numerous suggestions relating to class organization, lesson planning, and teaching methods are provided. The problem-solving method and creative games approach are given major emphasis.
Purchase Price: $240.

Title: "Teaching Games to Intermediate Children."
Details: 16 mm, 17 minutes, color, sound.
Distributor: Canfilm Media, 2450 Victoria Park Avenue, Willowdale, Ontario, Canada, M2J4A2.
Description: A companion film to "Teaching Games To Primary Children," it illustrates how individual partner and group activities can be used to teach games such as soccer, basketball, and softball. Numerous examples are provided to show how to apply the problem-solving method and the inventive games approach to upper elementary school children.
Purchase Price: $255.

Film: "Participation for All."
Details: 16 mm, 21 minutes, color, sound.
Distributor: Canfilm Media, 2450 Victoria Park Avenue, Willowdale, Ontario, Canada, M2J4A2.
Description: "Participation for All" is the central theme of this comprehensive film describing an elementary school intramural program for all grade levels, how to develop student leadership, and ways of modifying a variety of indoor and outdoor activities to maximize the use of all available space and equipment.
Purchase Price: $315.

Film: "Classroom Physical Education."
Details: 16 mm, 22 minutes, color, sound.
Distributor: Canfilm media, 2450 Victoria Park Avenue, Willowdale, Ontario, Canada. M2J4A2.
Description: A most useful and informative film for classroom teachers who do not have daily access to the gymnasium or playing field. It illustrates how the classroom can be effectively used to conduct fitness activities, yoga exercises, modified games, folk and creative dance, and many more exciting and challenging activities.
Purchase Price: $330.

Title: "Lifetime Sports in Education."
Details: 16 mm, sound, color, 17 minutes
Distributor: NEA, Washington, D.C.
Description: Demonstrates methods and techniques of organizing and teaching for large group instruction.
Purchase Price: $80.

Volleyball

"Volleyball for Boys," 11 minutes, Cornet Films

"Volleyball Techniques for Girls," 9 minutes, McGraw-Hill Book Co.

"Volleyball for Intermediate Grades," 26 minutes, UEVA, 221 Park Avenue South, New York, 10003 or 2450 Victoria Park Avenue, Willowdale 425, Toronto, Ontario, Canada

Touch Football

"Ball Handling in Football," 11 minutes, Encyclopaedia Britannica Films

Basketball

"Ball Handling in Basketball," 10 minutes, Encyclopaedia Britannica Films

"Basketball for Intermediate Grades," 28 minutes, UEVA, 221 Park Ave. South, New York, N.Y., 10003

"Basketball for Girls—Fundamental Techniques," 10 minutes, Cornet Films.

Soccer

"Soccer for Boys," 16 mm, sound and color, 23 minutes, UEVA or 2450 Victoria Park Avenue, Willowdale, Ontario, Canada

"Soccer for Girls," 11 minutes, Cornet Films

Softball

"Softball for Boys," 10 minutes, Cornet Films.

"Softball for Girls," 11 minutes, Cornet Films.

Track and Field

"Fundamentals in Track and Field," 26 minutes, Encyclopaedia Britannica Films.

"Track and Field for Intermediate Grades," UEVA, 221 Park Avenue South, New York, N.Y., 10003 or 2450 Victoria Park Avenue, Willowdale 425, Toronto, Ontario, Canada

"Sprinting and Hurdling: Young Athlete," 16 mm, 17 minutes, Educational Foundation for Visual Aids, 33 Queen Anne Street, London, W. 1.

"The High Jump," 16 mm, 12 minutes, Educational Foundation for Visual Aids, 33 Queen Anne Street, London, W. 1.

"Long Jump," 16 mm, 10 minutes, Rank Audio-Visual, Ltd., Woodger Road, Shepherds Bush, London, W. 12.

"Triple Jump," 16 mm, 10 minutes, Rank Audio-Visual, Ltd., Woodger Road, Shepherds Bush, London, W. 12.

"Shot Putting," 16 mm, 10 minutes, Rank Audio-Visual, Ltd., Woodger Road, Shepherds Bush, London, W. 12.

"Hold High the Torch," 16 mm, 29 minutes, color, sound, Association Films. (Story of the Olympics as carried out in the U.S.A. Shows how athletes are selected and trained.)

"Track and Field," filmstrip (sound or silent), Athletic Institution, 805 Merchandise Mart, Chicago, Illinois.

Swimming

American Red Cross, series of three films for elementary to advanced swimming, Washington, D.C.

"It's Fun to Swim" (1952), 11 minutes, black and white, sound, American Red Cross, Washington, D.C.

"Beginning Swimming" (1957), 11 minutes, color, sound, Cornet Films, Cornet Building, Chicago, Illinois.

"Beginning Swimming," Barley Films, Inc., 404 North Goodwin Avenue, Urbana, Illinois.

"Learn to Swim," Castle Films Division, United World Films, Inc., 1445 Park Avenue, N.Y.

Outdoor Recreation

Title: "Canoeing."

Details: 16 mm, 13½ minutes, color, sound.

Distributor: Canfilm Media, 2450 Victoria Park Avenue, Willowdale, Ontario, Canada, M2J4A2.

Description: Canoeing has become a very popular activity in the elementary school outdoor recreation program. This film describes the basic canoeing and safety skills and instructional techniques appropriate to upper elementary school-age children. Special features include animated illustrations of all major strokes and a boat-over-boat rescue.

Purchase Price: $202.50.

Title: "Orienteering."

Details: 16 mm, 18 minutes, sound, color.

Distributor: Canfilm Media, 2450 Victoria Park Avenue, Willowdale, Ontario, Canada, M2J4A2.

Description: Orienteering is a process of finding one's way across country using a map and compass. This film illustrates how children are taught to use a compass, read a map, and follow a designated course. Numerous orienteering games and activities are also included along with many helpful teaching suggestions.

Purchase Price: $270.

7. STUNTS, TUMBLING, AND GYMNASTIC ACTIVITIES

Written material

Bailie, S. and Bailie, A. *Elementary School Gymnastics.* St. Louis: Atlas Athletic Equipment Co., 1969.

Baley, J. A. *An Illustrated Guide to Tumbling.* Boston: Allyn and Bacon, 1968.

Dreham, V. L. *Head over Heels Gymnastics for Children.* New York: Harper & Row, Publishers, 1967.

Fisher, Hugo; Shawbold, Dean R.; and Wohlford, Paul R. *Individual and Dual Stunts.* Minneapolis: Burgess Publishing Co., 1960.

Keeney, C. J. *Fundamental Tumbling Skills Illustrated.* New York: Ronald Press, 1966.

Loken, Newton, and Willoughby, Robert. *Complete Book of Gymnastics.* Englewood Cliffs, New Jersey: Prentice-Hall, Inc., 1959.

Office of Superintendent of Schools. "Stunts and Tumbling for Elementary Schools." Sacramento, California: Sacramento County, 1959.

O'Quinn, G. *Gymnastics for Elementary School Children*. Dubuque, Iowa: Wm. C. Brown Company Publishers, 1967.

Ruff, W. K. *Gymnastics Beginner to Competitor*. Dubuque, Iowa: Wm. C. Brown Company Publishers, 1968.

Ryer, O. E. *A Manual for Tumbling and Apparatus Stunts*. 5th ed. Dubuque, Iowa: Wm. C. Brown Company Publishers, 1968.

Szypula, G. *Tumbling and Balancing For All*. 2nd ed. Dubuque, Iowa: Wm. C. Brown Company Publishers, 1968.

8. DANCE

Traditional Dance

Written Material

Ellefeldt, Louis. *Folk Dance*. Dubuque, Iowa: Wm. C. Brown Company Publishers, 1969.

Harris, J. A.; Pittman, A.; and Waller, M. S. *Dance a While*. 4th ed. Minneapolis: Burgess Publishing Co., 1968.

Kadman, G., and Hodes, T. *Israeli Folk Dance*. Tel Aviv: Education and Culture Center, 1959.

Kraus, R. *A Pocket Guide of Folk and Square Dances and Singing Games*. Englewood Cliffs, New Jersey: Prentice-Hall, Inc., 1966.

Kulbitsky, Olga, and Kaltman, Frank L. *Teacher's Dance Handbook, Number One, Kindergarten to Sixth Year*. Newark: Bluebird Publishing Co., 1960.

Latchaw, Marjorie, and Pyatt, Jean. *Folk and Square Dances and Singing Games for Elementary Schools*. Englewood Cliffs, New Jersey: Prentice-Hall, Inc., 1966.

Monsour, S.; Cohen, M. C.; and Lindell, P. E. *Rhythm in Music and Dance for Children*. Belmont, California: Wadsworth Publishing Co., 1966.

Murray, Ruth L. *Dance in Elementary Education*. 2nd ed. New York: Harper & Row, Publishers, 1963.

Mynatt, C. V., and Kaiman, B. D. *Folk Dancing for Students and Teachers*. Dubuque, Iowa: Wm. C. Brown Company Publishers, 1968.

O'Rafferty, P. *The Irish Folk Dance Book* (with music). London: Peterson Publications Ltd.

Robins, F. J. *Educational Rhythmics for Mentally and Physically Handicapped Children*, New York: Associated Press, 1968.

The Royal Scottish Country Dance Society. *Twenty-four Favorite Scottish Country Dances* (with music). London: Paterson's Publications Ltd.

Society for International Folk Dancing. *A Selection of European Folk Dances* (with music). 2 vols. New York: Pergamon Press, Inc., 1964.

Stuart, Frances R., and Gibson, Virginia L. *Rhythmic Activities: Series III*. Minneapolis: Burgess Publishing Co., 1961.

Vick, M., and McLaughlin, Cox R. *A Collection of Dances for Children* (card file). Minneapolis: Burgess Publishing Co., 1970.

Wakefield, E. E. *Folk Dancing in America*. New York: J. Lowell Pratt & Co., 1966.

Creative Dance

Andrews, Gladys. *Creative Rhythmic Movement for Children*. Englewood Cliffs, New Jersey: Prentice Hall, Inc., 1954.

Andrews, Gladys; Saurborn, Jeanette; and Schneider, Elsa. *Physical Education for Today's Boys and Girls*. Boston: Allyn & Bacon, Inc., 1960.

Boorman, J. *Creative Dance in the First Three Grades*. Don Mills, Ontario: Longman Canada Ltd., 1969.

———. *Creative Dance in Grades Four to Six*. Don Mills, Ontario: Longman Canada Ltd., 1971.

———. *Dance and Language Experiences with children*. Don Mills, Ontario: Longman Canada Ltd., 1973.

Eastman, M. *Creative Dance for Children*. Tucson, Arizona: Mettler Studios, 1965.

Mettler B. *Creative Dance for Children*. Tucson, Arizona: Mettler Studios, 1954.

Monsour, S.; Cohen M. C.; and Lindell, P. E. *Rhythm in Music and Dance for Children*. Belmont, California: Wadsworth Publishing Co., 1966.

Murray, Ruth L. *Dance in Elementary Education*. 2nd ed. New York: Harper & Row, Publishers, 1963.

Russell, J. *Creative Dance in the Primary School*. London: Macdonald and Evans Ltd., 1965.

Stanley, S. *Physical Education: A Movement Orientation*. 2nd ed. New York: McGraw-Hill Book Co., 1977.

Stokes, E. M. *Word Pictures as a Stimulus for Creative Dance.* London: Macdonald and Evans Ltd., 1970.

Taylor, C. *Rhythm: A Guide for Creative Movement.* Palo Alto, California: Peek Publications, 1974.

Thackery, R. M. *Music and Physical Education.* rev. ed. New York: Harper & Row, Publishers, 1963.

Wiener, J., and Lidstone, J. *Creative Movements for Children.* New York: Van Nostrand Reinhold Co., 1969.

Winters, S. J. *Creative Rhythmic Movement for Children of Elementary School Age.* Dubuque, Iowa: Wm. C. Brown Company Publishers, 1975.

Films

Title: "Rhythmics in Movement."
Details: 16 mm, 18 minutes, color, sound.
Distributor: Canfilm Media, 2450 Victoria Park Avenue, Willowdale, Ontario, Canada, M2J4A2.
Description: "Rhythmics in Movement" describes how the basic movement skills relating to games, dance, and gymnastic activites are taught to the accompaniment of music. The film illustrates how moving to rhythm begins with simple hand clapping and foot movements and progresses to partner and group routines. Numerous ideas relating to teaching strategies, use of small equipment and selection of music are also provided.
Purchase Price: $270.

Title: "Creative Folk Dance."
Details: 16 mm, 17 minutes, color, sound.
Distributor: Canfilm Media, 2450 Victoria Park Avenue, Willowdale, Ontario, Canada, M2J4A2.
Description: This film illustrates how folk dance activities can be taught using creative teaching strategies. Children are gradually introduced to each basic step and pathway through progress from individual to partner to group dance patterns. Numerous ideas relating to lesson plans, musical accompaniment, and teaching techniques are also provided.
Purchase Price: $225.

Title: "Building Children's Personalities with Creative Dancing."
Details: 16 mm, 30 minutes, color.
Distributor: Bailey Films, 6509 Lonpre Avenue, Hollywood, California.
Description: Shows how a skillful teacher can lead children through the phases of creative dance expression.

Title: "Learning through Movement."
Details: 16 mm, 32 minutes, black and white, sound.
Distributor: S. L. Film Productions, 5126 Nartwick Street, Los Angeles, California.
Description: Explores the multiplicity of learning concepts that a child can experience in a creative-dance class.

Title: "Creative Dance in the Junior School."
Details: 16 mm, 40 minutes, color, sound.
Distributor: County Film Library, 2 Walton's Parade, Preston, Lancashire, England.
Description: Illustrates progression of dance through the junior school (intermediate level); shows dances composed by children.

Title: "Music and Movement."
Details: 16 mm, color, sound, 13 minutes.
Distributor: Rank Audio-Visual Ltd., Woodger Road, Shepherds Bush, London, W. 12.
Description: A high standard of work from six-year-olds showing response to music and how the use of percussion and visual stimuli develop quality of movement.

Title: "Free to Move."
Details: 16 mm, 34½ minutes, color.
Distributor: Southern Film Production, Brockenhurst, Hampshire, England.
Description: The film illustrates the way children move and the relevance of this understanding to a child's total education. Shows excellent relationships to classroom and gymnastic activities.

Title: "Tinikling."
Details: 16 mm, 11 minutes, color, sound.
Distributor: General Learning Cooperation, 3 East 54th Street, New York.
Description: Instructions and teaching techniques for Philippine stick dances.

Title: "Discovering Rhythm."
Details: 16 mm, color, sound, 11 minutes.
Distributor: Universal Education and Visual Arts, 221 Park Avenue South, New York, N.Y. 10003.

Source of Records and Tapes

There are several outstanding record companies that have a wide variety of records and tapes for elementary school traditional, contemporary, and creative-dance programs. Unless you are purchasing a specific record, it is wise to write to several of the following companies, indicating your area of interest and requesting a catalogue. It is also important that you request that your name be kept on the mailing list in order to keep up with new releases.

—Bowmar Records, 622 Rodier Drive, Glendale, California.
—Burns Record Co., 755 Chickadee Lane, Stratford, Connecticut.
—Canadian Folk Dance Record Service, 605 King Street, West, Toronto 2B, Ontario.
—Folkraft Record Co., 1159 Broad Street, Newark, New Jersey.
—Educational Recordings of America Inc., Box 6062, Bridgeport, Connecticut.
—McGregor Records, 729 South Western Avenue, Hollywood, California.
—Folk Dancer, Box 201, Flushing, Long Island, New York.
—Israeli Music Foundation, 931 Broadway, New York.
—Columbia Records, 1473 Barnum Avenue, Bridgeport, Connecticut.
—Childhood Rhythms, 326 East Forest Park Avenue, Springfield, Massachusetts.
—Imperial Records, 137 North Western Avenue, Los Angeles, California.
—Square Dance Square, Box 689, Santa Barbara, California.
—RCA Victor Education Dept. J, 155 East 24th Street, New York, New York.
—Windsor Records, 5530 N. Rosemead Boulevard, Temple City, California.
—World of Fun Records, 150 Fifth Street, New York 11, New York.

9. MOVEMENT EDUCATION

Written Materials

Bilborough, A., and Jones, P. *Physical Education in the Primary Schools.** London: University of London Press, 1969.
Buckland, D. *Gymnastics.* London: Heinemann Educational Books Ltd., 1970.
Cameron, W. McD., and Pleasance, Peggy. *Education in Movement.* Oxford: Basil Blackwell & Mott, Ltd., 1965.
Cope, J. *Discovery Methods in Physical Education.* London: Thomas Nelson and Sons, Ltd., 1967.
Hackett, L. C., and Jensen, R. G. *A Guide to Movement Exploration.* Palo Alto, California: Peek Publications, 1966.
Halsey, Elizabeth. *Inquiry and Invention on Physical Education.* Philadelphia: Lea & Febiger, 1964.
Howard, S. "The Movement Education Approach to Teaching in English Elementary Schools." *American Journal for Health Physical Education and Recreation,* January, 1967.
Inner London Educational Authority, Educational Gymnastics.* London: 1966.
Kirchner, G.; Cunningham, J.; and Warrell, E. *Introduction to Movement Education.* 2nd ed. Dubuque, Iowa: Wm. C. Brown Company Publishers, 1978.
Laban, R. *Modern Educational Dance.** London: Macdonald and Evans, 1948.
Laban, R., and Ullmann, L. *The Mastery of Movement.** London: Macdonald & Evans, 1960.
Locks, L. F. "The Movement Movement." *American Journal for Health Physical Education and Recreation,* January 1966.
Ludwig, E. A. "Towards an Understanding of Basic Movement Education in the Elementary Schools," *American Journal for Health, Physical Education and Recreation,* March 1968.
Mauldin, E., and Layson, J. *Teaching Gymanstics.** London: Macdonald & Evans, Ltd., 1965.
Ministry of Education. *Moving and Growing.* London: Her Majesty's Stationary Office,* 1952.
Ministry of Education. *Planning the Program.** London: Her Majesty's Stationary Office, 1965.
Morison, R. *A Movement Approach to Educational Gymnastics.* London: J. M. Dent and Sons, Ltd., 1969.

*All books with an asterisk may be purchased from the Ling Book Shop, Ling House, 10, Nottingham Place, London W C 1.

Simons, W.M.M. "Educational Gymnastics—Its Meaning, Uses and Abuses." *Canadian Journal of Health, Physical Education, and Recreation.*

Stanley, S. *Physical Education: A Movement Orientation.* New York: 2nd ed. McGraw-Hill Book Co., 1977.

Wiseman, E. D. "Movement Education—What It Is and What It Is Not." *Canadian Journal of Health, Physical Education and Recreation,* March 1969.

Films

Series C contains four films that sequentially introduce the movement education approach. This series is specifically designed to be used as in-service films for teachers of grades one through six or for use in teacher training programs (produced in 1978).

Title (Film No. 1): "Introducing the Elements of Movement Education."
Details: 16 mm, 16 minutes, color, sound.
Distributor: Canfilm Media, 2450 Victoria Park Avenue, Willowdale, Ontario, Canada. M2J4A2.
Description: This film represents stage one in introducing the movement education approach. It describes how the safety skills and vocabulary of movement education are progressively introduced to primary and intermediate children. Brief sample lessons, problem-solving techniques, and numerous teaching ideas are provided.
Purchase Price: $240.

Title (Film No. 2): "Using Small Equipment in Movement Education."
Details: 16 mm, 16 minutes, color, sound.
Distributor: Canfilm Media, 2450 Victoria Park Avenue, Willowdale, Ontario, Canada. M2J4A2.
Description: The first part of the film describes how small equipment such as hoops, beanbags, and individual ropes are used in a movement education lesson. The second part shows how small equipment should be used to extend a child's movement potential and creative response. Ideas relating to task cards, stations work, and a variety of instructional techniques are also included.
Purchase Price: $240.

Title (Film No. 3): "Using Large Apparatus in Movement Education."
Details: 16 mm, 15 minutes, color, sound.
Distributor: Canfilm Media, 2450 Victoria Park Avenue, Willowdale, Ontario, Canada M2J4A2.
Description: This film describes how large apparatus such as vaulting boxes, climbing ropes, and balance benches are used to challenge and extend a child's physical and creative abilities. It also illustrates how to combine large apparatus with small equipment, how to use task cards in an effective and enjoyable way, and how to arrange a variety of large apparatus.
Purchase price: $225.

Title (Film No. 4): "Theme Development in Movement Education."
Details: 16 mm, 16 minutes, color, sound.
Distributor: Canfilm Media, 2450 Victoria Park Avenue, Willowdale, Ontario, Canada, M2J4A2.
Description: This film begins with a brief explanation of how to plan a short theme in a progressive and systematic way. In the second part, an extended theme of matching shapes is developed with a fourth-grade class through a series of nine lessons. Shows excellent use of small and large equipment.
Purchase Price: $240.

Title: "Movement Education—From Primary to College Level Programs."
Details: color, sound, 22 minutes, 16 mm.
Distributor: Universal Education and Visual Arts, 221 Park Avenue South, New York, New York, 10003, or 2450 Victoria Park Avenue, Willowdale 425, Toronto, Ontario.
Description: The film illustrates the role and emphasis of movement education in elementary, high school, and college programs. In the majority of scenes, typical programs are shown to illustrate the methods used, levels of performance, and differences in facilities and equipment. The film also shows a few advanced movement-education programs to illustrate the quality of performance that can be reached through this type of program.

Title: "Teaching Deaf Children Through Movement Education."
Details: 16 mm, sound, color, 16 minutes.
Distributor: International Tele-Film Enterprises, 221 Victoria Street, Toronto 205, Ontario.
Description: This film illustrates how the movement education approach can be used to teach deaf children. Adaptations are illustrated to show how movement challenges are presented to deaf children.

Title: "Teaching Blind Children Through Movement Education."
Details: 16 mm, sound, color, 12 minutes.
Distributor: International Tele-Film Enterprises, 221 Victoria Street, Toronto 205, Ontario.
Description: This is the companion film to the previous film. The film shows a similar method to teach blind children using the movement education approach.

Inexpensive Equipment

1. Skipping Ropes

To Cut Ropes:

1. Measure off the desired length of rope.
2. Wrap five inches above and below the cut mark with tape (plastic preferred; adhesive acceptable).
3. Place rope on small wooden block and cut rope in middle of taped area.

To Store Ropes:

1. Since there may be three or four different lengths of rope, dip the ends of the ropes in different colored paint to represent short, medium, and long lengths. (Dip about six inches.)
2. A simple way to store ropes is across or over a bar as shown above. The standard can be of any design with the top bar about four feet off the floor.

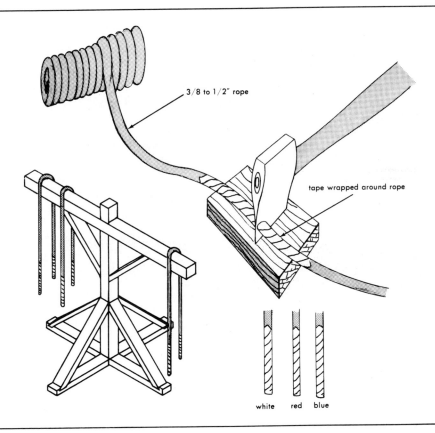

3/8 to 1/2" rope

tape wrapped around rope

white   red   blue

2. Horizontal Bar

General Features:

The following horizontal bar can be made at a cost of approximately fifteen to twenty dollars. It is designed for efficient assemblage and storage. The bolt as shown in Detail B prevents the bar from rotating while performing stunts. The bar is held firmly to the upright standard with a fixed 2¾" washer on the inside and a washer and bolt shown in Detail D. For efficient storage, the side support shown in Detail A may be drawn upward.

Designed by Bill Bressler
Drawn by Gary Sciuchetti

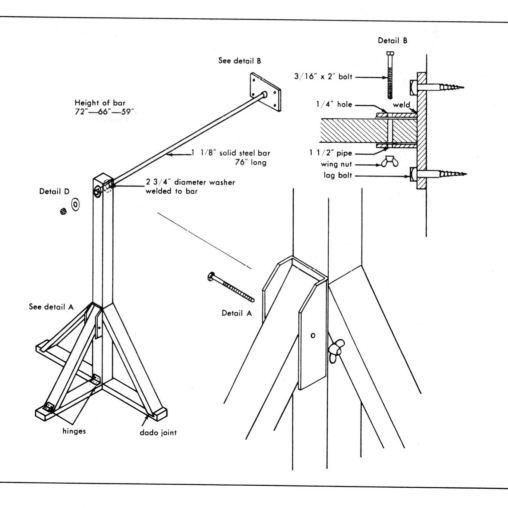

3. Balance Beam

General Information:
The diagram of the intermediate level balance beam is basically a 12' × 4" beam mounted on two sawhorses. Standard competition height for a beam is four feet; however, for intermediate level children, the height may range from 3½' to a maximum of 4'. It is also desirable to make the grooves for the low and high balance beams the same in order to mount the same beam on both standards.

A. Intermediate level

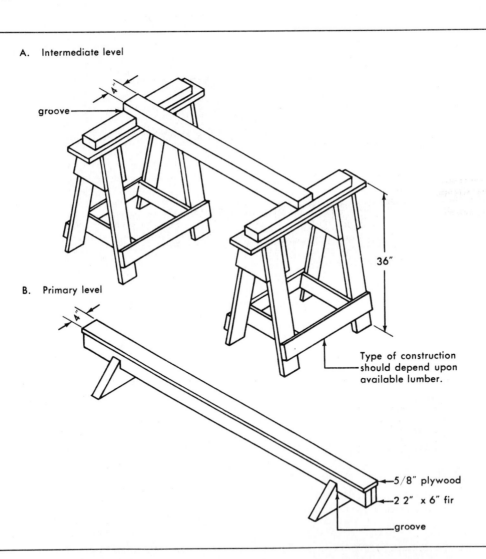

groove

4"

36"

Type of construction should depend upon available lumber.

B. Primary level

4"

5/8" plywood

2 2" x 6" fir

groove

4. Balance Bench

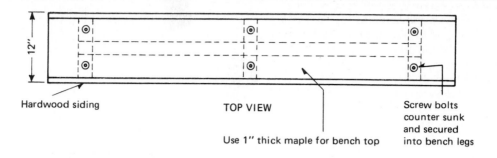

Hardwood siding

TOP VIEW

Use 1" thick maple for bench top

Screw bolts
counter sunk
and secured
into bench legs

12"

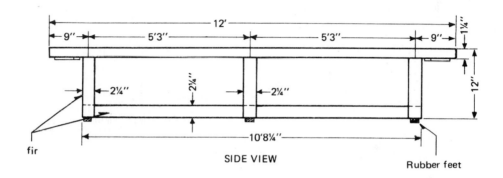

12'

9" — 5'3" — 5'3" — 9" — 1¼"

2¼" 2¼" 2¼"

12"

10'8¼"

fir

SIDE VIEW

Rubber feet

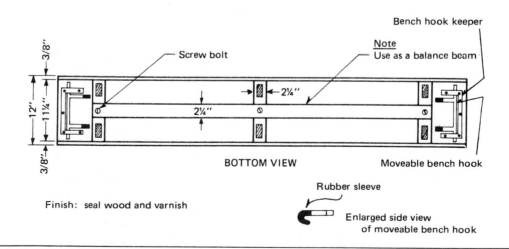

Bench hook keeper

Screw bolt

Note
Use as a balance beam

2¼"

2¼"

3/8"

12" 11¼"

3/8"

BOTTOM VIEW

Moveable bench hook

Finish: seal wood and varnish

Rubber sleeve

Enlarged side view
of moveable bench hook

B

5. Scooters

General Information:

An inexpensive set of floor scooters may be made from ¾" plywood and plastic casters. Cut 12" squares, round the edges and attach a strip of rubber around the outside edge. The latter strip prevents the edges from splintering as well as lessens the noise when scooters hit. A simple way to store scooters is illustrated above. The pole should be at least ¾" thick and firmly attached to the base.

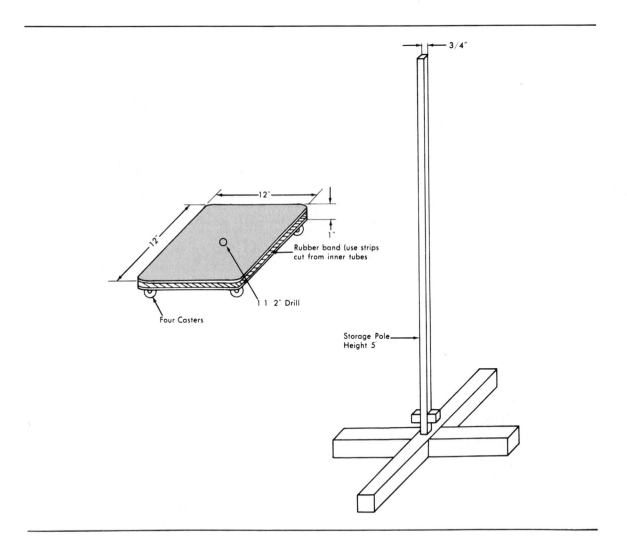

12"

12"

1"

Rubber band (use strips cut from inner tubes

1 1 2" Drill

Four Casters

3/4"

Storage Pole
Height 5'

6. Wands

General Information:
A set of wands (see Chapter 9 for appropriate lengths) may be made from old broom handles. Cut each broom handle off at the desired length and round both ends. Dip the end of each set of wands in different colored paint to facilitate each selection.

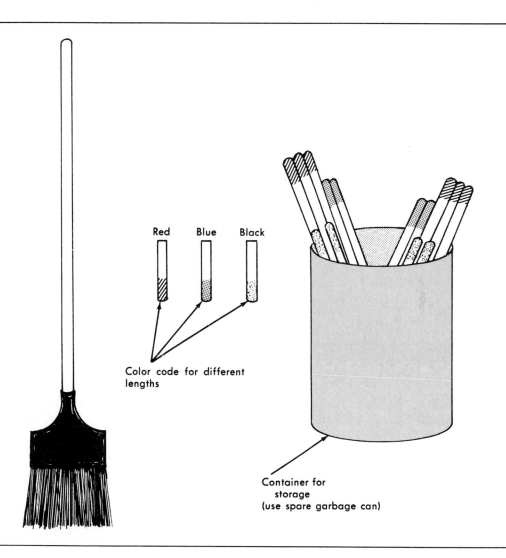

Red   Blue   Black

Color code for different lengths

Container for storage
(use spare garbage can)

B

7. Vaulting Box

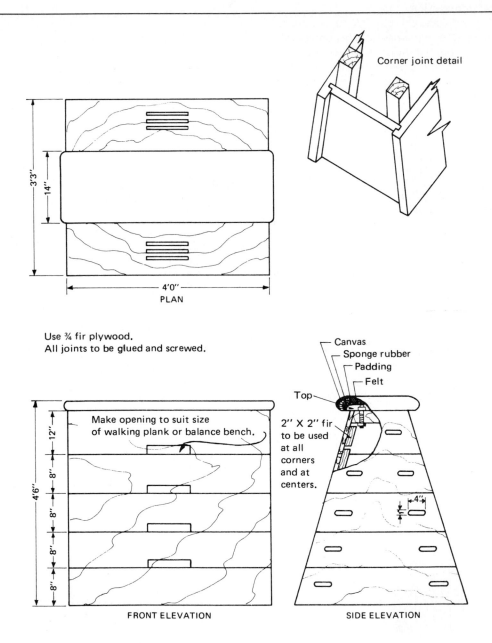

Corner joint detail

3'3"
14"
4'0"
PLAN

Use ¾ fir plywood.
All joints to be glued and screwed.

Canvas
Sponge rubber
Padding
Felt
Top

Make opening to suit size
of walking plank or balance bench.

2" X 2" fir
to be used
at all
corners
and at
centers.

4'6"
12"
8"
8"
8"
8"

4"

FRONT ELEVATION

SIDE ELEVATION

Finish: wiped white rez stain
shellaced and varnished.

8. Sawhorse

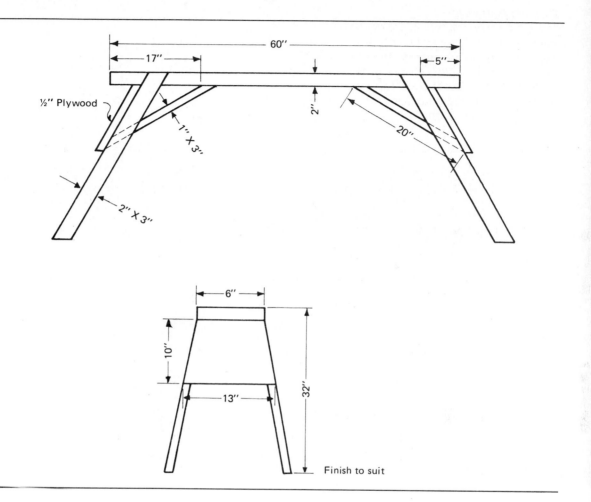

60″

17″   5″

½″ Plywood

2″

1″ X 3″

20″

2″ X 3″

6″

10″

32″

13″

Finish to suit

9. Jumping Boxes

General Features:
The jumping boxes shown below can be made for approximately fifty dollars, depending upon the number and size of each box. A minimum of three for each set is recommended. Do not cover top with rubber matting or cloth material. Sand all corners and, if desired, paint or varnish.

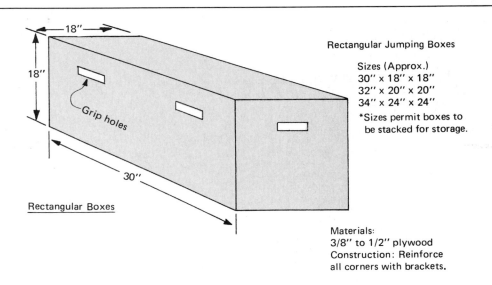

Rectangular Jumping Boxes

Sizes (Approx.)
30" x 18" x 18"
32" x 20" x 20"
34" x 24" x 24"
*Sizes permit boxes to be stacked for storage.

Materials:
3/8" to 1/2" plywood
Construction: Reinforce all corners with brackets.

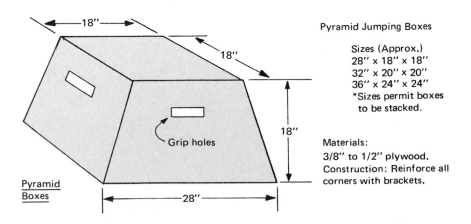

Pyramid Jumping Boxes

Sizes (Approx.)
28" x 18" x 18"
32" x 20" x 20"
36" x 24" x 24"
*Sizes permit boxes to be stacked.

Materials:
3/8" to 1/2" plywood.
Construction: Reinforce all corners with brackets.

10. Jumping Pit

How To Make:

The rubber tubes are placed on the ground as shown in the diagram and tied together. A tumbling mat is then placed on the top of the tubes. This provides a safe and comfortable landing surface. It can also be used indoors and outdoors.

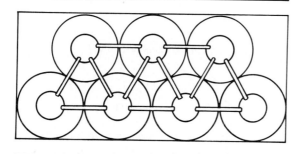

11. All-Purpose Game Bat

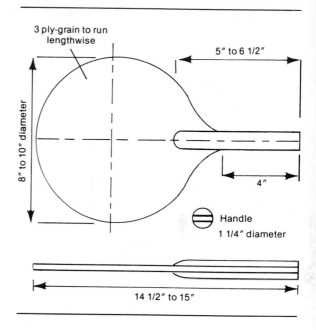

3 ply-grain to run lengthwise

8″ to 10″ diameter

5″ to 6 1/2″

4″

Handle
1 1/4″ diameter

14 1/2″ to 15″

Apparatus, Equipment, and Supply Companies

C

The following companies are listed on the basis of manufacturing and/or selling agility apparatus (indoor and outdoor), equipment (large tumbling mats, springboard, etc.) and supplies (hoops, beanbags, etc.).

Big Toys
3113 South Pine
Tacoma, Washington, 98409
or 18697 96th Street.   *Agility apparatus*
Surrey, B.C., Canada   *Outdoor apparatus*

American Athletic
Equipment Co.
Box 111
Jefferson, Iowa 50129   *Equipment*

American Gym Company, Inc.
Box 131
Monroeville, Pennsylvania
15146   *Equipment and agility apparatus*

Atlas Athletic Equipment Co.
2339 Hampton
St. Louis, Missouri 63139   *Equipment*

Mr. J. A. McLaughlin
Director of Industries for
Commissioner
Ottawa 4, Canada   *Agility apparatus*

Game-Time, Inc.
Litchfield, Michigan   *Agility apparatus*

Gym Master Co.
3200 So. Zuni
Englewood, Colorado 80110   *Equipment*

Gymnastic Supply Co.
247 West Sixth Street
San Pedro, California 90733   *Equipment and supplies*

The Delmer F. Harris Co.
P.O. Box 288, Dept. J
Concordia, Kansas 66901   *Agility apparatus*

Lind Climber Company
807 Reba Place
Evanston, Illinois 60202   *Agility apparatus*

**Madsen Gymnastic
Equipment Ltd.**
Unionville, Ontario   *Agility apparatus*

The Mexico-Forge Climbers
R.D. 1, Reedsville,
Pennsylvania   *Outdoor apparatus*

**Murray Anderson-Olympic
Gymnastic Equipment**
128 Dunedin Street
Orillia, Ontario   *Agility apparatus*

National Sports Company
360 North Marquette Street
Fond du Lac, Wisconsin 54935   *Equipment*

Nissen Corp.
930 27th Avenue, S.W.
Cedar Rapids, Iowa 52406   *Agility apparatus
and equipment*

Porter Athletic Equipment
Porter-Leavitt Co. MFGR
9555 Irving Park Road
Schiller Park, Illinois 60176   *Equipment*

A. G. Spalding & Bros. Inc.
Chicopee, Massachusetts
01014   *Equipment and supplies*

W. J. Volt Rubber Corp.
Subsidiary of American
Machine and Foundry Co.,
New York
3801 South Harbor Boulevard
Santa Ana, California 92704   *Equipment and supplies*

R. W. Whittle, Ltd.
P. V. Works
Monton, Eccles
Manchester, England   *Agility apparatus*

Creative Playthings Inc.
Princeton, New Jersey   *Playground apparatus*

Childcraft
155 East 23rd Street
New York, N.Y. 10010   *Climbing ropes and gymnasium
apparatus and equipment*

Glossary

The following words and phrases occur frequently in the instructional and intraclass physical-education programs. Separate glossaries are arranged alphabetically according to the following general categories.

Curriculum and Teaching

Accident
An unforeseen event occurring without the will or design of the person whose act caused it.

Apparatus work
The third part of a gymnastic lesson.

Classification index
A method of arranging equal groups for competitive purposes.

Classroom games
Games, relays, and contests that can be played in the classroom.

Concept
The degree of meaning a person possesses about something he has experienced.

Correlation
Relating one subject area to another.

Creative games
Games that are invented by children.

Creative playgrounds
A unique arrangement of outdoor apparatus (commercial or locally constructed).

Creativity
The degree of inventiveness of a movement.

Curriculum
The total experience within the physical-education program that is provided for all children.

Cumulative record
A method of plotting a child's performance (skill or physical-fitness items) at the beginning and end of each year.

Direct method
A teaching method in which the choice of the activity and how it is performed is entirely that of the teacher.

Dual activities
Cooperative and competitive activities between two children.

Equipment
Material or apparatus that is of a relatively permanent nature and would last, with repeated use, from five to ten years.

Evaluation
The subjective and objective assessment of program effectiveness and student progress.

Extraclass program
Cooperative and competitive programs between two or more schools.

Field theory
A theory that stresses that learning proceeds from comprehension of the whole to the identification of smaller parts.

Games of low organization
Activities such as relays, tag, and simple team games that involve one or more basic skills and a minimum of roles and playing strategies.

Humanism
A philosophy that asserts the dignity and worth of man and his capacity for self-realization through reason.

Indirect method
A teaching method that allows the children to choose the activity, as well as how and what they wish to perform within the activity.

Individual games
Low-organization games played by one person with or without small equipment.

Individualized learning
A system of teaching that adapts to each learner's individual abilities, needs, and interests.

In loco parentis
Acting in the place of the parent.

Instructional unit
The organization of material around a central activity or theme of instruction.

Intramural program
Competitive or club activities that are offered during nonclass time, on a voluntary basis, and within the jurisdiction of one school.

Introductory activity
The first part of a physical-education lesson.

Limitation method
A teaching method in which the choice of the activity or how it is performed is limited in some way by the teacher.

Method
A general way of guiding and controlling the learning experiences of children.

Modified teaching unit
A unit of instruction that emphasizes one type of activity and provides a minor emphasis in one or more other activities.

Movement training
The second part of a dance or gymnastic lesson.

Multiple teaching unit
A unit of instruction that includes two or more activities.

Negligence
An act, or absence of it, that falls below the standard established by law for the protection of others against unreasonable risk or harm.

Obstacle course
An arrangement of small and large equipment designed to improve physical fitness and skill development.

Physical education
That part of the educational process that contributes to the physical, emotional, social, and mental development of each child through the medium of physical activity.

Play day
An interschool event in which children from two or more schools play on the same team.

Relay activities
Activities that involve a race between two or more participants or teams.

Self-image
The feeling and/or opinions a child has about himself.

Sociogram
A technique used to study the relationships within groups.

Solid teaching unit
An extensive period of instruction that is devoted exclusively to one type of activity.

Specificity of skill
The differential ability of an individual to acquire and perform physical skills and movement patterns.

Sports day
A interschool competitive event in which teams represent their own schools.

Spotting
A method of assisting a performer in the execution of a difficult stunt or movement.

Station work
A technique of organizing the class into small working units.

Stimulus-response theory
A theory that stresses that learning consists of a strengthening of the connections (bonds) between the stimulus and the response.

Supplies
Material that is expendable within one or two years.

Teaching formation
A specific way of organizing the class, such as line, circle, or shuttle patterns.

Team teaching
The organization of teachers and students into instructional groups which permit maximum utilization of staff abilities.

Technique
A smaller part of a method.

Tournament
A method of organizing small and large groups for competition.

Structure, Growth, and Mechanics

Agility
The ability to shift the body in different directions quickly and efficiently.

Asthma
A condition of the lungs which causes labored breathing and wheezing.

Balance
The ability to maintain a stationary position or to perform purposeful movements while resisting the force of gravity.

Calisthenics
Conditioning exercises designed to improve physical fitness.

Circuit training
Repeating one or more exercises as many times as possible within a set time limit.

Diaphysis
The center of bone growth located in the middle of the long bones.

Endurance
The ability to continue a muscular effort or movement over a prolonged period of time.

Epilepsy
A disease of the nervous system which is characterized by seizures and convulsions.

Epiphysis
Center of growth located near the end of the long bones.

Exceptional child
A child who deviates from the normal intelligence, physical health, motor ability, or behavioral characteristics of the average or typical child.

Flexibility
The range of movement of a joint.

Force
The push or pull exerted against something.

Growth
An increase in size.

Hyperopia
Farsightedness, resulting in a condition in which distant objects can be seen clearly but nearby objects appear blurred.

Isometric exercise
Contraction of muscles involving a push, pull, or twist against an object that does not move.

Isotonic exercise
Contraction of muscles that involves both shortening and lengthening the muscle fibers.

Kyphosis
Marked curve of the upper back.

Linear motion
A movement in which the body or an object as a whole moves in a straight line.

Locomotor skills
Basic motor skills involving a change of position of the feet and/or a change of direction of the body.

Lordosis
An exaggerated forward curve of the lower back.

Maturation
The general progress from one stage to a higher and more complex stage of development. Maturation occurs as a function of time and is independent of experience.

Myopia
Nearsightedness, resulting in a condition in which distant objects appear blurred while nearby objects are seen clearly.

Neuromuscular skills
All motor skills that are under the voluntary control of the brain.

Nonlocomotor skills
Movements of the body that are performed from a relatively stable base.

Obesity
Eating more food than the body needs, resulting in formation of excessive fat tissue.

Overload
A performance of an exercise or activity that requires the individual to exert more than a normal effort.

Perceptual-motor responses
The process of perceiving a stimulus and translating the stimulus into a motor response.

Physical fitness
The state that characterizes the degree to which a person is able to function.

Physically gifted
To possess a unique talent or ability in physical activities.

Physically handicapped
A child who suffers from a disease or physical handicap.

Posture
The relative alignment of the body segments.

Power
The ability of the body to apply a maximum muscular contraction with the quickest possible speed.

Rotary motion
A movement that traces out an arc or circle around an axis or fixed point.

Scoliosis
A lateral curvature of the spinal column.

Slow learner
A child whose IQ is between 70 and 90.

Spatial awareness
The ability to move the body or its parts in specified directions.

Speed
The ability to perform successive movements of the same pattern in the shortest period of time.

Strength
The amount of force a muscle or group of muscles can exert.

Yoga exercise
An ancient Indian system of exercise performed slowly.

Movement Education

Agility apparatus
All types of indoor and outdoor climbing apparatus.

Apparatus work
The third part of a movement-education lesson, concerned with the application of movement ideas to large and small apparatus.

Asymmetry
A position or movement that is characterized by unevenness of one part of the body to its opposite side. Using a line drawn through the vertebral column, all twisting, curling, or held positions where greater stress is given to the limbs on one side, would be asymmetrical positions.

Balance
The ability to hold the body in a fixed position. (The common expression is "weight bearing.")

Body awareness
The way in which the body or parts of it can move (stretch, bend, twist, and turn).

Continuity
Movements following each other in succession.

Curl
An action that flexes or bends the body or its parts.

Flight
The ability to propel the body into the air.

Flow
The ability to link one movement to another with control and harmony.

Force
The degree of effort or tension involved in a movement.

General space
The physical area in which a movement takes place.

Introductory activity
The first part of a movement-education lesson involves general warm-up, lasting approximately five minutes.

Level
The relative position of the body or any of its parts to the floor or apparatus. Level may be applied to either stationary activity or position.

Movement ideas
A movement concept related to one or more of the basic elements of qualities, body awareness, space awareness, or relationships.

Movement training
The second part of a movement-education lesson, concerned with the development of movement themes and activities.

Pattern
The arrangement of a series of movements in relation to shape, level, and pathway.

Personal space
The area around an individual that can be used while he keeps one part of his body in a fixed position on the floor or apparatus; also known as limited space.

Qualities
Refers to how the body can move. It is the ability to move quickly or slowly, to perform light or heavy movements, and the flow with which one movement is linked to another.

Relationship
Refers to the position of the body in relationship to the floor, apparatus, or other performers.

Safety training
The ability of children to move and land safely and efficiently. In a broader context, it refers to the individual's safety on or around apparatus and to his concern for the safety of other participants.

Sequence
A series of movements performed in succession.

Shape
The image presented by the position of the body when traveling or stationary.

Space
The area in which a movement takes place.

Stretch
Moving the body or parts of it from a flexed to an extended position.

Symmetry
In movement education, symmetry describes a movement or balance position in which both sides of the body would look identical if an imaginary line were drawn through the middle of the body.

Theme
A central movement idea.

Time
The speed with which a movement takes place (quick, slow, sudden, or sustained).

Traveling
Moving in various directions by transferring the weight from one part of the body to another.

Turn
Rotation of the body and loss of the initial fixed point of contact (e.g., turning in a full arch).

Twist
One part of the body is held in a fixed position on the floor or apparatus and the rest of the body is turned away from the fixed position (e.g., twisting the trunk to the side and back).

Weight
The degree of muscle tension involved in the production of a movement, or the maintenance of a static position involving tension.

Wide
An action that moves the arms or legs away from the trunk.

Dance

Accent
The emphasis given to a beat in a series of beats in a measure.

Active couple(s)
The couple(s) who is designated to start the dance or to whom a part of the dance is addressed.

Advance
To move forward, usually with walking steps.

Allemande left
From a circle or square formation with all dancers facing the center, the boy joins his left hand with the girl on his left and walks once around counterclockwise and back to the starting position.

Allemande right
Same as allemande left only toward the opposite direction.

Arch
Two dancers join inside hands and raise their arms to form an arch.

Balance
In square dancing the usual movement following a "swing your partner." Partners face each other, join right hands, step back with the weight on the left foot and the right heel touching in front. Both partners may also bow slightly.

Beat
The constant steady pulsation that exists in a movement or a musical accompaniment.

Bow and Curtsey
The bow, performed by the boy, may be a simple nod of the head or an elaborate and pronounced deep bend of the trunk. The curtsey, performed by the girl, may be a simple nod of the head or an elaborate and pronounced deep bend of the knees and a graceful sideward extension of the dancing costume.

Break
Release hands.

Buzz
The weight is held on one foot while pushing with the other foot.

Chain (ladies chain)
In square dancing, the girls move across to the opposite couple, extending right hands to each other as they pass, then left hands to the opposite boy. The boy places his right hand behind the girl's back, grasping her right hand, and turns her one full turn counterclockwise.

Clockwise
Move in the same direction as the hands of a clock.

Contra or longways
Couples standing in a long line with boys on one side and girls on the other.

Corner
When facing the center, the boy's corner is the girl on his left and the girl's corner is the boy on her right.

Counterclockwise
Moving in the opposite direction as the hands of a clock.

Creative dance
The expression of ideas and feelings through unstructured movement.

Divide or split the ring
Active couples pass through the opposite couples.

Do-si-do
These words mean "back to back" and usually involve two persons facing each other. Two dancers walk forward, pass right shoulders and, without turning, move to the right passing back to back, then walk backward to their starting positions.

Folk dance
Dance patterns of past cultures.

Forward and back
This figure may involve one or more dancers facing each other. Both advance four steps forward (or three steps and a bow) and four steps backward.

Gallop
A sliding movement performed in a forward direction.

Grand right and left
This is a weaving pattern and usually follows an allemande left. Face partner and join right hands, pass, give left hand to the next dancer, and continue weaving around set.

Head couple
In square dancing, the head couple is the couple nearest to the music or caller.

Home
The original starting place at the beginning of a dance.

Honor
Salute or bow to the partner or other dancers.

Hop
Transfer of weight from one foot to the same foot.

Intensity
The quality or force of music or movement.

Jump
A light transfer of weight from one foot or from both feet to both feet.

Leap
A light transfer of weight from one foot to the other foot.

Measure
An identical repetitive grouping of underlying beats.

Open
Partners stand side by side with their inside hands joined. Girls stand to the boys' right.

Opposite
The person or couple directly across the square.

Phrase
A group of measures that fit together into a meaningful whole.

Promenade
Partners join hands in a skater's position and walk counter-clockwise around the set.

Reel
In a longways dance, the head couple moves to the center of the set and performs an elbow turn. The girl goes to the first boy and the boy goes to the first girl, performs an elbow swing, returns, and repeats action with partner. Pattern continues to the end of the line.

Rhythmic
Performing a variety of body movements in time to a specific rhythmic accompaniment.

Run
A transfer of weight from one foot to the other with a momentary loss of contact with the floor by both feet.

Sashay
This is the American term for the French term "chasse." These are sliding steps sideward.

Separate
Partners leave each other and move in opposite directions.

Singing games
A form of folk dance considered forerunners to the more complicated traditional dances.

Skip
A combination of a long step and a short hop, with the lead foot alternating after each hop.

Slide
A combination of a step and a short leap which can be performed forward, sideways, or backward.

Square
Four couples, with each forming one side of a square.

Square dance
A type of American-folk dance.

Star or wheel
Two or more dancers join right hands in the center of the set and walk forward or backward as directed.

Swing
A rhythmic rotation of a couple with a walking step, buzz step, two-step, or skip. The swing may be a one-hand, two-hand, elbow, or waist swing.

Tempo
The rate of speed of music or movement.

Varsovienne position
The boy stands slightly behind and to the left of his partner. While both are facing the same direction, the girl raises both hands to about shoulder height and the boy joins his right hand with the girl's right hand and his left hand with the girl's left hand.

Walk
A rhythmic transfer of weight from one foot to the other. One foot is always in contact with the ground.

Basketball

Backcourt
The half of the basketball court that is the farthest from the offensive basket.

Baseball pass
An overhand pass that employs the same basic techniques used when throwing an overhand baseball pass.

Baseline
The end line of a basketball court.

Basket
The circular goal located on the backboard.

Center
The middle position on the forward line, usually played by the tallest player on the team.

Defense
The team that does not have possession of the ball.

Drive
A quick dribbling movement toward the opponent's basket.

Fast break
A situation where the defensive team gains possession of the ball and moves the ball into a scoring position before the opposing team can recover into a defensive position.

Free throw
An unguarded shot that is taken from the free throw line. If successful, the team shooting scores one point.

Frontcourt
The part of the basketball court that is nearest the team's goal.

Jump ball
A situation in which two opposing players simultaneously gain possession of the ball and the referee tosses it up between the two players.

Jump shot
A shot that is taken while the player has both feet off the floor.

Lay-up
A shot that is taken close to the backboard. The ball is released off one hand and is gently placed over the rim or against the backboard to allow it to rebound into the basket.

Offense
The team that has possession of the ball.

One-on-one
A situation in which one offensive player tries to outmaneuver one defensive player.

Pivot
A player who has possession of the ball may move one foot while keeping the other foot in contact with the floor.

Post
The post player is normally a pivot player positioned near the key with his back toward the basket.

Rebound
A shot attempted at the basket which rebounds back into the court area.

Set shot
A shot taken from a stationary position.

Traveling
A player who takes more than one step with the ball without dribbling it.

Zone defense
A type of defense in which the defensive players are assigned a specific area of the court to guard.

Field and Floor Hockey

Attack
Players who are designated as forward line players.

Boarding
Holding a player against the wall.

Bully
A method of starting the game, after each goal, and after halftime.

Corner
When the defending team causes the ball to go over the end line, the attacking team is awarded a free hit from the nearest corner of the field.

Crease
The semicircular area around the goal area.

Defensive team
The team that does not have possession of the ball.

Dodge
A means of evading an oncoming tackler.

Dribble
A means of advancing the ball or puck with a series of short taps.

Drive
Hitting the ball from a moderate to a long distance.

Fielding
Gaining possession of the ball or puck.

Flick
A method of putting the ball or puck into the air.

Free hit
A free hit awarded to the opposing team after a breach of the rules.

High sticking
Raising the stick above shoulder level.

Obstruction
When a player runs between an opponent and the ball.

Offensive team
The team that has possession of the ball.

Offside
A situation in which an offensive player is in his opponent's half of the field and does not have possession of the ball as well as not having opponents between him and the goal line.

Roll-in
When the opponent causes the ball to cross the side line, a player on the nonoffending team is awarded a free roll-in at the point of infraction.

Scoop
A method of raising the ball into the air.

Tackle
A method of getting the ball away from an opponent.

Flag or Touch Football

Blocking
A legal method of stopping an opponent.

Down
A method of starting play after the ball has been stopped. In football, each team is given four downs to advance the ball ten yards.

Hike
The movement of the ball from the center player to the quarterback.

Lateral
A sideways pass of the ball.

Safety
When a defensive player in possession of the ball is trapped behind his own goal line. The attacking team is awarded two points.

Scrimmage line
The line on which each down begins. The defending team must remain behind this line until the ball has left the center's hands.

Spiral
A forward pass in which the football moves with a spiral-like action, with the point of the ball leading.

Stance
The starting position of a football player.

Touchback
When a defensive player intercepts a ball behind his own goal line and places it on the ground rather than attempting to run it out over the goal line. One point is awarded to the attacking team.

Touchdown
When a member of the attacking team carries the ball over the goal line or a teammate catches a ball while in the end zone. The attacking team is awarded six points.

Soccer

Attacking team
The team that has possession of the ball; also known as the offensive team.

Corner kick
A placekick awarded to the attacking team after the defending team has sent the ball over its own goal line.

Defending team
The team that does not have possession of the ball.

Direct free kick
A free kick from which a goal may be scored directly.

Feint
A deceptive movement to mislead an opponent.

Foul
An illegal act such as tripping or holding an opponent which results in a direct free kick being awarded the nonoffending team.

Heading
Playing the ball by striking it with the head.

Indirect free kick
A free kick from which a goal may not be scored directly.

Infringement
An illegal act such as being offside which results in an indirect free kick being awarded the nonoffending team.

Kickoff
A short kick taken by the center forward at the center of the field. The kickoff is used to start the game, at halftime, and after each goal is scored.

Offside
An illegal position of a player which occurs when he is in his opponent's half of the field and when there are fewer than two opposing players in front of him at the moment the ball is played by one of his teammates.

Penalty kick
If a foul is committed by the defending team within the penalty area, the attacking team is given a direct free kick from the twelve-yard mark and directly in front of the goal. All other players must be outside the penalty area until the kick is taken.

Punt
A kick that is performed by dropping the ball and contacting it with the top of the foot before it touches the ground.

Throw-in
A two-hand overhand free throw awarded to the team that did not cause the ball to cross over the sideline.

Trapping
A method of stopping the ball using any part of the body other than the hands.

Volley
A type of kick in which the ball is contacted while it is in the air.

Softball

Away
The number of players who have been put out ("one away").

Bag
Base.

Bases loaded
Runners on every base.

Box
The specific area marked and designated as the catcher's area, the batter's area, or the coach's area.

Clean the bases
A player who hits a home run with one or more teammates on bases.

Cleanup
The fourth, and usually the strongest, hitter in the batting order.

Diamond
The area inside the four bases.

Double play
A defensive play by the fielding team resulting in two outs.

Earned run
A run that is scored as a result of an offensive play and not as a result of an error committed by the defensive team.

Error
A mistake committed by the defensive team.

Fair ball
Any legally batted ball which is touched or lands in the fair territory.

Fan
A player who misses his third strike.

Forced out
A defensive player in possession of the ball touches a base before a runner, who is forced to move to that base.

Foul ball
A hit ball that lands outside of fair territory.

Infield
The playing area within and immediately adjacent to the diamond.

Innings
A division of the game in which both teams play until each has three players out.

Out
The retirement of a batter after he has three strikes or a base runner who is caught or forced out.

Outfield
The fair territory that is located beyond the infield.

Pinch hitter
Any substitute hitter.

Pop-up
A high fly ball that lands in or near the infield.

RBI
An abbreviated term to indicate the number of runs batted in by a player.

Steal
A player who advances to another base after the ball leaves the pitcher's hand and before the infield player can tag him with the ball.

Walk
This occurs when four balls are called on the batter. The batter advances to first base.

Track and Field

Baton
A short round stick that is passed between members of a relay team.

Float
An interval or period during a long run in which the runner has a relaxed stride with no increase or decrease in speed.

Front runner
A runner who performs best when he is ahead of his opponents.

Hash running
A team race with markers and hidden directions located along a route.

Heats
Preliminary track-and-field events to determine who will compete in the final events.

Jogging
A slow, easy run.

Lap
One complete circuit around the track.

Pace
The rate of speed the runner sets for a particular distance run.

Passing zone
An area on the track within which the baton must be passed.

Pole position
A runner who is assigned the inside, or curb, lane of the track.

Scratch
A foul committed by stepping over the scratch line.

Stride
The distance between the right and left foot imprints on a track. The measurement is made from the toe of the back foot to the heel imprint of the lead foot.

Volleyball

Block
One or two defensive players jump up at the same time as the spiker with their hands raised and facing the oncoming ball.

Dink
A deception drop volley that is executed from a spiked position.

Hitter
Another term used for a spiker.

Illegal contact
Any contact of the ball in which it comes to a visible resting position.

Net recovery
A fair move by a player to play the ball after it has been hit into the net by one of his teammates.

Setup
This is normally the second hit by a team and is directed to a forward player, who then may attempt a spike or a volley over the net.

Side out
A violation that is committed by the serving team.

Spike
A ball that is hit in a downward direction into the opponent's court.

Index

Game Activities

Basketball Games

Classroom Games

Field and Floor Hockey Games

Flag and Touch Football Games

Individual and Partner Games